CISTERCIAN STUDIES SERIES: NUMBER NINETY-FIVE

FRIENDSHIP AND COMMUNITY
THE MONASTIC EXPERIENCE, 350 - 1250

CISTERCIAN STUDIES SERIES: NUMBER NINETY-FIVE

FRIENDSHIP & COMMUNITY

THE MONASTIC EXPERIENCE 350 - 1250

by

Brian Patrick McGuire

CISTERCIAN PUBLICATIONS INC.
KALAMAZOO, MICHIGAN
1988

The work of Cistercian Publications is made possible in part by support from Western Michigan University through The Institute of Cistercian Studies

Available in Britain and Europe from
A. R. Mowbray & Co. Ltd.
St. Thomas House Becket Street
Oxford OX1 1SJ

Available elsewhere (including Canada) from

Cistercian Publications, Inc.
WMU Station
Kalamazoo, Michigan 49008

Library of Congress Cataloging-in-Publication Data

McGuire, Brian Patrick.
Friendship & Community.

(Cistercian studies series; no. 95)
1. Monastic and religious life—History—Middle Ages, 600-1500. 2. Friendship—History. I. Title.
II. Title: Friendship and Community. III. Series
BX2435.M37 1987 271'.009'02 87-6615
ISBN 0-87907-895-2
ISBN 9-87907-985-1 (pbk.)

Typeset by United States Type & Design, Grand Rapids, Michigan
Printed in the United States of America

Table of Contents

To Phyllis
and
in memory of Dan
first parents, then friends

PREFACE

FRIENDSHIP is hardly a subject which seems conducive to academic treatment, and yet if we look back on the history of western culture, we find friendship has been debated and discussed ever since the Greeks. Standard treatments, however, usually skip lightly over the Middle Ages, and monastic friendship has become a subject isolated within the special category of cloistered life. It is my contention that there is nothing odd or arcane about the friendships that are visible in the monastic literature of the Middle Ages: in the various ways of expressing friendship we find what can be recognisable in human terms, while at the same time we deal with a past culture which is, inevitably, different from our own.

At every step of the way I have been aware of the solid objection that friendship as human experience can only be detected through literary sources, whose authors were consciously aware of precedents and models in describing their bonds with other human beings. I have tried to take this dimension into consideration without resigning myself to the extreme view which makes every expression of friendship into a literary commonplace. Somewhere between lived experience and literary artificiality there is a middle ground, and there many of our authors functioned. It is easier to find this area when we take into consideration the fact that every monastic friendship was experienced in the context of a community. The history of friendship in the Middle Ages cannot be written without constant recourse to the overwhelming fact of community. As communities change, so do forms of friendship.

There are philosophies of friendship and there are lived experiences of friendship. Both are conveyed to us in literary terms, and all of these—literature, philosophy, and life—are interdependent. It might have been easier to write about changing views of friendship, but I have tried to read hearts and minds in a way that many historians might hesitate to undertake. But since my own childhood I have been fascinated with the subject and amazed at how relatively easy it has been for me to form friendships with women, while it seems relaively difficult in our culture to form close friendships with other men.

In the last few years an influx of refugees from the Middle East into Denmark has given me an opportunity to view and to experience at first hand the friendships possible in another culture. My work with refugees—while giving a chance for friendships—has also meant that the last chapters of this book were written in a quite different mental world from the first ones. A theoretical involvement with historical communities has been combined with practical involvement in the sufferings and hopes of refugee communities. At every step of the way I have sensed the strength of the background I have had in medieval life and experience. At the same time, however, I have been aware that I have been serving two masters: past history and contemporary politics. But the one commitment has led naturally and inevitably to the other, as if an old Europe of monasteries and friends could provide refuge and hope at a time when the West has tried to close itself off from the needs and sufferings of the rest of the world. In this new context I have felt renewed strength and inspiration from visiting present-day Cistercian communities in the United States and talking to their members about friendship. Problems and possibilities are similar today to those of the later twelfth century. Then as now, a new openness in human relationships is being replaced by a hesitant return to discipline and recourse to authority.

The period during which I have been preparing this book, 1982-87, has coincided with the spread of a new disease in the western world, Acquired Immune Deficiency Syndrome, popularly known as AIDS. This illness is now being compared to the Black Plague of the fourteenth century in terms of its potential for threatening our lives and culture. Whatever happens in the coming years, I hope that the contents of this book are not used in a polemic concerning sex versus friendship as part of the AIDS debate. In my mind, sexuality and the expression of human emotion cannot be separated. They are part of the same human impulse for warmth and unity. In sex as in friendship there are no simple answers: every human experience is different. AIDS is already influencing sexual behaviour and human interrelationships, and here the medieval experience might easily be misunderstood as 'proof' that celibate friendships are preferable to sexual relationships. Monastic friendships are obviously based on an avoidance of what we might call genital sexuality, but these friendships cannot be seen in individual, isolated terms. They flourished because they could grow up within loving communities. It is the aspect of community, not that of sexuality, which I hope provides the central interest in the pages that follow. Our culture is today in danger not so much because of the spread of disease as because of its failure to produce viable communities in which individuals can find meaning and inspiration in each other. Here the medieval monastic experience has something to tell us.

At every step of the creation of this book, I have been fortunate enough to be able to turn to distinguished colleagues whose guidance I have needed. Sir Richard Southern of Oxford, who once tutored me in the theology of Saint Anselm, has read early drafts of several chapters and has given invaluable advice. The late Beryl Smalley encouraged me to get on with the book at a time when I was ready to give it up. Peter Brown of Princeton has commented on some of the early chapters and has provided many helpful insights. I will always remember a conversation in his garden at Berkeley in 1982, when I was just beginning this work. He reoriented my view of friendship in antique society. Dom Jean Leclercq's contribution to this book can easily be seen in the bibliography. Where I go, he has already been. His brief notes, full of encouragement and suggested articles to read, are surely already legendary among medieval scholars. I am grateful to have benefited from the friendship of this monk in orbit.

Others who have made similar contributions are: John Benton at the California Institute of Technology; Robert Benson of UCLA; Walter Goffart at the University of Toronto; Giles Constable at Princeton's Center for Advanced Studies; Dom Alberic Stacpoole of Saint Benets, Oxford; Benedicta Ward at Oxford's Centre for Medieval and Renaissance Studies; Sir Kenneth Dover at Corpus Christi College, Oxford; Anthony Kenny at Balliol; the cistercian communities of the USA that I visited in the spring of 1986, especially Father Thomas Davis at New Clairvaux in Vina, California; and Kirsten Grubb Jensen and Graham Caie at the Medieval Centre in Copenhagen, constant friends and loyal critics as well as my colleagues at the Institute for Greek and Latin Philology.

Special thanks are due to my friends in Kalamazoo, especially to Rozanne Elder, whose careful and wise corrections and suggestions have caught many a slip and improved many a phrase that was descending into the depths of Dinglish, Danish English.

In spite of such good advisors, I am sure that there remain mistakes and oversights for which I am culpable. For these I ask for the reader's *benevolentia,* even if he or she cannot give *consensus.*

I dedicate this book to the memory of my father, Dan Francis, who died all too young in 1983 and whose friendship I miss, and to my mother Phyllis Evelyn, whose friendship remains one of the strongest bonds of my life.

B.P.M[c]G

Copenhagen
University
June 1987

INTRODUCTION

THE DEBATE ON FRIENDSHIP: ANTECEDENTS AND INTERPRETERS

PRESENT IN ONE WAY or another in all cultures, friendship seems to be a universal human phenomenon. Its very universality, however, makes it difficult to study friendship in a well-defined social and human context. Forms of friendship slip away from the intruding fingers of the historian. Literary considerations, silence in the sources, and especially a tendency to take friendship for granted: all these factors make harrowing and frustrating the attempt to 'isolate' friendship from other social phenomena. Already a half-century ago, one of the most attentive writers on the subject admitted:

> . . .when looked at more closely, friendship reveals itself as being quite complex in itself and very diverse in its areas. For a long time it has been regretted that our vocabulary concerning manifestations of the affective life is much poorer than that which concerns the intellectual life.[1]

The writer of these lines was a good theologian brought up on the teaching of Thomas Aquinas in its modernized form. He was used to dividing human life up into neat areas of classification. Here, however, he admitted from the start that great problems were involved. Today many historians might claim that the subject of friendship in itself defies analysis because it almost never can be narrowed down to a well-defined pattern of thought and behaviour in a given culture. To this contention the only answer is twofold: first, to try to deal with friendship in a clearly demarcated historical and cultural context; secondly, to recall that the humanities, if they are to concern themselves with human beings, must insist on dealing with areas of life that cannot be categorized and quantified. Every new generation will continue to contribute its own experience and insights.

My view of friendship in history results in part from my own experience of friendship. For the generation born in Western countries after the Second World War, friendship has been a major concern in life. This may be due to the fact that leisure time and material prosperity have let us deal with interpersonal relationships in a conscious way. At the same time my generation was brought up with an idealistic view of human bonds and a belief in the reality and power of love in spiritual relationships.

How does one get behind the abundant literary commonplaces or *topoi* about friendship to the people who formed them and to their feelings for each other? There are a number of approaches, all of which will be used in this work. First of all, I shall try to look at as much of the evidence as possible. Instead of limiting myself to one literary genre, such as that of letterwriting, I will include the descriptions of friendships found in chronicles, essays, monastic rules, and even poems, though the last present special problems because of requirements of form. Theoretical treatises are sometimes illuminating because they set up an ideal world which shows how the author's society visualized the possibility of friendship. Sometimes the very mass of the evidence provides an assurance that the historian is not being led astray by a brilliant piece of prose or poetry. Repetitions and commonplaces form a pattern that reveals to what extent authors are trying to impress each other and to what extent they may be reaching out to each other as persons and friends.

A second aspect of my approach will be, as already implied, its chronological and cultural limitations. By dealing with the period from about 350 to 1250 in the West (except for some initial remarks on the Eastern desert tradition), I will be able to look upon fairly uniform cultural wholeness in which the central ideals are clear to us, its heirs, and visible in the sources. In concentrating on the monastic sources, I limit this study to a world even more apparent and transparent than that of the much broader clerical milieu. At times, however, we will have to move outside of the monastery into the broader cultural stream in order to see the monastic development in its proper context. I stop at about 1250 because by then monastic-religious dominance in european culture had ended. Forms of friendship that brought cultural renewal and which reflect social change become more visible in other circles in the writings of Thomas Aquinas or in the non-clerical poets Dante, Boccaccio and Chaucer. Another book will perhaps someday be dedicated to the late medieval development.

A third characteristic in my method is its attempt to trace a development that is historical, for I see friendship not as a static phenomenon but as an expression of human binding that varies according to circumstances. These can be material factors such as the size and wealth of monasteries or the basis of their recruitment, or there can be intellectual considerations, such as the popularity of certain classical authors. Whatever the case may be, I shall argue that the very mention of friendship is significant: when monks choose to describe their lives in community in terms of individual friendships, then the literary popularity of the subject hints at the reality and desirability of genuine friendships.

This historical approach will be supported by a fourth element in my study: a consideration of friendship in the context of human communities. It is my contention that individual friendships cannot be understood outside of their relationship to the communities in which they are nurtured. In the medieval world practically everyone had a place and a role. No letter of friendship was written outside the context of the communities to which the correspondents belonged. This may seem a statement of the obvious, but we must make it in order to avoid concentrating exclusively on the personal bond and taking for granted the concomitant bond of community. It might sound more modern and more 'scientific' to talk about 'friendship and society', but for this writer medieval society was made up of a wealth of communities. My question has been to what extent close personal bonds found nourishment or obstacles within these various types of communities, especially monastic groups.

A final aspect of my approach is its attempt to relate the theory of friendship to actual practice. In both the Middle Ages and our own time, much that is written about friendship says little or nothing about everyday life. I do not delude myself by hoping that the following pages will provide a clear outline of any single friendship, for that would require a book in itself. There should at least be traces of the growth and development of several human relationships within a historical context. There is almost always a tension between theory and practice in monastic life and this can especially be seen when we deal with the practice of friendship. How far could friends go in cherishing each other when their main duty was to follow the Rule of Saint Benedict, which says virtually nothing about friendship? Ideals of closeness and sharing of self find their ultimate test in the monastery's well-defined sense of community and collectivity. In the monastic person-community conflict appears a microcosm of a dilemma as old as Christianity itself: how to love God and to love neighbour, and especially one or two neighbours. Practice and theory must be taken together in order to grasp medieval culture as a whole—and medieval people as individual persons within a collective culture.

A DEFINITION OF FRIENDSHIP

Before going any further we need to provide some sort of working definition for friendship. The classic statement of friendships comes from Cicero: 'complete identity of feeling about all things divine and human, as strengthened by mutual goodwill and affection.'[2] This definition attracted eleventh- and twelfth-century writers on the subject. Because so many of Cicero's terms are vague and invite quibbling and discussion, I would, however prefer to use a much briefer definition, which apparently first appears in the writings of Gregory the Great and soon gained celebrity, especially thanks to its inclusion in the magpie medieval encyclopedia, the *Etymologiae* of Isidore of Seville. According to Gregory and Isidore, a friend is the guardian of one's soul, *custos animi*.[3] By using this, rather than a more theoretical description of friendship, we can be more flexible about what its requirements are and less prone to reduce friendship to theory rather than practice. Being *custos animi* implies three elements in a relationship:

1) responsibility for another person's well-being and ultimate salvation
2) a knowledge of his or her inner life
3) a spiritual dimension

This bond does not necessarily imply equality or even mutuality. A monk can express friendship to another monk without ever receiving anything in return. Mutuality is, however, by no means ruled out and the guardianship can be reciprocal.

Today mutuality in friendship is usually taken for granted: the sharing of selves is seen as the foundation of friendship.[4] In the medieval sources we often know about only one side of a relationship, and so our more limited definition of friendship enables us to use the term in a less demanding manner. The idea of spiritual guardianship, however, opens the door to the bond of spiritual father and son, so important in the Egyptian desert and a model for monastic bonds all through the Middle Ages and beyond. When this responsibility is combined with contact to the feelings and inner life of another person, the spiritual dimension comes of itself. In knowing another person and taking responsibility for his or her salvation, the friend accepts a spiritual bond. In this way we do not have to add the usual modern proviso about 'celibate friendship', for in the monastic world celibacy is a point of departure for all community life. It is not a matter of immediate concern in friendship. The close bond, so long as it remains within the spirit of the monastic life, replaces any overtly sexual element by a tenderness and affection that can be physical without being genitally sexual. There is of course no absolute and sharp division between sexual expression and the manifestation of affection, but in a community with clear rules about chastity, there is usually a general consensus about limits and 'dangers'.

The medieval monastic word for friendship, *amicitia,* appears in our sources much less often than does the word for friend, *amicus.* It is appropriate that we follow Isidore and Gregory in concentrating on the living friend in order to understand the practices of friendship. Here we find the advantage and the pitfall of using words that also exist in our own time and culture. In speaking of 'friend' or 'friendship', one uses a term that existed a thousand years ago, unlike the tricky terms 'feudalism' or 'courtly love', which moderns invented to describe medieval patterns of life. The very sharing of terms between our age and an earlier one, however, makes it difficult to distinguish between our own experience of friendship and the medieval one. Two dangers appear: either we posit a facile similarity of all human experience, with no historical dimension, or else we conclude that the identity of vocabulary actually hides the fact that we know little or nothing about individual friendships in another age so different from our own.

Here it is essential to remember that the idea and experience of friendship were important for our ancestors and that we can follow the development of their concept of friendship by looking carefully at the places in the sources where friendship is mentioned. Friendship is always present, as are tears. But there are some periods in Western history where friendship is a subject of great interest, while in other periods and contexts it has been taken for granted or ignored. Perhaps the only complete history of friendship would also have to be a history of the modes of expressing grief in the West, for in lamenting over the dead friend, one describes what he meant in one's life.[5] There is no doubt that the great age of monastic friendship, the twelfth century, is also a period when there are floods of tears for dead friends. For the moment it is enough to point out that the way of describing friends and friendships varies from one period to the next. This variation in theme and the expression of experience we will follow through the available sources. My results may well seem limited and quite preliminary, but what follows can be looked upon as a point of departure for further and more profound studies which must consider more closely the various languages of friendship in their varying cultural contexts throughout history.

BIBLICAL EXPRESSIONS OF FRIENDSHIP

The major source for medieval views of friendship, besides lived experience itself, is the Bible, with its wealth of stories, sayings and teachings. In the Old Testament friendship is accepted as a natural aspect of human behaviour. When God speaks to Moses on Sinai, he is said to have addressed him 'face to face, as a man speaks to a friend' (Ex 33:11). The image reflects Yahweh as a personal being who deals with human beings in terms of human relations. The most detailed biblical description of friendship is found in the story of Jonathan and David. No explanation is given of how the friendship began. The first book of Kings (1 Samuel) merely records the event in the wake of David's defeat of Goliath.[6] The affection is expressed mainly in terms of Jonathan's devotion to David, his concern for David's wellbeing and safety. The two of them are described as making a pact, in latin *foedus*, an expression that may be behind a phrase later popular in medieval letterwriting, *foedus amicitiae.*[7] Jonathan's selfless friendship for the man who was to replace his own dynasty in the rule of Israel gained the attention of the twelfth-century writer Aelred of Rievaulx. But the bond between the two youths was often seen primarily in allegorical terms, as in the venerable Bede's interpretation of it in terms of the love between Christ and the Church.[8]

If one reviews carefully all the expressions used to describe the friendship between David and Jonathan, one finds remarkably little material in comparison to the steadfast legend of their friendship which permeates Western literature. There is not enough for us to see any development of friendship. The bond is presented as a fact. It guarantees David's physical survival despite the wrath of King Saul. Jonathan is the instrument of David's salvation, but only once are we told about David's feelings for Jonathan. This comes in David's lament after Jonathan's death. In the Vulgate translation, the one used by our medieval friends, there is a striking passage which compensates for much of the previous reticence:

> Doleo super te, frater mi Ionatha, decore nimis et amabilis super amorem mulierum. Sicut mater unicum amat filium suum, ita ego te diligebam.[9]

> (I am distressed for you, my brother Jonathan; very pleasant have you been to me; your love to me was wonderful, passing the love of women. As a mother loves her only son, so I was loving you.)

David describes his love in terms of that of a mother's love for her son, a surprising image in view of the fact that it was Jonathan who was David's protector. But the David who speaks these lines is the victorious future king of Israel and no longer the persecuted boy. There is a political dimension in the friendship of David and Jonathan. The involvement of Jonathan's father, King Saul, his jealousy of David, and his determination to make sure that Jonathan and not David is his successor: all these factors complicate the personal bond and make for a political triangle of jealousy/love. Jonathan's lack of interest in inheriting the crown is taken for granted. His whole life is centred on helping David, in making sure that 'the Lord be between me and you and between my seed and your seed forever' (1 Sam. 20:41) Personal and political motives are inextricably mixed here, for Jonathan's love for David is based on his sense of guardianship: "for he loved him as his own soul".[10]

The pact between them is sealed when Jonathan gives David his armour, sword, bow and even his clothes (18:4). The two of them weep and embrace each other after their separation. The personal story is set in the context of the development of the kingdom of Israel, which at the same time is the story of the salvation of the people of God, whose leader in his envy turns away from God and has to be punished.

David is a warrior hero in the mould of many an antique fighter, and his bosom friendship has parallels with that of classical pairs such as Achilles and Patroclus. In such warrior bonds, outer characteristics dominate: the sealing of pacts of friendship, heroic deeds, signs of love, declarations of attachment, but we are told little about the inner life of the friends. In the Old Testament story, however, there is sufficient commentary in the narration that we cannot be mistaken about Jonahan's feelings for David, while David's lament for Jonathan provides so concrete an image of love, that of the mother for her only son, that the friendship is portrayed in terms of reciprocity.[11]

At no time is there any hint of a sexual element in this bond. Here as in so much of medieval literature (and the latin Vulgate text can be seen as the central work of medieval literature), we must shed the accretions of the last century and realize that the question of what we call homosexuality was not an especially interesting or relevant topic for the people for whom such close bonds were important.[12] In the David-Jonathan bond as in so many others there is no explicit sexual dimension, and so the story could easily be integrated into the central tradition of christian spiritual friendship.

Other books of the Old Testament provide no similar instance of close friendship. The word *amicitia* is often used in the historical books to denote political alliances between different countries, a usage that will also be found in medieval Latin.[13] In the book of Job friends are used as an audience for the man whom God has allowed to be deprived of everything. Eventually even the friends are gone: *et quem maxime diligebam, aversatus est me* (Job 19:19). Here as elsewhere in the Old Testament friends are looked upon as a natural part of human society. A man needs his friends almost as much as his relatives. There is no need to defend the concept of friendship. Its practice is accepted without question. The problem in Job is not whether or not to believe in friendship: it is whether to believe in one's friends.

The Psalms say little about human friendships. Their main concern is the bond between God and his people, an angry, jealous but loving God to whom man can turn for help in need. God has his friends, who are rewarded.[14] The only mention of a human friend concerns the man who betrays a friend and becomes his enemy. This theme is present in many Old Testament passages: the fair-weather friend who in time of need is not there or who outrightly betrays his companion:

> It is not an enemy who taunts me, then I could bear it. . . But it is you, my equal, my companion, my familiar friend.
> We used to hold sweet converse together: within God's house we walked in fellowship.
> Let death come upon them: let them go down to Sheol alive (Ps 54:13-15).

Because friends cannot be trusted, only the Lord provides hope of salvation. 'But I call upon God, and the Lord will save me'. This idea of

God as our only help contributes to a major theme of christian literature: the search for a true friend who will never let us down often ends in our finding Jesus.

The passionate language of the Psalms with a bitter/sweet bond between man and God leaves open the possibility of substituting another human being for God and borrowing the expressions to describe human bonds that bring love and joy. Over the centuries the Psalms were a constant source of inspiration not only for describing the individual's yearning for God but also for expressing the strength of interpersonal human affections. One of the Psalms actually encourages the conception of a bond among likeminded men: *Ecce quam bonum et quam iucundum habitare fratres in unum* (Ps 133:1: Behold how good and pleasant it is when brothers dwell in unity). This line, perhaps more than any other from the Old Testament, provided a vision of a community of men who enjoy being each other's friends. It is an ideal to which we frequently will return: the good community makes for good friendships; where there is no conflict between individual bonds and the social structure.

The richest source for friendship in the Old Testament is its wisdom literature: the books of Proverbs, Ecclesiastes, Wisdom, and especially the Book of Jesus Sirach (Ecclesiasticus, as it was known in the Middle Ages). The very form of this literature, with its lists of brief sayings, makes it difficult to generalize about its contents. As elsewhere in the Old Testament there is an acceptance of friendship as a basic human bond, an important concern and a potential cause for disappointment and disillusionment. Proverbs even make the categorical statement that a friend loves at all times *(omni tempore diligit qui amicus est:* 17:17). The second half of this statement (in the Vulgate *et frater in angustiis comprobatur)* is not so absolute, for it makes the obvious point also accepted in classical literature that 'a friend in need is a friend indeed'. Jerome and later writers, however, stuck to the first half of the statement and insisted that friendship, in order to be true, must be indissoluble.

Proverbs provide much 'good advice' about how to keep friends: one is not to belittle a friend and to be trustworthy and keep his secrets (11:12). He who wants friends must be able to forgive and forget offences (17:9). Anyone who picks a fight with a friend will regret it

(25:8). Friendship requires openness (*meliora sunt vulnera diligentis quam fradulenta oscula odientis* (27:6). Friendship is connected to family in a striking saying: 'Your friend and your father's friend, do not forsake' (27:10). In the midst of warnings against the false friend and the flatterer, we find an assertion of the joys of friendship:

> Unguento et variis odoribus delectatur cor, et bonis
> amici consiliis anima dulcoratur (27:9)
> (Oil and perfume make the heart glad and the soul
> grows sweet on the good counsels of a friend).

Friendship is seen as an attractive goal in human life, a bond that is linked to that of the family but which is still independent of it, a potential problem for those who are not careful in distinguishing real from fair-weather friends, as well as a great consolation for those in trouble.

The most pessimistic of all the wisdom books, Ecclesiastes, provides a description of friendship that is remarkably positive and without any of the shadows to be found in the Proverbs:

Melius est ergo duos esse simul quam unum: habent enim emolumentum societatis suae.	Two are better than one, because they have a reward for their companionship.
Si unus ceciderit, ab altero fulcietur.	For if one should fall, he will be lifted up by the other.
Vae soli, quia, cum ceciderit, non habet sublevantem se.	Woe to him who is alone when he falls and has not another to lift him up.
Et si dormierint duo, fovebuntur mutuo: unus quomodo caleficiet?	Again, if two lie together, they can provide heat for each other, but how will one find warmth alone?
Et, si quispiam praevaluerit contra unum, duo resistunt ei:	And though someone might overcome a man who is alone,

funiculus triplex difficile rumpitur. (Eccles 4:9-12)

two will be able to withstand him. A threefold cord is difficult to break.

Here the advantages of companionship are seen in terms of the formation of *societas*, a bond that provides guidance, warmth, and defence. Practical, exterior advantages are listed, but a spiritual dimension is also implied. The content of the phrases may seem hardly extraordinary (what we today would call common sense?). What is attractive about the passage is its literary form, imagery and variation. In the midst of a world where all is vanity, the bond of friendship holds an almost unique place as the one aspect of human life that promises consolation and even joy.

One might expect a similar lyricism about friendship in the Song of Songs, but here the language is more exclusively erotic. There is one passage, however, where the beloved is called *amicus meus* (Song 5:16). As in the Psalms there remains the possibility that passionate language used to describe one form of bond can be transferred to another. In the sentence, 'I find him whom my soul loved: I held him and would not let him go' (3:4), the idea of fidelity in friendship can replace that of erotic love. As we will see in later discussions of friendship, the friend who loves at all times will not let his friend go, no matter what. In Aelred of Rievaulx the kiss of true lovers (Song 1:1) is seen in terms of the kiss of friends bound by a single law of friendship. This kiss is not a physical act but an expression of the heart's affection.[15]

Friendship among men is occasionally linked in the Old Testament with friendship with God, as in the Book of Wisdom, where we are told of the infinite treasure available for men who can be 'made sharers in the friendship of God' (7:14). In this striking passage, as in the description of Moses on the mountain, the unspeakable God becomes a being who can be approached in terms of human affection. This theme is also taken up in Ecclesiasticus, also known as the Book of Jesus Sirach, where the fear of the Lord is seen as the foundation of human friendship: *Qui timet Deum aeque habebit amicitiam bonam quoniam secundum illum erit amicus illius* (He who fears God will likewise have a good friendship because his friend will be according to the Lord: Si 6:17).

Here is a point of departure for spiritual friendship in the Christian tradition: the bond between two human beings is linked to their attachment to God. Because they are close to God, they can be close to each other.

The book of Jesus Sirach contains perhaps the most complete biblical description of the joys and rewards of friendship, a passage even today found in greeting cards and popular literature on friendship:

> A faithful friend is a strong defence.
> He that has found him has found a treasure.
> Nothing can be compared to a faithful friend,
> and no weight of gold and silver
> can countervail the goodness of his fidelity.
> A faithful friend is the medicine of life and immortality,
> And they that fear the Lord shall find him
>
> *Amicus fidelis protectio fortis,*
> *qui autem invenit illum invenit thesaurum.*
> *Amico fideli nulla est comparatio*
> *et non est digna ponderatio auri et argenti*
> *contra bonitatem fidei illius.*
> *Amicus fidelis medicamentum vitae et immortalitatis*
> *et qui metuunt Dominum invenient illum.* (Si 6:14-16).

Here the central expression is *amicus fidelis.* Once there is mutual trust and dependability, friendship has a foundation that is the most valuable possession in the world. With the faithful friend the sorrows of life can be endured. With the faithful friend we are on the path to God.

This lyric passage is counterbalanced by warnings against the fair-weather friend *(amicus secundum tempus suum)*, who lets one down when the going gets rough *(et non permanebit in die tribulationis:* 6:8). This concern appears often in the books of the Old Testament: superficiality in apparent friendship. The real friend is revealed not in prosperity but in adversity (12:8-9). *Fides* is the leading motif in Ecclesiasticus on friendship. An old friend should not be left, for a new one will not be the same. This is because a new friend is like a new wine that takes time to mature and acquire a gentle taste (9:14-15: *Ne derelinquas amicum antiquum: novus erit non similis illi).*

To a trusted friend, one can open the heart, because of the harmony *(concordatio)* that exists between the friends:

> Be faithful to your friend in his poverty so that you can rejoice with him in his prosperity (22:28). Blessed is he who finds a true friend (25:12). From his face I shall not hide myself and if evils befall him, I shall support him (19:31).

Ecclesiasticus does not analyse the content and meaning of friendship. It assumes that friendship is a foundation of human society and desirable for everyone. The problem lies in how to maintain friendship, and the solution in fidelity to the friend, come what may, and in union with the friend in God. Here we are close to hellenistic thought about friendship as a virtue, as we shall see when we look at Aristotle and his successors. The political-personal friendship of David and Jonathan in the Book of Samuel has been replaced by a more individualized ideal of spiritual friendship, but the emphasis on fidelity remains the same. The main interest of the writers of the books of the Old Testament was the progress of the people of God. As we move through the centuries from the Pentateuch to the Wisdom literature, there is more emphasis on the interior life of the individual and in his personal relationship with God and with other people.

Because of the late appearance and unsure position of Jesus Sirach's book in the cannon of Scripture, it never achieved the prominence that other wisdom books did. The first known commentary on it is attributed to Rhabanus Maurus, a carolingian writer whose interest in friendship is reflected in his remarks here as well as in other works.[16] There is no doubt that the friendship of David and Jonathan provided the most noticed and memorable Old Testament passage on the subject, but one should not underestimate the wealth, beauty, good sense, and authority of the Wisdom literature in treating friendship as a natural human phenomenon but also as a bond that could link good men to God. The individulization of the bond of friendship that can be seen in the wisdom books is indicative of a development in

Hebrew literature towards a broader, more universal context in a concern not only for God's chosen people as a whole, but also for personal relationships.

DUALITY ON FRIENDSHIP IN THE NEW TESTAMENT

The narration in John's gospel of Jesus's words at the Last Supper contains a central statement he was remembered as having made on friendship to his apostles:

> This is my commandment, that you love one another as I have loved you. Greater love has no man than this, that a man lay down his life for his friends. You are my friends if you do what I command you. No longer do I call you servants for the servant does not know what his master is doing: but I have called you friends, for all that I have heard from my Father, I have made known to you (Jn 15:12-17).

The commandment of love is based on Christ's willingness to show his love for us by dying for us. But it is important to realize that Jesus described his act of love in terms of an order, not a request. To be his friend, we *must* obey him. Not as servants, for we have a right to know what he knows from his Father, though even so there must be an element of acquiescence in order to make friendship with Jesus possible. 'You are my friends if you do what I command you': the christian imperative sweeps away any element of sentimentality in friendship and links it to a total commitment to the truth that is Jesus. Friendship with God, suggested a few places in the Old Testament, takes on a much more concrete, humanized form. But its content is by no means idyllic, for the message of Jesus is categorical: Love me, love one another, and obey me.

If we look at the Jesus represented in the four gospels, he appears a man who offered friendship only on uncompromising terms. He made it clear that there is no merit in loving those who already love us (Ma 5:46). Christian love *(dilectio* or *agapé)* is not the same as *amicitia,* for christian love is universal, not preferential. Only in loving one's enemies can one show oneself to be a true follower of Christ. In making this commitment the friends of the world have to change their ways and become friends of Christ, as Saint James pointed out in his epistle:

> *Amicitia hujus mundi inimica est Dei: quicumque ergo voluerit amicus esse saeculi hujus, inimicus Dei constituitur.*
>
> Do you not know that friendship with the world is enmity with God? Therefore whoever wishes to be a friend of the world makes himself an enemy of God. (4:4)

The friends of the world were well remembered in medieval monastic writers, for the process of conversion to the monastic life meant giving up such friends.

Strictly interpreted, the sayings of Christ leave little or no room for individual friends and friendships. Loyalty and devotion to Jesus become so important and central that all other human bonds are severed. As Jesus said, 'Whoever does the will of my Father in heaven is my brother and sister and mother' (Mt 12:50). We might add the term 'friend.' Today Jesus is usually seen as a man of peace, but he can also be remembered for the times when he spoke out for division and confrontation in the worldly order to realize his goal of union with the Father: 'I have come to bring not peace, but a sword. For I have come to set a man against his father and a daughter against her mother. . .'. (Mt 10:34-35).

This strict and uncompromising Jesus who requires that all bonds of sentiment be severed must be seen together with the Jesus who loved Martha and Mary and called Lazarus his friend (Jn 11:11: *Lazarus amicus noster)*. He wept for Lazarus and thus showed the Jews that he loved him: *Et lacrimatus est Iesus. Dixerunt ergo Iudaei: Ecce quomodo amabat eum* (Jn 11:34-35). The same Jesus made it clear that he especially loved his apostle John: 'One of his disciples, whom Jesus loved, was lying close to the breast of Jesus' (Jn 13:23). This is also the Jesus who in his parables used the word 'friend' in describing human relationships and took it for granted that people have friends (Lk 11:5). In the parable of the lost sheep, the man who has found the stray "calls together his friends and his neighbours, saying to them, Rejoice with me" (Lk 15:4-6).

Jesus demands our all-embracing love and yet can be seen in the Gospels as having accepted preferential loves. He allows for friendships as a natural part of human life. The uncompromising Christ who demands total devotion must be seen together with the gentle, understanding Christ. Both will play a role in the coming age. The friendship of Christ with Lazarus would enable coming generations of Christians to justify their own friendships. Christians could think of the requirement of separation from friends and family in the world in terms of their own choice of an ascetic life where they could find new spiritual friends and relations. Thus the friends of the world would be replaced in fellowship by the friends of Christ.

Jesus himself had promised that 'where two or three are gathered in my name, there am I in the midst of them' (Mt 18:30). Christian friendship provides a new family and new bonds of affection. The joyous language of Psalm 133 (to 132) about how good and pleasant it is when brothers dwell in unity could be used to describe the early christian communities of believers. This evocation of harmony lay behind the portrayal in the Acts of the Apostles of the one heart and one soul of the first christian community in Jerusalem (4:32). The *cor unum et anima una* image provided in the coming centuries a frequent point of reference for the projection or construction of a christian network of friends. At times the one heart and soul was seen in terms of the christian community as a whole, but during periods when individual friendships were looked upon as worthy pursuits, the phrase was also applied to them.

The early Christians called each other brothers, not friends. The family bond, not that of friendship, was chosen as the mode of expressing spiritual community. In the writings of Saint Paul there is much greater emphasis on group solidarity than on individual bonds. Paul himself, unlike Christ, does not reveal himself in terms of close individual friendships.[17] His goal was Christ alone, through the strengthening of the christian churches. In so doing he was willing to "become all things to all men" so that he could work for their salvation (. . . *omnibus omnia factus sum, ut omnes facerem salvos,* 1 Cor 9:22).

In calling upon Jesus Christ and the gospel for this metamorphosis of self, Paul provided a point of departure for what to this day remains a christian imperative: scaling down and proportioning individual loves for the sake of an all-embracing love of Jesus and his Father. In this total commitment, the Christian is willing to be friend to the person in need, to be critical of those who need to be criticized, to be gentle with those who cannot bear harshness. What gets lost is the person behind the transformation, the individual at the core of self-sacrificing love. Other people receive care and affection, while one's own personality and identity retreat into the background. The person who would save his life must lose it, but in so losing it he gives up his friends and concentrates on the commands of the one true friend, Jesus Christ.

In loving God and in loving his neighbour, and in bringing his neighbour to God, the Christian of pauline observance has little room for anything but the cause. This is putting matters on edge, because past history shows a great variety of interpretations of the christian message. But the fact remains that in the pauline version, the individual becomes a mere instrument for spreading the good news. As we shall see in so Christ-like a figure as Francis of Assisi, one can be a friend to one of the brethren who needs a friend without expressing one's own needs. This is why the medieval definition of friendship often does not go beyond that of the soul-guardian, for the christian approach does not necessarily include mutuality or sharing of like impulses and in some cases even legislates against it. In becoming all things to all men, the follower of Christ can come to believe that he cannot be a special friend to any particular man, at least not for long.

John on the breast of Jesus or Jesus at the tomb of Lazarus provided guarantees that friendship could not be banished from christian history. In the early Middle Ages, however, John's special attachment to Christ was attributed to his chastity. Among all the apostles, he was the one remembered as a virgin. Only in the eleventh and twelfth centuries, as we shall see in the writings of Anselm, did John's role in terms of friendship with Christ come into prominence. This development parallels a general awakening of literary and intellectual interest in friendship. The narrowness of the pauline approach and the hardness of some of Christ's sayings were softened by concentration on the humanity of Christ, a humanity that allowed for individual friends. For the early Christians what was most important was the establishment of communities of believers, while for their late-eleventh century successors Christianity was a fact of life, the very stuff of society. A firebrand religion, which had almost asked for persecution, had become a force of renewal at the core of a dynamic society. Within it sensitive and sensible men could describe spiritual yearnings in terms of bonds based on friendship and love.

CLASSICAL CONCEPTS OF FRIENDSHIP

Medieval writers on friendship drew on classical literature as well as on the Bible. Much of the eleventh-century rediscovery of friendship can and must be linked to the new schools and their interest in classical texts. Until the thirteenth century and even later, however, much of classical literature was not accessible to men of letters in the West. Through the writings of Cicero and especially his *De amicitia,* medieval clerics and monks did have a useful summary of the antique discussions about friendship. With Cicero as a point of reference for a medieval view of friendship that at times could disregard pauline absolutism, we can go behind him to the greek background from which Cicero's work emerged.

For both aristocratic greek and roman males, friendship was the most natural thing in the world.[18] It was the foundation of the state, the point of departure for all worthwhile human relationships. The presocratic Empedocles held that love/friendship (for the greek word *philia*) is what makes the world go round. Empedocles saw opposing forces of love and strife. Love brings things together in unity; strife separates them.[19] This idea attracted Cicero, who translated Empedocles's love as *amicitia.*[20] This concept of friendship as a glue binding men, cities, and the world together is prominent both in Aristotle's *Nichomachean Ethics* and in Cicero's *De amicitia.* For us it is a cliché belonging more to a pop song than to any description of the universe and of human society, but for Aristotle and his pupil Theophrastus (whose treatise on friendship is lost except for some fragments) 'friendship seems to hold states together' (1155a).[21]

Aristotle distinguished between friendships based on utility or mutual advantage, friendships based on the pursuit of pleasure, and friendships based on virtue. In doing so he provided a broad spectrum for friendship, even though he insisted that true or 'perfect friendship is the friendship of men who are good and alike in virtue' (1156a). Aristotle's analysis of friendship, which takes up two books of the *Nichomachean Ethics,* is a wonderfully clear and pragmatic exposition of the subject that never loses sight of the theoretical problems involved. He links individual friendships and their benefits to the whole life of the community. The famed passage in which Aristotle describes forms of government is merely a corollary of his description of the types of human bonds (1160b-1161a). For Aristotle individual relationships provide a point of departure for all societal bonds and even for the running of the state.

Aristotle characterizes friendship as a close personal bond. Friends need to live together in order to keep this bond alive. If they have to live apart for a time, the friendship can be endangered (1157b). Aristotle concedes the problem of flattery and falseness in friendship. He admits that social inequality can create difficulties, and he includes a long section on how to break off friendship when one party cannot accept the behaviour of the other (1165a). So much of what Aristotle says is what we today might consider 'common sense' that it would be easy to forget that he provided central definitions of human relations. There is, however, no specifically spiritual dimension in Aristotle's description of friendship. He sees it as a natural and inevitable bond in the world as it is. He indicates no desire to relate it to any god-given gift. But he does insist that in order to be happy one must have friends:

> It is said that those who are supremely happy and self-sufficient have no need of friends, for they have the things that are good and therefore being self-sufficient they need nothing further. . . . But it seems strange when one assigns all good things to the happy man, not to assign friends, who are thought the greatest of eternal goods. (1169b)

Aristotle, perhaps basing his theory on his own experience, sees the good life in terms of men living together 'and sharing in discussion and thought' (1170b). Here the conception of friendship is closely linked to the intellectual community, a dream that would deeply influence such late antique christian thinkers as Augustine. Friendship is exclusive and yet not seclusive: one can have only a few close friends but one can show good will to many people.

Aristotle merged political and personal friendships. The Greek *polis* provides a milieu in which male citizens know each other and are able to select a few close lifelong companions. For those who love wisdom and pursue truth, friendship can move beyond need and pleasure and become an exercise in virtue, though Aristotle does not insist that virtue excludes mutual benefits and enjoyment. He looks at the world he sees around him and accepts its order and chaos. Friends grieve for each other. They take as a blow the loss of a friend. They try to keep up a front with friends who have disappointed them but with whom they do not want to break openly. Friendship is one of the major forms of human contact: 'Men want to live with their friends, they do and share in those things which give them the sense of living together' (1172a). It is always to be sought: 'The presence of friends. . . seems desirable in all circumstances' (1171b).

No question of a sexual element entered his definition, for Aristotle dealt with relationships between mature men who were more or less equals in age, experience, and social position. Greek homosexual behaviour normally took place between an older and a younger man as an enjoyable pastime and as a part of the young man's upbringing and even military training.[22] It was this form of friendship which Plato took as his point of departure for the Socratic pursuit of goodness and virtue. In the *Symposium* the procedure is most clearly outlined: one advances from the individual beautiful young man to an appreciation of the beauty in all youths and then to beauty itself and on to the unchanging ideas.[23] There are many hints in the dialogues that Socrates himself was attracted by handsome youths, but his argument moves away from sexual friendship to the pursuit of an ideal where individual human beings become of secondary importance. This concept of reality in terms of hierarchy was merged with christian thought, along with the belief in divine ideas. The merger came at a very early point (it can be seen in Augustine most clearly but was probably already present long before him). The neoplatonic hierarchy dominated the medieval view of the universe until the thirteenth century.[24] Individual human bonds had to be joined and submitted to an all-encompassing good, the love of God. By the time of Augustine the greek point of departure in homosexuality had been forgotten or was ignored. The Western literature of the monastery, as we shall see, has almost nothing about homosexual behaviour. The main platonic dialogue on friendship, the *Lysis,* had no circulation at all in the West in our period, and so medieval writers on friendship had no way of knowing that the socratic model for friendship had grown out of a Greek practice that was unthinkable for most Christians.[25] Like Aristotle, however, Plato looked upon friendship as the pursuit of virtue. From all the convolutions and linguistic tricks of the *Lysis* dialogue, the point still emerges that friendship and virtue cannot be separated.

A much less exalted view of friendship is contained in the writings of Epicurus, who nevertheless had high regard for close personal bonds. For him friendship was a matter of personal need. 'Every friendship in itself is to be desired, but the first cause of friendship was a man's needs.'[26] Cicero disagreed with this point of view,[27] but the very vitriol of his attack shows that the epicurean definition exercised some attraction. In friendship Epicurus found a form of security for the individual. He even went so far as to say that wisdom is a mortal good, while friendship is an immortal one. Friendship and happiness are intimately connected: 'Friendship dances through the world bidding us all to awaken to the recognition of happiness.'[28] Like most other greek philosophers, Epicurus valued friendship highly. Until the late roman republic one might claim that friendship was traditionally looked upon as a solid foundation for human (i.e. greco-roman) society. There was nothing quite like it. Even if there were various definitions and much disagreement about its exact contents and function, privileged male Greeks and Romans were trained in schools where friendships were looked upon as desirable for every boy, every young man beginning a political career, every military leader, and every politically responsible citizen.

In the *De amicitia* Cicero summarized the antique discussion on the meaning, uses, and problems of friendship. In many areas he merely rephrases what Aristotle had said in the *Nichomachean Ethics.* At the same time Cicero is not nearly as precise and concise in his definitions as the Peripatetic. But the work is central for us because it was written in Latin rather than Greek and because it gave medieval readers a fairly brief, literarily attractive, easily understandable presentation of the place and value of friendship in human life. In his own time Cicero was something of an idealist. Though his description of friendship is down-to-earth and associated with everyday experience, he parted company with many of his contemporaries in insisting that friendship and virtue are intimately connected.[29] Cicero believed in roman aristocracy where good men could enhance each other's lives through close friendships. Much of what he says has to be seen in terms of political life in the late Roman Republic, but it would be an oversimplification to characterize Cicero's variety of friendship as purely political. Like Aristotle, he believed that men of virture seek each other out not because of need but because of the qualities within themselves. Only by sharing virtue can friends find genuine happiness in each other.

Cicero's teachings on friendship belong to the period when the roman constitution was collapsing. He wrote his essay in the last year of his life, after the murder of Julius Caesar, perhaps in an attempt to salvage the values of discourse and debate that he saw threatened in a tyrannical regime in which only flatterers could survive.[30] For Cicero as for Aristotle friendships and political life go together. The good state cannot exist without virtuous friends working together not only for personal satisfaction but also in furthering each other's public careers.[31] In this way they contribute to the quality of life in the republic.

This conception of friendship is perhaps extremely foreign to the individualistic Western world today, where we make a sharp division between 'private' and 'public' life. Our problem in reading Cicero is in this sense similar to that of the medieval monk, for whom the late Republican value of political discourse had no meaning at all. But in the Middle Ages scholars did not read classical treatises in the way that is common today, in relating them to their historical context. Each treatise was looked upon as a goldmine of appropriate quotations that easily could be separated from their context and used to enrich the christian world view of the writer. Aelred of Rievaulx, in describing how important the *De amicitia* had been to him in his youth, meant the passages in which Cicero praises friendship as the most important and attractive human bond, and one which is good in itself.[32] We seek what we need in what we read, but in the Middle Ages it was easier and more acceptable than it is for us to separate a well-expressed idea from its historical-cultural context and to use what was appropriate.

It is in this medieval sense that I shall try to sum up the teaching of the *De amicitia,* instead of making any further attempt to relate it to its historical background. Cicero's speaker, Laelius, begins by admitting that he felt sorrow at the death of his friend Scipio:

> Of course I am upset. I have lost a friend such as will never be seen again. Or so I must assume. For of this at least I am sure: there has never been a friend like him before.[33]

Here is Cicero's response to stoic and epicurean writers who prefer detachment and warn against emotional involvement in other people. For the medieval reader such lines could be seen in connection with Christ's grief at the death of his friend Lazarus. For cistercian writers such as Aelred or Bernard, a tribute to the dead friend provided a way to describe friendship in general.

Cicero makes it quite clear that friendship means living together and sharing everything. He speaks of a *societas* that emerges among close friends (4,15). Nothing is more fitted to nature than this state of friendship, he insists: *nihil est enim tam naturae aptum* (5,17). At the same time he refuses to elevate friendship beyond the capabilities of ordinary good men: *quae sunt in usu uitaque communi* (5,18). Unlike later writers, such as Montaigne, Cicero refuses to limit friendship to being a bond between only the most outstanding men. Here, however, he is on the verge of contradicting himself when Laelius enumerates the few celebrated friendships of antique history.

For the monastic reader there could be no doubt that Cicero's definition of friendship had a spiritual dimension, for it speaks of the divine *(omnium diuinarum humanarumque rerum:* 6,20). But it is not a cold, impersonal bond linked to some distant deity. In the virtue and practice of friendship is an element of sweetness and gentleness that makes intimacy joyful: *Quid dulcius quam habere quicum omnia audeas sic loqui ut tecum* (what could be more sweet than to have someone to whom you dare tell everything as if to yourself? 6,22) To give a framework for such friendship Cicero provides principles, which he alternatively calls *praecepta* and *leges*, as when he says that the first law of friendship is that we seek from our friends only what is right: *Haec igitur prima lex amicitiae sanciatur, ut ab amicis honesta petamus* (13:44). In this connection he speaks of limits or restrictions in friendship (*fines. . . et quasi termini:* 16,56). But in so doing Cicero rejects the one-for-one concept of friendship by which one gives only in relation to what one receives. Cicero's greatest concern, besides the pursuit of virtue, is that the friend be carefully chosen, for once made, friendship cannot be unmade, at least not in public, for this would be a great source of scandal to all: 'We must never make a friend whom we someday might come to hate' (16,59). Trust (*fides*) must be the foundation of friendship (18,65). If we have reservations about our friends, they cannot really be considered friends.

Friendship has its rights (*ius amicitiae:* 17,63). Here as often, Cicero does not precisely define what he means. The words *ius, lex, praecepta,* and *fines* leave the impression that the treatise can be used as a practical guide in defining the rights and obligations of friendships. To a certain extent this is true, but much of the argumentation is circular, and besides asserting the worth and value of friendship in human life and describing its connection with virtue, Cicero does not provide a full treatment of the content of true friendship. At many junctures the treatise turns into a condemnation of the travesties of friendship that appear in the life of the tyrant or the flattery which abounds in political and social life.

Cicero ends his treatise with Laelius' description of his friendship with Scipio (27,103-4). Having established the value of friendship in human life, Cicero uses an historically well-known friendship to summarize the ideal of the good life for the aristocratic roman male. This involves activities in common: shared military service, living together in country houses, and conversing on long walks, as well as traveling together. The very lack of 'romanticism' in Cicero's delineation of what friends do together makes friendship into an accessible goal for the socially privileged male.

In the clear prose of Cicero is the outline of a form of community (*societas*) that can greatly appeal to any group with common pursuits, especially those of an intellectual and spiritual nature. Friendship can pervade the totality of one's life. Cicero does not limit it to the 'private sphere'. It is agreement or harmony (*consensio*) in everything, whether human or divine. This definition secures a public dimension for friendship, and Cicero insists on what for us might seem unlikely, that political activities and private bonds come together for the public good in the lives of virtuous men. Friendship is thus the community of good men who contribute through their bonds to the quality of discourse and to the growth of virtue in society. If one scrapes away the background of roman republican life and thinks in terms of the monastic community, there are many of Cicero's concerns that are applicable: the problem of making friends, the fear of losing them, the desire to share everyday life with one's friend, and the question of how to cope with sorrow at the loss of friends.

Cicero's insights on friendship, his fragmentary rules and practical advice could thus become a central guide to the christian friend seeking a form of community but lacking in the Bible any detailed blueprint for friendship. Cicero could easily be christianized, so long as the uncompromising sides of Jesus and Paul were seen to leave room for preferential human bonds. If friendship was virtue, then close friends could be the instruments of each other's salvation within communities of love where friendship could flourish.

Cicero's language of friendship, if not his treatise as a whole, had a profound effect on medieval thinking. Yet the most popular classical definition of friendship came not from Cicero, but from the historian Sallust. Catiline, a notorious rebel against the roman state, in one of his conspiratorial speeches called friendship an agreement about 'willing and not willing the same things.'[34] The phrase was taken out of context and used perhaps because it was simple and direct. Its deceptive transparence meant that one hardly could forget the phrase once one saw or heard it. As with Gregory the Great's definition of friend as *custos animi*, Sallust's definition of friendship could appeal to everyone.

Horace's tribute to his friend Vergil as being the other half of himself (*animae dimidium meae*) also appears frequently, especially in carolingian expressions of friendship. [35] Other aspects of Horace's writings on love and friendship, such as his homoerotic poetry, did not become associated with the description of friendship. Medieval writers took what they could use from the classical heritage and made the best of it. When something in the classical heritage did not fit the purposes of the medieval writer, he generally ignored it. This selectivity might seem quite superficial to us, but it reflects a culture that was extremely confident about what is good, right and true.

One mini-treatise on friendship that obtained some circulation in the Middle Ages, especially after the cultural awakening of the eleventh century, was Seneca's critique of Epicurus.[36] Seneca wrote his friend Lucilius and asked whether Epicurus had been right in criticizing those (who must be Stoics), 'who hold that the wise man is self-sufficient and for that reason does not stand in need of friendships.' Seneca identifies the problem here as the Greek word *apatheia*, which roughly translated into Latin becomes *impatientia:*

> What we mean to express is a soul which rejects any sensation of evil; but people will interpret the idea as that of a soul which can endure no evil. This is the difference between us [Stoics] and the other school [the Cynics]. Our ideal wise man feels his troubles, but overcomes them. Their wise man does not even feel them. But we and they hold the idea that the wise man is self-sufficient.

Seneca thus identified himself with the Stoics. Through his letter collection to Lucilius and together with Cicero, he made Stoic thought easily accessible to Christian writers. For Seneca the wise man can live perfectly well without friends. Without them he can still be a complete person. Seneca rejected the teaching of Aristotle and Cicero and believed that the good man can and must be self-sufficient. He can thus 'endure the loss of a friend with equanimity' (*amissum aequo animo fert*). Cicero had admitted through Laelius that because of the immortality of the soul, a friend need not grieve for his dead companion because of death itself. But for his own loss he can rightly shed tears. Such grief was out of the question for Seneca. The friend confronted with such a loss must go out and find a new friend:

> He need never lack friends, for it lies in his own control how soon he shall make good a loss.

> *Sine amico quidem numquam erit. In sua potestate habet, quam cito reparet.*[37]

Seneca points out that the sculptor Phidias could always make a new work of art if one was smashed. Likewise the philosopher can refill the empty place left by the friend by making a new one. Friendship is a good exercise for the wise man not because he seeks individual friends for the sake of the friends or oneself, but because the experience of friendship in itself is valuable. Seneca even went so far as to say that the central delight of friendship lies not in having friends but in making them. As with the sculptor, the delight is in the creation, not the contemplation of the completed work.

Seneca as a Stoic thinker considered friendship as a spiritual exercise that enables the friend to serve another person, to help him, to do services that make oneself better as a person. The friend becomes merely the object of one's goodwill, not an equal, and certainly not an essential part of one's life. A certain emotional distance is to be maintained. Turning to a friend because one feels empty or incomplete would be to give up the stoic quest for self-sufficiency.

Seneca's concept of friendship can be seen in terms of what happened to the Roman state after the death of Cicero. His *De amicitia* can be looked upon as a last-ditch attempt to reassert the social and personal values of the *polis*, where members of the ruling class deal with one another in terms of personal bonds, edifying conversations, and the pursuit of a balance between ideal and real worlds. In Seneca's world the opportunity for such discourse is limited to rich men who cut themselves off from the machinations of a corrupt court where only sycophants get on and where friendship is impossible. The best thing a good man can do is to withdraw into himself and to cultivate friendships with like-minded men without entertaining any hope that such personal relationships will make a difference in the life of the state. The retreat of the good man from the political scene is thus paralleled in a retreat from the aristotelian-ciceronian vision of friendship as an essential part of the political life. Seneca's privatisation of friendship is an admission of defeat for the ideal of a complete friendship encompassing both private and public areas of human endeavour. Long before Seneca, even in the time of Aristotle, this ideal had been challenged, yet Seneca is important to us because his thinking was easily accessible in an easily readable letter that was available to the christian centuries.[38]

Like Seneca's form of stoic philosophy, Christianity can be interpreted in a quietist manner which abandons hope in the state's ability to do anything for the improvement of the human condition. The good Christian, of course, cannot believe in self-sufficiency, for he believes he is incomplete without Christ. But the other-worldly orientation of christian thought can isolate the individual from the life of human society around him and can distance him from any concern with the ways of the world. This helps explain how Augustine could write in his *City of God* that the sack of Rome was no great catastrophe, for the christian's kingdom is not of this world, and all things, like Rome, will pass away.

Concentration on the salvation of the individual soul can lead people to hold that we go to heaven alone, not in groups of friends. Here Stoic thought becomes a prop for the christian concept that the individual has nothing to gain by admitting a need for other persons, unless these people can be used as objects of and recipients for good works. Loving our neighbour in the stoic-christian sense means showing equal goodwill and generosity to all men, a noble ideal, but one that refuses to make distinctions among human beings. If this train of thought is pursued to its very end, then individual friendships are out of the question, for they distract from the individual's primary concern, the salvation of his own soul, and from the christian way of *agapé*, generalized love, rather than *amicitia*, particularized love.[39]

The Stoic, like the Christian, can experience catastrophes and evils in the world and yet still survive unscathed. In Seneca's anecdote of the man who loses all his family and friends and property but says 'I have lost nothing,' we find a roman version of Jesus's paradox that 'he who would save his life must lose it.' We must be prepared to give up everything and to be attached to nothing in order to become a good Stoic or a good Christian. The difference is that the former finds his strength exclusively within himself (*se enim ipso contentus est*),[40] while the Christian looks within himself to find the image of Christ and the promise of heaven.

The stoic strand parallels Christianity for a great distance but then separates itself, for the Christian, as we see already in the Acts of the Apostles and the epistles of Paul, also seeks salvation in community. Since every human being has an immortal soul, we cannot use each other only as objects for our own salvation. Personal feelings and attachments can have an independent worth in themselves. Augustine could never have agreed with Seneca that 'though the sage may love his friends dearly. . .often putting them ahead of himself, yet all the good will be limited to his own being'.[41] Self-contained Stoicism sees the individual alone in the world. Some forms of the eremitic life may do the same, leaving the individual alone with God. But for Augustine and the Western fathers, the ciceronian ideal of a community of sharing friends never completely gave way to the stoic ideal of the man who needs only himself.

Once there is community, there are politics. Even if the founders of the monastic life would have refused to express themselves in such a way, they realized that they needed a model for life. This had to be based not on individual self-sufficiency but on the development of the individual within a community that could help his spiritual growth. For Saint Benedict the goal and highest state in the ascetic way of life was that of a hermit. Most of us, however, he added, are beginners and need each other for mutual aid.[42]

THE PROBLEM OF CHRISTIAN FRIENDSHIP IN COMMUNITY

The classical world ended with the isolation of friendship from community. In Seneca's version of stoic philosophy, for all its attractive detachment, there was an admission that virtuous individual bonds could no longer contribute to the quality of life in political society.[43] The retreat into the mind may well have been the sensitive man's way of dealing with the horrors of arbitrary rule and widespread corruption. On the surface of life a polite and urbane tone could be maintained, as can be seen as late as the fifth century letter collection of Sidonius Apollinaris. But the merger of private and political life in bonds of friendship remained a nostalgic reminiscence and a literary topos instead of being a part of everyday life, as Cicero had insisted friendship must be.

While learned roman men retreated into their country estates and handed the state over to the army, new christian communities grew up in lower class milieux in the cities of the empire around the Mediterranean's shores. In these assemblies (*ecclesiae*), individual friendships are not visible to us, but we do know that they had as their model the community of believers in the first christian community in Jerusalem, which was remembered to have been of 'one heart and one mind'. Behind this ideal was the psalm verse about joy in community, an idealization of community life that provided a potential opening for individual friendships. When monastic communities began forming in the West in the fourth and fifth centuries, however, their model was not the euphoric group of brethren-friends of the psalm. It was the much more rigorously disciplined *schola*, the group of military or civil-service origins whose goal was learning and service to the master. The Rule of the Master, and especially its adaptation and abbreviation in the Rule of Saint Benedict, used this image as the point of departure for a description of monastic life.[44] In Augustine's descriptions of community, friendship among learned men and discussions that involve both mind and heart lay at the very centre of life. This is not the case in Benedict's Rule, which from the ninth century was to become the universal norm in the West. Benedict concerned himself chiefly with the relation between master and disciple, not that among equals.

Here we must backtrack a bit to basic principles, even at the risk of being repetitious. The christian commandment of love of neighbour could be interpreted in the stoic sense of universal good treatment of human beings, whether they be friends or enemies. In such a context, the love of individual friends becomes a potential distraction from a generalized and non-exclusive love of all men. In the monastic life there is even more reason that loves be maintained for all members of the community and for no particular member. The need for discipline in the monastery, as we shall see in John Cassian's writings, created a fear of the conspiracies that friends could foment against the community. Friendship and community had been seen in the aristotelian world as complementary; while in the monastic Christianity of the early centuries they could be looked upon as rivals. The solution of Benedict, to make the abbot the almighty father figure who made certain that the monks carried out the work of God, could easily make special bonds among the monks into a disciplinary matter. Cassian's concern with conspiracy is reflected in the initially surprising but quite understandable assertion of C.S. Lewis that 'every real friendship is a sort of secession, even a rebellion. . ., a pocket of potential resistance'.[45]

The question still remained for monks of the eleventh and twelfth centuries to answer: to what extent can and should the convert to monastic life leave old friends in the world and form new spiritual friendships? Should relationships within the cloister be forged in terms of *amicitia* or only in terms of christian charity, *dilectio*? To what extent can one take one's friends and relatives with one into the cloister, so that earlier family and school bonds are transformed and spiritualized? Varying answers have been given, both in the twelfth century and later.

The question of friendship is part of a larger christian and post-Christian debate on love and its place in the West and in the history of mankind.[46] If love makes the world go round, then can love keep the world from being blown to bits? Such a question was just as relevant for the medieval monk as it is for us, even if our predecessors had a different conception of the end of the world.[47] For them as for us the problem lay in how to reconcile a religion that commands us to love both God and all persons with our proclivity as individuals to seek out other persons for special loves of different kinds.[48] These unique loves make life worth living, unless one chooses to cut oneself off from the rest of humanity in following Seneca's advice and seeking self-sufficiency.

One radical strand of Christianity, found in the Egyptian desert already in the fourth century, favoured the way of *apatheia* or passionlessness and saw salvation as possible primarily for the man who could isolate himself from other men in order to be alone with God. In the absolutism of this approach there is a cold and terrible beauty. It remains a choice for anyone who seeks security and peace away from the unpredictability of other people and the arbitrariness of human loves.

In the West since Aristotle, however, it has been more common to seek a less exclusive form of life. The ideal has been to live in a good community where there is the possibility of close individual friendship. Christianity promises the community of the *ecclesia*, where commitment to Christ as saviour transforms us into friends of God and of his friends.[49] But here is the problem: in being Christ's friends can we be friends with anyone else? Is this not the one exclusive friendship which edges out all others? Is Christ not the only being worth our love, devotion and loyalty?

RECENT TREATMENTS OF SPIRITUAL FRIENDSHIP

Here I shall not provide anything more than a highly impressionistic and abbreviated review of recent literature on this great subject. One point of departure for contemporary treatment of friendship in the Christian life is provided by the *amitié* article in the *Dictionnaire de Spiritualité* from 1937.[50] Here Vansteenberghe relied heavily on neoscholastic terminology in describing the possibility of friendship and its practice, but his dry categories give way at the end of the article to a solid historical treatment of christian literature on friendship. This article, modest and unassuming and tucked away in an encyclopedia little known outside of specialist circles, provided a turning point in the theory of friendship.

In the 1920s and 1930s it was fashionable, at least in Catholic circles, to look upon friendship primarily in terms of the relationship between the individual and God: friendship with God. In one such treatment, Thomas of Aquinas's teaching was used in order to see the individual in isolation from other persons and to concentrate on the soul's preparation for the vision of God.[51] Relationships among people were purely secondary. Here we have 'just a few fleeting hours' seen under the appearance of eternity. Another work on the subject, *Gottesfreundschaft*, included some of the medieval writers, but their teaching was viewed almost exclusively in terms of the individual person's relationship to God alone.[52]

By dealing in a straightforward and concrete manner with friendships among men in the religious life, and also between men and women, Vansteenberghe opened up an experience of life that had been almost taboo in the monastic communities of the nineteenth and early twentieth centuries. Even in the 1950s Aelred of Rievaulx's *Spiritual*

Friendship was forbidden to novices at trappist monasteries in the United States, while a novice training to be a Dominican in Rome (who later left the church and became master of an Oxford college) was supervised even on walks so that he and his companions did not always choose the same partners and avoided getting to know each other too well.[53] This suspicion of 'particular friendships' is one strand in a spiritual tradition that Vansteenberghe squarely faced and rejected as a reason for forbidding close personal bonds in the monastic and religious life.

In 1945 the benedictine monk and medieval scholar from Clervaux in Luxembourg, Jean Leclercq, published a study of a Paris manuscript that contained a thirteenth-century letter collection.[54] Leclercq pointed out how such a collection cannot be looked upon as merely a model for students' literary exercise. It contains passages that point to letter-writing as a means of expressing personal friendships. From the scholastic milieu Leclercq pointed ahead to the humanists who were fascinated with friendship, for Petrarch made use of this same collection. More importantly for our purposes, Leclercq looked at the monastic milieu of friendships and letters from which the scholastic collection had evolved. Leclercq's assertion that such letters reveal something about individual human relationships pervades his later works, where much is devoted to the sources for friendship in the monastic life. His landmark study of the 1950s, *The Love of Learning and the Desire for God*, places friendship almost innocently within monasticism, without reference to the possible problems that individual bonds might create.[55] Leclercq approached friendship through the monastic flowering of letters in the twelfth century, when it was taken as a natural part of spiritual life and not regarded as a challenge to community life.

In the early 1960s several new contributions arrived which made the question of spiritual friendship more evident in the English-speaking world. I have already mentioned C.S. Lewis, whose *Four Loves* includes friendship and sees both its advantages and limitations. Lewis, as a Christian, took up a theme already found in the writings of E.M. Forster, who in the crisis year of 1939 bravely summarized the problem of reconciling friendship, personal loyalty, and devotion to a 'greater ideology':

> I hate the idea of causes, and if I had to choose between betraying my country and betraying my friend, I hope I should have the guts to betray my country. Such a choice may scandalize the modern reader, and he may stretch out his patriotic hand at once and ring up the police.[56]

Forster suggests the dilemma present in every system of belief in which there is supposed to be room for individuals and individual bonds:

> . . . . there lies at the back of every creed something terrible and hard for which the worshipper may one day be required to suffer, and there is even a terror and a hardness in this creed of personal relationships, urbane and mild though it sounds.[57]

Both the creed of Christ and Cicero's creed of friendship make absolute demands. For the Christian, friendship with God will always have to come first, but the problem is of course that one's beloved friend is physically and often spiritually closer than a God who can be so jealous and who through his Church can demand a total loyalty that at times can seem inhuman.

A facile development of this train of thought is found in the writings of the Italian sociologist Francesco Alberoni, who makes the blatant claim that the church has 'always' opposed close friendships among the clergy, not because of its fear of homosexuality but because of the fear that groups of men and of women in banding together will challenge ecclesiastical authority.[58] There is something to this conspiracy theory, going back to John Cassian, but the fact remains that personal friendships have been evident among many good Christians. God's friends, *amici dei*, can at times even be encouraged to be each other's friends.

Alberoni's assertion betrays a lack of interest in and knowledge about the history of friendship and friendships. In the 1960s Adele Fiske provided several individual studies that should by themselves have made it impossible for him to be so categorical about the church's opposition to close friendships. Looking at friendships from Cassian and until the mid-twelfth century, Fiske concluded that in this tradition the friend becomes a taste of paradise (*paradisus amicus*).[59] The problem with Fiske's studies is that they look in such detail at the language of friendship in each author that each is seen in isolation and the friends rarely come alive. They remain static and disparate entities, without a sense of any development in the practice and concept of friendship. Fiske was, however, a pioneer, whose work unfortunately has been available to few students of friendship.

At the same time as Adele Fiske's separate articles were being published, the Oxford historian R. W. Southern published his major work on Saint Anselm of Canterbury.[60] Here he devoted a special section to Anselm's friendships, with which I shall deal later. Southern's interest reflects a change of mood and concern that had actually come already in the 1930s, when he first worked as a research fellow. Friendship was becoming a worthwhile and acceptable topic for the historian, even outside of the Roman Catholic tradition. Southern was undoubtedly influenced by his teacher and friend, Sir Maurice Powicke, who maintained a life-long interest in Aelred of Rievaulx, and whose 1950 introduction to his translation of Walter Daniel's *Life of Aelred* remains one of the best presentations of Aelred's life and character.[61]

An interest which formerly had been limited to monastic and religious historians entered into the mainstream of medieval history writing. An historian of the future might well ask to what extent the friendships experienced in Maurice Powicke's circle in Oxford of the 1930s encouraged an opening to such an interest. The special intimacy and elitism of Oxford college life could have fostered sympathy and interest for the friendships of an earlier age. What is fascinating is not that young men and their teachers cultivated friendships—for such has assumedly been the case in school milieux throughout history—but that such friendships could provide inspiration and stimulus to historical study about friendship.

Southern's work influenced my own study of Anselm's friendships which I wrote in Copenhagen in 1972.[62] At the same time Southern supported Benedicta Ward in her important translation of the prayers and meditations of Saint Anselm, which for the first time made Anselm's powerful language of prayer in terms of intimate human bonds available to the public.[63] Another Oxford figure, Peter Brown, provided in his celebrated 1967 study of Saint Augustine of Hippo a biography that spanned the entirety of the man's life and work and considered Augustine's talent for surrounding himself with friends and building around himself a community, first pagan, later Christian, in which friendship and learning could support each other.

Within the Roman Catholic Church, the Second Vatican Council provided an impetus to interest in friendship in both contemporary and historical terms. The meeting of so many different talented people, from many faiths, in the Rome of the 1960s, made possible human contacts and new friendships that otherwise never would have been forged. A cistercian monk from Holland once described to me the excitement and sense of unlimited possibilities in the human relationships formed during those years in the cause of the renewal of christian life. Some of the participants in this movement ended by leaving the clerical or religious life because the needs and expression of love led them into marriages and other permanent individual relationships. Others stuck it out in their religious communities and today manifest, at least in North America, a lively interest in the subject of friendship inside and outside the monastery.

The spirit of the Second Vatican Council is well reflected in the Dominican Paul Conner's thesis, *Friendships between Consecrated Men and Women and the Growth of Charity.*[64] Here are optimism and hope in the possibility that men and women in the religious life can become more complete persons and enrich their spiritual lives through friendships. Conner deals openly with the question of sexual involvement. His frankness is indicative of the atmosphere of dialogue and debate that emerged from the ferment of the 1960s and which is still transforming religious life, especially in the Americas, where politics, community, sexuality, and the quest for God are seen as aspects of a total christian commitment.

Treatments like that of Paul Conner have only a limited historical perspective. They consider only to a secondary degree the long standing Christian debate about the language and practice of friendship. Spiritual friendships of the past are used mainly as exemplifications of the possiblity of friendship in every age. Such an approach opens up a deep and rich tradition within Christianity, but this needs to be seen in a fuller historical perspective. The australian monk Michael Casey has attempted to provide such a background in a well-written, clear article on the subject of spiritual friendship.[65] But in concentrating on patristic writers who praised friendship and in skipping over the problematic early medieval period, Casey does not pose an essential question: whether it is to the benefit or the detriment of the life of the community when friendship becomes a central factor in the lives of its members. Casey implies that christian thought and practice on the whole have supported friendship. The nuances and warnings of Vansteenberghe's careful article are replaced by a near-celebration of friendship. Like many other writers, Casey stops with Aelred of Rievaulx as the summary and climax of monastic spiritual friendship and does not ask what happened afterwards.

In the 1980s friendship has become almost a fashionable subject. With Alberoni's book friendship has come into the centre of a contemporary debate on how the individual can cope with the complexities of an impersonal society. Alberoni represents one extreme in his interpretation of the role of the christian church in the history of friendship: he sees its contribution as largely negative and prohibitory. At the other extreme is the work of James McEvoy, who knows intimately the writings of Aelred of Rievaulx and the learned, monastic context from which they emerge. McEvoy has written a classic article which argues that friendship and love are at the very centre of the christian experience of the world.[66] Here Dante, Cicero, Augustine and others are all employed to support the twelfth-century monastic view of friendship as an essential part of the spiritual life.

James McEvoy is aware of the 'reproach' among non-Christians that '. . .Christianity and the central importance of love in its theology, in reality destroyed the practice and the theory of friendship which the Greeks and Romans of antiquity so greatly favoured'. In McEvoy there is no conflict between the good of friendship and the highest good. His definition merges Cicero and Plato:

> Friendship is a growing, lasting union of minds, will and hearts. It is appreciated and cultivated for its own sake. It satisfies the fundamental needs of the human heart, by teaching it to want the good, the highest Good there is, for itself and for the friend. Through friendship we are saved from placing ourselves at the centre of things.[67]

However precise and attractive these remarks are, they do not reflect the mainstream of christian thought in the Middle Ages. As we shall see, the aelredian point of view that sees no conflict between individual friendship and christian universal love does not gain universal acceptance.

The difficulty of reconciling individual and general loves is best expressed in a brief but penetrating study by the american philosopher of ethics, Gilbert C. Meilaender.[68] Drawing upon historical examples, but without providing an historical context, Meilaender defines friendship as preferential love and insists on the possibility of personal bonds within the christian community. But he also deals with the problems and conflicts involved. Unlike E.M. Forster he does not consider friendship to be the highest good. As a citizen of a country which is so huge and complex that the individual has little voice in its affairs, Meilaender sees little importance in the aristotelian-ciceronian emphasis on friendshp in political life. He would rather have an impersonal state within which individuals have room to form friendships without a political dimension.

My criticism of this approach lies in my concern to see friendship in the context of community. Each individual friendship has a certain impact on the society in which it is formed. Conversely, the larger community and even the state as a whole have a significant influence on the quality, content and roles allotted to friendship. Friendship can and must be, by its very 'subversive' character, both political, personal—and spiritual. Despite its lack of historical context and its apolitical view, Meilaender's work provides a much-needed middle ground between McEvoy's paen to friendship in the christian community and Alberoni's rejection of its possibility.

In the coming pages I shall try to provide an historical introduction to the expression and practice of close personal friendships, especially in monastic life. I shall frequently turn to John Boswell's landmark study, *Christianity, Homosexuality and Social Tolerance.*[69] My interpretation might easily be considered a polemic against Boswell's view of medieval spirituality and human experience. It should already be clear that I consider the subjects of sexuality and of friendship to be separate ones, however many points of contact there might be. Like Alberoni, I allow for the possibility of a sexual aspect in some friendships, but in studying monastic culture I do not think that a general assumption of repressed sexuality provides much help or guidance. Boswell's work was necessary as a reaction to generations of medieval historians who preferred not to deal with the subject of male love. In the 1970s, this area of concern and interest took on a new visibility in Western countries. Now that there is more openness and awareness on this subject, it is possible to look at male interpersonal relationships in a larger context.

The goal for the history writing of the coming generation has already been formulated by the giants to whom we all are in debt: Marc Bloch, Maurice Powicke, R. W. Southern, Eileen Power, Georges Duby, Peter Brown, Giles Constable, and Jean Leclercq. In the work of these historians and the groups clustered around them, we perceive a desire to deal with whole human beings living in communities. Here the feelings of the individuals concerned are important and worth considering. A history of the expression of human feeling could easily become a history of literary clichés. Within the monastic context, however, it should be possible to write a history of human bonds in terms of friendship and society.

Here sexuality is one element among many that helps us to understand what people sought in each other. For me the problem has not been to separate what is 'sexual' from what is 'spiritual'. What expresses human closeness and what points to a clever writer at work? Ultimately the skilled writer may well be revealing his own feelings through his poised prose.

There is no single interpretation or view that can encompass medieval monastic experience. What I see is a familiar tension between what men are and what they want to be, for themselves and for each other. In seeking friends and friendship, medieval men and women sought self-knowledge, the enjoyment of life, the commitment of community, and the experience of God. In such people we find ourselves. Not in a distant mirror but through a glass darkly.

CHAPTER ONE

THE WISDOM OF THE EASTERN FATHERS

FOR THE ROMAN ARISTOCRAT of the late Empire, friendship was as natural and inevitable in social life as the acts of eating or breathing are in physical life.[1] Friendship among social equals contrasted with the carefully regulated life of patron and client. It provided an opportunity to express, in a controlled and dignified manner, shared values and experiences. The poems of Paulinus of Nola (353-431) for his teacher, Ausonius, provide an elegant witness to this elite world.[2] The poems idealize what these two learned aristocrats as pagans had once held in common.[3] What looks like passionate language must be seen in terms of the mode of expression of the day: 'I shall see you in my heart and grasp you with my mind/ Everywhere you will be present to me' wrote Paulinus to Ausonius without appealing to what might appear to be romantic love.[4] Paulinus looked back into the intensity of his youth and its discovery of classical literary culture through his friend and teacher Ausonius.

Any definition of friendship in Late Antiquity must take into consideration its social dimension. Friendships among roman male aristocrats existed in inter-personal relationships which the larger upper-class community recognized and accepted. The bonds between friends were no more exclusively private than the poems of Paulinus were.[5] Friendship manifested itself among aristocratic men as a semi-public agreement or concord (Cicero's definition is always in the background). Such male roman friends were mainly concerned with maintaining and enhancing their position in society by preserving and expanding the political influence and position of their families. For these aristocrats, friendships were bound up with the relationships that extended and strengthened the ties of kinship. At the same time these men sought attachments based on delight in sharing the same culture. In realizing such attachments roman men gained public recognition. Friendship existed for self, for family, and for community.

What happens when relationships of this type came to have lesser importance because of the new challenge of christian life and the breakdown of roman society in its classic form? When human contacts became regulated and directed by the desire for God, the friend of God could replace the friend of the kin group. Men could be each other's friends by sharing the same love of God. Paulinus found he had to break old ties with Ausonius, not because of guilt for any past sins, but because he, Paulinus, had entered into a new society. Spiritual kinship replaced blood bonds and socially useful or enjoyable relationships. As Paulinus wrote to Ausonius, any love between them had to be joined in Christ (. . . *in Christum conexa mente colendum*).[6]

For every Christian in the fourth century, the ideal of a harmonious life in community is contained in the Acts of the Apostles' description of the first christian community, its one heart and one mind, by which its members in unity and harmony shared all things (*cor unum et anima una* Acts 4:32). Individual bonds have no role here unless they can be integrated into community life. Paulinus had to part from Ausonius, but he could rejoice in the conversion of his old acquaintance, Sulpicius Severus, and try to mould him into a christian friend.[7] The friend within the new community was no longer concerned with shared cultural background, political ambitions or family interests. What mattered was integration of the persons into the worship and love of God. The general principle was established: every human bond that brings one closer to God is acceptable and even desirable, but likewise, every human relationship that distances the Christian from God is to be broken.

The question remains: to what extent are other people a help in reaching God, and to what extent are they a hindrance? Although no one would deny the second great commandment, love of neighbour, some fourth century Christians apparently experienced their neighbours as more an obstacle than an encouragement to salvation. The attitudes manifested in our sources vary according to the people behind them. Friendship of one kind or another seems in practical and everyday terms to be just as prevalent as in traditional greco-roman society. But the language and ideal of friendship had changed. For some writers, friendship in itself became a goal, while for others, it was not to be sought for its own sake.

Western christian fathers generally considered close friendships to be a positive element in the pursuit of salvation, while Eastern fathers often doubted the value of such relationships, especially within the special christian community, monastic life. Behind this typical East-West dichotomy, it is important to grasp the social roots of friendship. In upper class society, whether in the eastern or western Mediterranean, we shall see how it could be fairly easy to transform Roman *amicitia* into christian friendship. At other levels of the population, especially the village culture of Egypt, human friendships appeared as but one more form of entanglement from which the new friends of God had to flee.

THE SOCIAL BACKGROUND

If we turn to the writings of the desert fathers of Egypt, we find their requirement of *metanoia,* a total change of mind and life, meant not just a reorientation of the soul, but also a change in physical surroundings. Leaving the world of the village and going into the desert meant leaving behind all the obligations and emotional attachments associated with village life. Peace of mind was to be achieved by minimizing one's daily obligations to other human beings.

In this context the ascetic ways of the desert fathers must be seen. By living simply in terms of clothes, food and dwelling places, they eliminated the distractions of hard work which were necessary for the village men and their families to live decently. The desert fathers' attitude to marriage did not centre on sexuality. They were concerned with the problems created by the need to work first for a wife and then for children. 'If you cannot bear such weariness, stop wanting a wife'.[8] The man tempted by fornication who told his spiritual guide or *abba* that he would need ten wives to satisfy himself learned to his own chagrin that he could barely support even one.[9] From the description of his tired appearance, he seems to have had hardly any energy left to indulge his desires. The hard daily life of the village, its backbreaking work of cultivating the land, squabbles about water, boundaries, marriages—all these essential yet trivial matters the desert fathers could leave behind when they walked into the wilderness.

The family consumed heart, mind, and body of the fourth-century egyptian villager. But the Egyptian had the possibility of casting all aside and choosing something else. He could look to a christian alternative of a simpler way of life after repentance. Here the christian message did not contribute to the ideal of family life. Recent work on the family and the poor in the Eastern Empire during this period emphasizes a tension between, on the one hand, efforts to strengthen and solidify the family and, on the other, social and religious developments that undermined its position.[10] Close relatives intermarried in order to secure lands and wealth. The family from the fourth century onwards becomes a 'closed circuit for the distribution and conservation of material goods'.[11] At the same time heretical sects appeared which had no sympathy for marriage as a state of life but tried to further celibate forms of existence. At the moment when the upper-class family turned in on itself in order to protect its own interests, the ascetic movement challenged its centrality. The individual could resolve this tension by flight to the desert, the abandonment of the pursuit of family interests, and the substitution for them of an exclusive concern for his own salvation.

Sometimes the desert dweller could discover to his discomfort that his new spiritual brother in the eremitical life also happened to be his brother in the flesh. Or his wife might come to him with their two children and insist that he at least keep the boy, for she could not feed both of them.[12] As much as the village male wanted to escape from the requirements of everyday life, he could not prevent his brother, or his sister, from seeking the same safety. The Alphabetical Collection groups the Sayings of the Desert Fathers according to the individual fathers responsible for them.[13] This method allows us to see how different responses could be given to the problem of human isolation and contacts in the search for God. But the *abba* shared a general agreement that the bonds of physical kinship somehow have to be replaced by spiritual links. This shedding of old loves for the sake of new ones provides the pattern for all human contacts in the desert. The stern patriarch of village society gave way to the spiritual father whose word was wisdom and thus law. The older brother who had precedence in the village when the father died in the village also had his prerogative in the desert, but roles could be reversed.[14] A chronologically younger man might assume a position of authority if his wisdom and holiness merited it: 'From now on you are the old man and the father and I am the younger and the disciple'.[15]

Within the context of such permutations of kinship and authority the place of friendship emerges. Just as the old bonds of family had to be broken and replaced by new human relationships, so those of friendship could find alternative expression. When the desert fathers mention friendship, they usually mean friendships of the world, the world that has been left behind. Friendships could grow up in the desert, but they were not sought for their own sake but were forged in shared spiritual lives. We thus run into the paradox that the literature of Eastern wisdom says little about friendship in itself, except in a derogatory manner, while the lives of hermits, monks, and abbots are full of indications of friendships.

Desert friendships are not friendships in the sense of close human contacts recognized and accepted as such by the surrounding community. Desert society consisted either in the groups of hermits' cells, or else in cenobitic monasteries, with hundreds of monks, who still spent most of their time in individual cells. Both situations left little or no room for the cultivation of what we would call personal relationships. We read about moments of hospitality, many embraces and even kisses, and an endless stream of words of wisdom and advice given in an atmosphere of mutual concern. In all of these encounters, however, the individual was not encouraged to seek out one or more friends on a basis of equality. His most intense relationship was with the spiritual father, a vertical bond, while horizontal links were looked upon as either secondary or downright dangerous.

A late-twentieth century assessment of the distance kept among the men of the desert might be that they were afraid of homosexuality. The desert literature is surprisingly open about this subject, in admitting the possibility that men living in such proximity could become physically attracted to one another. In the strictures of this literature we find a reaction against the greco-roman tradition of male relationships with erotic content, but the main enemy is not sex but kinship. A father and his biological son could be suspected of homosexuality. Only when the son had destroyed his old identity and marred his good looks by defacing himself in a nitrate lake could the two of them live together in peace with their community.[16] Erotic links and kinship bonds are first confused with each other and then eliminated in a dramatic (and for us repulsive) manner.

Despite such anecdotes, the sources as a whole do not reveal any sustained concern with homosexuality. It may have become a problem for the desert dwellers when their form of life was in decline after 400.[17] If we count up the number of instances where the Greek Sayings mention homosexuality, we find it is not as great as the instances in which the problems of family bonds are recited.[18] Beautiful boys were to be kept out of the desert, for in both village and upper class life, boys could be considered to be sexually desirable.

The desert literature did not look upon homosexuality as an isolated phenomenon. It endangered the soul because it involved the death of self-restraint or *continentia.* This virtue involved more than sexual abstinence. It required the self-discipline of the individual in all matters of the senses.

A recent study claims that for Saint Basil of Caesarea (c.330-379), homosexuality was not an especially serious matter, for Basil deals with the trivia of gluttonous behaviour immediately after a section on sex with boys.[19] Here the modern historian reveals an unfamiliarity with fundamental monastic values. Homosexuality and gluttony are both manifestations of a soul in turmoil, unable to concentrate on God and turned instead to the worship of the body.[20] For the monk, sexual restraint is but one aspect of a much greater *ascesis,* the pursuit of the divine through the minimization of all that can distract and lead him away into purely human pursuits.

We can eliminate from our considerations any great fear among the desert fathers that friendships might lead to homosexual activity. The fathers did not equate friendship among males with sexual attraction, except perhaps among the very young. But they still had reservations about the value of friendship, for it could become a good in itself, and thus a distraction from the pursuit of salvation. In the rest of this chapter, I shall see to what extent the Eastern fathers in their writings integrated friendship as an ideal and a practice into their new world of spiritual bonds.

ANTHONY: CONTACT IN ISOLATION

Because of his historical position, Anthony (c.251-356) must be central to any consideration of Eastern monastic wisdom. But there are two Anthonys: the hero and the spiritual father. The hero can be seen in the portrait by Athanasius composed soon after the saint's death and quickly translated into Latin so that it became a model for Sulpicius Severus's eminently popular *Life* of Martin of Tours.[21] The second Anthony, the spiritual father, appears to a very limited extent in Athanasius's account, and is much more prominent in the sayings attributed to him which are part of the *Sayings of the Desert Fathers* or *Apophthegmata*. The first Anthony is the lonely hero who lives for decades in the desert, avoids all human contacts, and does constant battle with the devil. He is a man who has no need for other men, and so he becomes magnificent in his solitude and attractive to others because he is so difficult to reach. Like so many of the fathers after him, Anthony prefers isolation but eventually becomes surrounded by men who settle down in his vicinity in order to imitate his way of life and have him close by.

Athanasius was himself fleeing from persecutors into the desert, and so he had every reason to describe a hero who was attacked by demons and yet managed to triumph. The Anthony that Athanasius created was able to speak to Christians in both East and West. In the coming centuries, spiritual men would do battle with demons, either the invisible ones that brought temptation or visible ones in hostile foreigners who would overwhelm their lands and threaten their lives. Anthony showed that the individual could triumph against all odds if he willingly gave up everything and followed Christ.

Anthony was the new athlete of Christ, the winner who gained heaven because he asked for nothing except to be alone with God. The only friends mentioned in his *Life* are the angels with whom he spoke on his deathbed. They received and deserve the name *amici*, while his companions in the desert, who forced themselves on him, were *discipuli*, or, at best, *fratres*.[22] They are never personally close to him. Anthony's servant appears in the account in order to witness his miracles. The father's insight into the hearts of other human beings is mentioned not to show his love for them but to manifest his spiritual power. Anthony is a friend of angels and a friend of God, a brother to men, but not their friend.

Athanasius's literary recollection of Anthony concedes that he encouraged the brothers to 'console each other with talk' on spiritual matters.[23] Here we have the historical origins of the anecdotes that grew up about Anthony, and these expanded his role as spiritual father who provided words of wisdom. However much Anthony was admired for his years of isolation and spiritual battle as a desert hero, his attraction also lay in his having the words men needed. Many of the sayings attributed to Anthony in the *Apophthegmata* show how he made himself available to the brothers. In speaking to them, he insisted on the importance of involvement and concern for one's neighbour:

> Our life and death is with our neighbour. If we gain our brother, we have gained God, but if we scandalise our brother, we have sinned against Christ.[24]

When a man was scandalized at seeing Anthony enjoying himself with some of the brothers, the saint insisted that 'sometimes it is necessary to come down to meet their needs.' We see him being visited by three fathers once a year and discussing spiritual matters with two of them, while the third remained silent. Asked why, he replied, 'It is enough for me to see you, Father'.[25] The sayings attributed to him show how he made his inner spiritual life available for others. The man of miracles and the fanatical ascetic steps into the background. One finds a much more humanly concerned father than appears in Athanasius's account of a spiritual athlete's feats.

There is no contradiction between these two central sources for Anthony, his *Life* and his *Sayings*. But there is a shift in emphasis. Even in his most human moments, however, Anthony never makes a friend on his own level. He remains an authority, able to speak the words that guide men. The approachable Anthony is someone who has only temporarily emerged from isolation. Anthony's experience has no room for friendships of equality. His sons and disciples can grow into spiritual fathers and replace him. They can learn from example and experience to guide and counsel a new generation. But ultimately the desert requires that they be alone.

THE DESERT FATHERS: HUMAN CONTACTS AND ISOLATION

Towards the end of his life Anthony once again withdrew into solitude. His way of life showed the other desert fathers that however much they wanted to love their neighbour and serve him, their own personal salvation required a removal, sometimes temporary, sometimes permanent, from human relationships. The father who summed up this requirement most succinctly is Arsenius. Coming from the brilliant court of Theodosius, Arsenius must have known the tenderness and traps of *amicitia,* and his inaccessibility at times troubled his egyptian brethren. When one abba asked Arsenius why he kept away from his company, the answer was quite straightforward:

> God knows that I love you, but I cannot live with God and with men. The thousands and ten thousands of the heavenly hosts have but one will, while men have many. So I cannot leave God to be with men.[26]

One will; many wills. The contrast is revealing, for Arsenius wanted to be able to link his own will with God's single will. If he sought out the company of angels in his isolation, he could not make a wrong choice, whereas men would confuse him with the multiplicity of their purposes and intentions.

But Arsenius was not always sure of his own will. He left his cell in Lower Egypt because he 'was continually interrupted there'.[27] But eventually he returned to his disciples, and one of them protested, 'Your going from us has not been good for us, and many have not been edified by it'. Like it or not, Arsenius had become a spiritual father and guide for other desert dwellers. He could not simply get up and abandon his commitment to other human beings. He might bar his door to the stream of admirers coming to speak to him, but sometimes, when it was a question of a pious visitor's arrival, he would regret his avoidance. After his refusal to see the archbishop of Alexandria, Arsenius asked forgiveness, for as he said, 'I tasted neither bread nor water nor did I sit down until I thought you had reached home, to punish myself because you had been wearied through me.'[28]

Arsenius wanted to be left alone, but, like Anthony, the more he sought solitude, the more attractive he became to others. When a woman of senatorial rank came to see him, he was furious:

> Have you not heard tell of my way of life? It ought to be respected. How dare you make such a journey? Do you not realize you are a woman and cannot go just anywhere? Or is it so that on returning to Rome you can say to other women, I have seen Arsenius? Then you will turn the sea into a thoroughfare with women coming to see me![29]

When the woman returned to Alexandria and fell ill from the shock of Arsenius's rejection, Archbishop Theophilus comforted her by saying that Arsenius was not rejecting her spiritual needs but was simply being wary because as a woman, she provided matter for temptation to him. Other fathers confirm this outlook. It was not the individual women they were afraid of seeing; it was the image of woman that remained in their minds to provoke sexual temptation later.[30] Arsenius is quite explicit that he had no desire to cultivate with women any sentimental friendships of the type that Jerome was later to make and defend. He was not obsessed with sex. He was obsessed with the demands of solitude. It remained the basic condition for the inner peace he sought after a chaotic life.

Arsenius is an extremist, a man who chose the desert in order to reject completely the upper class culture from which he came.[31] For others, the desert actually improved their physical conditions and social status, as an anecdote probably based on Arsenius reveals.[32] Here a monk was shocked by the fact that Arsenius lived in a modest standard of comfort, but when the monk then contrasted Arsenius's former way of life with his present one, he realized that he had misjudged Arsenius completely:

> Woe to me, for after so much hardship in the world I have found ease: and what I did not have before, that I now possess. While after so great ease, you have come to humility and poverty.

The story ends with the assertion that the Egyptian became the abba of Rome's 'friend and often went to him for help'.[32] This is one of the rare instances in the Alphabetical Collection where a relationship between two desert dwellers is described in terms of friendship.[34] The Arsenius we meet in his own sayings would seem to have been the last person in the desert to forge a friendship.

The people whose visits Arsenius rejected were normally those who came from the cities and palaces that he had fled: the senatorial woman and the archbishop both wanted to show him their perhaps sycophantic admiration for his way of life, assumedly so that they could return home to boast of their accomplishment. But for a man who came from the native culture of Egypt, for whom poverty had been a way of life and whose straightforward manner brought a challenge to Arsenius's integrity, he made room for friendship. Arsenius had to define his own identity in terms of what he had left and what he was becoming. Even for a prickly Arsenius, friendship in the desert was possible. We hear almost nothing about the content of this relationship, for it is important only insofar as it reveals the wisdom of the father, not in itself. But friendship of this type provided no threat to Arsenius's choice of a life of solitude.

The more the desert fathers concentrated on cutting themselves off from each other, the more they came to know and understand each other. Distance gave room for meditation, which provided human insight and an awareness of differences among people. There is a story of the brother who went to visit Arsenius in the desert of Scetis and was struck by the man's aloofness. Yet when he visited abba Moses, he was received warmly.[35] One of the fathers asked God in prayer how it could be that 'for your name's sake the one flees from men, and the other, for your name's sake, receives them with open arms?' The answer came in a vision where two boats were seen on a river. In one was Arsenius, who sailed alone with God's spirit and was 'in perfect peace', while 'in the other was Abba Moses with the angels of God and they were all eating honey cakes'. The meaning in both stories is brilliantly clear: Arsenius obtained peace through solitude, while Moses approached God through enjoying the good company of others. They became as angels to him, and their presence by no means threatened his soul. Each father must find his own course in the desert or, to complete the image, on the spiritual Nile. Neither way, that of solitude or that of companionship, is in itself better than the other. Each way is good insofar as it leads to God.

Can the good ascetic eat honey cakes with his friends and yet be a spiritual father? Apparently yes, if these delicious foods accompany spiritual discourse, which makes one's friends become like God's angels, his messengers. At the same time, however, the eater of honey cakes must respect the choice of those who prefer to be on their own. There is room in the desert both for a Moses with his eager hospitality and an Arsenius with his avoidance of most human contacts.

Once the narrow confines and drudgery of village life (or of the palace) have been left behind, the horizons are limitless. The Alphabetical Collection contains an undercurrent of optimism according to which men (and sometimes women) by speaking to each other and by sharing with each other the wisdom of their lives, can help each other to heaven. It is here that we come closest to an ideal of spiritual friendship, without its ever being explicitly formulated. Because of the obligations of hospitality and of advice-giving, the brothers could take each other's needs into consideration. Interrupting the routine of their own ascetic discipline, they were obliged to respond to each other. Behind the anecdotes lies evidence for many friendships, however infrequently the word friendship is used.

One-seventh of the Alphabetical Collection is taken up by stories concerning Abba Poemen (The Shepherd). Although there are problems with his identity (for there may have been several fathers with this name), the sayings found here agree that the Poemen in question managed to bring several of his family members with him to the desert. According to Sister Benedicta Ward, 'the close ties of Egyptian monks with their families and their villages were constantly having to be broken in favour of the freedom of the desert'.[36] The point of many of these stories, however, is that old, now severed ties often were replaced by new ties *with the same people.* The biological brother had to become the spiritual brother. It was hard for Poemen to live in this new manner, for he could not ignore the old bonds. When he got upset that his brother Paesios had made friends with someone outside his cell, he reported the relationship to Abba Ammonas. The latter's response was sharp: 'Poemen, are you still alive', the old man retorted: 'Go, sit down in your cell; engrave it on your heart that you have been in the tomb for a year already'.[37]

This is the teaching of many of the fathers, based on the words of Christ himself. We must hate family in order to follow him (Luke 14:26). Poemen had to learn to forget or at least turn aside from blood bonds, for if he was concerned about his brother in the flesh, then he still belonged to the world, the village community where family members exist for each other and spiritual advancement is impossible. Even if his brother's *affectus* was undesirable, Poemen had no business asserting his position as biological brother in order to intervene in another monk's emotional life. The desert required above all *apatheia,* the total control of all passions, even when they seemed directed toward helping loved ones.[38]

Poemen had to break the old emotional bond with his brother, but he had the possibility of forging new spiritual bonds with him and with others. He provides one of the few instances in which *amicus* is used positively.[39] An old man known for his wisdom said he had no time for a visit from Poemen. When he persisted, the old man finally gave way and even became Poemen's friend: *factus est ergo amicus eis ex illo die.*[40] The plural pronoun, *eis,* makes it clear that it was not Poemen alone who approached and finally won over the old man. It was Poemen with a group of ascetic companions. This is not an individual friendship but an expression of how desert rivalries between speakers of wisdom were resolved. Poemen and the old man were potential competitors in the role, but Poemen showed humility by seeking out the old man and deferring to his wisdom. The point of the story is not friendship but humility.

The sayings attributed to Poemen distinguish sharply between kinship and spiritual bonds. When a magnate wanted Poemen's attention and was refused it, he imprisoned Poemen's nephew and said he would not release him until Poemen 'comes to intercede for him'. But the ascetic refused to do so, despite the pleas of his sister. His only answer to her was: 'Poemen has not brought forth any sons'.[41] Accused of having a 'heart of stone', Poemen retorted that he was dead to the world and could not be involved in its affairs. Yet in the next anecdote, Poemen invited to his cell a spiritual brother who had been driven away from a monastery because of his sins. Poemen 'embraced him and was kind to him and invited him to eat'.[42] Blood bonds counted for nothing, while spiritual ones demanded action. Poemen was not inviting a friendship of equality. He was acting according to his membership in the desert's spiritual brotherhood and expressing concern for a wayward brother in a manner that he could not show for his nephew. *Apatheia* required non-involvement with family and friends but did not preclude the duty of helping the weak on their way to God:

> Instructing one's neighbour is for the man who is whole and without passions; for what is the use of building the house of another, while destroying one's own?[43]

While many kinsmen of the desert fathers must have failed to grasp these altered relationships, a few relatives gradually came to understand what their severance from village and family involved. A relative of Poemen appealed for help for a sick child. She went not to Poemen, but to the other monks:

> I am related to Abba Poemen, and see the misfortune which has overtaken my child. Though I want to bring him to the old man, we are afraid he does not want to see us. Each time he hears I am here, he has me driven away.[44]

The brothers found a solution that spared both the child and the master. The boy was brought into the brethren, who blessed him, one after another, so that at last Poemen had to join them in the common act. In the context of community charity, he manifested miraculous powers and healed the child. In the anecdote he avoids showing preference to a member of his own family. He heals the child not because he is related to it but because he cannot exclude himself from participating in a community blessing.

One of the most striking anecdotes about Poemen concerns his refusal to see his mother. She beats on the door of the monastery and cries out:

> I want to see my children. What will happen if I do see you? Am I not your mother? Was it not I who suckled you? So I was troubled when I heard your voice.[45]

The mother missed not just Poemen but also his brother. The desert had broken up her family, and now she demanded some small contact. Poemen told her, 'If you refrain from seeing us now you will see us in the age to come'. The mother is said to have accepted the answer. This is no more than the desert fathers' imitation of Christ's relationship to his own mother once he had started his public life. However difficult it is for us to believe that Poemen convinced his mother by these words, the episode sums up the ideal of separation from village and family life that was essential for the egyptian monk.

Sometimes, however, ascetics did admit responsibility for mothers or sisters and saw to it that they were installed in monasteries. Some of the fathers were confident that kinship bonds could be transformed into new spiritual ones.[46]

How can one be dead to other people and yet be alive to them? The christian paradox is resolved in monastic *apatheia*, the removal of the passions in the pursuit of perfect peace. In normal social relationships, people can anger, excite, or disappoint each other. The eremitic response must be self-control: 'A man who lives with a companion ought to be like a stone pillar: hurt him, and he does not get angry, praise him and he is not puffed up'.[47] The brother who is beyond passion is also beyond anxiety:

> Whoever lives in the monastery should see all the brethren as one: he should guard his eyes and his lips; and then he will be at peace without anxiety.[48]

The oneness referred to here goes back inevitably to the ideal of one heart and mind in the Acts of the Apostles (4:32), but Paul was mainly concerned with describing how the early Christians held all things in common. The fathers of the desert took this expression to describe the ideal of peace of mind. This excludes the cultivation of close relationships with individual brothers within the community. Other persons, even those who share the spiritual life, were not looked upon as potential allies in the pursuit of salvation, except in special instances where they could provide guidance. In everyday situations, the desert dweller was not to concentrate on the people in the community whom he liked best. Other people are more often a distraction than a source of support:

> If you want to go to the monastery, you must be careful about every encounter and everything you do, or you will not be able to do the work of the monastery.[49]

Doing good to one's neighbour meant not getting involved with him. The giving of spiritual advice was limited to a privileged few. The majority of the desert dwellers were to sit in their cells or gather in silence for the common weekly exercises. They were to speak only when edification or advice were required:

> Flee from men, stay in your cell, weep for your sins, do not take pleasure in the conversation of men, and you will be saved.[50]

We are a long way here from Augustine's admission that he loved being loved, and yet the two statements both emerge at the end of the fourth century on the shores of the Mediterranean. Augustine could not imagine seeking God outside of the company of men, while the desert fathers found that they could not seek him without reducing companionships with other men to an absolute minimum. Augustine and the desert fathers provide alternative interpretations of the christian message. One looks on other human beings as an aid to one's salvation, while the other considers them a threat.

The desert fathers were not always as stern as Arsenius or Poemen. Some of the anecdotes even concede that a father could harbour greater love for one brother than another.[51] For all the desert dwellers, however, it was essential to get away from the demands of family and village. Because the pull was strong, the break had to be absolute, even if family members showed up in the desert and asked to share in the same way of life.

'The man who has learned the sweetness of the cell flees from his neighbour, but not as though he despised him', said Theodore of Pherme. Distance must be maintained, but there should not be contempt. This ideal could be realized if one lived with others but did not become attached to them:

> All the days of your life keep the frame of mind of the stranger which you have on the first day you join them, so as not to become too familiar with them.[52]

Self-restraint and caution, which people manifest when they are put into an unfamiliar situation, must be maintained later on. Only then can there be peace and harmony. Anger, the great enemy of every hermit and monastic community, will have no place, for mutual distance provides no occasion for it. Ultimately each brother is alone in seeking God, but at the same time each needs the other's advice and support. The bonds of friendship, like those of kinship, are restricted and submerged in the avoidance of passion. God is all, but other people are still present.

PACHOMIUS: PRECEPTS AND EXPERIENCE

Just as the eremitic fathers of Egypt thought little of friendship and preferred that brothers maintain a distance from each other, so too, the great legislator for cenobites Pachomius (c. 290-346) in his Precepts made clear his disapproval of closeness among the brothers.[53] The Precepts, however, express only one side of the Pachomian heritage.

If we look at the various Lives of this father, he seems to have enjoyed relationships that we could characterize as friendships. What was best known in medieval monasticism, thanks to Latin translations, was the Precepts, but in what follows I shall try to show how Pachomius, like Anthony, can be seen in more than one light.

Pachomius dealt in his Precepts with situations of possible sexual temptation.[54] He treated such matters in a specific and frank way. The brothers were not to hitch up their garments too high and expose their legs while they washed clothes.[54] They were not to ride on the same animal, unless they had permission to do so, for physical contact, it is implied, might occasion temptation.[55] Pachomius took into consideration a number of situations that give us an idea of daily life in one of his communities. In the prickly landscape brothers might get thorns into their bare feet and ask each other for help in pulling them out.[56] Even here, a banal everyday event could turn into an occasion for sin. Pachomius allowed young boys into his monasteries, and he was concerned that older monks might have 'friendships with those of tender years'.[57] Such bonds, which Jerome in his latin translation called *amicitiae aetatis infirmae,* are never directly said to have a homosexual content, but it is clear that Pachomius saw them as possible sources of sexual temptation.

If read in isolation, the Precepts suggest that Pachomius was very much afraid of homosexuality in his communities, and so discouraged special friendships. But if we read his Rule and letters as a whole, as well as the earliest biographies, we see the same pattern unfolding as with the desert fathers. Statements concerning sexual sin are only one part of a complex program seeking to maintain harmony and peace among individual monks and in the community as a whole.

Many provisions deal with the monks' relations to their kin. Relatives were allowed to visit a pachomian monastery, but under carefully regulated circumstances, and the gifts of food they brought were to be handed over to the porter, so no jealousy could arise (*Praecepta* §53). Brothers could visit sick relatives, but they were to have a trustworthy companion with them and during the visit stay in some monastic house or church (§54). If monks received anything from their parents, they were to use only what they needed on the way home, and what was left they were to deliver up to the housemaster on their return. Pachomius did not try to separate his monks from their kin as rigorously as some of the desert fathers insisted. His cenobitic life had more room for family bonds than did the eremitic existence. But he would not allow families to assume primary importance in the life of the brothers.

A sick brother was not to be taken care of by a relative (§47). When a young man entered one of Pachomius's monasteries, he was to be asked 'whether he can renounce his parents and his own possessions'.[36] Parents and property go together. They are part of the furniture of the world, and they are to be kept at a distance unless charity demands otherwise. Emergencies might bring visits to houses of women if a brother had there a mother, sister, or daughter, some relatives or cousins, or the mother of his own children (§143). One situation which might permit a visit was when an inheritance was to be settled.

Pachomius's concerns are summed up in his prohibition that one monk defend another in the monastery:

> If someone agrees with sinners and defends someone else who had committed a fault, he shall be accursed before God and men and shall be very severely rebuked.[59]

Pachomius does not distinguish between defending a relative, a friend, or a stranger. Such special pleading, no matter for whom, breaks up the unity of the monastery and is to be considered a grave threat not just to the spiritual lives of those involved but also to the community as a whole. This is one of the pachomian provisions integrated into the Rule of Saint Benedict.[60] It can hardly be accidental that Benedict ignored the several chapters dealing with occasions for sexual sin among the brothers but made use of this tenet.

Jerome translated into Latin not only the Rules of Pachomius but also his letters and those of his successor Horsiesios. We can turn to these for a fuller treatment of some subjects only lightly touched in the precepts. Many of Pachomius's letters contain a mysterious religious sign language. They say nothing about cloister friendships, but in addressing the leaders of one house, Pachomius speaks of the saints' work in terms of friends who have knowledge of the will of God.[61] The abbot and superior of the monastery are seen as responsible for the salvation of all the monks, but they are each other's friends. Once again we find that being a friend did not necessarily imply only friendships of the world. It could also describe the brothers of the cloister gathered in peace and unity. But there is no room for exclusive affections here. Like the desert fathers, Pachomius required equal love among the brothers:

> . . . so that, once conflicts cease, the tranquillity of peace return, and you be able to walk in it before God and men, so that you love all equally in serving God and concord.[62]

Equal love is the necessary antidote to conflicts among the brothers. Unequal loves breed tensions and disharmony, the reflection in the community of the passions of jealousy and competition.

Pachomius's successor as father of the monasteries, Horsiesios, repeated this provision in his Testament:

> Be careful, o man, not to love the one and hate the other, but show equality in all, lest by chance you love one whom God hates, and he whom you hate, God loves. For the sake of friendship, you are not to consent to anyone who is in error.[63]

Equality of loves is the only possible guarantee that man loves as God loves. *Amicitia* in this context is a negative term. As a bond between men, it encourages them to follow one another into error. Such friendships provide an independent standard of behaviour that cuts across the discipline of the cloister.

A pattern of attitude and behaviour begins to emerge from these sources. Men can be each others' friends in the cloister, but friendship for its own sake and as a goal in itself is dubious and undesirable. This may explain why *amicus,* in terms of a living, actual friend, can be used to characterize bonds in the cloister, while *amicitia* as a permanent relationship has a negative ring, echoing the carnal bonds of the world that corrupt the heart and create dissension within the spiritual community. When Horsiesios spoke of the friend of this world (*amicus huius mundi*) as being opposed to God, he was thinking of the attack in the Epistle of Saint James (4:4) on *amicitia*:

> Unfaithful creatures! Do you not know that friendship with the world is enmity with God. Therefore, whoever wishes to be a friend of the world makes himself an enemy of God.

There is a slight difference between the biblical text and the meaning which Horsiesios derives from it. Saint James was concerned with the total sum of relationships which ties a person to the world, while the desert writer considered worldly individual bonds of friendship. The biblical text does not condemn friendship in itself but is concerned with its too great attachment to the things of this world. The desert text, however, legislates against such friendships in themselves.[64] In latin translations Saint James speaks of *amicitia huius mundi,* while Horsiesios uses *mundi amicitias.* The difference between an abstract singular concept and plural friendships contrasts attachment to this world with individual corrupting friendships.

The moral exhortation of the Epistle against destructive passions of secular life is reformulated in a much more concrete provision. So that all the brothers shall be equal, there must be equal love among the members of the community.[65] One brother is not to defend another who is being corrected; no one is to receive gifts from relatives or close friends.[66] Only this way, insists Horsiesios, can peace and good will be achieved in the cloister. The *consortium* achieved among fellows on earth will make them sharers (*participes*) with the holy fathers in the future life. Here Horsiesios, as so many monastic writers, reverts to the image of harmony in Acts 4:32-33:

> In the Acts of the Apostles we also read the same: There was one heart and mind for the multitude of believers, and no one who said that anything was his own, but all things were in common to them.[67]

Mutual love means equal love for all brothers. Horsiesios allows no compromise here, for any nuances in affection let loose the passions and thus allow discord into the community.

The pachomian-horsiesian literature might seem to rule out all exclusive relationships. But if we turn to the First Greek Life (much of which was translated into Latin in the sixth century by Denis the Little), we find plentiful evidence of individual relationships based on mutual love and concern. Most prominent are spiritual father-son links, as between Pachomius's first master, Palamon, and himself, or between Pachomius and his successor Theodore. In a transition from eremitic to cenobitic forms of monastic life, such personal bonding is only to be expected. As leader of a number of populous communities, Pachomius did his best to look after the spiritual needs of individual members. When he had no time to do so, he would hand over a wayward boy to a proven monk for special care.

> Then Pachomius was patient with him; he called a great monk named Psenamon and told him in the boy's absence, "We know that you have labored in *ascesis* a long time. Now, for God's sake, take this boy and suffer with him in all things until he is saved. You know indeed how I am occupied with many affairs concerning the brothers."[68]

Pachomius seems to have institutionalized the father-son link, or at least to have approved its transference from the isolated world of a few cells around a master to the crowded daily existence of the new monasticism. He insisted on the importance of confessing one's temptations immediately to a spiritual guide.[69] On several occasions Pachomius's insight into other people, his ability to search hearts, is emphasized.[70] This not only shows his spiritual powers but also underlines the importance of spiritual interdependence among the brothers.

Hierarchical father-son links are by far the most prominent bonds in the biography of Pachomius, but he is also said to have had a good friend who apparently was not attached to any of the monasteries but who was able to use his influence to obtain a miracle.[71] Similarly the relationship between Pachomius's two successors, Theodore and Horsiesios, is described in terms of their equality and unity:

> . . . they two were as one man. Everyone marvelled at their life-giving goodness, for they had been trained by the Lord to be one.[72]

This description resembles that given in a letter of Archbishop

Athanasius to Abba Horsiesios on the death of Theodore. Such emphasis on harmony could have been intended by the biographer to explain away the fact that Theodore had originally been groomed by Pachomius to become the father of the monasteries but was initially set aside in favour of Horsiesios. Whatever conflicts lie behind the text, the pachomian world emerges from the account as one in which the requirement for equal love among the brothers left at least some limited room for individual relationships. Pachomius's biographer was much more interested in depicting him as a person in contact with others than was Athanasius in describing Anthony. Unlike the lonely hero who conquers devils and performs miracles (though he is also capable of doing so), Pachomius is seen primarily as a founding abbot, the man who institutionalized monastic life.

Pachomius's *Life* is a commemorative as opposed to a heroic biography.[73] The portrait of Pachomius reflects not only his own holiness but also his efforts to make his monastic settlements into permanent communities. This explains why the links between Pachomius and Theodore are so carefully described, and why the greek biography gives so much attention to Theodore's slow progress in inheriting the mantle of Pachomius. Pachomius, unlike Anthony, was almost never alone. He is seen at the centre of a movement that involves men in mutual dependence.

Pachomius cannot be without Theodore. While the older man appears as a saint and founder and therefore is difficult to view as a fallible human being, Theodore embodies the conflicts of the Pachomian movement. Like the desert fathers, he rejected his own physical family but he showed concern for the members of his new monastic family. Like Abba Poemen, Theodore had no time for his mother. When she came to visit and Pachomius at first insisted that he see her, Theodore's argumentation made him change his mind:

> 'The sons of Levi killed their own parents and brothers to please the Lord and escape the danger of his wrath. I too, I have no mother, nor anything of the world, for it passes.'
>
> Pachomius said to him, 'If you love God more than your mother, shall I prevent you? I shall rather encourage you.'[74]

Theodore also refused to give his biological brother any special attention, but when he converted to the monastic life, Pachomius asked Theodore to show him at least the concern owed every new recruit.

This anecdote about rejecting family bonds is followed immediately by one in which Theodore goes out of his way to give spiritual comfort and advice to a brother in the monastery. The juxtaposition could hardly be accidental. Theodore denied kinship to his physical brother (he 'refused to treat him as a brother'), while with his spiritual brother he shared himself. Theodore tells the recruit that he too could feel defeated when Pachomius criticized him harshly:

> 'You certainly know that this old man's (Pachomius') speech is abrupt beyond measure; and I do not know if I can stay here.'
> The brother answered, unburdening himself to him, 'Do you also experience this?'
> He answered, 'Even more so do I. But let us comfort each other until we test him once more. If he is good to us, let us stay; but if not, let us withdraw on our own to some other place and get relief'.
> And hearing this, the weak brother was strengthened.[76]

By showing understanding for the brother's hurt feelings and discouragement, Theodore made Pachomius's reprimand bearable. Here a 'big brother' figure mediates between a stern father and an injured son. Theodore resolved a potential conflict and reestablished peace in the monastery.

Through Theodore's experiences, we can see how he and Pachomius dealt with problems of kinship and loyalties. Pachomius sent Theodore with a brother who had received permission to visit his family, and Theodore showed sufficient tactfulness in a critical situation to ensure that the brother returned to the monastery. Pachomius accepted Theodore's actions as necessary. Theodore also explained to a brother the passage in Luke (14:26) about hating one's father and mother. This was more than a theoretical discussion. The brother 'often used to visit his relatives', but by confronting him with the gulf between the Gospel injunction and the brother's actions, Theodore managed to convince him to stop such visits.[77]

From this biography emerges the same values as are to be found in the *Pachomiana Latina:* an insistence that the cenobitic life requires the dissolution of all earlier human relationships and the maintenance of absolute harmony among the members of the new community. Necessary tranquillity can best be obtained through equal loves, with as few distinctions as possible. There is no explicit condemnation of friendships within the cloister, and there is no attempt to equate the emotions of friendship with sexual attraction. The pachomian literature is quite matter of fact about physical situations that might lead to sexual acts, and there is nothing sentimental or reticent in these hard-nosed descriptions.

The desert dwellers, whether hermits or monks, could be each other's friends while at the same time they were suspicious of the value of friendship. For these men and women, the elimination of all the soul's passions required a flight not just from sexual attachment but from all strong human emotions. What for the twentieth century might seem good and natural—the birth and growth of tenderness and warmth among people who like each other—was for Pachomius as well as the desert fathers a reversion to the limited and limiting world of the village or the city. There people concentrated on themselves and one another, and ignored God. As Abba Alonios said, 'If a man does not say in his heart, in the world there is only myself and God, he will not gain peace.'[78] In the pachomian world there had to be other monks, but asceticism required separation rather than community, loneliness and the inner journey undertaken within one's own cell. The desert might bloom with monasteries, but they were full of men who still were hermits at heart.

THE INFLUENCE OF BASIL

To Pachomius isolation was best, but community was the norm. In the writings of Saint Basil the Great (c. 330-379), community is exalted as desirable in itself.[79] Basil believed that since life in community gives men the opportunity to exhibit mutual love, it is a better means of salvation than eremitical life. His many spiritual tracts and *Long* and *Short Rules* contain a full description of the monastic community. It is not difficult to understand why he still to this day is the major mentor and guide of Eastern monasticism.[80] Both human understanding and spiritual wisdom are present in his advice. Basil gave himself time to explain the background for his ordinances. The *Long Rule* is more a spiritual treatise on the monastic life than a series of precepts.

Though Basil's program centres on community life, he agreed with the egyptian fathers about the need for cutting off 'the bonds of attachment to this life. . . through complete separation from and forgetfulness of old habits'.[81] Both the ties of family and all contact with the world are to be replaced by 'another world', and here Basil uses the words of Saint Paul, 'Our conversation is in heaven' (Phil 3:20). Any 'affection for this life' blocks the attainment of the goal of 'perfect renunciation'. Basil pointed to the precedent of the apostles themselves, who left not only their families but also their occupations, 'the very boat upon which their whole livelihood depended':

> Thus a man who is strongly seized with the desire of following Christ can no longer be concerned with anything pertaining to this life, not even with the love of his parents or other relatives if this runs counter to the precepts of the Lord, for in this case these words apply: 'If any man come to me and hate not his father and mother' (Luke 14:26). . .[82]

As in the case of Pachomius seen in his biography, Basil took literally Christ's injunction to cut oneself off from family bonds. One's family does not just provide a symbol of one's attachment to the world. It *is* one's bond to the world. A man works for it, loves for it, hates for it. All these energies must now be turned to the monastic community.

Basil's language is very close to that of the Gospels. He uses the parables of Christ to concretize his thought. The pearl of great price, for example, is to be treasured at all costs (Matt 13:45-6), and to obtain it, we must cut away 'the bonds of this material and transient life' and obtain 'freedom from human concerns'. This involves not just the removal of self from things but also from persons:

> How, indeed, can we gain either contrition of heart or humility of mind or deliverance from anger, pain, anxieties—in a word, from all destructive movements of the soul—if we are entangled in the riches and cares of a worldly life and cling to others by affection and association?[83]

Basil says nothing here about sexual attraction or temptation. The search for *apatheia* involves much more than refusing the impulses of the flesh (or, to use modern psychological terms, genital sexuality). Detachment means cutting away all the powerful emotions that stir the mind and unsettle the body. Peter Brown has shown how monks and hermits were concerned with checking the impulse of anger.[84] But anger was only one of the human passions that Basil considered dangerous.

For the Cappadocians as well as for the Egyptians, blood bonds were much more a problem than were ties of friendship. Basil's theoretical discourse on renunciation is followed by very concrete instructions on how men entering the monastic life should renounce property, not by handing it over in trust to undependable relatives but by giving it up to responsible persons who would distribute it to those who needed it.[85] Basil did not require that all possessions be handed over to the monastic community. His concern was to prevent relatives from coming around to bother his monks about their affairs. Kin are at best a nuisance, at worst a threat to the community:

> Superiors should not allow those who have been permanently admitted to the community to be distracted in any way—by allowing them either to leave the company of their brethren and live in private on the pretext of visiting their relatives or to be burdened with the responsibility of caring for their relatives according to the flesh.[86]

Unlike the egyptian fathers, Basil did not try to break all bonds between families in the world and the spiritual family of the cloister. He conceded that the monks have to take care of blood relations, but this is a task for the community, not for the individual monk:

> The parents or brothers of a member of the community, therefore, if they live piously, should be treated by all the brethren as fathers or other relatives possessed in common.[87]

Basil was more of a realist about human relations than Theodore showed himself to be when, in the biography of Pachomius, he tried to avoid all contact with his mother. For Basil the transformation of men from being members of a carnal family to participation in a spiritual one implied that individual kinship bonds become community ties. It is up to the superior to look after the needs of the monks' relatives who come to the monastery for help. He decides whether a man or woman is so 'entangled in the usual concerns of the worldly life' that the monastery can 'have no common cause with them'. Only relatives whose 'conversation will bring about the edification and perfection of the soul' are to have permission to talk with the brethren.[88]

Basil was concerned that relatives would talk too much about their daily lives out in the world. In this way they could lure the unsteady monk back into worries or anxiety about secular affairs. Basil did not, however, try to eliminate family bonds from the lives of his monks. Contacts were to be kept under strict control, but Basil believed that the community as a whole, under a good and watchful superior, can integrate individual family relationships into those of the community.

The section on relations with kin is followed by one 'on the proper way to converse with consecrated women'. Here also Basil leaves some latitude for relationships while retaining the principle: anything that disturbs the mind of the monk and distracts him from his inner life is to be avoided at all costs. Families can be upsetting, and female—or male—friends can also lure the monk away from his real business:

> [the monk]. . .will liberate himself entirely from all solicitude about giving pleasure to a woman, since he dreads the judgment of Him who said, 'God hath scattered the bones of them that please men' (Ps 52:6). Nor will he, therefore, cultivate acquaintance even with a man for the purpose of giving him pleasure, but he will hold discourse with him when it is necessary so as to manifest that zeal for his neighbour

> which every person is obliged to show according to the command of God.[89]

If a man seeks to gratify another man or a woman, then he is putting this person before God. But if he is concerned with speaking about his or her salvation, then the contact is legitimate. Once again we see how friendship in itself, as a matter for delight and enjoyment, is looked upon with the greatest suspicion, whether it be male-male or male-female. And yet the sexual element is not even considered. Basil wants to maintain 'the union of charity among the brethren' and so seeks to keep them safe from jealousy and resentment.

This principle of keeping a distance also applies within the cloister. Any monk entrusted with a position of responsibility is not to use it to punish those he dislikes or to reward those who please him:

> Now, the former course is an indication of fraternal enmity, the latter of particular affection, which is especially abhorrent because by it the union of charity among the brethren is torn asunder and is replaced by base suspicions, jealousies, strife, and a distaste for work.
>
> They who have the office of distributing necessary articles to the community, therefore, are duty-bound to be absolutely free from particular affection and from aversion . . .[90]

Basil's prohibition of 'particular affection' (*prospatheia* = *amor singularis*) is placed in the context of the relationships between those in charge and those under them. But what about friendships of equality among the monks? Do they, too, disturb the harmonious life of the cloister and split the community? A *locus classicus* in one of the ascetical discourses has been attributed to Basil but its authenticity has been challenged: 'particular affection should be banished from the monastery, for enmity is engendered by wrangling and particular friendship'.[91] The writer here insists on 'absolutely equal affection', thus echoing statements in the Sayings of the Desert Fathers as well as in the pachomian literature.

Even if its dubious authenticity means that this particular discourse is not Basil's own teaching, its message is close to that of Basil. Elsewhere he asserts:

> The brothers should maintain mutual love for each other, but not so that two or three at one time conspire and form cliques, for this is not charity but sedition and division. It is a sign of the evil behaviour of those who join together in such a way.[92]

Special relationships are viewed as an incitement to dissension in the community. Basil asserted the same principle as Pachomius and the egyptian fathers. We have returned to the precept of Poemen: 'Whoever lives in the monastery should see all the brethren as one'.[93] In order to obtain community discipline, everyone is to show equal love for each other:

> If they love the common good of discipline, those who do so will without doubt share a common and equal love towards all. But if they cut themselves off and separate themselves, they make a community within the community. This is a harmful pact of friendship, for it is different from that which joins them together in community.[94]

When particular friendships grow up, they create a divisive 'community within community'. The brothers should distribute their loves evenly not just for the sake of their own peace of mind but also for the peace of the community.

Equal love for all and the rule of discipline in everyday life implicitly exclude the formation of preferential friendships within the cloister. Like Poemen, Pachomius and Horsiesios, Basil calls for equal love for the sake of common discipline and a radically exclusive love of God. The question of sexual involvement is secondary to that of communal solidarity, even though Basil, like the Egyptians, is quite open about situations that might lead to homosexual involvement:

> If you are youthful in body or mind, fly from intimate association with comrades of your own age and run away from them as from fire. The Enemy

> has, indeed, set many aflame through such means and consigned them to the eternal fire, casting them down. . .on the pretext of spiritual love. . . At meals take a seat far away from your young brother; in lying down to rest, let not your garments be neighbour to his; rather, have an elderly brother lying between you. When a young brother converses with you or is opposite you in choir, make your response with your head bowed, lest, perchance, by gazing fixedly into his face, the seed of desire be implanted in you by the wicked sower.[95]

Basil understood human behaviour well enough to know that what looks like a spiritual affinity easily can provide an occasion for sexual sin.

Basil deals with homosexual temptations in far fewer passages than he devotes to particular affections, whether of kinship or of friendship. He is concerned with providing the blueprint for successful community life. For Basil, as for the desert fathers, homosexuality became a problem when young, attractive boys shared the ascetic life. Unlike some of the strictest desert fathers, Basil did not try to outlaw boys. He merely emphasized what is obvious: a monk cannot allow himself to become infatuated with a youth, for in so doing, he forgets his true purpose in being a monk. Love in community cannot be exclusive. It cannot concentrate on one body or one mind. It cannot desire to please one handsome young boy at the cost of the daily routine of prayer and work.

Basil is the first monastic writer in the East to be totally convinced that a common life provided the best way of bringing individual men to God. Almost everything he wrote for monks is concerned with the formation and preservation of community, and so friendship—or sexuality—can be only secondary. He insisted on the renunciation of carnal affections, which include 'things of our secret shame, ties of physical relationship, human friendships, and a mode of life that is inimical to the perfection of the Gospel of salvation'.[96] But renunciation did not mean isolation, as it often did for the desert fathers, at least for long periods of their lives. Basil saw community life as a permanent opportunity for the growth of love among the members, the charity of which Saint Paul speaks:

> . . . a life passed in solitude is concerned only with the private service of individual needs. This is openly opposed to the law of love which the Apostle fulfilled, who sought not what was profitable to himself but to many that they might be saved. (1 Cor 10:33)[97]

Basil's model was that of many other monastic writers: the community of mutual caring set forth in the Acts of the Apostles. This community cannot tolerate factions or divisions, and so exclusive relationships are forbidden in it. Experienced positively, however, such a community can be 'a good and pleasing thing. . . the dwelling of brethren together in one habitation'.[98]

THE EASTERN CONSENSUS

Basil's teaching on human bonds illustrates the agreement of the Eastern fathers that friendships had no positive social function in the eremitic or cenobitic way of life. Only a few statements reject friendship outright, and most of these speak specifically of 'worldly friendship' and mention friendships in the cloister only insofar as they manifest exclusive involvements that break up the unity and discipline of monastic life. There is no explicit celebration or approval of spiritual friendships. *Amicitia spiritalis* did not yet exist as a term used in monastic literature. In the fourth century *amicitia* still had too many overtones of greco-roman elite culture and the pursuit of worldly success to be drawn into a christian context: 'He lived his first years humbly and in poverty. . .Then he came into friendships and associations and received positions of royal trust. . . He was a friend of kings and governors and became accordingly rich'.[99]

And yet we know that the 'friends of God' could be each other's friends. In the desert the spiritual father had a recognized and necessary place. In the pachomian monastery it was not only acceptable but imperative for older monks to give guidance and advice to younger ones. The same ethic of interdependence is central in Basil:

> Nothing, indeed, is so compatible with our nature as living in society and in dependence upon one another and as loving our own kind.[100]

Is there a distant echo of Aristotle here? More likely a reminiscence of the Epistles of Paul encouraging Christian communities to live in harmony and mutual love. Within this context, Basil could write letters that express friendship with other churchmen, as Jean Leclercq has pointed out in order to counter the usual assertion that Basil opposed particular friendships.[101] Outside the monastic life, friendship had a place in the church. Even within the cloister, friendships existed. As Leclercq indicates, theory and practice of friendship are almost never the same.[102] Both have to be considered. Whether we look to the desert cell or to the pachomian community, we see monks being each other's friends. And at times they can even be friendly to women who have been hospitable to them or whom they help.[103]

How can we bridge this distance between the pejorative view of friendship and the fact that Eastern monks did form friendships? Friendship requires acceptance of the relationship by the community as a whole. Relationships among monks that helped lead them to their personal salvation and which did not disturb the unity of the community were acceptable. Friendship as an ideal in itself, however, the monks of the East did not usually countenance. Suspicious and sceptical, they were too close in time and place to the delights and rewards of *amicitia* in upper-class life or to the involvements and demands of blood bonds in village life.

In Eastern monasticism, asceticism almost always came first, whether it was the ascetic practices of the desert hermit or the ascetic tone of life within the basilian community. Only when the passions were removed and the monk was dead to all worldly ties could he begin to think about what still linked him to other people. The first great commandment gradually overshadowed the second. Basil sought a balance between the two loves, but he did not entertain the possibility that through first loving one's neighbour in terms of close friendships, the monk could find a pathway to God. Only equal love of all one's neighbours in a monastic community made it easier to love God. Basil would not have accepted that, in looking into another man's or woman's eyes, we find the image of God, and thus a being who is eminently lovable.

There was too great a chance that one's mind, or the devil, would play tricks and turn the other human being into an idol. The devil was always playing tricks on the monks of the East, who saw the world as a battlefield. God could not be friendship, for friendship was a selfish kind of loving, making life sweeter instead of making it easier to die to all that is human life so that one can live with God.

In the fourth century special relationships of close contact between two or more people would find no theoretical justification or official recognition in the monastic community. Human closeness caused unrest in the soul, unrest in the body, or unrest in the community. And yet there was hope that such bonds of the flesh and of human emotions could be replaced by relationships of spiritual fatherhood or brotherhood. The spiritual father guided his son, or two fathers could respect each other's virtue and learned not to compete with each other in asceticism. A certain distance was almost always maintained, and despite reference to ritualized embraces and kisses, there is little evidence of individual tenderness or affection. Physical touching, usually symbolic, illustrates spiritual harmony and is normally limited to greetings and partings.[104]

Friendship became in this context almost an accidental benefit of spiritualized human contacts. It was formed not because it was sought out for itself but because two or more men recognized in each other harmony and inner peace in christian love. Passions of the soul and feelings of personal devotion had no place in such relationships. Men who were dead to the world could not revive to the call of mutual affection without giving up their ascetic way of life.

MODELS FOR MONASTIC LIFE

In the fourth century, eastern Mediterranean secular culture was too evident and too alien for christian converts like Pachomius or the egyptian fathers to make it possible for them to think that they could be in the world but not of it. They had to get out, physically and mentally. They had to leave behind the *impedimenta* of greco-roman culture, of village life on the Nile, of family and kin with its overwhelming concerns and trivial obsessions.

Once the age of martyrs had ended, the individual might bear witness to Christ through what can be called the way of solitude. Very much alone, he minimized all human contacts. Anthony provided the ideal. At least for periods in their lives, most egyptian fathers followed his example. They cut themselves off from all contact with men in order to be alone with God.

Eremitic monasticism proved to be a way for the very few. Cenobitic monasticism attracted many more. As soon as people associated with each other outside secular society in order to find salvation, the problem arose in interpersonal relations: how does the individual interact with others while still dedicating himself entirely to God? Other people are perceived primarily as threat, or at best as challenge, and only rarely as help. The first response to this dilemma might be called the *way of asceticism.* Perfection of self is attained through the submergence of self in a community and by the performance of individual acts of self-denial. Total separation from family and friends is required. The new family of the monastic community exists not in order to create new bonds of affection but in order to provide a secure environment for the asceticism of the individual. Pachomian monasticism, though communal in form, was applied in an individualistic manner. As the author of the *Historia Monachorum* said of the pachomian community at Ammon and its monks:

> These live a very strict life: they wear sheepskin cloaks, eat with their faces veiled and their heads bowed so that no one should see his neighbour, and keep such a profound silence that you would think you were in the desert. Each one practices his own asceticism in secret: it is only for the sake of appearance that they sit at a table, so as to seem to eat, and then they try to avoid being observed by each other.[105]

While doing their best to ignore each other and each other's ascetic ways, the monks had nevertheless chosen to live together under community discipline. They wanted to recreate the isolation of the desert and yet were not hermits. Community life thus provided the individual with a means for becoming a better ascetic, but the most desirable way of life remained that of the hermit.

With Saint Basil and his emphasis on the positive value of community life, acts of asceticism were no longer individualistic and hidden. They became a community function, by which common discipline was seen as more valuable than acts of extreme self-denial. This manner of monastic life might be called the *way of harmony*. It became normative in the West with Benedict and many other legislators. It was generally sceptical about individual relationships and at times could see them as threats to the maintenance of community discipline. Basil's warnings against the formation of factions and special groups within the monastery left little room for any open and direct recommendation of close friendships.

Later in this book we shall see how the *way of harmony* could be replaced by a *way of friendship*. Special relationships that did not threaten the harmony of community life gained acceptance. While still requiring the same discipline for everyone, this monastic point of view looked upon friendships as contributors to a greater degree of perfection in the community through the encouragement friends give each other. The writings of the Western fathers, as we shall see, anticipate the way of friendship within monastic or quasi-monastic communities.

This more flexible norm eventually led to the conviction that friendships do not have to be limited to relationships within the cloister. Self-perfection through both community life and inter-mural friendships opened onto friendships outside the cloister, as with holy women. This ethic might be called the *way of brotherhood.* In any given monastic community at any time in history, all these ways of human binding probably existed, but for us what is interesting is how the literature about such bonds develops. What we look for is the celebration of friendship and open acceptance of it as a desirable goal in the monastic life.

Schematically the possibilities are as follows.

1. The way of solitude:

God
|
individual

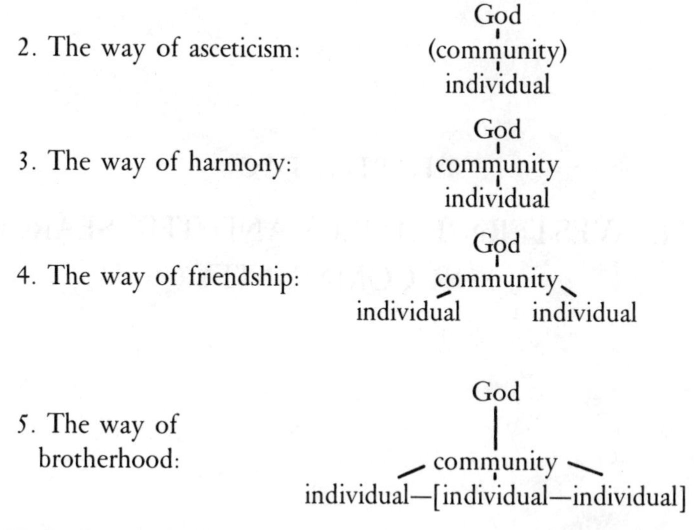

How does one follow Christ? Anthony answered differently than did Basil. But the wisdom of the East taught them both that the path to heaven did not lead through friendships, even among good men. In the West this point of view gained only limited response. Renouncing the world could still allow—and even require—the discovery or rediscovery of one's most beloved companions.

CHAPTER TWO

THE WESTERN FATHERS AND THE SEARCH FOR COMMUNITY

IN THE EAST friendship played only a limited role in the literature and practice of fourth-century asceticism. In the West in the closing decades of the fourth century, friendship became intimately associated with the new monasticism. However indebted the latin fathers were to greek and coptic experience, they showed independence of mind in picking and choosing the attitudes and practices that best fit their cultural needs and social situation.[1] An obvious point of departure is the concept of passionlessness (*apatheia*). This was central in the Eastern ascetic writer, Evagrius, yet absent in the works of his devoted follower, John Cassian.[2] Cassian and other Western writers did not incorporate the originally stoic idea that the ascetic must die to all passions and worldly involvements. They agreed that he must leave the world, but the Western writers looked upon the total break and separation from one's former life as an Eastern ideal that was commendable but not essential.

In the West asceticism combined forces with the development of the church as a pastoral organism.[3] There was little desire that the new monk or his community distance themselves from all human and pastoral concerns. Augustine has been called a passionate man.[4] He is hardly alone in giving expression to his deepest spiritual yearnings and combining them with active involvement with other people. In the East the salvation of the individual normally required, at least at one stage in life, a rejection of one's past and a flight into a totally solitary existence. In the West the experience of conversion also demanded a new life, but many old ties to the culture and habits of life could remain intact. However much men like Augustine and Paulinus assured each other that they had entered into a new existence, they were still aristocratic Romans. Their terminology was new. Their way of thinking was renewed. But their rhetoric as well as their manner of forming human bonds remained those of the upper class culture in roman Late Antiquity.

If the Eastern ideal required the killing of all passions, the Western ideal centered on the creation of community life, *vita communis*, within the christian context. However admired were the isolation, solitude, and extreme ascetic practices of the desert fathers in the West, there was general agreement that they were a special case. Sulpicius Severus sums up the Western argument: his description of Eastern hermits and monks was intended only as material for comparison with his beloved Martin of Tours. Martin emerges as the greater hero, not because his asceticism was greater, but because his miracles were more spectacular. These attracted men and formed the basis of a new christian community.

Everywhere in the West—in Italy, North Africa and Gaul—men and women at the end of the fourth century were forming quasi-monastic communities.[5] They read eagerly about the desert fathers, and many people went to Egypt, Palestine and Syria to see them for themselves. But when they returned, the communities they founded lay as often as not on the fringes of great cities and substantial towns. Contacts were maintained with the old roman community, now christianized, and it is often difficult to distinguish bishop from abbot. The Western fathers combined life forms in an almost naively optimistic manner. In the West one could be both chief pastor and ascetic. Augustine and Martin carried out both functions well. They could do so because of the monastic communities that they had formed. These men were not merely magnetic personalities able to attract other men. Unlike many of their Eastern counterparts, such fathers really did want men around them. Augustine could not be without his friends, but as he grew older, he realized that the best way to keep close to them and to live an ordered life with them was within a monastic community.

Western insistence on community life in order to stabilize friendships and to facilitate the practice of the new religion was connected with the social background of the participants. The leading church writers of the West came from upper class society. The monasticism they created was of an aristocratic type that was based on roman attitudes about friendship and alliances among good men. At Cassiciacum and at Thagaste, Augustine surrounded himself with people from his own class and background. Only at Hippo, after he had advanced further in the christian life, did he open his monastery to those from less favoured circumstances.[6] The poverty of Martin should not distract us from the fact that his publicist and the head of the community at Pruliacum, Sulpicius Severus, came from a well-heeled background, as did his magnificent friend Paulinus of Nola.

In the late Empire the practice of friendship had moved from the forum into the atrium of the aristocratic home. Many of those who frequented the home were now christian, and those among them who had been won over to an ascetic way of life often continued to live in these grand residences and to cultivate each other in friendship. The medieval monastery with its central cloister would be nothing but the atrium converted into a permanent residence for those seeking a life together in christian asceticism and friendship.

At the same time as upper class *amicitia* found expression in Western monastic friendships, the Eastern concern with homosexuality disappears from view. The Western fathers say almost nothing on this subject. Despite attempts early in this century by freudian psychologists to label Augustine's intense friendship of his youth as a homosexual one, most researchers would agree today that Augustine was not sexually attracted to other men.[7] He does not show any concern or even awareness that a passionate friendship between two men could become a homosexual relationship. Augustine is the complete heterosexual. His sexual orientation was expressed exclusively towards women. After his conversion, his refusal to have contacts with women, both in friendship and in sex, may well have strengthened an already strong emphasis on friendships with other men. But Augustine never associated his bonds with other males to his own sexual drive. He was fascinated with getting into friends' minds, as in the case of Alypius, whose motives Augustine delighted in exploring and describing. Augustine enjoyed matching his wits with his friends'. In Augustine's world men existed for friendship, women for sex. Friendship he considered a good thing, and sex usually not.

Augustine took the lead in forging attitudes towards friendship in Western monasticism. It would be incorrect, however, to claim that his own personal penchants were responsible for the Western lack of discussion about sex among men. It may well be the case that the fear of homosexuality went underground in the West. It can hardly be accidental that almost all the *apophthegmata* or sayings of the fathers in the Greek Alphabetical Collection that touch upon homosexuality are not included in the Latin Systematic Collection.[8] Some of those that speak vaguely of *fornicatio* could refer to sexual relations between men, but the Western version of the Sayings gives no indication that boys can be a source of temptation for men in the desert. It could be argued, of course, that silence could have been due to there having been no prohibition against homosexual behaviour, but such tolerance seems unlikely in view of a consistent rejection of every other form of sexual activity as being opposed to the monastic vocation.

Since there was no desert in the West to which men could withdraw, they formed communities in contact with the rest of civilization. At times they conceived of themselves as being cut off from their surroundings, but their roman roots were never far distant. The less isolated situation of Western monastic communities could have diminished the fear of getting too involved with a few individuals of one's own sex. In the East where a father could spend an intense day or two with one spiritual son and then see no one for a long period, homosexual fantasies could arise out of such encounters combined with the general habit of solitude.

In the West male sexual drives were projected on to women. They were seen as the central problem for men like Augustine, Jerome and Sulpicius Severus, who nevertheless all managed for periods in their lives to have close relationships with women without sex. However much the Western fathers' theorizing about friendship limited itself to male relationships based on roman ideals, almost all the Western fathers had strong and important friendships with women: Augustine at Cassiciacum with his mother; Jerome at Rome and Bethlehem with Paula, Eustochium, Marcella; Sulpicius Severus with his mother-in-law Bassula. The incarnation of christian conversion and the imitator of a new life in community, Paulinus of Nola, maintained a life-long non-sexual friendship with his wife Therasia, a relationship admired by and respected even by the sceptical Augustine.[9]

As soon as we turn aside from sex, misogyny, or marriage as our central concerns and look at the concept and practice of friendship among the Western fathers, a whole network of male-male and male-female relationships becomes visible. For these men and the women behind them, friendship formed the very breath of life, a point of departure for all spiritual life, and a necessary bond. Seldom if ever do the Western fathers express doubt about the value and utility of friendship. They had not had to flee stifling villages in order to find repose and truth. Their flight is from pagan roman culture of the cities to the blossoming christian roman culture of the same cities. For these men and women the transformation of self and the transformation of community provided fertile ground for the transformation of friendship from a purely natural phenomenon to a supernatural one: friendship in Christ.

AMBROSE OF MILAN: THE CONTINUITY OF THE ROMAN TRADITION

A closer look at Western fathers and their friendships should start, not with Augustine and all his complexity, but with Ambrose of Milan (c. 334-397). Simple and direct in his approach to friendship, Ambrose as bishop in 391 wrote on the duties of clerics, *De officiis ministrorum*, and dealt in his concluding paragraphs with the duties of friendship.[10] The work is important because it can be looked upon both as a restatement of roman classical values in a christian clerical milieu and as a proto-christian treatise on friendship. Ambrose provides a bridge between Cicero's *De amicitia* and Aelred of Rievaulx's *De spiritali amicitia*. Aelred not only took over sections of Ambrose's treatise verbatim, he also followed Ambrose's practice of substituting Cicero's use of pagan instances of friendship with corresponding examples from the Bible. Ambrose thus showed Aelred that a fully christian structure could be built on the classical foundation of friendship.

Ambrose based *De officiis* on the work of the same title by Cicero.[11] Like his mentor, he divided the treatise into three books dealing with uprightness (*honestas*), expediency (*utilitas*), and how the two could be combined in carrying out one's duties in life. Cicero had written for the politically active roman citizen, while Ambrose intended his work for his own clerics in the church of Milan, the up-and-coming members of a new ruling class in Western Europe. He was just as much concerned with human relations as with individual ethic. Ambrose, like Cicero, could not imagine men carrying out their duties in society without having friendships with each other. Cicero had said that friendship is to be valued but is not to be preferred to *honestas* (III. 43-46). Ambrose enlarged on these few statements in Cicero's *De officiis* and also borrowed ideas from his *De amicitia*, with the result that the closing chapters of his own Book III (124-36) make up a mini-treatise on friendship in the context of christian society.

Even if Ambrose was convinced that uprightness of life has priority to friendship, he saw no inevitable conflict between *honestas* and *amicitia*. One ought to correct a friend who is in the wrong, he states. He appealed to Proverbs 27:6, that the wounds inflicted by a friend are more bearable than the kisses of the flatterer (III. 127). Here as elsewhere in his exposition of the duties of friendship, Ambrose had no problem in finding christian wisdom to support and broaden the ciceronian ideal. Cicero had written of the joy one experiences in sharing oneself with a friend. Ambrose provided the example of the Hebrew boys in the furnace as well as that of David and Jonathan (131). Adversity produces a test for friendship (129) and a chance to show compassion for one's friend (130). Here the language of Paul about bearing one another's burdens (Gal. 6:2) and of Ecclesiasticus ('Even if evils should befall me because of a friend, I bear them': 22:31) are integrated into a defence of the value of friendship. Ambrose had no reservations about the utility of friendship, nor did he describe its limitations. Ambrose displayed unlimited optimism, not only holding that friendship is possible, but also believing that in spite of the demands of everyday life, trust, equality and commitment could be maintained among friends. He formulates a number of new phrases which perfectly balance old classical values with new christian ones and which seem to lessen the distance between them. In Ambrose there is a smooth continuity and easy transition from a noble ideal into a perfect one:

> For what is a friend, if not a companion of love, to whom you join and bind your mind, and so you are enmeshed, and you want to be made one from two with him to whom you entrust yourself as it were to another self, from whom you fear nothing, and of whom you seek nothing dishonourable for the sake of your own gain?
>
> Friendship has no element of gain in it. It is full of honour and of favour. For friendship is virtue, not profit. It comes forth not from money but from favour. It is not offered for sale at a fixed price but in mutual competition for the expression of good will (ch. 133).

What begins as a defence of the possibility of friendship in spite of the demands of political—or ecclesiastical—life ends as an assertion of friendship as common to both angels and men (ch. 135). In becoming friends of God by obeying his will (John 15:14) we become each other's friends. Christ has given us a formula for friendship:

> He gave the form of friendship which we follow, so that we do the will of the friend, so that we open our secrets to the friend, whatever we have in our hearts, and are not ignorant of his secrets.

In following the example of Christ, we learn how to be each other's friends. Just as he told us everything he had heard from his father, in making himself known to us, we should reveal ourselves and so make ourselves known to our friends: 'for a friend hides nothing' (ch. 135). The entire work of Christ Ambrose saw in terms of friendship between Jesus and his Father. This friendship is now offered to men. We are not just ordered to obey God. We are given his friendship and thus shown how to be each other's friends, by opening ourselves, by trusting our friends, and by forgiving them. The roman upper class ideal of *fides*, confidence and loyalty in the friend, is converted into christian trust in a God who never lets us down. Because God is true, friends can be true. Because God forgives, friends can forgive. Because God offers his friendship, we can be each other's friends.

Ambrose is not far from Aelred of Rievaulx's twelfth-century assertion that God is friendship, but he does not travel the full distance. He remained close to the maxims of classical roman friendship, and a harmonization of them with biblical sayings, without developing his ideas further. What is important to Ambrose is the lack of any tension between the ideal of friendship in roman and in christian cultures. The two worlds merge into each other in effortless harmony. Even the fear of betrayal in friendship and the fact that there was a Judas in Christ's life do not lead Ambrose to lose faith in the value of friendship. Because of it, he says, God can forgive. Ignoring the question of forgiveness for Judas, Ambrose points to the forgiveness extended by God to Job's friends because he had asked the Lord to do so (ch. 157 - Job 42:10).

Ambrose has a facility of language that makes it easy to penetrate his thought. His statements are transparent, and have nothing of the profundity of Augustine, nor are there his contradictions of meaning. For monastic readers like Aelred, Ambrose provided much of what they wanted and needed to hear about the benefits and duties of friendship. From Ambrose's other writings it is clear that friendship was not only a matter of theory for him. Several letters deal with friendship.[11] Even if at times it only has the status of a theme with which to begin remarks that soon lead elsewhere, there are several letters in which the experience of friendship has a prominent place. In writing to his teacher Simplicianus, Ambrose mentioned their old love.[13] To Bishop Sabinus, Ambrose combined a request for an evaluation of his recent writings with an assertion that such intellectual contact could strengthen the bonds of friendship.[14] Ambrose pointed to the importance of Saint Paul's letters to show how letters can strengthen the faith of Christians by making distant persons present to each other and clarifying their thoughts: '. . . in the letters of Paul is a certain image of his presence and the form of his work' (*ep* 47.6). Friendship through letters provided Ambrose with some of the richest moments of his life: 'I am never more in company than when I seem to be alone', he tells Sabinus, for at such moments he reads his letters. 'I am never more busy than when I seem to be most at leisure' on such occasions, he insists.[15] We know from the *Confessions* of Saint Augustine that Ambrose valued his solitude (VI 3). In Ambrose's own works we can see how he used that solitude in order to read and write not just theological treatises but also statements of intellectual friendship with colleagues.

The *De officiis ministrorum* and the letters alone might leave the impression that, for Ambrose, friendship meant a purely rational expression of shared beliefs. But Ambrose could also describe human bonds in emotional terms, as becomes apparent in a lament on the death of his brother, Satyrus.[16] In the first of its two books, Ambrose allowed himself to register the full extent of his loss, while in the second he concentrated on the hope of resurrection. The work confirmed the basic christian optimism about death, but it allowed Ambrose to represent without hesitation his own grief. 'What can be joyful to me without you, in whom was all our joy always?' he asks (I.34). 'What can I bear without you, such a companion of life, such a sharer of my labours and duties?' (I.35) Ambrose points out how Satyrus had spared him many practical tasks as bishop of Milan. Like Bernard of Clairvaux (who may well have used this lament as a model for his own),[17] Ambrose could not imagine carrying on his own spiritual life without the daily help of his now-dead brother (I.40). *Pietas*, *fides*, *jucunditas* are words that keep recurring, words that come directly from the late republican world of Cicero's Rome but still have rich meaning in the late imperial world of Ambrose's Milan. Ambrose will miss the brother who helped him hold together the fabric of the new church within the dying state in the West.

For Ambrose there could be no question of breaking off ties of kinship or friendship in moulding new christian communities. So long as family members and old friends followed him into the christian religion, he took their needs into consideration and himself needed them. In a treatise on virginity which he wrote to his sister Marcellina,[18] Ambrose supported community forms of life for both men and women.

Augustine tells of a monastery for men outside the walls of Milan, which was in Ambrose's care (*Conf.* VIII.6). The *De officiis* shows that Ambrose preferred that the clerks around him lived in community (II. 97-101). In his programme for the christian life, he used whatever he had at his disposal: the example of Eastern asceticism, the strength of upper-class loyalties, the literature of friendship from Cicero, and the bonds of family affection. Everything could be put to the service of the new christian community. Ambrose had no interest in thinking about inner contradictions or possible conflicts of loyalty. In Ambrose we find both a powerful roman bishop with no time for the intellectual and emotional enthusiasms of the young Augustine, and a loving roman brother and friend who believed in, accepted, defended, and used for himself the exclusivity and comforts of personal friendships.

AUGUSTINE: THE INEVITABILITY OF FRIENDSHIP

However much Augustine wanted to find rest in God, he could not live without his friends. This makes up an overwhelming fact of his existence, and he had the self-knowledge and honesty to acknowledge this need instead of denying it. In writing his Retractations at the end of his life, Augustine admitted that reading his own *Confessions* still could move him.[19] He was critical of his account there concerning his reaction to the death of his friend in youth, but he was displeased not with the feelings he had had at the time when it had happened but with the manner in which he had written about it. He could not accept the way he had reduced the matter to *declamatio levis,* an exercise in rhetorical delivery, instead of *gravis confessio*, the stuff of self-awareness. Even in shying away from his own prose, Augustine remained faithful to his dead friend and to his own reactions to the event.

Augustine considered all human things perishable, a realization that came upon him most powerfully when the young friend died (*Conf.* IV. 4). However much we may try to distinguish between various grades or degrees of friendship in Augustine's thought,[20] he consistently sought and engaged in friendships all through his life. He wrote that the only true friendships were those between good Christians,[21] yet he did not deny that what he felt for his friend was love, however incomplete:

> How well the poet put it when he called his friend the half of his soul (Horace, *Odes* I.3:8). I felt that our two souls had become as one, living in two bodies. . .[22]

The experience of the loss of the friend did not drive Augustine into a denial of friendship. It pushed him towards the realization that friendship has to be based on love of God, for only this love makes the other loves possible and enduring: 'Blessed is he who loves a friend in you. . . For he alone does not lose a beloved one, for whom all are beloved in him, who is not lost.'[23]

Augustine not only sought permanence in his loves: he needed protection from the terrible loss of his youth, and only in Christ could he find the *securitas* he required. For Augustine the dialectic between *securitas* in God and *fragilitas* in human affairs meant that every human involvement had to be seen as limited and limiting. The next step would have been to follow the fathers of the desert and deny the worth of human loves in the pursuit of divine love. But Augustine never went this far. His own human loves were too important to him: 'For he truly loves a friend who loves God in the friend, either because God is in him or so that God may be in him'.[24] Because of God, friendship is possible in spite of human weakness. One entrusts oneself not to the undependability of the friend but to the secure love of God. Even with a difficult man like Jerome, friendship can be possible for Augustine.[25]

Augustine points out that two human beings can never really know one another's hearts, and so no human friendship can be perfect.[26] He contradicted himself about whether or not friends have to enjoy each other's physical presence in order for their love to be complete.[27] He held himself back from friends who wanted to see him and be with him, as he did with Nebridius after their conversion and return to Africa.[28] And he reduced friendship to a matter of cultivating the right people in the influential circles and cajoling them into acting in the best way for the african church and by fighting heretics.[29]

Augustine manipulated friendship into a multitude of forms, but in the end he could not be without what he called *vera amicitia*, true friendship:

> . . . it is not true, unless you attach it in those bound to it with the love diffused in our hearts through the Holy Spirit, who is given to us.[30]

The definition is not easy, but it requires a divine presence. The result is a special bond between two or more human beings, who thereby become more closely attached to God.

From the very moment of his conversion friendship was essential for Augustine. In his *Soliloquies*, he speaks of a law of friendship in order to define how men know each other.[31] When Reason (*Ratio*) asked Augustine in their dialogue how he could obtain the highest good, he answered in a way that shows he could not imagine doing so without the companionship of his friends:

> But I ask you why you desire that those men whom you love either live or live with you.
>
> Aug.: So that we together in harmony can look into our souls and at God. So then it happens easily that he who is the first to find [truths], brings them to the others without any difficulty. (I.20 = PL 32:880)

Augustine here describes in christian terms a form of community life in the pursuit of truth. Earlier, he and his comrades had wanted to form a philosophical community patterned on classical antecedents, but the question of what to do with their wives/concubines had gotten in the way (*Conf.* VI. 14). Now at Cassiciacum he envisioned a community seeking truth, and reasoned that the man who first finds a truth will save his companions the trouble of looking for it.

This is a purely rational view of friendship as a life in community in the pursuit of intellectually perceived truths about the soul and about God. But when Reason asks Augustine what he will do if the members of the community do not want to join him in such an activity, his answer shows the strength of his desire for this fellowship in truth:

R.: What if they do not wish to seek these things?

A.: I shall convince them to want to do so!

When *Ratio* then objects that the very presence of the others might be an impediment to Augustine's pursuit, he has to concede this possibility. Reason wins the point that friends are present in such a way of life not for their own sake, but 'in order to find wisdom' (*propter inveniendam sapientiam*, I.20). Despite Augustine's admission, the impression remains that he could not imagine such a philosophical enquiry without the presence and participation of his friends. However intellectually he looked at this point in his life upon friendship, it had weathered the storms of doubt and conversion. Augustine conceded that he imagined this philosophical community as made up only of 'the fewest and most elect of those who love [wisdom]' (I.22). Later in the same discussion, however, he admitted to Reason that he would like to share the pursuit of wisdom with more people. Whatever happens, he cannot imagine life without friends:

> I love wisdom alone for its own sake, but I want other things to be present in my life, or I will be afraid to lack them for the sake of wisdom: life, peace, friends. What limitation can there be in love of such beauty, in which I not only do not envy others, but also seek more [friends] who will desire it with me, long for it with me, hold onto it with me and enjoy it with me. The more friends I shall have, the more can we love wisdom in common. (I.22 = PL 32:881)

The community of friends in the pursuit of wisdom is strengthened by an increase in numbers. Augustine linked wisdom with life, peace and friends. He could not imagine the study of philosophy as a lonely quest. Life in community (*vita communis*) was necessary even at the very moment of conversion, when Augustine immediately shared his new wisdom with Alypius, enabling him also to convert (*Conf.* VIII.12). Alypius became the first friend in Augustine's new community of wisdom. From this moment, a discussion on christian wisdom began.

From Cassiciacum in Italy to Thagaste and Hippo in Africa the philosophical community was enlarged and made into a christian and monastic one, where common life meant ascetic discipline, but where the ideal and practice of friendship were not neglected. The presence of this ideal accounts for the tensions evident in correspondence between Augustine and his friend Nebridius, who had chosen to remain with his mother on their estate near Carthage after Augustine and his friends had returned to Thagaste. Augustine never ordered him to come there, but he refused himself to go to Nebridius. He would not take Nebridius's special needs into consideration. Nebridius wanted Augustine's friendship for himself but would not sever the bond with his mother in order to join his friend. Augustine indicated in a most diplomatic manner that Nebridius had to choose between caring for his family and coming into the new community.[32]

Augustine's letters to Nebridius are among the first entries in his letter collection. Three of the friend's own letters are also included (*epp* 5, 6, 8). They give us invaluable insight into Augustine's concept of friendship as shown in the development of an actual relationship. We notice immediately that even though Augustine wrote intimately to Nebridius, telling him how he had enjoyed the friend's letter and had read it in bed after dinner, he made no direct statements about the intimacy of their friendship (*ep* 3). Friendship is implied but not spelled out. Only when Nebridius challenged Augustine and complained that he was too caught up in his many duties (*ep* 6) did Augustine show desire to share his life with Nebridius (*ep* 9). 'although you know my mind, perhaps you still are unaware how much I want to enjoy your presence'. Augustine defended himself against Nebridius's charge that he had done nothing to make sure that they could live together, but he left it up to Nebridius to make it possible for them to live in community. He did not try to minimize what he called Nebridius's 'friendly complaint' (*familiari objurgatione*, *ep* 10), but he was quite sure that it was Nebridius who had to surrender to his terms. Augustine would not budge from his other friends, for they had formed the community of christian *otium* he wanted and needed.

These letters eventually developed into an exchange of intellectual questions and opinions. Nebridius may have learned to accept limitations in his relationship with Augustine and a purely intellectual friendship. At times even this was almost too much for Augustine. He had to ask Nebridius to limit the stream of his enquiries, for he could hardly keep up with them (*ep* 14). Nebridius tried through letters to maintain the same intimacy with Augustine that they had had while they lived together in Italy. Now that they were separated, it was difficult for Augustine to maintain the quality and quantity of their earlier contacts. His preferred solution was one that Nebridius could not accept. Living together with Augustine would have involved separation from his mother. Augustine never openly criticized Nebridius for such a choice, but he made it clear to his friend that one particular friendship and its emotional commitments could not be preferred to an entire community of friendship and its all-encompassing expression of human needs for dialogue, enquiry, and the sharing of self.

This temporary resolution might eventually have led to conflicts and resentment, but Nebridius's early death (before 390) ended the relationship and the correspondence.[33] In his *Confessions,* begun in 397, Augustine mentioned Nebridius as one of the dearest friends of his youth (*amicus dulcissimus et mitissimus*, VIII. 6). When another of Augustine's boyhood friends had died, he had almost gone to pieces, but he had found comfort in the company of his friends. Augustine does not tell us how he reacted when Nebridius died, but once again he could rely on a community of friends, now even more tightly knit because of their christian faith. The more Augustine could count on his friends, the less he needed to address them in fulsome terms and with rhetorical flourishes.[34] As we have seen, the letters to Nebridius for the most part are direct and matter-of-fact. It is only when he addresses people with whom he felt insecure, such as Jerome, or people with whom he was getting acquainted through the medium of a letter, as Paulinus of Nola, that Augustine brought out the full register of affectionate address and expressions of friendship. For Augustine the truest friends did not need to be called friends. They knew who they were.

It might be tempting here to conclude that Augustine believed in and practised a purely un-emotional type of friendship, and this is true to the extent that the words 'emotional' and 'romantic' belong together. For Augustine friendship existed in order to cultivate and contemplate in common divine truth. We can get a good idea of what Augustine did not mean by friendship if we look at a letter from one of his most fervent admirers, Severus, who wrote of how he would like to suck wisdom from Augustine's breasts.[35] This letter, characterized as 'unmanly',[36] certainly used a form of expression foreign to Augustine's own way of communicating himself to Nebridius, Alypius, and other close friends. But Augustine replied politely to Severus. He could not accept all the praise being offered, but he did not take the correspondent to task for his enthusiasm.[37] Augustine must have understood that he was the recipient of the type of rhetorical display which he himself had once composed in Milan in praise of the emperor. He could still concoct such demonstrations as bishop of Hippo when he needed the favour of secular authorities.

We must distinguish between Augustine's letters of friendship for the sake of church unity and his declarations of friendship to express his own inner life. Even in the personal letters, he is more informative in stating what friendship involves for him as an abstract concept than in giving concrete descriptions of the content in individual friendships. For Augustine's own experience, we must turn to the *Confessions*. These provide a primary witness to a man who could not be without his friends, and who was led to Christianity because it offered him a basis for making fragile friendships into permanent loves. An incident that encouraged Augustine to take the last steps to conversion was the discovery of the lives of the desert fathers of Egypt. He felt a strong attraction to them, not only because of their asceticism, but also because he was told how their example had influenced the friendship of two roman officials and turned it into an eternal bond in Christ. The soldiers were so fired by their reading of the Life of Anthony that they saw in it the chance to escape the transitory and dangerous world of court friendships (and enmities) and to enter a permanent life of friendship with God. In converting to the christian faith they stood together and strengthened their friendship, just as Alypius and Augustine would do soon after the story was told them.[38]

It might be argued that after the death of his friend in youth, Augustine armoured himself against ever again forming so vulnerable and exclusive a relationship. He replaced an emotional friendship by intellectual ones within the context of a common interest in philosophy and learning. Such a description of Augustine's development is partly true, but it ignores the fact that for Augustine at all stages in his life, friendship was a basic human need that went beyond intellectual enjoyment. To be true, friendship had to be christian, but *amicitia* was still everywhere in human society. In describing the relationship between Adam and Eve, Augustine spoke of their friendship. It was this, and not any sexual relationship, which explained why Adam consented to Eve.[39] Here Augustine saw human affection and not the sexual drive as the basis for human behaviour.

In his *City of God*, Augustine summed up this conviction. In the midst of the confusion and disappointments of human society, what can give us greater consolation, he asked, than this 'unfeigned faith . . . and mutual affection of genuine, loyal friends'.[40] Yet friendship can be changed into treachery, malice and baseness. Besides this is the inevitable fact of the death of friends: 'how can it be that a man's death should not be bitter if his life is sweet to us?' The more friends we have, the more exposed we are to such disappointments. All this might seem to be leading to a conclusion similar to that of the desert fathers, that friendships have to be eradicated, but Augustine refused to take this last step:

> Anyone who forbids such sadness must forbid, if he can, all friendly conversation, must lay a ban on all friendly feeling or put a stop to it, must with a ruthless insensibility break the ties of all human relationships, or else decree that they must be engaged upon only so long as they inspire no delight in a man's soul.

For Augustine, as opposed to the desert fathers, it was undesirable that such human bonds be outlawed, and so he argued that we must accept the consequence: some friends will die, others will betray us, but friendships will remain and persist, despite a world filled with disasters and uncertainties. The passage can be read as Augustine's supreme statement of the instability of human society, but behind this assertion Augustine was convinced that whatever happens, friendships would continue to be formed and renewed.

Augustine tried to convince himself that one should find some consolation in the death of friends because death spares them 'those evils by which in this life even good men are crushed and corrupted'. He also insisted that 'we should prefer to hear . . . of the death of those we love than to find out that they have fallen from faith'.[41] Augustine may have been thinking of the arian Visigoths, the sack of Rome, the breakup of christian upper-class culture in the city of Rome, which he had once known so well. Even at his toughest, Augustine did not attempt to deny that friendship is a natural impulse that gives us joy and consolation. Augustine's belief in friendship explains his shock and disappointment at the news of the enmity between two old and famous friends, Rufinus and Jerome. In one of his most diplomatic letters, Augustine tried to smooth over his doctrinal differences with Jerome and then told him that he must find some way to be reconciled with Rufinus. The dissension between the two, he pointed out, had already caused a scandal in the church, but Augustine is also concerned because if these two openly fought, then friendship as an ideal was jeopardized. Augustine used some of the most emotional language to be found in any of his letters:

> . . . perhaps, as I am moved, as I grieve, as I fear, I should fall at your feet, weep as much as I can, plead as much as I love, now each of you for himself, now each of you for the other, and for others, and especially for the weak, for whom Christ died, who see you as it were in the theatre of life and in the greatest danger. (Ep. 73.8, CSEL 34:274)

On one level this appeal can be seen as a desire to maintain unity in the church. On another it is a defence of an ideal of friendship that was absolutely essential for Augustine's own life and value system.

As Augustine grew older, his individual friendships became less visible. In the monastery at Hippo, his community of like-minded serious pursuers of truth and a shared way of life fulfilled a desire he had had ever since his boyhood adventures. Augustine's critique in his *Confessions* of the intense friendship he had had as a youth has provided material for those who claim that he did not value friendship highly. But Augustine did not say or indicate that 'since all things mortal perish, we are better off not becoming too attached to anything or anyone except God'.[42] The sum of his teaching and his life is that since all things mortal perish, we must learn to use them as means to reach God and not as ends in themselves. We cannot run away from the need we have for one another. We cannot pretend that because God is the source of all creatures, we can cut ourselves off from his creation. Friendship began with Adam and Eve and continued into the catastrophic fall of the Western roman state, when it seemed as if the world itself might be coming to an end. As bishop of Hippo Augustine, consciously or unconsciously, may have stopped seeking intimate individual friendships, but he did not deny the value of friendship in his own life or in the christian life in general.

Augustine never wrote a formal *De amicitia*. Friendship was so much a part of his personal experience that his *Confessions* contained the sum of what he had to say on the subject. Unlike Ambrose he could not reduce the matter into a few well-turned paragraphs with no indication of problems and conflicts. Viewed as a whole, Augustine's 'doctrine' of friendship is an experiential one. Friends exist because we need them. In youth they exist for play and often lead each other into sin. In adulthood they can engage in the common pursuit of truth. Friendship is not a purely intellectual exercise, but at the same time it is too important to be reduced to purely emotional attachments. Friendship involves the entire human being in the lives, thoughts, hopes, and yearnings of other persons. It demands loyalty and can easily be disappointed. It may well include the pains involved in the death of friends. Friendship survives loss and reemerges in all periods of life. This is especially true about friendship founded on faith in Christ. Friendship, like Pauline love, bears all, not for the sake of suffering, but in the hope of delight: 'And so we bear up the more steadfastly under the evils of friends because their goods delight us and tie us to them'.[43]

A medieval reader of Augustine could hardly avoid the conclusion that being a friend of God by no means excluded being a friend to individual men, especially within the context of monastic community. An immensely popular biography of Augustine by Possidius showed not just a heresy-fighting bishop but also a leader of a community of friends sharing ascetic discipline and enjoying harmony. Possidius closed the biography by referring to the friendship he had enjoyed with Augustine for almost forty years, during which he had lived with him 'without any bitterness of dissension. .on close and sweet terms'.[44]

In the East the functions of monk and cleric were kept apart from each other. Those who lived in desert communities had no interest in serving the diocesan church. In the West distinctions were less sharp.

Augustine's fellow ascetics at Hippo became bishops of North African cities. Monastic community was contiguous with diocesan organization and authority. Similarly, the bonds of friendship in the monastic life become the bonds of the church against heretics and barbarians. Just as friends banded together in the roman community to influence public life, so too in the christian community of Late Antiquity friends sought each other out in alliances to protect and defend the true religion. For Ambrose friendship provided a language for bonds between men. For Augustine it was the very substance of human life and love.

JEROME: FRIENDSHIP AS RHETORIC

All that was disciplined and restrained in Augustine became violent rhetoric in Jerome. As far as friendship is concerned, two periods in his life left expressions of its value and importance for him and would have an impact not only on his own time but also on the centuries to come. Jerome had formed a community of friends at Aquileia, but for unknown reasons this group was split by dissension and recriminations. In the aftermath Jerome fled to the East, first staying at Antioch and then moving out into the desert of Chalcis (374-75). During this first dramatic exile, Jerome composed a number of letters, thirteen of which make up the first part of his collection (2-14), and almost all of which deal with friendship in terms of theory and as a reflection of Jerome's own needs. Most of these letters were addressed to other men who were involved in the attempt to live an ascetic life, and many of whom were friends with whom Jerome once had lived in Aquileia. About a decade later, while Jerome was at Rome (384), he began the second series of letters of friendship, this time for the greater part addressed to women (*epp* 22, 34, 45). Even though he addressed the ladies with affection, he was more restrained here in his statements of love and devotion. Some of the letters are pure expositions of biblical criticism. Ever aware of the impact of his writings on public opinion, Jerome had to defend his familiarity with women and hold standards of proper behaviour for an ascetic. These letters provide spiritual advice rather than giving indications of Jerome's state of mind, as the earliest letters of friendship had done.

While still at Antioch and before leaving for the desert, Jerome wrote, probably in 374, to Theodosius and other anchorites, asking them to pray so that he might have the strength to leave the world and live in the desert. 'How much I would like now to be with your community, this admirable fellowship', he asserts, 'even if these eyes do not deserve to look upon it, to embrace it with total joy'.[45] Jerome was preparing himself psychologically for the departure for the desert, which he insisted is 'more beautiful than any city'. Whatever had happened at Aquileia, he had become convinced that only by imitating the ascetics of the East could he live the spiritual life.

The subsequent letters reveal that Jerome did not really want the isolation of a hermit's life, but was constantly looking for friends from the West to accompany him in his search for Eastern self-denial. To Rufinus of Aquileia, he wrote that having heard his friend was in Egypt he wished to see and speak with him (*ep* 3). Jerome recalled biblical instances of the miraculous translation of bodies, as when Habakkuk came to Daniel. Jerome fantasized about the kisses and embraces that such a reunion would have permitted.[46] But since this is not possible, letters provided contact: 'These are my representatives, and I send them to meet you, for they are to join you in the bond of love and lead you to me'. The rest of the letter elaborates on this bond of love and mentions the people from the Aquileia community whom both Rufinus and Jerome knew. Some of them had apparently accompanied him to Antioch. Jerome mourned the death of one of them, Innocent, and praised in fulsome tones another, Bonosus, his foster-brother, who had withdrawn to do penance on a desert island where 'no blade of grass grows'.

Jerome admired the desert as a complete solution to the ascetic challenge, but the last lines of this letter show how much he counted on friends like Rufinus to join him in this new life; he ordered him to come because of friendship:

Charity cannot be bought.	Caritas non potest comparari;
Love has no price.	dilectio pretium non habet;

Friendship which can end was never true.	amicitia quae desinere potest, vera nunquam fuit. (CSEL 44)

These words were included to remind Rufinus that his presence was necessary to prove himself a true friend. This final flourish also reveals the highly-charged rhetorical structure of the early letters. As Jerome admitted years later about this period in his life, he had written letters with 'terse pointed epigrams at the end of each paragraph, put in to excite my audience to loud applause'.[47] In the isolation of his Eastern retreat, Jerome sought out not just Rufinus but an entire Western audience, men and women in their roman palaces who were interested in the ascetic life. These could admire a man who chose not just to describe Eastern heroic asceticism but also to live as an ascetic hero himself. Jerome sought to make fanaticism attractive. As an upper-class Roman, he needed to communicate with and to attract fellow members of his own circle.[48]

In his next letter (*ep* 4), Jerome asked a man whom he had never met, Florentius, to convey the previous letter to Rufinus, who had apparently returned to Jerusalem from Egypt. Jerome assured Florentius that he had already begun to love him, even though he did not yet know him. You are so deserving of love, he insists, that it would be a crime not to love you.[49] Again he is seeking friends from his desert solitude. Jerome had gone to Chalcis to be apart from men, but in every letter he pleaded for their company. Centuries later, men like Anselm of Canterbury would also declare their love and friendship for men whom they had never seen.[50] Jerome and Anselm dealt with people in terms of what they represented ideally and had little interest in individual people, their personalities and special characteristics.

A strong appeal often wins a positive response. Florentius must have written back, for in another letter (5), Jerome refers to his reply and provides what would become one of the standard expressions of the idea that the friend is present through the letter in spirit even if he is absent in body: *etsi corpore absens, amore et spiritu venio*. Behind rapturous phrases about how the friend's letters 'hasten between us. . . speak with us', Jerome was worried because Rufinus had not yet come. He did all he could to blow on the coals of a new friendship, but one cannot but wonder if the contact with Florentius at

Jerusalem was established chiefly as a means of getting information about Rufinus.

With the sixth letter in the collection, we find yet another indication of Jerome's fruitless efforts to attract men to him in the desert. To Julian, deacon of Aquileia, he excused himself for not writing and told him that a mutual friend, Heliodorus, had been with him but now had left. The main purpose of the letter seems to be to get news of old friends. To Chromatius, Jovinus and Eusebius, two of whom were brothers and also Western ascetics, Jerome replied to a letter written jointly by them. Once again the phrases of affection make up a number of general statements that could easily be lifted out of context to brighten any medieval monastic letter:

Those whom mutual love has joined together ought not to be separated on a written page.	Non debet charta dividere, quos amor mutuus copulavit. (*Ep* 7; CSEL 54: p. 26)

In the midst of some of his most polished language, Jerome claims he is ignoring the requirements of rhetoric:

> Perhaps you may wonder at my beginning thus afresh at the end of a letter. What am I to do? I cannot keep my heart from utterance. The brief limits of a letter force me to be silent, but my longing for your company compels me to speak. My words pour out in eager haste; my language is confused and disjoined; but love knows nothing of order.[51]

Jerome's love may claim to know nothing of order, but the letter is a carefully conceived attempt to maintain and enlarge contacts to the West. Jerome provided news of the spiritual progress of his sister, compared himself to the ascetic Bonosus, his foster-brother, and sent greetings to the mother of the letter's recipients. Most importantly, he described the visit of a mutual friend, Evagrius, to his hermitage. Once again a friend had come and gone. Jerome's main feeling for Evagrius, as well as for his correspondents, was *desiderium*, a yearning to share a way of life with a friend.

Letters substituted for friends who could not or would not stay, so Jerome could speak of the letter he had received as his most vital human contact: 'Now I talk to your letter, embrace it, and it talks to me, for it is the only thing here that knows Latin'. For the first time, Jerome mentioned his fellow desert hermits, and the reference is not flattering: 'In this place an old man has either to learn a barbarous jargon, or else hold his tongue'.[52] Jerome had gone East but could not stop thinking and communicating in the language of the West. He felt repelled by the uncouth desert dwellers, who lacked his education and refinement. In his solitude he sought human contact: 'Believe love when it tells you the truth: as I write this letter I see you before me'. He rejected the men who were close by and complained about the shortness of the letter he had received and the long stretches of sea and land between himself and his correspondents.

Another relationship that had to be maintained by letter was that with Niceas, also a subdeacon of Aquileia. He had accompanied Jerome to the East but had returned home (*ep* 8). Using the letter of Chromatius and Eusebius as a point of departure, Jerome insisted that these brothers by their letter had forced him to write. Jerome wishes to use this letter for the same purpose: 'Now that you have left us, would you not rather break off the recent friendship than let it fall into disuse, something that Laelius prudently forbids in Cicero?'[53] Under the scorching desert sun, and in growing hostility to the syrian hermits, Jerome referred to the rules of ciceronian friendship! This letter is shot through with a multitude of rhetorical weapons: cajolement, flattery, threats, the appeal to common experience. Jerome ends with one of his usual dramatic epigrams: 'I shall receive great comfort in my need if I receive the letter of a friend, even one who is angry'. Jerome begged for relief from suffering and bad company in his desire for the friend. He claimed not to care whether or not the friend was angry, so long as he communicated.

The subsequent letters (except for the tenth, which seems a simple request for books) all attempt to reestablish and strengthen links to friends and relatives in the West. Jerome conveys the impression that his friends had let him down, yet he also frequently hints that in the past he had in some way or another offended his correspondent and now wanted to make up for it. He appealed to the epistles of Saint Paul in order to describe the debt of friendship (*ep* 9). He referred to his miserable condition and physical suffering to point out how he had managed in spite of these to find writing materials (*ep* 11). He repeated his statement of the eighth letter that he preferred an angry letter to none at all (12). To his aunt Castorina he demanded some mode of reconciliation (13). In his usual prickly manner, Jerome was out for forgiveness. He brooded over the events of the Aquileia period and seems to have regretted the break it brought with his friends, relatives and companions.

To the monk Heliodorus, who had been with him in Chalcis, Jerome composed his most masterful phrases of friendship (*ep* 14). He reminded Heliodorus how he had tried to convince him to stay with him in the desert, and now told him that he should be able to see from the tear stains on the page how much he now missed him:

> Shall I keep silence? But what I wanted so much, I could not hide. Should I have pleaded more persistently? But you did not want to listen, for you did not love me as I you.[54]

We can almost hear the similar reproach William of Saint Thierry made to Bernard of Clairvaux centuries later: you do not love me as much as I love you.[55] Jerome used every weapon in his rhetorical armoury to make Heliodorus regret not sharing the life of the desert with him. Apparently he had followed Jerome to the East, but had postponed the decision to live with him in the desert. When Jerome left Antioch for Chalcis, he had promised to send Heliodorus a letter inviting him to join him. Now he was doing so, first cajoling and pleading on the basis of their old friendship, but soon changing to a tone of threat: 'Love must grow angry' (*ep* 14.2). Jerome calls Heliodorus a 'pampered soldier' who was unwilling to devote himself to winter training, and like any Egyptian desert father, Jerome insisted that as far as family bonds are concerned, 'the love of Christ and the fear of hell easily break such bonds as these'. The Christian must suffer, and any man who calls himself a monk must accept the definition of the word as someone who is alone. 'What are you, a solitary, doing in a crowd?' (*ep* 14.6). In this long and passionately argued letter, Jerome insists that a monk cannot be involved in the secular life of the church, but was to do penance and seek solitude apart from clergy and bishops. Jerome becomes almost lyrical in his praise of the desert in comparison to the cities of the Empire:

> O desert rejoicing in God's familiar presence! What are you doing in the world, brother, you who are more than the universe? How long is the shade of a roof going to confine you? How long shall the smoky prison of these cities shut you in? Believe me, I see something more of light than you behold.[56]

At last Jerome had admitted to himself and to his audience that becoming a desert dweller required separation from the world. And yet in asserting this truth and allying himself with the full force of egyptian asceticism, Jerome was seeking out the companionship of a close friend! He was moreover addressing groups of friends and former friends and new admirers in Italy who shivered with delight at his maxims and heroic religious prose.[57] In a letter written in 394 to Heliodorus's nephew Nepotian, after Jerome had settled down to a less daunting life at Bethlehem, Jerome said he regretted his letter, which had been written 'with youthful fancy', when he was 'still fired with enthusiasm for the teachings of the rhetoricians'.[58] Jerome could condemn both the violence of his language and his sentiment that the life of the hermit was the only desirable one for the good Christian. He had learned to accept the need of the secular church for good priests and bishops.

After 385 Jerome found at Bethlehem in its community life the peace and creative expression that the desert had not been able to give him. Behind his attempt in the mid-370s to impress and enthrall his audience with the power of his rhetoric lay an appeal for human contact and love, an attempt to share himself with other people in a common pursuit. It may sound banal, but behind the acuity of Jerome's language and his vaunting of sacred history we find a scared human being repeatedly driving away the people he wanted and needed.

What matters for our purposes is not so much the personality of Jerome but the mark the expressions of this personality left on the monastic literature and consciousness of Western Europe. His finely-hewn phrases, his tears, his exhortations to the monastic life—all would be copied and remembered, consciously and unconsciously, over the coming centuries.[59] Jerome spoke of his friendships in a direct, naked manner. He never could count on his friendships as Augustine could and so he could not write letters of friendship where the basis of friendship was assumed and not stated. Jerome's exaggerated statements and elegant formulae—however insincere and overwrought they might strike us—could for a medieval monastic writer combine power of literary expression with an attractive commitment to the ideal and practice of friendship within an ascetic community.

In between the desert of Chalcis and the community of Bethlehem came Jerome's contacts with the aristocratic women of Rome in the years 382-85.[60] Jerome's concerns are best summarized in his famous Letter 22, to Eustochium, Paula's daughter, written in 384, two years after his arrival at Rome. This is one of Jerome's fullest statements on the requirements of the ascetic life, and here he reverts from his earlier emphasis on solitude and isolation from the world and comes to emphasize the importance of virginity. Looking back on the battles of the desert, he now claimed that his main problem had been sexual desire, not loneliness. Indirectly, however, he revealed to Eustochium that he had been unable to cope with a way of life which cut him off from other people with whom he could share himself. As the recipient of the letter, Eustochium represented the pious, aristocratic women who would devote themselves to God's service under Jerome's tutelage for the rest of his life. Jerome may claim to regret that 'I am not now what I once was', but he had chosen to leave the desert, involve himself in the affairs of the church, and attach himself to the community of women who had been following him at Rome from a distance.

In his protests against men and women who lived together and claimed they had no sexual contact (*ep* 22.14), Jerome asserted that there can be friendships between good men and women if men can function with undisputed authority as spiritual advisors. Jerome did not concern himself with the other side of the relationship: the dependence that the men develop on the warmth and understanding of such women, but the letter itself is a witness to this experience in his life. With Marcella, Eustochium and her mother Paula, Jerome managed to form a network of friendships which he had failed to maintain with men. He formulated no more bold statements on the requirements of love, no phrases charged with tension between emotional content and rhetoric. Jerome no longer had to be assertive about his friendships because devotion and loyalty were guaranteed. His women were more patient than his male friends.

Jerome's advice and experience of friendship are not consistent in all his letters. But in Chalcis, at Rome, and at Bethlehem, friendship was a matter of primary concern. Jerome's great enmities and hatreds can be understood only on the basis of his intense friendships and loves. Always seeking, seldom finding, Jerome could no more than Augustine or Ambrose consider abandoning the ciceronian ideal of friendship transformed and heightened in the fellowship of Christ and through the language of Saint Paul. When he tried to become an Eastern ascetic and hermit, Jerome ended up reasserting and reformulating in attractive terms the Western latin ideal of friendship. Even in writing the life of the first desert hermit, Paul, Jerome left his western imprint by dwelling on a friendship central in Paul's life.[61] The climax of the hagiography comes when Paul meets Anthony and they form a friendship. Athanasius's description of Anthony is given a new dimension, not just in order to show the superiority of Jerome's hero to Anthony, but also to assert that even in the desert friendship is inevitable. Jerome may have been projecting his own needs on his subject, but he insisted that the ascetic ideal and the search for friendship could be combined. However contradictory it might have seemed to an Eastern observer, for whom classical culture had to be removed to make way for the ascetic life, Jerome remained true to Cicero. Even if his dreams shook him out of his fantasy that Cicero and Christ could be reconciled (*ep* 22.30), Jerome managed like Ambrose to combine the classical ideal of friendship with the pauline concept of life in community. Jerome's actual experience of community with other men brought little harmony or unity, but the historical reality of his life with conflicting periods of ascetic separation and passionate involvement in the life of the church did not capture the imagination of future writers. What mattered for them was Jerome's language, especially that of the earliest letters. Once separated from the sordidness of his personal experience, these letters provided a rapturous language of friendship, building on classical models and integrating them within a christian universe.

In analyzing Jerome's early letters, the historian of monastic friendship, Mother Adele Fiske, claimed: 'The tone of these letters is one of rhetorical violence and of genuine self-pity; in them *amicitia* is already divisive'.[62] Looked at in terms of the effect such letters could have had on Jerome's contemporaries, the charge is fair. But if we consider the letters as expressions of Jerome's new language of friendship, they emerge as a central literary inspiration for the expression of friendship in medieval letters. Augustine lived his friendships but in his letters wrote very little about them. Jerome could rarely live up to his friendships but was a master at projecting them into his letters. Because of the very forcefulness of his language, Jerome made a central contribution to the medieval monastic language of friendship.

PAULINUS OF NOLA: FRIENDSHIP AS DISAPPOINTMENT

The most complete expression of the christian ideal of friendship in the context of roman upper class culture in the West occurs in the letters of Paulinus of Nola (353-431).[63] Especially in the letters he wrote to his friend Sulpicius Severus between 395 and 400, Paulinus combined the most faultless Latin with a total confidence that friendship and the christian religion could be in harmony with each other. As in Ambrose of Milan, there is no hesitation or doubt in Paulinus. Unlike Jerome, his was a sunny personality, giving out warmth to a world from which he expected gratefulness and the reflection of his ideals. Both Paulinus and Sulpicius Severus came from rich land-owning families in Aquitaine. They had had a similar education. They converted to Christianity at about the same time. Externally they were spiritual twins, and Paulinus could rejoice in his first letter that he could transform an old bond with Sulpicius into a christian friendship.[64] Just as he had had to leave his pagan friends, so now he could share his new life with an old friend in a friendship renewed.

If Paulinus's letters were nothing more than a collection of well-turned felicitous phrases, they would deserve only limited attention. But in Paulinus patristic friendship takes on a dramatic dimension, for he was disappointed in one of the central friendships of his life. By tracing the development of his letters to Sulpicius, we can see in a christian correspondence the development of friendship from early intensity to later reserve and distance. Just as Paulinus's first letters are superb expressions of all that friendship can be between two christian men, so his later ones provide poignant documentation of disappointment in great expectations.

The first letter in the collection has been dated to 395 and was sent to Sulpicius Severus from Barcelona. It is addressed, appropriately, 'to the most beloved brother according to the common faith' (*carissimo fratri secundum communem fidem*). From the start the tone of christian friendship is set. Because Paulinus and Sulpicius shared the same faith, they could share each other. He encouraged Sulpicius to come and visit him: 'But what shall I say about the distance? If you desire us, the way is short; long if you neglect us'.[65] Subsequent letters from Paulinus (the replies of Sulpicius have been lost) all elaborate on this theme. Paulinus wanted Sulpicius to come and visit him. He never considered the possibility that he might go to Sulpicius. Sulpicius made innumerable promises to come and broke them all. At first Paulinus accepted the excuses given, but eventually his patience ran out.

The second letter from Paulinus to Sulpicius was sent about eighteen months later, from Nola in Campania. Paulinus and his wife Therasia had settled down in a chaste relationship to serve at the shrine of the martyr bishop Felix. 'Do you think it has to be excused, most beloved brother', writes Paulinus generously to Sulpicius, 'that you did not come to us as you promised and we hoped?' From the first the problem is clear: Sulpicius had not kept his promise. Paulinus thought of every possible excuse that could be made for Sulpicius's behaviour. It does not matter that you left your body at home, he insists, for you have come to us in spirit and in word. Even in body you were not entirely absent, for you joined yourself to us through your servants.[66] Sulpicius had become a beloved brother, one with Paulinus in Christ (*frater vere sancte merito dilectissime et in Christo nobis unanime*). These words celebrate a new stage in friendship, and assert a continuing desire to share that friendship in physical proximity. Paulinus indicated that he still expected Sulpicius to come: 'so that which you wished, you do not stop wanting, and you maintain your immutable decision to come to us'.[67] The latin word for decision here is *sententia*. This is more than the promise (*sponsio*) mentioned at the beginning of the letter. It is a firm resolve, an intellectual decision, a moral commitment. In every way possible Sulpicius is reminded of what the two friends share with each other because of the bond of faith. They are 'members of one body' now in the church, and everything they do and experience, even their sicknesses, unites them.

Now Paulinus writes to Sulpicius in order to give him 'solace'. 'So that we meanwhile hold on to your letters, until we see you, as you have promised, and as we never stop hoping from the Lord' (*ep* 5.12). Subsequent sections develop the theme of reunion: how pleased Sulpicius will be with the quiet of Nola after the confusion and conflicts of Rome (5.13), how all of Campania had come to visit him while he was ill, and now it was Paulinus' turn (14). He fantasizes about how Sulpicius will come, not alone, but together with his spiritual brothers (15). He even uses the language of the Psalms to express the joy which he anticipates at their reunion:

> When you and I shall at the same time return mutual embraces, rightly let me say to all of you in calling out: this is truly the day which the Lord has made. Let us exult and rejoice in it, for it is good and joyful for brothers to dwell together. (Ps. 117:24 and 132:1)

The language seems almost overwrought at times, but there is none of the undercurrent of aggression and resentment that we found in Jerome. In a postscript Paulinus excuses himself for writing a long letter, which exceeds the bounds of rhetoric, but 'in dictating it while I think of you and am wholly in you, I speak to you as present despite the long distance, and forget to put an end to my talk'.[68] Jerome could not have expressed the idea better: friendship not only overcomes physical distance but also breaks the literary limitations of a letter.

Sulpicius Severus was favoured with some of the most passionate statements of christian love of friendship that exist. In the summer of 397, Paulinus wrote him that his love was like the medicine of life for him. Their old worldly friendship had now become a 'spiritual kinship', a phrase that introduces the theme that one's true mother and brothers are those who share the same faith (*ep* 11.1). The words of Christ (Matt. 12:48 'Who is my mother and who are my brothers?') are used here not as they were construed in the egyptian desert to disassociate oneself from all former human bonds, but instead to assert the reality of new bonds: 'All the more strongly you are related to me in family than those whom flesh and blood alone join to me' (11.3). What does it matter to me, Paulinus asks, if my family is unkind or my brother negligent or my friend forgetful, so long as I have all these reminders of the bonds of love from you alone. The passage reaches a climax with the words of Acts 4:32:

> To us our brothers and friends and neighbours were good and outstanding; but it did not please the Lord that we were with them, for he chose you to give to us an inseparable brother and a most beloved neighbour, whom we deservedly love as we love ourselves, since we have one heart and one soul with you in Christ.[69]

Paulinus did not try to minimize the importance of the old bond between himself and Sulpicius. He asserted that this had now been strengthened and made perfect, for now they were joined to Christ in a christian community of brothers. Paulinus summarized perfectly the Western idea that roman friendship can be transformed into christian brotherhood, based on sharing of the ascetic life, without there being any drastic break with the past. Once individual Christians have converted, they can reestablish contact with each other and transform former bonds into new alliances to spread the message of the Gospel lived in terms of an ascetic brotherhood.

The letter ends with some indication that Paulinus, in spite of his glowing prose, was losing patience with Sulpicius for not coming. He had heard that Sulpicius was not enthusiastic about sharing Paulinus' modest monastic quarters. He criticized him for backing away from the very ideal of poverty he praises so highly in his newly-completed *Life of Saint Martin* (*ep* 11.13). Paulinus was beginning to admit publicly the difficulties and deviousness of Sulpicius Severus.

Paulinus was incapable of deceit. However polished his literary style, he wrote what he thought and felt. The salutation of the next letter, written a year and a half later, at the end of 398, says everything:

an austere *Paulinus Severo*, with no titles of affection. Paulinus describes how long he had been suffering, as summer went by and then winter closed off travel over the Alps, in the hope and expectation that Sulpicius would come. 'For almost two years you have tortured us, suspended in daily expectation of the sight of you' (*ep* 17.1). Paulinus reveals the doubts about Sulpicius that had been growing in him during the intervening months. He still hoped to see him, but he could not think it was physical weakness rather than laziness or lack of interest which kept Sulpicius away from Nola. In the course of a summer Sulpicius had gone several times to gallic shrines, but the shrine of Felix at Nola he had avoided (*ep* 17.4). If he failed to live up to the promises Paulinus had made to Saint Felix on his behalf, Sulpicius would be committing a grave offence, *delictum*. Here the language of the letter becomes legalistic, speaking of *causam istam* between Felix and Sulpicius, with Paulinus as the saint's lawyer. In modern terms, Paulinus could be said to have transferred to the martyr his own frustration and anger with Sulpicius for not keeping his promises. In Paulinus's mind, Sulpicius had shown contempt for what was dearest to Paulinus in daily life, the cult of Felix. In concentrating on Martin, Sulpicius had snubbed both Paulinus and Felix.

Sulpicius Severus never came. After Paulinus grew openly angry with him (*ep* 22) and apparently stopped writing, Sulpicius grew sufficiently concerned about their relationship to appeal to Paulinus to show greater love for him. Paulinus wrote back that he could not love Sulpicius any more than he already did. This would be like asking the sea to overflow its boundaries (*ep* 23.1). The old bond of friendship is reasserted here, but the amount of passionate language has drastically cooled. In the following letters Paulinus treated Sulpicius more to intellectual discussion than personal declarations. This development has been seen in terms of Paulinus' learning to become 'more the master of himself, more detached from contingencies, more disposed to look at facts in an objective manner'.[70] This is a generous interpretation by a man who knew the writings of Paulinus intimately, Pierre Fabre, who has pointed out that in 399-400 Paulinus went through a spiritual crisis. Its exact content remains something of a mystery, but when it was over, he distanced himself from the tenderness and open sharing of his former letters of friendship.[71] He seems to have withdrawn more into the community he had created at Nola. Never did he deny or regret the hopes and ideals of his early days, nor did Paulinus, like Jerome, question the ways in which he had expressed them. Paulinus had invested a great deal of himself in Sulpicius, and he had often been disappointed. Not only had Sulpicius failed to keep his promise to visit and share his spiritual community. Sulpicius even accused Paulinus of holding back the messengers Sulpicius had sent him. In point of fact, these messengers had originally come from Paulinus (*ep* 27.2) and were supposed to return to him.

Why did Paulinus bother with Sulpicius, who seems to our eyes to have been so undependable in his human contacts? Paulinus sought out Sulpicius as any good roman male would seek out a neighbour from the same social and educational background and with the same interests. The adoption of Christianity only strengthened the social bond of *amicitia*. In moving from a less perfect to a more perfect form of friendship, Paulinus had unlimited expectations from the old-new alliance. He may have been naive in his hopes, but his reactions are perfectly understandable in the context of his personal and cultural renewal. The more he distanced himself from his former teacher Ausonius, the more he needed friends like Sulpicius, who seemed to represent an ascetic form of Christianity that had room for both spiritual heroes and friends.

Like Jerome and Augustine, Paulinus was looking for community. In building a fellowship of faith around the shrine of Saint Felix, he wanted to establish new links with an old friend and to attach him to this shrine. Sulpicius, however, wanted to use Paulinus not as a living, close friend, but as a representative of a glorious new Christianity, a man to be imitated, a trophy in his collection of friends.[72] A gap yawned between what Sulpicius wanted and what Paulinus sought. The first, like Jerome, coveted both friendship and literary distinction. The second, like Augustine, achieved recognition at an early age and concentrated on transforming his classical heritage into a living christian experience of friendship.

Paulinus had his wife Therasia always in the background. Her presence is as important for the community of Nola as Monica's was at Cassiciacum.[73] One cannot appreciate Paulinus' spiritual development from being the great celebrant of christian friendship to becoming the reserved and careful bishop of Nola without remembering that Therasia was there at every step of the way. Once again we see that a male-male friendship was limited and failed to live up to expectations, while a male-female bond, even if much less visible to us, could underpin a man's life and endure.

Paulinus was celebrated and well-known in his own age not only because he was a rich, learned and gentle Christian. He was an attractive friend because he stood at the centre of a living community of Christians united in the cultivation of a saint, Felix, who was a potent friend of God. Sulpicius wanted to do in Gaul what Paulinus had achieved in Campania. His competitiveness with setting up his cult and his single-minded concentration on moulding his own ascetic community at first surprised, then hurt and angered Paulinus. The subsequent distance that grew up between the two has been called a 'spiritualization of friendship'.[74] More accurately it could be called a process by which Paulinus learned from disappointment to protect himself from concentrating too much on certain friends. His early letters express a dream of christian friendship, while reality turned out to be something else. He was perhaps too prolix in his enthusiasm, too long-winded in his self-assertiveness, and too complicated in his style to be attractive to monastic audiences, whose literary stamina could not match his. But twelfth-century Cistercians were to copy these letters and provide one of the main manuscripts for the modern edition.[75] Paulinus may have been disappointed in friendship; he may have had to transfer his feelings from individuals to the community as a whole and to Saint Felix in particular as his invisible friend. But Paulinus like Jerome had created a literature of friendship that would be available for later monastic friendships.

SULPICIUS SEVERUS: FRIENDSHIP AS OBSESSION

As Paulinus cannot be seen without Therasia, so too behind Sulpicius Severus (*c.*363-*c.*420) we find a woman, his mother-in-law Bassula, who remained with him after the death of his young wife. A single letter, apparently sent to her at Trier, suggests her role in his life.[76] Outwardly it is a playful, almost coy letter, in which Sulpicius smilingly threatens her with legal penalties for divulging his writings on Martin to others before he had finished polishing their language. He describes the death of Martin, on the condition that no one else read the account. Behind these phrases is Sulpicius's ever-present desire to publicize himself and the cult of Saint Martin. There is also, however, a hint of closeness and companionship with a woman who did her best to make both Sulpicius and Martin better known. According to Jacques Fontaine, one of the most thorough students of Sulpicius, the letter shows that Bassula 'played an important role' in his life.[77] She probably made it possible for him to live well in his ascetic community at Primuliacum in the south of Gaul. A mission to Trier she undertook is mysterious; she may have gone to the emperor's court in order to advance Sulpicius's interests. The letter indicates Bassula's eager resolve to spread Sulpicius's writings and further her son-in-law's reputation. He could count on her. With his male friends Sulpicius at times revealed a mistrust bordering on paranoia. He often doubted their loyalty and devotion. With Bassula he had no such problem. The mock accusations of the letter and its familiar tone indicate that here was one person he felt he could trust.

We find again a late antique christian writer for whom friendship was an essential part of life. Indirectly Sulpicius expressed friendship to the woman in his life, and directly he expressed friendships with male companions, as well as with the saint whose cult he publicized. Sulpicius Severus's biography of Martin describes his first visit to the saint and how well Martin treated him. The friend of God became the friend of Sulpicius. Paulinus was included in this intimate circle because Martin himself had pointed out to Sulpicius 'the case of his excellency Paulinus'. There, Martin kept exclaiming, 'there is someone for you to follow. There, he cried, is someone to imitate'.[78] By naming Paulinus in the description of his visit to Martin, Sulpicius bound more closely both the living friend and the dead one. He projected the image of a community of friends united by their christian asceticism. His function was to make known their way of life. In the *Dialogues*, Sulpicius starts his description of egyptian fathers and of Martin's miracles by dwelling on the friendship between himself and Postumianus, who has just returned from the East:

> I embraced this most affectionate of men and kissed his knees and his feet. For a moment or two we were overwhelmed; then we took a turn together, shedding tears of joy.[79]

What is emphasized here is not the manifestation of physical affection, for the scene is highly stylized and probably represents Sulpicius's visualization of how the reunion between friends ought to have been. Sulpicius is making the point that he, Postumianus, and with them Gallus, all share in the cult of Martin. The stories Postumianus told of his travels prove that even the egyptian fathers cannot measure up to Martin in spiritual prowess. As Jerome made his Paul the Hermit greater than Athanasius' Anthony, Sulpicius would make his Martin greater than any desert father.

This aspect of Sulpicius's work is so blatant that it can obscure an underlying theme—almost an obsession: friendship and betrayal. The First Dialogue returns several times to the obligations and involvements of friendship. Postumianus tells Sulpicius how in Egypt he had had a dream in which he saw Sulpicius calling him back to Gaul (Dial. I.1). Sulpicius replied that all the while Postumianus was in Egypt, he was close to him in mind and thought: 'your love completely occupied my thoughts, which were with you day and night'.[80] The first Dialogue begins with a scene of old friendship renewed and ends with Gallus drawn into this alliance because of his association with Martin. 'Any friend of Martin's is a friend of mine', we almost hear Postumianus saying. Sulpicius thought it essential to tighten bonds to the aristocratic Christians around him through strengthening the cult of Martin. Before the conversation turned to the egyptian fathers, Sulpicius engaged in a rhetorical *praeteritio*, referring to other friends who had betrayed him, but refusing to go into detail, especially about one:

> . . . he was once a friend of mine and . . . I had an affection for him even when he was supposed to be my enemy. At the same time, when I have been silently turning the situation over in my mind, it has been

> a very sharp sorrow to me that I have almost completely lost the friendship of such a wise and pious man.[81]

By leaving this alienation so tantalizingly vague, Sulpicius manages to place his own personal alliances with other leading christian authorities on centre stage. All through the description of Postumianus' voyage, we wonder about this lost friend and what might have happened. This must be what Sulpicius wanted us to do! For Sulpicius the cult of Martin is also a cult of friendship, an alliance of like-minded churchmen sharing ideals. In the midst of describing his travels, Postumianus reverts to the theme of Sulpicius's disappointment. Postumianus mentions two old men whom he met in a monastery. They had been there for forty years and were praised by the abbot and all the brothers, for they never had been angry with each other. At this point Gallus is supposed to have looked at Sulpicius and exclaimed, 'Oh, I wish that a certain friend of yours—I would rather not mention names—were now here. I would like so much for him to hear about that case'.[82]

At regular intervals during the rest of the first Dialogue we are treated to debate and discussion about the duties and involvements of friendship. There is a section on male-female relationships. Like Jerome, Sulpicius is critical of close attachments between men and women following the ascetic life, and yet he believes that such relationships are to some extent possible.[83] Martin provides the example of the man who kept women at a distance but who also managed to attract them to him and allowed them to serve his needs. Postumianus here becomes the spokesman of Sulpicius in summarizing the lesson Martin provides in his dealings with women:

> . . . if we were in the habit of following in the footsteps of Martin, we should never have to defend ourselves against charges of kissing and should not have all that scandal talked behind our backs.[84]

Again gaining attention by pretending to keep a distance, Sulpicius refuses to join in this discussion, but he reveals that his statements on the matter have unsettled some people: 'I stirred up such hatred against me among all women and all monks that the two armies of them have solemnly declared war on me'. But Sulpicius has already made the necessary point through his friend: 'You may allow a woman, if she is married, to wait on you, but not to rule you, to wait on you but not to sit at table with you'. Thus women can go to men to seek advice, and they can also provide practical services for men. Sulpicius and his friends preferred to believe that it was the woman who needed spiritual advice, and saw confirmation of their views in the case of Martha and Jesus, or a roman empress and Martin. In conceding a place, however unequal, to women in the lives of ascetic men, Sulpicius left the door ajar to spiritual friendships between men and women.

Martin is everywhere on the surface of the *Dialogues*, but underneath is a constellation of friends and enemies cooperating with Sulpicius or working against him in spreading Martin's cult. Thus friendship in true roman fashion becomes an alliance for a personal cause. The second Dialogue ends with the mention of a friend, Pomponius, who had betrayed Sulpicius and left for Palestine, where he had died. Sulpicius addresses Postumianus and tells him that in returning to the East, he should visit the grave of this man, pray, and shed tears there:

> Tell him [Pomponius] that if he had only been willing to listen, at one time to you and at any time to me, and had imitated Martin rather than one whom I will not name, he would never have been so cruelly separated from me. He would not now be covered by a heap of alien dust . . . Let them gaze upon their handiwork, those who took revenge on him in the hope of injuring me . . . All this I sighed out in a voice choked with sobs, and all were moved to tears by my laments.[85]

At the end of the second dialogue, as at the beginning of the first, Sulpicius draws attention to himself and his friendships. While the opening of the *Dialogues* is characterized by the tenderness and joy of reunion with a friend, the closing is marked by sorrow at the loss of a friend, and by an attack on the enemies of Sulpicius who are responsible for the alienation of Pomponius. Exact events are never specified, but once again we experience how Sulpicius demanded total loyalty, feared betrayal, and was angry with whoever did not comply with him. Behind all these concerns are undoubtedly the vicissitudes of Sulpicius's own community of friends at Pruliacum, however obscure this group must remain to us because it is kept almost out of sight by Sulpicius's self-absorption.

Even if the personality that emerges from these polemics is not attractive, the Letters and Dialogues, as well as the Life of Martin, made an enormous impression on medieval monastic audiences.[86] Here as in Paulinus of Nola, the cult of the saint as invisible friend is tied firmly to the community of visible friends. But Sulpicius did not lose himself in the high-flown prose of Paulinus. His Latin was more succinct, less artificial, and more accessible than the difficult images of Paulinus and the tortured periods of Jerome. Sulpicius dealt with friendship in terms not just of idealization or disappointment, but also considered the alliance it forges between good men in a common concern. He echoes Paulinus, but he was able to express more concisely the belief that the friends of God (or of a saint) become each other's friends, while those who refuse their cause and friendship become the saint's enemies.

Paulinus had hinted at this dark side of friendship in his charge that Sulpicius was not being faithful to Saint Felix. In the *Dialogues*, Sulpicius returned frequently to unnamed former friends who refused to share in the cult and example of Martin and thus challenged Sulpicius and his noble pursuits. The language of christian friendship in Sulpicius, like the language of roman friendship from which it descends, makes apparent alliances among men of power. The power that was once rational and political has now become spiritual and ecclesiastical. It is difficult to keep categories of power separate, however, for the habits and manners of roman society continued in the powerful churchmen of the fourth and fifth centuries in Gaul. Here the ascetic and monastic ideals of Egypt and the East became part of a Western roman ideal of friendship and power in the church.

JOHN CASSIAN: FRIENDSHIP AS HARMONY

If friendship remains a constant undercurrent in Sulpicius Severus, it assumes a well-ordered monastic role in the writings of John Cassian. His *Institutes* and *Conferences*, while not monastic rules in themselves, were of immense importance in shaping the normative monastic literature of the following centuries. Benedict recommended their reading in the monastery.[87] Any medieval monk who thought about friendship could have turned to Cassian's famous sixteenth Conference on friendship. Yet if we look first at the *Institutes*, it seems as if we are in the Eastern tradition, for Cassian is quite specific that the monks are not to go off on their own together, nor are they to hold hands, and here he is specifically concerned with the younger monks:

> The greatest care is to be expended in making sure that none of the brothers, and especially the young ones, is found to be keeping to themselves, even for a moment, or going off anywhere, or holding each other's hands.[88]

In the next passage Cassian explains that monks who indulge in such practices are to be punished because of 'suspicion of conspiracy'. The sexual element in such relationships is not brought into the open or dealt with directly. As in the writings of Saint Basil, we are still very much in the province of concord in the cloister, where exclusive relationships harm solidarity. But the word *conjuratio* is new in this context and indicates an immediate threat to the peace of the community. The danger in Cassian's eyes lay not so much in holding hands but in hatching plans and schemes when monks go off by themselves and keep exclusive company. A subtle difference exists between Pachomius' heavy-handed prohibitions of any sensual contact and this more general warning about conspiracies.

Turning to the Conferences, we find resonances at the basilian-pachomian tradition which frowned on intimate friendships in the cloister. At the same time, however, there is a certain limited opening to friendship. In the sixteenth Conference, Cassian introduces the wise abbot Joseph of Egypt, who knew Greek, enabling Cassian and his companion Germanus to speak to him directly rather than through an interpreter. In the very first chapter, Joseph asks them if they are brothers (*germani fratres*), and they reply that they are joined not 'by bodily but by spiritual brotherhood':

> . . . and we from the beginning of our renunciation of the world, both in our pilgrimage, which was extracted from us to obtain a spiritual term of military service, as in our desire for the coenobitic life, which we always shared in union with each other.[89]

Cassian's Conference on friendship is set in the context of his own friendship with Germanus. Theory and practice complement each other. All warnings about the mutilation of cloister discipline, and the Eastern fear of homosexuality vanish in the warm sun of companionship. Cassian came from the Eastern desert but went west and settled down in Marseilles in the year 415.[90] He soon founded monasteries there, and so, like Sulpicius Severus, but with more lasting results, joined Western and Eastern traditions and provided a foundation for the spread of monasticism in the West.

What did Cassian mean by friendship? Any investigation of the *Conferences* in the light of twelfth-century descriptions of intimate friendship is doomed to disappointment. After an initial description of the types of friendship and its indissolubility (in ch. 2-5, where Cassian draws on classical models), he concentrates on describing how friendship provides harmony in the cloister. In chapters 6-12 and 15-28, Cassian uses abbot Joseph in a pedantic series of counsels about how to avoid conflict and anger among monks. Not for a moment does Cassian hint at anything resembling the close friendships within a small community that were idealized in Sulpicius Severus. Monastic friendship has come to resemble Basil's 'common charity', which is nothing more than a consistent effort to keep everyone on good terms with everyone else, so that none of the monks feels left out or harmed or threatened by anyone else.

John Cassian's Conference on friendship would have been better entitled *De concordia in claustro* than *De amicitia*. Amid all the discussions of how to deal with anger, any trace of affectionate bonds among the monks disappears. After the first promising beginnings in the presentation of the good friends, Cassian and Germanus', friendship is reduced to a rather innocuous relationship. An awareness of Cassian's cool, rational types of love and friendship in the cloister brought Owen Chadwick to write in 1950:

> . . . the discussion turns or deteriorates slowly and willingly into an advisory and useful debate upon the acqusition of peace in a community by the renunciation of self-will: and love of the neighbour has been restricted once again to a spiritual exercise. It is not surprising that throughout his books he quoted a familiar text not once, 'Thou shalt love thy neighbour as thyself'.[91]

From this indictment we can defend Cassian on two points. In the first place, he was writing about love solely in the context of community. In the second, many of his provisions about 'renunciation of self-will' are eminently practical insights into how to make a community function. When Cassian quoted the New Testament, he did not include the admonition to love one's neighbour, but he dwelt carefully on Paul's statement in his first letter to the Corinthians (13:7), on how love is patient and long-suffering.[92] Cassian, moreover, made use of the description of the early christian community from the Acts of the Apostles (4:32):

> There was one heart and one soul in that group of believers, and no one claimed that anything he possessed was his own, but all things were held in common.[93]

It is this sense of harmony within a community of love that Cassian wanted to analyze and secure. Cassian was not concerned with how one monk can love another with affection but with how a community of monks can manage to live together in peace.

The second point in considering John Cassian's ideal of friendship is that since we are dealing with a community concept of love in Cassian, then he was bound to be concerned with types of behaviour that threatened such a common ethic: the anger and resentment that so easily grow up in a relatively closed community; one member can become irritated with the words or actions of another or feel that his needs and interests are not being provided for. Here Cassian's advice is eminently practical. One is not to hide anger, but to bring it out into the open. Cassian points out that *ficta patientia*, even more effectively than silence, can provoke one's brothers to anger. Anger must be dealt with immediately and must not be suppressed, for then it turns into real poison.[94] What appears at first as an uninspiring description of basic principles of behaviour turns out to be a subtle treatment of the ways and wiles of asocial attitudes threatening community solidarity.

Cassian provides a bridge between Eastern and Western monasticism. His work was to become ever more useful in coming centuries, when *concordia* became so important for the survival of communities. But Cassian also left seeds for the later growth of close friendships. In two chapters tucked into the midst of the discussion on wrath and dissension, Cassian deals with their opposite, the love behind the *unanimitas* and *concordia* he seeks. In his fourteenth chapter, *De gradibus charitatis*, Cassian briskly defends the maintenance of different degrees of friendship within the cloister. He uses the classic example that Jesus preferred John among the apostles, although he loved them all. John the Apostle, he says, was more worthy of the Saviour's affection because he was a virgin, and on this basis one can speak of the rightful ordering of love:

> This is truly the ordering of love, which hates no one, but loves certain people more because of their merits: although it loves all in a general manner, this love nevertheless chooses some of these whom it ought to embrace with a particular affection. Again it singles out, from among those who are foremost in love, a few who are cherished above and beyond the others.[95]

Here we find none of the *Institutes'* strictures about not holding hands or not going off on walks together. Cassian deals at the end of this Conference with the danger of conspiracy from brothers who join together in associations that have nothing to do with friendship in its true sense. But when he speaks of a friendship based on christian love, Cassian does not suggest even the possibility of sexual attachments or selfish cliques. For a brief moment, he shows an unqualified optimism that lifts him out of his immediate concern with anger and ill-feeling and legitimizes a more intimate and personal relationship than anything Pachomius or Basil ever accepted. The writings of other Western fathers have already shown that such friendships existed, but they are now being placed in a stable monastic context. Carefully disciplined friendship that does not threaten community is seen as an acceptable part of the discpline of the cloister in the West. Cassian set a precedent which, however incompletely expressed in his own writings, would be of immense importance in the coming centuries. He provided a patristic foundation for monastic ideals and human relationships within the cloister.

BENEDICT: FRIENDSHIP AS A POSSIBILITY

To illustrate the influence of Cassian on medieval monasticism, we can turn to the basis of monastic life in the West, the Rule of Saint Benedict. There already in the second chapter is the provision that the abbot is to make no distinction of persons in the monastery: 'He is not to love one more than another, *unless* he finds one who is better in good actions and in obedience'.[96] This echoes Cassian's point that one monk can be loved more than another because of his virtues. What appears in the first half of the sentence as a clear prohibition of abbatial favouritism turns into an opening for special friendships, at least between abbot and deserving monks. Benedict was not so much concerned with love and friendship, however, as with the correct ordering of life within the monastery: 'But if the abbot, for just reason, thinks fit to do so, let him fix anyone's order as he will'. In justifying this principle, Benedict uses the language of Saint Paul, 'for there is no respect of persons with God' (Rom. 2:11). As so often in monastic literature, the Epistles of Paul are used to express the community ethic at the base of all coenobitic life.

Aside from this concern about the abbot's having friends, Benedict does not explicitly mention love or friendship in the cloister, but there are other provisions which remind us of Eastern monastic rules and of Cassian's writings. This is especially the case when Benedict specifies 'how monks are to sleep' (RB 22). He insists that the young monks are not to sleep in the same part of the common dormitory but should have their beds distributed among those of the more senior monks. The monks are also to sleep singly in their beds and to be dressed, and a candle is to be kept burning all night. These provisions have been seen as an attempt to keep the younger monks from having sexual contact with each other.[97]

At least in conscious terms, Benedict's concerns may not have been sexual. Benedict says that the monks are to sleep in their clothing, 'so that they always be ready, and once the signal is given, get up without delay and hasten' down to matins. The night light can be explained as a comfort to youths afraid of the dark—and to make it easier to find the way when the time came to get up for matins in the middle of the night. There can be little doubt, however, that separate beds were intended to make it difficult for monks to have sexual contact with each other. Compared with those of Pachomius these provisions are much less explicit in indicating danger of sexual expression in the cloister. Like so much other Western monastic literature, the purpose seems to have been to foster order and discipline in daily life rather than to forestall sexual relations. The separation of the young from each other can be seen primarily as a way of keeping them from forming cliques, talking in their beds, breaking silence, and thus disturbing the gravity of daily life.

Benedict, like Basil, was mainly interested in the community of the cloister and its strict ordering. Unlike Basil, however, he did not legislate against close friendships among the monks. Aside from the case of the abbot and the most virtuous monks, Benedict did not deal with the subject of preferential bonds at all. But in recommending the daily reading of the Conferences of Cassian, Benedict implicitly approved of Cassian's point of view that close friendships could lead to dangerous cliques. Another indication of Benedict's attitude is his prohibition against anyone's attempt 'to defend another in the monastery':

> Care must be taken that no monk venture on any ground to defend another monk in the monastery, or as it were to take him under his protection, even though they may be connected by some tie of kinship. Let not the monks venture to do this in any way whatsoever, because it may give rise to most

> serious scandals. But if anyone breaks this rule, let him be punished very severely.[98]

Benedict leaves no doubt that covering-up for one brother by another threatens the unity of the monastery and thus is a serious offence.

> Whoever consents to those who sin and defends anyone committing a fault, he will be accursed by God and man and is to be punished most harshly.[99]

By using the words *tueri* and *propinquitas consanguinitatis*, Benedict betrays that Pachomius was his source. In the monastery the bonds of kinship must be dissolved. Otherwise the brothers form cliques based on family relations and interests. Such groups, Benedict was aware, cover up for monks who break the Rule and disobey the abbot and give rise to the hated conspiracy against which John Cassian warned, a travesty of true friendship. Benedict's interpretation and clarification of Pachomius actually underlines one of the most essential Eastern concerns: the danger of transferring to the cloister the loyalties that exist in the world outside. No one is to take the monk under his special protection in the monastery, for he is subject only to the abbot. For Benedict the best insurance against factions was a single principle of order, the authority of the abbot.[100]

Pachomius was worried both about sexual temptations and family distractions, while Benedict reveals only the latter fear, that old bonds of lay society with family and preferences will flourish in the monastery and undermine the abbot's position. Monks are not to receive letters or gifts without the abbot's permission; such gifts from the outside are linked to the monks' families:

> On no account shall a monk be allowed to receive letters, devout tokens, or any small gifts whatsoever, from his parents or other people, or his brethren, or to give the same, without the abbot's permission.[101]

Benedict's silence on the subject of monastic friendship can only be understood in terms of what he did say about contacts within and without the monastery. The main principle was that of the abbot's supremacy, and whatever he allowed was not only acceptable but also commendable. So the monks could be friends with the abbot (and probably also with each other); they could write letters to each other (which we know they did); they could even give each other small presents. The abbot set the tone of life, and if he were interested in monastic friendships and felt they could be integrated into the discipline and daily life of the cloister, then Benedict's Rule allowed room for them. Benedict left many of the details to the abbot's judgment. He was not overly specific about the petty matters of monks' lives and did not include all the scrupulous details that some Eastern rules provided. He was a legislator who knew that the best collection of laws limits itself to general principles and does not deal with all possible cases.

Benedict did not treat personal contacts among the monks, except insofar as they could threaten the stability of monastic life. When he did lay down the law, it was to quell a threat to the abbot's authority by cliques of favouritism and privilege. These were under no circumstances to be permitted. The bonds of the secular family were to be severed for good, for these could pose an even greater threat to peace within the cloister. Biological brothers in the same monastery were not to look out for each other's interests and family feuds were not to extend within the walls of the monastery. In excluding relationships based on protection and defence, Benedict did not go as far as some of the Eastern fathers and demand equal love for all community members.

GREGORY THE GREAT: FRIENDSHIP AS CONSOLATION

The roman bishops and abbots who inherited the legacy of Rome and Christianity could look to the tradition of friendship as a source of consolation in the midst of troubles. In the *Dialogues* of Pope Gregory the Great from the 590s, it might at first seem there is no room for the delicacies of anything resembling the friendships of Late Antiquity.[102] The Benedict who is described in the *Dialogues* is another Martin or Anthony, a spiritual hero who could take on all demons. The heroic Benedict discovers that his monks tried to poison him, and somehow survives in a monastery surrounded by hostile peoples outside. Gregory conveys a sense of an age of invasions. The evil arian Lombards had taken political power in northern Italy, and what is needed is men of God who were just as ruthless as their enemies, not sentimental friends speaking of the sweetness of friendship.

In the midst of decay and the heroic fight to maintain the Catholic faith and its churches in Italy, Gregory was himself very much concerned with friendship. Just as Sulpicius Severus had begun his *Dialogues* with a tender scene of friendship, so too Gregory chose to begin his *Dialogues* by describing how he as pope after a day of tiresome secular business, turned to a friend. Feeling sorrow and 'deeply dejected', Gregory noticed that his deacon Peter had entered. 'He had been a very dear friend to me from his early youth and was my companion in the study of sacred Scripture.'[103] Peter asked why Gregory was so downcast, and the pope replied by stating the classic christian dilemma between the active and the contemplative life, how the one at times excludes the other. Gregory revealed how much he missed the quiet cloistered life, and recalled the active spiritual men of Italy and their extraordinary powers. So begin his *Dialogues* as a conversation arising out of an old friendship that goes back to the monastery. It is this friendship which gives Gregory relief from onerous papal duties.

This poignant passage we can see as a literary device to introduce the mini-biographies and miracle stories that make up the Dialogues. The introduction could be dismissed as pure embroidery, just as the opening lines from Sulpicius might be looked upon as nothing more than an artificial creation. And yet in both instances we hear echoes of friendships within a monastic way of life, relationships fondly remembered and made memorable in prose that spoke to successive generations of monks. Literary devices need not rule out genuine emotional content. A successful literary structure only underlines that the writer has taken his scene from personal experience. This, I think, is the case in both Sulpicius Severus and Gregory.

Gregory as pope sentimentalized his cloister days. At the same time he spread the Rule and cult of Saint Benedict. In all these ways Gregory contributed to an institutional foundation for spiritual friendships. In this as in so much else, Gregory became one of the founders of the Middle Ages. In Benedict he was favouring not an overwrought abstraction about love and friendship in the monastery, but order and orderliness in a disorderly society, only a few of whose members could deal with the chaos around them. In Gregory the Great's Italy, practical men like Benedict had immediate and basically simple solutions worth remembering. There was neither time nor psychic energy for anything else.

Another Gregory, the bishop of Tours in the seventh century, found that his main preoccupation as bishop was not friendship but feuding. In the pages of his *History of the Franks* most moments of affection are followed by hatred and murder.[104] Only in the cloister did stability and continuity sometimes make it possible for human relationships to be idealized and looked on as sharing love with God. Gregory of Tours sought the stable, well-ordered community where human bonds led to love, not to violence.

THE TRIUMPH OF FRIENDSHIP IN COMMUNITY

Gregory the Great and his Benedict were both, like the other Western fathers of this chapter, roman aristocrats who adapted their upper class culture to the requirements of a changing society. Ambrose made the effort seem painless and effortless. Augustine retained the foundation of ciceronian *amicitia* throughout his life. Jerome and Sulpicius Severus were concerned more with loyalty (*fides*) than with friendship, which remained central no matter what happened. Paulinus and Sulpicius Severus concentrated friendship in a new community around a saint, but also transformed noble roman ideals into an enduring christian love. Even John Cassian, whose models for monastic life were taken from the East, was not far from Cicero when he spoke of monastic friendship. Benedict above all was very much the roman legislator who avoided matters of the heart but concerned himself with discipline of the group. With Gregory the Great at the threshold of the Middle Ages we are still in the company of a roman aristocrat who, like Cicero, could look to friendship as a source of comfort and consolation in a time of troubles.

The medieval monastic forms of friendship to which we will now turn spring from roman upper class friendship. This background helps explain why so little hesitation about it existed in the West. Just as

Ambrose and Augustine did not have to give up their educations and backgrounds in becoming Christians, but could feel that they were completing themselves, so too they could maintain their friendships and remould them within christian communities. At the same time they could combine monastic and clerical ways of life. Service to the church and the ascetic ideal were not separate, as was the case in the East. The cleric could live in a monastic community in North Africa in a way not possible in Egypt. The West did not demand the total separations and clear distinctions on which the East insisted. The aristocratic roman teacher became the christian bishop leading a community of friends in monastic discipline. The ascetic movement and pastoral care joined forces in the West in a way that benefited the church and stimulated monastic life. Gregory the Great sums up the developments of almost three centuries, and in his *Pastoral Care* and his *Dialogues* he passed on to the coming centuries his conviction that friendship, ascetic life, community, and pastoral work could all be combined.

In the midst of a weakening social structure and the disappearance of the very urban society that had made such alliances seem possible, the leading writers of the Western church remained optimistic about new forms of community. In Augustine's very rejection of the roman state and its failed institutions was formed his secure belief that friends and kin together could manage to form christian communities. Monastic discipline left ample room for friendship among individual members. Augustine was not being naive about human limitations and weaknesses when he recommended this arrangement. He was legislating into history what he had experienced in his own life with his friends and companions. Lesser lights like Paulinus of Nola and Sulpicius Severus agreed with him in insisting that alliances of friendship were necessary so that good Christians could become friends of God and spread the cult of the saints and the ascetic discipline of the church. As Paulinus wrote to Augustine (*ep* 6.2): we are not starting a new friendship but taking up again, as it were, an old love.[105] The boundaries of the acceptable and the feasible were constantly shifting, but they seldom left friendship outside. Even in his coolest letters, Paulinus had a good word to speak for friendship. Even in his bitterest enmities, Sulpicius dreamt of what friendship might be like.

With such powerful advocates of friendship as Jerome, Augustine and Paulinus, friendship in the West might seem inevitable as a desirable form of human expression within christian love and community life. But late medieval and post-reformation monastic experience demonstrates that things could have turned out differently, that close individual friendships could have been banned from the start. The fact that Benedict did not do so is not due simply to John Cassian's idealization of friendship. Even though Benedict was literarily and ascetically influenced by Cassian, his indirect acceptance of friendship mainly reflects the fact that as a good roman aristocrat, he could no more outlaw friendship than deny the impulse of men to band together in communities for support in the ascetic and contemplative life. Neither tendency needed justification. The only reservation involved guarding against the proclivity of men in groups to split into factions and dissolve community.

On the foundation of classical tradition the structure of christian friendship was built. Cicero's roman examples were replaced by christian ones, and around the maxims of the Old Testament, the friendships of Christ in the Gospels, and the letters of friendship to christian communities from Paul, a new literature of friendship grew up. Its content indicates a lack of distance between Western monks and the 'old' culture. The monk did not have to leave everything and flee to the desert. As often as not he walked a few miles away from his home town, as to Marmoutier near Tours, or even remained within the town walls, as at Hippo in North Africa. Bonds of kinship and friendship could be transformed and strengthened in the new society. The old order was losing its strength and attractiveness, and the flight from the world could be reduced to mental separation.

Here male-female friendships often had an important role. The ascetics' rejection of sex did not preclude a cautious opening to chaste relationships between men and women. The Western fathers feared women as sexual objects because they were afraid of their own sexuality. They insisted that women had to abandon their procreative function and remain virgins. If they did so, they could play a central role in the spiritual life of churchmen, even though only a few women were given the literary prominence in this new christian culture that their social and emotional positions deserved. Just as later in the Middle Ages, women provided the foundation of many spiritual friendships, but they rarely got credit for their self-offering. *Amicitia* remained, in spite of social reality, a matter for men alone. In this area as in so many others, classical roman attitudes passed into a medieval framework.

In the East, John Chrysostom (d. 407) held marriage in high esteem and was terrified by male homosexuality.[106] In the West Augustine gave the married a very limited role in the church and showed no special concern about homosexuality. He was certain that men would thrive in an ascetic community. The difference between Chrysostom and Augustine is representative of the way the East separated while the West integrated. Eastern writers made absolute distinctions between ways of life within the christian brotherhood; Western writers combined the desert and the city in a new monasticism. If the East made the desert a city, the West brought the spirit of the desert to the city. The ideal of a life in common for philosopher-aristocrats became the monastic community of friends at Hippo for Augustine or at Bethlehem for Jerome. In both contexts women were allowed on the fringes so that they could serve the needs of men, both spiritual and material. However we might today look upon such an arrangement, the Western fathers made one central point from which their medieval heirs could benefit: they insisted that love of an individual neighbour was not necessarily a dangerous commitment. Men could embrace each other, and sometimes even women, in a common movement towards God.

CHAPTER THREE

THE MONK AND THE WANDERER: VARIETIES OF EARLY MEDIEVAL FRIENDSHIP

BEDE AND BEOWULF: LOOKING FOR FRIENDSHIP

IN MOVING from Late Antiquity to the early Middle Ages to trace expressions of friendship, we can begin at no better place than the writings of the Venerable Bede (*ca.* 672-735). In clear latin prose Bede sums up the events and attitudes of his age in monastic terms. If we look at Bede's description of Gregory the Great, the pope who sent Augustine the missionary and monk to England, we sense an immediate contrast between Gregory's own description, in the start of the *Dialogues*, of his sadness, and Bede's account of the pope's frame of mind. Gregory had written of how, after his election to the papacy, he had turned to a friend and recollected the spiritual comfort and solace of monastic life. Bede is attentive to the monastic theme, while he lets Gregory's close friend, the deacon Peter, drop out of the scene.[1]

Bede sees Gregory in purely monastic terms and ignores the theme of friendship in Gregory's account. He recalls that when Gregory had been envoy in Constantinople, he had taken a few fellow monks with him from his roman house and established a common life for the sake of brotherly love (*gratia germanae caritatis*). Bede's passage is rich in the language of community and brotherhood in self-discipline. There are no individual friendships, no moments of contacts and closeness between one monk and another. Fraternal loves, while not explicitly excluded, are not mentioned. Bede adapts Gregory to the needs of northumbrian monasticism, where monks and their communities were the bearers of roman christian culture. In Bede's eyes, Gregory established roman Christianity, with its universal quality. Bede then has good reason to ignore Gregory's moment of fatigue, self-doubt and appeal to a friend. What he chooses to remember is the need for community (*consortium*) and the exercise of discipline leading to heaven (*caelestis exercitia vitae*).

Amicitia is a word found fairly often in Bede's historical works, but it is used in a political rather than a personal context. When Benedict Biscop, the founder of Bede's monastery at Jarrow, returned to Britain after a visit to Rome, *amicitia* describes his approach to the king of Wessex: 'He came to confer with the king. . .whose friendship he had made use of not just once before and by whose benefits he had been aided.'[2] Here *amicitiae* is used almost as a synonym for *beneficia:* friendships give benefits, rewards, gifts and concrete material help. When largess was impossible because of the king's recent death, Benedict turned to his native land of Northumbria and found the monastery of Wearmouth. There he had found favour with the king: *gratiam familiaritatis*.

The word *familiaritas* is used in Bede and other medieval writers to associate the idea of friendship as an alliance between two individuals with the concept of the close bond found among kin. A *familiaris* can be a companion or a relative. At times it can be impossible in early medieval monastic literature to distinguish between kinship and friendship.[3] As in Late Antiquity, the point of departure for the development of human bonds lies in the closeness of family members.

Bede accepted this state of affairs and reflected it in his work. In a letter written in 734, Bede encouraged Archbishop Egbert of York to call on royal power for help in maintaining the standard of religious life: 'He will make sure to aid you with a firm intention and especially because you are his most beloved kinsman. . .'. Here the expression *propinquus illius amantissimus* might possibly mean that Egbert and the king were close friends, but a stricter reading indicates that they are relations.[4] The very ambiguity of the language here underlines the early medieval situation. In a society where structures of governmental administration had almost disappeared, it was personal bonds among men that maintained order in society.[5] These bonds were strongest among those of the same blood, and so friendship could function as a spiritualized kin bond.

Almost anywhere we look in early medieval society men are looking for bonds that will not break. The most complete expression of this search is the anglo-saxon poem, 'The Wanderer,' where the lordless man is also the man without a friend:

> Seeking unhappy the hall of
> some prince and friend,
> Where far or near I could
> find one to know me
> And comfort me left
> alone.—But he who has
> tried can tell forth
> How bitter is sorrow for
> companion
> To the man with not a
> friend on earth![6]

The wanderer awakens from a dream in which he has been doing homage and embracing his master. He finds only the cold reality of the wind-swept sea. The poem takes us into a world that is far from the monastic community life of Bede, and yet its sense of isolation and apartness from other human beings runs parallel to the desert fathers' ethos of exile from the world and lonely battles against the devil. The poem ends with the hope of a heavenly fortress, the same protection that the monastery could offer on earth:

> Happy is he who keeps his faith: his anger starts not
> abroad
> Till the sequel he can finish with his sword.
> Well it is for him who looks for a merciful hand

From the Father in heaven, where for us all the fortress stands.

Could the wanderer find friendship? In the Beowulf poem, the hero's exploits establish a somewhat official friendship between the king, Hrothgar, and Beowulf. Friendship is maintained through an act of vengeance: 'it is better for a man to avenge his friend than to mourn him long'.[7] After the reprisal, Beowulf is promised not only fame but also friendship. In Hrothgar's words, 'I shall keep my promise of friendship with you, as we agreed not long ago. You will become a sure and lasting comfort to your nation and a help to mankind.'[8] Beowulf reflects the search of early medieval men for order through heroic exploits, the alliance of friendship, and feasts in well-lit halls. Friendship is seen as being established to seal pacts of loyalty, and to cement personal ties that easily could be broken in a moment of anger, mistrust or misunderstanding.

Bede lived a life of stability in contrast to that of the wanderer. In his *Life of Saint Cuthbert* (*Vita Cuthberti*), however, he showed a similar concern to that of the Wanderer's author for the bonds among men that can enable them to cope with a harsh and ungenerous world. After Cuthbert had been bishop of Lindisfarne for a few years (685-87), he realized that he was close to dying. There was a priest named Hereberht who lived alone at Derwentwater in what today is the Lake District. This man would come to Cuthbert once a year for advice. The relationship between saint and hermit is described in terms of spiritual friendship: 'They were bound to each other by the bond of spiritual friendship' (*spiritalis amicitiae foedere copulatus*).[10] This phrase distinguishes the attachment of Cuthbert and Hereberht from the political friendships that are the usual form of individual associations in Bede. Because he was aware of the tradition in which friendship means political alliances, Bede had to find a term to make it quite clear that men can be close in friendship for non-political motives.[11]

It has long been assumed that the first appearance of the term *spiritalis amicitia* comes in the letters of Saint Boniface and his disciple and successor Lull. Here, however, Bede uses the term several years earlier.[12] His use of it is important not only because it points to an earlier application of the term but also because it shows how sensitive Bede was to the need for precision in expressing the varieties of friendship. Bede summarizes the early medieval development, in which friendship can be expressed in many different ways, most of them secular, but with at least the possibility of spiritual union.

In Bede's description of Cuthbert, blood relationships, power and influence have no role. Only the need of one man for another's help and guidance counts. As soon as Hereberht heard Cuthbert was at Carlisle, he went to visit him. When Cuthbert told him that this would be their last meeting, the hermit broke into tears and begged him not to leave him alone: 'Remember your companion'.[13] The term *sodalis* which is used here has a more spiritual ring than *amicus* would have had in Bede's vocabulary. He shies away from identifying the traditional word for friend with the spiritual relationship exemplified here. In the story the hermit and the bishop die on the same day so they can be together in heaven.

Bede says that Hereberht first had to experience a long and painful illness so that he could be sufficiently cleansed to enjoy heaven and be equal to Cuthbert. There is the point of the story: Cuthbert was on so exalted a spiritual plain that his companion had to suffer greatly to reach his level. But the story could not work if the friends had not been seeking closeness and a sharing of self.

Within the life of the monastery Bede was much more interested in collective discipline than in individual bonds, but the story of Cuthbert and Hereberht is not the only indication that friendship could have some importance for him. We see this in Bede's description of a visit by an abbess of royal lineage to Cuthbert. When she asks about the identity of the next king, Cuthbert does not reject her as being impertinent but answers her question indirectly.[14] Bede was not fond of this curious woman but respected her for the love she showed Cuthbert.[15] There is no mention of the word friendship, yet the scene is intensely personal and intimate. At another time Cuthbert sought out this woman, Aelfflæd, in order to speak with her: (*et ipsam videre atque alloqui*).[16] Once again she is so concerned with Cuthbert's power of prophecy and becomes almost a nuisance who refuses to leave the man of God alone. Even if Bede's portrait of the woman is unsympathetic, the hagiographer still portrays a bond between a spiritual man and a noble woman and sets it firmly in the context of monastic life. Politics, visions and friendship are all combined here. The purpose is, as almost always in hagiographical literature, to show the powers of the saint. Indirectly, however, we are shown that Cuthbert and the abbess were on close terms.

In Bede, a sensitive register of his age, we discover a central spiritual bond of the early Middle Ages: friendships between men and women in a monastic context. In the rather stiff greetings in Bede's letters, friendship seems a rhetorical formula.[17] Anecdotes from the *Life of Cuthbert,* however, attest to the receptivity of the age to closeness between powerful churchmen and almost equally powerful noblewomen. Cuthbert needed the abbess as a source of revelation for his spiritual powers just as much as she needed him for his advice and prophetic information.

Bede's letters cannot place us within the daily relationships of cloister, but they can provide at least a glimpse of a world of friendly relationships, often in the context of intellectual bonds. To Bishop Acca of Hexham Bede sent his commentaries on various books of the Bible and prefaced them with letters speaking of his friendship (*amico pectore*). Bede looked upon Acca as an inspiration to his work. It is impossible to say whether the two were close friends in any modern sense of being men who know each other's habits, thoughts and lives well, but Bede insists that Acca's frequent exhortations and prayers maintain him in his efforts. This is why he is most beloved of all bishops for Bede.[19] Here the language of friendship provides a description of the bond among scholars. As we will see in the letters of Rhabanus Maurus a century later, such terms of affection are the trademark of a scholar rather than the language of an intimate friend. It is, however, impossible to distinguish the two completely. The scholar needs the patron. The friend needs the intellectual bond.

So long as we do not reduce friendship to a purely emotional relationship, it becomes clear that many types of friendships were expressed in early medieval life. For both the wanderer and the monk, human bonds can be described in a number of ways. The literature of the monastery, however, lacks clarity about how individual relationships and monastic structure can coexist and complement each other. This problem is connected with the fact that the monastic institution itself was not carefully defined. Each monastery or group of houses went its own way, and so it is impossible to study friendship during this period in a purely monastic context.

In the early Middle Ages it can often be difficult to see whether those who write about friendship are expressing themselves as monks, scholars or courtiers. Friendship is just as ill-defined and ephemeral as monastic life itself. Those who advocate friendship use many different forms of expression, and these vary just as much as does the content of monastic life as a whole.

SOCIAL AND LITERARY BACKGROUND

Behind Bede is the latin literature of friendship which persisted while the society from which it sprang disappeared. The landowners of the period, whether bishops or laymen, expressed themselves to each other in the language of friendship.[20] As Sidonius Appolinaris wrote to a friend in the 470s:

> I learned with pleasure that you have been made governor of the province. . . first because you are a friend, secondly because you are a just man, thirdly because you are severe, and fourthly because you are a neighbour.[21]

Sidonius had someone to whom he could go for help in matters important to him. This he says quite bluntly.[22] He hoped to use the new governor in his own circle of influence, just as his roman ancestors had done. The very breeziness of this letter (and there are others much like it) points out how friendship means connections and alliances for political purposes.

We might turn up our noses at this practice, but Bede would have understood it and showed how it functioned in the anglo-saxon kingdoms several centuries later. In the decades after Sidonius, Bishop Avitus of Vienne (c. 450-518) wrote letters of friendship, brief greetings to influential churchmen and nobles mentioning the ecclesiastical feasts of the year.[23] Roman landowners had often been replaced by barbarian, but there is no difference in the way they were approached. A bishop needed to have no qualms in using the formulae of friendship and expecting beneficial results.

When we turn to the poems of Venantius Fortunatus (c. 530-603), we remain within this same environment, except that here both Gallo-romans and 'barbarians' received his writings. Fortunatus played the literary man who expressed all the right things to important nobles and church officials. He remembered their birthdays and their favourite dishes. Invited from court to court, he made a grand tour of Gaul and Burgundy, apparently to his heart's delight.[24] But for Fortunatus the commerce of friendship for pleasure and literary recognition was not enough. At Poitiers he found the formidable Radegund, once queen and one of the few survivors of the thuringian royal family. She had established a monastery and appointed the aristocratic woman Agnes as abbess. Fortunatus was won over completely by the grace and beauty of their way of life. The relationship he established with Radegund has been described as that of a slave serving a nun.[25] This may have been one of the poet's many literary poses. In expressing his devotion, however, Fortunatus changed his poetry. What had earlier been dainty products for appropriate occasions become memorable expressions of sharing in a world of flowers, gifts, sympathy, understanding and affection.[26]

Venantius Fortunatus was more than a court poet. In the early Middle Ages, he is the first we meet to celebrate friendship in monastic surroundings. It is significant that some of his most prominent friendships were with women. Although he never became a monk himself, his function at Poitiers seems to have been as administrator for the monastery.[27] His poems make it clear that during Lent his beloved ladies would withdraw from his sight.[28] He is a monastic friend in the sense that he identifies himself with the cloister and concentrates on its inhabitants. The simplicity and directness of his poetry to Radegund and Agnes would have been impossible had they lived at court. For these royal ladies in their monastery, Fortunatus could concentrate not on grandeur and power but on the objects of everyday life: eggs, violets and meals together:

> In what the mother loves, the brother also desires
> So that while we take food and whatever we say,
> If you do the same, then I am twice filled.[29]

In his declarations of affection to Radegund and Agnes, Fortunatus does not call himself their friend. He is someone who loves them (*amans*).[30] They are mother, sister, beloved. Abbess Radegund has given birth not only to Agnes but also to Fortunatus, and Fortunatus even describes how they both have taken milk at her breasts.[31] However exuberant he may seem in his language, he keeps control of his affection.[32] Perhaps the term *amica* would have evoked something too familiar and sensual, a roman idea of the girlfriend? More likely Fortunatus followed the roman conception that *amicitia* existed only between men. As a matter of course he distinguished his devotion to these two extraordinary women from what he felt for his male friends.

Fortunatus' poems of *amicitia* are much more conventional than the linguistic fireworks of those made for Agnes and Radegund. Some of his declarations of friendship, which use the poem as a sign or pledge of friendship (*pignus amicitiae*), are vague and appear to be purely laudatory exercises.[33] But to Sigoald, a companion provided by King Sigibert when the poet first came from Italy, Fortunatus expressed what looks like genuine affection for a man of political importance but was important to Fortunatus as an object of love: *magnus honore tuo, maior amore meo* (X 16). To Rucco, a deacon when Fortunatus had known him but afterwards a priest, Fortunatus composed the most complete expression of male friendship that we have prior to the letters of Saint Boniface and of Alcuin. He describes their separation but insists on how their love binds them together:

> The Seine holds you back, while the Atlantic binds us
> One love draws together those separated by their lands.[34]

We are fortunate to have a second poem to the same man after he had become bishop of Paris (576-91). Here he is called Ragnemod, so Rucco must have been an intimate name that Fortunatus shared with him:

> Great father of the country, dear to me in the name
> Rucco, holding thy inmost heart in love.
> Whatever friendship we shared of old,
> Grow ever in my affection.[35]

Whatever friendship we once had, assures Fortunatus, will continue to develop. There is to be no forgetfulness (*oblivio*), only an increase in closeness.

This may have been wishful thinking, and there is no doubt that Fortunatus was a flatterer who could impress any vain austrasian count with his art. As was aptly pointed out many decades ago, in the autumn of another world, Fortunatus' expressions of friendship belong to the 'good tone' of social relations among the aristocracy of the time: *ein Kennzeichen aristokratischer Gesinnung.*[36] And yet by his poems to Rucco-Ragnemod, to his companion Ligoald, and especially to Radegund and Agnes at Poitiers, we enter into a neoplatonic world of spiritual friendships. Love is based on invisible bonds among men and women that disregard distance and never age. The theme of separation/closeness becomes one of the guiding motifs of Fortunatus' poetry.

Such a theme was not new or 'original'. Pain in parting for those who love can be found in the Bible as well as classical literature. But Fortunatus developed the ideas both literarily and spiritually. He contrasted geography with union of hearts, and he made Rucco at his altar in Paris more present to his listener than the raging of the Atlantic Ocean. Venantius Fortunatus tried to unite emotion and rhetoric in pure poetry. Augustine's neoplatonic teaching about the soul's yearning for security in the friend took on poetic expression.

Fortunatus did not share the depths of Augustine's vision of existence, nor his sense that ultimately friendship is insufficient and that the true comfort is to be found only in God. Fortunatus was the first of a number of early medieval writers to posit a direct link between friendship with men and friendship in God.[37] These writers lacked the depth of vision and sense of limitations in human relationships so apparent in Augustine.

For Fortunatus' audience, poetry assured the continuity of the world they knew. Friendship was a necessary expression of that poetry. Long after the collapse of roman society that Augustine had anticipated, there was still hope in human relationships—and in the written expression of the content of those relationships.

Early medieval attention to language is apparent to us especially in Aldhelm of Malmesbury (639-709). Aldhelm set a linguistic standard greatly appreciated by the anglo-saxon world in the coming century.[38]

He never wrote about friendship in detail but in a number of places in his works he mentions it. In dedicating a work on metrics to a king of Northumbria, he tried to describe his bond of affection with the king.[39] Let love not grow cold through separation, he pleaded.[40]

One would hardly imagine that a work dealing with difficult principles of poetic metre would provide themes about friendship, but the literary device of a dedicatory letter allowed Aldhelm to expatiate on the bond of friendship. In the few letters we have from him, many only fragments, there are similar phrases that in themselves are innocuous but which will turn up in eighth-century works. Such is the case with a letter to an abbess advising her *ex intimo cordis cubiculo* to allow the bishop to baptize a certain man.[41] No special affection is indicated here, for Aldhelm may only have been extravagantly polite. But the very floridness of his prose provides fertile soil for terms of friendship and love that were later to service anglo-saxon monks and nuns looking for models for the expression of their own affection.

In his closing letter to the abbess, Aldhelm calls her a hundred times loved; no, a hundred thousand: *decies dilectissima/immo centies et milies.*[42] How literally we should take Aldhelm's effusions is less important than how they affected the minds and hearts of those who would read him in subsequent generations. In a time when learning was at a premium, the written word deserved the highest respect. In his letters and especially in his treatises, Aldhelm encompassed the learning of his time.

What unites Aldhelm in the seventh century with Sidonius Apollinaris in the fifth and Venantius Fortunatus in the sixth? All three considered friendship a topic important to define and express. Their rhetoric of friendship is more than 'mere rhetoric'. It is there because friendship mattered to them. Sidonius wrote of friendship in order to maintain life-preserving links among members of his class at a time when he needed every friend he could get. Venantius Fortunatus used the language of friendship first as a way to get to the top but he eventually put it into the service of the rich and intimate world he discovered with Radegund. Aldhelm could use friendship as a way of making his solid learning palatable and attractive to his audience. Finally in Bede in the eighth century friendship could take on a spiritual dimension in a monastic community. Here, as so often, Augustine had already said it all: 'The friend is to be loved freely because of himself and nothing else'.[43]

The writers of the early Middle Ages did not look with special interest at Augustine for their language of friendship. They were satisfied with mastering the latin language, finding the right words and using them in appropriate context. Latin for them was an object of fascination. The teacher tried to imbue his pupils with a sense of the mysteries of this foreign but necessary language. At this meeting point of roman reminiscences, platonic visions and fragile experiences of friendship, Venantius Fortunatus could describe his bonds of love in terms of plums, chestnuts, milk and eggs. For him these lowly and delicious foods provided a seal on a happy and lasting friendship with Agnes and Radegund. Aristocratic and monastic figures at one and the same time, they point the way to new forms of friendship in coming centuries.

THE IRISH CONTRAST

Ireland nurtured monastic culture in the early Middle Ages, especially in the sixth and seventh centuries, and so it is to Ireland that we must turn in tracing the ideal and practice of friendship.[44] At first we seem to have returned to the egyptian desert, to the ascetisism of Pachomius, which looked upon familiar relationships with the utmost suspicion. In the Rule of Saint Columban (c. 543-615), the brothers are forbidden to have any extraordinary contacts with one another without specific permission.[45] Youths are to be especially careful about talking out of turn even when addressed. Punishment is to be meted out to a monk who speaks to someone who does not share a cell with him. If a monk holds the hand of another, he is also to be punished.[46] One wonders whether Columban had not read through the Rule of Pachomius carefully. Like his egyptian predecessor, he aimed at minimizing all contact with old friends and with blood relatives.

The egyptian association of the dangers of blood links with those of friendship bonds is maintained here.[47] Relatives were not to try to recruit their kin to the same monastery.[48] Columban himself is praised in his *Life* for abandoning his mother. She had tried to block the door on his departure, but he ordered her to stop grieving, 'saying she never would see him again in this life'.[49] When Columban became a monk at Bangor under Comgall and then went to Gaul with twelve companions, their chronicler emphazies their unity as a community, not their individual friendships.[50] For the irish monk as for the egyptian hermit, *conversio* meant giving up everything having to do with family, friends, and position in the world. At times even the community of the monastery became intolerable, and Columban sought solitude away from the brethren. In so doing he made himself into a new desert father in the Eastern tradition.[51]

The models of early medieval irish monasteries with which archaeologists have provided us make it apparent from the buildings themselves that community life never became completely dominant on the island.[52] The individual cells of monks were grouped together in a common area, but within this space the monks could easily have maintained an eremitical existence. Community exercises—prayers, eating and teaching—could still have taken place, but human contacts were regulated not so much by a common discipline as by the ascetic ideal that monks outdo each other in prayer and fasting. Irish monasticism brought the spirit of the egyptian desert to the rocky coasts and isolated corners of northern Europe.

Early irish monasticism had little interest in individual friendships among equals. Closeness could exist only with the abbot or with the father-confessor. In Ireland this figure, the *pater confessionis*, emerged to provide a supplement to the practice of collective confession.[53] To him the individual monk could turn in his guilt and shame for advice and comfort. Such a father-confessor or spiritual director is often described as *anmchara*, a 'soul-friend'.[54] The soul-friend approached in function the spiritual father of the egyptian desert. When Saint Medoc was walking by the Irish Sea with his fellow monks, he remembered that he had forgotten to ask his master, David, to tell him who his confessor was to be in Ireland. He walked across the sea to discover the man's identity.[55] Told that the holy man Molua would be his spiritual guide, he returned to Ireland without taking his cymbal along, so when he discovered it was missing, he crossed the sea once more on foot to retrieve it!

Saint Molua also appears in a story about Saint Comgall, the founder of Bangor abbey near present-day Belfast. Comgall told Molua that, 'My soul-friend has died and I am without a head and you are without heads: for a man without a soul-friend is a body without a head'. Molua advised him to find a new soul-friend: 'Take Christ's Gospel to yourself and let someone lift it up before you and kneel to it until you get a soul-friend out of it'. Comgall chose Molua, for he was holding the Gospel book.

Closeness also developed when monks brought up youths in their monasteries. A bishop and an abbot were both said to have loved a youth greatly. He 'was called their foster-son' (*alumpnus eorum*), for he had spent his life from boyhood with them.[57] In the individual cells of the Irish monastic foundation, boys could grow up in the same room with single monks.

In the germanic languages friend at root means kinsman, while in Irish and Welsh it derives from the word for foster-brother.[58] Here and with the father-confessors or soul-friends, friendship normally linked a spiritual father and son, not two equals who sought each other out for mutual sharing and affection. This again is close to the practice of the egyptian desert, when eager neophytes would cultivate venerable fathers so that they could train in asceticism.

Monastic encouragement of close father-son bonds and discouragement of ties based on equality can be rooted in a fear of homosexual relations. We have noticed this in the tightly-knit egyptian communities, where even a donkey ride could be dangerous, if two men were sharing the donkey! The same concern seems to have existed in irish monasticism. The *Penitential* of Saint Columban contains many penances for sexual sins. Several of them are clearly identifiable with male homosexual acts.[59] An ascetic life based on individual self-discipline seems to require strong prohibitions as a safeguard, while more collective forms of monastic life, great monasteries with a variety of personal and social relationships, show less fear of homosexuality, as we will see in the carolingian world.[60]

For all its rigours, however, irish monasticism does not absolutely preclude spiritual friendship among equals. The *Life* of Saint Columba, the first abbot of Iona (c. 521-97), by his successor Adamnan, several times uses the word *amicus* in an approving monastic context. In prophesying the death of the priest Ernan, Columba called the man his friend.[61] Describing the relationship between the two saints Columba and Columban, Adamnan calls Columban friend of the abbot of Iona.[62]

Despite the not infrequent use of the word *amicus*, the noun *amicitia* does not appear. This may be accidental, but it may also indicate that Adamnan looked upon *amicitia* as a secular phenomenon outside the monastic ideal. Monks could be each other's friends in pursuing the spiritual life, but personal friendship was not in itself attractive to them. Adamnan knew that every great and powerful lord had a company of friends about him (*in ejus comitatus, quasi unus de amicis*).[63] These friends could be helpful in time of war as allies. They were often one's blood relations. As Saint Comgall told Columba while they washed their hands, the fountain from which their water came would one day be unfit for human use, for 'my friends according to kinship and your relations according to the flesh' would fight at the place and pollute the water with their own gore.[64]

As we learned from Bede, the friend as political ally is a far cry from the spiritual friend. Men can be each other's friends in monastic life, but friendship is based on blood bonds. Kinship brings conflicts and bloodshed as often as union and harmony. Friendship cannot be a worthy ideal so long as it is dominated by this secular ethic. At rare moments two saintly men can be each other's friends because they are equals, as were Columba and Columban, but most monks' friends are on different levels and must maintain a necessary distance from each other.

THE ANGLO-SAXON MISSIONARIES

Irish monasticism generally discouraged friendships of equality in the cloister. The anglo-saxon Bede suggested the possibility of spiritual friendships, while Boniface (c. 675-754) confirmed this acceptance and clarified its development. There may have been (and probably were) monastic friendships all along, but the letters collected by Boniface and his successor, Lull of Malmesbury (c. 710-786), make them visible to us. Usually remembered as a missionary rather than as a monk, Boniface like his irish predecessors was brought up in a monastic environment. After he left home Boniface looked to the monasteries of his country of birth for both spiritual and material assistance.

If we did not have Boniface's letters and had to rely solely on the *Life* by Willibald, we would be able to say little about the role of friendships in Boniface's life. Willibald looks upon friends in the traditional lay sense of "friends of the family". When Boniface at the age of seven wanted to gain entrance at the monastery of Exeter, his 'friends' are said to have been standing about and listening to his bright answers to the abbot.[65] These can only be the representatives of his family. Once he joined, his fellow monks are not called *amici* but *fideles confamiliaritatis illius viri*: faithful men in the fellowship of the monastery.[66] At the monastery of Nursling, where Boniface went to improve his education, he is said to have lived in *contubernia*, a roman military term suggesting camp life. Boniface becomes the perfect example to all the brothers, giving advice to men directly and to women indirectly through his writings. He is famous for his mildness. All these qualities fit nicely into the portrait of Boniface as a saint.

Saints' lives in the early Middle Ages give scant place to individual friendships, or to other individual traits in the saint. Only with the pope are bonds of friendship formed (*amicitiae foedera*), but these are seen more in formal than in personal terms.[67] When we are introduced to Boniface's friend Lull, he is called *fidelis in Domino comis*: Boniface's faithful companion in the Lord.[68] It is the devil, not the saint, who has friends in this hagiography.[69] When we hear echoes of the phrase from the Acts of the Apostles (4:32) about how the early christians were of one heart and mind, Willibald is talking not about a community that shares friendship but one that participates jointly in martyrdom.[70]

In this *Life*, as in so many others of the early medieval period, friends (*amici*) are those who create short-term political alliances, while companions in the monastic or missionary life are given other titles, such as *sodales* or *comites*. Even when Boniface foretells his coming martyrdom to Lull, the moment does not lead to any expression of closeness. Boniface hurries away from Lull's tears to other business.[71] The friend is not to share his feelings: the great spiritual hero must remain untouched by signs of weakness.

Here we are functioning within the rules of traditional hagiography, where anecdotes and the smallest details contributed to the portrait of a man who acts like a saint and has done so from the start. In the early Middle Ages hagiographers concentrated on making their saints into heroes, elevated above and beyond all other people, including their closest associates.

When we go behind the saintly facade, however, and look at the letters of Boniface and Lull, another set of values emerges.[72] It becomes clear that the literary genre of hagiography has deliberately submerged individual traits richly evident in the letters. Here at last we are on the homeground of monastic friendship.

The earliest letters in this collection contain large numbers sent to Boniface. Many of them come from anglo-saxon abbesses. The abbess Egburg addresses Boniface by his english name, Wynfrid, an indication that the letter was written just after he went to the continent, so it can be dated 716-18. Her fulsome salutation calls Wynfrid her 'holy and true friend', adding every flourish that could be learned from the school of Aldhelm.[73] Her elegant turns of phrase are heavily dependent on Aldhelm.[74] The letter is a pastiche of borrowed phrases, and yet the result is more than an elementary exercise in stringing quotes together. Egburg uses the knowledge of past writers in order to make her letter into *pignus amicitiae*, a token of friendship.

Egburg tells Boniface in the letter that his love for her has the sweetness of honey. Even if she could not for the moment be with him, she embraced him as a sister.[75] He had become her father as well as brother, for especially since the cruel death of her brother, Boniface had been the man she loved the most. Not a day or night passed without her remembering what he had taught her (*memoria magisterii tui*). She trusted Boniface would not forget the friendship which he had had with her brother. Even if she was unequal to her brother in learning and merits, she was not unequal to him in her love for Boniface. Egburg emphasises family relationships: her own physical link to her brother, Boniface's spiritual bond with him, and her taking on of that link now that her brother was dead. She mentions her sister, who had gone on pilgrimage to Rome and remained there. Egburg borrows a phrase from the *Aeneid* to express her grief: 'Everywhere there is grief, everywhere fear and everywhere the image of death'.[76] Egburg contrasts her own situation with that of Boniface. He can look forward to a high place in heaven while 'I still in this veil of tears. . . weep for my own sins'. Her one consolation is the thought of seeing Boniface. As the storm-tossed sailor desires port, the thirsty fields rain, the anxious mother her son, so she waits for Boniface's return. Egburg has borrowed an expression of yearning for an absent loved one directly from one of Jerome's letters.[77] It is the letters of Jerome, not the works of Augustine, which provide apt expressions for friendship in the anglo-saxon and carolingian age of friendship from about 700-850.

In the remainder of the letter Egburg asks for Boniface's prayers and some token of his affection, either relics of the saints or some of his writings, 'so that in them I shall always have your presence'. The letter adds a postscript from another friend, Ealdeorcth, who reminds Boniface of the 'friendship you once promised' and asks to be remembered in his prayers. He reminds Boniface that 'even though we are separated in body, we remain joined in memory'.[78]

If we analyse the letter's borrowings from classical authors, from church fathers, and of course from biblical texts, we discover that it is a composite of classical and christian literary traditions of friendship. The only surprising element in the letter is the postscript from an otherwise unknown man who speaks of a promise of friendship in the past.

This letter shows how important the language of friendship could be in eighth-century anglo-saxon monastic life. Egburg used the phrases at her disposal to tell Boniface how she loved and needed him. Not satisfied in conceding the inevitability of his absence, she demanded some token of his affection. The fact that this letter was preserved in the Boniface-Lull collection indicates that the men behind it—ultimately Boniface and Lull themselves—approved of such expressions of need for friends.

If Boniface had remained in England we might never have had such a collection of letters. The missionary impulse provided a base for these expressions of love and friendship. This is a far cry from the political friendships of gallo-roman landowners or the circumscribed descriptions of friendship in irish monasteries. In these letters we are put into contact with a tradition that may have existed for a long time before it becomes evident to us. Anglo-saxon missionary friendships however, make visible spiritual bonds of affection in Western Europe. Such impulses find form at this time because monks, nuns and missionaries had absorbed enough of the classics, the Bible and the church fathers to be able to employ their phrases to convey their own desires and ideals in the language of friendship.

Women could write to men and their writings could be recorded by men because they occupied a place in society that they rarely achieved later on in the Middle Ages.[79] They had freedom to express themselves directly to spiritual men whom they admired. Moreover they could expect men to answer and to respond to their religious and intellectual needs. The new literature of spiritual friendship is at least in its anglo-saxon phase a literature that has room for the expression of love between devout men and women.

Another important letter to Boniface is dated to about the same time (719-22) as Egburg's letter. Abbess Eangyth and her daughter, after an elaborate salutation, thank Boniface for his letters, and tell him of all the pressures of the world from which they suffer.[80] This he can see, they insist, from the tear-stained page: a literary device that can be traced to one of Jerome's most renowned and passionate letters.[81] The nuns never quite specify the troubles they experience but indicate that they have to do with the situation of monasteries. They describe their poverty and attacks by the king, and then they bemoan the loss of friends and compatriots.

Almost all our relatives are gone, Eangyth and her daughter Bugga complain. There remain only one sister, a very aged mother, and a brother's son, and he is handicapped by a grudge the king has against his people. This leads them to express the need for an *amicum fidelem* like Boniface who can advise them, for what can be sweeter than to have someone to whom you can tell everything as to yourself? This last phrase is taken from Pseudo-Seneca and comes originally from Cicero's *De amicitia*.[82] Eangyth and Bugga expanded beyond the sweetness of friendship by saying that the faithful friend is someone in whom one can have even greater confidence than oneself: *amicum fidelem et talem, in quem confidamus melius quam in nosmet ipsos*. They had looked for that faithful friend for a long time, they insist and 'now we have found him in you: . . . *invenimus in te illum amicum*.' Here Cicero's concept of friendship has been united with that of the faithful friend in the Book of Jesus Sirach (6:14-16).

The letter closes with another phrase from Jerome: 'A friend is long sought, hard to find, difficult to keep.'[83] This adage was to be one of Alcuin's favourite quotations. It is Jerome at his most epigrammatic, and such facile phrases were welcomed and repeated in anglo-saxon and carolingian letters. This literature deserves new attention as a striking manifestation of the cult of friendship between anglo-saxon nuns and men whom they sought out as advisors and confidants.[84] But it should not be thought that such bonds were totally spiritual and selfless. Eangyth and Bugga's letter also asks Boniface to look out for a relative who was having troubles with the king. The two women appeal to Boniface to help a family worn out by failures and defeats. He was to become not just a spiritual friend but also their father in need.

Bugga appears in several later letters. She congratulates Boniface on his success in Frisia and sends him fifty shillings and an altarcloth (*ep* 15). He writes back, perhaps much later, and says that if she cannot obtain peace of mind at home, then she can make a pilgrimage to Rome (*ep* 27). But she is to wait until the saracen threats have diminished. Having been in contact with an anglo-saxon woman who already was at Rome, Boniface tells Bugga that this friend, 'our sister Wiethburga' will send her a letter of invitation (*litteras invitatorias*) when the time is right.

Boniface's answer to Bugga's query is sensible, diplomatic, and affectionate. He calls her not just his dearest sister, but also 'mother and sweetest lady', who is to pray for him.[85] He does not use the word *amicitia* with her. He describes their bond as *fidem antiquam.*[86]

Another female correspondent was Lioba, who was related to Boniface on her mother's side. Asking for prayers for her parents, she reminded Boniface of the 'former friendship which you once joined with my father. . . in the West Country'.[87] For the male bond Lioba uses the term *amicitia*, but for her own link to Boniface she expresses herself differently. She uses the language of family and asks him to become her brother: 'I am their only daughter and would that, though unworthy, I could deserve to have you in the place of a brother'.[88] Here protective kinship provides the basis for closeness between man and woman. In order to seal the bond, Lioba sends Boniface some verses about the Trinity. Much of the language is taken from Aldhelm, and there is no evidence of literary independence or theological insight. If we regard Lioba together with Boniface's other female correspondents, Bugga, Eadburg abbess of Thanet, and the abbess Eangyth, a pattern emerges of fervent declarations of friendship from anglo-saxon women of noble or royal background to missionaries from England to the continent. Using a language that can be traced back to Aldhelm, these women made use of Boniface and his successor Lull in order to express a need to be taken seriously in their hopes, fears and plans. Such women took up the language of spiritual love and made it possible for men to reciprocate.

Boniface himself summarizes the bond of spiritual love in a letter to Abbess Eadburg of Thanet dated between 742 and 746. He describes how he is tied to her by the golden chain of spiritual love: *aureo spiritalis amoris vinculo* (*ep* 65). Lull wrote to the same Eadburg of the 'spiritual kinship which is joined between us'.[89] Terms of physical kinship are used even though there are no family ties. Such terms are spiritualized. This happens also in letters to men: *spiritalis germanitas* to Archbishop Egbert of York (*ep* 75); *spiritalis adfinitas* to Archbishop Cuthbert of Canterbury (*ep* 78). In a letter to the abbot of Saint Denis, Boniface used the phrase *spiritalis amicitia*. Boniface wanted to distinguish his request from any attempt to gain purely material favour.[90] Since the letter actually asked the abbot to obtain the good graces of the king, Boniface's term seems a far cry from Bede's intimate type of spiritual friendship.

Although they were not above inviting friendship for political purposes, Boniface and Lull also wrote letters with a less utilitarian content. In this vein Lull wrote to an abbess and a nun in England about the need for spiritual friendship. This is unusual because churchmen did not usually address women in terms of *amicitia*.[91] Archbishop Bregowin of Canterbury, writing to Lull to tell him of the death of the beloved Bugga, reminded him how he and Lull once at Rome had had a conversation about making a pact of friendship.[92] Here we get behind the literary screen that letters make between people who are distant from each other. Letters allow the writer to express himself in ways that he might never use when face to face. The mention of a *conventio amicitiae* indicates some type of agreement to become friends, an agreement by no means 'conventional'. It could have sprung out of a single intimate conversation or have been the result of a long period of acquaintance. Bregowin does not specify, but for him friendship is a fact and not a mere literary convention. His very confidence in referring to the pact of friendship without specifying its content indicates that he assumes he will be understood by his correspondent:

everyone knows what friendship is, how important it is, and how friendships are made.

Letters merely state what already exists between friends. They are a useful vehicle as reminder, comforter, renewer. Old friendships can be revived in letters, as when an unnamed monk recalls for Lull the *antiquam amicitiam* they had as monks at Malmesbury. The abbot there used to call you 'Lytel', he says as a sign that he is the friend from those days.[93] Just as the anglo-saxon nuns sent pepper and cinnamon to the missionaries (as well as liturgical vestments), so too a monk conveyed a poignant reminder of past days in order to forge a new link.

Read as a whole, the Boniface-Lull letter collection indicates that friendship was lived fact as well as literary convention for the anglo-saxon community of the early eighth century. The letters were written for utilitarian as well as spiritual reasons: to ask for favours as well as to get advice and comfort. Nuns described their trials to Boniface, and he provided a full account of his troubles to an old friend, Daniel, bishop of Winchester. It is the custom of men in distress, he says, to seek comfort from those bound to them in friendship.[94] Boniface tells of false priests with whom he has to deal. He would like to break off all contact with them, but since he needs the patronage of the frankish court, he cannot isolate himself completely. After requesting advice, Boniface asks for a book left by his former teacher and mentions the gift he was sending, a bath towel 'not of pure silk but mixed with rough goat's hair to dry your feet'. He adds that he had heard Daniel had become blind and hoped that in his affliction he 'may see more clearly with the eyes of the spirit'. This is a letter of affection and trust in which Boniface expresses himself tenderly to a man whom he respects.

Daniel wrote back with the same undercurrent of affection but with almost none of the conventional terms of friendship (*ep* 64). Only in his farewell to Boniface as a hundred times dearest (*centupliciter carissime*) do we find a suggestion of the aldhelmian rhetorical tradition. Otherwise Daniel limited himself to replying to Boniface's concerns, telling him that it was necessary to have contact with evil men in order to convert them (remembering how Christ associated with sinners), and reminding him that evil is to be found in England as well as Frankland:

'We are afflicted by the same scourge of sorrows'. Daniel responds to Boniface's query with straightforward advice that would be easy for Boniface to follow. The anglo-saxon bishop at home maintains a link with the anglo-saxon missionary in exile. The bonds of friendship are strengthened by the fact of separation and by the need to seek each other out for comfort and advice. More than a revelation of the conflict between Boniface's strict ideas and the lax ways of the frankish church, the letter shows the importance of a language of friendship in early medieval missionary-monastic culture. In moments of geographical separation and cultural alienation, the evidence of friendship in the Middle Ages is found in letters and poems. We know almost nothing of the relationships Boniface had with his fellow missionaries. Only when he looked back to his cultural and religious roots did he make his own desire for friendship visible.

Sprinkled among these letters we find manifestations of another type of friendship, that between communities in fellowships of prayer.[95] Mortuary rolls are sent from one monastery to another to transmit the name of the dead 'to all friends in the neighbourhood' (*omnibus circumquaque amicis*, *ep* 55). Boniface asked the abbot of Monte Cassino to join him in a community of prayer. They were to exchange the names of each other's deceased (*ep* 106). Abbot Eanwulf asked Bishop Lull to share a list of deceased brethren for whom the monks can pray (*ep* 119). In this letter spiritual communion and *amicitia* are combined. Collective bonds strengthened individual friendships. Bishop Lull could be asked by a deacon and a woman to be joined with them in a community of prayer: *inter ceteros fideles vestros amicos in commune benigne suscipiatis* (*ep* 129). Behind such a statement lies a list of friends for which a community prayed, a list that constantly grew and which was kept up to date. As an abbot wrote to Bishop Lull, your friends are those for whom you pray, this *familia Christi . . . per omnes amicos vestros* (*ep* 133). Such bonds of prayer in Christ were usually much more a collective phenomenon rather than a place for individual friendships. The friends of the community, however, could include men and women who were genuine friends and not only patrons or colleagues. The family of Christ could include almost every type of kin, friendship and community relationship.

The writers and recipients of these letters were aware of a difference between the spiritual friendships (even if the term was still rare) of the missionary and monastic life and the worldly friendships of political and social advancement. The priest Wigbert, after returning from England, wrote Bishop Lull to ask him what he should do: 'I confess to you that no worldly position that is in conflict with your will, no secular friendship could keep me here. I love you among all men,' he insists, 'as God is my witness.'[96] Lull has rarely attracted in later periods the attention Boniface gets. He missed martyrdom and lived on to intrigue for the archbishop's pallium and for the body of his dead companion.[97] His prose is far less attractive than Boniface's. Aldhelm's style has a last revival in his letters. But he does seem to have collected the same loyalties as Boniface did.

The Boniface-Lull collection of letters evidences the language and practice of friendships among anglo-saxon missionaries and the people whom they left behind in England. The most powerful of many expressions of the yearning and pain created by the separation from loved ones occurs in a series of three letters at the end of the collection. In them a nun, Berthgyth, complains to her brother that she has not seen him for a very long time. In the first letter her words are simple and direct, with no apparent literary borrowings.[98]

> What is it, my brother; why have you delayed so long
> before coming to see me? Why do you not think that
> I am alone in this world and have no other brother
> or relative to care for me?

In the second letter, the brother is called Balthard, apparently a missionary who ended as first abbot of Hersfeld. Biblical language as well as aldhelmian flourishes are used for literary support. But the message is still simple: 'Now then I ask you, my beloved brother, that you come to me or make me come, so that I can see you before I die, for your love has never departed from within me'.[99] In the final letter (148) Berthgyth recalls how as a child she had lost her parents. Now again she feels abandoned, and her hope is that her brother will come to her, so that she can die 'there where the bodies of our parents rest'.

What is surprising is not so much the fact that a woman in the eighth century felt such pain at the absence of her brother but that Lull, or the compiler of this collection of letters, found such statements worthy to be included among the letters of Saint Boniface and Lull. The compiler may well have seen what is apparent also to us, that Berthgyth's insistence on a link between family loves and those of friendship repeats a theme present in the early letters to Boniface by anglo-saxon abbesses. Berthgyth has no need to apologize for wanting to embrace her brother or to die at the tomb of her parents. Friendship and kinship are regarded as natural facets of the loves that men and women have for each other.

In an age of separations, it was important to express friendships. The wandering missionary settled down to become a parish priest, a monk, an abbot or a bishop, but he did not forget the sister or former companion left behind. He was not allowed to do so, for in their letters such people insisted on maintaining and renewing old bonds.

Absence in itself is no explanation, even if it does not make the heart grow fonder. Anglo-saxon, as opposed to irish, culture was more receptive to friendship because it was less affected by desert asceticism with its warnings against loves among kin and loves among friends. Anglo-saxon writers could go directly to the biblical sources for friendship in order to substantiate their own desires. As Boniface wrote in a letter:

> It is written in the book of Solomon: Happy is the man who finds a friend, with whom he can talk as if to himself. (*ep* 79)
>
> (Scriptum est in libro Salomonis: Beatus homo qui invenit amicum, cum quo possit loqui quasi cum semet ipso.)

The happy man who has found a friend is, however, more than a biblical reminiscence. The second half of the quotation comes originally from Cicero (*De amicitia*, 22) with its assertion of the joy of talking to one's friend as oneself. It is combined here with Ecclesiasticus 25:12 in order to state that friendship is an attractive human condition.

Did Boniface know that he was quoting Cicero here? It is not clear, but the easy combination of a classical and a Christian source shows how a christian language of friendship could be developed without any concern for the pagan roots of the conception. The expression of friendship was what mattered, not its defence or legitimacy.

CAROLINGIAN VARIETY

In the Carolingian Age, a small elite group set the tone in a self-conscious and narrowly-based cultural revival.[100] If we look at the literature and trace its indications concerning the practice of friendship in this period, from about 770-850, we discover a great variety of ideas rather than a synthesis of them. Carolingian writers combined and renewed all that went before them in the language of friendship: the tradition of secular friendship for political advantage, the classical view of friendship in purely human terms, and the christian platonic conception that friendship is a path to the Good. In conscious borrowings and unconscious echoes of classical and patristic authors, the Carolingians showed mastery in applying a heritage they greatly appreciated.

My original point of departure for research of the Carolingians was the impression that they developed a language of friendship attractive in form and skillful in manner, but in essence produced nothing more than rhetorical froth. After a review of the available materials, which are abundant and lead into almost every corner of carolingian life, I have to concede that there is more here than literary exercises and showmanship. The poems and letters of this period point to friendships among monks, churchmen and lay nobles. The language of friendship indicates little interest in the type of male-female bonds visible in the anglo-saxon period. We move into an almost exclusively male world.

An element of homoerotic delight is discernible in some carolingian literature. This is a far cry from any sign of tolerance towards homosexual behaviour. But the warmth and tenderness of Boniface's missionary world grows even richer and more luxuriant in expressions of love for men. Carolingian multiplicity should be looked upon in itself, not as a pale reflection or pure imitation of classical and patristic friendship, and not as a premonition of what is to come centuries later. It manifests a world far more subtle and creative than traditional textbook treatments might lead us to believe.

Only in the letters of Agobard of Lyons do we meet what appears to be a purely rhetorical expression of friendship. A letter to Archbishop Ebo of Rheims begins with a long and tortured sentence about how

Ebo had offered his friendship to Agobard. This is apparently pure politeness. *Piam amicitiam* is a phrase used to build up to the archbishop's final request.[101] It means more a favour or a gesture than a personal relationship between two people.

If we compare this text with some of Einhard's expressions of friendship in his letters, we realize that the declaration of friendship could be more than a matter of form. For Einhard, friendships exist to help one get on in the world of court and privilege. He asked an abbot 'in mercy and friendship' to provide for a certain man who had been in his care.[102] Einhard gives no hint of a religious content in his friendships. They involve bonds of loyalty, mutual favours, or concern for the weak. In one of the most striking letters Einhard tells how a certain count had asked him if he would approach his friend (the recipient of the letter) to remove the pigs he had pastured in the count's territory. The friend was asked to let the pigs be fattened so that the count could buy them for a reasonable price when they were ready to be slaughtered. 'For he, knowing our friendship, thought I could obtain this from you'.[103] Einhard does not use words to conceal his intention. He openly equates friendship with favours. When he writes to a certain bishop, he protests his undying loyalty but makes it clear that he expects the bishop, who apparently was close to the Emperor, to make it easier for him to come to court.[104]

In Einhard we see a carolingian Sidonius Apollinaris, perhaps far less subtle in his ways and certainly less able to maintain his predecessor's classical standards of language. In becoming an abbot, he became like Sidonius, essentially a great land-owner. He was never a monk, was married, and so his writings on friendship can hardly be seen in monastic terms. Like Sidonius, Einhard turned to friends not for comfort and delight but to gain favours at court and to provide for those to whom they owed loyalty or protection.

At the centre of carolingian friendship is not Einhard but Alcuin (c. 732-804), who brought with him from York in the early 780s the anglo-saxon culture that he had inherited ultimately from Bede. Friendship was a matter of vital concern for Alcuin, an expression of the christian love of neighbour. His letters and poems deal with almost every nuance of love, and so it is important to understand what it is he is saying. Expositions of carolingian culture traditionally quote one of his letters to Bishop Arno of Salzburg in which Alcuin says he wishes he could be taken by the hair like the Old Testament prophet Habakkuk and put into the presence of his distant friend so that he could kiss and embrace him:

> With my lips pressed not only on your eyes and ears
> and mouth, but also on each of your fingers and toes,
> I would kiss them not once but many times.[105]

One historian warns against using such a statement as anything personal, while another sees in Alcuin's letters 'an element which can scarcely be called anything but passionate'.[106] Both interpretations, that of literary typos and that of erotic passion, take us only a short distance in understanding what Alcuin meant. To us his language might seem sensual, but he was not engaging in some sexual fantasy. Alcuin wanted to see his friend, and and his images are meant to convey that desire. Just as such desires must not be set in a purely erotic context, so too they must be taken as more than expressions of token loyalty among carolingian churchmen. Alcuin is telling his friend that he loves and needs him, not in a sexual sense and not in a political one, but in terms of a close personal bond.

For Alcuin friendship is the lifeblood of existence. Only in the network of friends did he find the peace and meaning which he sought in his life. Unlike Augustine he seems only rarely to have found limitations and boundaries in his friendships. Unlike Paulinus of Nola, he rarely indicates that friends have let him down. To us Alcuin may seem far too glib, a carolingian Pangloss spouting didactic truths of christian love. But behind all the rhetoric and posing there is a friend, a friend to whom a few other men were of great importance in his own life.

Most of the letters we have from Alcuin's hand date from the last decade of his life, so we get to know a man in his late 50s and 60s who had left the crises of youth far behind him.[107] But it is clear from the letters that Alcuin had made many friends in England who continued expecting him to share friendship after he had gone to the Continent. Writing to the bishop of Hexham and his community, Alcuin encouraged the priests to pray and study. He told them how he desired their spiritual friendship, a rare term in Alcuin. He reminded them of their old bond of friendship.[108] This seems to indicate more a community of mutual prayer than any close friendship, but Alcuin here as in many other letters to England, points to the importance of old ties. To the bishop of Lindisfarne, Hygbald, Alcuin wrote of the friendship they once had formed. This is not a loose expression. Alcuin says that it was 'once joined between us with specific words'.[109] In many such letters, Alcuin shows concern with establishing communities of prayer that would remember him. But with the head of such communities he at the same time renewed personal relationships that could go far back into the past.

To many of his correspondents Alcuin offered friendship and love. But Alcuin distinguished among degrees of friendship. To an important official of King Charles he wrote in a manner that reveals political motives.[110] To Ricbod, archbishop of Trier, Alcuin overlooked the man's power and influence to excoriate him for loving Vergil too much. Alcuin insisted that the world could not separate what God had joined in them. He asked the archbishop why he had kept himself at a distance. It would be better to be poor and have his friend closeby than rich and have him at a distance.

> Where is that sweetest conversation between us,
> where is your happy face which I used to look upon,
> where that bond of love?[111]

For more than a year, Ricbod, whom Alcuin calls Macharius, had not written. What sin had the father committed so that the son had forgotten him? Or does Macharius think these days more about Vergil than about Alcuin? If Alcuin's name had been Vergil, then he would even have been before the archbishop's eyes: *O si mihi nomen esset Virgilius, tunc semper ante oculos luderem tuos.*

Alcuin plays with words and with nicknames: Maro for Vergil, Flaccus for himself, Macharius for his friend, and one can almost see him smiling behind the reproaches. The letter is so elegant and self-aware that one thinks of the phrases of Jerome, which exercised a special attraction on Alcuin because of their striking simplicity and linguistic balance.[112] But Alcuin lacks Jerome's vitriol. He is almost always kind, and even when critical, he tries to be gentle.

An almost classic expression of friendship comes from the years just before Alcuin was made abbot at the monastery of Saint Martin in Tours in 796. This is a letter of advice and apparently has no political overtones. A new friend is not like an old one, he insists, and reshapes Jerome's statement that the changeable friend is no friend at all.[113] Alcuin wants to share the secrets of his friend's heart, to know everything within him. For the moment he can communicate himself only by letter. As a flame can be seen but not touched, so love can be perceived in a letter but can not really be felt, for it exists in the heart of the writer. Like sparks scattered from a fire, love reaches out through the letter. Since Alcuin has found true charity in his brother, no distance will keep him away. Alcuin then turns these expressions of love into a christian statement of love, declaring that friends are bound to one another in Christ. Through love for him their love will last forever.[114]

This elaborate series of statements on love of the friend and love of Christ is followed by much good advice, ending with the recommendation that the friend read Gregory's *Pastoral Care,* and a request for his prayers. The letter could have been written to almost any cleric Alcuin knew. There is nothing in its contents that makes the friend into a particular person by describing his habits of referring to any shared past experiences. The problem thus arises: is Alcuin writing a letter of such powerful literary imagery simply in order to show his prowess at the art? Is he giving good advice because he knows that the letter will be read by many priests and he thinks they all should read Gregory?

In his letters (as elsewhere in his life) Alcuin did best as the perennial teacher. He could not pass up an opportunity for conveying good advice and guidance. The best way to distinguish between Alcuin the teacher and Alcuin the friend is by concentrating on the individual friends whom he addresses in his letters. With Arno, who became bishop of Salzburg in 785, we can trace a friendship from 790 onwards. In dozens of letters, Alcuin shows remarkable consistency in his desire to see the friend, talk to him, counsel him, and find comfort through him. In almost none of these letters is there any hint that Alcuin used Arno for political purposes, even though the bishop of Salzburg was an important figure in Charlemagne's imperial projects and a loyal defender of an outpost of the Empire. Alcuin seems oblivious to or uninterested in Arno's connections. He wanted Arno's attention for himself.

We have many of these letters because they apparently were put together in a collection by the monks of Salzburg prior to Alcuin's death.[115] The community, or Arno himself, must have realized the prestige that so many communications from the great teacher and churchman gave them. In another smaller collection of Alcuin's letters, to Adelhard, abbot of Corvey, Alcuin expressed a tenderness of affection, but there is not the consistent demonstration of warmth we find in the Salzburg letters.[116]

Alcuin's letters to Arno combine affection and news. In 798 he wrote that he had been expecting a message from Arno (*ep* 146), who had been on mission at Rome, apparently for King Charles, and Alcuin calls him his eagle, *aquila*, for whose flight back over the Alps he has been waiting. He provides news of himself. He will be going to Aachen in July but does not quite know where he will go afterwards. His descriptions of itinerary make use of images of birds. A light tone is maintained, but there is no doubt that Alcuin very much wants to see his eagle. When Arno receives the letter, Alcuin asks him quickly to send another so that he can know what his eagle is about to do with his 'little birds', which must mean the people in his pastoral care.[117] Alcuin asks about the actions of the roman nobility towards Pope Leo III and expresses interest in saints' relics 'with which you can console your Albinus'. He adds his own news: he is plagued by age and fever, but it is all to the good that he is afflicted so he can increase in the strength of faith. All Spain, he adds in this jumble of news, is in the grip of the Adoptionist heresy. In closing he returns to the image of his eagle, 'Live happily rejoicing in the love of Christ with all who are yours, most loved eagle' (*aquila carissime*).

This letter sets the tone for the dozens of missives that followed in the next four years, until 802. We can follow them almost month by month, these separate moments of hoping and pleading that Alcuin and Arno can find a time and a place to meet. Usually Alcuin was disappointed. Only once does a letter indicate that the two actually succeeded in seeing each other, and then Alcuin complains about the brevity of their meeting.[118] Alcuin shows impatience, frustration, disappointment, but he never seems angry with his correspondent. In the process emerge some of the most affectionate phrases of friendship between two men that any medieval letter collection contains. At times Alcuin stops his flow and begs Arno's forgiveness for the lack of discipline in his language:

> I have spoken these things in some rapture, venerable brother, and I have not done so with the order required by the limits of a letter, but out of affection, as required by the inmost impulse of my heart. But you, sweetest father and my companion, patiently bear the tears of my heart. And keep within you what you have heard from me.[119]

Alcuin emphasizes the unusual structure of his letter in order to underline the intensity of his affection.

These letters are not pure declarations of love. Alcuin looks to Arno for news about court activities, military expeditions, and the conversion of pagans. We have none of Arno's letters, but at times he must have provided little or no information, for Alcuin complains about this lack in his replies. Arno does not seem to have considered all his queries coupled to expressions of love as anything inappropriate. More than once Alcuin indicated that Arno had himself complained that Alcuin had not written him.[120]

The letters show something of the importance Alcuin felt with the problem of maintaining contact with friends through letters. In September of 798 Alcuin wrote Arno that he had sent him a letter through the latter's clerk, whose name Alcuin had forgotten. He believed he had dispatched it on 26 July, and he still did not know if it had arrived. Alcuin's July letter had asked about Arno's movements: he wanted to know when he could hope to see Arno come into Alcuin's district.[121] Alcuin was hurrying now to Tours where he probably would spend the winter. As in so many letters to Arno, Alcuin uses a language of intense affection.

> Would that my eagle come to pray at Saint Martin, so that there I could embrace those gentlest wings and hold him whom my heart loves nor let him go until I could bring him into the house of my mother

> and he kiss me with the kiss of his mouth, and we rejoice together in ordered charity.[122]

The images of the mother's house and kisses are taken directly from the Song of Songs (Sg 3:4, 1:1). The last phrase, *ordinata caritas*, shows that this is not a declaration of romantic love in any modern sense. Alcuin's love for Arno is put into the context of brotherly love and the love of God. The great carolingian researcher Heinrich Fichtenau once complained that Alcuin mixed up the varieties of love and failed to distinguish between human and divine loves.[123] But Alcuin knew exactly what he was doing: in human loves he saw the image of divine love that makes all love possible.

Examples could be multiplied, for the alcuinian literature is vast. Fortunately we are not limited to the letters of Alcuin himself. Dümmler's collection of Alcuin's correspondence also contains a few stray letters from other sources. One of them, to Arno of Salzburg from Angilbert abbot of Saint Riquier, was originally in the Salzburg manuscript with Alcuin's letters. It belongs there not only because of the addressee but also because it too employs the language of friendship.[124] The abbot quotes from the Old Testament book Ecclesiasticus on the importance of a faithful friend (Si 6:11-16). He writes to Arno as a *fidelissimi amico* whom he had praised before King Charles at court. Angilbert has news of politics concerning the monastery of Saint Amand that affects Arno, but everything is couched in terms of friendship. Angilbert plays with kin roles just as Alcuin did when he in letters to Arno called him father, son, brother and friend.[125]

Alcuin's letters have been well mined for political information, but they have seldom been taken seriously as expressions of love and concern for other men. Perhaps all the nicknames that Alcuin fostered at the carolingian court are a bit embarrassing for historians looking for subtle motives and self-interest among men of power. But Alcuin is not some early Polonius, full of good will and close to the seat of power but ignorant of what is really happening. It is apparent from his letters to Charlemagne that Alcuin did follow closely the political and military vicissitudes of empire and kept himself well informed. Alcuin realized, moreover, that his friendship with the king brought immense benefits not just to himself but to those around him.[126] But his relationships with other men, such as Arno, do not have to be seen exclusively in a political light. Alcuin liked the company and conversation of other men. He liked writing to them in familiar terms.[127] He delighted in composing letters of recommendation 'to all friends in Christ' to speed messengers on their way.[128] For Alcuin life was friendship, from the friendships of York to those of the court and those of Tours. During the 790s, his letters reveal a network of friendship which stretched across carolingian Europe.

These are not monastic friendships. Even after Alcuin became abbot at Tours in 796, he continued to write to his friends as their beloved 'Albinus' and not as the abbot of a powerful monastery. The network of friends is extra-monastic: it was based on the clerics who became bishops and abbots (often both at the same time) in order to administer the Empire. Arno, for example, became first bishop and then abbot, and finally, in 802, was appointed one of Charlemagne's key itinerant officials, *missi dominici*. During the reign of Charlemagne, the religious and secular were so closely intertwined that intellectual figures like Alcuin could be attached to monasteries and yet remain laymen, even if monastic ideals were important to them. Only after the death of Charlemagne did there emerge an ascetic monastic life that distinguished itself from the broader aristocratic and international scholarly milieu that Charles fostered with the help of men like Alcuin.

Alcuin liked men, and he had at his disposal a language of christian platonism with spiritual embraces and fires to convey to his male friends a passion that invariably remained controlled and dignified. Alcuin combined classical ideals of friendship, the rhetoric of Jerome's letters, and biblical images with the christian conviction that friends are united in Christ.[129] There are no qualms or hesitations in Alcuin, and so 'explaining' his love for men in terms of homosexual attraction has no meaning. The one letter that has been used to show homosexuality among Alcuin's friends, and to indicate that he did not take the matter too seriously, does not necessarily treat this phenomenon at all. Alcuin wrote to a friend in Britain that he had heard how people giggled at the friend's fault, which is clearly one of the flesh. Alcuin found it disturbing that a man of his age was plagued by such a sin, and hoped that his friend could purify himself so that he could lift up 'pure hands' to the Lord.[130] The reference to purity of hands suggests that the sin is masturbation, a habit that Alcuin says his correspondent had never been able to break and one that he as a youth never should have developed in the first place.[131]

In another letter that deals similarly with sins of the flesh, the nature of the sin is not even hinted at.[132] Alcuin's letters reflect no special concern for sexual matters. We are a long way from the strict views of Saint Columban and his irish monks. Alcuin's main concern in his letters of friendship is to use every facet of language in order to underline his loves. He seems himself to be sufficiently innocent and unworried by sexuality to use the most sensual images. For the pure all things are pure! Only when Alcuin is in danger of losing a friend does he lose his calm surface and plead passionately for understanding (*ep* 58). But even here Alcuin never approaches the acerbity of Jerome or the disillusionment of Paulinus.

Alcuin shows little linguistic restraint in his letters to men, while in writing to women he used less enthusiastic expressions of affection. Like his anglo-saxon predecessors, he did not use the word *amicitia* in addressing women.[133] Even to his most faithful and devoted correspondent, Charles's sister Gisla, Alcuin maintains a polite distance that shows he places relationships with women on a different plane from those with men. In a letter to Gisla Alcuin admitted that he had made 'a bond of charity' (*pactum caritatis*) with her.[134] In the year 800 he wrote that he had sent her part of a commentary on the Gospel of John (*ep* 195) and that he at Charles's order was emending biblical texts. Gisla wrote back a much warmer and quite elegant letter to Alcuin full of biblical allusions and sufficiently clever to move Alcuin to include it in the preface of his completed commentary. As the tongue of the speaker penetrates into the ear of the listener, Gisla wrote, so the pen of the writer proceeds into the eye of the reader and gains the interior of the heart.[135] Gisla's images are related to those of Alcuin, but they do not reflect Alcuin's usual language to women. She seems to sense his hesitation, for she reminds him of the example of Jerome, who did not spur the request of holy women in Rome. The great distance between Rome and Bethlehem was no problem for him when his female friends wanted his attention, and so Alcuin should oblige Gisla, who is geographically much closer to him.[136] The comparison is well made and shows that Alcuin's style, based on Jerome, had found an imitator in this powerful and extraordinary woman. She managed to obtain an answer from him. I can deny nothing to love, he wrote, but he used the term *caritas* rather than *amicitia*.

Gisla can be looked at as a successor to the royal or aristocratic anglo-saxon abbesses of the early eighth century. When Boniface had replied to their letters, he addressed them as equals worthy of sharing his friendship. Alcuin, despite his respect for Gisla's royalty and learning, offered her none of the passionate embraces and rich biblical images of love that he extended to Arno or to his other close male friends.

Alcuin's letters leave many unanswered questions concerning his motives and feelings for his correspondents. He is personal only to a limited extent. Like every medieval letter writer, he knew that many eyes and ears would see and hear the fruits of his efforts. But even if the primary purpose of such letters was didactic, they give us an impression of a personality which is more than a string of clichés. These are the letters of an old, often tired man, looking for comfort and consolation in men whom he rarely saw.

Alcuin shared with Charles a dream of forging a political unity based on personal relationships and undivided loyalties. This, the dream of the coming centuries, had some possibilities at a time when governmental structures were flimsy. Alcuin's emphasis on the bonds of friendship and his constant repetition of the themes of distance/closeness and faithfulness/unfaithfulness in friendship may indicate political as well as personal awareness of the fragility of human bonds. The popular historian Eleanor Duckett speaks in a rare analytical moment of a 'lack of confidence' in Alcuin.[137] His desire to have everyone love him and his fear of making enemies perhaps reveal a sense of the weakness of the structures maintaining his life and the Empire itself.

At times it can seem as if Alcuin was a man who never stopped writing letters and poems of little depth or originality. Alcuin could devote himself to obvious reflections and become little more than a pocket philosopher. But Alcuin was more than a superficial house intellectual. Even Fichtenau admitted in his harsh evaluation of religious life among carolingian court intellectuals that Alcuin at moments could envision Christianity as a religion of inwardness.[138] Behind the slick facade we find a man who sought to compensate for his own incompleteness by gaining and keeping trustworthy friends. From the austrian marches to the north of England Alcuin looked for friends to pray for him, to share their news, to visit him and worship with him at the tomb of Saint Martin.

Alcuin is a centre from which many clusters of friendship emerged. One of his most visible disciples is Rhabanus Maurus (776-856). Educated at Fulda, he eventually became Alcuin's pupil at Tours before he returned to his monastery and became abbot there. Of his letters we have only his rather stiff and formal dedications of his many works commenting on most of the books of the Bible.[139] But from his hand we also have a collection of poems that take up many of the alcuinian themes we have seen in letters. One of the focuses of Rhabanus' affection, and that of other carolingian literary monks, was the abbot of Saint Gall, Grimald, whom Rhabanus could address as a source of strength, a safe shore, and landing place for the wreck of his life.[140] The poem may have been written after Rhabanus had had to abandon the abbacy at Fulda for political reasons and before he returned to a position of power in 847 as archbishop of Mainz.

Most of these poems cannot be ordered chronologically, and so they can only be looked upon as generalized expressions of the importance of friendship in Rhabanus' life. A monk who in his prose works appears to be a cool scholar turns out to be an advocate of alcuinian attachments, seeking to bind a friend to him through his verses.[141] Sometimes the recipient of a poem is a bishop, sometimes it is Rhabanus' own abbot at Fulda, Eigil.[142] With the priest Gerhoh, who may have been librarian at Fulda or a neighbouring monastery, Rhabanus played with the idea of the power he had over the books. Because of the keys at his disposal he had access to the wisdom that books provide (XXIII). Through books the friend could be praised. Both books and friend are related to the love of Christ. Samuel, a priest and perhaps a monk of Fulda, who from 841 became bishop of Worms, received the largest number of poems of friendship (XXV-XXXI). 'My mind follows you and also my song of love', he wrote. 'Remember me as I do you.'[143]

A poem of friendship presents many more problems than does a letter of friendship, for the poem is usually more abstract in its message and more attentive to form. But there is no doubt in the poems to Samuel that this friend was important to Rhabanus, not just as some idea of friendship, but in terms of a relationship with a living, individualized person: 'Don't reject your comrade; a friend always loves', he insists (XXVIII). Remember me when you are at the altar, he asks as Alcuin might have entreated his friends, and then he appropriately recalls the teaching of his master Alcuin:

> What once master Albinus rightly taught,
> May this heart hold and this deed prove
>
> (Quod quondam docuit Albinus rite magister,
> Hoc pectus teneat, hoc opus omne probet.)

Rhabanus sees himself in his declarations of friendship as faithful to the memory of Alcuin. His heart carries the teaching, and his work realizes it. Like Alcuin, Rhabanus can relate his own love for a friend to the love of Christ:

> You have pleased me, may you please Christ in heaven
> Be loved to the saints as you are dear to me
> As you are my one and only, may the one author of life protect you
> One among many [in heaven] you are my one and only.[144]

Like Alcuin Rhabanus enjoyed playing with words: oppositions, parallelisms and various images are frequent. Rhabanus is more abstract in his description of love than Alcuin. The sensual and almost physical descriptions of Alcuin's love for his friends are replaced by a constant juxtaposition of love of friend with love of Christ. Christian platonic friendship is brought here to a new level of immateriality.[145]

The poems of friendship are only a small part of Rhabanus' work, but they suggest that it would not be fair to claim that outside of Alcuin the theme of friendship was not frequently or profoundly expressed in other carolingian writers.[146] There is a certain truth to this assertion in letter collections but not in poetry. Friendship may not be a dominant theme in Rhabanus, but it is still an evident and persistent one. In the friend he looks for permanence and comfort, for the friend always loves and is always to be loved (*semper amicus amat, semper aman-*

dus erit: XXII). The absolutism of this statement recalls the maxims of Saint Jerome about friendship. There is no sense of any boundaries or limitations. Loving a friend is a way to love Christ and to anticipate the loves of heaven.

One of the most brilliant students of Rhabanus Maurus at Fulda in the late 820s was Walafrid Strabo (809-49), who became teacher of Charles the Bald and finally abbot of Reichenau (809-49). His early death means that all his poems were written before he was forty. His poetry has a platonic quality in direct descent from the work of Alcuin, and yet it is fundamentally different in context from both Alcuin's and Rhabanus' work. In Strabo we encounter a new formulation of the carolingian concept of friendship, for he writes on the subject without any direct reference to the christian faith. God and the afterlife are presupposed in his poetry, but in such a vague manner that he could at times almost be referring to roman religion.

To the cleric Liutger, Walafrid writes: 'As the rose is to the soil, as fish to water, as air to the birds, so your face is dear to me, my little one.'[147] There is nothing of Alcuin's union in Christ, nothing of Rhabanus' anticipation of the approaching happiness of heaven. One has to remind oneself that these lines may have been written when the author was an abbot with perhaps a hundred monks under his charge.[148]

Are these poems the fruit of a rare leisure hour's dalliance for a too busy abbot seeking relief from duties? It is hard to think of them as mere trifles, for in Walafrid even more than in Rhabanus, we sense an undercurrent of urgency and need for the friends addressed: 'I am yours, be mine, for what each of us had belongs to the other/ So I am your other self, and you are mine'.[149] Such language is in a superficial sense not far from that of late twentieth-century pop songs! But there is no sentimentality, only a constant search for faithfulness and loyalty in a relationship. 'Be to me a far greater friend, I ask, than I deserve', Walafrid insists to Godescalc, the recipient of some of the most complete statements of friendship.[150] The thoughts and actions of the one friend are constantly being interwoven into those of the other. 'Father and brother, unique part of my mind' (*meae pars unica mentis*), Walafrid declares in an echo of Alcuin, which in turn recalls the Odes of Horace.[151]

In Walafrid Strabo, carolingian poetry of friendship reached a literary zenith. Word play and intimate terms of affection sometimes make translation into modern language almost impossible. As Adele Fiske has pointed out, the addresses of Strabo to the subdeacon Bodo have to remain in Latin:

> Candide, care vale, carissime semper ubique
> Pusio candidule, candide pusiole.[152]

The conceptions of smallness and whiteness are juxtaposed here. The words are a point of departure for the expression of unity and intimacy between friends. In this neoplatonic universe the friend is very much an individual human being, but he is also lifted up to a universal plane. Christian elements are implicit but the pagan classical heritage is prominent, not just in terms of literary borrowings, but also in the sentiment expressed. Without ever having read Plato's *Symposium* Strabo has converted its spirit into poetry.

Yet another variation of carolingian friendship can be found in the letters of Lupus Servatus, abbot of Ferrières (805-62). He was taught by a disciple of Alcuin and then was sent to Fulda to be educated under Rhabanus. Once again Alcuin and Rhabanus provide points of departure for the carolingian literature of friendship. But just as Strabo had little need of christian terminology to elucidate his loves, so Lupus could convey himself in intellectual and political terms without the passionate personal involvement of his predecessors. He is perhaps best known for his letters of comfort and consolation to Einhard on the death of his wife.[153] These letters can be looked upon as the attempt of an eager young scholar to find a means of access to the most respected teacher of his day. Lupus spoke of the *ius amicitiae* to justify his desire to commiserate with Einhard, but soon he turned to questions about grammar and arithmetic. Lupus could insist that the law of love and friendship required Einhard to reply to such queries.

Lupus has been a perennial favourite among modern carolingian scholars because he was himself a scholar, a man capable of finding time amid all his duties as abbot and even warrior to copy and compare manuscripts and to contribute to the preservation of precious classical writings.[154] Many of these activities Lupus carried on by letters in which he used formulae of friendship, but the content of the letters reveals that it was manuscripts he sought rather than friends. For Lupus as for many a single-minded scholar, individual human beings can be mere instruments for the conveyance of learning. Lupus knows how to use them to the right effect, and when political involvements blocked his research and writing, he was willing to use political friendship to help him out. Last year, he wrote in 837, with the help of friends, he had been led to the presence of the emperor.[155] The friends are there in order to facilitate influential connections.

Lupus expresses himself in his loyalties and pursuits more intensely than did Walafrid Strabo or Rhabanus Maurus. He can write letter after letter in order to obtain the return of a daughter cell to his monastery. He searched the empire for the manuscripts he needed to collate so that he could improve texts. For him friendship was mainly a utilitarian arrangement, a means to an end, as he reveals in a letter to the abbot of York, Altsig, to whom he turned because he hoped the works of Bede and Quintilian might be in the library there:

> I seek your friendship, so that we can care for each other through holy prayers and also in other useful services.[156]

Even to his closest friend Marcward, abbot of Prüm, Lupus wrote briefly about his pleasure in the abbot's safety after an expedition and then concentrated in detail on how Marcward was to arrange sending a trustworthy monk to Fulda to ask the Abbot Hatto for a manuscript of Suetonius (*ep* 91).

Thanks to Lupus we have good texts of several classical works. Lupus led a busy life and felt sometimes obliged to keep potential visitors away from Ferrières. If they did come, he warned, they would be given hardly a moment of his time.[157] For anyone who tries to combine a life of research and writing with the demands of an active life involving contacts with people and even a modest exercise of power, it is easy to understand Lupus' impatience and his willingness to make use of friends to obtain help from other monasteries and at court. Lupus is close to Einhard in at least one respect: both valued the ideal of friendship and in daily life used these contacts to get things done.

We have come a long way from Alcuin, who rarely can be seen, even in his letters to Charlemagne, to have used friendships for the sake of personal gain. Alcuin was more privileged than Lupus. He was at the centre of events, while Lupus was on the fringe. Alcuin apparently was able to build up a considerable personal fortune, while Lupus' letters several times indicate money problems that must have been embarrassing and enervating.[158]

After Lupus friendship begins to disappear from view. We can pause at the great monastic reformer Benedict of Aniane (c. 750-821). Like the Alcuin who wrote letters of friendship to him, the second great monastic Benedict was interested in spiritual friendship.[159] We have some pages he wrote on the subject, difficult to interpret because of a faulty manuscript, but apparently mostly borrowed from one of the sermons of Augustine.[160] Benedict may have believed in the possibilities of male friendship within the cloister but there seems to be little correspondence between these optimistic descriptions of friendship and the text of the various monastic rules formulated during his lifetime.[161] These are for the most part concerned with outward behaviour, liturgy, discipline, all important enough in the monastic life, but hardly good soil for the growth of friendships. Benedict thus reflects an interest in friendship typical of his own generation, but he did not try to integrate the ethic and practice of spiritual friendship into the monastic life. Like Alcuin and so many other carolingian writers, he celebrated the ideal of friendship, but did not indicate how collective practices of monastic discipline could make room for individual friends.

Carolingian friendships are of every type, from the most intense particular bonds to purely self-interested alliances, with room for many variations in between. Unlike anglo-saxon friendships they are almost exlusively male in their expression. They point to a male-dominated culture where women did not have the political prominence and spiritual significance that they may have had in anglo-saxon England. If there is one theme that unites carolingian letters and poems of friendship, even Benedict's brief remarks, it is loyalty. In both secular and ecclesiastical society men were looking for other men who would be faithful to them. One sees time and again the lines from the Book of Ecclesiasticus (ch. 6) about the *amicus fidelis*, or Jerome's epigram about how hard it is to find and keep friends, and how easy it is to lose one.

The letters and poems of the age are full of news about wandering, travel, departures and arrivals. What could Alcuin have written about if his beloved Arno had remained settled at Salzburg? Arno was at Rome, on campaign against the Avars, at the court of Charles, and (all too rarely for Alcuin) at Tours. Such movements provided the background for literary expressions of friendship. After about 850 these disappeared. What had been built up around a few brilliant individuals could not persist once they were gone. Carolingian fragility is usually seen in terms of the empire's structure, but we can also detect it in a lack of social and institutional framework for human bonds. Carolingian friendship was based on an intellectual community that did not find a more permanent monastic context in which to express itself. This would have given it a more stable form. Even if many friends were abbots, they wrote to each other not as monks but as intellectuals or politicians eager to win each other's support. Only in Rhabanus Maurus do we find a monk-abbot for whom the experiences of monastic life were important in defining his relations with his friends.

For these carolingian writers the bond of friendship joining men to God could be an individual one. Individual friends, however, were not usually attached to communities, except when writers asked each other for prayers and inclusion in lists of brethren kept in monasteries or other religious foundations. There was little awareness of how personal and intellectual involvements could be made possible by the collective discipline of the monastic life. Not until monastic rules and lives came to emphasize a union of love and discipline would it be possible to unite the requirement of community with the desire for personal friendships.

CHAPTER FOUR

THE ECLIPSE OF MONASTIC FRIENDSHIP c. 850 - c. 1050

THE BRIEF AGE of carolingian political unification, with its literature of friendship in poems and letters, was followed by two centuries difficult for any medieval historian to interpret. In the midst of material destruction appear foundations of a western european age of confidence and growth. Amid disparate sources the historian finds hints that carolingian thought and literary expression continued, but at the same time post-carolingian writers could not reach the same level of latinity.[1] After the letters of an Alcuin and the poems of a Walafrid Strabo, it can at times seem as if this period offers little material to document friendship. It is impossible to find a monastic writer who gives special attention to friendships within the cloister. Friendship can nevertheless at times be found just beneath the surface of the hagiographies and letter collections available to us. As so often in this study, it is necessary to accept that friendship is a natural human phenomenon, evident in all types of social life. Our task is not to prove its existence. It is to point out the moments in Western history when friendship was described and discussed as desirable in itself and as an incentive to the christian life.

Monastic legislators of this period, unlike their eastern predecessors, made no attempt to outlaw close friendships in the cloister. They do not indicate in any overt manner a fear that exclusive relationships will lead to scandal or to homosexual loves. Inside the monasteries we hear about *sodalitas* or *familiaritas* or some other term indicating that individual bonds were seen primarily in terms of the spiritual life of the community as a whole. Outside the cloister *amicitia* can be named in various contexts, usually as a bond among men of power in the church or in lay life. The word rarely has religious overtones. It is mainly a secular practice, a way of lubricating the relationships of the world. So far as I can detect, the phrase *amicitia spiritualis* does not appear in our sources. At moments, especially in the writings of Gerbert of Aurillac, the ideal of spiritual friendship comes into sight. Gerbert, however, never goes into detail about the monastic content of friendship. In the post-carolingian period, from the end of the ninth to the beginning of the eleventh centuries, monastic friendship was in eclipse. A darkness temporarily obscures human bonds but does not completely blot them out for us.

The monks of the tenth and early eleventh centuries emphasized the virtue and importance of collective love. They saw love and harmony as growing out of participation in community. The link between the *concordia* essential for the group and the *caritas* emerging here is beautifully expressed in a hymn about charity that goes back to the ninth century:

> Since we therefore are joined in oneness
> We should then be careful not to become divided
> in spirit.
> Evil controversies and quarrels must stop,
> So Christ truly will be in our midst.
> Where charity is true, God is there.
>
> For us charity unites even those absent from each
> other
> Just as discord separates even those present to each
> other.
> We must all sense that together we are undivided
> So that we in being joined together not be divided
> Where charity is true, God is there.[2]

The language is clear and simple, replete with allusions to New Testament expressions on charity. There is nothing in the hymn about friendship as a form of love, for the ideal of the christian community in perfect peace with itself receives emphasis here.

It would be too easy to relate this concern with the collective life to the concrete dangers to which monastic communities were exposed in the ninth and tenth centuries. Cowering men afraid of the next onslaught of the Vikings could be said to have needed the collective security of monastic life. But the language of the hymn says nothing about fear and the flight from the world.

This poem of charity belongs very much to an age when the loves of the individual were seen in terms of the concerns and requirements of the community. A parallel manifestation of this search for concord is evidenced in the reforming decrees of Benedict of Aniane for monastic houses. Only in unity could there be peace; only in peace, love. There was no room here for individual experience or expression. God is present in the good community, and so the individual must seek him there:

> Ne et simul congregati dividamur
> Ubi caritas est vera deus ibi est
>
> (So that we who are joined together be not divided/
> For where charity is true, there is God.)

Another example of the spiritual tendencies of this period comes from the liturgy of Cluny and deals with the Trinity. Here the great mystery calls for praise and worship, but no attempt is made to describe the relationship of the individual monk to the triune God.[3] Only in a later age, as in the theology of Richard of Saint Victor, could the interreactions of the various persons of the Trinity inspire meditation on the place of personality in God's scheme. At Cluny it was not so much a personal God whom the community greeted in worship as the ineffable, unfathomable reality of divinity. God is beyond and above the perceptions of the individual monk, who can only put himself safely into the midst of the community in order to acknowledge Him. The individual monk had no need to think about his personal bond to God or his own understanding of the workings of the Trinity. The collective act of worship, in which words are sung not for the sake of intimacy but to express what the individual cannot grasp, is what mattered.

The contents of our carolingian hymn as well as that of eleventh-century cluniac liturgy are in agreement that God is sought through a community effort. Only in the act of worship can God be given anything of what is due him. One worships together with one's neighbour, but not in order to get to know him or God any better. Outside the realm of the liturgy the monk maintained silence much of the time. If he broke silence in order to be able to form bonds of friendship with fellow monks, he might be in danger of losing his soul to the devil.[4] The impulse to friendship could be looked upon as the beginning of the road to hell.

If these considerations were all that we could find in the literature of the period, we would have to conclude that friendship disappears completely from sight. But in historical sources one seldom finds quite what one thinks one is looking for. As we shall see in the following pages, monks could in some cases be each other's friends. But in their ways of expressing friendship they showed some hesitancy and reserve.

FRIENDSHIP AT SAINT GALL

The great monastery of Saint Gall managed to scrape through the breakdown of carolingian power with much less damage than most other monastic houses suffered. In the carolingian age it had become a cultural centre renowned for manuscript illumination, poetry, and building.[5] Saint Gall has become more accessible to us recently through the imposing and beautiful volumes on the Plan of the monastery published in the late 1970s.[6] This Plan, which probably dates to the early ninth century, was never realized, but there were certainly facilities for art work and for writing at Saint Gall that any monastery would have envied. For our purposes it is important to realize that Abbot Grimald (841-72) had been a pupil of Alcuin, or at least as a youth had been in contact with the literary culture that Alcuin fostered.[7] The poetry of several carolingian intellectuals was dedicated to him. His 'little garden' at Saint Gall became a nostalgic centre for gentle men dedicated to learning and to their pupils.

While Grimald is known to us mainly through the poetry and writings of others,[8] his contemporary, Notker the Stammerer (c. 840-912), can be seen in his own letters and poems, as well as in episodes from the *Casus Sancti Galli* written by Ekkehard IV of Saint Gall more than a century after Notker's death. In both the contemporary and the later sources Notker uses a language of friendship comparable to what we have found in carolingian sources. Notker's way of describing friendship continues carolingian forms. In writing to Salomo, who had been his pupil at the monastery's school but then (between 878-84) had made his own way in the world, Notker laments the loss of a pupil whom he dearly loved.[9] It was bitter for him to acknowledge that he had been deprived of a young man whom he had considered his friend, but who apparently was more attached to a girl who had become a nun:

Tardius invento citius defraudor amico
Si tamen hoc ultra nomine dignus eris.[9]
(I am deprived so soon of the friend I found so late
If you will be worthy at all of this name any more).

Notker continues about his own disappointment for almost twenty-five lines before he could admit that Salomo had made his choice and before he wished the best for the youth. Before that point he laments: 'Now I am rejected, for another man is being loved' and 'I follow you and with tears I drench your bed'.[10] Notker's regrets are almost unrestrained. One wonders who this man was and what could have been the bond Salomo had with him. It is likely that he is none other than Salomo's uncle, under whose care Salomo placed himself after he left Saint Gall. The young man was on his way up in the world, and Notker had to resign himself to this fact by the end of the poem. Before then, however, he could even threaten pursuit: *Persequar et temet fune ligabo, fugax* (Let me go after you and bind you, my fugitive).

This image of Notker, who apparently hardly ever left his monastery, out on the road chasing a runaway friend, seems more fantasy than substance. But Notker used the concept of pursuit to illustrate the seriousness of his own involvement in Salomo. The poem belongs to the rich carolingian tradition of declarations of love for absent friends and expressions of desire that they return to the love. Notker's love for the rich and attractive Salomo may have a homoerotic element, but his way of expressing his need points also to the strong literary culture that flourished under Notker at Saint Gall.

In a letter to Salomo and his cousin Waldo, dated 878-84, Notker expresses in a more controlled manner his sense of having been abandoned by his pupils.[11] He had learned to love the apostles and had obtained 'the friendship of confessors and virgins, the companionship of the patriarchs and prophets', he says, and thus he had learned through the saints to have friends on this earth who belonged to his own surroundings (*temporales et locales amicos*). 'I love you in Christ as he himself witnesses', he adds.[12] Notker calls the youths back to Saint Gall by telling them how much he wanted to share the beauty of the place and its liturgy with them. But after twenty-five lines or so, he admits defeat and turns to giving information and good advice. His hope is expressed at the very close of the letter: *O si vos videre merear!* (If only I deserved to see you). No matter how he dresses his language in moral exhortations and scriptural quotations, Notker still betrays pain and loneliness in the absence that Salomo and Waldo had inflicted on him.

This is not a letter of conversion, in which an abbot or a monastic teacher tries to convince a wayward youth to return to the monastery.[13] Notker concedes implicitly that the two young men had gone out into the world to start a brilliant career. The purpose of the letter seems to be the same as that of the poem: to insist that his former pupils consider their teacher's devotion to them and that whatever they do, they remember him. In another letter, Notker reminds Waldo and Salomo that since their childhood, they had been learning prose and poetry, and now, as they are about to cross the Alps, it is up to them to use these skills to keep in touch.[14] At least to some extent, Notker apparently did continue to receive Salomo's attention. The main indication is a so-called 'fur-coat poem' (*Pelzgedicht*) that was written probably in the 880s before Salomo reached the zenith of his career in succeeding his uncle and namesake as bishop of Constance. Notker writes to Salomo as a munificent friend who had sent him a gift which he always would have around him: and which would care for him:

> But this ornament accompanies me night and day

> Embracing me it takes care of me, protects and cherishes me.[15]

Salomo may have been trying to compensate for the break with Notker years earlier. Notker seems to have been appeased and to have accepted what Salomo was willing to give of himself.

In the writings of Ekkehard IV in the eleventh century, Notker appears not as an isolated teacher and friend but as a member of a circle of friendship.[16] Ekkehard is so far in time from the events he describes that no single fact he provides is trustworthy. But the general outlines of his description of the intellectual life of the monastery and its practical problems are useful for a glimpse of Saint Gall. Ekkehard writes vividly, and many of his anecdotes are unforgettable. As he says himself, he draws on the tradition of the elders of the cloister.[17]

Ekkehard was just as fascinated with Salomo's person and works as Notker was. He describes Salomo as a product of the external school of the monastery and a man who, despite his success in the world, could not keep himself away from the place that had brought him up. He would come at night to the monastery and be let in by the three friends Notker, Ratpert, and Tuotilo. They would engage in the 'holy trick' (*sanctam fraudem*) of providing a cowl for Salomo so that he could participate in the liturgy.[18] When the practice was found out, there were long discussions among the monks about what to do with this powerful man who wanted to wear their garb but not become one of them. Finally a place was provided for Salomo to enter the monastery where he could don the cowl. Notker and his friends, with their tolerant view of the matter, had triumphed. Salomo was finally persuaded to become a full-fledged monk of Saint Gall. Despite this status, Salomo was soon called away to court, and when he returned to Saint Gall in 890, it was only to take the position of abbot, which he held together with his episcopal title.

Salomo befriended not just the monks of Saint Gall but also Archbishop Hatto of Mainz. This relationship seems to have been more than a political bond. Ekkehard speaks of the two as *sodes*, his word for *sodales*. He tells how the two friends enjoyed trying to trick each other. After one successful prank by Hatto, Salomo arranged that the news of his own death be brought to Hatto. This would oblige the latter to carry out the terms of an agreement they had made. Hatto believed reports that came from merchants returning from Italy and spent a great deal of money on alms and on a magnificent tomb for Salomo. When Salomo returned from the dead, as it were, Hatto was shaken, but Salomo insisted that his friend's efforts had not been in vain:

> 'But please give me permission to speak out, my beloved friend! I want you to know that you acted well and rightly. The alms given before one is dead are more worthwhile to God than those which follow.' . . . And so finally they resumed their original friendship with the agreement that they would not deceive each other again, either in a prank or in any grave matter.[19]

Hatto went to Constance and was received festively by Bishop Salomo. The coffin made for the bishop was given over to the body of the martyr Pelagius that Salomo had brought back from Rome.

Ekkehard constructs a scene of tender reconciliation replete with embraces and kisses (*amplexatus sodalem . . . osculis rogat*). The chronicler does not use the word *amicitia* for the relationship. His terms *sodalis* and *sodalitas* are apparently intended to indicate the spiritual content of the bond. When Hatto died in 913, Salomo kept his promise to look after his friend's soul, and this time the spiritual companion was called *amicus*.

This tale of friendship mainly provides information about relics brought back from Rome and objects of art made at Saint Gall rather than giving a description of human relationships. Ekkehard finds 'holy deception' entertaining and amusing. He was interested in the friendship of two men, but it is only one theme among many in this description of the magnificence of Bishop Salomo's life. It may only be a coincidence that Hatto is not given the status of *amicus* to Salomo until after his death. At any rate, Ekkehard does allow us to perceive the imprint of a close human relationship that in some respects grew out of the learning and culture of Saint Gall.

Amidst Ekkehard's accounts of Saint Gall at the end of the ninth and the beginning of the tenth centuries, we find the friendship of Notker the Stammerer, Ratpert the poet and Tuotilo the artist:

> Concerning Notker, Ratpert and Tuotilo, pupils of his [Iso] and Marcellus, since they were indeed of one heart and soul (Acts 4:32), we begin to narrate in one group of stories how the three acted as if they were one, as we heard from the fathers [of the monastery].[20]

These three were of one heart (*unicordes*), and yet they were different from each other. Ekkehard spends many lines in showing how they each have their own areas of artistic creativity, and he provides here a sense of the cultural riches of Saint Gall at the end of the ninth century. During the night all three of them used to meet in the scriptorium and collate texts.[21] They did so with the prior's permission, he adds. There was to be nothing conspiratorial about their friendship.

Ekkehard does not call the three *amici*. They enjoyed a friendship so obvious that it does not need the word *amicitia* or any other specific name. When Ekkehard later described political bonds in his *Casus*, he used a standard vocabulary of friendship. Friends are those on the outside of the monastery who will help the monks in need, political allies, relationships, good bishops. A monk is a friend to another in one episode 'because of lineage and because of nobility of character'.[22] Both mattered at Saint Gall. Notker and Tuotilo never address each other as *amici* but yet they use terms of endearment, such as *mi anime*, my soul, and call each other beloved (*amabili suo*).[23] When lay or clerical protectors appear, however, whether they be relations or friends, the chronicler is not hesitant to use the word *amici*. In Saint Gall, and apparently also elsewhere in the Western Europe of the tenth century, friends are those who will look after one's physical well-being in dangerous surroundings.

It is perhaps misleading to attach too much significance to the use of a word to express friendship. But Ekkehard is fairly consistent in looking at *amici* as those out in the world to whom the monastery's population is attached, while friends in the cloister either have no special appellation, or else are described in some general term of love, such as *unicordes*.[24] More significant than the individual words is the fact that Ekkehard provides no examples of a group of close friends at Saint Gall after the time of Notker, Ratpert and Tuotilo. A few episodes hint at bonds of individual friendship among monks. None of these, however, is singled out again to show a strong and fruitful alliance inside Saint Gall.

Ekkehard's distance from events requires caution from the historian, but the prominence given to Notker's circle of friends combined with Notker's own passionate letters and poems indicates that friendship was important and acceptable at Saint Gall at the end of the ninth century. Notker's language reveals a platonic, highly intellectual variety of friendship conceived in terms similar to those used by the great carolingian monastic poet Walafrid Strabo for Abbot Grimald.

Notker does not herald a new age of monastic friendships. He and those around him provide a last manifestation of carolingian friendships. In scenes of affection and tenderness among the monks from later in his chronicle, Ekkehard does not single out any single members of the community. In a description of the monks' reaction after a visit by the emperor, who exonerated them from charges made against the monastery, Ekkehard writes how the monks touched, kissed and hugged each other. The *hilaritas* is shared among all the monks. There are no special friends here, only a community which felt relieved that it could continue in its established ways. In responding to outside criticism which had preceded the emperor's visit, the monks could reassert the importance of their collective life. Individual monks had become mere actors in a common drama that required no starring roles.

FRIENDSHIP AS ENMITY: RATHERIUS OF VERONA

From late carolingian culture to the ottonian revival after 950 is only a matter of decades. The troubled life of Ratherius, bishop of Verona (c. 890-974), brings us into the very heart of the Ottonian Age. Ratherius was first deposed but then restored to the bishopric of Verona, thanks to the brother of the german king and new emperor, Otto I, the archbishop of Cologne, Bruno.[26] Ratherius's letters provide us with one of the few source collections from the tenth century that allow more than a biographical sketch of one of its important participants. His is no easy personality, and the vitriol of Ratherius's attacks on others has, for better or worse, inspired psychohistorical analysis.[27]

Ratherius's distance from any ideal of friendship is to a great extent the result of his personality. But his flight from friendship is also an expression of what happened in the tenth century when social bonds and human affection were squeezed out by fear and rivalry. Ratherius is not only a unique individual with a basic lack of trust in his fellow human beings. He failed in his life to experience institutions or ways of life that provided good soil for the growth of bonds of friendship.

In a letter written at Como, dated to 936 or 937, Ratherius makes it clear that friends are those who help a man in trouble (*interventu amicorum vitam et libertatem obtinuerim*).[28] This is a secular ethic of friendship, made more apparent in a long letter of conversion to the Doge Peter II of Venice telling about the duties of a monk. Ratherius warns about friendships with lay people (*amicitia secularium*), which for a monk can only be distractions. He warns against cultivating friendships with the enemy (*inimici amicitias*), and against having contacts with former relatives, for the monk is dead to such bonds.[29] Here in undiluted form is the teaching of the East. Friends are more dangerous for their flattery than enemies are in their hostility. There is no possibility that worldly friendships can be translated into monastic bonds. Potential enemies are everywhere and the monk must flee from them into his silence.

The central biblical passage in these considerations of Ratherius is from the Epistle of Saint James (4:4): 'Whoever wishes to be a friend of this world is made an enemy of God'. Friendship is thus enmity, for friendship is seen only in the context of worldly involvements. The theme of the friend as enemy appears in an appeal to the pope for help in which Ratherius explains how Count Milo of Verona had acted as if he were Ratherius's best friend:

> And so he assailed me in the most clever manner,
> so that practically everyone in the kingdom thought
> he was my very best friend.[30]

The evil will find the way to one another to do evil, Ratherius insists to Bishop Hubert of Parma. 'The likeness of their desires always gives rise to an equality in their effects; human friendships seek like minds and wills in agreement with each other.'[31] Once again *humane amicitie* are considered harmful to the good man. The language echoes Cicero, perhaps through the filter of Ambrose's *De officiis*, but the classical or patristic echoes are distorted. Friendship is conspiracy!

In defending the use of a donation to his diocese to rebuild the church of Saint Zeno instead of extending it to help the poor, Ratherius wrote in 968 to a cleric that those who would persuade him to do the latter were not friends but his greatest enemies.[32] Ratherius one time addresses his correspondent as a friend (*o amicissime*), but present company excepted, he looked upon all friends as deceivers. To Ambrose the chancellor of Otto I, Ratherius explained the reasons for his conflict with the clergy of Verona. Ambrose, Ratherius insisted, had broken God's law by forging a bond of friendship with these clerics who hated God: *Set his, qui oderunt Deum, amicitia iungeris*.[33] Once again friendship is perceived as an alliance that endangers men's souls and leads them away from what is good and right. Ratherius uses Sallust's popular definition of friendship as wanting and not wanting the same things. If this is what friendship is, he insisted, then he could not be friends with such men, for there were no shared desires between them and himself. They had always sought opposites.[34]

In his letters, Ratherius presents friendship as either an impossible ideal or a means of conspiracy against the good and holy. Men who befriend each other become enemies of Ratherius and of God. Ratherius never hinted that friendship might lead to heaven instead of to hell. Friendship meant political alliances that conspired against his vision of the church. Ratherius may have been a crank, even a disturbed personality, but his letters describe friendship as irreconcilable with the life of the christian bishop or monk. As Ratherius wrote to the doge of Venice, the monk must leave all friendships of the world behind him. He left no door open to new bonds of attachment in the cloister.

This rejection of friendship may reflect Ratherius's personal quirks, but he also was drawing on the tradition of the egyptian desert. The desert mentality provides a constant factor and point of reference in Western ascetic experience. It reappears regularly, as in the accounts of hermit saints such as Guthlac of Croyland, who found their salvation in severing bonds with other men. In tempting Guthlac, the devil is described in an eighth-century biography as his friend. This false friendship, *pseudo-sodalitas*, is typical for the devil, who also tried to allure Christ by promising all the world's delights.[35] Once again he twisted the truth to entrap a man of the spirit. Guthlac as he is portrayed by his biographer, Felix, and Ratherius, as he conveys himself to us in his letters, share a disregard for the spiritual worth of human relationships. Both detect the devil behind most human activity, and so they search out a zone of loneliness and apartness in their own lives, to protect themselves from the devil's wiles.

The eclipse of friendship that takes place in the letters of Ratherius is not so dramatic in other tenth-century sources, but in various lives of bishops, friendship is similarly limited. Bishop Ulrich of Augsburg (923-73) hinted at friendship only when he spoke with the monks of Saint Gall in seeking their advice.[36] Otherwise friends played the role of political counsellors. Ulrich was closely attached only to one person, his nephew Adalbero.[37] In the Life of Bruno of Cologne by Ruotger, this magnificent archbishop is perceived as a loner.[38] He warned against too intimate talk (*nimiam . . . colloquii familiaritatem*).[39] After he was elected to Cologne, his friends were those who loved the emperor, his brother, on whom he concentrated his love.[40] Bruno chose as *familiares* those who could serve Otto. Ruotger's portrait of Bruno is intended to show the harmony possible when society was run by two wise and brave brothers. The biography is a panegyric to the sanctity of the ottonian order. A single friendship emerges between the two pillars of the new establishment, but it is an ideological relationship which for the biographer sums up the unity of the regime. Alone in his greatness, Bruno is matched only by Otto. There is no sign of any community of canons where he might find friendship. 'We have always felt one and the same thing', Otto is supposed to have told his brother, in a distant echo of Sallust's definition of friendship.[41] Here there is mutual understanding, but friendship within religious or clerical communities is practically invisible in the episcopal and hagiographical sources of the tenth century.

THE OTTONIAN SYNTHESIS: POLITICAL FRIENDSHIPS WITH A MONASTIC TONE

Gerbert of Aurillac, who became Pope Sylvester II (999-1003), sums up in his life the complexity of the ottonian experience and provides the evidence for most of what can be seen of tenth-century friendship. Gerbert is not ususally considered a monastic figure, but, as Jean Leclercq convincingly argues, he had come from a monastic milieu. In his letters as abbot of Bobbio in Italy and again later in life, Gerbert remained close to the language and principles of the Rule of Saint Benedict.[42] Whether or not Gerbert in fact ever was professed a monk is of little moment. He was steeped in the monastic tradition, and so his statements about friendship can be looked upon as, at least in part, a monastic expression of this ideal.

The collection of his letters begins with a disastrous year when he was at the great monastery of Bobbio, 983-84, and ends in 997 just before he was appointed by Otto III to be archbishop of Verona.[43] We never get to know the young Gerbert. He was in his forties when he came to Bobbio, and his papal letters were formed by the demands of a chancellery and have nothing personal about them.[44] For about seven years in the 980s, however, we can follow his concerns as teacher at Rheims and assistant to Archbishop Adalbero. In 991 Gerbert himself became archbishop, but his title was challenged and he was preoccupied with having to defend it. It is in letters from the earlier period, from about 983 to 989, that Gerbert best reveals his personality, and from these his fullest statements of friendship emerge.

At Bobbio, Gerbert as abbot demanded that a renegade noble return stolen possessions of the monastery. He appealed to friendship's laws (*leges amicitie*), a friendship clearly secular in kind and providing leverage to an abbot in need of assistance (*epp* 3-4). To his patron Archbishop Adalbero in 983 Gerbert wrote how he missed him, but he expressed himself through a mosaic of classical tags that interpose a shield between his own feelings and what he says in the letter. At Bobbio, Gerbert's friends lived outside the monastery, and they existed to provide help.[45]

Writing to a monk at the imperial court who seems to have had some influence, Gerbert could 'rejoice in the friendship of such a great man' (*ep* 21). A similar phrase is used for a lady at court.[46] Friendship existed for political but not scholarly favours. When Gerbert wanted a book, for example, he did not appeal to *amicitiae* to justify his request (*ep* 24).

There is no doubt that Gerbert during this period 'ghosted' many of Archbishop Adalbero's letters. The imprint of his language of friendship is apparent in many of them. When the archbishop asked Bishop Notger of Liège to look after a friend's interests (*amici causam*)[47] we hear Gerbert echoing the language of Cicero's own letters: friends are for influence, patronage and favours. The world of the ottonian court in Italy attracted Herbert. He did what he could to gain entrance to it, even though in 984 he had to vacate the abbacy at Bobbio and return to Rheims to teach (*ep* 37). He did his best, however, to keep in touch. The same year he asked a deacon, Stephen, for information about the situation in Rome. Gerbert pointed out that it was Stephen's duty not to keep anything from a friend: *nos tibi amicos celare non debebis* (*ep* 40). Affairs of the heart are not at stake here. Matters of church and state held the attention of Gerbert, who wanted to keep abreast.

The letters reveal Gerbert as a political climber. He used his gift for language and made use of expressions of friendship in order to get to the top. The letters also show Gerbert as an intellectual who used a network of friends to get hold of books he needed. In one letter to this effect, he points out quite unashamedly that he does not identify with those who would separate what is virtuous from what is useful in friendship. He agrees with Cicero that the two belong together in the best and most complete friendships.[48] Variations of this phrase (*honestissimas atque sanctissimas amicitias*) were to appear in many letters over the following decade and establish beyond all doubt the central source for Gerbert's formulation of friendship, Cicero's *De officiis*. Friendship is good because friends could help Gerbert get books!

There is something attractive about Gerbert's forthright way of combining the good with the useful. He was no cynic out to flatter every powerful man or woman who came his way. But he wanted his place in the ottonian order, and he did his best to advance beyond a scholarly life at Rheims. Gerbert sought more than fame and fortune, however; he remained devoted to the monastery of Aurillac. A letter to a monk Raimund asks him to come to Rheims.[49] 'By how great love we are bound to you is known to Latins and foreigners who share in the fruits of our labour', he wrote. To Abbot Gerald (*ep* 46) he asserted that he felt privileged to know such a man: 'I do not know whether divinity has granted anything better to mortals than friends, if only they are the ones who seem suitably sought and suitably kept'.[50] The purpose of this letter is not clear. Gerald was praised for the advice he gave, but the text makes no reference to any particular problem Gerbert may have had. Here as in other letters to the Aurillac community, Gerbert took on a bond of friendship that lasted a lifetime. Writing to a Bernard at Aurillac, he recommended as teacher of music at the monastery, Constantine of Fleury, who was 'intimately joined to me in friendship' (*michique in amicicia coniunctissimus*, *ep* 92). Gerbert would have known that friendship alone is no guarantee of intellectual excellence, but he counted on the trust the monastery had for him as one of its loyal 'old boys'. To point to the function of a network of friendship does not demean it. For once in the dark tenth century (dark to us because we lack sources), the bonds of loyalty and affection in a monastic context become visible.

In such personal exchanges *amicitia* is used in a monastic context. In most of Gerbert's correspondence, however, he used the word to describe the bonds among churchmen and secular rulers necessary for the maintenance of peace and order. Gerbert wrote in the name of Archbishop Adalbero to the bishop of Verdun and to a count asking them to effect an alliance between Hugh Capet and the Emperor Otto III and to win Hugh's friendship.[51] To Sigfried the son of the Count of Luxembourg, Gerbert wrote that he had visited Sigfried's imprisoned relatives. Gerbert was trying to encourage a potential alliance with the upcoming Hugh Capet: *si Hugonem in amicitiam vobis*. . . (*Ep* 51). Gerbert did what he could to advance the cause of the future royal family of France. Even to his own archbishop Adalbero, Gerbert insisted on this same goal: 'Hugh's friendship ought to be actively sought after, and every effort should be exerted lest we fail to make the most of this friendship, which has been well begun'.[52]

Friends exist to form alliances. On Adalbero's behalf, Gerbert requested that an abbot come to Rheims because of friendship. One must obey old friends, he insisted, when they had proven themselves faithful (Ep 81). Gifts sent by the empress to the church at Rheims are described as a pledge of friendship: *pignus vestre amititie circa nos* (*Ep* 85). In these letters friendship is almost emptied of any purely personal content. It becomes a manifestation of alliance among good and loyal sons and daughters of the church against disloyal ones. Ecclesiastical and royal politics require the cultivation of friendship, and in Gerbert's language of *amicitia* we find little to remind us that this is a christian writer nurtured in monastic life and not some latter-day Sidonius Appolinaris seeking political allies in the crumbling world of Late Antiquity.

Gerbert at one moment sings the praises of friendship in the cloister, and the next makes it a ploy of pure lay politics. Can we reconcile such different uses of the same word? In a letter from the abbots of Rheims to the monks of Fleury over a disputed abbatial election at Fleury, Gerbert's basic principles emerge. We belong to one community, Gerbert insists as the spokesman of the abbots. This most holy fellowship and most chaste friendship were being threatened at Fleury: *hanc sanctissimam societatem castissimamque amicitiam* (*ep* 95).

The viciousness of a few men threatened the existence of a fellowship of friendship: *fidelium una societas*. Three concepts are linked in this letter: community, faith, and friendship. The mutual faith of members of the community produces a state of friendship.

If friendship exists best within an ordered life in community, then friendship is a collective practice. There is no place in this scheme for individual friendships! Gerbert never makes this distinction specific, but it is a natural result of his train of thought. Even if we admit that Gerbert is simply being pragmatic in appealing for concord at Fleury, he makes friendship into a generalized social bond here rather than something individual and interpersonal. In Gerbert's scheme friendship makes the world go round not because individuals love each other as friends but because communities function through the harmony that friendship provides.

There is no purely monastic ideal of friendship in Gerbert's letters. His point of departure is classical. Friendship holds society together, and he was not particularly concerned to show how this also happens within the cloister. Holy friendship can send King Hugh Capet to the byzantine emperor (*ep* 111). In writing such letters for his masters, Gerbert was not abandoning monastic ideals. He was positing an ideal in a world where friendships were preeminently practical.

Gerbert's most detailed idealization of friendship appears in the opening or *exordium* of a highly rhetorical brief he wrote at Rheims in 995 in order to defend his treatment of Adalbero's successor, and his own rival and predecessor as archbishop of Rheims, Arnulf. Without *casta societas* and *sancta amicicia*, Gerbert says outright, the world would collapse: 'From where would arise families, from where cities and kingdoms, unless stabilized by association and friendship'.[53] The ideas can be traced easily back to Cicero, but Gerbert takes a further step in postulating world order as a result of friendship. All goods emerge from the greatest good, God, and within the great good of society and friendship we find God's ordering of an eternal law of friendship (*amiticie aeterna lege*). This is a sweeping platonic visualization of friendship.

However cosmic such a concept of friendship may be,[54] it is only one aspect of Gerbert's all-purpose view of friendship. If friendship makes things work, then it is just as important in political struggles as in monastic life. There is no room in Gerbert's scheme for any special type of monastic friendship. Friendship is so grand and universal that it cannot be seen in one context alone. It is the source of order among men and at the same time something men always seek and rarely find.

A talented man, respected teacher, and leading ecclesiastical advisor, Gerbert ultimately realized his greatest desire and came briefly into the company of the emperor, Otto III. Gerbert's alliance was furthered by his idealization of friendship as a political virtue. Gerbert made holy friendship a social necessity and a political program. But on a personal level, it is difficult to see the presence of individual friendships in Gerbert. Only a few phrases indicate anything of his devotion to Archbishop Adalbero. The letters the two exchanged indicate little about any close bonds.[55] Similarly we have no idea from Gerbert's letters whether he had any genuine friends at the ottonian court. The people to whom he wrote were often on the fringes of events. Gerbert's purpose in writing letters seems to have been to widen his circle of political contacts, not to form personal friendships.

The magnificent ideal of 'most holy friendship and firm association that will remain with us forever' and the actual experience of Gerbert's life seem to have little in common.[56] Despite his rhetoric of political friendship, Gerbert for most of his life remained on the fringes of the social institutions he wanted to affect: the archbishopric of Rheims, the imperial administration, the papacy, and monastic life. After a struggle he did gain his archbishopric and finally the papacy itself. He had convinced the Ottonians that his golden pen was worth keeping close by. But in spite of the brilliance and clarity of his letters, Gerbert remains obscure, more a collection of pleasing ideas than a person. His letters rarely allow us to see anything of Gerbert as a teacher at Rheims. He looks upward and outward from Rheims, and his daily activities, most of his pupils, and his theories about education, remain a questionmark. Only once do we find him inviting a friend to Rheims and this was someone who seems to have no political significance but who was owed hospitality because of what Gerbert calls the right of friendship (*ius amititie*).[57] In you we seek rest, he wrote, a yearning also expressed in some of the letters to the monks of Aurillac.[58]

Gerbert's vision could attract rulers, but at Bobbio as abbot, at Rheims as archbishop and at Rome as pope he was unable to convert his principles into action. He speaks to us immediately in his clear Latin with straightforward classical reminiscences. But as with most diplomatic missives meant for many ears, his letters are more form than matter, attractive pieces of art, but a false trail in the history of friendship. Gerbert may well have been a friend, but this part of his life is not visible in his letters.

However difficult Gerbert is to characterize, it is clear that in the upper regions of ottonian culture, the ideal of friendship was attractive. Gerbert's ideal is more ciceronian than christian, but this is not always the case in ottonian sources. In the *Life* of Bishop Adalbert of Prague (born *c.* 956), written by John Canaparius shortly after Adalbert's martyrdom in Pomerania in 997, friendship takes on some christian elements. Once again we deal with a bishop and not a monk, but again a bishop who owes much to his own experience of the monastic life. This monastic dimension is enlarged by the fact that the biographer was himself a monk of the monastery of Saints Boniface and Alexius at Rome.

John Canaparius tried to show Bishop Adalbert living like a monk. As a member of an ascetic house, he wanted to glorify this way of life. He described Adalbert's monastic practices when he was bishop of Prague and added that he shared these with his brother, Gaudentius, and with a certain man who had been blind from birth. These were joined to him in the greatest friendship (*amicissima familiaritate iunctos*).[59] We notice here that he makes *amicus* into an adjective and as his noun uses the more monastic-sounding word *familiaritas*, apparently to indicate life in community rather than individual friendships.

In 990 Adalbert left his post and travelled to Italy, where he visited Monte Cassino. Advised to settle down in a monastery, he continued until he found a celebrated monastic figure, Nilus, in a monastery near Bari in Capua. Nilus was known for his adherence to the Rule of Saint Basil. In tears and on his knees, Adalbert asked for help: 'Seek the city of Rome', Nilus answered. 'There you will come with a good angel leading you and you are to greet the abbot Leo, who is our dearest friend'.[60] Having sought a spiritual father who belonged to the Eastern tradition, Adalbert found himself steered back into his own culture, to a monastery that was open to Eastern influence but which followed the Rule of Saint Benedict. Nilus' good advice suggests a network of contacts among Italian abbots, who could refer recruits to each other: Monte Cassino, Capua, and Rome. Two houses at Rome were named as possibilities. Nilus left it up to Abbot Leo to decide what was best for Adalbert.

At this point Adalbert lost two of the companions who had been with him. Only his brother Gaudentius stuck with him. Described as a brother twice over, in spirit and in flesh, Gaudentius had been from childhood Adalbert's most faithful companion (*fidissimus comes*).[61] Once again the word *amicus* is not used. Elsewhere Nilus is said to provide friendly consolation (*amica solacia*), but there is no indication, direct or indirect, of any spiritual friendship.

After Adalbert and Gaudentius had joined a monastery at Rome, the bishop was recalled to his duties at Prague. In about 995, however, he managed to return to Rome and his monastery where they 'all loved him, but above all his abbot' loved him.[62] This passage echoes the Rule of Saint Benedict's provision in chapter two that the abbot is to love no monk more than any other, except on the basis of virtue. Because of Adalbert's virtue he came to deserve the love of the monks and especially the abbot.

When Otto III arrived in Rome in the summer of 996, he became acquainted with Adalbert and made him an intimate (*familiarem*: once again the word *amicitia* is avoided). If we remember how fond Gerbert was of this term we might suspect our monastic biographer of deliberately avoiding a word that in his time had a too secular ring. Gerbert wanted to portray Adalbert as the emperor's counsellor on a purely spiritual level. John Canaparius mentions only heavenly conversations. Otto and Adalbert seem to have been together almost all the time, for Adalbert is called his 'closest companion . . . both at night and during the day, like a most attractive chamberlain'.[63] The latin expression *dulcissimus cubicularius* almost defies translation into terms understandable in our culture. Bedroom-mate would be a travesty of the phrase, but chamberlain implies a servile status that was not intended here.

This linguistic problem indicates the distance between our two cultures. As the historian Karl Leyser points out so well in a work on medieval politics and culture, the personalities of the twelfth century are comprehensible to us as people, while those of the tenth elude us.[64] Certainly the content of Otto's and Adalbert's friendship can to us seem forced and exaggerated in the way it is described. But for the biographer there was no problem. Here are spiritual father and son, who happen to be the emperer, and when they part, they exchange kisses and embraces 'not without grief'. In this quasi-liturgical ceremony the individuals are subsumed into fixed roles. But at the same time we find a great monastic friend who could convey his asceticism and learning to leading political personalities of the day. Adalbert in this account becomes for Otto the spiritual counsellor that Gerbert had aspired to be.

In Adalbert's final return to martyrdom at the hands of the 'barbarians' of Eastern Europe, the biographer makes no attempt to deal with this event in terms of bonds of friendship between Adalbert and those who die with him.[65] Adalbert is seen primarily as a great spiritual hero. His end was foreseen by Abbot Nilus in a letter to John Canaparius:

> May you know, sweetest son, that our friend (*amicus noster*) Adalbert walks with the Holy Spirit and that his present life will come to a most happy end.[66]

There is nothing striking about the prophecy in terms of the requirements of hagiography as a literary genre. But why is Adalbert called *amicus* instead of *familiaris*? This may be due to the fact that he was soon to become a saint, and thus a friend of God. As such he could become a friend to the men who loved him in life. This development recalls Notker's letter to his two young friends: first he had learned to love the saints as friends, he said, and thereby he came to love his friends on earth. John Canaparius seems willing to concede Adalbert as a friend only when he is poised on the brink of sainthood through martyrdom. The next step would be to consider the friendship of the saints to extend to one's friends in the world, and to strengthen such bonds.[67]

Some loose ends remain. The view of friendship in Adalbert's *Life* is fragmentary and allows no firm conclusion.[68] Adalbert was clearly loved by monks in his roman monastery as a friend, but their friendship for him is only expressed in our sources after he was dead. Once again friendship within community dominates individual bonds. Adalbert is said to have had a special friendship with his brother Gaudentius, but this remains unsubstantiated and shadowy. The entire roman monastic community may have loved Adalbert deeply, but the text does not make individual relationships visible. A person-to-person bond with the emperor is revealed, but here political considerations may be involved. The emperor's support was essential to roman monastic communities, as it had been for Gerbert at Bobbio, for without him greedy laymen could disturb peace and occupy abbey properties.

Inconsistency in tenth-century expressions of friendship and descriptions of it reflects a lack of clarity about the place of friendship in the christian life. Gerbert saw no problem: friendship existed everywhere in harmony and stability, but only as an ideal, for in reality there was little concord in his life. At the opposite end of the spectrum is Ratherius, for whom friendship endangered human salvation because it usually resulted from the workings of the devil. In between Gerbert's optimism and Ratherius's pessimism is the more moderate John Canaparius. His Adalbert is not particularly interested in friendship, but once in a while his narration provides a glimpse of monks who enjoy making spiritual use of each other's fellowship. John does not go into detail, and so it is difficult to use him to say anything definite about the actual practice of friendship at the time.

Even the rich sources from Saint Gall say very little about the existence of friendship in the cloister after the death of Notker and his circle. For all that Ekkehard tells about disputes and factions at Saint

Gall, he gives almost no hint of any special relationships and mutual concern among individual monks. An easy explanation would be that with frequent fires, barbarian attacks, imperial intervention, and jealous outbursts from bishops and other monasteries, the monks of Saint Gall had little time to cultivate friendships. But a 'no creativity in chaos' theory could easily be turned on its head. In just such a period of challenge a new emphasis on the value of loving bonds in the community could have manifested itself in our sources. But the Notkerian idealization of friendship in the school of Saint Gall and among its beloved pupils brought a carolingian development to an end and was not a point of departure for an ottonian monastic revival. Friendship disappears as a literary form in monastic literature because monks turned to other matters. Because the monks were human beings, they must have had their friendships. But in the literary productions of the period from about 950 to 1050, we can see there was only a limited interest in describing and celebrating the value of friendship.

REFORM MONASTICISM: FRIENDSHIP SUBORDINATED TO ASCETICISM

The best point of departure for seeing what tenth-century reformed monks valued in their lives is the biography of John of Gorze.[69] This incomplete work, for all the obscurity of its latinity, provides a vivid account of John's background, his pursuit of a reformed monasticism, and his life at the refounded monastery of Gorze near Metz in what today is northeastern France. The writer, John, abbot of Saint Arnulf in Metz, uses his saint as the most perfect example of a new asceticism. In the words of one expert on the tenth century, Ludwig Zoepf: 'The work is a piece of propaganda for asceticism, which has found its most brilliant representative in the personality of John'.[70]

The question for us is whether this renewal of asceticism left any place for friendship. The story of a small, devoted band of men striking out on their own to follow Christ could easily contain elements of spiritual companionship. The biography in many instances provides us with first-hand materials about this group. The anecdotes are lively and detailed. They indicate intimate knowledge of John's words and actions. In the prologue John of Metz reflects on John of Gorze's holy companionship (*sancta familiaritate*).[71] And yet this is the only characterization of their relationship. John of Gorze, for all the rigour of his asceticism, remains an obscure figure whose inner life his biographer makes no attempt to expose.

John of Metz was aware of the unknowability of his subject. John 'hid within himself in all ways' and lived 'as a hermit amid the crowds'.[72] This last phrase, similar to an expression in the contemporary *Life* of Bruno of Cologne,[73] may have been fashionable in the tenth century to make saintly heroes inaccessible. But the characterization fits with later descriptions of a man who kept to himself, had no intimate conversations with his fellow monks, and did not encourage them to come to him about their problems. At the centre of the biography there is a great silence, and it seems a literary device. In Zoepf's words, John of Gorze had 'richly developed inner life, which remains almost completely hidden even from those closest to him'.[74]

If John was so isolated, it might seem pointless to look more closely at his biography to seek traces of monastic friendship. But it is worth seeing why there is so little about human bonds. After all, John did talk to and live with several hermits before he finally helped form the group of ascetics who refounded Gorze. The biographer shows John as a member of a community and not just as an isolated figure. The biography can in fact be used as an early history of the Gorze that, after being refounded in 933, became one of the leading reform monasteries of the Upper Lorraine.

One might conclude from the absence of friendship that John of Gorze and his namesake at Metz were intent on fostering a variation of Eastern monasticism in the pachomian mould, where entrance to the monastery meant loosing all bonds with the world. Yet John of Metz describes with approval how John of Gorze took care of his mother in her old age and settled her near the monastery so she could mend the monks' clothes.[75] John is by no means portrayed as a monk far from the world. John of Metz praises him for his attention to the monastery's external affairs. His function is to make it possible for the abbot, Einold, to concentrate on the monks' spiritual life. John's position is never given a formal name, but he performed the duties of cellarer, with a great deal of independence. His abilities in the affairs of the world become so well known that he was chosen in 953 to go on an imperial diplomatic mission to the caliph of Cordova. Here he worked to establish *amicitia* between the two powers.[76] Some of John's intimate conversations with the caliph indicate that he did have a capacity to influence other men directly through words of advice and friendship. This may be literary windowdressing, of course, to show the power of Christians over Islam. But it is significant that the one moment of near-friendship in this biography comes when John was thousands of kilometres away from his own monastery and among pagans, not his monastic brethren.

John of Metz names the Easterners Paul, Hilarion, Macharius, and Pachomius as fathers worthy of imitation, but then added Western bishops such as Martin of Tours and Germanus of Auxerre, as well as John the Almsgiver. In their *amica dulcedine* and *suavitate* John found models to imitate.[78] John of Gorze combines Eastern asceticism and Western pragmatism, withdrawal from the world and involvement in the life of the secular church. The biographer aptly uses the Eastern figure of John the Almsgiver as a synthesis of these two directions. This admirable saint, whose life was available in Latin, managed to combine concern for the spiritual and material needs of his neighbours with an extreme asceticism.[79] He provided a spiritual and literary model for John of Gorze, who worked among men and yet kept apart. He was a good businessman, administrator, cultivator of land, and builder. Despite all these practical demands, he lived so sparsely that he ruined his health by fasting and by showing no concern for the type of food he did eat.

Because John of Gorze could be so many things to so many different people, it is significant that he nevertheless was not seen in the role of friend to any of them. Instead, his abilities and extreme life style seem to have caused jealousy and dissension among the brothers.[81] John was not at the centre of a community of love. He was a provocation to his fellow monks, and he had to prove himself to them time and again. His holy way of life and strict liturgical observances did not bring him closer to the other members of his community.

There are no miracles here and few literary concessions to the genre of hagiography.[82] We are allowed to look into a decisive period of monastic growth and see there the resentment, anger and competition one of its leading personalities could cause. None of these disturbing elements is offset by generous moments of friendship: John of Metz saw in his spiritual hero no capacity for friendship. Lacking a dimension of intimacy, John of Gorze made no attempt to share his inner life with others. He was praised, in fact, because he kept so much to himself.

To concentrate on the absence of friendship would be to ignore the versatility of this portrait of a monastic reformer and the men around him. John of Metz's main concern was to show how men like John of Gorze were able to reestablish a material and spiritual basis for monastic life. This theme makes this biography one of the fullest and dearest accounts we have of the new monastic order in the tenth century in places like Cluny, Gorze, and Canterbury.

For John of Gorze's contemporary, Odo, the second abbot of Cluny (927-42), we are fortunate to have a greater range of materials to investigate the place of friendship, even if his biography does not measure up in quality or detail to that of John. We have Odo's moral poem on the history of salvation, the *Occupatio*, his biography of the knight Gerald of Aurillac, and finally John of Salerno's account of Odo's own life. The *Occupatio* is an impressive work of seven books tracing the history of salvation and revealing especially in the third book a concern with chastity and sexual sin.[83] Homosexuality is named as one of the greatest vices, but the destruction of Sodom and Gomorrah is seen as the result of a whole catalogue of sexual sins and not of homosexuality alone.[84] There is no reference to friendship, except in a citation of James 4:4:

> Whoever loves the world, the love of the Father does not fill him. By this friendship he is made worthy of the wrath of the Judge, because he prefers what is base to the beautiful, the vile to the precious. He who befriends this world is an enemy of the Father. . . [85]

The word *amicitia* occurs in the entire poem (so far as I can find) only in the unfavourable context familiar to us from Ratherius of Verona. Friends of the world are by definition God's enemies. There is no suggestion that we can become God's friend or friends to good men, for friendship is seen as a distraction from the right and the holy. David is mentioned in several places in the poem, but never Jonathan, and so there is never anything about their friendship. Nor do we hear about John the Apostle and his closeness to Jesus.

One cannot criticize an historical source for not including what interests the historian! Once again, however, we meet either a negative attitude towards friendship or complete indifference to it. Odo's concern in describing the Last Supper is to tell not about Christ's love for his apostles, but about how the bread and wine he offered on that occasion help strengthen virginity.[86]

This theme of sexual abstinence is just as evident in the biography of Gerald of Aurillac (855-909), whom Odo apparently had not known, but whom he wanted to commemorate as a type of the christian knight.[87] Odo describes Gerald as an outstandingly attractive man, whose neck was so well-shaped that his vassals wanted to kiss it. He is also loving and much loved (Bk. I, ch. 30), and he was especially close to Duke William of Aquitaine, the founder of Cluny (ch. 32). This bond is described in terms of the 'sweet fellowship' (*dulci contubernio*) and 'great veneration' (*ingenti veneratione*) William had for Gerald. The knight is made into something of a living saint, looked upon with awe. His physical and moral attributes make him an object of admiration, but not a friend who is present and accessible to others. His relationship with William at one point is described as *amicitia*, but the context indicates this was a political bond which was supposed to guarantee peace in Gerald's lands.[88]

At one moment spiritual friendship seems present. In doubt about his vocation, Gerald spoke to Bishop Gausbert of Rodez, who convinced him that it was better for him to be in the world and serve men: 'for this lord Gausbert was most beloved to the man of God, and because of their holiness they shared a great fellowship with each other'.[89] The word used is *contubernium*, which already in classical Latin indicated friendship, while retaining its origins of military camp life and comradeship. But these few lines about the two saintly men's friendship are included in the account only to show how Gerald found his true call to be a good count, to found monasteries, and to show charity to all. His relationship with the bishop is of secondary importance.

But Gerald was not another John of Gorze. He did have friends, normally called *familiares*. A priest, also named Gerald, was *charus et familiaris* to him. When they met, Gerald spoke to him in an intimate manner and asked what they were going to eat together:

> He spoke like this on account of the easy relations that this priest had with him. But with pleasure the priest replied, 'If it pleases your piety, my lord, you shall not go away fasting. Nevertheless I have only bread and wine to put before you . . .'.[90]

All this, not surprisingly, provides the setting for a miracle: the priest found a fish that turned up in good biblical fashion to take care of hunger. Such incidents are intended for the requirements of the genre of hagiography, where miracles are part of the proof of saintliness, but they still indicate that for Odo companionship with other men was not just the dangerous worldly bond he described in the *Occupatio*. But it is never a primary theme. Gerald was a friend to good men, but Odo thought it far more important to show how he lived chastely and supported the interests of the church. The cluniac abbot might be accused of drawing a portrait of a layman that suited perfectly the interests of the reformed monastery. But the new knight was at least allowed human bonds that suggest the possibility of friendship.

The military language prominent in Odo's biography of Gerald of Aurillac is also evident in John of Salerno's biography of Odo. He is seen as a soldier of Christ who exchanged one form of military life for another. But in this account, which at times attempts to reproduce Odo's very words to John of Salerno, there is very little about the fellowship of military service, whether secular or spiritual. John's portrait is so chaotic and disorganized that a later monk of Cluny attempted to give it chronological unity.[91] But John remembered individual episodes vividly, as once when Odo paid an overprice for berries and was pursued by a grateful crowd. In John's words:

> When I had distributed alms, I asked him what was the purpose of the berries and where he had got them. He answered with such merry words that I have never heard the like, nor hope to. He made us laugh till we cried and were unable to speak to one another.

> With the tears still streaming down my face I leant forward and begged that we might no longer be burdened with the berries. . . . [92]

The scene is as vivid as Ekkehard's description of how Saint Gall's monks could laugh together. John of Salerno enjoyed telling of the comraderies and even intimacy which easily could grow up in a group of monks on a long trip.

Although mutual appreciation and joy are here, John does not make any explicit conclusion about his friendship with Odo. There is no indication of any privileged relationships between Odo and any of the monks of Cluny. Like almost all commemorative biographies from this great abbey, the *Life of Odo* concentrates on his external actions and says little about the internal life of the monastery. The only monk who attains some closeness to Odo is John himself, who regretted that he was able to 'be associated with him for less than two complete years'.[93] For all his attachment to Odo and despite the moments of laughter with him, John does not characterize their relationship in terms of *amicitia* or even *familiaritas*. Odo brings joy to his companions, even laughter, but they are not his intimates. The closest they can come to him is to kiss his clothes in secret. Already in life, he was a spiritual relic, not a personal friend.[94]

The abbot remains a grand and isolated figure. His great friendship in the biography is not with any living monk but with a dead saint, Martin of Tours. John is especially careful to include various indications of Odo's devotion to Martin, perhaps because he wanted to show the cluniac abbot as a latter-day Martin reforming monasticism and attracting men to the cloister while at the same time able to direct the affairs of the secular church.

This is not a new desert biography. Like John of Gorze, Odo is seen as providing for his parents.[95] He made sure that they joined monasteries. John of Salerno sees him as taking the responsibility for his parents' salvation. Odo shows ascetic qualities, but his practices are not nearly as austere as those of John of Gorze. He is drawn as an attractive, talkative man, and at moments John of Salerno characterizes him as a friend for individual men. The hermit Adhegrinus spoke to Odo of their old fellowship (*sodalitas antiqua*), but the point of the story is not to describe friendship but to tell of a vision of Saint Martin the hermit had had.[96]

Such a commemorative biography of a dynamic abbot provides a magnificent witness to the revival of monastic life in the tenth century. Reforming monks appear as saints, not as friends. Being a saint in the tenth century hardly left literary room for being a friend. Whatever traces of friendship are apparent to us, they were clearly secondary for the biographers themselves. The pattern repeats itself in the earliest lives of Dunstan, archbishop of Canterbury, the great english monastic reformer.[97] John of Gorze, Dunstan of Canterbury and Odo of Cluny are all seen as men of spiritual power, isolated from their contemporaries in order to express a special relationship with God. Saints like Martin of Tours can be mediators between them and God, but in human relationships these men are elusive figures.

Although tenth century heroes are situated within monastic community, their ascetic practices, self-inflicted discipline, and reforming zeal reach beyond the normal practices of community life. To judge whether these portraits are accurate or fair is less important than to understand that these great monastic figures made this impression on their surroundings. The new fathers of monks had returned to the desert, to miracles, fatherly advice, and ascetic feats. But this time the desert could not keep out the requirements of a new society that needed such men of spiritual power in its midst.

NEW LEARNING AND A NEW INTEREST IN FRIENDSHIP

Fulbert of Chartres (c. 970 - c. 1028) provides us with some of our first indications of a revived interest in friendship. As bishop of Chartres from 1006 until his death, Fulbert at the same time trained in the liberal arts men who became celebrated (or notorious) for their learning.[98] In the letters of Fulbert and of his assistant Hildegar we not only catch hints of friendship: we also discover traces of a community of friends in ready contact with each other. This element of two-way communication marks Fulbert's correspondence decisively off from Gerbert's, even if the two men are separated by only a few years in time. Gerbert spoke of cosmic friendship but had few friends; Fulbert spent little time describing friendship but can be seen surrounded by disciples who considered themselves to be his and each other's friends.

The new learning of the eleventh-century cathedral school and not tenth-century reformed monasticism first articulated friendship as a conscious and important matter for men in the church. Because Fulbert's circle considered for the most part of secular clerics, it might seem inappropriate to include in our monastic overview his witness to the practice of friendship. But Fulbert and the abbot of Cluny, Odilo (994-1049), were on close terms. This bond points to a new willingness in monastic circles, as we shall see, to consider friendship a valuable part of the Christian life. The evidence at this stage is limited, but friendship as a literary theme is present in both the letters of Hildegar of Chartres and the biography of Odilo of Cluny. Cluny in the early eleventh century was no enemy of the new learning, nor was it unreceptive to new ways of expressing human bonds.

In the earliest letter we have from Fulbert (dated to 1004), he wrote to the abbot Abbo of Fleury that he was repaying him for his friendship 'by offering. . . my eternal fidelity'.[99] He used the word *amicitia* instead of *familiaritas*, *sodalitas*, or another expression that might suggest a bond between communities rather than individuals. So effusive is the rhetoric that one wonders how much real friendship was involved. But it is a breakthrough that *amicitia* was found fitting to describe a bond between a cathedral teacher and the abbot of the monastery where Benedict of Nursia himself was buried.

A more convincing indication of friendship in Fulbert's life comes in a letter of 1008 to a former clerk or student in which the bishop explains why he had kept himself at a distance:

> Do not be troubled, my son, or let your heart fall away from its love and trust in us, for my soul did not abandon you.[100]

The flowery language, full of scriptural reminiscences, hints at tenderness for the student who is being 'recalled to the hospitality of a friendly breast'. Fulbert asks the man to come and visit him. We have no idea who the student was or why there were problems. But Fulbert took on the role of a spiritual father who had 'followed the Lord's example in disguising his face for a little while', but now revealed his love openly. The letter provides insight into the loyalty that Fulbert inspired in his students. Fulbert's attentiveness to his pupils encouraged them to return to Chartres to see their former master and speak to him not only of intellectual matters, but also those of the heart.

This same involvement and even need for others are apparent in a letter from Fulbert to Odilo of Cluny, (abbot, 994-1049). Fulbert thanked Odilo for his generosity and affection shown in receiving him, (*ep* 49). He asked for Odilo's advice and help, but he did not specify the nature of the problem he faced. In answering, Odilo praised Fulbert for following Christ's example in inquiring about himself, but said he could not be the judge of Fulbert's soul.[101] In the politest possible way Odilo backed away from acting the role of spiritual counsellor. Fulbert may be his 'dearest brother and fellow priest', but the relationship had limits. 'You know best what you are in need of', Odilo insisted, and so the letter ends in a brush-off.[102]

This letter provides a striking indication of the limitations of any language of interpersonal relationships in the monastic world of the early eleventh century. Fulbert wanted comfort, reassurance, and advice, but Odilo would only point out that he did now know or wish to plumb the depths of Fulbert's soul. His most profound thought was plucked from Isidore of Seville: 'No one can run away from himself'.[103] This concept derives from Seneca and ultimately from Stoic philosophy. Such a reply indicates that Odilo wanted to leave the task of analysis to Fulbert. Despite his affection, Odilo maintained a distance.

In writing to another monk, probably cluniac, in 1021, Fulbert conveyed his greetings to Abbot Odilo:

> I am quite well and both eager in mind and ready in body to serve you more faithfully than anyone except that holy archangel of monks, Odilo, to whom I in no way presume to compare myself.[104]

The Cluniacs liked this description of Odilo and used it in their biography of him.[105] Fulbert, however, was unwilling to go into detail about what he owed his friend. Like Odilo himself, he avoided expressing intimacy:

> If I should try to tell what his love has done for my soul, I should seem to be attempting to express the inexpressible.[106]

Odilo is an archangel of monks and much loved (though not an *amicus*). Just as Odilo maintained that one friend cannot sit in judgment on another, so too, Fulbert cannot describe the good influence of one friend on another's inner life. Two churchmen praise and admire each other, but maintain a respectful distance.

Such expressions of friendship, subtle and bombastic at one and the same time, are difficult for us to interpret. In spite of what might be purely literary modesty, as well as a conscious sense of distance, these letters do acknowledge the existence of an interpersonal bond. Fulbert's letters to other correspondents also show devotion. To a bishop in Hungary he mentioned his love which he wanted 'to flourish in the depths' of the prelate's heart. He had never seen the man before and would probably never meet him, but was replying to a request for a copy of Priscian. Fulbert was replying graciously and warmly to a fellow teacher (*ep* 82). In commending a student to the archbishop of Rheims, Fulbert called the youth 'my dear one' (*hunc carum nostrum*), who deserved to be loved and honoured like a brother in the flesh (*frater uterinus*; *ep* 76). There is nothing here about friendship, but Fulbert's recommendation may help explain why his former pupils felt such loyalty to him. The best pupils became not only spiritual sons, but merited 'love and honour no less than' brothers in the flesh. Preference in the world based on physical kinship had to give way to a new system based on personal spiritual ties. A new network of human relationship was being laid out.

Fulbert reveals to us his involvement with other people in far more intimate ways than Gerbert did. The acceptance, admiration and recognition Gerbert sought Fulbert seems to have possessed from the time when the correspondence begins in 1004. The cleric responsible for collecting the correspondence, Hildegar, added a number of his own letters. He was a close associate with Fulbert at the school of Chartres, and from 1024 to 1026 his stand-in as treasurer of the church of Saint Hilary at Poitiers. Despite Fulbert's promises and reassurances, the bishop never managed to get there to assume his duties as treasurer.

Instead he engaged in a lively correspondence with Hildegar. For the first time since Boniface we have both sides of an exchange. We gain a first-hand impression not only of a great figure of the church but also of some of the lesser personalities around him. We can watch the way two men firmly fixed in place and time deal with each other.

In 1024, shortly after Hildegar left for Poitiers, Fulbert wrote briefly: 'Your absence often reminds me how important your presence was'.[107] The letter is full of good advice, some of it taken from Cassian's *Conferences,* one of Fulbert's favourite texts. Fulbert is concrete and detailed in his instructions, for he is dealing with a man whom he knows well and who has need of precise instructions. If we had no letters from Hildegar, it might appear that Fulbert was dealing with an efficient administrator, a right-hand man, now doing a troublesome but necessary job for him, and acting as liaison with Duke William of Aquitaine.[108]

But Hildegar himself in writing back to Fulbert uses the very language of tender relations that we see elsewhere in Fulbert's correspondence. Already a subdeacon and scholar of Chartres, he had in late 1022 or early 1023 written to a friend, Siefried, reminding him that he had been promised a horse. However practical the letter, it is not just a pastiche of clerical formulae. It is written by a friend to a friend (*amicus amico*). 'I treated you as one of my very best friends when you stayed with us here', Hildegar insisted.[109] Now it was up to Siefried to treat Hildegar well. Hildegar says that friendship is for practical purposes as well as for its own sake (*non propter se tantum sed et propter utilitatem*).[110] We return to the ciceronian considerations so familiar in Gerbert. In a second letter he appealed to the same friend in holy friendship (*per sanctam amicitiam*). Mutual usefulness now became an outright demand. Whatever Hildegar's actual feelings for Siefried, he dealt with him by using a language of friendship, its obligations and commitments in order to procure the horse he had been promised. What in Gerbert was cosmic has in Hildegar become mundane, part of an everyday world of human relationships.

With these two letters in mind we can hardly be surprised that Hildegar did not write to Fulbert in the same business-like manner that his master normally used for him. 'I am afraid I am so prone to anger that I will lose your favour', Hildegar fretted. Once again Cassian's monastic writings provide a point of reference, this time his

Conference on anger. Counting on the strength of his relationship with Fulbert, he wrote:

> I confess with a simplicity that is free of flattery that I have enjoined my inmost soul to love you above all mortals; for by the care of God's grace I have been subject to your teaching since my childhood, nor to anyone have I ever revealed so many secrets of my conscience, for though to others I have revealed some, to you I have revealed all.[111]

Such language is redolent of twelfth-century confessional literature, but this letter was written in the 1020s and sent to the same Fulbert who earlier had wanted to share his soul's secrets with the abbot of Cluny. Here we find an intimate tone foreign to Gerbert's cosmic scheme of friendship. Willingness to discuss one's interior life is one of the preconditions for friendship. This need to bare the secrets of one's heart appeared already in the monastic segments of Adalbert of Prague's hagiography. In Hildegar, however, a hint becomes a full-blown declaration of love.

Hildegar does not call Fulbert his friend. *Amicus* he reserved for Duke William of Aquitaine (*ep* 105) and the word retains a secular meaning, indicating a bond between a cleric and a layman. Hildegar's intimate letters to Fulbert are few. Usually he wrote in a chatty, familiar manner, provided the news of Poitiers, repeated a standard request that Fulbert come, and asked for news of Chartres. A typical letter often closed, however, with a clear statement of Hildegar's affection for the friends he had left behind at Chartres: 'Please convey my greeting to Sigo and Hilduinus: the one is my soul, the other half my life', he asserted, borrowing from Horace, but in one sentence summarizing the affections of a community of scholar-friends at Chartres.[112]

Hildegar's letters from after 1025 are in the same vein, with news, advice, the hope of reunion, and the assertion of close bonds. Hildegar calls Fulbert his *vitae dulcedo*, once again a phrase that can hardly be translated into a modern European language, because for us it would indicate romantic love.[113] Here it is one more term to describe what Fulbert and Hildegar share as master and pupil. Hildegar probably also wrote the letters from Duke William of Aquitaine in the collection. Here terms of friendship are used liberally. 'I am accustomed to believe my friend', the Duke writes to the bishop of Vercelli: *quia meum est amico credere* (*ep* 113). Friendship is trust. For Hildegar it is important in politics as well as in personal life.

Towards the end of 1025 or early in 1026, it became impossible for Fulbert to continue holding the office of treasurer at Saint Hilary without visiting the place. Hildegar was becoming ever more impatient with a separation that seemed almost permanent. He spoke of himself as Fulbert's *necessarius*, which might mean friend, but more implies a patron-client relationship.[114] The correspondence begins to take on the quality of that between Paulinus and Sulpicius Severus: the friend is asked when, if ever, he would come. Being without him was unbearable. Hildegar does not miss Fulbert alone. He also addresses Fulbert's secretary Sigo, *tuumque Sigonem*. It is Chartres, the cathedral, its school, and his community of scholars and friends that drew Hildegar back home.

In another letter, probably from the spring of 1026, Hildegar details the political news, pleasant or not. He asked forgiveness for his forthrightness, which was a result of 'devotion rather than impertinence'.[115] Elsewhere Hildegar mentioned Duke Willam's friendship with Fulbert.[116] Hildegar frequently returned in his letters to the subject of friendship and loyalty. In the world he shared with Fulbert, the bonds of friendship, personal, social and political, were a matter of primary concern and were worth writing about.

In the summer of 1026, Hildegar finally returned to Chartres, and Fulbert made the necessary excuses to Duke William for his neglect of Poitiers (Ep 119). Some unspecified action of Hildegar's had earlier upset Fulbert, who had reproached him for delaying his promised visit to Chartres. Once Hildegar did come, however, he stayed for good. The letters stop. Fulbert eventually resigned his post at Poitiers, and not long afterwards he died. As a source of inside information about Fulbert's political career, these letters provide little, for they are too vague about his projects. But as witnesses to the love and loyalty he could engender in a pupil like Hildegar, for whom Chartres' scholarly and episcopal community had always been home, the letters are invaluable. Hildegar reveals much more his own needs and hopes for friendship than does Fulbert who maintains a certain distance from his pupil. But if we compare a letter of Fulbert to Hildegar to a letter by Fulbert to another bishop, we realise that Fulbert maintains towards Hildegar a relaxed tone and directness missing in the other letter.[117] Fulbert does not formulate an ideal of friendship, as Gerbert did. Instead we find evidence for actual bonds of friendship, which we failed to do in Gerbert's letters. Hildegar considered these connections the most important part of his life. As he wrote to Fulbert in 1026 shortly before his return to Chartres:

> Unless you force me to, I can in no wise bear being permanently absent or away any longer from serving God's loving mother [the church of Chartres] and you; and as the heart pants after the fountains of water (Ps 41:2), so I long to be more fully instructed by your teachings, which are more precious to me than all gold and silver and even life itself.[118]

How did the great Odilo of Cluny fit into this new expression of affection among churchmen? The evidence of the letters in the Fulbert collection is inconclusive. Odilo is addressed with great warmth, but his answer was hesitant and restrained. If we turn to Odilo's other writings and look at his biography of his predecessor, Maiol (954-94), there is no evidence for any special interest in friendship.[119] Odilo follows the cluniac tradition in placing great emphasis on chastity in the individual monk rather than on bonds of love in the community. He points out that Maiol remained a virgin all his life.[120] Before his own conversion, he 'had frequent conversation and spiritual association' with monks of a nearby monastery (*frequens habebat colloquium et spiritale contubernium*). But this contact is described only as part of Maiol's preparation for monastic life. There is no doubt that *spiritalis suggestio* led Maiol to the cloister. One of the elder brethren, Hildebrann, is especially singled out for his "sweet talk and spiritual ability to convince". When Maiol finally decided to become a monk, he left 'the worldly company both of friends and of relatives'.[121] Here as so often in monastic literature, friends belong to the world and have to be abandoned when one becomes a monk.

The portrait of Maiol takes on a form that by now is almost conventional in cluniac writings. He is physically attractive. Everyone loved him, especially the emperor, and so he became lovable both to God and to men while at the same time being the 'leader of the monastic discipline' (*princeps religionis monasticae*). This is a bold claim for any abbot, but probably a fair assessment for the role Maiol had, and Odilo envisioned for himself, in the reform of monasteries. Individual friendships are missing, except with the emperor and his wife.[122] There is no room for particular friendships, inside or outside the cloister.

This conventional description of a cluniac abbot by Odilo is repeated a half century later when Odilo himself is portrayed (after 1049) by the monk Jotsald. He draws on standardized cluniac virtues for Odilo. He was impressive in appearance, graceful in body (the sign of an aristocrat), attractive to kings and emperors.[123] Jotsald incorporates phrases about unity of soul and body from the Acts of the Apostles (4:32) but uses them to describe not the harmony within monastic community but the concord Odilo reached with princes.[124] He himself is a spiritual prince, lifted above mundane concerns.

All this is what one might expect in the life of such a powerful churchman. Could there be room in so vast a career for the theme of friendship? Odilo's biography does in fact include descriptions of his friendships. A bishop named Sancius, for example:

> . . .was so joined to him in friendship (*amicitiis*) and showered him with such gifts that he came to Odilo from afar and decided to be made a monk by him.[125]

So attached was Odilo to this bishop that he arranged that after his own death two brothers of Cluny should visit in his monastery, give him relics of Odilo's clothes and describe how his life had ended, and comfort him because of his old friendship (*antiquam amicitiam*).

Another friend was Fulbert of Chartres, Odilo's *praecordialis amicus*.[126] The terms *amicus* and *amicitia* which were used so sparingly in tenth-century monastic accounts are now acceptable not only to characterize relationships among men in the world but also for bonds between abbots and churchmen. Tenth-century spiritual men were admired for being alone and apart. A century later they are described as having friends and companions. The hagiographical pattern had changed, and behind a literary alteration lies a changed attitude towards friendship.

We see Odilo as using his travels as abbot of Cluny to forge a network of friends. Jotsald writes of a very good friend (*familiarissimus*) to whom Odilo was so closely joined that when Odilo realized he was dying he went to Rome to see the friend.[127] This man, Lawrence, archbishop of Amalfi, illustrates Cluny's attractiveness to great men in the church. These include the popes, who are to have considered Odilo as a 'second Solomon' and both 'friend and father'.[128] These friendships with churchmen in high places are meant to reflect credit on Odilo, but this new language of human relationships in hagiography introduces individual friendships instead of merely claiming that everyone loved and admired the abbot.

In describing Odilo's relationship to the community at Cluny, Jotsald did not single out any of the monks as recipients of Odilo's special love. Unity remained the highest goal. The monastic prince and father could permit himself to be a friend only when he was dealing with men outside his own monastery. Some of Odilo's friendships were monastic, however, as with his fellow reformer, William of Dijon. The two became inseparable friends.[129]

William of Dijon and Odilo are said to have shared 'the same quality of affection' for the humanity of Christ, an early instance of the personal affection for Christ as a beloved friend that was to find its fullest expression in the twelfth century. Odilo, who in Jotsald's first chapters seems to be yet one more conventionally great abbot of Cluny, turns out to have both an inner spiritual life and an interest in personal friendships. The abbot who as biographer revealed little about his predecessor's friendships turns out himself to have been remembered in his own biography as a friend. William of Dijon, who in the *Life* composed by the cluniac historian Ralph Glaber was described as a man of action, is portrayed in Jotsald as someone who shared himself spiritually with a friend.[130]

Why this change of emphasis in cluniac hagiographical literature? The various cluniac practices which were collected into the constitutions compiled after 1050 left little room for friendship at Cluny or its associated houses. The youths of the monastery were never allowed to be alone with each other or with their master. A system of guardianship made sure that idle conversations could not take place, especially at night when monks went out to the latrines.[131] The Eastern fear of homosexuality is not specified. Youths were to be guarded not to avert intimacy but in order to maintain the collective discipline of monastic life: the same spirit that is in the Rule of Saint Benedict itself. The monks were given periods in the day when they could converse with each other about spiritual matters or important practical affairs.[132] The long-standing myth that Cluny was totally dominated by the liturgy has long since been challenged.[133] It is clear that not all the monks were in choir all the time, and the routine of a monastic day with its varied activities left time for the cultivation of friendships. In Cluny's first century we hear almost nothing of such relationships, while in the life of Odilo they rise just above the surface. The change in the literary treatment of friendship indicates that attitudes also were changing. *Familiaritas*, *sodalitas*, and *contubernium* were giving way to an acceptance of *amicitia* without an exclusively pagan, classical or lay resonance to the word.

Did the circle of Fulbert at Chartres in the early eleventh century provide the impulse which after 1050 enabled the biographer of Odilo at Cluny to portray friendship as a desirable bond among holy men in the church? I find no immediate link, aside from the fact that Fulbert and Odilo wrote to each other, and that Jotsald's account points to an awareness at Cluny that the two men were close. Jotsald may in fact have made more out of their relationship than it really deserved. But here, as so often, an attitude is just as important as a concrete historical fact. Jotsald's interest in the Fulbert-Odilo friendship shows that the literary expression of friendship, so obvious at Chartres-Poitiers was not limited to the secular church. It spilled over into the monastic world when Jotsald claimed Fulbert was Odilo's dearest friend (*praecordialis amicus*). This phrase, which to us might have a sentimental ring, was for Jotsald an indication of strength and of sanctity. Good men sought out each other, admired and helped each other, and so they became each other's friends.

THE TRANSITION IN BAVARIA: FROUMUND OF TEGERNSEE

Despite many signs of a new interest in friendship at Cluny after the middle of the eleventh century, the very lack of personal letters and poems in the cluniac literature makes it impossible to detect individual friendships within the cloister. For these we need a monastic correspondence equivalent to that of Fulbert and his former pupils. This exists in a collection from the bavarian monastery of Tegernsee, the first part of which contains the letters and poems of the monastic teacher Froumund from 982-1012, while the second part contains materials from the following decades, until about 1050.[134] Here the words *amicus* and *amicitia* are still used mainly for bonds between the monastery and churchmen or laymen who could provide material advantages for the monks.[135] But the content of letters sent from one abbot to another (and almost certainly written by Froumund in his own abbot's name) indicates bonds of friendship were accepted as normal and desirable in monastic life. When Abbot Gozpert (982-1001) addressed Abbot Ramwold of Saint Emmeram in Regensburg, for example, he spoke of his thirst for the abbot and the monastery which he had left. 'We desire to be refreshed for a while by the most pleasant conversation of the brethren.'[136]

Froumund delighted in teaching young boys in the monastery, and one of his longest and most ambitious poems concerns his longing for his pupils when he was away from Tegernsee.[137] His interest was not always purely paedagogical. In a striking poem to an otherwise unknown youth called Pabo, whom Froumund had met at the celebration of Candlemas, his language has a passionate intensity that recalls Alcuin's poetry for men whom he loved:

> Hail, brother ever sweet to me in love
> Sweeter you are to me than the taste of honey
>   in my mouth
> The liquid knows not how to love, but love
>   grows sweet and into the heart
> It enters and joins in its pact to the other's breast[138]

Because we have only a few such lines from Froumund's pen, it would be foolish to try to characterize the kind of love he is describing here. We need only point out that he is reviving terms of devotion and loyalty in a form we have not seen since the Carolingians. No longer do we have the abstract philosophical statements of a Gerbert: here are flesh and blood and a network of friendship whose members are impossible to determine, but they are there: 'Do not let yourself think that my care for you has grown lax, for there still burns in me towards you an unquenchable flame of charity, which your fervent love lit in my heart'. The phrases are from a letter whose sender and recipient are not named, but it was almost certainly written by Froumund, who described how he looked on his unnamed correspondent's 'face with the eye of love'.[139]

At times Froumund reverted to traditional language of bonds among monks, the *germanitas* that linked one community to another (*ep* 40), and we can see that often a declaration of love could mean an expression of the bond between a community and an individual more than between two persons. This is the case when Abbot Gozpert and the other brethren of Tegernsee write to a 'beloved son' who apparently once had been a pupil at Tegernsee but later had done well in the world. The abbot is merely interested in getting some contribution from the man by reminding him of his duties to his *alma mater*. Thus when he reminded him of his 'former friendship' (*priorisque amicitie*), he meant a collective rather than an individual bond (*ep* 46).

This collection of letters and poems is especially valuable because it contains so many different elements reflecting monastic life and sentiment: there are descriptions of practical matters for the monastery as well as accounts of how a tireless teacher tried to get his pupils to behave. A poem by Froumund to his pupil Ellinger (who would twice hold the office of abbot at Tegernsee) excoriates the youth for his laziness and tries to provoke him into some kind of reaction. Froumund charms and threatens at the same time, promising that Ellinger will feel better about himself if he becomes productive and himself starts writing poetry.[140] At no point does the teacher admit any special love or friendship with Ellinger, but there are commitment and even intensity existing behind the playful surface of the poem.

The collection has probably received no attention from historians of monastic friendship because most of its indications of friendship or love within the cloister do lie beneath the surface of the text. Only at moments does Froumund allow himself to state the nature of his bond with his correspondent. To a friend who had entered the monastic life, apparently at Cluny, Froumund promised continued devotion: 'Through all regions we have sought you in sorrow', he insists, 'But now we rejoice greatly because we hear that you have found rest in the quiet of a monastery'. Any good monk would rejoice in another's entrance into the monastic life. But in the midst of pious considerations Froumund speaks of his own situation:

> What then? Even if I, unworthy man, have been ordained a priest I have not forgotten you: from now on, whenever I think of myself or my affairs, I shall never and in no place forget you.[141]

Amicus is never used, but it would be absurd to deny that the relationship described between the two monks was one of friendship. Froumund wanted to assure the man that even though his own state has been changed through his ordination, he had not changed in his devotion to the man, and even though the friend has made himself less accessible by going into a monastery that apparently was far away from Froumund, the latter would not forget him. Froumund would in fact make every effort to visit him. Monastic stability or not, monks of the early eleventh century like Froumund intended to get around to see their friends!

One of Froumund's friends we know by name, Reginbald of Saint Emmeram. The two seemed to share intellectual interests, and Froumund wrote to Reginbald assuring him of his love and then in the next sentence asking him to send along a book he needed (as *ep* 79). The second part of the Tegernsee collection allows us to see some of the responses 'the most beloved brother Froumund' received from Reginbald (*epp* 100-102). These letters are invaluable because they allow us to conclude that Froumund was not alone in using a language of love and friendship. He may have been responsible for the cultivation of such a style at Tegernsee, but he got a similar response from Saint Emmeram. As Reginbald wrote to him: 'Even if the exterior man in me is unable to see you because of the great distance separating us, still the interior part of myself recalls you in the contemplation of your intimate love'.[142] In this formula Reginbald reminds us of the expressions typical in Jerome's letters, which may have been the source of inspiration.

Froumund apparently won loyalty from the pupils who became his friends. The same Ellinger whom Froumund once had cajoled and threatened one day wrote to him *intimo affectu cordis* when he had learned that his master had become a priest. Ellinger assured him that 'my love for you will always burn deep in my heart and will always rejoice in your success'.[143] The letter conveys congratulations, but also a penitential tone and a request for forgiveness. Here it is impossible to be precise about the relationship of Froumund with given individuals. But the collection as a whole points to a monastic milieu where the language and probably also the practice of friendship had gained a certain prominence.

The editor of this surprising volume compared Froumund's admonition to his pupil Ellinger to one of Notker's poems to his Salomo when he left Saint Gall.[144] In both cases poetic statements convey the pain of the teacher whose pupil refused to do what he considered best. Personal affection for the attractive youth is mingled with an awareness that any teacher-pupil relationship requires some authority and some distance. But if Froumund is expressing himself in a way close to that of Notker, could it be that there is no break at all between the end of the ninth century and the early eleventh century in terms of the practice of monastic friendship? Has our eclipse of monastic friendship been more apparent than real?

More likely monastic friendships did continue throughout the tenth century, even though they are not visible to us. But the historian looking not for universalisms about friendship but for evidence of change in human modes of expression must note that Notker had no immediate followers and that almost a century passed before monks again penned words about devotion, loyalty and love. This revived language of friendship appeared towards the end of the ottonian cultural revival, and in a monastery and a part of Europe intimately involved with the ottonian reforms.

Between Saint Gall and Tegernsee, there is a chronological gap. In between is a new ascetic movement which initially showed no interest for friendship. However familiar the new language of friendship is when it appears at Tegernsee, this monastery and its mode of expression are no throwback to the late ninth century. Because of Froumund, we can date to the end of the tenth century a revival and renewal in the monastic expression of friendship. Tegernsee is not an isolated phenomenon, for, as we shall see in the next chapter, the bond of the monastery with Saint Emmeram provides a continuing manifestation of monastic friendship.

Despite the importance of the Tegernsee collection of letters and poems, it lacks one central element that the cluniac and chartrian materials do contain. At Tegernsee Froumund wrote of his love and devotion to his friends, but he seldom called them friends. The language of human bonds is still traditional, with *amici* usually being looked upon as those in the lay life who served the monks' interests. In this respect Froumund was cautious and conservative in a way that Hildegar chose not to be.

In these pages we have seen how the tenth century, usually described in terms of collapse or barest survival of christian life and culture, actually produced several monastic writers of interest. Friendship maintained a limited appeal in Notker the Stammerer's circle at Saint Gall, where carolingian ways of expressing friendship persisted. In John of Gorze and the first abbots of Cluny in the mid-tenth century, friendship exercises less apparent attraction. Later in the century, Gerbert of Aurillac and Adalbert of Prague revived the ideal, but with only a vague concern for monastic forms of friendship. After the death of Odilo of Cluny, monastic friendship becomes visible.

The renewal of a language of friendship within the monastic context came first at Tegernsee in Bavaria and shortly afterwards at Chartres with Fulbert and his pupil. It may be only accidental that these two places seem so significant in this process; letters from here have come down to us instead of someone else's collection. But between Tegernsee and Saint Emmeram is an indisputable link, which was to become important in the writings of Otloh of Saint Emmeram, and between Fulbert of Chartres and Odilo of Cluny, the great master of students and the archangel of monks. These two central figures hesitated to use the language of friendship, but their disciples were less reserved. Both Jotsald of Cluny and Hildegar of Chartres replaced monastic *familiaritas* with *amicitia*. The ideal of personal friendships became just as attractive as the collective friendship bringing harmony to a community apparent in the carolingian hymn to charity.

Why do men alter their ways of speaking to each other and about each other? How does the rather bloodless ideal of cosmic friendship in Gerbert manage to find form and life in Froumund's poems or in

Hildegar's letters? We could mention stronger links within international society, greater mobility, and respect for learning and stylistic skill. But we could also argue that this slow opening to new forms of friendship required a reinterpretation of the christian gospel, one that saw human relations as just as important as ascetic feats. When Odilo started thinking about Christ's humanity, perhaps he also began to consider the bonds of love among human beings. Friendship, inside and outside the cloister, could begin to take its place as a means of expressing and realizing human love in order to attain the love of God.

CHAPTER FIVE

REFORM AND RENEWAL: NEW IMPULSES TOWARDS FRIENDSHIP c. 1050-1120

THE LITERATURE OF FRIENDSHIP increased significantly in the last half of the eleventh and the first decades of the twelfth century. Letter collections, rare in the period 850-1050, became common. Hagiographies began to deal in detail with closeness among human beings. Even theoretical works about monastic discipline began to mention friendship.

This change by no means limited itself to the monastic world. Wherever we find literary men, we usually also discover signs of friendship. This new opening to the practice and ideal of friendship did not come abruptly after 1050. From the end of the tenth to the end of the eleventh century, friendship as a literary form grew up in a slow and often obscure manner. Both before and after 1050, many transitional writers expressed interest in friendship while at the same time holding back from embracing the ideal wholeheartedly. Sometimes the earlier sources reveal more than later ones. The letter collection of Froumund of Tegernsee from the early eleventh century has much more to say about friendship than do the letters of Peter Damian from the years after 1050.

Peter Damian nevertheless did find room for friendship in his life and writings. The excitement of reforming the church and sweeping away moral abuses still allowed for the sweetness of friendship. Peter made friendship sound so natural and inevitable that it is easy to forget how different a view of the matter he might have had. His energetic pursuit of monastic reform could have led Peter Damian to require the severance of human bonds for the sake of ascetic withdrawal. But Peter was an optimist about human and social renewal. The retreat from all passions, so important in the literature of desert asceticism, never came to prominence in the West. By the eleventh century the models for christian living in community were Augustine and Ambrose, not Pachomius or Basil. Saint Anthony the Great was admired as a hero of the desert, and the monks of the West vied to fight devils as he had done. But they did so, not in isolation, but in community.[1] It was in community that they sought out friends to help them on their way to heaven.

LITERARY AND SOCIAL IMPULSES: CHANGES AND CONTRASTS

Before we deal with the evidence provided by individual monks and their lives, we should look at the literary development of the concept of friendship. Here the various *Lives* of the tenth-century english monastic reformer, Dunstan of Canterbury (909-88), shed light on the way the ideal of friendship was described both before and during our period.[2] In one of the earliest accounts, from about the year 1000, a monk of Glastonbury, Wulfred, is said to have appeared after his own death to Dunstan. In describing this vision, the author mentions in passing that Wulfred had once been close to Dunstan, having been in life his loving companion: *familiaris amator*.[3] The language has both classical and monastic overtones. *Amator*, borrowed from a ciceronian vocabulary, indicates a friend (*Atticus* 1:20), while *familiaris* implies the group friendship of monastic life. A modern translator would be content with the term 'friend', but this would not quite capture the nuance. The two did not enjoy a simple friendship. Their bond included the collectivity of the monastic community.

In the third *Life* of Dunstan, written by Osbern, precentor of Christchurch, Canterbury, either while Lanfranc was archbishop of Canterbury (1070-1089) or shortly afterwards, nothing new is said about Dunstan's vision of Wulfred. The earlier statement about love is expanded to emphasize that this relationship had begun when Dunstan and Wulfred were children. The new formulation individualizes the bond and makes their friendship unmistakable: 'Whom he as a boy had known. . . and had always loved in holy closeness' (*sancta familiaritate*).[4] Here we are just a step away from the ideal of spiritual friendship, for *sancta familiaritas* could be translated in this way, even though the term does not have the same sense of individual friendship that *amicitia* would convey.

A few years later Anselm's biographer, Eadmer of Canterbury, recast the *Life* of Saint Dunstan and described the bond with Wulfred in terms of the 'holy fervour of holy love'(*sancto sancti amoris fervore*).[5] Eadmer is something of a reactionary here. He kept closer to the vague language of love found in the early eleventh-century biography than to Osbern's clear statement about friendship. Eadmer mentioned spiritual love without being specific. Like his master Anselm, he was fond of juxtaposing apt expressions and balancing phrases, while he marked his distance from Osbern by not using *familiaritas*.

The development of a language of friendship culminates in the first decades of the twelfth century with William of Malmesbury, who was more specific about the relationship between Dunstan and Wulfred: 'His name was Wulfred, a deacon, a youth, and joined to Dunstan since boyhood in holy friendship'. (*Is erat Wilfredus nomine, diaconus ordine, adolescens aetate, Dunstano jam inde a pueritia* **sancta** *devinctus* **amicitia**.)[6] *Familiaritas* has disappeared. There is no longer any ambiguity about whether the relationship is based on membership in a religious community or on an individual's own special love. William of Malmesbury chose *amicitia*, but in order to make clear that he did not mean a classical and purely secular form of friendship, he added *sancta*.

The change from *familiaris amator* to *sancta familiaritas* and *sanctus amor* to *sancta amicitia* might seem at first only variations on a theme. But the expressions used to characterize the bond between Wulfred and Dunstan reflect changing views of friendship among holy men from the early eleventh century to the early twelfth. Dunstan's various biographers apparently had no new evidence about the relationship. They refashioned their descriptions of Wulfred and Dunstan according to their own view of how a saint relates to other men in the process of his salvation. Holy friendship is much more specific and individualized than holy love. William of Malmesbury saw Dunstan as a man who cultivated spiritual friendship.

Each age has its own heroes and remoulds the heroes of the past according to its own needs and interests. The solitary Dunstan of the year 1000 became the spiritual friend of the twelfth century. In this literary transformation we see how monastic life began to deal openly with the phenomenon of individual friendships among members of the community.

Dunstan's first biographers may have shied away from describing his bond with Wulfred in terms of pure friendship because this relationship had secular overtones. Such an association can be seen in a letter dated to 961 from a count of Flanders to Dunstan. What starts as a selfless declaration of friendship ends as a request that Dunstan secure the english king's friendship with the count. You know, he wrote;

> . . . how much I want to be your friend in every way...but I ask you to see to it that the same kinds of friendship exist between me and your lord the king as our predecessors once had when they were allied to each other.[7]

Here the bond of friendship ensures a useful alliance. Dunstan was asked to secure it not because he was a saintly man but because he had power at court. Just as we saw earlier in the letters of Gerbert of Aurillac, friendship is used as another way of expressing political alliance. There is nothing underhanded about this transaction, but it reduces friendship to a bond with only a very limited religious dimension. Friendship remains at best a secular ideal among men who need each other's help and influence and not a christian ideal that enhances the quality and content of the spiritual life. It may have been for Gerbert the glue that holds the universe together, but in this form it did not bring men to salvation.

How could such a one-dimensional view of friendship give way to the rich spectrum of expression that becomes apparent by the early twelfth century? First of all, the number of men who were able to express themselves in terms of friendship had to increase. Such a change required the appearance of new centres of learning and a curriculum that encouraged stylistic excellence. This is precisely what happened in monastic and cathedral schools from the end of the tenth century onwards. After a lull of a century, carolingian plans for cathedral schools began to be realized, while at the same time monasteries took a more active educational role.[8]

Youths who attended such schools, whether monastic or secular, received a basic training in latin grammar. After they had learned simple latin phrases, such as those taken from the *Disticha Catonis*, they might be encouraged to practice writing letters.[9] The *ars dictaminis* was once thought to have been invented at Monte Cassino in the 1070s, but recent research shows that the origin of letter-writing as an art cannot be limited to any one centre. The eleventh century brought a revival in schools and learning that encouraged letters.[10] From the post-carolingian letter collections at which we already have looked—those of Ratherius of Verona, Gerbert of Aurillac, and Froumund of Tegernsee—it should be apparent that such writers were well-trained and practiced in their art. Even in the tenth century, then, masters of schools must have had a technique for training the few pupils they had.

In the eleventh century the number of pupils increased drastically, especially after about 1050, and school training became more formalized. More textbooks and exercise books become visible to us. By the twelfth century Bologna seems to have become a centre for the *ars dictaminis*, a good foundation for more advanced legal training. The art of letter-writing grew up in a changing society that required men able to express themselves in precise terms so that they could enter the exacting fields of law or theology, or so that they could draw up deeds and charters at courts or churches.

Some of the models used in the new primers of letter-writing might make it seem as though communications were intended mainly for the purpose of getting money from patrons, relatives, or old friends.[11] One variation after another is suggested, and letter-writing meant the ability to put together a jigsaw puzzle, with phrases that are pre-cast, ready and waiting for the player. In reality medieval letter collections contain elements far more subtle and varied than the manuals would lead us to believe. The collections that have survived seldom betray the immature and literarily dependent schoolboy,[12] but almost always provide evidence of some independence of mind. The five elements of the classic medieval letter (*salutatio* or greeting, *captatio benevolentiae* or expression of goodwill, *narratio* or description, *petitio* or request and *conclusio*)—all these can usually be found but are not in themselves important for our analysis.[13] More central to our purpose is the way in which various literary centres in the eleventh century dealt with the concept of friendship in new contexts. The variety is almost infinite, and since only a fraction of the letters written during this period has survived, we get only a sample of the independence of this literary form. Letters of friendship in this period express in renewed ways human feelings and bonds among persons.[14]

Although the following pages will take us away from purely monastic friendship, the secular church and its new learning form an essential point of departure for subsequent monastic developments. In the eleventh century it is impossible to segregate the monastic from the cathedral school. Already in the case of Gerbert of Aurillac, we saw how the same man started at one type of school and ended up at the other. A man who had been well-trained by a cathedral master might end up as a monk teaching grammar, including *dictamen*. Monastic stability seems to have been more an ideal than a reality during these years, as in the career of Otloh of Saint Emmeram (c. 1010-1070), who spent his life at several different german monasteries.[15] Otloh was educated at the great monastic centre of Tegernsee in Bavaria, but his family did not intend him to become a monk there. After this early training he spent some time at home. Only then did he have to make up his mind about his vocation. Had it not been for rivalries and jealousies with the local cathedral clergy, Otloh indicates he might have never returned to Tegernsee. We will return later to Otloh's life and works, but first we must look at contemporary letter collections.

The earliest group of letters from a cathedral school comes from Worms.[16] It contains materials mostly from the second quarter of the eleventh century and shows how developments at the school of Chartres under Fulbert soon were paralleled in Germany. By no means all of the letters deal with friendship. Some are devoted entirely to church business. A number of them, however, reflect the educational activities of Wolzo, the master of the cathedral school under Bishop Azecho (1025-44).

In one of the letters with much material about friendship, a pupil complains that Wolzo had listened to the accusations of the writer's enemy. On the text of a passage from Ecclesiasticus (6:8) about the fair-weather friend who will 'not persist in the day of tribulation', the young man insisted:

> You have not maintained in wholeness the friendship between us which was established rightly on a foundation, because you have listened to my enemy...and this not only: in many ways you have confirmed everything that he said.[17]

Because of Wolzo's sympathy towards the accuser, the clerics of the church (at Worms?) had turned against the letter-writer, who repeated his charge more emotionally: 'O God, God, wherever I look, whom shall I find as a faithful friend to me?'[18] Wolzo might retort that he did not act against the pupil, but for the sake of the youth. But was this really necessary? Did it really suit Wolzo to see that the writer was punished in such a drastic manner? The language is strong, verging on polemic. The biblical concept of the faithful friend gives way to Cicero's in *De amicitia:* 'Thus far I have loved you because of virtue, because of what Tullius teaches, that we also love those whom we have never seen.'[19] But now, he adds, he shall love his teacher only because of fear. The implication that virtue now has disappeared and only fear remains is not a declaration of enmity, but an assertion that friendship, once possible between pupil and master, had been ruined by the accuser.

This passionate letter is followed by another from the same correspondent, who now uses both Cicero and the Gospel of Saint John to offer Wolzo reconciliation and renewed friendship. He says he had written not so long ago in anger, but this should now be forgotten. He recalls the words of Jesus recorded by John 'while reclining on his breast and drawing forth the sweetness of nectar from his love'.[20] This is the earliest letter I have found in which a writer appeals to the apostle John's physical closeness to Christ at the Last Supper as an image of love and friendship. Passages follow from Cicero on how the good find each other in friendship and how all human beings need its gift. After these questions from the *De amicitia*, the writer adds that he could call on even more witnesses to friendship such as Solomon, Paul, the lives of the saints as well as sayings of the pagans.[21] But the point is that love must persist. If it is changeable, then it is the love of children, always ready to turn into anger, never stable. The letter ends in a plea for friendship both as concept and reality for writer and his correspondent.

This is a letter of reconciliation in which the writer insists on mutual love without fear. The overtures are balanced so perfectly against the outrage of the first letter that one wonders whether the two might be the fruit of a school exercise, perhaps by the master Wolzo himself. In the first he would have shown his students how they could show anger against a friend who had let them down; while the second letter provided the formulae, both christian and pagan, for a reestablishment of friendship.

It is impossible to determine whether such products are 'real letters'. The modern editor of the collection argues that the letters were indeed sent.[22] For our purposes, what matters is that the writer freely draws on both pagan and christian conceptions of friendship without contrasting or distinguishing the two. Friendship was seen as a natural and essential human impulse, something so important that it merited a central place in a letter. These letters are able to balance a very personal message with a general statement on the meaning of friendship. Whether sent or not, the letters are more than a dry grammatical exercise. They provide a view of how human relationships function within the context of christian society. The writer expressed, and encouraged others to express, anger at being accused behind his back, and hope that in spite of the breach, new understanding would be possible. Friendship and letter-writing belong together in the cathedral schools of the eleventh century.

In the seven or eight other letters that deal with friendship in the Worms collection, we find further instances in which Cicero and the Bible are combined to provide a synthesis of views on the meaning and content of friendship (as *ep* 11). Friends are asked for help or favours.

The master of the cathedral school is requested to take good care of a youth encharged to him (*ep* 19). A recipient is asked to exert influence so the letter-writer can obtain an office (*ep* 20). We even find the scholars of Mainz declaring *amicitia* to their colleagues at Worms (*ep* 26). Here we detect an older type of friendship, one we found in Gerbert and in earlier monastic forms, a collective bond between two communities having little individual content.

In the Worms collection friendship is taken for granted as a way of life without any distinction between christian and pagan friendship. The letter writers make friendship into an ideal that can fit into any kind of collective way of life. There even is a striking letter of friendship from the Bishop of Worms to an apparently powerful superior of a woman's monastery in which he defends spiritual love among men and women and then asks for a favour that only she can grant because of her political influence.[23]

Letters from the school of Hildesheim found in the so-called Hanoverian Collection belong for the most part to the third quarter of the eleventh century. While the Worms collection deals mostly with the school's external relations, the Hildesheim letters have more to say about the problems and interests of the school's pupils.[24] The letters of friendship do not refer so often to specifically christian statements on love. The writings of Cicero appear to be almost the sole inspiration for the language of friendship here. This difference in emphasis from Worms (when christian and pagan language are mixed), may reflect the intellectual orientation of the master, the saxon Bernhard who wrote many of the letters in the collection and lived at Hildesheim from 1076 to 1085.[25] Appropriately enough, he died as a monk in 1088, another case illustrating the short distance between the cathedral school and the traditional monastery in eleventh-century learning and life.

In the Hildesheim letters, old political friendships are combined with new spiritual bonds. A letter from Henry IV to Bishop Hezilo (1054-79) asked that a political ally be loosed from the bond of excommunication. Henry is brief: 'the friend has few words, for in showing good will he proves himself to the friend'.[26] A saxon prince asserted to the same bishop that nothing is more joyful in this life than the friendship of good men. The words have the ring of Cicero, but they are not a direct quotation: 'Friendship is always to be cultivated, always to be renewed': *amicitia semper est colenda, semper est innovanda* (*ep* 34). The benefits of friendship are enumerated. It joins those who are separated, and it provides a pledge of love through letters giving expression to the bond.

These formulae of good will, or *captatio benevolentiae* according to the requirements of *dictamen*, are followed by the news that the nobleman's wife had given birth to a son. This *narratio*, or fresh news, gives way to what appears to be the purpose of the letter, a request (*petitio*) for unity in the fight of the church against the simoniacs. 'Don't hesitate to defend the portion of Saint Peter', the nobleman concludes in a rousing cry to the bishop of Hildesheim.

The letter has been dated to the years 1076-79, the outbreak of the Investiture Controversy under Pope Gregory VII. It shows vitality, optimism and confidence, as well as somewhat naive and facile sentiments. Again it is not important to determine whether the nobleman himself wrote the letter or even if he ever meant it to be sent. Friendship was being used as the foundation for the message of the letter, the deliverance of the church from the hands of the simoniacs. The mandate of reform and the ideal of friendship are combined in a natural, almost inevitable, manner.

Because the letter deals with politics, it is fairly unusual in the collection. Most of the time we are closer to education than to politics in the scholarly milieu of Hildesheim. An older student in France wrote to a younger one, apparently at Hildesheim. He thanked the Hildesheim scholar for a letter sent at Easter and said that this made the occasion a double feast for him. His flowery language is literarily pretentious in a way the nobleman's letter was not:

> For in leaving you I was drawn as it were as a captive in my mind into the grave and destructive darkness of Egypt and since I could find out nothing about what happened to you, even though I often made many enquiries, I was wandering through the difficulties of the evil and hostile desert and was in different states of mind.[27]

The imagery of the desert is enhanced by the assertion that the arrival of the friend's letter had brought its recipient into the promised land. In semi-ecstatic language, almost nothing is spared to indicate the importance of the bond of friendship: 'If sometime you would make me joyful in your bodily presence, I would embrace you, speak with you and exult in joy, joyful in exulting. . .'[28] The friend laments the present separation and in language reminiscent of Cicero, asks how much longer this pain must last: 'For how long am I to be cut off from you my lord and most beloved?' He wants one thing only, to be refreshed by the friend's 'most pleasing and sweet taste'.

As a probably young student absorbed in composing literarily ambitious letters, the writer put few restraints on himself. How much genuine feeling lay behind his utterances? It is impossible to tell for certain, but in the same decades, similarly intense declarations of love are to be found, as we shall see, in the letters of Saint Anselm at the monastery of Bec. This type of letter writing cannot be dismissed, merely because of its style as a reflection of an immature personality. Such letters express the attachment of a new seriousness to explicit statements of friendship in the scholar's life. It was not enough to mouth a few phrases from Cicero and then get on with the self-serving business of the letter, as at Worms. At Hildesheim the milieu of the school encouraged passionate friendships, or at least the *language* of passionate friendships.

The sincerity of this super-charged letter is made more likely by the writer's eagerness to give practical help to his friend. He informs him that he is doing everything possible among 'Franks, Normans and Germans' to recommend the recipient's intellectual abilities. 'Even if I have no talent myself', he says, 'I am doing everything in my power to see that you advance to some high office' (*ad quodlibet culmen gradiaris honorum*, *ep* 36). Closely associated with the loyalty of friendship is a conviction that ability will be rewarded. In such a brazen letter we get a hint of a job market for scholars, a raw world with great opportunities through a network of clerics dedicated to furthering their own and each other's interests.[29] This all begins, not surprisingly, with school friendships. An 'old boy' system becomes just visible here because the number of centres for education had greatly increased, and more source material survives to provide documentation for such a system. Its ideology was made explicit through the expression of friendship.

To give good advice was part of the expression of friendship. The older scholar warned the younger one that he was to stay away from a certain Heribert. Not only did this Heribert fail to apply himself to his studies while at Beauvais: he also blocked others in their careers because of his 'petulance and insanity'. Anyone who tries to study under him, the writer warns, will gain more shame than honour. The diatribe against Heribert ends with a quotation from Vergil, and an awkward poem describing the correspondent's devotion. He asked to receive a letter in return by Pentecost: 'These things are for you alone', he closes. 'Think seriously about what has been said.' Was the writer signaling that the letter was not intended as a general statement containing warning and advice which could have been sent to anyone? The writer indicates he was very much involved in his friend's career and in his feelings for him. The letter is so rich in content that it might be interpreted in many ways, but I think it is a letter of friendship from one scholar committed to another.

Another letter dealing with friendship (*ep* 37) uses at length Cicero's teaching in order to remedy a conflict between two friends. The writer purports to be a pupil at Hildesheim in the time of Bishop Hezilo (1054-79), but there is always the possibility that the letter was 'ghosted' by the teacher Bernhard: 'I am amazed that you have called me your one friend', the letter opens, 'for in reality you have treated me quite badly'. The false friend had abandoned the letter-writer, and his kind words now seem to be 'the flattery of your mouth, not of your heart'.[30]

The friend's great closeness had ended all too abruptly. Everyone else had known that the friend was going to leave the area, but the writer had not been told. 'Truly I thought you were a man, not a stone, a faithful friend and not some Burgundian', he complains, levelling his lowest blow, no doubt!

After all these charges, the writer borrows some material from Cicero: his definition of friendship, the assertion of how sweet life together can be for friends, and his conviction that friendship makes men of different virtue and rank each other's equals. In his letter passion is kept under much tighter control than the one we examined previously, but beneath the surface there is nearly the same intensity. The requirements of friendship are summed up in the desire to be with the friend, the attempt to reach some kind of understanding with him, and the fear that he will not be loyal.

Cicero as so often provided the necessary formulae for maintaining friendship that would last. It is a secular ideal, even though the writer at one point refers to Saint Paul: 'But as the apostle writes to the Galatians [4:20], I could wish to be present with you now to change my tone, for I am perplexed about you'. The quotation has no religious overtones in this context but is particularly apt for the writer's situation. He needs the presence of the friend. Only in direct contact could he express himself. The writer picked an apt phrase from the New Testament, and yet chose exclusively pagan texts to describe the content of friendship and the best way of living. A formalized declaration of friendship between the two men seems to have existed at some point, a pact that now had been broken. The writer indicates his own uncertainty at how to end the letter. He did not know whether or not to add kind words when the friend has been so unfaithful to him, but he did not want to close in anger. The matter was left undecided. Now it was up to the friend to reply.

Like today's greeting-cards-for-every-occasion, the Hildesheim letters contain messages for every possible situation. The variety of the contents suggests that certain types of letters were included because of literary quality, the prestige of the correspondent, or the various subjects they treated.[31] Problems of human relations and friendships / enmities were included as a legitimate and worthwhile subject matter. In this selection no attempt was made to limit the subject of friendship to purely theoretical discourses. Concrete problems emerged: recommending each other for good jobs, misunderstanding intentions and news of the friend heard at second hand.

One of the most striking letters in the Hildesheim group was probably composed by a pupil there and sent to another student (*ep* 48). The writer says he remembers having been called 'not only your beloved, but rather your most beloved' (*non tantum dilectum, sed potius dilectissimum*). 'You promised to me not what you possessed but your very self' (*non tua sed te mihi obligasse*). The writer recalls the happiness that the two once had together and which he wanted to share again.

The language of exclusivity in love might sound sentimental in translation, but behind it is a firm belief in the value of friendship. The two men had known each other since boyhood. They had studied together, and now one of them had gone off on his own. For years he had been saying he would go to Saxony to be a soldier, but now the friend had decided to return to his studies. If this is true, the letter-writer insists, then the two of them could be together again. The friend should return to his companion 'so that the love which grew up among us so well when we still were small now be made more solid through a more mature strength in accordance with our ability'.[32]

At this point a concrete request is formulated. The youth's former master had finished his commentary on the Psalms and was about to begin lectures on the epistles of Saint Paul. The letter-writer asked his friend to come with him to attend the course. The errant friend was apparently staying in the place where the two had grown up, for he had conveyed the news that the writer's parents were in good health. It is not made clear why the two friends had gotten separated in the first place, except for the fact that the one had dreamed of a military career, without apparently doing anything about it. But the writer insists that if his friend intends now to continue his studies, then they can be together in these pursuits: 'I wish and desire that you be part of these, if it pleases you'.

In this appeal we come very close to the ideal and the reality of eleventh-century friendships in a scholarly setting in Germany. There is no great difference between these letters and the declarations of friendship at Chartres in the first decades of the century, except that the german materials are more articulate and specific. Certainly they are more long-winded. Fulbert of Chartres seems to have encouraged pupils like Hildegar to be succinct. From one cathedral school to another, the letters of friendship vary, but a pattern emerges that is different from the one we found at Tegernsee in the last chapter. There poetry and letters were mixed into a collection that looked back to the elite and exclusive friendships of the carolingian age; at Chartres, Worms and now Hildesheim, writers looked upon friendship as a manifestation of normal and natural bonds with each other in everyday life.

The spiritual flights of Alcuin have given way to down-to-earth job hunting. For this, friends are important, even essential. Fundamental needs for company and contact may remain the same, but the literature of friendship has become more prosaic and receptive to secular language.

Church and lay society were looking out for well-educated clerics. It was no longer a question of 'making it' at some prestigious, artificial centre, such as carolingian Aachen had been. Now there were many different possibilities, even on the fringes of Europe at Hildesheim. Cathedral schools did their best to train articulate young men who could deal with theological argument through communicating well with each other in speech and writing. An important bond cementing this new society was the language of friendship, sometimes taken directly from Cicero. No limits were placed on the ways friendship could be used to bring men together to administer and enhance this new world. Friendship was worthwhile, and so collections of letters of friendship were made in the manner of *exempla* for future generations of scholar-clerics.

NEW FORMS OF SPIRITUAL EXPRESSION

The rebirth of friendship in the eleventh century resulted from the revival of learning and a new, or renewed, need for scholars. Friendships were characterized as a natural manifestation of the ideals and pursuits that students and teachers shared. The cathedral schools of Chartres, Rheims, Beauvais, Worms and Hildesheim might seem to have dominated the new language of friendship, but the early eleventh-century collections from the monastery of Tegernsee warn against seeing friendship as a practice exclusive to the secular clergy. So long as centres of learning were in contact with each other, monastic revival and the revised curriculum could unite to foster the articulation of friendship.

Monks did not accept uncritically the view of friendship that could be obtained from the classical writers who were studied in the cathedral schools. If Tegernsee reflects the friendship literature of the carolingian age, abbeys like Bec, Fécamp and Saint Emmeram anticipate new ways of expressing friendship, monastic revival and reform in the eleventh century increased them. The West fed once more on the literature of Eastern asceticism, but monastic writers used desert fathers' sayings not to encourage each other to cut off all human links but to form communities in which men could deepen and intensify their interrelationships. Monastic expressions of friendship in the late eleventh and twelfth centuries go together with the clerical concern with friendship we already have seen. Friendship was looked upon as part of christian ascetic life and not as a temptation away from it.

This monastic reorientation appears in three celebrated writers of the period: John of Fécamp (d. 1078), Otloh of Saint Emmeram (c. 1010-1070), and Goscelin of Saint Bertin (d. soon after 1099). These three monks did not write in detail about friendship, but they provide evidence for growing attention to the spiritual content of human relationships. These men also provide important signs of a renewal of religious language essential to the intense spirituality of the period after about 1050.[33] The first of these writers, John of Fécamp (d. 1078), combined in prayer-like theological treatises a new depth of feeling with rhythmical cadences of language. From here there is little distance to the content of the prayers and meditations of Saint Anselm (1033-1109).[34]

John of Fécamp was not at all positive about the worth of friendship. In a lamentation for the peace and solitude he had lost, he spoke to *solitudo* as something chaste and pure: 'Who has taken you away from me, my beloved?' he asked. John regretted the type of life he had to lead as abbot at Fécamp, 'among this crowd of brothers, where I daily give offense in many matters'. His only way out was withdrawal into the self, where he would find the 'secret of solitude'.[35] Monastic life of the community seems only a distraction from the solitude necessary for true meditation. The flight into isolation recalls the attraction that italian hermitages exercised on men like Romuald of Ravenna (d. 1027) and his publicist, Peter Damian.[36] John wants to get away from it all, to the solitude that is his only true friend, now so far away: 'Alas how far I have been removed from your holy company, my friend!'

If we had only this powerful lament, it might seem that John wanted to separate individual monks so that they could live as spiritual hermits, mentally as well as physically apart from each other. Friendship could have no part in such a scheme. But John is not so one-dimensional. He opens another work, structured as a letter, with praise for the charity of his correspondent. His soul rejoices in this love as Mary's did over the conception of Jesus within her. The birth of charity for another person is an occasion for joy. John adds that Christ had united him with his correspondent so that he could be aware of him all the time:

> What is sweeter or what more beautiful than that amid the shadows and great bitterness of this life we can aspire to divine sweetness and eternal blessedness?[37]

John did not use the word friendship. He does insist, however, that his own salvation and that of the friend are closely linked. 'I have written this letter', he closes, 'so that you may always have me present and so that through the letter you can know more fully and surely how much I love you.[38] John did not use the language of friendship common at Hildesheim or Worms, but he was still willing to refer to his own need for contact with beloved ones. John concentrated exclusively on self-fulfilling love, while friends of the secular schools also promise each other material benefits.

John belongs to the same monastic tradition of friendship which we will find in Anselm of Bec. Both sought to enlarge the vocabulary of spiritual experience, to enrich the content of communication between man and God, and at the same time to reenforce the spiritual bonds uniting men dedicated to the same purpose. John stood at the threshold of a new humanism. Without ever using the word *amicitia*, his prayers and meditations provide a point of departure for a new world of spiritual friendships in the cloister.

In Otloh of Saint Emmeram (c. 1010-1070), we find another aspect of monastic spirituality particular to the eleventh century. Otloh was eager to draw on his own personal experience to provide an example to other monks and men of the church.[39] This openly autobiographical form had not been so much in use since Augustine, and it has provoked widely differing interpretations of his behaviour and writings.[40] At times in his *Liber de suis temptationibus*, he became so caught up in telling about his own religious turmoil that nothing else seems to have found room in his consciousness. Otloh and the devil are locked in a battle of wits and grace, with God intervening at last to provide a message of comfort and hope.

Otloh would seem to have been alone in his trials. A review of his works, however, shows that he in fact was very much dependent on friends in the cloister. He tells us in detail about a noble monk, Henry from Reichenau, whose visit to Saint Emmeram (probably in 1053) provided Otloh with a willing partner for theological discussions. He calls Henry his special friend (*mihimet specialis amice*).[41] Some of the questions that Henry poses are very close to those that Otloh says he himself had pondered as a youth. In the long run, Otloh could not keep up the dialogue form and dropped it for the sake of pure exposition. Otloh's work nevertheless emerges from a specific encounter of two monks who matched each other intellectually. It is not just theology that comes alive in Otloh's writings. It is also a dialogue of minds seeking insight through each other.

Otloh did not dwell at length on such friendships, but it is easy to stumble onto them. Such is the case when he describes with pride all the books he had written and where he had sent them: 'to certain friends in Bohemia I sent four books; to a certain friend in Padua, one book; to the monastery of Tegernsee, two books. . . .'[42] Who are these friends? If Padua was already an educational centre in the eleventh century, Otloh may have been trying to impress some master. But it is also possible that Otloh was in contact with a youth whom he had once taught at the school of Saint Emmeram and who had gone on to Padua for further education.

Were Otto's friends at Padua monks? Since most of the other names in the list are of monasteries or of individual monks, some of these friends were probably also monastic. Otloh did not feel called upon to explain how he used the word *amicus*. It was not a controversial matter to have friends outside the monastery with whom one shared learning and labour. To expand on the renowned formulation of Jean Leclercq, the 'love of learning and the desire for God' made possible and necessary bonds with other men who pursued the same goals.

Otloh adds little to the literature of monastic friendship, and yet his willingness to point to such friendships is of great importance. Despite the demands of his own inner conflicts, Otloh still had the resources to compose a *Liber Proverbiorum*, probably his most popular work during the Middle Ages. Maxims and sayings from the Bible provide an easily accessible collection of proverbs as a substitute for the well-known epithets of pagan writers. Many concern friendship, as the warning in the Epistle of Saint James (4:4) that a friend of the world becomes an enemy of God. I find no trace of Cicero in this collection, but Otloh cannot resist the temptation to provide a variant of Sallust's celebrated definition of friendship: '*To want and not want the same: this is firm friendship*'.[43]

Otloh's search for an exclusively christian ethical code was both personal and literary. At moments he reveals in great detail his reactions to events in his life that have moral significance. After excoriating a pupil in class in front of the others, he felt remorse. Otloh had no idea what to do: whether to seek reconciliation with the youth and shame himself in the process or else to wait for some sign of God's will.[44] In his lack of certitude Otloh reveals that the teacher in a medieval monastery school by no means always played an absolutist authority role.

Otloh was rescued by the youth himself, who came and asked to be forgiven for protesting the punishment he had been given. But the boy made it clear that in the future Otloh should address him in private before making his offence a public matter! Otloh was overjoyed and greatly relieved. His bond with the pupil is by no means described in terms of friendship, but the incident reveals that Otloh's self-doubt and sense of isolation may have been due not just to his own special personality but also to the lack of a fully-formed code of behaviour for the new monastic school of the eleventh century. In such a fluid social situation, the role of friendship could be looked upon in various ways, some positive and some negative. Otloh and his contemporaries were openly seeking a context for describing and experiencing close human relationships.

In several instances Otloh gives vent to the traditional monastic suspicion of friendship as a link with the world. In the account of his temptations he admits he was mistaken in worrying about getting the advice of his friends and relatives before entering the monastery.[45] Friends are defined as those who belong to the old secular world. Ties to them endanger conversion to monastic life. Elsewhere (in the *Liber de cursu spirituali*), he warns against following the advice of friends, 'lest by chance because of friendship or some temporal help', we get into a situation in which we risk damnation.[46] Almost anything in this life can turn into a temptation to evil, including 'the adulation of friends and other men'.[47]

A synthesis of Otloh's ideas on friendship is contained in his description of Saint Wolfgang (d. 994). His *Life* had already been written by the monk Arnold at Saint Emmeram, but Otloh was asked to improve it.[48] His composition can be dated to between 1037 and 1052, and its sections about the bishop of Regensburg's early life were apparently taken not from Arnold but from other sources, most of them presumably oral. According to Otloh's narration Wolfgang at Reichenau's monastery school met another pupil named Henry. This youth convinced Wolfgang to come with him to his hometown of Würzburg, where his father, the city's ruler, had employed an outstanding italian teacher. Wolfgang went, but he did not obtain the teacher's favour because Wolfgang knew more than he did! This rivalry between pupil and teacher parallels the experience of Otloh's own youth. There is no doubt that in Wolfgang's life he found much with which to identify. When Wolfgang wanted to enter a monastery, Henry convinced him not to do so:

> For if he had not been pulled back by the request of his friend Henry, with whom he had a close comradeship (*familiare contubernium*), he would have renounced all secular desires.

In normal monastic ideology, the friend who holds his companion back from conversion to a monastery is no friend at all. But Otloh accepted Henry's need to have Wolfgang close to him, at least for a while longer:

> But thinking carefully that charity does not seek what is its own, but what belongs to the other person, he put off the decision for a while.[49]

Meanwhile Henry was made archbishop of Trier by Otto the Great and asked Wolfgang to accompany him. Once again friendship had its rights: 'He resisted for a while, but since he could do no good this way and did not want to be rebellious, he set forth with his friend'.[50] Once in Trier, Henry did everything to show the strength of his love for Wolfgang (*internae dilectionis vim*), but Wolfgang accepted only the position of a teacher of youths, finally becoming the head of a community of clerics.

In Otloh's narration friendship implies rights, and Wolfgang is seen to have shown charity by thinking of Henry's needs rather than his own. Human bonds have limitations, however: called home to save the family fortune, Wolfgang hesitates. Even though the Scriptures order obedience to parents he can cite Matthew (10:37) 'whoever loves his mother or father more than Christ is not worthy of him.' Saint Jerome's vitriolic letter to Heliodorus on the ascetic life, perhaps the most famous letter of conversion, provides a final assurance that family and friendship must give way to the monastic life.[51] Wolfgang also thinks of John the Baptist, who left his parents and to avoid being polluted by living among men went into the desert. So begins Wolfgang's monastic career at the reformed monastery of Einsiedeln under its english abbot Gregory, 'who as a youth had left fatherland, parents, and also the woman to whom he was married and had flown to the monastery',[52] another exile from friend and family.

Being a monk was only one stage in a career that eventually led Wolfgang to a powerful bishopric. Otloh may have been especially interested in this man's life because in it he could see his own conflict between wanting to be well-known and celebrated for his work while embracing an ascetic ideal. One result is an ambiguous attitude towards friendship. Wolfgang is praised for his loyalty to Henry as a friend, but also for his lack of loyalty to his own parents. The violent rhetoric of Jerome at his most uncompromising provides support for Wolfgang's decision to break family ties, and yet Otloh still defends the ties of love and friendship among church men. Seeking friends himself and yet feeling isolated from the rest of the monastery because of his problems of faith, the young Otloh may well have felt that friendship was only a distraction and even a danger for the soul, one more diabolic ruse. But he still admitted a need for friendship in the life of a 'man of God', as he called Wolfgang. Once old friends and family were left behind, new friendships could grow up among like-minded monks. These did not necessarily endanger advancement in spiritual life.

In Otloh's ambiguous attitude towards friendship as well as in his anguish about how to treat his pupils, an insecurity of character is evident. There is no reason, however, to reduce Otloh to a purely psychological case study. He was a literary man who carefully reshaped his source and at the same time drew on his own inner life. The writings of the Fathers exercised a great influence on his conviction that at some point the man who seeks God through the ascetic life has to break bonds with other men. This realization could have led to the assertion that if Christ asks us to leave everyone else in order to follow him, the new way of life excludes affectionate human bonds. Otloh did not take this step. He embraced the West's less rigorous attitude towards involvement with other people within the ascetic life. The reform of the church did not require the dissolution of all friendships and a retreat into solitude for those who wanted to achieve closeness to God. The increase of learning and the excitement of spiritual renewal increased the opportunities for men like Otloh to travel to various monsteries, to make contacts with monks and clerks interested in the same theological problems, and to express themselves to each other in terms of christian friendship.

The last member in our group of eleventh-century monks whose works touch on friendship is Goscelin of Saint Bertin.[53] He travelled to England from his flemish monastery to become secretary to Hermann, bishop of Ramsbury (later Sherborne). After Hermann's death in 1078, Goscelin was forced to leave the area and wandered for some time before settling down at the monastery of Saint Augustine, Canterbury. In the years 1082-3, he wrote a *Liber confortatorius* to Eve, who had been a nun at the abbey of Wilton. For unknown reasons she had left the monastery and gone to France, where, near Angers, she finally settled as a recluse. As C.H. Talbot has aptly pointed out, the first of the three books in Goscelin's work is more a description of his own pain at his loss of Eve than any attempt to comfort her.

The violence of Goscelin's emotions in the early part of the *Liber* may indicate that he had been in love with Eve. But his disappointment could also stem from the fact that she had left England without consulting the man who had been her spiritual advisor and who had watched her grow from child to adult in the monastery. Goscelin may have experienced the pain of a surrogate father whose only daughter runs away from all the plans and good ideas he had for her. Various passages from the first book could support both theses, but as with Otloh our purpose is not to provide an explanation for the behaviour of one individual in the eleventh century but to show his writings as a reflection of a new wave of sentiment and open involvement in human bonds.[54]

Goscelin in no way restrained himself in describing his feelings for Eve. She was the great love of his life:

> O soul more beloved than light, your Goscelin is present with you; in the inseparable presence of the soul, he is here with his better part, in that with which he could love you, separately, which no distances on earth can keep away. . .[55]

The central message of the first book is that, even though Goscelin and Eve have to be apart for a time, they will be united forever in heaven: 'where we never ever can be separated'. Goscelin longs for that reunion and describes it in almost ecstatic terms. The bond between them is Christ. Goscelin reminds Eve of what they already had shared. He asks her to think of how it was when he was with her at Wilton, and how they had spoken togetheri He would exhort and console Eve and pour the love of Christ into her. The thought is interrupted by Goscelin's tears and sobs.[56]

In the following pages there are both tears and friends. Saint John, for example, is seen as the friend (*amicus*) of Christ when Jesus gave Mary to John. Goscelin recalls the tears that Augustine's mother shed for him, an indication that he was influenced by the *Confessions* as a model for expressing spiritual and human bonds. Surprisingly enough, however, the word *amicitia* is used only in the secular sense, as of the friendship of the flesh and of the world, which is vain and faithless. There are also examples of friendship to be found among the infidels, but when it is a question of a christian union, Goscelin prefers the expression *beata sodalitas*. Here Christ is the centre.[57]

Without providing a detailed description of christian friendship, Goscelin manages to link firmly his own love for Eve with their unity in Christ. He asked her never to forget his own birth in Christ. He recalled Eve as a little girl and looked forward to once again holding her in his lap—in paradise. His language borders on a bloodless eroticism when he reminds Eve of his physical as well as spiritual self. Goscelin wanted her to know about his pain, and yet he accepted the finality of their separation. How rare to find even two souls united and dwelling together forever, he remarks and recalls the friendship of David and Jonathan. What was more beloved to Jonathan than David? The one gave up his kingdom for the other, and yet they had to accept that they could not live together. Biblical examples of friendship reflect the situation of Eve and Goscelin.

What did Eve think about all these passionate statements? She is silent, as are so many of the women in history whose existence is known only through what men wrote. One suspects that her flight from England may have been inspired by a desire to get away from so dominating and dependent a figure as Goscelin.

Like Otloh of Saint Emmeram, Goscelin was better known among his contemporaries for his competent and attractive hagiographical writings than for his more autobiographical work. Without the *Liber confortatorius*, Goscelin would appear to us as a talented monastic figure who used his abilities to travel far and wide to make himself appreciated by polishing inadequate biographies. The first book of the treatise to Eve, however, provides a different picture of Goscelin. Here we see a man who had shared his religious and emotional life with a girl he loved. Such a one-sided communication hints that in the later eleventh century male bonds with women in the religious life could be just as important as men's friendships with each other. In a striking letter in the Worms collection (*ep* 45), a bishop wrote to a nun that he could see no reason why men and women could not have such friendships. He pointed to the renowned cases from Late Antiquity such as that of Jerome with Paula and Eustochium. This bishop, like Goscelin, knew well his patristic literature. Goscelin drew on various lives of desert saints, including that of Saint Mary of Egypt. From these he might have concluded that friendship has no place in the christian life. But, like Otloh, he was unwilling to go the full distance with the desert fathers and conclude that because human relationships are limited and bring sorrow, they are basically distractions from the true end of monastic life. Because Goscelin placed his hope in an eternal reunion in heaven, he could accept the worth and content of what he had once shared with Eve on earth.

Neither Goscelin nor Otloh nor John of Fécamp defined the meaning of friendship. Yet in their writings we find that friendships contributed to their monastic lives in terms of learning and spiritual-emotional exchanges. Goscelin cannot be understood without his Eve, Otloh has to be seen with his Henry, while John of Fécamp's friend remains anonymous but still very much present in one of his letters. The intense personal spirituality of John, the autobiographical self-awareness of Otloh, and the injured love of Goscelin all contain in them the potential for friendship as a part of monastic life. They all expressed hesitation about the value of close human bonds. The ascetism of the East exercised an enduring attraction on them. Yet friendship was too important to be dismissed as something undesirable because it could be a danger to the monk.

THE REFORM OF THE CHURCH AND THE EREMITICAL MOVEMENT

The great renewal of church life in the second half of the eleventh century known as the Gregorian Reform produced a literature of polemic that marks the first great public debate in Western European civilisation.[58] The pope for the first time addressed letters to all of Christendom, or to the faithful of an entire realm, while the supporters of the emperor replied by formulating an alternative theory of the relationship between church and crown. This new level of articulation might seem at first to have nothing to do with friendship, and yet the atmosphere of polemic also fostered the clarification of human bonds. The very same set of letters from Hildesheim, after 1050, that speaks so eloquently about the content and meaning of friendship also deals with the need to reform the church and fight against the enemies of the pope. In the Hildesheim letters friendship and reform go together, as we saw in a saxon prince's letter to the bishop. Here friendship undergirds papal reform. The one is inconceivable without the other.[59] Similarly Henry IV himself appealed to the idea of friendship in order to ensure an ally.[60] Discussions of loyalty engendered talk on friendship. This is to be expected, but we also find that friendship, seen as a necessary human bond, was linked up with church reform, made into a duty for all the faithful.

In the monastic sources also, friendship was identified with reform. But in this case it is the reform of monasteries, not that of the secular church, that provides a foundation for a new interest in expressing friendship. Men remembered mainly for their ascetic and administrative feats reveal a capacity for engaging in and describing friendship. The main figure here is Peter Damian (1007-72). Articulately afraid of homosexuality in the church and favouring the eremitical way of life, Peter might seem an unlikely champion of monastic friendships. But his life and writings show receptivity to friendship.

Damian did not idealize friendship to the extent that we shall see Anselm and his circle doing. His writings have to be carefully gleaned to find relevant passages. This is worth doing, however, for the contents contradict or at least modify an intrepretation of him as a man beset by the trauma of childhood and isolated from other human beings.[61] Peter Damian preferred the eremitical above the cenobitical life. He valued withdrawal from the world as the best way to salvation. He feared the sensuality and worldly learning that surrounded him as a youth in Northern Italy. And yet from this background he was able to distill a confidence in spiritual bonds among men in the church. He had friends and wrote letters of friendship, not in the ciceronian style of the cathedral schools, nor in the ecstatic manner of a Goscelin or an Anselm.[62] But what he wrote in his austere, straightforward way are letters of friendship.

Peter Damian strikes the reader of his works as a disciplined man, whose strong inner life did not preclude involvement in the affairs of the church.[63] His unhappy childhood and strong fear of sex gave him the necessary material to become an eleventh-century Jerome, torn by the violence of his needs and desires, at one moment calling for eternal friendship, at the next rejecting it. Peter Damian achieved a serenity that Jerome never gained. He combined opposites in his own life and in the church. In him there was room both for withdrawal and involvement, for the eremitical and the cenobitic way, for the loosing of all kin bonds and the fastening of new spiritual ties. Damian made sure that the eremitical movement that started in Italy and soon spread north of the Alps did not become fanatical and isolated from other groups working for the reform of the church. In 1043 he was elected abbot of an insignificant eremitical community at Fonte Avellana and made this his platform for his involvement in reform.

The collection of Damian's letters is divided up according to the different groups to whom he wrote, and we can turn immediately to the sixth book, reserved for his letters to monks. To the monks of

Fonte Avellana, Rodulph and Ariprand, he wrote in detail about his illness. The unity of friendship, he insisted at the start of the letter, justifies our informing each other about both our successes and our problems. This statement forms a perfect opening expressing good will, *captatio benevolentiae*. It might seem that Damian is showing off his rhetorical abilities:

> It is appropriate in an intimate friendship that one brother write another about both his successes and his adversities, in that our spirit shows compassion when we are told of reverses, so too they can rejoice together when we have success.[64]

If Damian always wrote such statements of friendship to his correspondents, one would think it likely that no feeling lay behind them. But this is an unusual declaration from his pen, and since we know that Ariprand for a period had been his secretary, and that Damian wrote other affectionate letters to him, this declaration of friendship was probably intended in a personal and not a general sense for the two hermits of Fonte Avellana.[65] What follows appears to be a frank letter, among the most personal in the collection, where Damian at times looses himself from linguistic restraints and uses a language of tenderness:

> These things, my most beloved, I as a friend have described to you, as it were my accomplices and friends, and I have summarized the course of my illness to you, who in the closest friendship are like brothers from the same womb.[66]

Damian here used the traditional monastic term, *familiaritas*, while *amicitia* sufficed at the opening of the letter. He considered the two as synonyms for describing his relationship with Ariprand and Rodulph. Concerned not only with giving them news of himself and evidence of his affection, Peter sent them a youth to whom they were to give special care and attention. His two friends were held responsible for whatever happened to the boy. Friendship implied obligations of a personal nature. Peter's letter was probably heard by the entire community at Fonte Avellana, but it addressed Ariprand and Rodulph, who gained the immediate benefit of his affection and bore the burden of responsibility for Peter's charge.

Peter Damian placed friendship as a high priority in cenobitic as well as in eremitic life. Most of what he wrote about it, however, describes not its enjoyment but the dangers which surround its appearance. In writing on the perfection of the monk, Damian warned against those who appear to show friendship but actually deceive other members of the community.[67] He uses the phrase *veritas amicitiae*, which indicates that Damian believed in the possibility of friendship in the monastery, even while warning against a counterfeit variety. For Damian this threat was a real one that easily could creep into his own life. Once when given a present by a papal legate, he refused to accept it as a sign of friendship. This cannot be bought by us as people who live in the world, he insisted, for 'whatever among the brethren is legitimate, he can possess freely'.[68] Lester Little interpreted this incident to emphasize Peter Damian's fear that in accepting a gift he would be risking 'an affective response to someone who was reaching out to him'.[69] This may be true, but on a more prosaic level, Peter's reaction is consistent with the principles expressed in his *Liber gratissimus* that since God's grace is a free gift, then the services and sacraments of the church cannot be bought. By making friendship also a free gift among churchmen, Peter Damian emphasized its worth and even its sanctity. He was not so much in doubt about the positive value of affective ties among men but he was wary about combining friendship with political favour.

Often when Peter uses the word *amicitia*, he is referring to collective bonds rather than individual ties among members of a community. *Amicitia* can be a synonym for *confoederatio*, the unity of the brethren in concord that is a necessary condition for a good community.[70] In writing to Abbot Hugh of Cluny after his visit there in 1063, Damian did speak of his friendship, but in a rather legalistic sense: 'I return to the right of old friendship for your love' (*in jus veteris amicitiae pro vestra charitate reduco*).[71] Friendship with Hugh was only a part of Peter's new devotion and loyalty to Cluny.

In this same letter Peter warned that friendship must be exclusive and selective. We are to reject from our friendship those who bring darkness into our lives:

> Rightly therefore we have contempt for the friendships of the world or of its prince, and with these we are to have in contempt any bond of society, so that we are not joined to darkness and deprived of light.[72]

The language is reminiscent of the Epistle of Saint James (4:4): '. . .whoever wishes to be a friend of the world makes himself an enemy of God'. Damian, however, made the contrast more vivid by adding a biblical story. King David, on the death of a neighboring king took pity on the man's son and sent his servants to express his grief, as the father once had done for him. The new king, Hanon, seized David's servants, cut off half their beards and ripped off their clothes, then sent them away (2 Samuel 10). In Damian's eyes, David asked for a pact of friendship, but Hanon rejected it by his insults. In recent events at Cluny, one of whose monks, Andrew, had left in order to join forces with men who were the monastery's enemies, Peter sees a similar abrogation of the bond of friendship (*foedus amicitiae*).[73] The parallels between Old Testament and modern events can at times seem rather strained, but Peter's message is clear: friendship is a necessary bond among human beings. Those who break it are to be excluded from all friendship and protection. Appropriately he ends the letter by expressing his desire to share the life, or at least the prayers and other spiritual benefits, of Cluny. In this letter friendship emerges more as a social and religious virtue than as an expression of personal bonds. His friendship with Abbot Hugh is an alliance with the cluniac community as a whole.

In letters to the monks at Fonte Avellana and at Cluny, Peter Damian evidences bonds of both personal and collective friendship. Despite the strong influence that the eremitical life of the East had on him in his conversion to Fonte Avellana, Damian could not imagine a world without friendship. He signals the opening of a new age of friendship in monastic life. Even if his statements on the subject are fragmentary and scattered, his reluctance to eliminate friendship from the reformed monastic or even eremitical community is in itself of great importance.

Peter Damian is only a transitional figure in this context. He did not embrace the idea, for example, that Christ is our friend. In a sermon on the feast of Saint John the Apostle, Damian recalled the special love John had for Jesus and the moment at the Last Supper when he lay on Christ's breast (Jn 13:23). Peter saw John's relationship with Christ as a means by which the apostle-evangelist obtained wisdom.[74] The touch of Christ is not so much proof of friendship as a guarantee of divine understanding. John's intimacy with Christ Damian understood as a result of his being a virgin, and in this manner, an example to the reformed clergy. John strengthens the conception of sexual abstinence among those who are close to Christ.[75] Peter Damian never forgot his main effort in church reform: ensuring the chastity of the priesthood, and so he transformed John not into Christ's special friend but into a chaste priest who was rewarded by Christ with love and closeness. Damian even went so far as to claim that once John lay on Christ's breast, he absorbed a divine power that wiped out all sexual impulses.[76]

Here we come to grips with Peter Damian's concern with sexual morality. Now that John Boswell has made the arguments of Damian's attack on clerical homosexuality accessible to a wider public, there is a danger that Damian will be perceived primarily as an apostle of repression against homosexuals in the church.[77] There is no doubt Damian was in earnest about punishing priests who engaged in any kind of sexual activity. But it is also clear that the man to whom he sent his work, Pope Leo IX, refused to go as far as Damian asked in campaigning against homosexual priests. Almost no echo of this concern is heard in Damian's later writings. Why at the end of the 1040s did he show such fear of homosexual priests, only to drop the subject after the papal response? One possible explanation is that he found other matters to be of far greater urgency, such as the question of simoniacal priests or the problem of priests who lived with women and had children.

In *Contra gomorrhianos* as well as other writings, Damian is quite open about human sexuality. He lived at a time when churchmen were not yet sure how to apply general principles of morality to sexual matters. In the fruitful chaos of the eleventh century, a consistent church code for human behaviour did not yet exist. Before Damian could condemn homosexuality, he had to define what it was and, even more importantly, to ask the central question about what it is that attracts one man to another.[78] Damian's query on this point indicates some awareness on his part of the man who seeks out other men for sex or tenderness or both. His formulations point in either of two directions: to a man who knew what he was talking about, or to someone for whom the phenomenon was so foreign that he had to ask how it possibly could happen. Either way Damian does not echo the eastern fear that close friendship among men and boys in the eremitical or monastic life will lead to homosexual loves. Damian's idealization of monastic friendships, even of an individual nature, makes it likely that in his own life he experienced strong friendships with other men and did not see such close relationships as the source of sexual temptation.

We have moved so far in this chapter from the friendships that grew up among students and masters in cathedral schools to those that could be encouraged in the new reformed monasticism of the eleventh century. Such a development was by no means inevitable, for the wave of asceticism could have emphasized the egyptian desert's extreme fringe, which demanded total separation from all human bonds. In a letter collection dated to about 1100 from a monk of an english abbey to a friend at Fécamp in Normandy, we find the literary wealth and personal self-confidence of this monastic celebration of friendship in formulations concerning theory and practice.[79] The Fécamp collection would not have been possible without the letters of Peter Damian, the spiritual writings of John of Fécamp, and the experience of Anselm of Bec and his circle.

THE MONASTIC RESPONSE: THE ANSELMIAN REVOLUTION c. 1070-1120

Peter Damian supported monastic friendship by allowing for it and, especially, by not warning against it. Anselm of Bec and Canterbury (1033-1109) made friendship not just possible but also desirable and attractive for a circle of monks and churchmen in Normandy and England from the 1070's onwards. More than twenty years ago R. W. Southern explained Anselm's letters of friendship in terms of the special qualities of his mind: Anselm's platonic bent reduced all human reality into ideal images; his powerful declarations of love reflected a desire to unite all his friends in monastic community; his physical expressions of affection were linguistic devices representing the realization of his ideal world.[80] Southern's explanation provided a basis for my own attempt to reinterpret Anselm's relations with his friends as we see through his letters, while a careful article on Anselm by Adele Fiske goes through the language of the letters and shows exactly how Anselm characterized friendship.[81] So much fundamental work has already been done on Anselm that in the following pages I shall use him and his writings for a look at a network of monastic friendship where Anselm was the centre. He appears as the inspirer and promoter of new ways of talking about friendship. Anselm and his followers contributed to a veritable revolution in the expression of human sentiment. This change is closely tied to the triumph of monastic reform movements in the late eleventh century.

Before we look at Saint Anselm's circle, however, it is necessary to consider his unique personality and writings. John Boswell's treatment of anselmian language suggests the saint may well have been homosexual. I once tried to show that Anselm's bonds with other men were homoerotic as opposed to homosexual.[82] He loved men, and in terms of the human bonds, his world was composed only of men, but there is no evidence that he was a repressed homosexual. Today in rereading the sources I would add the proviso that here as in so many other areas of Anselm's life and thought, he defies characterization or neat definition. Any 'final' analysis slips away into the sands of uncertainty, for Anselm himself is an elusive figure to our lesser minds and more limited hearts.

I would nevertheless still argue that Anselm had one great love in his life, the young monk Osbern at Bec in Normandy, and that Osbern's death when Anselm was prior there was a terrible blow for him. In his earliest letters, from the beginning of the 1070's, Anselm wrote the monks who had left Bec for Canterbury with Lanfranc and described his love for Osbern with an intensity of pain that exceeds his expressions of love for other monks in these same letters. This can be seen especially in a letter dated to 1071 and addressed to Gundulf at Canterbury. The phrases meant for Gundulf convey devotion and loyalty, while those describing Anselm's love for Osbern suggest that the two were bound by a much greater intimacy.[83] Anselm's biographer, the Canterbury monk Eadmer, had a sometimes troubled relationship with his subject and gives few direct indications of Anselm's friendships. But Eadmer does mention Osbern, who provides an example of how Anselm could treat difficult young novices by combining kindness with harshness.[84] Osbern becomes so real, especially in the way Eadmer describes Anselm's sorrow at his death, that the *exemplum* reveals much more about Anselm than it intended. Using a biblical phrase, common in hagiography, Eadmer claims that after Osbern's death, Anselm became 'all things to all men'.[85] Never again did Anselm have a favourite monk to whom he showed special devotion. Instead he concentrated on many different monks, even though his followers vied with each other to take over Osbern's preferred position. Anselm intended his letters of friendship to be read aloud to all the Bec monks at Canterbury, even though he addressed his letters to individuals among them.

The exact nature of Anselm's bond with Osbern cannot be determined, but it seems possible and even likely that Anselm as prior and teacher did become strongly emotionally attached to this attractive and spirited young man. After he had won Osbern over to monastic life, Anselm tried to discipline him by keeping a distance from him. Anselm may also have been disciplining himself. Only when Osbern lay dying and after his death could Anselm reveal to his surroundings the intensity of his feelings for the young man. Monastic friendship almost got out of control, for it lead to the brink of obsession and exclusivity. But so far as we can tell from Eadmer and from Anselm's letters, he kept his emotions under control. The first letters of friendship can be regarded as spreading out to many monks the feelings that Anselm had once reserved for the young Osbern.[86]

The experience of Osbern provides a context for the letters of friendship from the 1070's and the early 1080's. But they are by no means merely witnesses to the transference of one emotional bond into many. The letters are a monument to a renewed and deepened monastic celebration of friendship. Anselm's vocabulary of friendship has from the start a completeness not seen since the writings of Saint Augustine or the letters of Alcuin. Every possible nuance of *amicitia* is exploited in order to describe the bond, and there is almost no dimension of spiritual intensity left untouched. Anselm's linguistic abilities are well-known. He juxtaposes phrases, uses alliteration, strings together words with the same endings, and is acutely aware of the sound of a sentence as it is read aloud. This is true for all his writings but seems especially to be the case in his letters and his prayers. Already John of Fécamp emphasised word rhythms and repetition in order to build up a climax, but this technique was now used to describe love of friends as well as love of God.

Writing to a monk called Henry, Anselm placed the words 'friend' and 'advice' almost in apposition to each other in order to underline that Henry was to take heed of his friends' advice:

> Therefore your friend in counsel speaks to you of these matters, most beloved, since I hear that in a certain matter you are making plans against the counsel of your friends.
>
> (Ideo tecum haec, dilectissime, loquitur *amicus tuus de consilio* quia de quodam negotio audio te disponere *contra amicorum tuorum consilium.)*

The two words *amicus* and *consilium* are placed together and correspondingly at the end of phrases. Anselm here sets the tone of friendship and advice in the remainder of the letter and at the same time establishes that he is writing to a friend and not just to a monk who is to be obedient to him.

Here, as elsewhere in Anselm's writings, a closer investigation of linguistic parallels and precedents would indicate that the writer has absorbed the culture of the past and could surpass it without allowing his reader to see any immediate dependence on his predecessors. We catch only distant echoes of carolingian writers on friendship, and even though Anselm knew his Augustine, his formulation of monastic friendship is very much his own.[87]

As Southern pointed out in *Saint Anselm and his Biographer*'s classic section on the letters of friendship, Anselm's language was often misunderstood. His contemporaries interpreted his expressions of love as indicating a desire for geographical closeness and a promise of frequent communications. Anselm began many letters by explaining why he had not written, and often his tone of self-defense indicates that he was answering recriminations. We almost always lack the letters of his correspondents, but Anselm's own replies are usually enough to indicate that his combination of spiritual presence and distance was not always appreciated.

There could often be a gap between what Anselm's correspondents understood him to say and what he really meant. This divergence helps us understand the place of monastic friendship at Bec in the 1070's. Anselm's friends had no firm cultural or linguistic background according to which they could interpret his words. When Anselm wrote to one of them but said that the same expression of love applied to another monk, his friends at Canterbury were unable to see that he was expressing an ideal of friendship rather than his personal feelings for any one of them. For Anselm had no problem in distinguishing soul from body, individual from community, heavenly reality from earthly. Every physical image was meant in his vocabulary as a symbol of spiritual reality. Unlike Goscelin of Saint Bertin, Anselm did not expend great effort in describing a heaven where at last he would be able to enjoy his friends to the fullest. Anselm agreed to such a conception, but his main concern was neither earthly or heavenly friendships. He looked at friendship as a way to enrich the content of monastic life, which Anselm considered the best and often the only way to reach paradise.

One reason why Anselm could so easily be misinterpreted is that he kept assuring his correspondents that they were in his thoughts all the time. The words *conscius* and *conscientia* appear often in Anselm's letters of friendship, as when he wrote Gundulf (*ep* 16):

> Pressing and pressing upon me is an awareness of another's awareness, that is of myself, so that my letters fly and sail more often across the sea to him, as if they were wishing to learn of the state of my friendship.

This mental bond, which meant awareness and identification of self with the other person, allowed the two friends to be constantly in each other's presence. The point of the letter is to remind Gundulf that since this is the case, he really does not need to keep asking Anselm about the state of his soul and their friendship! Gundulf can get to

Anselm best by withdrawing into himself and looking into the depths of his soul. For here, in himself, he will find Anselm's soul: *o tu altera anima mea.* Anselm made this statement not just as a figure of speech. It expressed theological truth and contrasts with Augustine's idea that in looking within himself, he finds God. Now the journey into self-awareness brings the seeker also into the presence of an intimate friend, for the friend is really a part of his deepest self. The bond of friendship is complete when one human being can identify so much with another that the two souls become identical. The idea could be pushed to an extreme and reduce human individuality, just as Augustine's discovery of God in the human soul could have become a form of pantheism. But Augustine always kept away from such an easy conclusion, and Anselm never investigated these frontiers in his letters. In his *Cur Deus Homo*, however, the common identity of all men and women provided the necessary theological basis that enables Christ's act of self-sacrifice to apply to us all.

Anselm sought unity in human bonds, and so it is vain to look to him for an articulation of human differences as a basis for the formation of friendships. Anselm loved his fellow monks precisely because they, like him, were dedicated to the same learning, the same discipline, and the same loves. Anselm ignored diversity and individuality in order to assert the unity of human experience, especially in the cloister. His doctrine of the identity of friends may be looked on as a convenient way of putting off friends who wanted particular attention and frequent letters. But Anselm after Osbern's death consistently emphasized that friends' consciousness of each other does not require frequent contact or even the regular exchange of ideas. Everything that is in the one friend is to be found in the other, and only in the pursuit of self-knowledge can true friendship reach its purest expression.

As a corollary of Anselm's doctrine of the inward awareness of friendship, one friend cannot tell another what it is exactly he feels for him. Writing to Gundulf, Anselm remarked that everyone who came from him said that Gundulf wanted Anselm's letters. 'In this I know quite well that you expect nothing else than to read of the mutual affection of our love', Anselm admitted.[88] Anselm did not mean that Gundulf's love was asleep and needed to be awakened by letters, nor did his own love need similar encouragement. The letter, though not essential, provided a guarantee of love that is permanent and lasting. Gundulf ought to have realized, Anselm adds, that he could not provide a full explanation for his range of feeling (*affectus*): 'by what words or letters can your love or mine be described?' After these reflections, Anselm could allow himself to criticize the friend who asked for too much:

> And yet you insist in a pushy way that I do what cannot be done. Let our mutual awareness be enough, for by this we are conscious of each other and how much we love each other.[89]

This is one of the harshest passages in Anselm's letters of friendship. Eventually Gundulf stopped receiving explicit declarations of affection from Anselm. Perhaps Anselm tired of Gundulf's impatience for attention, but his conviction that genuine friendship must not make demands probably also was present here. Anselm insisted that consciousness of the other person does not engender emotional need for news of the other. Since friends by definition share each other's minds and hearts, they do not need always to point to what they have. Anselm's cool distance in the midst of what look at first like passionate letters of friendship can probably never be completely explained. One wonders at times if he really needed people's presence and affection. There is in him something of the desert father who attracts people only to drive them away. One must remember, however, that Anselm wrote from Bec, where he was at the centre of a fruitful intellectual and spiritual milieu. Friendship for him was only one means of expressing his vocation as a monk and not an individual human need requiring constant attention. A final consideration lies in Anselm's concentration on his immediate environment at Bec: for those monks who had left it behind, it was important for Anselm that they found friends in their new homes rather than in looking back to Bec as a unique place for friendship.

Inward awareness of the friend rather than outward expression of friendship meant that for Anselm the spiritual benefits of friendship rather than its enjoyment came first. It was therefore important for

Anselm that his friends did well in living out their monastic vocations rather than that they were physically present to each other. This attitude is apparent in the way Anselm dealt with a young monk, Maurice, who from the time he was sent from Bec to Canterbury tried to return to his Anselm. At first Anselm seems to have encouraged Maurice, but when he realized that the Archbishop Lanfranc was not in favour of the change, Anselm began to hedge. At the time Anselm was just completing his *Monologion*, with fresh and daring ways of describing God's existence. He may have wanted not to make an issue of Maurice's problems and thus jeopardize Lanfranc's approval of his intellectual work (*epp* 60, 64, 69, 74, 77).

Speculation about Anselm's relationship with Lanfranc adds an extra dimension to a consideration of his hesitation to retrieve Maurice. Anselm's attitude was that so long as Maurice did well at Canterbury and found friends there, it was not necessary to bring him home. Anselm expresses this idea in elevated spiritual terms and with his usual intensity:

> It is a long time since we have paid call on each other through letters, since we have no hesitations about the strength of our love for each other and since we greet each other through the words of our messengers when we get the opportunity. But in order that our love itself not seem at any moment to grow cooler, I think it a good idea that occasionally it be seen to burn hotter through written contacts, which are like sparks leaping forth from us both.
>
> But since in desiring you, who also desires me, I cannot have you with me, I still love you not less but more, for I see that you are so beloved by those who are greater and better than I that they will not let you go. Thus I understand that you are all the more

> worthy of love. So it comes about that I am not quite sure whether I should rejoice in the fact that you make yourself lovable or grieve because I cannot enjoy one so lovable.[90]

Here Anselm states a doctrine central to his concept of monastic friendship and love: what is important is the state of loving within a monastic community, not the personal affection between one monk and another. That Maurice has made himself an object of love in his new community was of primary importance for Anselm. Consequently Anselm could not let his own love for Maurice stand in the way of the love that had grown up between Maurice and the brothers of Canterbury:

> But since I know that you ought to be loved by me not so much because of myself as on account of yourself, the question is resolved, and it is certain that I ought to rejoice more in the fact of your praiseworthy way of life than I can allow myself to feel sadness at your physical absence. For the first quality is within you, the second within myself.[91]

Anselm compares and contrasts presence and absence, but the central contrast he makes is between his own personal, subjective desires and the objective state of Maurice's soul. The second is always more important than the first. Always basing human and divine behaviour on the rock of rationality, Anselm had to conclude that what matters is not individual feeling but the fact of living a good life leading to God:

> I always desired and did my best to see that you would be lovable to God and to good men, and I made an effort that you be aware of me so long as you were with me: and that desire has not grown cold even though my effort could not continue after you no longer were with me.[92]

Maurice's 'lovability' to good men and to God outweighs any consideration of Anselm's own feelings, and so an almost mathematical formula can be set forth as conclusion to Anselm's logic and as a universal maxim for all friends:

> You cannot be wherever you are being loved:
> but wherever you are, you can be loved and be good.
>
> (Verum non ubicumque amaris, esse potes: sed ubicumque sis, amari et bonus esse potes.)

Anselm was neither shrugging off his own responsibility for Maurice nor telling him that he now belonged to other people. He closes the letter with a formula, 'saving our reciprocal desire for each other, as reciprocal love requires' (*salvo tamen mutuo nostro, quia exigit mutuus amor, desiderio*). Anselm did not deny that he wanted to be with Maurice and Maurice with him. Human feelings still count, but what decides the matter is an awareness of how best to live in the love of God and men. In being loved and being good, Maurice had found a place at Canterbury, and for the time being he was to stay there.

As is so often the case, Anselm's words are open to a multiplicity of interpretations, and one cannot leave behind the nagging suspicion that he wanted to keep a difficult friend at a distance. But Anselm's response fits perfectly into his intellectual system. What matters is what our lives become in interaction with those around us in everyday life. There is a suggestion here of christian existentialism, *avant le mot*. Anselm felt responsible for Maurice, but his code of conduct meant that he could feel justified in ignoring Maurice's desires. It was Maurice's monastic life that Anselm considered primary, even though he did not exclude from it the love they shared as friends.

However much Anselm subordinated the subjective desire for the friend to the monastic stability, he still thought that the practice and ideal of friendship had a place within monasticism. Christ becomes the cornerstone of both community and of friendship, and there can be no implicit conflict between individual and collective bonds. In Anselm's prayers the saints are addressed as friends of Christ. John the Evangelist is remembered specifically for his physical closeness to Christ. As Benedicta Ward has written, 'Perhaps this is one of the earliest instances of this picture of Christ with the beloved disciple being detached from the whole setting of the Last Supper and being used as an instance of friendship'.[93] Peter Damian had used the image to symbolize John's wisdom and purity, while for Anselm the moment expressed friendship. The saints are addressed as the 'compassionate friends of God', who in turn can have compassion on Anselm the sinner. In Anselm's second prayer to John, Jesus and John, because of their love for each other, are almost obliged to share themselves with Anselm:

> I believe and know that you love each other,
> but how can I experience this,
> if you do not grant what I ask of you both?[94]

The language of the prayers of Saint Anselm is close to that of his letters, where a salutation can in itself be a prayer:

> To the lords and brothers and dearest friends Herluin, Gundulf, Maurice: brother Anselm in ascending from virtue to virtue to come to Christ, the highest virtue of God. (*ep* 51)

At the same time Anselm fulfills the requirements of *dictamen* (and abrogates them by always putting the name of the friend before his own), he explains and deepens his concept of friendship among monks from the same community who are separated from each other. The overwhelming theme is unity of the spirit.

The renewed and deepened language of friendship to be found in Anselm's prayers and letters is not cluttered with feudal imagery of subordination and loyalty.[95] In writing a letter concerning the call to the monastic life, Anselm uses traditional images going back to Sulpicius Severus of the good christian monk as the soldier fighting a spiritual battle against the devil.[96] But when Anselm addresses his friends whose vocations are not in danger, his language emphasizes their equality of station. Alcuin considered fidelity (*fides, fidelitas*) the primary bond of friendship, while Anselm took this for granted and subsumed it into monastic community. Alcuin cultivated one-to-one friendships with men all over Europe and could not count on the permanency of institutions to which these men belonged. Anselm in every letter of friendship assumed the presence of an active, even thriving monastic community to which he sent his love. At the same time as he wrote to individuals, he addressed communities. Stability and loyalty he could take as a point of departure for personal bonds. Anselm's monastic world of friends was a much more solid one than Alcuin's.

It is only when a correspondent was putting himself outside this inner security that the traditional image of a split and warring world reappears.

Anselm's Circle

With few obvious predecessors and with a highly philosophical view of friendship, Anselm in his independence and originality of mind eluded his contemporaries and at times invited misunderstandings and hurt feelings.[97] But Anselm's ideal of friendship nevertheless gained an audience more responsive to him than that which dealt with his theological definitions of the Redemption.[98] Theologically he could be inaccessible, while his expressions of friendship were too exciting to ignore. Anselm struck a chord in his listeners, and their response shows us that the age and the milieu were receptive to the idea that monks could be each other's friends in working towards a more ascetic community. Today Anselm's theological solitude wins our respect and admiration, but for his contemporaries who were excited by his plain talk and clear moral examples, he was by no means a lonely figure. They did their best to follow his lead.

However little Anselm's teacher at Bec, Lanfranc, appreciated his brilliant pupil's new theological language, Lanfranc made use of a similar vocabulary of friendship in letters composed while he was archbishop of Canterbury.[99] Anselm and Lanfranc differed in personality and outlook, but they shared the same delight in describing the bonds of friendship among monks. 'To my lord, father, brother, friend Anselm', Lanfranc could write, thanking him for taking in his nephew at Bec.[100] This youth Lanfranc says he loved 'as my soul', not a very original phrase, yet one that could have been plucked from one of Anselm's own letters. Anselm's answer is reassuringly delicate. It provides an opportunity to mention the monk Maurice, 'whom you have separated for your own sake from him by whom he is loved more than anyone else, and whom he loves more than anyone else'.[101] Anselm seems to have been doing his best to hint that Maurice might want to return to him: 'Judge for yourself what you owe him'.

Lanfranc may have written so affectionately to Anselm in order to match his style, but the archbishop could express himself in the same manner in asking Gilbert Crispin, monk of Bec and then of Caen, to take good care of his nephew. Lanfranc sent a cross with relics to Gilbert as a 'token of eternal friendship' between Gilbert and his nephew.[102] Lanfranc wanted to create a special bond between an older and a younger monk because of his love of the latter. He made it clear that he felt responsible for the youth's spiritual as well as material well-being. In Lanfranc's letters, bonds of family and friendship are intermingled. As we have seen in earlier chapters, kinship and friendship bonds are often intertwined in monastic life, despite a clear theme emphasizing conversion as abandonment of family and friends. Lanfranc makes clear what often is only suggested in other contexts: every monastery was a network of close family ties of both spiritual and biological kinds. He told Gilbert Crispin that he considered his nephew Lanfranc to be Gilbert's brother because Gilbert's mother, who had become a member of a monastery for women at Caen, 'as has been told me, deigned to call him, Lanfranc's nephew, her son'. Lanfranc linked up the monastic worlds of Canterbury, Caen, and Bec on the basis of friendship as well as that of blood relations. In the monastic context the two can be interchangeable: brothers in the flesh became spiritual brothers, and spiritual brothers became as closely linked to each other as brothers in the flesh could be expected to be. 'I said he was your brother', Lanfranc insists to Gilbert, 'because I really want and ask that he be so'.

A new monastic generation represented by the nephew cemented the bonds that had long existed between Lanfranc and Gilbert:

> . . . so that you may love me in every age of your life, as you were accustomed to loving me in boyhood and youth.[103]

The balancing of the phrases as well as the sentiment recall Anselm's style so strongly that one might ask who influenced whom. Lanfranc may have been influenced by Anselm's explicit mode of expression, but there is also the possibility that both of them can be seen as products of a long development in the preceding century's schools where expressions of friendship had been highly valued and cultivated. In any case it was Lanfranc who in the early 1060s had provided Anselm with the linguistic and theological training necessary to combine a rhetoric of friendship with a theological understanding of it. The few letters of friendship ascribed to Lanfranc make clear his care and precision in expressing his loves and loyalties. His phrases are balanced and tailored to the particular correspondent. In writing his nephew and the nephew's companion at Bec, Lanfranc summarized a conception of continuity and growth in friendship with a succinct simplicity that even Anselm could not quite match:

> Since you loved each other in the world in a godly manner, as I believe, I ask that you beseech God that with his help, you may love each other in that holy vow which you have taken.[104]

Lanfranc saw a natural transition between the good friendship of secular life and that of monastic community. The taking of vows did not demolish the earthly bond, so long as this was linked to God. Becoming monks makes the two into even closer friends, for they now are each other's brothers:

> Let the one be a solace to the other in trouble, the one is to take on the example of the holy way of life of the other. Show humility to all, and check your tongues in salvific control from all slander.[105]

After centuries of ambiguity about the relationship between secular and monastic friendships, Lanfranc made it seem obvious that two men could be each other's friends both before and after they embraced the monastic life. Instead of worrying about the dangers and distractions of the friendships of this world, he saw the possibility that these are divinely guided towards monastic friendships.

Lanfranc did not reserve the language of friendship for the monastery alone. He considered *amicitia* a bond that could be established between two men from the time they got to know each other. Unlike Anselm, Lanfranc was not afraid of combining kinship and monastic bonds in making friendships. Anselm did his best to keep his family at a distance, while Lanfranc at least with his nephew did his utmost to make this surrogate son into a friend to good monks. More work needs to be done on the letters of Lanfranc and their linguistic and philosophical links with Anselm's letters. There is no doubt, however, that Lanfranc and Anselm agreed that the language and practice of friendship had an important role in the monastery.

A similar orientation can be seen in the context of Gundulf's *Life*. This monk of Bec became bishop of Rochester (1077-1108) and was one of Anselm's staunch allies after he became archbishop in 1093.[106] In describing the friendship between Gundulf and Anselm, the biographer uses phrases that could have been taken from one of their letters:

> In such great friendship he was joined to Gundulf that he would say he was another Gundulf and Gundulf another Anselm, and he would rejoice at being thus named.[107]
>
> (. . . tanta Gundulfo est amicitia vinctus ut se alterum Gundulfum, Gundulfum vero alterum Anselmum diceret et vocari gauderet.)

This bond is also expressed in terms of the *cor unum et anima una* of the Acts of the Apostles (4:32). What appears in the Bible as a mainly social bond by which all things are held in common is now used to describe a personal friendship.[108] Anselm is said to have provided the words, while Gundulf offered the evidence of his tears.[109]

The *Vita Gundulfi* was composed between 1114 and 1124, more or less a decade after the deaths of Anselm and Gundulf. The author, as the modern editor points out, uses this commemorative biography to criticize conditions at Rochester. In so doing he gives us his version of what monastery friendships do not involve:

> Far from their hearts or tongues to detract from their priors or brethren. They were not vexed as so often happens with complaints about food or drink or clothing.[110]

The content of monastery life and talk (*confabulatio. . . claustralis conversatio*) leads not to the complaints but to an ever stronger asceticism.

The sweet converse of friendship (*dulcia colloquia*) was not limited to the contact between Gundulf and Anselm. In bonds with other men, Gundulf found more opportunities for friendship. The *Vita* indicates that Gundulf and Anselm continued their friendship after they became bishops, something not evident in Anselm's letters of the time. Whenever the two had a chance to meet, the author claims, Anselm would speak about the fire of divine love, while Gundulf would listen.[111] The account is full of traditional elements of a commemorative biography: good works, self-denial, conflicts with the devil; but the element of friendship introduces a new theme into hagiography, a sign of Anselm's literary and personal influence in the early twelfth century. However much the biography intended to use Anselm's prestige to increase Gundulf's, it is significant that friendship achieves such literary prominence. For centuries hagiographers had dwelt only rarely on friends and friendships among men from monastic backgrounds. Now they began to do so.

Another bishop who seems to have been influenced by anselmian enthusiasm for friendship was Herbert of Losinga, bishop of Norwich (d. 1119). The collection of his letters seems to be little known, but since the nineteenth-century edition was reprinted in 1969, it has become more easily available.[112] To Roger the abbot of Fécamp (where Herbert had been a monk), Herbert wrote of the bonds of father and son that still united the two, and then added a practical *petitio*, a request for a copy of Suetonius (*ep* 5). To another abbot he mourned over not being able to see him: 'I get light from the eyes of my friends', he insisted and then asked for texts with letters of Augustine and of Jerome, a solid indication that those who formulated the new literature of friendship were drawing on the patristic heritage (*ep* 10).

Anselm's letters as archbishop of Canterbury tell little about any attempt he may have made to cultivate friendship with the monks there. They seem in many respects to have resented his ways and to have contrasted him unfavourably with his predecessor Lanfranc. Does this perhaps mean that the anselmian practice of intimate friendship can exist only in relatively small and isolated monastic communities? Herbert's frequent letters from his travels to his monks at Norwich, however, make the bonds of friendship at a large cathedral-abbey seem both possible and real. To brothers who pursued courses of studies he encouraged hard work and ceaseless dedication but also offered his friendship. 'Friendship does not deserve anger when it tells the truth', he assured a scholar whose verses he had criticized (*ep* 30). To another he says, 'If you love yourself and wish to enjoy my love', then the student was to complete his study of Aristotle before Herbert returned home! Herbert prods and insists. His letters have a prosaic quality about them that makes them much less exciting in content and form than those of Anselm. But they share his assumption that human bonds are based on friendship. These have a place within the cloister as well as outside of it. To brothers of the church at Norwich as a whole, he spoke of the one heart and soul as representing the unity of community. 'Everything is to be done in common so that there is no place for individuality' (*singularitati*).[113] Nevertheless Herbert wrote to Ingulf, the prior at Norwich, a brief letter that conveys a special bond of friendship:

> I am going to court, almost without horses and without money, but God will be my companion. I hand over the church of Norwich and my work on the church to you, and I commend you to God. If you need anything, get hold of it, and when I return, I shall repay everything to your creditors. Peace be to you and to all the brethren who in humility and truth keep with you the observance of our rule in our house.[114]

Friendship based on trust is implicit here without any florid declarations of love. In simple language this dynamic bishop who began building the great cathedral of Norwich handed over responsibility to a man in whom he had confidence and for whom he obviously cared greatly.

Several of the letters do not reveal much information about the identity of the recipients. But even when we cannot establish the precise historical circumstances, the language of friendship is still very much evident. To a Robert whom he calls brother and son, Herbert warned against a tendency to make new friendships without being loyal to old ones (*ep* 33). Cherish your old friends, he advised, for then Herbert would be to Robert the friend he once had been. Herbert, just as Anselm and Lanfranc, believed that friendship holds human society together. Like Anselm, Herbert linked human bonds of friendship to unity with the saints. In a prayer made for the Queen (who must have been Henry I's Edith), Herbert addressed Saint John the Apostle as a friend of Christ.[115] Herbert prayed that he would be able to come with John to the heavenly feast 'in effable sweetness and sweet ineffability' (*ineffabili dulcedine atque dulci ineffabilitate*). Such a construction could have come from a prayer of Saint Anselm. Herbert's exact debt to the prayers and letters of Anselm remains to be established in detail, but here probably is a man aware of the revolutionary language of the archbishop of Canterbury and able to adopt some of it to his own needs at Norwich.

Even in the letters of the great abbot of Cluny Hugh (1049-1109), Anselm left his mark. Despite the many biographies we have of Hugh from the medieval period, we actually know very little about his personal life and thoughts.[116] We do know, however, that meeting Anselm in exile at Marcigny, near Cluny, had a strong influence on him. To Anselm he wrote a letter that underlines the importance of contact among monks and shows how Anselm's own words could enhance such bonds: 'Who could ever be so inhuman that after he had experienced the sweetness of your talk, he would not receive and venerate you as the angel of God?'[117] Such an exclamation makes it clear that however much Anselm spoke of friendship in his letters, his talks and sermons with monks both at home and abroad may have been still more moving and exciting for his listeners. The sweetness of his talk made men love him, partly because he encouraged in monastic life a dimension of spiritual friendship.

WHY FRIENDSHIP NOW?

The sources we have examined in the preceding pages make it clear that the ideal and practice of monastic friendship developed gradually in the course of the eleventh century. From the last decades of the tenth century onwards a constant stream of writings took up this theme and dealt in ever greater detail with it. Friendship emerged as a major theme of monastic life. To note this development is not enough: it is also important for the historian to ask *why* or at least *how* it could happen. In the course of this chapter I have indicated some explanations for its development in this period:

The cathedral schools and their literary pursuits

It is here that the new interest in a language and celebration of friendship first can be seen. During this period monks and scholars were almost interchangeable in a society where there were lively contacts between the two environments. It was natural for the new interest in Cicero and in the expression of ideas about friendship to travel quickly from the secular cathedral to the monastery school. Men who received their first literary training at cathedral schools later joined monasteries. In this way they brought with them the enthusiasm of their masters for writing about friendship and discussing its content.

Interest in deepening the content and quality of spiritual life for the individual

Carolingian prayers and spiritual writings emphasized the community's worship of an omnipotent God, while eleventh-century prayers and meditations from the cloister paid more attention to the meeting of the individual monk or cleric with a saint who would bring him to God. The saint was seen as a friend of God and so became a potential friend for the monk. The saints as *amici dei* supported a view of friendship that emphasized the worth of human bonds as part of the scheme of salvation.

The Gregorian reform and a new literature of debate in the church

This movement, with its polemics, brought a greater articulation of intellectual and religious matters in terms of theological speculation and in descriptions of letterwriting as a means to express friendship. The need to choose sides and find allies encouraged communities and individual monks to seek each other out and to define what their bonds involved. Heightened controversy encouraged a heightened statement of tenderness and unity among men in the church.

The phenomenon of Saint Anselm and his language of friendship

As prior at Bec Anselm maintained through letters his links of friendship with his monks after their departure to Canterbury. This new literature inspired many imitators and admirers. It reflects the desire of monks to write about interpersonal bonds and the links between individual, community and God.

A more dynamic and mobile society

People seek out friends when they leave a traditional way of life and enter into one that is not so well-defined or determined. For the youths who entered the cathedral schools of the eleventh century, friendship was not just a matter of convenience. It was a necessity so that they could make their way in a competitive and fluid society. This new mobility and chance for social advancement made friendship attractive and important in everyday life.

All these developments may in retrospect seem so obvious that they hardly need repeating. But things could easily have gone differently. Peter Damian's fear of homosexuality in the church might have developed into a full-scale persecution. Instead the apparent lack of concern in clerical circles about homosexuality, described by John Boswell, meant that churchmen for the most part concentrated on other matters of discipline during the period of the gregorian reform. Monastic writers show practically no interest in the possibility that monks might end up loving each other physically if they got to know each other too well. This is a view that I do not find in the vast eleventh-century literature of monastic friendship. Monastic authors of the time read the Lives of the Desert Fathers, but they did so in Latin, where there is almost no trace of the fear seen in some of the greek collections that the brethren might become sexually attracted to each other.

The anselmian revolution in the expression of monastic friendship was only a partial victory for a new tenderness in the description of interpersonal bonds in a religious context. The Anselm who to us looms so large in his letters and prayers never achieved great prominence in Western Europe. His prayers managed to get into continental cistercian circles, but his letters of friendship are to be found almost exclusively in an english or norman context.[118] However well the monks of Fécamp, Caen, Bec, Canterbury, and Norwich cultivated monastic friendship, they lay on the periphery of european events and cultural trends. Cluny seems to have been little affected by Anselm. Only a direct meeting with Anselm awakened Abbot Hugh to the attractiveness of a man seeking spiritual truths in a new mode of fraternal intimacy.

By its very definition, monastic friendship seems to have been doomed to extinction after a brief moment of acceptance. Anselm's letters had a direct effect on only a few churchmen. The main thrust in the reformed monasticism of the late eleventh and early twelfth centuries was towards greater asceticism, which idealized desert isolation. From Italy eremitical movements spread into France. Even Anselm before coming to Bec had thought about becoming a hermit. As a monk at Bec he wished at times that Lanfranc his prior would order him into the forest to live alone.[119]

Despite the pull of solitude, monastic friendship did not die out. It was to enjoy its most complete expression in the twelfth century. Instead of insisting that men break all bonds in becoming monks, the reformers of this period from 1050 to 1120 used the human family and human friendships as models for a new society of the cloister. Friendship would not just survive. It would flourish and come time and again to the surface of monastic lives and texts. The contribution of the eleventh-century reformers to this development was much more profound and solid than their twelfth-century successors perhaps even realized.

CHAPTER SIX

THE AGE OF FRIENDSHIP: NETWORKS OF FRIENDS 1120-1180

THE TWELFTH CENTURY in Western Europe, especially in England and Northern France, brought an age of friendship. Bonds between men became a matter of great experience, discussion, debate, and description. At the forefront of this enthusiasm for expressing friendship were the Cistercians, a new order of monks which in reforming the observance of the Rule of Saint Benedict became the monastic innovators of their day. Their first members at Cîteaux in Burgundy betrayed no special concern for close personal bonds, but once Bernard arrived there with his band of friends, the question of friendship became a matter of general concern.

To tell the full story of this development towards more explicit forms of friendship would require a treatment of the lower aristocracy, the knights, from which the Cistercians drew so many of their members. The skillful and sensitive analyses of monastic culture of Jean Leclercq would have to be combined with the best pages from George Duby's characterization of feudal society.[1] Rather than spreading myself in this way, I shall limit myself to the phenomenon of monastic friendship as it is visible to us in texts which mention it. We will have to make forays from the monastic world into that of the secular church, for many monks enjoyed friendships with non-monks. One motive behind such friendships lay in a desire to convince such people to become monks. Many apparent letters of friendship were inspired by a desire to encourage vocations to the monastic life.[2]

The popularity of these vocational letters in the collections of the period points to a dynamism in twelfth-century religious friendship. In this period monks were not content in considering their own odyssey from home and family to monastic life as sufficient in itself. Since they were members of an almost aggressive social and religious movement, many monks felt both inspired and obliged to convince fellow family members as well as friends of childhood and youth to follow them into the cloister. Social, personal and biological bonds came to be looked upon as a source of strength and expansion. The old battle between the world and the cloister ended in victory for the monastery, which accepted a role as a centre not only of ecclesiastical culture but also of social and spiritual ferment.[3]

As we have so often seen, it is difficult to distinguish between friendship as a purely literary phenomenon and as a part of everyday life and experience. The gentle opening of a polished monastic letter, its *captatio benevolentiae*, is the perfect place for niceties about wanting to be with the friend and feeling pain at his absence.[4] To some extent it can be argued that the very existence of such phrases is of more than literary significance. By picking up classical expressions and combining them with biblical language of love and longing, monastic writers looked for ways to include close human bonds among the desirable goals of their lives.

Twelfth-century monastic writers were so adept in their facility of literary expression that they could convey almost any message they wanted in a convincing manner.[5] Appropriate passages from Paul, Jerome, the Acts of the Apostles, or even the words of Christ, were within easy reach for these well-practiced writers. The language of the Psalms and that of the Song of Songs, as we shall see, became a primary vehicle for what appear to be passionate declarations of love and devotion. As also happened in the carolingian period, the reader can wonder whether such able writers were more in love with their own facility of expression than concerned about the well-being of the person to whom they wrote.

In this period it was much easier than it had been a century earlier to exchange letters. Practical hindrances to this form of communication had been reduced. Trade, pilgrimages and church meetings meant that many more people were probably moving about in Western Europe than had been the case since the first christian centuries. The amount of movement in medieval society cannot be measured, but eagerness to go on crusade, to discover new lands, and to take risks affected the monasteries and encouraged monks to increase contacts with each other. At the same time it became easier to put down one's thought on expensive parchment. More of it was available for cistercian houses, whose branches in Yorkshire specialized in sheep production. Monasteries could also afford writing materials at a time of generous donations. Most of the precious parchment was still used for recording gifts and property transactions, but scraps were available for brief letters of friendship. Monks also delighted in exchanging texts of theological works and biblical commentaries, and such contacts could also be facilitated at a time when there were the necessary resources.

Busy abbots who had no time to write their own letters painstakingly by hand found a growing supply of clerics. Cistercian houses attracted young men from parisian and other schools and could draw on the best secretarial help of the age in drawing up letters.[6] These were sent across Europe, thanks to the new order's network of connections between mother and daughter houses and because of the yearly meetings of the General Chapter. An increase in the amount of business because of shared concerns among the many new houses meant more frequent personal contacts. Here the 'older' monasteries, such as those loosely associated with Cluny, were by no means excluded and often had intellectual, administrative, and friendship bonds with monks from new houses. Friendship and business could be combined in the same letter whether one was Cluniac or Cistercian.

Several of the letter collections from this period have the mark of being self-conscious products. Writers asked for letters to be sent back to them so they could include them in their files.[7] Given an increased interest since the eleventh century in *ars dictaminis* as a literary genre with clear rules and with the opportunity for able writers to establish a reputation, it might seem pointless for us to attempt to extract from letters of this rich and complex period an element of living and lived human friendship. The wealth of the collections, however, provides some assurance that they contain reflections of a personal side to monastic life. Collections grew in size to such an extent that they no longer include only 'representative' letters. Often they are so complete that they allow us to trace the development of a friendship through a succession of letters to the same correspondent. These collections also contain both copies of letters sent and letters received in answer.[8] Writers express an entire register of human responses: anger and disappointment as well as praise and delight in the friend.

Such factors supply an element of variety, even of unpredictability, in the collections, something familiar to any modern observer of human relations. Forms are essential in such exchanges, but they do not necessarily blot out all traces of individuality. Ultimately the monks whom we meet in the twelfth century convey themselves to each other not only as representatives of traditional or well-defined ideologies, but also as individual human beings. In twelfth-century letter collections the elite artificiality of carolingian epistolary exchanges does not return, for the message of friendship usually required just as much attention as the literary structure. In what follows I shall be able to do no more than to suggest a very few of the human relationships implied in the letters. Letters which by themselves deserve careful literary analysis will be given what may seem like superficial treatment. At times I can depend on solid textual studies, but just as often I rely on editions that cry out to be redone. No matter how much we need detailed studies, the historian must at times synthesize on the basis of the abundance of materials we already have.

At the end of this chapter I shall make a schematic attempt to relate the triumph of friendship to its social background and to consider some reasons for the articulateness of this century in european history. Friendship formed one part of a much larger development in Western civilisation: the integration of classical and christian culture into a new *urbanitas* or urban culture.

THE SUCCESSORS OF SAINT ANSELM

Although Saint Anselm never founded a clearly-defined school of followers, he did have a profound emotional and intellectual effect on many who knew or read him. One of his immediate followers, Elmer, monk at Christ Church, Canterbury in the early twelfth century, held office as prior from 1128-37.[9] His small collection of letters is by no means a landmark in monastic friendship, but, as Jean Leclercq has pointed out, they provide us with 'little-known witnesses' of monastic life on a more ordinary level than that of an Anselm or a Bernard.[10] Many of the recipients of Elmer's letters cannot be identified. Some must have been fellow monks, while others were lay persons or members of the secular clergy. Almost all of them are addressed with great affection and enthusiasm. To a monk named William, Elmer recalls 'sweet talks' that 'concerned the salvation of our souls, when we would stimulate each other through reciprocal exchanges to love of the eternal city.' This recollection, of course, only augments the pain of separation. But writing to a friend eases the pain:

> What then? If I cannot be with you in bodily presence as often as I would like, then ought I not be with you at least in letters? For it is certain that our writings join us to each other, and pious speech fashioned in a simple style inflames our inner hearts to divine love.[11]

The expression *stilo simplici* reveals William's literary awareness and may be a devotional formula of humility, what Curtius calls a *Bescheidenheitstopos.*[12] These beginning sentences serve as a fitting *captatio benevolentiae* and provide a point of departure for a meditation on how to increase the two monks' shared devotion to Christ.

Equally skilled in literary terms, but perhaps a clearer manifestation of friendship, is a letter to a certain Geoffrey, who was renowned for writing poems, (*ep* 9). These Elmer received with great affection and joy, reading and rereading them, not only for their content but also because they showed love towards him. Elmer describes how his reply was interrupted by a sudden pain, which threatened to stop him. This may be one of the headaches about which he elsewhere complains.[13] The 'infirmity' was warded off by the comforting sense of the friend and the act of writing him. There are many edifying thoughts about the desire for heaven, but the correspondent is not forgotten. The letter does not become a mini-treatise on the next life. Elmer looks forward to 'crossing over' to these spiritual joys together with Geoffrey. So, as he ends his letter, words fail, but 'the affection of our love for you will never cease'.[14]

Elmer's spiritual message is carefully and completely integrated into his declaration of friendship. He did not just give good advice to people who we might guess were his friends. They very clearly were his friends! For Elmer affection and advice belong together in this life, so that friends can enjoy each other both now and in the next existence (*ep* 10). All the separations and misunderstandings of the present will give way to the 'one and simple intention in the sole love of the heavenly fatherland', as he insists in a letter of conversion to Giffard, apparently a rich layman.

At times Elmer indicates that he has not met his correspondent.[15] Sometimes he is ambiguous about the relationship. In several instances, however, he makes it clear that his letter of friendship was based on an established bond. This is the case with a Robert, whom he reminds of their old intimate conversations (*familiari colloquio*). Now he wants Robert to join him in the monastic life. Biblical citations are mixed with ciceronian language to produce a power of expression that rivals that of Anselm himself:

> I cannot tell you, my most beloved, with what sweetness, with what efficacy of spiritual desire, my mind embraces your soul in the intimacy of holy love, when it remembers gently your goodness.[16]

Elmer's theme of the abandonment of this world and the joys of the next is present to some degree in most of his letters. His words do not allow us to penetrate very far into his own mind, nor do they provide details about his personal relationships. But he clearly used the language of friendship to describe his bonds with other people whose lives he wanted to share in the monastery.

Far more specific about the content of his friendship, and enmities, was an anonymous writer at Bec in the mid-twelfth century.[17] Leclercq has suggested that some of his letters were written to fellow monks of his own house, for the writer sometimes implies that his recipients were physically present but were unable or unwilling to speak with him.[18] The anonymous of Bec is much less visibly influenced by the style of Saint Anselm than was Elmer of Canterbury. He paid homage to Anselm not as a great letterwriter but as one of the revered abbots of his house, along with Herluin and Lanfranc.

To an unnamed friend (*ep* 2), the Bec writer started a letter by referring to the love of David and Jonathan (1 Kings 18:1). He also held up pagan friendships as important to remember, such as that of Pylades and Orestes. The conclusion is obvious: if non-Christians could love each other with such intensity, then we Christians can love much better. Love can be a relief to the soul: *maximum animi est refrigerium*.

Apparently the correspondent had taken the first step by offering his friendship to our writer: 'by a wondrous expression of love you decided to form a friendship with me'. He responded in describing his vision of friendship. In one and the same letter he seems to be writing of his individual friendship and of the collective charity of the cloister, or that intended for all Christians. The reality of the individual relationship is brought out in another letter to the same friend, which is entitled a 'letter of consolation' (*ep* 3). The Bec writer tells his friend why he had delayed writing him and how he understood his correspondent's pain at their separation and his long silence. Friendship like love is a happy state when every day, and every hour, it brings opportunities for extended talks, but it is still wondrous that after long periods of separation, love suffers no injury.[19]

The anonymous of Bec says he wrote not so much for the sake of his correspondent, whose love he trusted, but for the sake of those who might read the letter. This admission of the public audience of a letter is reenforced with a final request: do not pay more attention to rhetorical form than to content. The Bec writer excoriates those monks who when a letter arrived at their monastery were mainly concerned with discussing its literary elegance (or lack of it) instead of its 'spiritual meaning'.[20]

In another letter of consolation (*ep* 4), the Bec writer comforted a monk who had been sent away from the monastery to one of its priories. He insisted that the friend was to bear his own trials, but at the same time he offered love and friendship. The friend also had the solace of having two people with him to keep him warm, he added.[21] Apparently the monk had not left Bec alone but had gone to the priory with two companions. Although he had been torn from the breasts of his mother (Is 28:9), the monk would survive at the new priory. But the Bec writer admitted that it also was hard for him to console himself at the loss of his brother.

Sweetness, comfort and good advice: such saccharine elements make one wonder to what extent the monks of Bec and Canterbury spoke to each other about the full range of their feelings. One indication that they sometimes may have covered a broader spectrum, and with little restraint, comes in a letter from the anonymous of Bec to a monk who is described as his rival. In passionate language he describes all that he had done to get this brother to love him. This man could have been joined to the anonymous writer's heart if he had only wanted such closeness, but instead he had tried to slander him. 'You claim you would love me if I stopped cutting you down', our writer says and insists that he never had detracted from the rival's reputation. Other people may call him names and make accusations, but he, the writer, had never done so. When the rival does evil towards others, why does he feel evil towards the writer and think that it is because of him that other people think badly of him?[22] The Bec anonymous insists that he had often taken his correspondent aside to win him over and had even wept, but to no avail. He had asked for witnesses who had heard him denigrating the rival, but none had come forward.

The letter becomes harsh and uncompromising in tone. The brother who had been attacking the writer is said to have no spark of charity in him *(ut nullam caritatis scintillam in se ualeat admittere).* His words and actions do violence not only to the writer but also to the very body of Christ. Since this monk loves no one, no one can love him in return. Friendship and community belong together, and the opposite of friendship, enmity, provides a threat to the community as a whole and to the whole fabric of salvation in the monastic life in Christ.

At the end of this extraordinary letter the Bec writer claims he had had to restrain his anger, but he had already released a great deal of it. Twelfth-century fondness for letters of friendship here can be seen as allowing something rare in carolingian collections: the production and conservation of letters dealing with failure in friendship. The combination of declarations of love and enmity strengthens the case for arguing that such letters reflect actual human relationships in the cloister. This letter could of course have been intended as a model for the literary expression of anger and disappointment, but its existence points to a new publicity and openness about interpersonal bonds among monks. Our Bec writer may have been addressing a fellow monk in his own community. Whoever the recipient was, the letter itself points to monastic concern in this period for clarifying human bonds.

While Elmer of Canterbury wrote most of his letters of friendship to encourage conversion to the monastic life, the anonymous writer of Bec wrote either to those who already were monks or to those whom he realized would not become monks. In this second category we find a letter to a scholar named Richard (*ep* 7). The Bec writer says that even though he as a monk had to concentrate on 'the one thing necessary' (Luke 10:42), the ascetic life of prayer, he still had a place in his life for love towards those whose lives resembled his own.[23] Whatever he wrote to Richard, he said, would have to convey a sense of the life of the cloister (*claustrum redoleat*).

The Bec monk was answering a lost letter from Richard. The scholar had apparently expressed a desire to become friends with our monk, who in turn was eager for such a relationship and emphasized that it was something natural. It should be evident, he wrote to Richard, that their mutual love was not due to written law, the biblical commandment of love. There was also a natural law commanding it. Love between human beings is looked upon as a natural phenomenon, something that monastic life completes and does not destroy. The monk could reach out to those in the world who are also concerned with spiritual and intellectual matters. Richard should know that he had one person 'in the monastic life from whom without doubt you can benefit as your true friend'.[24]

This brief review of a few of the letters in the anonymous of Bec's collection can give only a cursory impression of his richly-varied ways of expresssing his relationships with other people. This multiplicity of bonds, monastic and secular, underlines the abundance of the twelfth-century material as compared to that of earlier centuries. The flexibility and enthusiasm of monks for forming and describing relationships also points to a change in a conscious attitude towards friends and friendship. Before the eleventh century, except for a few anglo-saxon and elite carolingian writers, monastic culture and manifestations of friendship made insecure partners. After the end of the eleventh century the cloister became a focal point for a variety of spiritual friendships anchored in christian love. This impulse of friendship spilled out of the cloister and into other areas of medieval life.

At times the content of a letter does not indicate whether it was being sent to a monk or not. The Bec writer emphasizes in one letter (*ep* 8) that there is a natural affection which provides a bond among all men and links it to the love of Christ. In this letter spiritual friendship required mutual consolation and could be formally declared in a pact of love (*pactae dilectionis propositum*). The main sign of friendship, however, is unity of will persisting between friends, providing they maintained devotion to God, for they could confide in each other as if in other selves.[25] When friends grow old, their love remains untouched by age, grows younger, and never knows eclipse. There is a lyrical element in this letter that borders on what we might call romantic love. The expression of friendship is, nevertheless, always under careful literary and ethical control.

In the anonymous of Bec's letter, friendship becomes more personal than Anselm would have allowed. Anselm distanced himself from his friends to keep them from loving him too much as an individual. The anonymous of Bec did not keep this distance. A friend in England named Clement wrote our monk and said he could not be happy in merely reading the letters of friendship he wrote to others and which apparently were circulating (*familiares. . . ad amicos epistolas*, *ep* 9). He wanted something for himself. The Bec writer obliged him. How could he deny, he asked, that in Christ he belonged completely to his friends? He mentions talks the two once had had. Such a reference indicates that the Bec writer really did have close contacts and not just ghostlike friendships at a distance. The letter is the response of one friend to another, using the friendship and the epistolary genre to convey something important to the recipient: a story of a failed attempt to share love with another monk at Bec. The writer seeks consolation in Clement's declaration of love: 'Would that I could find at last someone onto whose breast I could cast myself, after having shed all my hesitation'.[26] This total surrender of self he can make to Clement, for whom the Bec writer defines friendship in sallustian terms, to will and not will the same.[27]

Speaking of a 'law of perfect love between brothers', the monk of Bec nevertheless warns Clement against ignoring his vow of stability and coming to him at Bec. However personal and attentive our writer was with Clement, he still set clear limitations in monastic life on contact among friends. He also had to disappoint Clement in his request for a copy of a sermon by Peter of Poitiers. The Bec writer had been unable to copy it because severe headaches had almost kept him from writing at all. Although the Bec writer dutifully ends by quoting from the Rule of Saint Benedict, the line Clement might have taken to heart had already come earlier: 'What else can I say to you? In Christ I love you, simply and truly': *Quid aliud tibi possum dicere? In Christo te diligo, hoc breviter et veraciter*.

The power and beauty of these letters are increased by the ability of the Bec writer to turn from generalities about love to specific concerns. To a friend who was possibly at his own monastery, he apologized profusely for sign language he had used that apparently was misunderstood as a slight. First he had tried to talk to the friend, the Bec writer insists, but the man had rejected him. The two were becoming a laughing stock for their rivals (*ep* 13). The friend might claim that this was a small matter and that he was unnecessarily disturbed, but the Bec writer still asked forgiveness for a crime he said he had not committed: 'Sighing, I composed this letter', he claimed, and begged the friend not to be angry with him any longer.[28]

Every monastic friendship involves the possibility and frequently the reality of jealousies and rivalries. These can hardly be avoided in a tightly-knit community. But our Bec writer insists that individual friendships have a secure and rightful place in the monastery. Friendship is based on a natural human need for love which is strengthened and heightened in a christian community. The cold fear of the desert about human attachments has retreated into the background. Medieval monastic discipline provided a structure to make friendship possible, while a new interpretation of the individuality of christian love made it eminently desirable.

Another member of Anselm's circle, but one less closely linked with him than the Bec monk or Elmer of Canterbury, Hildebert of Lavardin, was born in 1054 and became bishop of Le Mans from 1097 and archbishop of Tours from 1125 until his death in 1134. Hildebert, a literary genius in his own right, seems to have admired Anselm greatly. His collection contains several letters to and from Anselm. In one (*ep* 6) he complains, as did many of Anselm's correspondents, about a lack of replies. The rarity of your letters, Hildebert pointed out tartly, might be made up for if you composed longer ones! Hildebert announced that he hated statements which, just as they ought to begin to give delight, come to an end. He would rather forget Anselm completely than to feel that his difficult friend thought only occasionally about Hildebert.[29]

Hildebert of Lavardin was not a man to mince words. He needed to hear from Anselm and made use of the anselmian theme that it is hard for friends to be separated from each other. To another friend, who had been away in Rome, he spoke in ciceronian terms of laws of friendship (*amicitiae legibus*, cf. *De amic*. 44). Like many other writers of this period, he assumed that friendship is such a well-defined human relationship that it can be subjected to certain rules:

> For this agreement of minds exists between friends, so that nothing is kept apart from each other, and there is nothing that belongs to the one rather than the other. One will makes all things to them as one republic. Here you should know that I act according to the laws of friendship when I return to you in memory, when I am near you in my sense of compassion, when I take up your cause in prayer.[30]

Whether the friend is present or absent, one experiences everything with him. But presence brings joy, absence, sorrow. In the letter Hildebert expressed his joy because his correspondent had returned safely from Rome.

Hildebert bridges the chronological gap between Anselm, who died in 1107, and Bernard, who entered Cîteaux in 1112. Hildebert corresponded with both of them on terms of friendship. Writing to Bernard in about 1130, he asked him to accept the archdeacon of Trier, Gebuin, who sought to join his fellowship: 'We desire with desire that he be received into the holy place of your spiritual companionship'.[31] Hildebert was a secular cleric, but one who rejoiced in helping make a fellow cleric into a monk. Bernard replied in showing his gratitude: 'What I am is yours'.[32]

In an extraordinary letter showing great understanding about a certain monk's sexual problems, Hildebert evidences his interest in monastic life.[33] Like Elmer of Canterbury and the anonymous writer of Bec, Hildebert used the language of friendship to express his bonds with other people, both lay and monks. The 'one republic' of friendship in which he believed was based on a meeting of classical ideas of friendship with a new christian language based on optimism about the worth of close human relationships.

Hildebert was sufficiently learned in the classics to draw on them directly when he wanted to define the content of friendship.[34] At the same time he composed conventional sermons on monastic life, so that the concept of one heart and mind (Acts 4:32) meant the collective love of the cloister and not any individual relationships.[35] At moments, however, Hildebert described spiritual friendship as the most important relationship in his life, as he did when he required it from Anselm. Hildebert illustrates how the newly-articulated monastic concern for friendship could be shared by those who loved monks (or former monks) but were not themselves monks. When one remembers that many monks who converted as adults had gone to school together with men who remained secular clerics, it is understandable how the converts of the cloister shared with other 'old boys' from school a language of friendship.[36]

Before the twelfth century, friendship had not been considered an especially meritorious state of being for good Christians. Christ himself had said in the Sermon on the Mount: 'If you love those who love you, what reward have you?' (Mt 5:46). In the twelfth century, love of friends became a central concern in treatments of christian love. Anselm, in answering Hildebert, claimed that if we are to love our enemies because of God, then we can at his command love our friends all the more.[37] Such love requires more than vague good will. As Hildebert wrote to a friend on behalf of a dean from Tours who had been unjustly treated: in practice and in need, we are taught to flee to the help of friends (*ep* 39). In an almost anselmian substitution of one human being for another, Hildebert asks that, 'When Ralph comes to you, know that in him I speak to you . . . knowing that I speak for him more devotedly than I do for myself'.[38]

Hildebert provides a human and literary link from the world of Saint

Anselm to that of Saint Bernard. He admired the work of Anselm and even imitated it in his own manner.[39] For all his frustrations with Anselm he still believed in the value of friendship. Hildebert, Anselm and Bernard did their best to talk about God and to talk about human friendship. The christian message did not exclude the one for the sake of the other.

The homoerotic expression of friendship

Among Anselm's followers, there was no need for clear distinctions between spiritual and physical love, for the possibility that friendships among spiritual men would turn into sexual relationships did not exist. This innocence characterizes most of the manifestations of friendship in the twelfth century. It would be typically twentieth-century misuse of medieval sources to translate the intense language and practice of friendship into evidence of repressed homosexual behaviour. But this is not to deny that there were clerics and monks during this period for whom male friendship and love could have a sexual dimension. John Boswell has dealt with some expressions of this type of friendship.[40] In what follows I shall try to provide a more nuanced interpretation of a few of these men, for Boswell at times reads their poetry too literally and does not allow for the element of literary freedom that can be present.

Baudri was abbot of Bourgueil in northern France from 1107 until his death in 1130.[41] We have a fairly large collection of his poems, and in several of them, he writes of friendship and love with a homoerotic element. Several times he condemns homosexual love as a 'greater crime which violates nature'.[42] Baudri almost had to say this in order to escape the censure of his fellow monks. Much more importantly, he on several occasions indicated that his poetry was not autobiographical and that he merely imagined various situations for the sake of literary novelty.[43]

The personal question still arises, a product of our own century's concerns: 'was he or wasn't he', 'did he or didn't he', 'does he or doesn't he'? In the next chapter, on Aelred of Rievaulx, we will have to answer as straightforwardly as possible. Baudri's sexuality, however, is not nearly as important to his concept of friendship as his secularization of the ideal. Baudri's contribution to friendship lies not in his attachment of it to physical love, at least in fantasy, as in his tendency to write about friendship in purely this-world terms. Baudri's friendships use the monastic milieu as a necessary background, but the bonds he celebrates have very little to do with the monastic life as a quest for personal and collective salvation. The monastery merely provides Baudri with a setting for a community of learning and poetry. He encouraged a small group of men to take on the monastic habit together with him in order to pursue literary studies in common.

Baudri's poems concern more the joys of writing poetry together than the enjoyment of male beauty.[44] The letter of conversion to monastic life becomes a poem of conversion to scholarly life in the monastery. He needed the talk and presence of his friends.[45] In his poems Baudri ranks his friends from one to ten and demotes one so that he can promote another. If we can take the poems in any literal sense, he seems willing to move a new friend a notch up to fourth place after a single impetuous meeting.[46]

While such a system might seem puerile (the schoolboy debate of who is one's best friend), there is still a virility in this poetry. Its strength of form and concentration on the idea of friendship reveal the importance of friendship in Baudri's literary world. To a friend who kept promising he would come but did not, he could be sharp: 'either I shall throw your words to the winds, or loyalty will protect these words'.[47] The bond of friendship (*foedus amicitiae*) is made manifest through the poem.[48] The strength of a single poem might so win over an enemy that Baudri could be accepted as number ten in the hierarchy of this man's friends.[49]

It is perhaps remarkable that a man who occupied the office of abbot in a significant monastery could in his writings ignore this role and describe friendship with little religious content. Human friendship provided an end in itself for Baudri: it offered, as it were, its own reward. Baudri wished in one letter that he had been able to take its place so that he could experience the presence of the friend in the same way that the parchment of the letter itself felt the friend's touch. 'Then I would explore your face and mind.'[50] The letter had become a mode of physical contact, not in the traditional sense of representing the friend but in a more sensual manner of being an object that the friend would touch.

To what extent is this poetry a product of literary imagination and to what extent does it reveal Baudri's emotional life? Since his constant theme is his need for friends and his desire for them to come to be with him, it does seem that Baudri had a great emotional dependence on other monks and scholars. His poetry served as a means of contact with them. To a monk named Maiol he promised he would do anything because he loved him so much.[51] Baudri had been impressed by the man's education, the sweetness of his ways, the nobility of his blood, as well as the nobility of his bearing. One meeting was not enough. Now Baudri insisted on more conversations (*altera colloquia*).

In much monastic literature, a monk may be addressed as a friend in the salutation of a letter whose purpose seems to have been to make contact with a group within the monastery or with the community as a whole. Addressing the individual monk was a matter of convenience. This can be seen in several of Anselm's letters, where he cultivated a circle of friends and not a personal friend. With Baudri just the opposite seems to have been the case. He could acknowledge a monastic community but used contact with it only in order to draw closer to a single monk.[52] Even if the monastic institution is very evident and necessary for such a poem, the content of monastic life, its disciplines and ideals, are almost completely missing. This is not the glorification of Ganymede, as Boswell would have it. Baudri sought to characterize chaste homoerotic relationships in a monastic setting but in secular terms.

An element of play also characterized Baudri's friendship poetry. We see it in the way he changed the rank of his friend Teucer. This enjoyment of literary games is combined with a naive self-awareness that recalls something of the flavour of carolingian friendship poetry. The friend's presence provides a source of joy and the inspiration needed to write more and better poetry. Life becomes art, so that Baudri makes it impossible for his readers to penetrate to any definition of who the artist really is. Baudri's vital, humanistic poetry may result from sexual repression, but it also shows how the monastery could shelter a sensitive and creative man. In our context of monastic friendship, Baudri's work points towards a secularization of the language and practice of friendship.

Like Baudri, Marbod, bishop of Rennes (d. 1023) delighted in writing about male love and friendship while at the same time he claimed to be attached to the monastic life.[53] It is important to read his poetry as a literary product dependent on models and pointing to them. In praising the beauty of a boy and criticizing him for his coldness, Marbod was alluding to a poem by Horace in which the point is not that the boy denies others his favours but that he is so puffed up by pride that he forgets how quickly he will lose his beauty. Marbod's moral has been translated as 'while you bloom, adopt a more becoming demeanor', implying that he should give way to the persistence of his suitors. But if we look at the latin words and their context, the phrase *ergo dum flores, maturos indue mores* has a completely different connotation. Marbod's point is that the boy should act in a more mature way by being less caught up in himself and in his transient beauty. He is not 'denying the beauty of his body' to other men out of viciousness of character. It is his coldness and distance which come to negate the beauty of his body.[54]

Marbod, like his beautiful boy, enjoyed parading in front of his readers the joys of physical love, only to pull away. In a *Dissuasio amoris venerei*, he described the deliciousness of sexual desire and a predicament with a boy whom he pursued while a girl whom the boy was after wanted Marbod. The passage does not have to have an autobiographical interpretation but must be seen as a literary construction for a typically augustinian complaint about the errors of love. Sexual attraction is full of deception.[55]

Marbod of Rennes is an outstanding writer, but his poetry was not intended as anything more than a form of artistry. He drew on the materials of his life and times in order to describe the joys and disappointments of human love. Western Europe in the early twelfth century had room for bishops who could write such poetry without losing their position in society. Even though Marbod shows some caution about revealing his sexual life, more so than Boswell indicates, the bishop contributed to and benefited from contemporary interest in writing about male relationships. I can see no direct links, however, between, on the one hand, Marbod, Baudri and other writers who played with homoerotic themes in the early twelfth century and, on the other, the monks who developed the genre of letters of friendship.

Geographically they were close to each other. Psychologically the distance can be bridged in terms of a common fascination with male love. But the point of divergence is the question of where christian love takes its place in the phenomenon of friendship. In the love poetry of Marbod and Baudri, christian expressions are only superficial glosses, for it is the enjoyment of poetry as an art rather than its contribution to monastic community that takes first place. For the network of monastic friends which will become apparent in the mid-decades of the twelfth century, christian phrases and images are the very substance of the language of friendship. Marbod and Baudri remain outside this development, harbingers of a new secular expression of friendship that came in the later Middle Ages.

The persistence of the conservative view

Besides writing homoerotic verse, Marbod of Rennes also composed a pious poem in praise of the monastic life. Here there is nothing about passionate friendship, only the assertion of the traditional bond of community in the monastery. Similarly, in writing the life of an important monastic founder, Robert of La Chaise-Dieu, he says nothing about friendship.[56] Medieval writers were dependent on the genres they used. In love poetry they were attentive to the classics; in hagiography they had other models.

In general the view of friendship in monastic circles remained untouched by the secular and erotic undertones of early twelfth-century literature. At the same time the conservative view persisted that allowed only a limited place to friendship in the cloister. The monk Orderic Vitalis from Saint Evroul in Normandy (1075-1141) is one of the stolid conservatives of these years who shows by his silences as well as by his open concerns how small a role *amicitia* could play in the monastic consciousness. Describing the reform of the monastic order under Dunstan in tenth-century England, Orderic emphasized the primary role of monks, as fighting against Satan and persevering in the Lord's battle.[57] He remembered Saint Anselm as a man of letters and never hinted at his letters of friendship.[58] Friends are mentioned only when he had hopes of getting them to join the monastery. After they came, they were not called friends any longer.[59] In a rare use of the word *amicitia,* Orderic refers to a political alliance.[60] Orderic saw contemporary figures in ways that have no room for the place of friendship in their lives. Peter the Venerable, whose friendships we will soon consider from his letter collection, was acquainted with Orderic, but the monastic historian never hints at this side of the abbot of Cluny, whom he had probably met there in 1132 at an assembly to reform cluniac statutes. Orderic mentions Peter in order to criticize him for not being more careful with the venerable traditions of the monastic order and for trying to imitate the Cistercians.[61]

Orderic did not like abbots who renewed monastic language or statutes. In his own life there was only one renewal: that of the boy who in tears left his family and friends in order to enter a monastery, where he found that the members of his new community treated him well:

> I left my fatherland and parents and all my family members as well as friends and acquaintances . . . among strangers I found every form of kindness and friendliness.[62]

One notices the word *familiaritatem* here. In a dictionary of classical latin it can be given the meaning of 'friendship', but in medieval monastic context it often means more 'companionship in community' in a general sense, with no special resonance of individual friendship. This is the sense I think Orderic intended here, for he related his own experience to that of the generations of monks for whom going into the cloister meant giving up all family and friends in offering themselves to a community where individuality was lost.

Even monastic literature which gives friendship a certain prominence often made clear that such strong individual bonds can not survive the requirements of community life. In the engaging biography of Saint Stephen of Obazine (d. 1159), the first book, written in 1166, tells how this dynamic founder of a whole congregation of monastic houses started out his ascetic life together with a friend. This was Peter, a priest who is described as Stephen's *socium et sodalem*.[63] Their relationship is not described in any detail, but for much of the first book Peter is very much evident in the background, sharing with Stephen first the life of a hermit and later contributing to the foundation of monasteries. He and Stephen lived for a time in a little hut, where they 'day and night' prayed and sang without ceasing.[64] Here they also scourged each other in penance.

One day Stephen and Peter disagreed about who was to head their new monastery. Neither of them wanted to take on the burden, and so the one recommended the other. Eventually Stephen was forced to take the post.[65] At this point Peter made clear that he expected to be given the abbacy at a daughter house of Obazine. Stephen had no intention of appointing him, and the two friends broke totally when it was discovered that Peter on his own was collecting funds to finance his move from Obazine. Stephen dismissed him. His decision is explained in terms of Peter's naïveté: he was unaware of the illicitness of his action and gullible enough to believe those who tried to deceive him into thinking that Stephen wanted to make him an abbot.[66] As part of a hagiography of Stephen of Obazine, this account may well be an apology for the saint's decision not to share power with his friend Peter. Regardless of the historical accuracy of the narrative, one thing is clear: friendship could not survive. The requirements of funding new monasteries left no room for special considerations for an old friend.

Stephen had to be strict towards Peter, our author insists, in order to provide an example for others.[67] There could be no favouritism, not even towards the man who had been together with him since the first stirrings of his vocation. The old monastic fear of particular bonds and ensuing jealousies comes to the surface here.

It might be objected that with Orderic and the author of Stephen of Obazine's *Life*, we are dealing with a different literary genre than previously in this chapter. It is quite true that letters and poems are more suitable vehicles for conveying images of friendship than are histories and hagiographies. But we need turn only to Orderic's distinguished predecessor, Bede, to find mention of friendship in his hagiography of Saint Cuthbert. As we pointed out early in the preceding chapter, the benedictine historian William of Malmesbury, almost contemporary with Orderic, had room in his writings for terms of friendship. The inevitable difference between two literary forms does not provide a full explanation for the persistence of the conservative view into the twelfth century. Some monastic literature continued to look upon friendship in traditionally limited terms. This attitude has always been present in monastic life. Individual friendship and the community life are seen to exist in a state of tension, even when the monk seeks friends outside his monastery. Friendship is not necessarily an aberration in monastic existence, even though after the medieval period it came sometimes to be interpreted in that way.

In the main monastic tradition friendship had had only a limited or at best an implicit place. Friendships have existed as a matter of course, but no lyricism or special attention has been afforded them. The monk's job has been to pray, not to write letters of friendship. But during periods of dynamism, optimism and the growth of individual and community consciousness, friendship comes into its own. Everything seems possible. Opposites can live together, even if only for a short while. In the twelfth century we see this happening for some monks and clerics. For a few decades friendship takes its place in the vanguard of monastic learning, reform and self-expression.

A MID-CENTURY NETWORK OF FRIENDS: TROYES, CLUNY AND CLAIRVAUX

In the letters that circulated in the 1140s and early 1150s between the monasteries of Cluny, Clairvaux, and Montier-la-Celle, just outside of Troyes, friendship seems to be everywhere. The abbot of Cluny from 1122 to 1158, Peter the Venerable, developed warm friendships with both benedictine and cistercian monks. The benedictine Peter of Celle, who became abbot of Montier-la-Celle in about 1145, wrote to monks at Clairvaux and other monastic houses as his 'dearest friends' with whom he wanted to spend more time. Even Bernard of Clairvaux, whose literary abilities sometimes make his sincerity suspect, manages to convey a sense of the obligations and duties of friendship as well as a genuine need to maintain contacts on an intimate level with those whom he calls his friends.[68]

How did this network of monastic friends come about? Unfortunately the letter collections of Bernard as well as of Peter the Venerable do not give us many glances into the early years of their abbacies, the 1120s and 1130s. The letters abound for the period after about 1138, the year that Bernard's brother Gerard, Clairvaux's cellarer, died. Peter of Celle we can follow only from the time he became abbot. There is nothing to show us a relatively young monk developing a new language of friendship, as did Anselm when he was prior of Bec writing to the monks who had left for Canterbury with Lanfranc.[69]

The Cistercian Order, founded in 1098, does not evidence in its first years any great interest in friendship. Some writers have emphasized the importance of the *Carta Caritatis* as a bond of love among the monks of the New Monastery which became Cîteaux. This gave them a legal basis rooted in mutual love.[70] A close inspection of the document reveals much more about early twelfth century monastic concepts of order and regularity than about bonds of closeness among the earliest Cistercians.[71] Bernard's abbot at Cîteaux, Stephen Harding, however, shows elsewhere that he had mastered traditional benedictine language of friendship between communities.[72] At the same time Stephen must have been keenly aware of the young Bernard's talent and abilities. Only with Stephen's permission could the persistent young nobleman have been allowed to enter monastic life with some thirty of his friends and family members.

When Bernard entered Cîteaux in 1112, he brought his world with him: the young men with whom he had grown up and with whom he had lived a quasi-monastic life on the family estate at Châtillon for six months before making Cîteaux their permanent retreat.[73] Bernard could not tolerate the thought that any of his close school friends might not come with him. He pursued one of them, Hugh of Vitry, and even cried through the night next to him in a narrow bed, a story whose details were almost too physical for Bernard's biographer William of Saint Thierry to include when he polished Geoffrey of Auxerre's *fragmenta* for a biography.[74] But William did understand what was special about Bernard, his uncanny ability to attract young, intelligent and sensitive men to him. William shared with these admirers of Bernard their desire to gain his love.

Like Anselm, Bernard often disappointed his followers by giving them something less than the love for which they asked. Unlike Anselm, Bernard met their objections directly, as he did with William of Saint Thierry, who accused Bernard of not loving him as much as he, William, loved Bernard.[75] Love requires self-knowledge, Bernard answered. William's complaint, he argues, had to be based on William's assumption that he knew both himself and Bernard. This only showed how little William really knew his own self. Bernard's reply may have been a clever way to answer William's complaint, but it shows how Bernard accepted as a fact that a friendship existed between him and William.

To be a Cistercian of the clarevallian line after the death of Stephen Harding in 1134 was to follow Bernard in everything, to be tantalized by the totality of commitment he required, and to believe that practically the whole world had to become Cistercian in order to be saved. Yet conversion to the monastic life no longer meant leaving friends and family. Male friends and family members were encouraged to accompany the recruit into his new life. This may explain the cistercian relish for letters of conversion. Clairvaux was the gate of heaven, and all those whom the monk had loved in the world were encouraged to participate in its community. The bernardine conviction of salvation in the Cistercian Order thereby contributed to the spread of the literature of monastic friendship.[76]

Clairvaux's passion for proselytizing drew on an acquaintance with the expression of friendship present in classical authors. Many of the early Cistercians had gone to school and read these writers. In Bernard we find resonances of Cicero's *De amicitia*: sometimes there are passages close to direct quotations, but usually only indirect formulae.[77] The Cistercians did their best to demean their education and to hide their debt to classical culture, but it is very much present, even in the first generations.[78] Clairvaux was at the same time sensitive to developments at Cluny. Bernard's attacks on the Cluniacs in the 1120s are much better known today than his later expressions of friendship with Peter the Venerable. This elusive relationship, I am convinced, developed into a real friendship, with moments of hope, anger, trust, fear and mutual need.[79]

In Peter the Venerable's letter collection there is a great jump between a letter he wrote to Bernard in the late 1120s defending cluniac practices and indicating only a superficial acquaintance between the two abbots, and a letter from 1137 where the tone is much warmer and Peter writes as if the two were old and intimate friends.[80] Peter had met Bernard at Pisa in 1135 and this may have provided a point of departure for their later relationship. Peter speaks of his devotion and love for Bernard. God knows how much he loves Bernard, even in the absence of his body, for now the two had been apart from each other such a long time that Peter no longer could picture Bernard in his mind's eye. Nevertheless, Peter insists that he remained close to Bernard: 'My soul adheres to you and can no more be separated from your love' (. . . *adhesit anima mea tibi, nec ab amore tuo ultra diuelli potuit*). In the meeting at Pisa, Peter claims, Bernard had won him over completely. Now they belonged to each other, he says, a love that is mutual in Christ and the only love that never ceases.

Some of this language could be dismissed as the verbiage of good relations between two immensely powerful abbots. But Peter's use of the term *amicitia* is supported by his plea that Bernard not reply to his letter by the oral communication of a messenger. Instead he was to send his own letter. Throughout the correspondence of Peter and Bernard, there are many moments when the one or the other claims he is owed a letter. The two abbots kept tabs on each other's signs of good will and sympathy. On a human level they appear as two friends who were constantly misunderstanding each other and then being reconciled again. Amid the recriminations that the letters sometimes contain is the hint that the two men did need to hear from each other. If their only bond had been shared monastic affairs, they could have made do with oral messages or briefer and more business-like letters. If they had been interested in writing memorable statements on monastic life to each other, they could have kept to a minimum the initial statements of affection, as was the case in the first letter between them, Peter's defense of Cluny from the late 1120s (*ep* 28).

Bernard replied to Peter's letter of 1137 in the spring of 1138 in a manner that is affectionate but formal.[82] A few years later, in late 1143, he wrote a much more personal letter to Peter. The abbot of Cluny had apparently complained about a lack of letters from Bernard. Now the abbot of Clairvaux turned the tables and accused Peter of not responding to his letters:

> So you are pleased to jest? Courteously and kindly I would admit, if I could be sure you were not ridiculing me. . . . It is not so long ago that I greeted you

> in a letter with all the respect that is your due, yet you never answered one word. And it is not long since I wrote to you again from Rome, but even then I did not get a reply. Are you therefore surprised that I did not presume to trouble you with my trifles when you got back from Spain?[83]

Bernard was offended and made it clear that the fault (*culpa*) in neglecting to write was not his own but Peter's. At the same time he used the situation to point to a need for openness in friendship. Friends must not harbour their resentment or criticism. Since charity believes all things (1 Co 13:7), it necessarily removes all suspicion. The combination of Paul on charity with Cicero's insistence on openness in true friendship (*vera amicitia*, cf. *De amic.* 44) came genuinely to Bernard. From Cicero he also drew an optimism about the possibility of strong and idealistic friendships between powerful men. The message is conveyed in a rhetorical framework which never gets in the way of the meaning, as it does in Jerome. *Invectio* at the start clears the air and makes way for reconciliation. 'Being recalled I am happy to return, happy to be recalled', Bernard wrote Peter, who was still asked to realize that he had offended Bernard. In a christian spirit of brotherhood and in the conviction of honesty in friendship, Bernard could respond to Peter's invitation.

Bernard addressed Peter both as an individual friend and as the abbot of the most important monastic centre in the West. Both roles are present in the writer's consciousness. Bernard provides news of his health and may indirectly also be indicating his willingness to solve a dispute between Cluny and Cîteaux over payment of tithes. The institutional background for the letter is only implied. Bernard's main point was to reprimand a friend and then to embrace him wholeheartedly:

> If I had perhaps grown cold towards you, as you reproach me for having done, there is no doubt that cherished by your love I shall soon grow warm again. I welcomed your letter with open hands. I have read it and reread it greedily and gladly, and the more often I read it, the better pleased I am. I must say I enjoy your fun.[84]

Bernard claims to have been surprised that Peter could maintain a safe and pleasant middle ground between being ridiculous and being gravely serious. Bernard may himself have wanted to be able to use such a mild tone, but the strength of his passions would not let him. Bernard's response, however, provides an impression of the sensitivity Peter must have shown Bernard in the lost letter. Peter had apparently criticized him for neglect of their relationship, but at the same time he had joked with Bernard in a gentle way. Uncomfortable at such jesting, Bernard still knew enough about the art of writing letters and the person of Peter the Venerable to detect affection behind it.

Peter's personality and attachment to Bernard become apparent in his reply to this extraordinary letter. He first apologizes for his delay in writing back to what he calls the friend's attractive and happy letter.[85] He imagines Bernard thinks his silence due either to laziness or contempt for his friend. But this is not true! Peter takes up nothing more eagerly or reads more carefully than Bernard's letters. The delay is partly due to the bearer of the letter, who had left it at Cluny while Peter was staying nearby at the women's monastery of Marcigny. When Peter came home and found the letter, he kissed it fondly, something he never did to anything else except the holy Scriptures.[86] Reading and rereading the letter, he felt ever greater affection for Bernard. He would have written back immediately but somehow could not do so, and time slipped away.

There is no doubt that Peter was a genius at literary expression and could make almost any account of his actions convincing. A proof of his sincerity lies more in his attitude than his words. He wanted to respond directly to Bernard's objections instead of denying them. In almost every line he combines respect for the passionate abbot with affection for a friend. Peter did not, moreover, meekly surrender to Bernard's charges. He explained his actions to Bernard, who he assumed would listen. As far as Peter remembered, it was he who had written first, while Bernard was at Rome, and so he regarded Bernard's letter as a reply to his own and not as a letter that required an answer. As for the second letter Bernard had mentioned, Peter had no recollection of it at all, and this explains why Bernard got no response. Peter examined Bernard's word *culpa* and said it could not apply to him.[87]

In a remarkable exegesis of Bernard's letter, Peter quotes whole passages to show that he knew what Bernard had been thinking but insists that Bernard had misunderstood his actions. He also gives Bernard a clear signal of his own intention. In the rest of the letter, he promised he would refrain from playing with language but would write in all seriousness. To Bernard's possible reply, that the abbot of Cluny was fond of joking, Peter admitted he did like play, but only with Bernard and not with others. Peter was afraid of discarding a serious tone with others and making his words seem empty. But with Bernard, he insisted, he was not afraid of being misinterpreted, for from Bernard he sought one thing only, love. Peter leads up to a magnificent conclusion:

> And so it is always something sweet for us to speak with you, and to keep a honeyed sweetness between us in our love through joyful talks.[88]

Because love and trust exist between the two friends, they can savour humour and the enjoyment of skilful language. These create an atmosphere of sweetness or *dulcedo*, a term that is often associated with spiritual friendship in this period.

This statement is followed by an eloquent plea for concord between Cistercians and Cluniacs. Bernard's and Peter's personal bond is woven into the nexus of relationships between members of the two Orders and the misunderstandings that had grown up between them. This development might seem to indicate that the personal remarks at the letter's opening are nothing more than a rhetorical flourish, a clever *captatio benevolentiae*, before the important institutional business at hand. We have gone through this section of the letter carefully here in order to show that Peter was not just flattering Bernard. He was addressing him frankly and directly, responding to what he had written, and confronting Bernard with his misconceptions of Peter's intentions. His approach can hardly be looked upon as a conventional and sugary *captatio benevolentiae* before the substance of the letter. Personal remarks are integrated into the relationship of the two Orders. As Peter pointed out to Bernard, as friends they could not remove one another from their hearts, but at the same time they had to act as fathers to their own monks.[89] Peter is subtle, careful and diplomatic in describing differences between the two orders over the payment of tithes and a disputed election of the bishop of Langres. But he places the relationship between Cistercians and Cluniacs in the context of a personal bond, at times even seeming to imitate Bernard's language of fire, water and love taken from the Song of Songs:

> For as concerns the love which I by now from old times have kept in the secret of my heart for it, it seems to me that many waters cannot quench love, nor can rivers drown it.[90]

Of all monastic writers who grace the twelfth century, Peter the Venerable manages to provide descriptions of friendship that are most convincing to a modern reader. The abbot of Cluny could draw on biblical imagery without drowning in it and combine the language of scriptural love with that of classical friendship. Thanks to the work of Giles Constable, we are aware of many of the sources on which Peter drew, while others remain unidentified. The notes to Constable's already classic edition of Peter's letters convey to us a twelfth-century humanist monk who had at his command an immense amount of christian and pagan literature and who was able to pick and choose the expressions that suited him best in any given situation. Peter's only fault by late twentieth-century standards is a tendency to repeat himself and to go on for what seems too long with the same subject. Even here, however, his relaxed development of thought can be attractive.

The importance in Peter the Venerable's life of friendship as an end in itself is most immediately apparent in his all too few letters to his secretary, Peter of Poitiers. The first letter cannot be dated more precisely than at some time after 1134, when Peter of Poitiers entered the service of the abbot of Cluny.[91] Both Peters were attracted by life in a hermitage, away from material cares and worldly distractions, and at some point Peter of Poitiers, at least temporarily, seems to have left Cluny for such an existence. Peter the Venerable addressed him as 'special' and 'dearest', and at first he seems to accept that his friend and helper had chosen solitude: 'I rejoice in your quietness', he writes, 'I take joy in your peace.' Peter the Venerable feels he is out at sea while Peter of Poitiers has come to a safe port, and yet the abbot is happy for him. His love is such that he prefers Peter of Poitier's well-being to his own needs.

Once the abbot has shown his concern, he changes his tone and takes advantage of a 'privilege of friendship' in order to criticize Peter of Poitiers for caring only for himself and thinking so little about his friends. He stops himself, and insists: 'let me not feel thus towards your heart, towards which I am used to feeling the same as towards my own'.[92] Peter the abbot wanted to know more about his friend and what he is doing. He insisted he favoured Peter of Poitier's self-chosen exile from Cluny. What one sentence concedes, however, the next takes back. Lamenting that he was so caught up in worldly affairs that he had no time to think of heaven, he pleaded with Peter of Poitiers to come back to him so that the two of them once again could talk together: 'Come to me then quickly, so that I can believe in the confidences of a friend and trust what I did not dare to entrust to an unfaithful letter'.[93]

Weighed down by the many obligations of being abbot, Peter the Venerable looked towards Peter of Poitiers as a receptacle for his worries and as a confidant. The letter as a whole is split by a contradiction between the abbot's claim to accept his friend's choice and his demand that the friend return to him immediately! This lack of coherence is best explained by Peter the Venerable's divided desire between wanting to live with his friend's choice and needing to have him with him. Love is not logic, and Peter the Venerable may have deliberately written his letter to reflect the conflict within himself.

A second letter helps explain why Peter the Venerable needed Peter of Poitiers so much. Peter wrote it in early 1134 from the parisian house of Saint Martin-des-Champs. Peter, as he was fond of doing in several of his letters, describes his recent travels. He had just spent Christmas at the cluniac foundation in Paris. 'Placed here I remembered you: no, I didn't even forget you for the briefest moment. For the more joyfully I embrace you when present, the more painfully I bear your absence'.[94] Peter of Poitiers remained in the mountains, while his friend kept to the valleys. He prayed that God would deliver him from the mess around him, and he asked for Peter's prayers. This was not enough, however; the abbot wanted his beloved Peter of Poitiers himself. He borrowed the words of Paul to Philemon (1:19): 'You owe your own self'. Peter asks his absent companion to remember all that they had experienced together. How could he ever find someone more like himself? With Peter of Poitiers he could plumb the depths of the Scriptures or of secular literature.[95] This monk had also spoken to the abbot more intimately than anyone else about spiritual matters. He could revive the abbot when he was tired out by worldly cares. Once he had spoken briefly with his Peter, the abbot writes, he could return to his work, comforted by the nourishing food Peter gave him. Peter the Venerable asks whether Peter of Poitiers had forgotten what they had experienced together, all their frequent and fervent conversations: *frequens illa et feruens collatio*:

> How often we closed the doors and admitted no other mortal within, having only him for a witness who never is absent to those who share their thoughts and words. Then we engaged in all-consuming conversation about the blindness of the human heart and its hardness, the snares of various sins, the many traps of demons, the abyss of the judgments of God, how terrible he is in his counsels over the sons of men, how he has mercy on those he wants and is hard on those he wants, and how a man does not know whether he is worthy of love or of hate. We would also talk about the fearful burden of our vocation, of the conferral of human salvation through the Incarnation of the Son of God and his Passion, of the fearful day of final judgment, of the incomprehensible harshness of the divine verdict by which he punishes the evil forever, of his unspeakable mercy, by which he hands over an eternal reward to the good.[96]

I have translated the passage in full because it suggests better than anything else what monks talked about when they revealed themselves to friends. At first look it might seem that Peter was only mentioning the conventional topics that belonged to all edifying contact that good twelfth-century Christians would have had with each other. What can be personal in such a review of the teachings of the christian faith? Such concerns belong to the *conversatio* (in both senses of 'talk' and 'way of life') every good benedictine monk tries to maintain. What is revealing for us here, however, is the context in which such talk is set: not in the bosom of the community, but in a private place, where two monks were alone with each other, sensing that Christ, as he promises, was in their midst (Mt 18:20). In this situation seemingly impersonal subjects become intensely personal. Instead of speaking in the abstract about heaven and hell, the two Peters could relate to each other their own hopes and fears, their visions and dreams of judgment, heaven and hell, as well as their own sense of sin, guilt, and failure, and finally their trust in God, who had given them to each other for mutual help and guidance.

Intimate talks of this kind must have inspired Anselm's monks to write to him with longing and urgency after they had left Bec for Canterbury. Such talks must have moved Bernard's friends and relatives to want to go with him into the monastery. A whole new vocabulary grew up in twelfth-century monastic spirituality in which bonds among monks are described in new ways, as when the abbot began to characterize himself as a nurturing mother.[97] In this development Peter the Venerable reveals how the monastic father figure who spoke of ultimate matters with his monks as a community and with outsiders also could seek responses and mutuality in an intimate and semi-exclusive friendship.

Peter the Venerable, one of the most public figures of his age, was attracted by the call of the desert—but with a friend. He wrote to Peter of Poitiers about how they had made a hermitage together in the midst of men. This, the abbot claimed, they had experienced not only at home at Cluny, but also on the journeys that they had made together. In all things Peter the Venerable found in his friend 'alone and almost singly that definition of true friendship':

> . . . this is to will and not will the same [Sallust, *Catilina* 20:4], so that nothing which displeased you could please me, nor displease me which pleased you, and as is read in a certain writer, we are not two in two bodies but one single soul would seem to be in our bodies.[98]

Sallust's definition of friendship, probably the most popular one in medieval literature, is integrated with another description, the idea of one soul, which recalls the key passage in Acts 4:32, concerning the one heart and one soul of the early christian community in Jerusalem. But here the one soul is that which two friends share.

After this reminder of what the two Peters share, Peter the Venerable follows the same procedures as in his earlier letter to Peter of Poitiers and criticizes him for letting down his friend. The time for accusations had come (*sed iam tempus est querelarum*), he said. Peter of Poitiers had abandoned the pact made between them. The friend had left his friend, the intimate his intimate, the disciple his master, the monk his abbot, the servant his lord. Peter the Venerable does not try to conceal the fact that in several respects Peter of Poitiers could not be his equal in the cloister. As a monk of Cluny, Peter of Poitiers had to obey his lord abbot. But Peter the Venerable was more interested in pointing out his own sense of abandonment than in insisting on his authority:

> Behold when I work, you rest; when I watch, you sleep; when I cry out, you are silent; when I fight, you are unoccupied; when I travel the earth, you remain on your mountain.[99]

In almost every line of this extraordinary letter, Peter the Venerable insists that Peter of Poitiers pay attention to his needs, return to him, and make a place of solitude, a true hermitage, for the two of them, at least within their hearts, where only the voice of God can be heard.[100]

Peter never actually used his authority and ordered his secretary home, as was his right to do. We have to remind ourselves that the writer is the mighty abbot of Cluny, for the main role that Peter the Venerable assumes is that of friend appealing to friend. He adds a new dimension to Christ's words about leaving everything for his sake and cutting ourselves off from father, mother and friends (Mt 10:37). Just as we must distance ourselves from those who threaten our own salvation, whether they be friends or relatives, so too we have the right to appeal to those whom we need in order to work for our salvation. The letter is a new step in the articulation of monastic friendship as an integral part of the process of salvation, and yet it does not depart from traditional language. The contents draw heavily on biblical imagery. They borrow the language of Jerome in their passion for the life of the cloister. Peter nevertheless conveys as a natural step in the spiritual life the practice of companionship that excludes the rest of the monastic community. He insists on a place apart, an opportunity for spiritual talk and tears.

The abbot of Cluny was not appealing to anything even vaguely equivalent to our modern concept of privacy when he asked for solitude with his Peter. Privacy could hardly exist in a world where people ate, slept and worked in common rooms. Peter was, however, seeking a mental space not accessible to others, a state of intimacy for two people who loved and understood each other. This necessary retreat made it possible to return to other people in a refreshed and strengthened state. Peter the Venerable, in asking for an exclusive bond with Peter of Poitiers, accepted that he could not order a friendship because he was abbot, and he knew that he could not cut his friendship off from his relationships with others in the community. In writing a letter of friendship he was making his individual bond public to others.

The letter is keenly aware of the place of community. Peter reminds his correspondent that there is much to weep about, for he passes on news of the death of Gerald Le Vert, who had held office at Cluny. This reference brings the letter back to Cluny's everyday life. This reality can be integrated into the friendship of the two Peters. Peter needed to have someone to whom he could describe his tears at the death of a monk for whom they both cared and whom they would miss. This letter reveals a great deal about how rich and complex twelfth-century monastic friendship could be. It sought out individual bonds but did not cut them off from the integrity of the community.

One more cluster of letters around Peter the Venerable and Peter of Poitiers underlines the same interchange between individual friendships and community life. It started when Peter of Poitiers wrote from Cluny to Peter the Venerable and his companions, who were staying at some distance from the monastery in a forest retreat. At least for short periods, Peter the Venerable seems to have been able to realize his ideal of life in hermitage. This time Peter of Poitiers could not join him because of a foot ailment. His letter is simple and brief, referring to the tasks the abbot had given him and expressing hope that his foot would get better. He closes with a greeting for Peter the Venerable's 'fellow hermits and companions'.[101] In replying the abbot quotes Horace and speaks of his desire that Peter could be 'our fellow hermit' (*coheremita noster*). He sent him a hymn he had written for the feast of Saint Benedict and pointed out how those traditionally sung on this day were full of errors of fact about the saint's miracles. The language the two Peters use with each other here is more restrained and business-like than in their own letters. This may be because Peter of Poitiers was now back at Cluny after his separation from the community. Peter the Venerable no longer had so much reason to pour intense feelings into a letter when he knew that Peter of Poitiers was doing what he wanted and needed.

In this correspondence Peter the Venerable's companions in retreat jumped at the chance to try their skill at writing to the favoured secretary. Three monks had letters included in the collection. All make light of the idea that they are living as hermits or philosophers in the woods. The abbot's comrades say they would like to share their life with Peter of Poitiers, for they are cowled poets (*cucullatos poetas*).[102] Peter of Poitiers, taking the hint, wrote back to Peter the Venerable admitting that the group was not just one of hermits but also of philosophers and poets. He wanted to be with them but could not, and he was grateful for Peter the Venerable's 'truly sweet and piously joking letter'. Here the abbot is said to have gotten revenge for the slight in Peter of Poitier's earlier use of the words 'forest' and 'hermitage' in describing the situation of the abbot and his companions.[103]

Much of this is wordplay, but it reveals what cluniac friends sought in their relationships: a chance to share the enjoyment of expressing themselves with care, intelligence and humour. An element of affection is implicit in this exchange, and there are moments of teasing that may approximate the content of verbal exchanges at Cluny and with Peter the Venerable. In his response to the abbot, Peter of Poitiers could also be serious. He pointed out how much it meant to him to be able to discuss hymns and language with the abbot: 'You well know how sweet it is for me always to talk to you about such matters'. When he was at Cluny and the abbot was away, Peter felt very much alone: 'Even if many are present and the whole world makes a commotion, without you I really feel that I am lonely.'[104] At the end of the letter he asks Peter the Venerable to keep the letters he has sent him, for the writing of them has given him much consolation (*tanti solacii*).

He embraces the abbot's letters and preserves them.

A letter of friendship is an expression of self that lasts. It gives comfort when it is written, when it is read, and when it is reread, by the writer, by its immediate recipient, by those in his circle, or by others. Both the letter and its response are worth preserving and collecting. This is not just a pious formula: it is a policy declaration whose result is apparent in the collection that has come down to us of the abbot of Cluny's letters, which also includes some of the letters sent to him. This great collection Peter of Poitiers helped to make.[105]

Peter the Venerable's letters to Bernard point to a diplomatic and utilitarian relationship which contains an element of personal friendship. The letters to Peter of Poitiers reveal a more intimate friendship based on intellectual and emotional sharing in the cloister and outside. Another series of letters, between Peter the Venerable and Bishop Hato of Troyes, record the author's patient efforts to bring a learned and articulate ecclesiastic into the monastery. These, however, are more than idealized letters of vocation. Once again, we meet the variety of Peter's thoughts on friendship and his desire to share himself with a friend. Conversion to Cluny was but the natural conclusion of such a relationship.

In the first letter we have, from mid-March 1138, Peter explains why he preferred to write Hato rather than send an oral message. One heart had to speak to another (*cor vestrum ex corde meo*) instead of being conveyed through the mouth of another. As wines frequently transferred from one container to another lose their strength, so words that are transmitted by the ears of strangers to the hearts of others often get jumbled. Their content of truth is altered and diminished. Since each of us knows his own heart best, he can convey himself more truly than can anyone else.[106]

Peter was convinced that aside from direct contact, personal letters are the best vehicle of communication, for in them "the mind converses through its own self": *per se ipsum animus colloquatur*. This may seem obvious to us, even if in our time the telephone has won out against the personal letter as the most convincing (and easy) means of contact from a distance. Peter's defense of the value of a letter in terms of its authenticity and immediacy is, however, not a commonplace in classical or monastic literature.[107] As so often Peter was widening the vocabulary of friendship. He could have chosen to limit contact with correspondents to what his messengers could convey by word of mouth. For those to whom he wanted to express his inner self, however, such a mode of communication was inadequate because it did not reproduce the genuine Peter.

Hato replied that he wanted to restrain the intensity of his language but could not. He appealed to the augustinian 'love and do what you like'. This he claimed because he was writing 'in a special way to a special friend' (*singulari amico singulariter*).[108] The letter ends with a fulsome greeting from Hato's secretary Nicholas, monk of Montiéramey, the first reference in Peter's collection to a man whose own friendship we will consider later in this chapter.

This exchange sets the tone for a rich correspondence. Peter did his best to attract Hato to Cluny, but the bishop managed until 1145 or 1146 to elude him. In a letter to Hato that cannot be dated more precisely than to some point between 1122 and 1146, Peter the Venerable used Cicero's definition of friendship as consent. He managed also to weave in a passage from Gregory the Great and then to add his own conclusion, that consent is possible only when friends convey their feelings openly to each other, when they are sure they are loved or hated. Here as so often, Peter builds consciously and openly on his sources and then draws his own conclusion.[109]

For Peter friendship requires reciprocal self-knowledge. Peter explains that he had read in a recent letter of Hato's that an ex-monk had claimed Peter's love for Hato had grown cold. He insists that this is not true. Peter seeks nothing in life more avidly than friendship, for nothing else could be more attractive, more fitting, or more useful. Cicero again is close to the surface here, with his maxim that life has nothing sweeter than having someone with whom one can speak as with to one's own self (*De amic.* 22: *Quid dulcius quam habere* . . .).

Having established that friendship is essential in life, Peter goes on to assure Hato that his feelings have not cooled. But Hato's love for Peter seems to have become tepid, he insists, if the bishop can write as he does and believe false words! In almost bernardine fashion, the attack is reversed on the attacker, at least for a moment. Peter claims that he can address Hato so harshly because he knows he can count on the mutual love between friends.

The letter moves from recrimination to explanation. Three reasons are given for Peter's failure to reply to Hato's three letters: illness; the haste of the bearer; and finally the press of business. Peter had intended to write Hato about many matters, but now he thought it best to speak to him in secret rather than to publish his thoughts in letters. This reference to the way letters were read by others than the recipient underlines how medieval letters were intended not only for the person addressed but also for a larger audience. Peter claims he wants to avoid this inevitable publicity and so hopes that the bishop would not let distance or his duties hinder him from coming to Cluny for a visit. Nothing, he claims, would make the Cluniacs rejoice more than even a brief visit by so intimate a friend, so desired a father. Peter related his friendship with Hato to the bishop's relationship to Cluny as a whole. Individual and community bonds are still closely linked. Peter wanted to speak to Hato in secret, but he wrote him a public letter that described their friendship. By answering the criticism of those around Hato and by bringing the monastery of Cluny into the letter, Peter involves both church and community in a personal friendship.

The relationship of Hato of Troyes and Peter the Venerable repays close study because we also have the bishop's response to Peter. He uses the same type of language as did the cluniac abbot, thus indicating that the images and concepts of friendship were by no means monastic property in this period. The growth of a language of friendship that we witnessed in the eleventh century had benefited both secular clerics and monks. First Hato describes friendship in general terms, with echoes of John Cassian and Jerome in the conviction that true friendship never ceases.[110] Like other writers of the period, he borrows the ciceronian concept of laws of friendship. These preclude any lapse or forgetfulness in a friendship. All this is not a paean to Peter. It is an overture to criticism of him for failing to write:

> Where are your frequent letters, where your regular consolation, where your usual eloquence, by which you used to revive your old friend?[111]

Peter's answer is affectionate. He tells Hato that he is like the bellows which can rekindle a dying spark and make it burst into flame. Peter claims his silence is occasioned by a love so strong that it cannot be conveyed in words. This assertion might seem groundless were it not for the intensity of expression already shown in the Hato-Peter correspondence. Another reason for his failure to write, Peter adds, is that Hato had not kept his promise to come to Cluny. Once again, Peter turned the tables and complained about a friend who had been complaining about him: 'Where is that devotion, where is that affection. . . ?'[112] The letter becomes an exhortation to conversion. It was probably sent together with a letter to Hato's secretary and chaplain, Nicholas of Montiéramey, in which Peter asked Nicholas to do his best to convince Hato to carry out his original intention (*ep* 87). Other letters follow, and then a gap interrupts the correspondence until a letter appears just before Hato's entrance into Cluny in 1146.

This final letter Peter builds around the maxim that a new friend, as new wine, becomes more pleasant to drink as it grows old. The new wine delights the drinker but frustrates because of its bitter aftertaste, while an aged wine is gentler and smoother. 'Thus plainly and completely in you, beloved, I see how Solomon's words are fulfilled.'[113] The image is appropriate to all the problems Peter had had in getting Hato into Cluny. Now the relationship had aged and Hato was obliging Peter. *Conversio* and *amicitia* are linked as they often must have been in monastic life.

Does friendship find expression here only because it is used for the sake of conversion? The question could easily be reformulated: is not conversion attractive because of friendship? Cluny could become a new home for Hato because his friend Peter was Hato's imminent entrance into Cluny as a completion of their friendship. The wine of friendship had reached the ideal age, and Peter could enjoy his friend to the fullest. What the youth of friendship did not give, let at least its old age confer (*quia quod non dedit amicitiae iuventus, conferret saltem senectus*).

In writing of Peter the Venerable, I feel at times as the medieval letterwriter who apologizes to his readers for breaking the boundaries of literary convention and going on for too long. It is hard to be brief when there is so much material in these letters, a fine balance between appropriate quotations, striking images, and an undercurrent of concern with individual friendships in a monastic context.

A final letter from Peter's collection perhaps summarizes its disparate elements on friends and friendship. Addressed to Geoffrey, archbishop of Bordeaux, in mid-1143, this letter at one level is a business letter entrusting to the archbishop the care of cluniac houses in France while Peter was away on a journey through Spain. The appointment of Geoffrey as *conservator*, however, is shown to be the result of Peter's relationship with him as a trusted friend. When thinking of various cares, Peter begins, he sometimes comes to think of friendship, and which friends he prefers to others.[114] In penetrating the depths of his soul, Peter finds that the archbishop of Bordeaux is to be ranked below almost no other friend, and he is to be preferred to almost all others. It is not his ecclesiastical rank that gives him such importance: it is friendship in Christ that joined him indivisibly to Peter.

Peter uses the term true and spiritual friend (*in spirituali et uero amico*). His association of the friendship with Geoffrey to friendship with Christ is perhaps the most concise expression in his letters of the christian content in true friendship. Christ is the mediator, the midpoint, between two friends.[115] Peter gives the relationship a chronological context, pointing out that he has known Geoffrey and felt close to him ever since they had met on the way to La Chartreuse (*Carthusiense iter*). Now their closeness made it impossible for them to be absent to each other: 'For I think I cannot be absent where you are, nor where I am, can you be absent' (*Nec enim me absentem puto ubi uos estis, neque ubi ego sum vos absens esse potestis*). The linguistic device of chiasma is here so perfect, the intertwining of friendship and affairs so natural, the rhythm of the letter so right, that one cannot help being suspicious. How could two so powerful men, solidly established in their own lives, regard each other in terms of real friendship? The *Confessions* of Augustine or the letters of Anselm seem to make spiritual friendship an experience of relative youth. And yet Peter's language here matches what he used with his closest friends, such as Peter of Poitiers. The genuine sentiment behind Peter's expression is suggested by the fact that there are no other great figures, except for Bernard, whom he addressed in such terms. The journey to La Chartreuse may have given the two men a chance to become friends. One must remember what it could have been like for two men to meet each other on the road, where their daily lives would have been far away and there would have been time for good talk. In sharing the destination of a carthusian house, they gained an aspect of religious pilgrimage in their journey. The dimension of power politics does not necessarily preclude such a friendship. In the twelfth century power and religious devotion often combined in natural and spontaneous ways. Mutual need for each other's benefits could well have been combined with a meeting of minds and hearts on the road to La Chartreuse.

PETER OF CELLE AND HIS CIRCLE

In Peter the Venerable we have met an idea that had great currency in the twelfth century, that friendship is governed by certain laws that make it a predictable and dependable practice in society, especially in monastic society. This concept goes ultimately back to Aristotle's *Nichomachean Ethics* with its division of types of friendship as utilitarian, pleasurable, or virtuous. The belief in the possibility of the virtuous friend permeates Cicero but did not have an easy time in coming to the surface of late antique and early medieval descriptions of monastic life. Here friendship was seen as something worldly and as a potential danger to community life. Yet in every network of human relations from the eighth century onwards we have seen evidence that friendship bonds could be present in monastic communities. These indications become more specific and detailed in the period after about 1050, and in writers such as Baudri of Bourgueil the *foedus* or *pactum* of friendship is looked upon as a natural human phenomenon that fits into the monastic life. Several writers refer to laws of friendship which require friends to maintain regular contact with each other. This was an extension of the ciceronian view (*De amic.* 40) that friendship has no place for base deeds done by one friend for the sake of the other. Cicero's single law of friendship became a point of departure for formulating a number of laws or rights that touched on aspects of friendship, which came to be seen as a social and personal bond that could be integrated into the strictest forms of the christian life. Twelfth-century writers such as Peter the Venerable were convinced that friends have a rightful claim on each other's time and inner lives, even within the context of monastic community. This view was quickly attached to the idea that friendship makes up one manifestation of genuine christian love. Instead of threatening the monk's love of God or his love for all the members of the community, friendship on a personal, individual basis, if it is kept within its rights and laws, can enrich the monastic vocation.

With Peter the Venerable we found a complete integration of classical literary statements of friendship with christian ideals of love. Less classical in tone and more heavily dependent on biblical language was his contemporary Peter of Celle. His collection of letters summarizes what might be called the benedictine tradition of monastic friendship. What we first noticed at Saint Gall, Tegernsee, and Saint Emmeram, is expressed most fully in the letters Peter wrote, first as abbot at Montier-la-Celle outside of Troyes in the years between 1145 and 1162, and between 1163 and 1181 as abbot of the important house of Saint Rémi at Rheims.[116] Peter's letters need a modern edition: the Migne one is the latest and most accessible but lacks an apparatus of references, essential in making letters immediately understandable in terms of context and models.[117] Even in their critically unsatisfactory state, however, the letters of Peter of Celle form a *tour de force* displaying an abbot's friendships with other monks and with secular clerics.

Peter emphasized friendships in almost all his ecclesiastical relationships, even where they would seem to have no place. When Peter wrote Hugh, archbishop of Sens, to defend the marriage of his nephew, he insisted that every legal case should perish which brings about the downfall of friendship.[118] As a monk Peter felt no qualms about continuing to show open concern for his relatives' affairs. Monks had for centuries been involved in the affairs of their biological families, but here Peter boldly defended such entanglement and gave no attention to the clearly formulated requirement of the Gospels that those who follow Christ must give up everything, including kin bonds (Luke 15:25-33).

For Peter of Celle, friendship, family and monastery were all bound up in each other. He asked Alan, bishop of Auxerre, a Cistercian from Clairvaux, what hope of friendship could remain in him when Alan refused to believe what he said about his nephew's marriage. Despite his anger and sense of injury, Peter still offers the hope of a 'dawn of resurgent friendship' with Alan.[119] Peter writes to him not so much as to a bishop but as one of Saint Bernard's monks. Peter had probably known Alan before his episcopal election. He pressed their relationship for all it was worth, while championing his nephew. In Peter's defense of the marriage in the face of a charge of consanguinity, kin bonds and friendship triumphed against legal scruples and scriptural casuistry. In these first letters in his collection, Peter of Celle did his best to make friendship the basis of human relationships, a magnet that was to draw bishops to him and make them do what he wanted. Friendship was to triumph both in the nephew's marriage and at the monastery of Celle!

To John, bishop of Saint Malo in Britanny, apparently also a Cistercian, Peter wrote in the same intimate, familiar manner. Charity is patient, he began, recalling Paul (1 Cor 13:4). Such love, however, was driving Peter to impatience.[120] John's messenger had approached Peter with news from John by word of mouth, but there was no letter from John. Peter asked how John could have contacted him in such a way. He named several reasons which might explain John's failure to write. If the cause of famine, he asked, was it customary that when Britanny lacked bread, then it also lacked heart?[121] Peter conceded that there had been a famine, but he refused to see how a famine of virtue necessarily followed. He allowed that John had episcopal duties but asked if these could keep him from dictating letters: 'What hinders you from composing friendly letters?' (*amicales litteras*). Having dismissed all other excuses, Peter could imagine only one reason: plain neglect of one's friends. He knew he was being hard, but John, he insisted, deserved it.

If there is one theme that characterizes these letters and other twelfth-century letters of friendship, it is an insistence on regular contact between friends as a necessary condition for friendship. Peter of Celle never hesitated to prod John on this point, even if his efforts apparently bore little fruit. In his next letter Peter was less barbed but just as demanding, despite the fact that John in the meantime apparently had written to him, though we have no copy of the letter. But this reply had not been enough for Peter, who insisted on speaking in person with John. He could think of nothing else. Peter wrote that he could never be satisfied with contact only by letter with one whom he loved with no limit. 'My monastery is your people; our people is yours; my soul is yours.' This statement intermingles personal and institutional bonds in a way Bernard and Peter the Venerable would have understood and approved.[122]

Peter did his best to define and redefine his bond with John. He said that their love 'glues together our souls'[123], a phrase that seems meant to evoke the love of Jonathan and David for one another. Peter calls himself John's 'one and special friend' (*unicum. . . et specialem amicum*), only to add that if John failed to come to see him, he would diminish the fullness of their love.[124] Peter gave John of Saint Malo many ultimata. One wonders if they had any effect. The abbot of Celle expresses himself with the impatience and haste of the lover who needs and even craves his beloved. There are not many monastic friendships in the twelfth century which are appropriately described as passionate, but this is perhaps one. It is in fact a term Peter himself used in trying to arouse John's sympathy for his predicament after a serious fire at Saint Aigulf, a priory of Celle: 'But we cry after you: we want to awake your compassion for us through our passions'.[125]

Like Peter the Venerable, Peter of Celle used the cistercian concept of laws of friendship to describe what a close relationship requires. Friends must be open with each other about their needs, 'for a friend is said to be aware of all counsels as well as a willing helper in all matters'.[126] The fire at Saint Aigulf and Peter's misery become a point of departure not just for soliciting John's sympathy but for demanding that he show how true a friend he was.

The demands made on John may not have had the desired effect. In the next letter he sent, which may or may not be in chronological order, Peter inquired bitterly if John was still alive or whether another bishop had taken his place at Malo. He, Peter, had heard nothing from him.[127] The satirical pose seems to be yet another means for provoking John out of his silence, but a more drastic manoeuvre than soliciting sympathy. Peter turned from bitterness to a long theoretical discourse on truth and lack of falseness in friendship, but then like his namesake at Cluny he made his discourse personal by addressing his correspondent directly:

> I regret, father, the failure you have shown in the last two years to remember me, and the decease also of our friendship, which lasted for four days but has been, as it were, buried for a long time.[128]

The expression *amicitiae quatriduanae* may tell us how long it took for Peter and John to become friends, or how much time they had once spent together, perhaps at Celle. These lines provide a fascinating indication of what was required to initiate a spiritual friendship. A fews days of companionship was enough for a man as impulsive and spontaneous as Peter of Celle.

Once Peter attached himself to another man, he could not let go. He asked John what blocked their friendship. Were there mountains between them or the sea, or some great chaos? Charity could overcome all barriers, he insisted (1 Cor 13). It cannot be quenched even by the sea (Sg 8:7).[129] In echoing Paul and the Song of Songs, Peter of Celle shows keen literary sense. Direct address, images from nature, biblical resonances, all are used to lead into an apostrophe of love itself, which ends, 'now let it speak, nay rather let him come. . . for my soul desires you, and your friends desire you'. This language comes from the Song of Songs: show your face and let your voice sound in my ears. In almost erotic language, Peter called on his spiritual friend to come to him.

The final letter in the series develops similar themes. Peter pleads with John to regard his affection and reciprocate, instead of despising it.[130] The correspondence ends inconclusively, leaving many questions unanswered. But it provides evidence of the manner in which Peter of Celle attached himself spiritually and emotionally to other men, whom he needed to see and hear from regularly. Material self-interest is not apparent in these letters, only the plea of one man to another in the language of christian spiritual friendship.

Reading other letters of friendship in Peter of Celle's vast collection helps explain his attachments. Peter treasured the visits, short or long, of intelligent and articulate men to Celle. They talked about spiritual matters, discussed intellectual problems, and spent a happy time together. This seems to have been the case with John of Salisbury, whose classical training and secular humanism might seem to have made him an unlikely candidate for a monastic friendship. But Peter apparently got hold of him at the right moment, when John was 'at the nadir of his fortunes' and settled for a temporary position as Peter's clerk at Celle until he could return to England to enter the service of Archbishop Theobald of Canterbury.[131] Once back in England, John of Salisbury began to write Peter and did not disappoint him as his namesake at Saint Malo had done.[132] He wrote regularly and kept Peter well informed about affairs of the english court, as well as joining Peter's campaign to collect money for new buildings at the church of Saint Aigulf after the fire. The abbot of Celle's letters to John reveal a special mixture of personal tenderness and theoretical reflections on love and friendship, but they also contain news of the monastery. John's responses are more business-like and more cleverly expressed. They excel at eminently readable passages of gossip, just as his historical works do. John indicates only indirectly the affection he felt for his former benefactor and good friend. But there is no doubt about the strength of his feeling.

Sometimes we have letters of both correspondents, and this rare situation allows us to see more clearly the language and practice of monastic friendship and how flexible it could be. When Peter of Celle sought and obtained letters from John, he seems to have been satisfied with an analytical tone that had little of his own sweetness of style and mind. John for his part was pleased to receive light-hearted epistles with ancedotes about wine and drinking that still contained strong moral advice straight from the cloister.[133] In John of Salisbury and Peter of Celle court and monastery addressed each other in different styles but still in terms of close friendship.

Peter of Celle asked a great deal from his friends and friendships. He wanted his closest friends to spend time with him at Celle or at Rheims, where Peter sheltered John for most of the turbulent years 1164-70 when he was in disgrace in England. But when physical proximity proved impossible, Peter required frequent letters.[134] Once John became bishop of Chartres in 1176, Peter felt let down. He contrasted John's silence with the communicativeness of the good old days. He wrote John describing a pile of letters he had in front of him. They bore witness, he said, to the closeness they once had had with each other.[135] By now John had not written for a whole year. There could be no possible excuse for his negligence. Certain unnamed men had visited Peter at Saint Rémi, and levelled charges of favouritism and partiality against John. They sought Peter out not because he was the powerful abbot of Saint Rémi but because he was looked upon as the friend and advisor of John, someone who might have some influence on him. Peter insisted in his pained letter to John that he did not want to believe the accusations, but John would have to give him good reasons for not doing so. In another letter from the same period, Peter openly showed his anger at John's silence. He said sourly that he knew John must have been busy, a remark similar to the ironic tone used earlier with John of Saint Malo. But the bishop of Chartres may have retorted with reassuring signals, for in a third letter Peter showed a willingness to be reconciled to John of Salisbury. It is easy to forgive the errors of friends, Peter concedes, when they happen by accident and not on purpose.[136] John had received Peter's legate Bernered of Saint Crispin in an inhospitable way but he would be forgiven when he came to Rheims and admitted his fault. A sudden frost cannot kill an old root (*Radix enim longaeva pruina subdita non arescit, neque marescit*).

One wonders how it must have been for John, now a bishop buried in duties, to be called upon to answer such letters and ordered to go visit his friend. Peter of Celle shows the same strength of will and conviction of his own righteousness as Bernard of Clairvaux, even if on a lesser scale. He was not interested in excuses. He believed in friends and friendships and would accept no half-hearted substitutes! This is the general attitude of twelfth-century monastic writers: a lack of willingness to compromise their principles, at least in public. This is perhaps the reverse side of the tenderness or *dulcedo* that is so evident in monastic literature of friendship. When friends loved each other, they did so in a visible way. They referred to concrete obligations in friendship, the *leges amicitiae*. When friends disagreed or let each other down, accusations came forward in force. Irony, bitterness and disappointment came to the surface. Twelfth-century monastic friendships can at moments remind us of the nineteenth-century marriages immortalized in the swedish playwright Strindberg's plays dealing with the search for love and the numbing pain and bitter anger of unanswered love. In both cases, the description of human relationships cannot be reduced to literary conveniences or brilliant collections of contemporary vocabulary. Here we get close to the heart of an age because we meet the hopes, dreams and disappointments of human beings.

Peter's loss of John of Salisbury as a loyal companion may have been partially compensated for by a close relationship he formed with John's brother, Richard. To him Peter wrote with a passion that exceeds even the intensity of his declarations to John of Saint Malo. In a joint letter to Richard and John, which is a response to the news that Richard had taken the habit of an austin canon, he addressed Richard specifically with the words 'I rush to kiss your face'.[137] This was the aged abbot of Saint Rémi writing in the early 1170s, and yet friendship and its formulation were just as central to him as they ever had been in his correspondence.

Peter's later letters can at times be easier to understand than his earlier ones in terms of friendship. To a certain extent he cuts back the apparatus of biblical language and imagery for the sake of a more direct personal expression of his thought. At times he is subtly humorous. He asked John to remember how they used to make jokes together. Peter had complained once about the size of the reliquary of the then archbishop Thomas Becket.[138] Now he asked John to visit Thomas's tomb for his sake. He claims to feel insulted because John had apologized for keeping for a little longer a book Peter had lent him. 'You were with us for such a long time', Peter insists, 'and I am amazed, nay horrified, that you have such limited confidence in me'. At the end of the letter he asks John to greet Richard tenderly.[139]

In such chatty, affectionate, yet direct letters, we come close to spiritual and emotional bonds among medieval churchmen. These bonds formed through visits to each other, small tokens of affection, a rich classical and biblical vocabulary of friendship in letters, and the sharing of news and gossip. At moments it might seem rather superficial, a little spice over the bland routine of everyday life in monasteries or cathedral chapters. But we have only to turn to the ecstatic language of Peter's last letter to John's brother Richard and his references to kisses and embraces to see the trust and intimacy that Peter sought in the fullness of his friendships.[140] Here we see that in Peter's life, friendship did not take a back seat to the monastic profession. He could require that Richard, even if he now also led a regular life, placed him, next to his brother John, as the one he loved the most. In Peter of Celle's letters, everything is suffused with the light, language and practice of friendship. His emphasis on its centrality explains why Peter can be so hard on friends whom he thought had let him down and disregarded his love for them.

A final friendship worth looking at in Peter's letters is that with abbot Bernered of Saint Crispin Major at Soissons. He is in evidence during Peter's abbacy in Rheims (1162-80). From Peter's letters to John of Salisbury at Chartres, we know that Bernered represented Peter during this period (*ep* 120). Bernered not only was entrusted with Peter's correspondence: he was a beneficiary of it. 'The nights are dearer and more useful to me than the days', Peter wrote Bernered, for his days were full of business, while long winter nights gave him time to refresh his body as well as his soul.[141] Spiritual renewal came not only through thinking about heaven but also in remembering friends. Peter would have written more, but Hugh, his secretary, had taken only a small piece of parchment for the letter, so he had to end.[142] He asked Bernered to keep his letters and so indicated that in writing Bernered he was expressing something about himself that he wanted to be permanent. Once again a letter of friendship combines a personal with a public statement. Peter was evidently planning a collection of his own letters, and yet he had apparently not planned this individual letter well enough to provide himself with all the space he might have used!

Peter wrote briefly both to Bernered and to his brethren at Soissons that he could not come to celebrate with them the feast of the monastery's patron martyrs, Crispin and Crispinian: 'Behold the symphony and choir, behold there a holy assembly of friends, but where am I and what am I?'[143] Another letter to Bernered mentioned trouble at Celle with the abbot who was Peter's successor, and abruptly ends for lack of parchment (*ep* 99). Brief messages of this type are fairly frequent, but when Peter sat down to compose one letter, he must have made sure he had enough writing materials to develop his thoughts about love. How could it be, he asked, that love burns more strongly for friends who are far away than for those who are under our very eyes? His answer is simple and convincing: love can be calm when the beloved is present. In his absence it worries about whether the friend is still alive, healthy, sad, happy, fearful or secure.[144] This long list of worries, says Peter, stirs up the flame of love and increases its heat. Love slumbers when the beloved is present. 'Believe me', Peter insists, 'I have experienced it' (*Experto credendum est*). Such a sentence summarizes the wisdom of twelfth-century monasticism in terms of the spiritual life.

At Troyes, Rheims, Cluny and Clairvaux, a network of monastic friends becomes visible to us. This group of friends we will trace in further detail in the next pages in order to see its fragility. For the moment, however, it is the soundness of many of the observations these monks made about friendship that interests us. Absence can indeed make the heart grow fonder, as Peter claimed, and this may well be at least partially due to concern for the welfare of the absent friend. Friendship was not, however, an unselfish commitment. It also involves need and even utility. None of our writers denies that friends sometimes call on each other for moral and even economic support.

In its monastic context friendship is also linked to the existence of collective forms of life. One or two monks can be singled out for special love, but only when the integrity of the community has been acknowledged and the personal bond poses no threat to stability and order. Peter's letters make it clear that he considered friendship possible between men of different rank and station: the abbot and his secretary, the abbot and a bishop (who may once have been a monk), the monk and his friend or relative who remained in the world. To dismiss such bonds as mere literary formulae manipulating people into behaviour pleasing to the writer would be to deny the presence and attractiveness of christian humanistic ideals in the monastic culture of the twelfth century.[145] From the language of love to the practice of friendship inside and outside the cloister among spiritual men is not such a great distance. Spiritual men were encouraged to friendship by the Scripture and its exegetes whom they had heard since childhood: first in the liturgy, then in school, and eventually in reading church fathers in larger segments. Classical authors complemented christian thoughts. It is no accident that Seneca and his letters to Lucilius became one of the most popular works in the cistercian libraries of the twelfth century. Seneca's self-assured tones of affection fitted perfectly into a monastery environment with room for the expression of love in friendship.[146]

THE RISK OF FRIENDSHIP: NICHOLAS OF MONTIÉRAMEY-CLAIRVAUX

Lively relations between Celle, Cluny, and Clairvaux were encouraged and furthered in the years from 1146 to 1152 by a figure who is mainly remembered for betraying the confidence of his friend and abbot.[147] Nicholas first became monk at Montiéramey, a cluniac house near Troyes, and then secretary to Bishop Hato of Troyes, whom we met earlier. In 1146 he converted to Clairvaux, where he made himself indispensable to Bernard. Eventually he even was given a small office all to himself. In 1152 it was found out that Nicholas had removed Bernard's abbatial seals from the monastery. Nicholas was disgraced. Bernard pilloried him in letters to half of Christendom. Here was a false monk whose conversion to the heavenly troupe had failed.

Because of the disgrace of 1152, some interpreters of Nicholas have looked upon him and his letters of friendship with suspicion. His expulsion from the loving company of Saint Bernard, however, should not in itself call into question the sincerity and enthusiasm of his early years, with his many declarations of love and friendship. In the period from the mid-1140s to the early 1150s, Nicholas served as an important link between Cluny and Clairvaux, and as a bond of love between Peter the Venerable and Bernard. At the same time he was a close friend of Peter of Celle and acted as a ghostwriter for many monks at Clairvaux who wanted to have appropriate letters of friendship composed for their contacts in other monasteries or in the world. Despite the brevity of his clarevallian career, Nicholas managed to sum up the promise and the limitations of the practice of intimate friendship in a monastic context.[148]

The best approach to Nicholas is through his relationship with Peter of Celle. In this friendship, much less dramatic than the violent exchange with Bernard, Nicholas revealed an enormous capacity for creating a climate of love which depended more on mutual enthusiasm than on understanding. In a typical letter, he tells Peter of Celle that he loved him more than he loved himself: 'I have committed theft because of you, for I have stolen myself from myself for your sake'. Nicholas explained that in becoming a monk he had sought solitude and silence. He had put aside the writing pen. Now he had taken it up again because of Peter's eagerness (*aviditatem*). He was combining utility with affection in his friendship by sending the abbot of Celle copies of Bernard's works, as Peter had asked for.[149] Nicholas insisted that his task as a monk was to weep and keep silence. He knew well the desert tradition and especially Jerome, whose rhetorical extravagances fitted Nicholas' personality. Peter of Celle warded off Nicholas' reference to cistercian silence by claiming that Nicholas could do his editing without talking. Nicholas demurred: who experiences more turbulence than the one who edits texts, he asked: *Quis enim magis in turba est quam ille qui faciendis dictaminibus implicatur*?

Jean Leclercq has singled out this letter as evidence of the confusion Nicholas created between his own works and those of Bernard. At one moment he wrote as if he were the author of the works involved, while at the next he was the humble secretary recording the words of the holy man.[150] A tone of impatience, self-importance and even short temper marks this letter: 'Hurry up and write back in a hurry', Nicholas insisted, 'and send copies to me and for my collection' (*opus meum*). 'In accord with our agreement, have them copied'.[151] What started as a simple letter of friendship becomes infinitely more complex and ambiguous, an indication of an arrogant and perhaps devious personality.

Nicholas seems to have functioned at times as secretary-at-a-distance for Peter of Celle, who valued him highly. He told Nicholas he rejoiced in his letters, for in him he had found a true friend (*veraci amico*) to whom he could extend his love. 'Even if I show a lack of learning in my style when I write back, I do not lack the knowledge of how to love you in return', Peter asserted to Nicholas: 'I know whom I ought to love, why, how much, and for how long'.[152] Through Nicholas Peter could express his link to the entire community at Clairvaux: 'These are your, no rather, my Clarevallians' (*tui immo mei Clarevallenses*). A collective and a personal bond combine harmoniously. Peter and Nicholas were bound to each other by a special mutual love, enhanced by the collective love of the cloister.

Nicholas responded in kind: 'Before ever I saw you, I loved you'.[153] After hearing about Peter, Nicholas finally got the chance to see him. Then came the 'secret of mutual closeness, and from unequal persons friendship made equal minds'.[154] Nicholas chose every word with exquisite care. He ranked *familiaritas* (a shared relationship) at a level below the highest *amicitia*, which implies equality. Having made this opening declaration of love, he confided to Peter that there was a problem between them. Because love involves trust, he could be open. Some letters Nicholas had handed over to Peter to be given to a monk named Lecelin had somehow got into the hands of Nicholas's former abbot at Montiéramey. He asked how this was possible. Here as elsewhere Nicholas indicates that he used letters to convey personal confidences and even secrets, a practice that departed from the usual one according to which letters involving friendship were meant for a general audience, even though they contained a personal message. Nicholas wanted friendship and fame through his letters, but he ended seeing enemies on all sides. On the one hand he sought to make his literary prowess known, while on the other he was afraid of compromising his reputation. The confusion of his proper role and identity which brought about his disgrace in 1152 is here already in view.

In another letter, perhaps from the same period, Nicholas offered only sweetness and light.[155] He had recently been bled at Clairvaux and so had a respite from his secretarial duties. This had given him a chance to think of his Peter, how ardently he loved him and was loved by him. Nicholas describes an inner dialogue he had had: now it was time for him to write to him whom his soul loved, he had said to himself: *quem diligit anima mea* (Sg 3:2). The phrase, taken from the Song of Song's ecstatic love poetry, was a favoured one in this circle of friends and one used for example by Bernard in describing Peter the Venerable's love for Nicholas (*ep* 389). This introduction leads to a soliloquy on the abject condition of man, including a borrowing from Seneca's famous twenty-fourth letter to Lucilius about how we die daily: *quotidie enim morimur*. Nicholas was taking time off from his usual busy life in order to imitate the style and thoughts of the men he loved: Peter of Celle and Bernard. As he pointed out, the strongest proof of his love lay in the fact that Peter had been allowed to descend far into the depths of his soul to receive his friendship.[156]

The thoughts in the bulk of this letter may not seem very profound in a twelfth-century monastic context. Nicholas remains the imitator who took on the forms and fashions he found around him. But the letter's central message remains: Nicholas wanted to give something of himself to a man he loved. He was stepping outside a daily routine in order to offer a part of his self. The combination of literary skill and uninspiring thoughts can make his sincerity suspect, but Nicholas can be seen here as trying to achieve the tone of love and the sharing of consciousness so important to literary monks of this period.

Peter of Celle must have respected the content and intent of Nicholas's message, for in his response he complimented Nicholas for what he had written but also criticized him for his philosophical and theological speculations.[157] Thus began an exchange of letters that reveals a great deal about the limitations and problems of monastic friendship cultivated through letters. Even though Peter continually assured Nicholas of his affection for him and called him half of his soul (*dimidium animae meae*) in recalling Horace (Odes 3), Nicholas could not accept criticism of the content of his exposition. Intellectual prowess, literary style and the bond of friendship were all entangled in Nicholas's responses. When Peter challenged his theological interpretations, Nicholas felt Peter also was showing him that his friendship was not true. Nicholas appealed to the laws of friendship. He pointed out that he was obliged to write what he thought and felt, for if he did not express himself, then friendship would be harmed. 'Now I have hidden myself from the faces of those seeking me in a most secret and remote place, with only a few brief interruptions, so I could speak directly to you instead of dictating a letter.'[158] Nicholas had figuratively and perhaps literally taken refuge in solitude in order to write a letter uninfluenced by the presence of others, even of a copyist. Embarrassed by Peter's challenge, he asked for secrecy and admitted he had kept his letter away from the curiosity of other monks.[159]

Peter of Celle wrote back, echoing Cicero and the Song of Songs, with an effusive declaration of love that nevertheless leads to a reassertion of his own definitions of divine nature and life.[160] These are the very definitions that Nicholas had already had problems in accepting. Here appear the limitations inherent in using a letter of friendship for the sake of theological exchange. Assertions of love get in the way of intellectual definitions. Language strains at the requirements of rigid categories. Emotion conveyed in careful stylistic devices and rational argument arranged in a subtle progression of thought have difficulty in finding each other in what becomes polemic of love: 'O my sweetest, were you asleep when you read our letter? Perhaps you were occupied and so are not to be blamed?'[161] Peter's almost patronizing tone shows he was angry that Nicholas had misused his statements and given them meanings he had not intended. Where did I deny that the body lives, that the soul is living, and that God is life, he asks, citing Nicholas' assertion that had started the argument. It would be more useful, Peter suggests, if we were to stop all this argumentation and keep silence. So he orders Nicholas not to write again.

What Nicholas had started using as a literary image, a comparison of various forms of life, had provoked Peter into taking Nicholas literally and pointing out the theological implications of his words. Nicholas had replied by citing various authorities and had thus revealed an acquaintance with platonic philosophy.[162] But the letter of friendship, and perhaps the friendship itself, could not stand the strain. There are no more letters between Peter as abbot of Celle and Nicholas as monk of Clairvaux. The absence of further letters in itself proves nothing, but it hints that Nicholas had at least a temporary falling out with Peter.

Peter of Celle took Nicholas of Clairvaux's letters seriously, both their declarations of love and their theological content. Nicholas tried to be all things to all men, to please, to impress, and to immerse himself in the currents made by deeper men around him. William of Saint Thierry gives us a vital clue to his character by telling us about the monk Nicholas at Clairvaux, who must be our Nicholas, who had gone to Bernard to obtain the gift of tears.[163] Not satisfied with converting to the Cistercians from the Cluniacs, Nicholas wanted to be able to weep for his sins as a monk was supposed to do. He was not content with the fact of conversion: it had to be visible in the very functions of his body, and the other monks had to know about it.

Much of what Nicholas did he came to regret. A weepy, overwrought letter from him at Clairvaux back to his abbot at Montiéramey apologizes for his arrogance and bad behaviour towards him (*ep* 40). While not specific, Nicholas says enough to indicate that his dramatic choice of Clairvaux caused hard feelings at Montiéramey. It was perhaps no accident that Hato the bishop of Troyes who employed Nicholas in the early 1140s eventually went to Cluny, while Nicholas entered Clairvaux. Hato sought a quiet retirement together with his friend Peter the Venerable; Nicholas wanted the passion and total commitment of monastic life with Bernard.

Nicholas apparently got what he bargained for, and much more.

As Bernard's secretary, he became indispensable, and his final break with Bernard can be explained partly by the huge burden of work Bernard placed on him. Nicholas acted as more than Bernard's secretary: he became his alter ego, sufficiently trusted to be heeded when he warned Bernard that his other secretaries were misinterpreting the abbot's intentions in their versions of his letters.[164] The exchanges of letters between Peter the Venerable and Bernard concerning Nicholas reveal that by the late 1140s Nicholas had become indispensable to both abbots. Bernard needed Nicholas to maintain a steady flow of his correspondence and in the editing and copying of his writings; Peter the Venerable sought Nicholas out in order to have a friend to discuss intellectual matters and to inform him of the newest developments in the cistercian world. At the same time Nicholas proved to be of eminently practical value to the two abbots, both sought his presence also because they needed him emotionally. Bernard writes fondly of how sweet it was to withdraw into privacy with Nicholas in order to read Peter the Venerable's letters, while Peter in turn could not bear the thought of spending an Easter without having Nicholas with him.[165] The usually disciplined and diplomatic Peter almost sacrificed his sense of propriety and control in a passionate appeal not only to Bernard but also to several of his other good contacts at Clairvaux in order to get permission to have Nicholas visit him at Cluny. He reminded Bernard how many of his own monks he had given up to him. Now he asked for Bernard to lend him this one for a little while!

In the years from 1146 to 1149, Nicholas acted as a centre for the practice and expression of friendship at Clairvaux and as a link with friendships at Celle, Cluny, and elsewhere. Because he was not abbot but only secretary, Nicholas could speak openly and represent the thoughts and feelings of the brothers of Clairvaux in a way that Bernard could not. Thus we find Bernard writing to a former prior of Clairvaux, explaining that he had not been able to convince the pope, the cistercian Eugenius III, to let him go back to his beloved Clairvaux. Eugenius had insisted that the man take a post as abbot of the cistercian house near Rome. As father abbot, Bernard could only exhort his former monk to obedience, whatever his personal feelings. Nicholas, writing to the same man, could allow himself to express pain and yearning for the friend who had so unhappily been taken away from him and their community of love at Clairvaux.[166]

The letters that Nicholas collected before he left Clairvaux make it clear that he prided himself on being a representative of the monks, someone who could articulate their hopes and desires. Many of the letters were written by Nicholas on behalf of Clairvaux monks. The prior, Gerard of Peronne, used Nicholas to clear up a misunderstanding between Clairvaux and the abbot of Celle. In Nicholas's letter on Gerard's behalf to Peter, he distinguished between *familiaritas* and *amicitia*, insisting that since true friendship existed between Gerard and Peter of Celle it could not be upset by some minor suspicion.[167] In such letters Nicholas uses favourite commonplace phrases, as the almost sensual enjoyment friends can have in each other's presence (*vivae voluptatis*, taken from Seneca, *ep* 35 to Lucilius). Friends can be distant in body but close in heart; monks can cultivate mutual concern (*affectus*); friends belong to each other (*tuus sum* . . .). Several of these expressions come from letters in Bernard's own collection, and these shared expressions suggest that Bernard and Nicholas collaborated in writing many of the letters traditionally attributed to Bernard alone.[168]

If this is true, then Nicholas' role with Bernard could at times have resembled his literary relationship with other monks in Clairvaux: Nicholas supplied them with the necessary language to transpose their thoughts to the page and convey their feelings and concerns to those outside the abbey. Many of Nicholas' letters written on behalf of other monks are messages urging conversion, telling of the delights of Clairvaux and encouraging the correspondent to join in the monastery the monk who loved him. Here Nicholas frequently confronts the old conviction that entering the monastery means breaking old bonds. Going into monastery, he insists, does not mean giving up human attachments.[169] In making this assertion Nicholas followed the lead of his beloved Bernard, who could not bear having any of his family members excluded from his new spiritual family. Nicholas gives explicit expression to this implicit departure from traditional conversion. In bringing along friends or summoning them later on in letters, the monks contributed to the growth and expansion of Clairvaux. Nicholas was willing to confront the old attitude and contradict it openly. *Apatheia*, passionlessness, had given way to a conscious and articulate involvement in other human beings, so that human relationships could be transformed, heightened, bettered, intensified in the cloister.

How far we have come from the words of the desert father Alonios: 'If a man does not say in his heart, in the world there is only myself and God, he will not gain peace'.[170] In one of Nicholas' most personal letters of conversion, he describes to a nobleman named Walter how the latter's letter had come to him and how he had read it in his little writing room at Clairvaux, where one door opened on to the cell of the novices.[171] In this tiny office Nicholas had entered into solitude, but not that of the desert, for in going into himself, he recalled how he and Walter had once been close and how while in the world they had experienced being two souls with one mind: *animae due, animus unus*. Now he wanted Walter to return to him and give himself back to Nicholas: 'I would see the half of my soul living according to my will in the midst of my Clarevallians'.[172] Nicholas did his best to make Clairvaux sound attractive, a community full of brilliant and well-born young men. He used the example of the brother of Louis VII, Henry, who had not been able to keep away.

> If Walter did not come, Nicholas assures him, he would continue to love him: I shall maintain friendship, for once it is given and received, it lasts until death and after death in Jesus Christ, so that whatever I have, whatever I am, and whatever I can be, is yours.[173]

Bernard himself could not have expressed the idea better. At such moments it is almost superfluous to distinguish between Bernard and Nicholas on the subject of friendship. Nicholas' language may be more hyperbolic than Bernard's. He may have used classical reminiscences, especially from Seneca's letters, more obviously than did Bernard. Nicholas devoted time and effort to composing letters of friendship in a way that Bernard in the 1140s could not have done because of the press of business. For both Nicholas and Bernard, however, friendship made up a major occupation in life. It existed outside the cloister but became complete there because the monastic community could provide the best conditions for leading the friends to eternal life together. For friends who remained in the world or lived in other monasteries, letters provided a bond, however insufficient. As Nicholas said in a sentence that should be the retort to any scholar who would reduce medieval letterwriting to an art without any content of human emotion: 'The absences of friends would be intolerable if it were not for the remedy of letters'.[174]

In Nicholas the one heart and mind of the early christian community in Jerusalem described in the Acts of the Apostles (4:32) became the love shared by close friends within the context of community.[175] Nicholas' ability to combine a desire for close human bonds with religious language and experience may have been what attracted Bernard and Peter the Venerable strongly to him. Perhaps because he was not an original thinker himself, Nicholas could formulate in his writings the thoughts and phrases that summarized the desire and yearnings of a dynamic and optimistic community. The Clarevallians, as Nicholas and Peter of Celle both called them, sought to make their house into a magnet of love drawing the best and brightest young men to them, and then sending them out to found monasteries in all corners of Europe. Nicholas provided a bridge between Clairvaux and Cluny in this process. His humanism and enthusiasm for intimacy brought him to Peter the Venerable, while his intensity of language and secretarial abilities won over Bernard.

At times even the most sympathetic modern witnesses to Nicholas have difficulty in accepting the enthusiasm he generated. The able editor of Peter the Venerable's letters, Giles Constable, has characterized parts of a letter from Peter to Nicholas as 'affectionate verbiage'.[176] Peter in such passages hardly tries to restrain himself. Thanks to the intense, personal language of the Psalms and the Song of Songs, his way of expressing himself could fit into the monastic language of friendship. Peter's violent language indicates that monastic friendship was more than a collection of neat phrases. It was a living relationship between men who invested a great deal of themselves in expressing themselves to each other.

After 1152 the days of intoxicating love were over for Nicholas.[177] The course of his fall from grace has been carefully traced elsewhere. We need here only to point to a little-noticed late letter from Peter of Celle, as abbot of Saint Rémi, to an unspecified Nicholas. This may be evidence that years after the disgrace, Peter accepted Nicholas back into his affections. The letter's playful, loving language would befit a relationship of distance and closeness.[178] Certainly Peter lived long enough and was sufficiently tolerant to have given Nicholas a second chance. Otherwise Nicholas seems to have become a flatterer and sycophant of the type he had always threatened to be but never quite became while he was at Clairvaux. Looking for a generous employer, he collected his own works and those of others. In new letters he churned out the old phrases, but monastic friendship had been replaced by pure adulation.[179]

The life and letters of Nicholas provide ample warning against any simplifications about the expression of friendship in the twelfth century. In his career we find: a desire to please, a need for attention, the pursuit of love pure and simple, a fear of rejection, and disappointment and anger at being misconstrued and misunderstood. Did Nicholas mean what he said about love and friendship? Certainly Bernard took him at his word, and the violence of his rejection of Nicholas indicates the intensity of the abbot's feeling for him. Nicholas' disgrace brings us to a major problem with exclusive relationships in the monastery, especially with the abbot: a trusted monk comes to expect special privileges and rights, a status that can never be made official or permanent in the give-and-take of community life. Nicholas deliberately made himself indispensable to Bernard and got to the point where he considered himself to be a second Bernard. As Peter the Venerable wrote to Bernard in asking to have Nicholas with him, 'I shall see you, holy brother, in him; I shall hear you through him'.[180] Nicholas apparently took such language literally.

His experience exposes a risk in monastic friendship. It could create expectations and even demands that exceeded the capacity of abbots such as Peter the Venerable and Bernard of Clairvaux to honour them. Peter did his very best to comply with Nicholas' desire to spend time with him at Cluny, but in the process he may have compromised his position at Clairvaux by making use of his contacts there to influence Bernard.[181] For his part, Bernard was willing to trust Nicholas implicitly so long as he kept up with his correspondence. Holding a position of responsibility and gifted with literary abilities, a man like Nicholas who identified with those he admired found it hard to distinguish between himself and Bernard. The network of friendship in which Nicholas functioned so well for a while turned out to be a delicate structure, dependent on a self-discipline, maturity of behaviour, and a discrimination that Nicholas did not have. As for Bernard, he wanted and needed friendships, but they had to be secondary to his goal of expanding the Cistercian Order and reforming the Church.

Was Bernard ever really a friend with anyone, in the sense of sharing part of himself with other persons for the very sake of such sharing, instead of using them for other purposes? With Nicholas it is hard to say, for both men seem to have been willing to deceive themselves about what they were giving and what they were taking. But with Peter the Venerable, Bernard seems to have had an implicit understanding that friendship indeed existed, yet only so long as Peter was willing to make the major effort, offering compromises on practical points of difference and doing his best to placate Bernard. In a period of financial and ideological crisis, Cluny naturally needed good relations with the progressive and prosperous Cistercians. There was every practical reason for Peter to seek out Bernard.

Too many moments of affection, mingled with threats and promises, nevertheless appear in the Bernard-Peter correspondence to reduce it to political manipulation. The variety of thought, emotion, and stylistic expression to be found in these letters makes it all but impossible not to see them as witnesses to personal relationships. In the case of Bernard's bond with William of Saint Thierry, we cannot ignore his descriptions of life with Bernard at Clairvaux, when the sick William was invited to spend time with his friend, who also was ill.[182] Bernard emerges as a man of will in the presence of a friend willing to make allowances for him out of love and devotion. Peter the Venerable and William of Saint Thierry both understood what being Bernard's friend required: generosity, gentleness and very great patience.

'As I have depicted myself in the letter, so I am, except in the respect that the hand is less able to express the affection of the mind.'[183] So began Bernard a striking letter to an unknown friend. He goes on to describe friendship in the same certain and uncompromising terms that Nicholas used: 'I am yours and will be so as long as I live'.[184] This literary similarity might call into question the genuineness of descriptions of friendship in Nicholas or Bernard. But their agreement when describing the presence and relevance of friendship in their lives points to a common language of friendship and love inside and outside the cloister. This shared expression developed in the first half of the twelfth century. Supported by eleventh-century controversies and advances in learning, the twelfth-century monastic practice of friendship insisted that friends need each other's physical presence, even though letters can to some extent compensate for absence. Friends were friends forever: 'I embrace my new friend from of old, for true friendships do not grow old, or they were not true', says Bernard in rephrasing Jerome's 'friendship which can cease was never true' (*ep* 3) and adding a new dimension. Friends could be addressed in a sensual language taken directly from the Song of Songs. 'I will hold him and not let him go', Bernard assured a friend with all the conviction of the biblical text iteself.[185] The collective heart and mind has become a single love shared by two friends.

Nicholas described Clairvaux after he first saw it as a paradise.[186] Despite the element of rhetorical exaggeration, Clairvaux must indeed have seemed like heaven on earth to the young, sensitive and bright men who came there from all over Europe in the decades from 1120 onwards. Clairvaux did not stand alone, however, as a guarantee that *familiaritas* in the cloister would lead to *amicitia*. Traditionally benedictine Celle, reformed Cluny, and even the courts of bishops like Hato at Troyes offered similar opportunities for the development of individual friendships based on common bonds. Except with Nicholas it is usually impossible for us to penetrate individual monasteries to see how abbots related to their own monks. But through the letters monks of different houses wrote to each other, we can see how the benedictine, cluniac and cistercian abbots of the period could count on a rich network of intellectual and emotional as well as quite utilitarian exchanges. These all occurred in the context of friendship, a living bond seeking new literary forms, a state of mind and heart that we can never pin down and explain completely.

FRIENDSHIP IN A SOCIAL CONTEXT: FAMILY, MONASTERY, CITY

The cistercian family provided an ideal place for the development of a common language and network of friendship. Commitment to the monastic life required an intensity and totality that managed to transform the loves of the world into those of the cloister. The spiritualization of human bonds became more important than the practice of self-denial and asceticism. Like Augustine, Bernard could not be alone. However much he complained about the crowds seeking him out at Clairvaux, his withdrawal from others meant being with his beloved Nicholas in order to read letters of friendship from men like Peter the Venerable.

In late Republican Rome, Cicero considered friendship a matter of course in social life, a natural phenomenon that could be seen within his city's governing class. Cicero fought the widespread conviction that friendship existed basically for profit. Those who think of friendship only in terms of gain, he wrote, 'deprive themselves of the opportunity to experience for themselves how powerful, how wonderful and how all-embracing this kind of relationship can be'.[187]

Augustine could not have the same confidence in the naturalness and inevitability of close human bonds. In a lament contained in the *City of God*, he praised the virtues of friendship but also warned his readers that they could not count on their friends. We can lose them in war or famine or, even worse, experience their treachery. 'Certainly we would rather hear that our friends were dead', he reflected, than experience betrayal.[188] Augustine's words reflect the uncertainties of life in Late Antiquity, when the Roman Empire was becoming less a reality than an ideal, and when old mediterranean bonds were threatened by invasion, war and the collapse of old codes of loyalty.

In the early Middle Ages—the period from about 500 to 1000—the same sense of the impermanence of human bonds persisted. Friendship and the protection of a generous lord provided the highest goals for The Wanderer in the eloquent anglo-saxon poem. This ideal, however, was only a memory of better times. The wanderer had to awake from a dream of kissing his master to the reality of 'the fallow sea stripped by cold winds'. In a world where 'man is short. . . kinship short', the best solution for many an anglo-saxon scholar was to enter into the cloister to find the only hope in the poem, 'the Father in heaven, where for us all the fortress stands'.[189] The monastery of the period offered protection from the evil, not friendship with the good. Even in the twelfth century this attitude is still visible in the traditional language of Orderic Vitalis.

There are moments in the earlier period (the so-called Dark Ages) when friendship was present in an impressive way in monastic culture. This was the case in the eighth century in the circle of Boniface and later with some of the learned Carolingians. Especially in the latter case, however, friendship existed only among a few intellectuals who used the cloister as a place of study to which they withdrew in the fashion of roman gentlemen retiring to their landed estates.

With the eleventh century revival of monastic life and the growth of society, friendship took on a new importance and gained a language that was more accessible to a broader group in the monastery. But at the same time as friendship became a subject celebrated in monastic life, the monastery was losing its central position in the development of Western thought and life. Peter of Celle described this loss of attractiveness for the monastic milieu when he wrote to John of Salisbury about the delightful life in Paris which John had arranged there for himself among his friends:

> You have chosen, my most beloved, a most attractive exile, where joys abound, even if they are empty, where there is a much greater abundance of bread and wine than in your fatherland, where there is a ready flow of friends, and where the dwelling together of comrades is by no means rare. Who else besides you will not think of Paris as a place of delights, a garden of fine plants, a field of first-fruits? Laughing you still told the truth, that where there is more and fuller bodily enjoyment, there is true exile of souls, and where decadence reigns, there miserably the soul becomes a slave and is afflicted. O Paris, how well suited you are for capturing and deceiving souls![190]

The intellectual centre easily came to compete with the monastery as a place to find friends. The friends of the world, in the sense of the Epistle of Saint James (4:4), could lure an attractive and learned man like John away from the 'friend of God', men like Peter himself, who dearly wanted to hold on to him. Peter remained confident, however, that John would maintain his spiritual friendship and follow

Peter's advice. Paris held him for a while, but John did in fact return to England, joined the company of the archbishop of Canterbury, cultivated friendships, and eventually returned to his Peter, at least for a time.

Peter of Celle reflects the hope and belief that spiritual bonds could win over material ones. Like Cicero, he believed in the benefits of a friendship that did not limit itself to personal gain. Peter knew that monastic friendship had to compete with delicious new opportunities for personal bonds and clerical careers that Paris provided: 'O Paris, how well suited you are for capturing and deceiving souls!'

For the first time in the West since Late Antiquity, the city was seen as a place for advancement and wealth. Urban centres were attracting the best young men of the new generation. This story is a well-known one for medieval historians, but it has to be seen in the context not only of learning but also of friendship.

Human history deals with both individuals and groups. The history of friendship in the Middle Ages tells how the bonds of the family were reestablished and renewed in the bonds of the monastery. This form of monastic family, embracing learning, religious experience, and human emotion, was quickly challenged by the success of new communities of scholars and clerks in the city. For a short time in the mid-twelfth century, monastic and urban centres complemented and strengthened each other. Apparently the new monasteries could recruit more than the number of young men they wanted and needed in order to expand. Religious houses could also take in scholars who had become too controversial for the outside world. Abelard became a monk long before he withdrew to Cluny. Peter of Celle continued to form friendships and maintain contacts with some of the most influential men of his time when he moved from Celle to urban Rheims to become abbot of Saint Remi on the outskirts of the town. Monasteries continued to be crucial cultural centres, with a wealth, stability and permanence that city schools lacked.

The rural aristocracy of Champagne, Burgundy, the Rhineland, and the Low Countries willingly sent many of their younger sons to cistercian houses.[191] There they wrote letters of conversion to school friends, encouraging them to take the same step. The monks turned what they had learned about love and friendship in classical florilegia and scriptural texts into a specifically christian set of principles. The monasteries themselves became small centres of learned culture and friendship. No longer isolated oases of learning, as they had been in carolingian times, monastic houses were linked up with each other in ways that encouraged personal bonds among individual monks and abbots. Here it was not only houses of the same order whose members maintained contact. The friendship network had no respect for such divisions.

Some monastic writers tried to combine their description of friendship with a language of analytical discourse, as in the case of Peter of Celle and Nicholas. But the spacious language that grew up in the rural monastic setting combined poorly with the precise categories of urban investigations. The love of learning belonged to both rural monastery and city school, but the link between learning and human affection could only be made explicit where intellectual culture, community and individual bonds drew on each other. Bernard of Clairvaux, Nicholas of Montiéramey, Peter of Celle, Peter the Venerable, and all the lesser lights of these years formed a language of friendship that could not flourish amid the tensions, conflicts and competitiveness of the new european city.

CHAPTER SEVEN

AELRED OF RIEVAULX AND THE LIMITS OF FRIENDSHIP

IN HIS LIFE and writings Aelred of Rievaulx summarizes the literature as well as the yearnings of the previous centuries.[1] Aelred communicated to his surroundings as the monastic friend *par excellence*, willing to share himself with other monks in an intimacy both frank and direct.[2] At the same time he linked this closeness to his attachment to the human Jesus and to a loving God. Aelred's two central works on love and friendship, the *Speculum caritatis* (Mirror of Charity) from the early 1140s, and the *De spiritali amicitia* (Spiritual Friendship) from the early 1160s, reveal a man who understood his own need to engage in the augustinian search to love and be loved (*amare et amari*). What is surprising about Aelred is not his friendships but his willingness, even eagerness, to spread to others the good news of his loves. In Aelred friendship formed not just one aspect of monastic life; it became a major part of it and an indispensable step on the path to God. In Aelred's writings we move away from scattered references in letters and biographies and take hold of whole treatises in which friendship has a primary position.

Aelred's writings on friendship, as Adele Fiske has pointed out, follow directly from Cicero's *De amicitia* as well as John Cassian's Sixteenth Conference.[3] Cassian, however, did not take time to define friendship except to point out the danger of conspiracies among cliques in the monastery. Aiming at the *apatheia* of Evagrius and the other Greek-influenced desert fathers, John Cassian was willing to concede only a limited role to friendship. His hesitation about the worth of individual bonds among monks continued to be felt through the centuries. Even though Cassian's contemporary Augustine wrote a great deal on the subject, he had similar reservations about investing too much of one's self in friendship. The friend of his youth to whom he had been most closely attached he lost, and this experience contributed to Augustine's sense of the fragility of human bonds and the need to transcend them in divine love.[4]

Aelred absorbed this literature, compared and contrasted it with the experience of his own life, and defended the worth and necessity of friendship in human life, especially in the monastery. He might be thought to have disregarded the problems such relationships involved for the rest of the community. As we shall see, however, Aelred knew what he was facing in terms of jealousy and misunderstandings. He had sufficient conviction about the value of friendship in itself to choose the pagan Cicero's essay on friendship, the only complete model available to him, as a point of departure for his own exposition. This dependence on Cicero has led to the charge that Aelred merely provided a christian facade for Cicero's thoughts.[5] If one counts up the number of passages taken from Cicero, this view seems reasonable. But if one looks at Aelred's work as a whole and at its audience, then it becomes clear that the direction of Aelred's thought is quite different from that of the *De amicitia*.

Aelred's *De spiritali amicitia* is not just a vaguely christian and monastic medieval exposition of friendship. It is the distillation of Aelred's life experience into a set of rules for friendship, according to the twelfth-century conviction we saw in the last chapter that such a human bond can be regulated by certain norms.[6] These limitations would, in Aelred's mind, safeguard monks who wanted to integrate everything in their daily lives into the love of God. Aelred was convinced that loving one's fellow human beings and choosing among these loves a few individuals as friends could help the monk (or any Christian) to the love of God.

Aelred's christian neoplatonism envisaged a continuous movement, from physical loves to those of the mind and heart and thence to the threshold of God. Even Augustine, the great model for Aelred's thought and life, separated decisively the love of one's fellow human beings from the love of God. Aelred saw no gap. In advancing from love to love we advance ever closer to God, in whom we become one with our friends. Aelred provides the fullest medieval unification of the two great commandments of love. In his life and writings he sees nothing to fear when one sets forth on the path of friendship with other members of the monastic community. Because God is also friendship, loving the friend in the context of community means also loving God.

AELRED'S YOUTH: LOOKING FOR LOVE

Our main source for Aelred's youth is the prologue of the *Spiritual Friendship*:

> When I was still just a lad at school, and the charm of my companions pleased me very much, I gave my whole soul to affection and devoted myself to love amid the ways and vices with which that age is wont to be threatened, so that nothing seemed to me more sweet, nothing more agreeable, nothing more practical, than to love and to be loved.[7]

The most important word for Aelred here is *affectus*, whose translation here as 'affection' is inadequate because the term implies more than temporary, unstable impulses. The place of *affectus* provides one of the main themes of Aelred's *Mirror of Charity*.[8] Here Aelred defines *affectus* as a spontaneous and pleasant drawing of the mind itself to another (*spontanea quaedam ac dulcis ipsius animi ad aliquem inclination*, *Sp.Car.* 3:31). One notices immediately the term *dulcis*, one of Aelred's favorite terms, impossible to translate into modern English as 'sweet' because that word has become so maudlin in describing human attachments.

In an excellent treatment of the prologue to *Spiritual Friendship*, James McEvoy suggests the translation of *dulcis* as 'rewarding' or 'attractive', depending on the context.[9] The word 'pleasant' perhaps provides a better sense of the non-commital quality of an experience that is *dulcis*. There is no moral content or judgment here, only the notation of a movement from one human being towards another.

Aelred registered the impulses of his own soul in a masterful way. The cistercian school of spirituality, with its emphasis on experience, encouraged him to look within himself and to record what he found. In Aelred the autobiographical element, present to a greater or lesser degree in Bernard of Clairvaux, William of Saint Thierry and other contemporary writers, becomes explicit and detailed. However much we might argue about the accuracy of Aelred's recall of his boyhood situation, the fact remains that he thought it important to remember and write about it.

Augustine provided Aelred's guide and model. The language and spirit of this whole passage are permeated with reminiscences of Augustine's *Confessions*, its sense of the sweetness of life and the attractiveness yet horror of sin.[10] The rest of the prologue, which continues in this vein, has been so carefully analyzed by McEvoy that it would be superfluous to try to improve on his treatment. Aelred tells how he wandered among various loves and friendships, not knowing any true law of friendship (*uerae amicitiae legem*), until he came upon Cicero's treatise. At first he found joy in having a set of norms, but after his conversion to the monastic life, he discovered that only Sacred Scripture gave him fulfillment and sweetness. The language of Augustine is more than mere literary embellishment. As a master of Augustine's language, Pierre Courcelle, has conceded: 'A Cistercian so profoundly nourished on the *Confessions* of Augustine could relive episodes of his own life with him and present them in conformity with Augustine's writings'.[11]

After Aelred's conversion, he found time to look for christian writings that also dealt with friendship. Finding none as specific as Cicero, he decided to write his own account of friendship, integrated into monastic life. This would be spiritual friendship, as he said in his Prologue, with rules for a chaste and holy love. Throughout his life, Aelred did his best to turn Cicero's law of friendship into a christian norm that took into account what Cicero took for granted but which was essential for the monk, chastity. Here as in other areas he wanted a formula and boundary for friendship: *forma* and *meta.*[12] How much of himself could the youth or the monk invest in loving his fellow men and selecting one or two of them for the special love of friendship? The pattern Aelred establishes in the Prologue to the *Spiritual Friendship* reveals the thrust of his early life. Other passages in the work, as those describing his stay at the scottish court, only underline the initial impression of a young man singularly caught up in love and closeness with other men.

Aelred's father was a priest who had been treasurer of the church at Durham and then moved to Hexham when the Gregorian-Norman reforms of the clergy reached the North of England by the beginning of the twelfth century. In the words of F.M. Powicke, whose knowledge of Aelred's background and public life is unsurpassed:

> His family was well-to-do, well connected and prominent in the neighbourhood of Durham and Hexham. This strict Cistercian came of a long line of married priests, learned, respectable, conscientious. If there were many such families in Northumbria, it is easy to understand why the movement for a celibate clergy made such slow progress in the eleventh and twelfth centuries.[13]

There is no evidence for any conflict between Aelred and his father, who eventually accepted the new monastic regime and died as a Benedictine of Durham. Since we know nothing about Aelred and his mother, we are effectively spared any easy psychological explanations for Aelred's sexuality. Aelred lets himself appear to us regularly and consistently as a human being who wanted and needed the companionship of other men and who was not particularly interested in women. He seems to have to use his own life as an *exemplum* so others could see it was possible to rise from the desires of the flesh to the fulfillment of the spirit. Whether Aelred used himself consciously in such a way is a debatable point, but as a consummate judge of the interior life in himself and in other men, it seems likely that Aelred did know what he was doing in giving his audience a first-hand view into the fires and passions that had almost consumed him before they became spiritualized.

Aelred was most frank when writing to his sister in the *De institutione inclusarum*. In giving her advice about maintaining chastity in her life as a recluse, he revealed much more about himself than about potential threats to female purity:

> Remember, if you like, that filthiness of mine for which you so often pitied and corrected me, the girl the boy, the woman the man. Recall now, as I said, my rottenness when a cloud of lust was emitted from my slimy concupiscence of flesh and from the gushing up of puberty, and there was no one to snatch me away and save me.[14]

Aelred speaks of himself as being seized and drowned in an 'abyss of evil deeds'. The sweetness of human attachments and the impurity of physical desires are inextricably mixed into each other, and he remembered quite clearly the "fire with which I was burned". 'I lost my purity', he confesses, while his sister is commended for keeping her virginity. Here Aelred admits as openly as he could in the language of his time and his social position that he had physical experience of sex in loves that were considered to be grossly impure: *convenientesque in unum affectionis suavitas et cupiditas impuritatis*.

During this period Aelred lived in a typically adolescent state of confusion, with extremes of depression and exaltation that he describes in the *Mirror of Charity*. One particular autobiographical passage indicates that Aelred at one point felt so low that he thought of suicide. In the section that leads up to this assertion, Aelred best characterizes his state of mind:

> The chain of my worst habit bound me: the love of my blood overcame me, the bonds of social grace restricted me and especially the knot of a certain friendship, delightful to me above all the delights of my life. The gracious bond of friendship pleased me, but always I was afraid of my offence, and I was sure that it would be broken off at some time in the future. I thought about the joy with which it had begun, and I awaited what would follow, and I could foresee the end.

> I realized that its beginning was reprehensible, the middle state offensive and the end would inevitably be damnation. The death I awaited terrified me because it was certain that punishment would await such a soul after death. And men said, looking at my circumstances, but not knowing what was going on within me, 'Isn't he doing well! Isn't he though!'[15]

Aelred was remembering his period at the court of King David of Scotland. A success in the world, celebrated at court, holding a position of trust, he was riddled by guilt and doubt.[16] This is a typically adolescent state of mind, but the Aelred who lived it was not fifteen years of age but twenty, a grown man by the standards of his day, the companion of knights, courtiers and administrators. How could the inner and the outer Aelred be integrated? The man who sought friendship and love had to reconcile his needs to the moral code of the church, which strictly condemned all sexual relations outside of marriage.

At no point does Aelred say outright: I slept with another man. His autobiographical passage, however, points to a sexual element in the friendship he mentions. Aelred indicates how he had experienced his friendship as being of too great importance in his life. He realized that his attraction had created a bond that was a nightmare for him. He had to escape. Grave consequences loomed before him: guilt, certainty that he would go to hell, fear that he would soon lose the friend anyway. Amid the intrigues of court life, Aelred may have had reason to be afraid of whispers and slander. Certainly Aelred was afraid of sin and its consequence in terms of eternal damnation.

To ask whether Aelred actually 'had sex' with another man reflects perhaps our concerns more than Aelred's. For him what was important was not the act but the fire of desire that consumed him. It is in this sense that his expressions 'love of the blood' and 'worst habit' must be seen. In classical Latin *consuetudo* can mean any habit. For Augustine it implies a habit of sin.[17] The *pessima consuetudo* in Aelred suggests some individual sinful habit, one linked to the impulses of the blood or heat within him, something that came 'gushing up' in his adolescence. It is likely that he was referring to masturbation.

Elsewhere, in Aelred's letter to his sister and even in his justly celebrated *Pastoral Prayer*, Aelred mentions the same 'bad habit' as still being a problem for him.[18] In giving good counsel to the recluse, he advises her to commend her chastity to God in bed at night and then to examine her conscience. If she awakes and is tempted, she is to think of holy virgins who were martyred for their chastity. No matter how often she is tempted, she should know that 'he who looks upon our hearts and bodies is present, and it is under his eyes that whatever you do or think takes place'.[19] Surely Aelred was writing just as much about himself and his own temptations as about his sister and any she might experience.

The historian John Boswell has called Aelred 'gender-blind' and claimed that he put homosexual relationships on the same level as heterosexual.[20] Such a view contributes to Boswell's thesis that there existed in the decades before about 1150 a degree of toleration towards homosexual activity. Insofar as Aelred indicated that he had to cope with a sexual desire for other men, Boswell's interpretation captures one aspect of the special quality of the earlier part of the twelfth century. Autobiographical openness on the subject of homosexuality would have been unthinkable in the next century. But Aelred at no point is 'modern' in accepting homosexual love. He maintained the traditional view of medieval theology that sexual contact among men is morally more reprehensible than between men and women: '. . . that crime is to be detested by which a man goes mad on a man or a woman on a woman. It is to be judged more damnable than all other crimes'.[21] Aelred does not go into detail, but it is clear that he leaves no opening either to tolerance or to a sense that one form of human sexuality is the same as another. Homosexual love represented for Aelred an especially direct way to hell.

In condemning genital sexuality as sinful and vicious, Aelred still believed in tenderness, affection and touching, and in being open and talking intimately about one's personal life. At the same time he did not feel pain or guilt for appreciating physical beauty in other human beings. Beauty was worth seeking so long as the pursuit did not lead to sin, for an attractive human being can also be virtuous and thus increase one's own virtue.[22] Instead of being afraid of the impulse within himself, Aelred by the end of his life, when he completed his *Spiritual*

Friendship, became convinced that he could use this attraction towards others to become spiritually closer to other human beings and thus closer to God.

CONVERSION: DEALING WITH THE IMPULSES OF SEXUALITY

Aelred's transference of sexual energy to spiritual fire came in the aftermath of the conversion to the monastic life at the age of twenty-four. The man who introduced Aelred to the young community of Cistercians at Rievaulx in Yorkshire was Walter Espec, a nobleman whose castle was located at nearby Helmsley. Aelred described him with unreserved admiration: 'keen of mind, prudent in counsels, reserved in peace, provident in war, always maintaining friendship with his comrades and faith with kings'.[23] Aelred is attentive to Walter's physical characteristics: he was a big, solid man, impressive to those around him, a man in command. His devotion to the christian faith summarizes Aelred's ideal of being 'noble in flesh but more noble in christian piety'.

Walter Espec had founded Rievaulx in 1131, a community whose attractions Aelred could not resist. Aelred's biographer, Walter Daniel, tells of the visit by the young official of the scottish king to the monastery. The next day, on the road leading north to Scotland, now a paved highway on the crest of the hill above Rievaulx, Aelred wanted to turn back to the monastery.[24] The crucial decision of whether to descend the hill or continue north Aelred left up to his companion-servant on the journey. Such a gesture, whether or not it actually was made in the way Walter Daniel describes, summarizes Aelred's thoughtful courtliness, a quality that easily could be converted into the practice of christian charity. Aelred did not want to ruin the career of his servant, as other entrants to cistercian life did, apparently heedless of the consequences for those who served them in lay life.[25] The agent of the king of Scotland was willing to forget his mission, but not the man who was attending him.

Walter Espec's role and Aelred's gesture to his servant provide needed perspective on this sensitive and seemingly tortured young man. He was a success: the distinguished priest's son who by his own doing had become a respected member of court. Whatever Aelred felt guilty about, he was capable of filling a trusted position as royal messenger to a key figure in the aristocracy of the english North. And yet Aelred was willing to give it all up, so long as his servant gave the final word!

Cistercian writers loved spectacular conversions.[26] This is certainly one of them. Aelred reminds his listeners and readers, however, that he did not live 'happily ever after' in the cloister. There was a long period of transition in learning to overcome the impulses of his body and mind. In finding a community of men at Rievaulx, Aelred found a possibility for loving other men without guilt and with great joy. Now he had to learn discipline in this love and in this new way of life:

> I know a monk, who at the beginning of his life as such, both because of natural drives, and because of the violence of his evil habit, and because of the suggestion of the clever tempter, feared that his chastity was in danger. So he set up against himself, and against his flesh, an overwhelming hatred, and he desired nothing more than that which tormented him.[27]

This passage is most probably autobiographical. Aelred tells his sister what he had to go through in terms of fasting and other forms of self-denial to cool the heat of his body. 'For often feeling these forbidden movements', he would whip his body and overcome 'fire by fire' (*incendium incendio*). When all this was not enough, he would prostrate himself before the feet of the image of Christ and pray.

Eventually victory came, but when the physical symptoms were quiet, illicit affections invaded Aelred's heart. The life Aelred experienced must at times have been a hell on earth:

> My God, what crosses, what torments that wretched one suffered until at last there was imparted to him a delight in chastity, so that he could overcome all the desires of flesh which could be felt or imagined.[28]

The passage would seem to indicate that Aelred first had to deal with the habit of masturbation. Once this was under control, he found himself still fantasizing about erotic friendships with men. He threw himself into ascetic observances, including (as Walter Daniel mentions) cold water baths in the freezing current of the Rye.[29] This hagiographic detail recalls Gregory the Great's *Life* of Saint Benedict in the second book of his *Dialogues.* It does not in itself provide proof of any special sexual problem for Aelred, but together with his own description of battles with the flesh, the icy bath is highly suggestive. Aelred seems to have had what we would call a strong sex drive and had the greatest difficulty in bringing it under control. His self-denial was not just the pious practice of the saint who belittles his own holiness. It was a necessary means to keep the fires of his body at such a low point that he could keep from masturbating or fantasizing scenes of sexual love.

It is not common in treatments of Aelred to devote so much attention to his sexuality as such. The traditional silence among scholars before John Boswell about this side of Aelred recalls Aelred's own caution. As he said to the novice who sometimes appears in the *Mirror of Charity*, it is best not to be too specific about sexual matters. Otherwise the novice might get the wrong food for thought.[30] Aelred does not go into detail, but he says enough about himself that we can sense how his problems were not just the result of an over-zealous and scrupulous conscience. To remain chaste, Aelred had to struggle constantly. He saw the habit of masturbation and its accompanying sexual thoughts as a barrier to total integration in the life of the cloister.

As novicemaster at Rievaulx from the early 1140s, and later on as abbot, Aelred coped with the same problem in other monks. He told his sister about one of them who in his youth (*pueritia*) apparently also took up the habit of masturbation. Eventually he gained control of himself. Burning for chastity, he refused himself even what was necessary for his body in the monastic life.[31] No one heard a single superfluous word from his mouth. He kept his eyes downcast, for fear of contact with others and of divine judgment.

This may have been the friend of Aelred's mature years whom he describes at the end of *Spiritual Friendship*.[32] Here as in his own case, Aelred was convinced that in order to maintain chastity, all bodily functions had to be restricted. The friend died of a stomach ailment. Aelred too suffered the results of his extreme asceticism and died fairly young after much suffering. Bernard also is remembered for ruining his health in his pursuit of perfection. Cistercians of this kind sought the unrestricted asceticism of the Desert Fathers. They did so, however, not by maintaining a distance from each other but by asserting the value of banding together and even of forming special bonds so that they could help each other. Aelred loved his friend. He watched his development. He counselled him as best he could. He integrated him into a loving community. One of Aelred's favourite phrases from the Psalms was the first line of Psalm 132 (133): 'Behold how good and pleasant it is when brothers dwell in unity'.[33]

In his *Mirror of Charity*, Aelred excoriated bishops and monks who surrounded themselves in their homes by family members and at the same time lived in a Sodom and Gomorrah of their own making. They collected effeminate youths who would strut about in tight garb and make their homes into male brothels.[34] Aelred was keenly and painfully aware of the possibility that even well-meaning spiritual men could become so fascinated with attractive, attentive youths that they could be tempted to form sexual bonds with them. Such men would willingly receive troubled young men into their care but soon discovered that they could hardly be together with youths of this type without feeling a form of titillation.[35] One type of attachment, Aelred explains, easily leads to another. We have to be constantly on our guard against the impulses of the flesh.

It might seem that a man with Aelred's awareness and fear of sex in an all-male world would have been inclined to deal with the conflict by warning against all forms of bonding among men. This was the solution of the more extreme Desert Fathers, while Aelred continued to believe in the possibility of spiritual friendship. He discarded *apatheia* or passionlessness as a goal in itself and insisted that love could be pure. Since human relationships concerned with either physical desire or hope of gain did not deserve the name of friendship, *amicitia* by definition remained untouched by the sins of the world.[36] In striving for true friendship, the monk was necessarily seeking God and the presence of God in those he came to love.

In Aelred's dialogue on *Spiritual Friendship*, this progression from human to divine friendship takes place in a way both natural and inevitable. This is what Aelred as abbot of Rievaulx argued, seeking to convince his monastic audience that friendship was a goal worth pursuing and not a danger to the solidarity of the community. A few passages deal with the question of sexual attraction in the stages of friendship.[37] For the most part, Aelred was optimistic about the path to friendship and is steadier and more consistent in his analysis than earlier in the warnings of *Mirror of Charity* (which belongs to the early 1140s, while the *Spiritual Friendship* was begun in 1147, when Aelred became abbot at Rievaulx, but was not completed until shortly before his death in 1167).

Did Aelred deliberately or even naively ignore the problems that arise when men live together in a tightly-knit community and are constantly aware of each other's comings and goings and states of mind and heart? Aelred was in reality very much aware of the conflicts latent in a cloister, where men of all ages are dedicated to a spiritual ideal but have to live in the face of physical realities. As he wrote to his sister, he might have spoken to his fellow monks: 'I want you never to be secure but always to be afraid'.[38]

THE CISTERCIAN WORLD OF FRIENDSHIP

The young Aelred at Rievaulx in the early 1130s seems immediately to have caught the attention of an older monk, Hugh, who was a close friend of a young and attractive monk, Simon. Aelred found to his delight that the two of them willingly opened their friendship to include him.[39] All this Aelred revealed ten years after the events of his conversion, when he wrote the *Mirror of Charity*. Simon was a friend gained because of likeness of character and interests. Aelred writes of how Simon appeared to him at the time: a vision of male beauty in the bloom of early manhood: 'Who would not be amazed at this tender and delicate youth, outstanding in his parenthood, beautiful in his appearance. . . .'[40] Aelred indicates in his description that Simon was inspired to come to Rievaulx by the *boy* Jesus, who wanted this youth (*puer*) to be part of a monastic community. So the three were made one: the boy Christ with the youths Aelred and Simon.

Another triangle was formed when Aelred and Simon joined forces with the older and more experienced Hugh. He had an enormous influence on Aelred. When Aelred in the early 1140s as novicemaster started putting together materials for his book on love, he composed some parts 'in the manner of letters' for Hugh, who had become prior (whether at Rievaulx or at one of its daughter houses is not made clear). Aelred speaks of Hugh in the familiar formula of friendship available since classical times, according to which one's own identity becomes merged in that of the friend:

> But in deciding to take up the present work, I considered some matters with myself, while some I thought about as it were with myself—no, rather even more with myself—because I dictated them to be expressed in the manner of disparate letters for the most reverend prior Hugh, who is of one mind with me, and who is more with me than I am with myself.[41]

The language leaves open the possibility that Hugh at the time was still at Rievaulx and that the communications were not real letters, only formed as letters. This mode of contact would have enabled Aelred to get around the rule of silence and have given him as well a chance to formulate his thoughts more precisely than he could have done in conversations with Hugh. His tribute to the prior is, at any rate, a perfect example of how in Aelred's view the friend becomes the most real part of one's self. Aelred draws here on the passionate language of the psalms as well as that of the Song of Songs and shows closeness to the language of Bernard of Clairvaux.

Bernard surely recognized an eager pupil and follower in Aelred when the young english monk visited Clairvaux in the early 1140s on his way to Italy to sort out the twisted case of the election of the archbishop of York. Thanks to the historian of spirituality André Wilmart and his detective work with a letter now attributed to Bernard, we now know that it was he who asked Aelred to write on the subject of love in the monastic life and in the christian life in general.[42] Aelred may well have been already formulating some ideas on his own, but it is Bernard who gave him the necessary impulse for what is generally recognized as his best and most complete work. Aelred had claimed that because of his early life he knew more about kitchens than about writing rooms, *scriptoria*. Bernard swept aside this excuse. He liked a man who wrote from the experience of his heart and hands and not on the sole foundation of speculative knowledge. Bernard's letter cannot be used as evidence of any personal friendship between Bernard and Aelred, but the *Spiritual Friendship* points to another friendship Aelred formed at Clairvaux, with the sacristan named Gerard, who has been confused with Bernard's brother of the same name, who was Clairvaux's cellarer.[43]

Already at this time, Aelred demonstrated to his spiritual fathers at Clairvaux an ability for making friendships and a talent for writing about love. But Aelred could also draw on the inspiration Bernard gave him. Aelred's lament in the *Mirror* for his dead friend Simon is patterned on Bernard's description of his sorrow, penned a few years earlier, on the death of his brother Gerard.[44] While not as brilliant a writer as Bernard, Aelred managed to convey intensely his own personal loss. Aelred was not indebted to Bernard's language alone. He also had his eyes fixed on Augustine's lament for a dead friend in the *Confessions* (IV:4).

Augustine provided Aelred with a way to express the need for love and friendship present in every human life. As a good Cistercian, Aelred obeyed Bernard's command to write about love. The result was something different from anything Bernard ever wrote about friendship, for Aelred, far more than Bernard, followed the augustinian autobiographical model to teach his fellow monks the trials and pains of life. What we know about Bernard has for a great part been communicated to us through other men or comes only indirectly through his letters, for Bernard was not eager to reveal his motives and inner conflicts. What we know about Aelred, we know for the most part from his own words, not from his biographer Walter Daniel. Aelred conveys himself immediately to us and so belongs directly to the augustinian tradition. He is more open about himself than any of the french cistercian or benedictine friends. He makes it possible for his monastic audience to reach out to him as a person.

AELRED'S EXPERIENCE OF FRIENDSHIP

At the end of the first book of the *Mirror of Charity*, Aelred paused in order to lament the death of Simon, his early friend at Rievaulx. As in Bernard's lament for Gerard, what is made to appear as an interruption in the text we can be sure is actually an integral part of it. Even more than in Bernard's case, Aelred provides an exemplum of human love by describing his own love and loss.[45] This is not the place to review Aelred's literary devices and phraseology or to compare them with Bernard's, even though a complete study of cistercian friendship would have to do so. But what is central here is the impression Aelred gives of the content of his friendship with Simon. He makes it clear that he found Simon attractive in every way. On him he could concentrate an enthusiasm and delight that he later, in writing of Simon in the *Spiritual Friendship*, considered to be the result more of impulse than reason.[46]

Simon, as I mentioned in the beginning of the last section, is described by Aelred as having been handsome. Cistercian literature does not normally give attention to a young monk's physical attractiveness. Walter Daniel says that Aelred himself was admired for his 'beautiful countenance' (*pulcher et decorus aspectu*), a passage borrowed from the first book of Samuel (16:12) in describing the young David. This description the monastic historian David Knowles imagined would not have pleased the strict Stephen Harding, one of Cîteaux's founders.[47] But by the 1130s, the uncompromising asceticism of the earliest Cîteaux had given way to acceptance that there must be an ascent from physical to spiritual beauty. Bernard himself furthered the attitude of a new cistercian generation that accepted a refined sensuality of the spirit expressed in its passion for writing well.

Bernard's letter to Aelred indicates that he saw him as an attractive young man who, in choosing the monastic life, showed how asceticism, community, and human and divine loves could be reconciled in one another. It is a tribute to Bernard's perceptiveness that he realized Aelred was the man to describe how human loves and the ascetic life could be combined in the new cloister. Tenderness, gentleness, tears and even embraces were all possible in a monastic community of the new order.

Simon's family and background remain obscure in the details.[48] Aelred's description, however, makes it clear that he, like Aelred, came from a well-off and well-connected family. Again like Aelred, Simon was sensitive, attentive and affectionate. The two seem to have been very close, in spite of the restrictions monastery life placed on friendly conversations. Perhaps such limitation even strengthened the bond between the two youths:

> At the same time when the authority of our order kept us from speaking, the expression in his face spoke to me, his way of walking, and also his silence. For his face was chaste, his gait dignified, his speech weighty and his silence without bitterness.[49]

Elsewhere Aelred says that friends have to be able to share each other's secrets, and so it has been asked how this would have been possible for young monks with so limited opportunity for talking together.[50] How could Aelred and Simon have found out about each other's backgrounds, their reasons for choosing the monastic life, their problems in adjusting to it? Aelred's silence on this subject perhaps suggests that he shared with Simon more a non-verbal than a verbal relationship. The two recognized each other as kindred spirits, were keenly aware of each other, and occasionally dared study the other's face, as at chapter, if one or the other were called upon to speak. The very fact of enforced distance within such an intense way of life could keep the friends in a state of anticipation and joy at the fact of each other's presence.

Aelred indicates that the friendship was never really tested. Simon died too young for the two monks to have a chance to get to know each other over a span of years. Their relationship might for us suggest a teenage romance in which boy and girl almost never dare to speak to each other and yet are in love. There is an element of such youthful love in Aelred's feelings for Simon. Here it is essential, however, to realize that we can describe their friendship because Aelred himself in *Spiritual Friendship* tells about it in a way that allows at least partial translation into terms of modern experience. We profit from Aelred's self-awareness as it had developed in the last decades of his life.

We will return to the question of silence in monastic friendship. For the moment it is sufficient to point out that as abbot Aelred showed great understanding for such incomplete relationships. While in the first book of *Spiritual Friendship*, begun in the 1140s, he had little trust in the value of relationships based on pure enjoyment of each other, he conceded to Walter Daniel in the early 1160s that adolescent forms of carnal friendship had a use and meaning if they later could lead to spiritual friendship:

> . . . this friendship, except for trifles and deceptions, if nothing dishonorable enters into it, is to be tolerated in the hope of a more abundant grace, as the beginnings, so to say, of a holier friendship.[51]

Here Aelred shows the possibility of an ascent from one form of friendship to another so that friends 'may, with purer affections, mount to loftier heights'.

Aelred had nothing to regret in his friendship with Simon. It was not a perfect friendship, but Aelred was on the way to the divine love that he also sought. Like Bernard defending his tears for his dead brother Gerard, Aelred protested against those who might judge his attachment to the now-dead Simon to have been too physical. Both Aelred and Bernard departed from the tradition of the desert that the monk was to break off all kinship and friendship bonds. Aelred's activities later in life actually underline how he maintained the political and ecclesiastical bonds of his biological family in order to serve the interests of his spiritual family at Rievaulx.[52] Aelred even managed to modify Christ's words about hating one's mother and father (Luke 14:26) by distinguishing between love based on reason and that founded on emotion. In Aelred, family bonds always mattered.[53]

At Simon's death Aelred could release some of the emotion that he had so carefully guarded in life.[54] His eyes could no longer look on Simon's sensitive face, his ears no longer listen to Simon's wise words in chapter. Here Simon had admitted his faults to the community and thus showed Aelred and the other monks that he had the same problems they did in living in harmony with the Rule. Aelred's relationship with Simon was both a private and a public matter, a combination difficult for us to understand in an age and culture where these spheres normally are kept carefully apart. In the monastery every thought, word, or action was a matter of concern for the entire community. Aelred could share his friendship with Simon with other members of the community and yet maintain a personal bond, a privilege to which he felt entitled so long as it did not jeopardize the harmony of the community. What seems a paradox of the personal and the communal in the same social relationship was for Aelred and other twelfth-century monks a matter of course. In the end all the tensions and contradictions and imperfections would be resolved in an act of union between human and divine loves.

Aelred speculated a great deal about the bond between physical signs of love and their spiritual meaning. For him the symbol of the unity of love was the kiss. In the *Spiritual Friendship* he takes the opening line of the Song of Songs, 'Let him kiss me with the kiss of his mouth', and distinguishes three types of kiss: bodily, when the lips meet; spiritual, when spirits are joined; intellectual, arising from unity of spirit that gives understanding, when grace is poured into the soul through God.[55] The bodily kiss can be a sign of reconciliation, as when two men become friends after having been enemies. The kiss can also be a sign of peace, as before communion in the Eucharist, or a sign of love, as between bride and groom, or between friends, who offer and receive it after a long absence. As Aelred warns, the kiss can be misused in lust. In such cases, 'to be kissed is nothing else than to be corrupted' (*adulterari*).[56] Aelred obviously had his mind here on Christ's remark about the man who commits adultery in his heart. Inner consent is equivalent to the act itself (Mt 5:27-28).

Aelred walked a fine line between an ascetic flight from other people and cultivating individual bonds in the cloister with an intensity that might easily have led to scandal and repression. Aelred in his writings does not deny the possibility that sexual love can overwhelm two people who seek contact with and consolation in each other and in Christ. The *cor unum et anima una* had become a description not only of harmony in community but also of individual friendship.[57] Aelred completed the transformation of friendship's language that had been taking place since the eleventh century.

Uniquely among twelfth-century monastic writers on friendship, Aelred deals with physical manifestations of friendships in terms of how they can be used or misused. He distances himself from spiritual writers on the Continent, who either saw no problem in the manifestation of signs of affection or who may have avoided the subject deliberately. Here as elsewhere we realize Aelred's special sensitivity, his eagerness to define the limits and possibilities of friendship. As Aelred made Walter Daniel say in *Spiritual Friendship*, 'I want you to establish for me a clear boundary for friendship'.[58]

Aelred wrote this work as a monument to his own efforts to combine monastic life in community with intimate personal relationships. At the end he described at length the second great friendship of his life. This was with another young monk who also was dead by the time Aelred wrote. He never tells us the man's name but describes how he had brought him 'across the sea', perhaps from France or Normandy. Eventually Aelred appointed him subprior at Rievaulx.[59] This office and its practical business would have given the abbot ample opportunity for daily conversations with his friend. The young monk had not been enthusiastic at the prospect of office. He told Aelred he did not want to be privileged in this manner. Trying to displease the abbot, he also told him quite frankly what he thought about him. Aelred, instead of getting angry, was only happy that one of his monks, and especially the one he had wanted to be his friend, had taken the risk of being open with him. This exchange became a breakthrough in the friendship which allowed Aelred to come to share all his inner thoughts and concerns with the friend:

> But his freedom of speech and spirit only led our friendship to its culmination, for my desire for his friendship was lessened not a whit. Perceiving then that his words had pleased me, and that I answered humbly to each accusation and had satisfied him in all these matters, and that he himself had not only caused no offense but rather had received more fruitful benefit, he began to manifest his love for me even more ardently than theretofore, to relax the reins of his affection, and to reveal himself wholly to my heart. In this way we tested one another, I making proof of his freedom of utterance and he of my patience.[60]

Aelred's enumeration of the stages of friendship, from election, to probation, admission and enjoyment, seems foreign to an age where friendship is usually looked upon as something that just happens.[61] Aelred had the position, authority and experience to allow himself to test the young monk and to determine whether he was fit to be entrusted with his secrets. In Cicero, Scripture, and the Church Fathers, Aelred found models for ideal friendships. Most importantly of all, he had a great need to enrich his life with such relationships. He wanted to spend time with someone with whom there would be no pretence, no deception, with whom everything was out in the open.[62] The subprior was not only the abbot's friend and confidant. He also had an active role at Rievaulx in 'heading off emergent scandals'. Aelred does not specify, but his words imply he needed help with internal dissensions, a subject to which we will return later in this chapter.

'Was it not a foretaste of blessedness thus to love and to be loved?' asks Aelred in describing this the last great friendship of his life.[63] As ever, he saw the pathway from human to divine love as clear and uncluttered. The love Aelred had for the brethren at Rievaulx, his special love for his subprior, and his love of God merged to provide him a sense of the love for which he yearned in heaven, where all would be his friends in loving God. Aelred looked upon Rievaulx as a garden of friendship and love:

> The day before yesterday, as I was walking the round of the cloister of the monastery, the brethren were sitting around forming as it were a most loving crown. In the midst, as it were, of the delights of paradise with the leaves, flowers and fruits of each single tree, I marveled. In multitude of brethren I found no one whom I did not love, and no one by whom I felt sure I was not loved. I was filled with such joy that it surpassed all the delights of this world.[64]

In such a vision of friendship the individual friend helped Aelred as abbot to live up to the requirements of community life. Because he loved one monk in a special manner, Aelred had more love for the other monks, all of whom he loved. This idealized picture of monastic life may correspond ill with what we otherwise know about jealousies and internal divisions that easily could beset cloisters.[65] But Aelred is here speaking on the basis of a lifetime of experience in terms of what he felt was possible and desirable. He worked so hard to realize friendship that he became convinced that he made it possible within his own community.

DIFFICULT FRIENDSHIPS

Although Aelred believed in the worth of friendship, he did not pretend it was easy to keep close friendships alive and healthy. Aware of Jerome's maxim that a friendship that can cease was never a friendship, he preferred Cicero's assertion that a friendship can become such a burden in one's life that it has to be slowly dismantled.[66] After the period of disengagement, former friends have still an obligation to show each other special love and loyalty. The bond must never cease, a former friend has a right to maintain a distance in order to protect himself.

Aelred's confidence that friendship either endured or could be gently dissolved, but not abruptly ended, is especially evident in the sections of *Spiritual Friendship* where he admitted that some of the friends he had were difficult personalities. He insisted nevertheless on the value of their friendships. Aelred made use of the dialogue form of the work to introduce some of his monastic friends to us and to reveal their reservations about each other. Despite Aelred's warning against taking as friends men who are unstable or inclined to anger, he used the monk Gratian in the dialogue to point out that one or two of Aelred's friends were of this type. As Gratian said to Aelred:

> A few days ago that friend of yours, whom many think you prefer to all of us was, so we thought, overcome by anger, and said and did something that everyone could see displeased you. Yet we do not believe or see that he has in any degree lost favor with you. Hence we are not a little surprised that, when we speak together, you will not neglect anything that pleases him no matter how trivial it may be, yet he cannot bear even trifles for your sake.[67]

Aelred's answer was simple. The man was dear to him and, 'having received him into friendship, I can never do otherwise than love him'. But Aelred also explains that in the particular case being discussed, his own position as abbot was stronger than that of the friend, and so it was easier for him to be tolerant. Aelred preferred to maintain peace instead of insisting on his rights in a matter whose exact content is not described but where he found no 'dishonour being involved. . . confidence. . . violated, or virtue lessened.'[68]

Another participant in the dialogue, Walter, was clearly not happy with Aelred's explanation. He said he did not understand how Aelred could have coped with a friend of this type. Earlier in the dialogue, Walter had mentioned yet another friend of Aelred's. This man, unable to control his anger, had sometimes hurt Aelred. The abbot's reply to Walter's charge is quite meek: some men have a bent towards anger but do their best to restrain their passion. When they fail, we should bear them patiently.[69] Later on, however, Aelred revealed that such a friendship is by no means a one-sided relationship. A single look from Aelred could quell the anger of a friend who had learned through him to gain mastery over himself:

> Indeed, he about whom we are now speaking, preserves the law of friendship toward me in such a way that I can restrain an outburst at any time by a mere nod, even when it is already breaking forth into speech, so that he never reveals in public what is displeasing but always waits till we are alone to unburden his mind's thought.[70]

Even though Aelred seems on the surface to have reproduced ciceronian advice about what to look for and what to avoid in a friend, he adapted his model according to christian patience and forgiveness. This process can also be seen in great detail if we consider the dialogue of the last two books of *Spiritual Friendship* in terms of what it reveals about the personality of the Walter who is so significant here. We can assume that Aelred was using aspects of a personality and conveying it in his work, contrasting it with the more pleasant ways of the monk Gratian. There is generally agreement among scholars that the irascible and suspicious Walter of *Spiritual Friendship* is the Walter

Daniel who defended Aelred fiercely in his biography, while the Gratian of the dialogue, unlike Walter or the Ivo of Wardon present in the first book, cannot be traced as an historical person.[71] Gratian may be a composite or type of the monk who wanted to please everyone. Aelred thus took Walter Daniel as one of his own friends from late in life and used him as one type of friend, the suspicious but sharp-witted one. Walter was placed in a dialogue with a monk whose name, *Gratianus*, betrays his character, one seeking grace or favour.

Walter had been introduced to us at the start of the second book on friendship as an impatient brother whom Aelred had noticed while the abbot had been dealing with practical matters: 'You were turning your eyes here and there, rubbing your forehead, running your fingers through your hair, and frowning angrily'.[72] Walter, like so many others, was jockeying for Aelred's attention. He was openly jealous, even contemptuous, of laymen, whom he called 'agents of Pharaoh', perhaps representatives of the king, who had been taking up Aelred's time. As a practical man and the offspring of a well-placed family, Aelred insisted that such visitors were to be well treated, for the monastery needed their good will. Now that they were gone, however, he could enjoy all the more the *solitudo* he had been given. For us today solitude means being alone with oneself. For the fathers of the egyptian desert, it had meant apartness from other men in order to cope with oneself. For Aelred, as for other twelfth-century monastic writers, *solitudo* meant the chance to spend time with one's intimate friends.

To what extent does Aelred's carefully constructed scene of his recourse to his friends represent life at Rievaulx, the character of Walter Daniel, and Aelred's relationship to him? However little we know about the historicity of the scene, it reveals a great deal about Aelred's sensitivity towards his friends. He noticed and commented on Walter's facial expressions and body language, just as in the first dialogue he did with the monk Ivo. Aelred as abbot of Rievaulx had been visiting the daughter house of Wardon where Ivo lived:

> Just a little while ago as I was sitting with the brethren, while all around were talking noisily, one questioning, another arguing—one advanced some point on Sacred Scripture, another information on

> vice, and yet another on virtue—you alone were silent. At times you would raise your head and make ready to say something, but just as quickly, as though your voice had been trapped in your throat, you would drop your head again and continue your silence. Then you would leave us for a while, and later return looking rather disheartened. I concluded from this that you wanted to talk to me, but that you dreaded the crowd, and hoped to be alone with me.[73]

In the presence of Aelred the abbot, monks did not imitate the egyptian fathers by keeping their eyes down in order not to be distracted by each other's faces.[74] Aelred looked at the monks whom he loved and accepted that some of them had special needs requiring something more than the animated conversation of the community. They were to be taken aside and talked with on their own terms.

Friendship was a serious business, but even amid the demands of monastic life, it could be enjoyable and pleasant:

> . . . affability in speech, cheerfulness in countenance, suavity in manners, serenity in the expression of the eyes [are] matters in which there is to be found no slight relish to friendship.[75]

Such cheerfulness (*hilaritas*) was by no means always present in aelredian friendship. In the first book of *Spiritual Friendship*, where Ivo of Wardon was present, Ivo quickly yielded to Aelred's warmth once he received his full attention, while in the second and third books, Walter Daniel showed irritability and scepticism. He challenged Aelred, refused to accept his definitions, threw in unpleasant remarks, chided Gratian, and objected to Aelred's optimism about other people and their goodness.

Aelred seems to have enjoyed the situation, while Gratian admitted that he needed Walter's acute questions to penetrate the subject more deeply.[76] As with the friend whom Aelred made subprior and who opened his heart to the abbot by criticizing him, Aelred had ample room in his life for the type of friend who spoke his mind and never tried to please. Walter Daniel was a difficult friend, but in Aelred's mind he was worth having. However much Aelred sought and enjoyed a pleasant face and good manners, his desire for friendship extended to the Walter Daniels of the world as well as to the Gratians. Aelred believed in and practiced a variety of friendship not at all visible in Cicero's definition: a bond where urbanity and ease were secondary, and where closeness could grow in challenge and crisis. This development led to complete acceptance of the friend and total self-revelation to him in the context of love of Christ that embraced the two friends completely. .

FRIENDSHIP IN HISTORY

Throughout his life Aelred looked upon the friendship of Jonathan and David in the Old Testament as a model or 'mirror for true friendship'.[77] In this relationship Aelred saw a total disregard for gain. Jonathan was willing to let David become king because he had but one desire, to be his friend: 'You will be king and I shall be second after you' (1 Sam 23:17). Despite the connivings of his father Saul, Jonathan's devotion to David could not be impaired: 'So long as the son of Jesse lives, your kingdom will not be established', insisted Saul (1 Sam 20:31). Aelred asked how anyone on hearing such words could keep himself from hating the cause of his own loss, but not Jonathan.

Another dimension in this Old Testament friendship is the presence of physical affection. In the *Mirror of Charity* Aelred brings together in a single description two separate visits of Jonathan to David in hiding. At the first meeting there had been kisses and tears, while Aelred also mentions hugs (*amplexus*), which are not in the Vulgate.[78] On a second visit, Jonathan uttered his memorable words about being second after David (1 Sam 23:17). Here is Aelred's conflation of the two meetings:

> Amid embraces and kisses, when they shed tears for each other and through loyal crying showed their loyal affection, the pact was again renewed when Jonathan said. . . .[79]

Aelred chose to recall the two events as a single one. The unitary picture fits better into Aelred's vision of a total friendship between Jonathan and David, where manifestations of love could be physical and where unselfishness was total.

For Aelred the friendship of Jonathan and David was a model for the friendship of his time. He drew a lesson also from the closeness of John the apostle to Christ. He pointed out that Christ's special love for John did not mean that the beloved disciple had to be chosen for the highest office in the church.[80] Friendship must not determine the selection of suitable candidates for office. The life and words of Christ provided a pattern for every abbot who wanted to take good care of the flock entrusted to him--but who also sought individual friends.

Aelred's wealth of examples from christian revelation and history meant that he could drop Cicero's examples taken from history and instead limit himself to instances from the Bible, especially the Old Testament. For Aelred friendship has a history closely bound up with the economy of human salvation. God's love for us makes possible an infinite variety of human loves, including friendship. This love, however, is different from love of neighbour because we choose our friends, test them, depend on them, even die for them. Aelred's model for perfect friendship is, not surprisingly, the early christian martyrs, for they carried out Christ's maxim that there is no greater love than to lay down one's life for a friend.[81] Faith and loyalty had no limits in Aelred's world of friendship. The classical ideal of the friend made in political or military life was transformed into that of the monastic friend bound in a way of life characterized by free choice (*ordo voluntarius*).[82] The difference was that the classical scheme involved only two men, while the christian one set these men into the context of a community of love.

Aelred trusted in the experiences contained in autobiography, history, Scripture, and the classics. His teaching is, as it has aptly been called, an experiential one.[83] He sought and found God in the impulses of his own heart and in the experience of men whom he knew through his reading or daily contacts. Aelred's teaching and observation are not limited to some narrow personal context.[84] Aelred sought to know himself in the augustinian manner of looking inside himself to find

God. He was confident he here would find the image of God. Unlike Augustine, however, he also trusted friends and friendship enough to turn to them to find God. Augustine's reservation about friends who die or betray each other had been replaced by an insistence that in the course of a lifetime a few friends will be faithful. Even those who die leave behind the memory not only of sorrow and a sense of loss but also joy in having experienced so much with them:

> I recall now two friends, who although they have passed from this present life, nevertheless live to me and always will so live.
>
> . . . with the dispelling of all anxiety by reason of which we now fear and are solicitous for one another, with removal of all adversity which it now behooves us to bear for one another. . .[85]

Aelred looked forward to the reunions of heaven, but at the same time he turned aside from the hesitation Augustine expressed in the *City of God* (19.8) about the worth of friendship. There was nothing to worry about. Ultimately we will all be friends in the God who is Friendship.

THE CONTEXT OF FRIENDSHIP

On the basis of Aelred's writings, we can gain a fairly good idea of the context in which he sought his friendships. As novicemaster he engaged his novices in the type of dialogues contained in the *Mirror of Charity*. The first book of the *Spiritual Friendship* shows the abbot, assumedly shortly after his election in 1147, visiting a daughter house and seeking out a monk who was not satisfied with talking to Aelred until he could be alone with him. The last two books of the same treatise provide a nuanced picture of a small community of friendship within the larger community of monks loving each other. Here Aelred shows how he used his office as abbot to give his monks leave to speak about themselves.

Aelred's refuge from community life was not the pleasure of being alone with himself. His solitude was the enjoyment with Walter and Gratian of discussion that was both personal and abstract. At times Aelred suggests how difficult it could be to achieve or maintain this self-chosen isolation from the rest of the community when Gratian warns:

> The cellarer is coming: if you grant him admittance, you will have no opportunity of proceeding further. But see, I am guarding the door; do, Father, go on as you have begun.[86]

No doubt this potential interruption was added as literary embroidery to the discussion. At the same time, however, it reflects the real dilemma of monks who wanted to cultivate interpersonal relationships, an area of life which is only implicitly dealt with in monastic rules and routines. If the cellarer had walked through the door, he would have had the right to Aelred's ear. We imagine that he saw the three monks huddled together and realized that his business would have to wait until a more opportune time, when the abbot was not so caught up in his favourite subject.

Bernard of Clairvaux leaves us with the same impression of withdrawal into the secrets of friendship in order to savour with his Nicholas every word of a letter just arrived from Peter the Venerable. Friendship needed secrecy and a secret place. For Aelred the exchange of the heart's secrets formed an essential part of true friendship. Such revelations only take place in an undisturbed atmosphere, even though the content of the monastic day is always present in the dialogues' background. As Aelred told the others at the end of the second dialogue, 'An hour has already passed, and these others who have just arrived are, as you see, hustling me off by their impatience to other business'.[87] Friendship had to take into consideration the requirements of the community. The next day, however, time might again be found in order to take up the discussion. Literary artifice is woven into the requirements of monastic routine. Aelred's dialogue takes on an immediacy and a concrete setting rare in medieval dialogue forms.

As for the persons involved in the dialogues, we have already looked at the personalities of Walter Daniel and Gratian. The novice in the *Mirror of Charity* is not so well nor so consistently described. At one point, when Aelred is talking about sexual temptation and describing images of filth (1:76), he pauses to say, 'I see your embarrassed face', and promises he will spare the novice any detailed descriptions. Even in this highly abstract and theoretical treatise, Aelred addresses a person who shares the monastic life with him.

Aelred spoke in his written works to living persons who remain inseparable from the ideas propounded in them. To deal with discipline for female recluses, Aelred composed an extended letter to his sister in the manner of Jerome's famed twenty-second letter, to Eustochium.[88] Another bond which he enjoyed and which supported his literary activity was with Gilbert Foliot, bishop of London, to whom Aelred dedicated a work.[89] In this letter Aelred once again invited a friendship, defined it, and set limitations to it. Gilbert had been a benedictine abbot before becoming bishop. Aelred sought to engage a colleague in the Rule of Saint Benedict in yet another dialogue, this time through a collection of sermons based on Isaiah: '. . . so I have been made desirous for you, not only in order to be noticed by your grace, but also, as I foolishly would say, I dare to aspire to your very friendship'.[90] In such a letter Aelred comes close to the mode of expression of friendship that we have seen so often in the continental literature: the common pursuit of intellectual-spiritual goals in which friendship is a boon to shared learning. If other letters had survived, they might have revealed more examples of this quest. But this was only one aspect of Aelred's search for friendship. His central interest was focused on making friendships within his own cloister.

Aelred used almost every possible approach in establishing friendships. His flexibility, versatility and receptivity did not, however, amount to the uncritical naïveté of a Gratian, wanting to be everyone's friend and showing little, if any, critical reserve. Aelred aimed at matching his own impulses and yearnings with the wisdom of the friendship tradition. He had a keen eye for the sayings and exempla of the Scriptures, the Fathers, and the pagan writers, as he called them, that could be used to strengthen his analysis and exposition of friendship. One notices how he used Ambrose of Milan's explication on friendship in his treatise *De officiis* to a much greater extent than he did Jerome's letters of friendship with their clever maxims and facile assertions about the context of friendship.[91] Ambrose was hardly an original thinker. His advice was not specifically intended to apply to monastic life, but Aelred preferred his measured, moderate view of friendship instead of letting himself be carried away by Jerome's passionate hyperbole. Aelred's borrowings from Ambrose are so straightforward that they have attracted little attention.[92] Yet they provide a valuable indication of the common-sense tone Aelred wanted to set for friendship. It involves both reason and affection, he pointed out. It is not some wild impulse, what we today would label romantic.

Similarly out of the Wisdom literature of the Old Testament, Aelred carefully dug maxims about friendship that reflected the experience of men seeking a meaningful order in life. The earthbound yet idealistic provisions about the friend who loves at all times (Proverbs 17:17), the medicine of life (Si 6:16), and the possibility of reconciliation with a friend (Si 22:27): these sayings balanced off the dizzying kisses and embraces from the Song of Songs which transform friendship into a type of God's own embrace (*Spam*. 3:22). For the first time in the history of medieval writings on friendship, the literature of the Old and New Testament is used as a whole, transformed into a complete statement, and integrated into Cicero's own exposition of friendship.

The result may seem so obvious and straightforward that some observers have claimed that Aelred merely recast Cicero, but the result is much more than a superficially christianized *De amicitia*.[93] Aelred provides a treatment of the role and practice of friendship within the twelfth-century cloister. Because Aelred is so broad-ranging and yet at the same time maintains a strict discipline in balancing good sense with eternal hopes, his work seems easily adaptable to non-monastic contexts.[94] It is Aelred, not Cicero, who makes friendship seem something so timeless and universal that one is tempted to ignore its historical context. But if we do consider Aelred's message in terms of the community of the cloister, the sayings of Scripture and the christianization of the classical tradition, then the breadth of its achievement in establishing a spiritual and institutional basis for friendship becomes evident.

Aelred's vision of the possibilities of friendship was based on conscious choice and not on unconscious wishful thinking. For Aelred the community of heart and mind described in the Acts of the Apostles (4:32) easily lent itself to a description of intimate personal bonds. To those who might dismiss Aelred as a starry-eyed dreamer who expected the best from his people and projects, one can point to his warnings about how friendship can sour, how it can turn into physical desire, lead to misunderstandings and hatreds, and bring tears as well as joy. For all his sensitivity and delicacy, Aelred was a man of the world who knew about hatred and jealousy, fights and divisions. Daily he felt the impulses of his own flesh. At times he may well have longed for tournaments and the companionship of courageous knights. He had proven in his youth that he could function well in such a world and win popularity.[95] He had chosen, however, the quiet of Rievaulx. Here too he found divisive factions, jealous monks and troubled souls, but he never gave up his pursuit of a new form of noble monastic culture where friendship was allowed a central role in bringing men together in the common pursuit of the one eternal friend, Jesus.

AELRED AS A SPECIAL CASE

Aelred was fascinated with male beauty and with youth. The attraction he felt towards other men he was eventually able to gather into an all-embracing love culminating in the love of God. Here he could gain strength from the christian religion's concern with Jesus as God-made-man. While so much of later medieval religious devotion concentrated either on Christ as child or Christ as crucified, Aelred followed the impulses of his own life and wrote a treatise on Jesus at the age of twelve. It was assumedly meant for the same Ivo, monk of Wardon, who was his conversant in the first book of *Spiritual Friendship*.[96]

In Aelred's literal reading of the passage in Luke about how Jesus was lost for three days by his parents and then found in the temple, he provides us with a description of the young boy Jesus as a beautiful, physical person, so attractive that old men kissed and young men hugged him: *senes osculantur, amplectuntur juvenes*.[97] When Jesus travelled with Joseph and the other men from Nazareth to Jerusalem, 'they all cry out with the deepest affection that he kiss me with the kiss of his mouth' (Song 1:1). The use of this passage from the Song of

Songs to describe male attachment to Christ the youth is highly unusual, if not unique, but Aelred did not hesitate to take this and other phrases from the Song in order to show how delightful and attractive the boy Jesus was:

> And to the boys who long for his presence but do not dare to intrude on their elders' confabulations it is very easy to apply the words: 'Who will grant me to have you as my brother, sucking my mother's breasts, to find you outside and kiss you?' (Song 8:1) 98

Aelred indicates concern about the physical well-being of Jesus during his three-day disappearance: 'Who took care of food and drink for you? Who made your bed? Who took off your shoes? Who warmed your youthful body with ointments and baths?'[99] When Mary finds Jesus in the temple, Aelred makes the scene one of explicit affection. Mary is said to have spoken as in the Song of Songs (3:4): 'I found, she said, him whom my soul loves: I held him and shall not let him go'.

Aelred's fascination with physical contact with Jesus perhaps explains his inclusion of the story of Mary Magdalene at the home of Simon the Pharisee, a scene that, strictly speaking, does not belong to this adolescent narrative at all (Luke 7:47). But because of the kisses that Jesus got on the way to Jerusalem and from his mother in the temple, Aelred found it appropriate to mention another time Jesus was kissed, 'Kiss, kiss, kiss, o holy sinner, kiss those most lovely feet, so sweet so beautiful'.[100] The absence of Jesus gives the 'greatest pain'.[101] His presence even in the tenuous contact when one's tears touch his body, gives the greatest joy: 'I sought your face, your face, Lord, I ask for' (Ps 26:8). Much of this exposition is devoted to contemplation on the symbolic meaning of the boy Jesus's actions, but even there the language of religious sensibility verges on the erotic. Each image can be traced back to the language of the Bible. But Aelred jams them together in his message of love on a spiritual level in an atmosphere heavy with the scent of a beautiful body and warm kisses.

Only a man who combined extremes of physical and spiritual longing could describe Jesus in such a manner. Aelred could write about the boy Jesus in this way without transgressing what was acceptable in monastic writings. Such a treatise belongs to the special atmosphere of twelfth-century monastic life, when experimentation in language and thought was welcome. Here as elsewhere Aelred's writings can be used to see what he is saying about himself. As a youth he was fascinated by the beauty of other youths; as an adult monk he concentrated on the beauty of the boy Jesus. When he wrote about kisses and embraces, he could do so without hesitation or guilt. In his works Aelred conveys himself to us in terms of what he himself had experienced. By the time he wrote about the young Jesus, Aelred had little to fear from his own sexual drives. Jesus had become his love. As he made clear in the *Mirror of Charity*, we must seek to concentrate on the flesh of Jesus the drives that otherwise would be directed towards the flesh of other men.[102] One great passion took over and consumed all others, but instead of destroying his involvement in other men, the love of Jesus made human loves stable, permanent and part of the unity of the community.

In evaluating Aelred's contribution to the literature of friendship, we must distinguish between our own attachment to him and the role he actually played in the development of medieval monastic friendship. As David Knowles already implied in some masterful pages on Aelred, the man is unique in monastic history.[103] No other monk tells us quite so much about himself. No other medieval writer invests so much of himself in discussing friendship and friendships. Because Aelred devoted his life to friendship and made his involvement so explicit, he departed from the tradition whose fullest expression we until now have seen in Northern France in the mid-twelfth century. Peter of Celle, Bernard of Clairvaux, Peter the Venerable, and Nicholas of Montiéramey made friendship one of the major themes of their writings. On the basis of what these monks put into their letters of friendship, we can assume that the practice of friendship was important to them. But their commitment to friendship was not as great as Aelred's was. This difference in degree may help explain why we find few indications of friendship between Aelred, with his circle of friends in Yorkshire, and the Cistercians on the european continent.

Here it might be objected that if we had Aelred's lost letter collection, it might reveal that he did have a lively correspondence with leading continental monastic friends. Aelred's biographer, Walter

Daniel, describes his abbot's letter collection as containing the official communications of a man involved in monastic businesss and political affairs rather than one expressing love and friendship to other monks.[104] Another indication of the psychological distance between Aelred and the monastic friends of the Continent is the fact that most of the manuscripts of his work circulated in England. Only in the Low Countries did some cistercian house get hold of copies of *Spiritual Friendship*. The well-provided library of Clairvaux acquired only a single copy of the work, and then not until the thirteenth century.[105]

Why such relative restraint in the medieval response to Aelred's writings on friendship? The answer to this question lies in Aelred's apartness as friend and writer on friendship. Aelred belongs to the european monastic friendship tradition but was not in its mainstream. In making this claim I may well call down upon myself the wrath of scholars and students today who rightly value Aelred's life and thought. Here I would like to be as autobiographical as Aelred allowed himself to be. His *Spiritual Friendship* is what drew me to the subject of monastic friendship. In going back to the origins of the tradition, I have been looking for the roots of Aelred's mode of expression. This search has brought me to see Aelred's work as a side-growth from the writers on whom he based his exposition. So familiar was Aelred with his sources that the reader easily assumes he is loyally rendering their content. He does not misuse his sources, but when they are put together in his personal framework the result varies from anything to be found in Cicero, Ambrose, Augustine, Jerome, or John Cassian.

The appearance of many familiar formulae of friendship can hide the fact that Aelred is specific about friendship and individual friendships in a way we have not before met among late antique or medieval writers. Aelred insists on the natural and inevitable place of friendship in human life. In the spiritual community of the cloister he sees the possibility for friendship to reach new spiritual heights. What was so obvious for Aelred was not at all apparent for his contemporaries. For the continental Cistercians and Benedictines, friendship was still mainly a mode of intellectual contact through letter. Although friends embraced when they met and enjoyed each other's company, they usually felt a certain hesitancy and reserve about their need for each other. Even so loving a friend as Peter the Venerable, in whom this sense of distance is almost gone, by no means made friendship in community the major theme of his works, as was the case for Aelred.

Aelred's pursuit of friendship can almost never be reduced to an intellectual meeting of minds. He insisted on telling his readers about the actual friendships he had had, how he experienced them, even how his friends had exchanged glances with him. Aelred's loves were immediate and open, with no hesitation, guilt or fear that friendship might become a problem, an exclusion, or even a temptation away from the discipline of monastic life. No wonder that even as late as the 1950s, the great trappist monastery of Gethsemani in Kentucky forbade the reading of Aelred's *Spiritual Friendship* to novices and young monks![106]

In recent years a great deal has been talked and written about Aelred as a homosexual.[107] Since the social, political, religious and personal status of gay people in the last decades of the twentieth century still poses a very real question to the christian churches, as well as to Western society as a whole, one can hardly deal with Aelred's sexuality without inviting anger and reproaches from one group or another. The time has come, however, to deal plainly and openly with Aelred's sexuality, for it is connected to his search for friendship.

As I indicated earlier in this chapter, Aelred as a youth either had or was strongly tempted to have sexual contact with other men. He apparently had a problem with masturbation that plagued him after he entered the monastery. Even when he gained control of his physical sexuality, Aelred was attracted to sensitive young men. In spite of this way of looking at Aelred, I find difficulty in giving him the name 'homosexual', for this word did not exist in his age and is of modern coinage, a product of the nineteenth century's increased awareness of the role of sexuality in individual personality. I experience the same problem with the word 'gay'. Despite the efforts of the historian John Boswell to anchor the term in medieval literature, this is also a word from our times and not one that helps explain any medieval phenomenon.[108] The absence of the name does not in itself rule out the activities covered by it. Our problem is that 'homosexual' and 'gay' reflect a model description of men who seek out and desire other men sexually, while the medieval word 'sodomite' deals only with sexual activity and was used exclusively in terms of sin.

Can we not assert in all simplicity that Aelred at some point in his youth became aware that he was sexually drawn to attachments with other men? He gave his heart and perhaps also his body to other youths. He also experienced an intense romantic friendship which became an unbearable burden for him because of the pain, fear and guilt it caused.

Aelred loved other men. He spent much of his life in converting his sexual drive into a spiritual embrace of other men. He sought to integrate all the facets of his being into love without any sexual activity, which he considered to be a form of carnal concupiscence.[109] To many a modern observer, this effort may appear to have been a tremendous waste of human energy. One must at least concede that Aelred seems to have succeeded. He got to the point where he could cultivate friendship without considering sex as a central factor or potential threat. In Aelred's definition of true friendship, as in his life experience, sexual contact and spiritual love cannot be combined.

Aelred's special version of friendship, combining its theory and practice, as well as advocating openly its worth, can be partly explained by his personality. He needed to be with other men. The emotional bonds he shared with them he was able to heighten and spiritualize so that after his conversion to monastic life, his loves did not manifest themselves in terms of sexual attachments. Aelred underwent a lifelong process of conversion. Even in old age he could write with contempt, and perhaps with a spark of pity and envy, about aged gay men who felt they were past an active sexual life and so could dare sleeping in the same bed and embracing each other because they did not have to fear that such closeness would lead to sexual acts.[110]

Aelred had chosen a way of life that excluded most physical and all genital manifestations of love. His emotional makeup fitted him for the cistercian life, even though he can by no means be looked upon as a typical Cistercian. These monks in their heady early years ruled out the presence of women in the lives of monks.[111] They allowed themselves only each other for spiritual help, consolation and friendship. Aelred could take comfort in cistercian success in ridding the surroundings of women and the care of women. Like Bernard, he was not anti-woman, but a-woman. An all-male world made strong emotional and spiritual bonds among men natural, even desirable. Cistercian writers eager to use sensual images from the Old Testament, especially the Song of Songs, also contributed to a supercharged atmosphere. This intense mid-century cistercian spirituality combined with Aelred's own personality to make possible a life based on friendship and friendships. Other Cistercians also lived and wrote in terms of friendships, but Aelred alone conveys to us so strong a passion for such spiritualized attachments to other men. With Bernard and the Clairvaux monks whom we know through Nicholas, there is no question of resolving a sexual desire in a spiritual bond. With Aelred there is. Aelred thus appears more as a saint for our times than as a representative of the development of medieval friendship as a whole movement. His apartness has not been understood. Recent discussions of spiritual friendship still see his writings as the crowning development.[112] For us they may be a high point, but not for the monks of the twelfth century.

THE LIMITATIONS OF FRIENDSHIP

Like Cicero, Augustine, Ambrose, and various twelfth-century monastic writers, Aelred set out to define a law of friendship, to draw up rules and discern limits to its practice. In theoretical terms and in his own life, he did amazingly well. From his writings, it seems that Aelred succeeded in becoming a whole person, who could combine the impulses of his sexuality with the demands of everyday life and a desire for union with God in eternity. Friendship and community were the two ingredients that bound these diverse elements together and integrated Aelred's life after the first difficult years at Rievaulx.

The history of friendship has to account for more than individual friends and their writings. We need to see how friendship functioned in the social contexts from which our writers emerge. In Aelred's case there are many hints that his programme by no means was a total success. Within his Yorkshire monastic world, Aelred's pursuits engendered jealousies that brought divisions to the monastery and led to open scandal after his death. Already in the remarks of Walter Daniel in *Spiritual Friendship*, we hear hints at scepticism in the community towards the abbot. In Walter Daniel's biography of Aelred, this resistance to the abbot's views and methods becomes much more specific. Even though in the *Life* Walter plays down Aelred's friendships and gives the reader no idea of how closely attached Aelred was to some of his monks, he does make it clear that some of the monks resented his friendships and preferences. When Aelred was elected abbot in 1147, a group of monks accused him of ambition. Later others questioned his asceticism.[113]

This resentment might have been due to Aelred's living apart from the rest of the community the last ten years of his life because of his arthritis, which may have partly been due to the extreme asceticism of his first years at Rievaulx. Into his little hut he would let his favourites come, where they could talk of spiritual matters, hold each other's hands, and have frank conversation with Aelred.[114] This 'monastic free zone' could hardly have pleased the monks at Rievaulx who were not encouraged to visit Aelred. In a community of several hundred monks and lay brothers, no more than an elite few could be admitted to the abbot's special chamber. Those who never got an invitation must have felt very slighted indeed.

Once while Walter Daniel sat alone with Aelred in this room, a monk entered and tried to throw the abbot on the fire:

> O you wretch, now I am going to kill you, now I am going to destroy you by a hard death. What are you doing, lying here, you impostor, you useless silly fellow? You shall tell no more of your lies, for now you are about to die.[115]

It is a stock theme of hagiography to show the opposition which a saintly figure has to meet in the course of his life. This contributes to the picture of a physical or a psychological martyrdom. The attack of the angry monk, however, is more than an isolated incident thrown in to include the theme of martyrdom. Real resentment towards Aelred is evidenced by the fact that Walter had to add new materials to his biography in a vitriolic epilogue written in the form of a letter. This was intended to meet criticism that rained down on Walter's *Life* of Aelred.[116]

Here he had depicted Aelred as living like a monk at the court of King David of Scotland. Rumour protested that Aelred at the time had hardly been chaste. Similarly his description of the beauty and whiteness of Aelred's flesh when his clothing was removed after his death drew protests. Walter had to admit that he was following Sulpicius Severus's account of Martin of Tours, and so he indicated that he was exaggerating what he actually had seen.[117]

The use of a hagiographical cliché again points to Walter's own involvement in defending Aelred's memory. Walter was fascinated by Aelred's boyish beauty and innocence in the same way as Aelred himself had been with Simon's. After Aelred was dead, Walter could allow himself to express what he had had to hold back while Aelred was alive:

> I was not able to restrain the kisses which I gave his feet, though I chose his feet lest feeling rather than pure affection should reproach me: the beauty of one who sleeps rather than the love of one who lies as he lay.
>
> Whenever I think of him then, I am still overcome by joy and wonder at the gracious recollection. And when do I not think of it? When do I not brood on that sweetness, that beauty, that glory?[118]

Walter was careful to defend and explain his enthusiasm for Aelred as a physical being. He may have wanted to assure himself and his readers that his attachment to Aelred had no element of forbidden sensual enjoyment. Walter's awareness of a sexual element in Aelred's reputation is reflected in a vision of Aelred which he describes a monk having had shortly before the abbot's death. Here Aelred's body was seen as gleaming all over, except for a 'tiny cloud' about his navel. Although Walter does not say so directly, this imperfection might symbolize the sins of Aelred's youth. Because he had sinned through his genitals, this part of him could not be as brilliant as the rest of his body, so long as he was still alive.[119] Monks could hold hands at Rievaulx, but they knew that the abbot earlier in his life had not restrained himself in his loves. All of this is conveyed in a subtle and indirect manner, but Walter's account hints that some monks still felt that Aelred was undermining the community because of his preferences for some of them rather than others. Resentments were very much on the surface when Walter wrote his biography and especially afterwards, when he had to add his apologetic letter.

Aelred's friendships required flexibility in monastic life. He described bonds among monks from the abbot's point of view. He had the advantage of being entitled to speak with the monks at any time he chose.[120] What of the choir monks who normally had only a few minutes a day to get together for conversation in large groups? If two or three went off on their own, what might have been thought of them?[121] Aelred's description of the development of friendship can thus be almost too personal and too special as a recommendation for the monastery as a whole. He wrote as an abbot who devoted a part of his life to this pursuit, and who willingly tested individual monastic candidates to see whether they were suited to take on the role of the abbot's friend and confidant.

The Rule of Saint Benedict had indicated nothing about such a potential friend of the abbot, and for good reason. The abbot had to be the father of all and to treat all equally. In his sermons Aelred reveals himself as a perceptive, insightful abbot father, not as a special friend.[122] The continuing study of this literature and the discovery of new collections will in coming years bring to light new sides of Aelred.[123] We are perhaps only now beginning to plumb some of the depths of his personality and seeing what it was that made him so loved and hated in the same community.

For this study, however, it must suffice to point out that in the Rule of Saint Benedict there was the possibility that the abbot might show special favour to those of outstanding moral character. Aelred could have appealed to this provision. At the same time he nevertheless insisted that friendships were possible and desirable among all the monks of the monastery, even the younger monks. What he had shared with Simon and Hugh in his early days at Rievaulx he wanted to be possible for their successors.

Aelred believed in complete friendships that could be articulated on every level except that of genital sexuality. In asking for so much he assumed the existence of a monastic climate which was generous, tolerant, and yet firmly disciplined, a rare combination in any human community. Aelred's scheme required a charismatic figure who could be all things to all men and reconcile the various factions in the monastery. As Benedict's Rule indicates, the abbot is at the very centre of cloister life. His choice of special friends could easily bring charges of favouritism. Aelred was aware of this danger and warned in his *Spiritual Friendship* against elevating one's friends to office. But even if the abbot restrains himself, other monks might be aware of the intimacy that friends enjoy with each other and with the abbot. The 'outsider' might become hypersensitive to open signs of affection and attention expressed from abbot to monk. Aelred does not deal with how jealousies can be prevented in such a situation.

Aelred's successor at Rievaulx, Ernald, commissioned a work on the history of the times by the augustinian canon at nearby Newburgh, William.[124] Keenly aware of the religious reform movements of his life and a great admirer of the founding of cistercian houses at Rievaulx and Fountains, William of Newburgh devoted not a word to Aelred.[125] Writing at the end of the twelfth century, he may have experienced the aftermath of Aelred's regime that we find in Walter Daniel's apology and in other sources for Rievaulx: runaway monks, outside intervention, and doubt about the consequences of Aelred's friendships for the community as a whole.[126] William's silence in itself proves nothing, but it hints at the next monastic generation's lack of enthusiasm for some of the ideals which Aelred articulated. He believed that spiritual friendship could be integrated into the life of the cloisters. He sought a loving community and turned away no one who sought admission. His successors had to live with the consequences. Evidence for a reaction against Aelred is not abundant, but what there is makes it at least clear that his regime of toleration and special bonds ended with his death.

Aelred's life and work do not in themselves sum up the history of monastic friendship. His formulations both articulate the hope of spiritual friendship and threaten its practice. Aelred pushed the requirements of friendship beyond what most monastic communities would allow because he made personal bonds so explicit and necessary as part of daily life.

Aelred was a master of love, but the intensity of his loving created resentment, even hatred, from those who felt excluded or incapable of response. In his time and in our day, Aelred remains a controversial figure, simply because he insisted on loving and being loved, on being disciplined and being free, on giving to and taking from others, and in combining everything in God and man in one complete dynamic of love. Sensitive man, dedicated monk, devoted abbot, true friend—and source for scandal as Jesus himself had been in his time—Aelred sought and gained in his own lifetime the friendship without which he could not live. He combined loving other men with loving God in the human and approachable Jesus to whom he reached out in his community of love. Aelred of Rievaulx enriches the history of friendship but does not complete it.

CHAPTER EIGHT

CONTINUITY AND CHANGE: THE PERSISTENCE OF FRIENDSHIP 1180-1250

THERE WILL ALWAYS be friendships. What changes is the manner in which the idea of friendship and individual friendships are described. After about 1180 friendship lost its prominence in the spiritual and religious literature of Western Europe. This development was partly due to new interests and concerns among those who could express themselves in writing. The end of the twelfth century and the first decades of the thirteenth brought a more rigid intellectual discipline, often described by the word 'scholastic'. Out of the schools of France and England during these years there emerged the universities of Paris and Oxford.[1] These institutions manifested a canalization of intellectual effort far removed from the eclecticism and diversity of monastic theology in method and breadth of interest. Such a development can be seen as a natural result of the insistence expressed among earlier twelfth-century parisian scholars, such as Hugh of Saint Victor, that one must 'learn everything'. The pursuit of universal knowledge required categorization, definition, and regulated forms of intellectual discourse. The methodology removed the element of personal experience so characteristic of monastic theology. In such a context, where collections of *epistolae* gave way to *summae*, it might seem that there could have been only limited interest in the literary expression of bonds of friendship among men in the church.

After about 1180, monastic culture began to lose its central position in Western learning. The great age of the cistercian fathers was over. In spiritual literature the figures we meet are of the second rank in mode of expression and originality of thought. The best minds of the time (and perhaps the most sensitive hearts) were dedicating themselves to getting ahead in the schools through a method of learning and expression that had no place for personal statements about the worth of friendship.

In dealing with friendship as a human, existential phenomenon and not just as a mode of literary expression, we have the chance to be just as concerned with what such 'secondary' figures have to say as we were in the mid-twelfth century with the 'greats'. Our task is almost easier now, for the writers of the late twelfth century did not have the literary skill to make it difficult for us to distinguish between style and meaning, as was so often the case with masters of style such as Bernard of Clairvaux. The outstanding authors of the new age, such as Peter the Chanter, were concerned with other areas of life,[2] but friendship continued to be written about among the less prominent figures. Friendship in fact became more apparent and widespread in the monastic landscape than it had been in mid-century. In 1150 indications of friendship in letter collections and treatises were limited to England and northern France. The last decades of the twelfth century and the first of the thirteenth brought manifestations of friendship in the urban culture of northern Italy as well as the Rhineland. Here the cistercian movement continued to flourish and to provide new soil for monastic friendships.

Since my study uses literary sources as representative of life and mentality, judgments about the sources have to take into consideration the amount of material that has been lost. What looks to us like sustained or even more widespread interest in friendship may also be a result of the fact that monasteries became better in these years at collecting and preserving their letters. The variety and geographical distribution of the extant sources, however, point to the strength of friendship as ideal and practice in the spiritual life. Even though we are limited to the top of history's iceberg, and even though most personal friendships have left no literary trace, enough material is visible to banish the idea that monastic friendship declined or disappeared from view after the death of Aelred of Rievaulx.[3]

After 1180 there were no longer only a few great centres of friendship on the Clairvaux-Troyes-Cluny axis as were visible in mid-twelfth century. In the Low Countries, southern England, northern France, Italy and the Rhineland, we find evidence of friendship. Parisian regular foundations such as augustinian Sainte Geneviève seem even to have provided a new clearing house for an international network of friendship because of the diverse clientele that made use of such houses as places of learning. At the same time, a new interest in and concern with the 'spiritual direction' of women, the so-called *cura mulierum*, as well as attentiveness to female visions and revelations, also seem to have fostered male-female bonds in monastic circles.[4] Some of these manifest a degree of sharing and exchange which allow us to call them friendships.

In some quarters, especially in the new Franciscan movement, there was uncertainty and even doubt about the worth of close human bonds. An Order which brought pairs of religious men out into contact with the world, as we shall see, had no interest in close individual friendships. The other Order of friars, the Dominicans, reveals both male friendship and male-female bonds. When one looks upon development as a whole, the impression is one of *varietas*. There is no longer a characteristic way of expressing friendship in terms of a bond that enhances community, as friendship had been seen in the time of Bernard, Peter the Venerable, and Peter of Celle. Nevertheless friendship and friendships continued to be written about as an integral part of christian spiritual life.

DERIVATIVE EXPRESSIONS OF SPIRITUAL FRIENDSHIP

Aelred of Rievaulx had a number of imitators, and thanks to Anselme Hoste's excellent edition, one can see almost at a glance how they used his *Spiritual Friendship*.[5] In every single case, they shortened his text, left out individual and personal examples, and attempted to make a theoretical treatise out of what had been an artistic and spiritual whole treating monastic life and human experience. It is easy to understand why Aelred's treatise was dissected in such a manner. He had written clearly, had been careful with his definitions, and had made a statement so complete that it was easy to excerpt essential bits and leave out qualifications, exemplifications, and personal remarks. As Anselme Hoste commented on the efforts of the english augustinian canon Thomas of Frakaham in turning *Spiritual Friendship* into a *Mirror of Spiritual Friendship* (*Speculum spiritalis amicitiae*): '. . . from a dialogue full of flavour and vibrant with life, he knew only how to make an arid treatise'.[6] Hoste is correct in emphasizing a distance between dialogue and treatise. Aelred's words take on life because he set his treatment in a plausible monastic milieu, where monks talked to each other and revealed personality, disagreements, and variant interpretations. Hoste blames 'the spirit of scholasticism' for 'drying out' such a rich source of life.

I would prefer not to look upon some vaguely-defined and all-pervasive scholasticism as the culprit but instead would point out how the generation after Aelred sought to combine the learning of the cloisters with systematized moral and theological statements, which also could be useful outside the monastery.[7] Aelred's monks had time to discuss, to reflect, to react to one another, while Thomas of Frakaham was writing for Augustinians who were actively involved in contemporary efforts to reform the church and reach the laity. Here the new generation of Cistercians was much more in tune with Thomas than with Aelred, for monks now accepted the papal charge to preach and lead crusades against heretics.

Aelred's work was abbreviated and simplified not because he was outdated but because the essence of his teaching was found relevant and useful in a new setting for friendship. A constant exchange took place in this period between established conceptions of spiritual friendship in a monastic context and the requirements of human bonds in the secular church, where canons, monks and clerics met each other. Here Peter of Blois, the magpie cleric about whom R.W. Southern has written so evocatively,[8] combines the contradictions. He was attracted, especially late in life, by the warmth and interiority of cistercian spirituality. Peter spent the later decades of his life in writing bishops, abbots, monks and clerics about the moral needs and intellectual issues of the contemporary church. His letters bear witness to his principles, as well as to a ceaseless search for preferment and favour. In one and the same writer we find devotion to spiritual relationships among men, pursuit of material goals, and a vein of moral indignation. All these are combined with an exceptional talent for hurting other people's feelings and enunciating one's message tactlessly.

If we first consider Peter of Blois's *De amicitia christiana* and *De charitate dei et proximi*, written later in his life, between 1191 and 1200, it is immediately apparent that the first section is an extract of Aelred's *De amicitia spiritali*, while the second condenses the *Speculum caritatis*.[9] Peter never names Aelred, but in the preface common to the two works, he makes it quite evident that he is borrowing from somewhere. His only deception is to make it appear he makes use of several authors, for he says he is collecting nectars of different flowers.[10] As in other abbreviations of Aelred's writings, Peter leaves out the abbot's emphasis on the experience of friendship and turns the dialogue into a short treatise. Aelred is doctrinalized. This development may signal a decline from Aelred's rhetorical standard of expression, but Peter's attention to him also manifests a continuing interest in friendship as a subject worth writing about in the idiom of the times.

Peter's own concept of friendship emerges in his letters in a way the rigid form of the *De amicitia christiana* would not allow. Like so many other twelfth-century writers, he saw a *lex amicitiae*, which required friends to help each other in need. In a letter that can be dated to before 1184, Peter as archdeacon of Bath admitted to the prior of Canterbury, William, that although he knew him only slightly, they had already become good friends. 'And so our conversation lasted only a moment and our acquaintance was brief, but it bound me to you in a tie of charity, so that I can think of you as wholly mine'.[11] Friendship requires concrete assistance. Peter asks William to do his utmost to help the bearer of the letter. The problem at hand is not specified, but Peter makes it clear that the obligations of friendship do not allow William to refuse his request. If William does not comply, Peter can only conclude that William had deceived him when he in the past seemed to indicate his friendship:

> Perhaps I am deceived, and you will not respond equally to my affection, but it would be rude of you to waver in friendship, for your words, deeds, face, manner and all else promised that you would be an effective and stable friend.[12]

You promised me friendship, Peter persists. Now you must deliver! The words *inurbanum* and *efficacem* hint that friendship, instead of being seen as the manifestation of spiritual love in a christian context, is looked upon as a practical alliance that cultured men make with each other in order to get on in life. Friendship is here a question not just of keeping one's promises but also of being a polished and cultivated person. Even though he is writing to a monk, Peter is asking him to realize the values of urban life: culture, kindness and mutual service to a friend. Just behind the letter stand the ideal and practice of friendship from Cicero.

Peter claims that sincere affection does not need rhetorical prefaces and illustrations.[13] Often, however, his letters are consummate exercises in the *ars dictaminis*, with clever *captatio benevolentiae* openings that say something pleasant, often concerning friendship.[14] As so often in the literature of friendship, it can be difficult to know what to do with such a statement. One solution is to turn to the letters where Peter describes the value of friendship and then reveals his anger at being let down. He may well be revealing the importance in his own mind of friendship as a bond that protects him from the wiles of the world, a necessary antidote to a world of courts, intrigues, schemes and betrayals. This is the case in a letter to his 'dearest friends and associates', the dean of Chartres and the archdeacon of Blois (*ep* 49), where he deplores the evil done him by the canons of Chartres, whom Peter had thought were his friends. In order to despoil him of his position at the cathedral, they had tried to slander him. The loss of temporal things, the death of friends, afflictions of the body, Peter claims, are not as bad as such a betrayal (a thought that comes directly or indirectly from Augustine's *City of God* 19:8). Since one's friends are a part of oneself, their separation means a split in one's very being: 'Are not my friends my inner self, whom I cherish and who take care of me in a sweet commerce of services, in an identity of affections?'[15]

An element of rhetorical exaggeration can dominate Peter's letters, especially in such a message of disappointment and loss of faith: 'Without the consolation of friends, life for me would be death'. Behind the melodramatic language is a man who wants to create a world in which the bonds of friendship provide him with honours, recognition and acceptance in a cultivated way of life. Peter aspired to lucrative offices, but the quirks of his character, his inability to restrain himself, and perhaps the very overeagerness of his letters seem to have kept him from getting his desire. With his contradictory manner and idealism mixed with opportunism, he emerges as a plausible human being who both wanted to get ahead and who believed in friendship. Obviously Peter kept for his collection only letters that he believed would reflect well on his thoughts and style, but there are enough letters to reveal both the complexity of his personality and its idealistic bent, seeking out and occasionally also finding friendships with other men.

To a friend at the cistercian abbey of Aulnay, Peter wrote reminding him of an old friendship, even stronger than a blood link: 'That affection of love has bound us since youth. Neither blood nor nature can transcend our kinship'.[16] The friend had helped Peter both in illness and in other difficulties. He had been 'a most faithful aid, a most attentive comforter', while Peter had always made the friend's misfortunes his own: *Ego etiam tua semper infortunia mea feci*. The friend, apparently in a letter to Peter, had admitted he was not satisfied with being a monk. He desired a stricter way of life so he could avoid the temptations of the world. At the same time, however, the cistercian friend had asked Peter for the love poems Peter had composed in his youth so that they could provide 'solace in the midst of a tedious way of life'. Peter refused the request: 'Leaving out these more lascivious poems, I am sending you a few which I composed for you in a more grown-up style, so they perhaps can relieve your boredom and edify you to salvation'.[17] The two friends had once composed poems and exchanged them with each other. Now Peter resumes the practice but insists on a 'more mature' content.

Despite the general view of conversion to the monastic life as a break with one's past, Peter accepted it as natural for an old friend who had entered religion to turn to him for advice and help. His letter reflects the development we saw earlier in the twelfth century: the maintenance of early friendships after conversion to the monastic life. Bernard took his friends with him, while Peter's friend could appeal to him from the cloister for the renewal of a youthful bond. The warm response he got from Peter indicates that such a request was fully acceptable in the context of their new lives. As always, Peter wanted to appear as the friend who knew what was best, but the important (and easily overlooked) aspect of this letter is how it treats friendship as a natural human phenomenon, one which can be transformed in the spiritual life but which precedes it. Friendship is formed before conversion and persists afterwards. Instead of telling friends to put away childish affections, Peter welcomed the renewal of friendship in adulthood and used it to provide moral guidance for the friend. Old love poems were replaced by uplifting new ones.

However much Peter was caught up in himself and in his search for recognition and position, he had time and energy to pay tribute in his letters to the value of friendship. To a correspondent in France, he emphasized a desire to see his native land because of his need to see his friend. Everyone else in his fatherland had abandoned him, and he had been forced to find his home elsewhere. 'Among friends and brethren, you alone showed yourself to be a brother and friend to me, and I could not repay your favour even if I filled you with gold and silver.'[18] Here as elsewhere Peter expresses himself in strong, even hyperbolic, terms.

With almost every letter in the collection it is fairly easy to understand why it was preserved by Peter for a larger public. As Southern has pointed out, Peter began to collect and publish his letters because they were his one means of maintaining contact with influential churchmen and of impressing them with his knowledge and talents.[19] 'Look at me', Peter seems constantly to be saying, in effect calling our attention to the fact that he was a second-rate cleric who never quite got the recognition he wanted and thought he deserved. Peter sought to impress his audience with firm moral statements on the condition of the church. He included letters showing his opposition to forcing women to enter religious life, while he encouraged those already there.[20] Simony and other ecclesiastical abuses received his condemnation.[21] Peter sought credit for correct moral ideas. At the same time he was taken aback when someone was reported as having spoken against the english king, while he himself excoriated an influential archdeacon for glorying over his purity of conscience.[22] One cannot help calling Peter an opportunist, a man always looking for an opening, a way to find the favour of privileged rulers of church and state. His reputation never quite lived up to his expectations.

In the midst of this network of friends and influential contacts, Peter did not try to hide what he was about. Writing to his 'beloved companion and friend, Master Philip', he pointed to friends as an acceptable reason for giving preferment in the church. Philip, he said, had been too harsh on the archbishop of Canterbury, who had suspended a clerk, Ralph, from his position in his court and had then reinstated him out of compassion. Prelates, Peter points out, can show favour to their subordinates simply for the sake of friendship: *ob simplicem amicorum gratiam*. Pointing to such behaviour in the great pope Gregory himself, Peter warned: 'Do not then in such a hateful manner accuse in my lord something that is a daily habit of kindness among men'.[23] Here friendship is seen as primarily a natural human practice without any necessary spiritual element.

Peter had a practical motive in defending the archbishop whom he served. Almost every one of Peter's letters could be reduced to his pursuit of some political or ecclesiastical preferment. But if we admit the realities of late twelfth-century life, the difficulty of finding a living in the church solely on the merits of one's literary talents, as well as Peter's lack of influential family to support him, he emerges as more than a crass opportunist on the make. Peter of Blois represents a new breed of wandering scholar, seeking a place to settle and a milieu in which to be creative. He is an almost familiar figure for our age: the underemployed academic who knows he has to sell his wares to the highest bidder but who wants to maintain a sense of dignity in applying his talents.

One means by which Peter apparently managed to maintain his self-respect was through writing about friendship as an ennobling factor in human life. Friendship he insisted, is a contract, which exists by natural right.[24] Its foundation thus has no specific christian element, for Peter sees friendship as integral to human society and as subject to human laws. In the rest of the letter, however, Peter adds a christian dimension to his good advice. The friend should study Scripture to find enlightenment.

To John dean of Rouen, elected bishop of Worcester in 1196, Peter wrote of an old friendship between them: 'I ask you in that social bond of friendship, which we long ago contracted'.[25] The matter at hand concerned exactions being made to finance an expedition to Jerusalem, and Peter warned him not to require too much. Friendship obliges. It allows one friend to criticize the other. It lasts for a long time. It involves mutual faith. Friendship can go into hibernation but can later be revived, as Peter wrote to Odo of Sully when he became bishop of Paris in 1197: '. . . may it grow strong in the exchange of mutual love and the contract of friendship'.[26] Peter's motive is transparent. His search for a generous patron was by now directed towards Paris, for as he wrote Odo, he had been having a difficult time in England. Odo was instructed to think not only of his friendship but also of his episcopal duty to show magnanimity.[27]

Peter looked after himself, but he also showed concern for his family. To a nephew who had just been elected abbot, Peter gave traditional advice but also showed affection and care for his well-being.[28] He borrowed from Jerome's letter to Paulinus a phrase about the strength of the living voice as opposed to the medium of the letter.[29] Peter thus identified his literary efforts with the epistolary tradition of Jerome. Like his predecessor he wanted to reach out to the christian world through his letters and to present in them his needs, criticism, and links with other good men.

If Peter is seen only as a manipulator of medieval *dictamen*, he can appear to be a sham, a charlatan, a maker of pretty phrases of love and friendship. But in the context of his struggle for recognition and place in a competitive society he was remarkably successful at taking the ideal of spiritual friendship out of its sheltered monastery context and converting it into a literary and human ideal for life in the secular church. As he wrote to Master Alexander Nequam of Saint Albans congratulating him on entering the augustinian canons at Circencester:

> With every part of my soul I rejoice in your conversion and in your new way of life. From the very first time when I got to know you I loved you, not for your face, not for your money, but for your virtues in the Lord of virtue. For it was your learning and

> the outstanding reputation of your achievement that brought us to your friendship, saving the saying of Cicero, who in his book on Friendship writes that in the course of several centuries there had scarcely been four pairs of friends. Today, truly, friends are multiplied beyond number. For love has been diffused in our hearts, love which alone is the true seasoning of friendship.[30]

Here as we saw earlier, conversion to the monastic life does not for Peter mean the loss of friendship or separation from a friend. Alexander's entry is a joyful occasion, for it provides a chance to take stock of an old friendship in order to renew it in a new context.

Peter casts aside the caution and exclusivity of Cicero and turns to christian revelation and the action of grace to point to the prominence of friendship in his own age. His message is one of measured optimism. In spite of exiles, frustrations, thwarted aspirations, he can celebrate the simple fact of friendship. From the time of the early church, the bonds of affection expanded into a unity of minds, he insists, so that now there is one heart and soul among the community of believers: *ut jam tunc multitudinis credentium esset cor unum et anima una* (Acts 4:32). Individual friendship is linked with the wholeness of the christian community. Friendship has become an achievable goal for all christians because it is available to all who share in the fellowship of belief.

As a master of epistolary form, Peter of Blois used his talent to seek out his fellow churchmen as friends. His ideas about friendship grew out of personal need, hope for advancement, and concern for individual friends. So long as we allow the utilitarian motive to be part of the reality of friendship, Peter can be seen as a friend who at moments leaves the monastic and spiritual context and accepts a secular conception of friendship that still keeps christian overtones.

When Peter's letters are looked upon as a whole, however, they do not suggest that he was associated with a group of close friends. No names reappear often enough to allow us to trace the development of individual bonds. Peter's friendships of youth appear in later letters when he turned to old and perhaps half-forgotten friends for some service. Such was the case in 1192 when Peter wrote to Conrad, archbishop of Mainz. He addressed the prelate as an old school friend because they had lived in the same residence hall and so had 'contracted the rights of a collegial friendship' (*socialis amicitiae jura contraximus*).[31] Now Peter needed Conrad to help him to secure the release of King Richard from captivity. If it had not been for Peter's apparent desire to use his connections to improve his political standing, one can imagine there would have been no such letter to Archbishop Conrad with a *captatio benevolentiae* dwelling on old comraderie.

Likewise Peter turned to friends at court to help him regain an archdeaconry he says he had lost over a false accusation. Pity has a rightful place in the 'contract of friendship' he pointed out.[32] Once again friends are sought out because of a well-defined practical motive. This does not prove that Peter was fickle in friendship, but indicates that the bonds he formed with others were of a superficial kind. The letters provide no evidence for any development of his friendships later in his life.

The younger Peter may have been more idealistic. His first letter collection was not put together until the 1180s, when Peter would have been in his early 50s.[33] If any letters of friendship from his youth had survived, Peter did not consider them to be sufficiently important to be included in his collection. In it we meet a myriad of individuals who are called friends and who are asked to live up to the obligations of friendship. But we see almost nothing of the tensions, reciprocal demands and compromises of friendship. Peter leaves us with a one-dimensional view by which it is tempting to dismiss him as a collector of literary sayings about friendship but not a real friend. The accumulated evidence of the letters as a whole, however, argues that Peter not only believed in friendship in human life but also cultivated friendships in his own life. Yet these can be only dimly perceived. Peter is ever looking back to earlier friendships on which he wanted to draw, but when he dealt with the present it was his enmities much more than his friendships that dominated his attention.

Another source for studying friendship in this period, and one that provides food for thought about the link between literature and life, is the collection of letters attributed to the papal notary Transmundus, who ended his life as a monk at Clairvaux.[34] Transmundus compiled a *summa* on the art of letterwriting. In most manuscripts this is followed by a letter collection which manifests his link to the cistercian world. Transmundus' collection was intended as a formulary with illustrations of good epistolary style for the sake of imitation. The fact that Transmundus was allowed as a monk of Clairvaux to continue the kind of literary activity in which he had engaged at the papal court indicates a continuing interest in late twelfth-century cistercian circles in the *ars dictaminis*. This is hardly surprising in view of the fact that Bernard had been a consummate letterwriter, but it is worth noting that many of the model letters contain more than formalized general expressions of friendship. These letters contain names, salutations, and various details that indicate they may have been copied from real letters of friendship sent by Cistercians to each other.

Eighteen letters of friendship have been identified in the Transmundus collection. Some of them might have been authored by the compiler himself.[35] Of these letters only four deal with requests, so the remainder look as though they were letters of 'pure friendship'. The letters' content recalls the letters drawn up for Clairvaux monks half a century earlier by Nicholas of Montiéramey. A monk writes to a friend now at another monastery and rejoices that letters can bridge the gulf between them. To a friend who has been made prior at another monastery, the writer says how much he misses him. We find familiar material about monastic separations that bring pain and sorrow, which can be lessened through a closeness made possible by letters. Several of the letters in the Transmundus collection are vehicles of personal contact, religious edification and encouragement in hard times.

In pointing out a derivative quality in the expressions of friendship found in Aelred's compilers, in the letters of Peter of Blois, and in the formulaic letters compiled by Transmundus, we may seem to indicate that the expression of friendship had 'declined' from a higher plateau attained in the age of Saints Bernard and Aelred. But the late twelfth-century development can just as well be interpreted as showing an extension of friendship's language and expression to a larger group of men in the church: monks at Clairvaux who wanted to write letters of friendship but needed models to imitate, clerics struggling for position in the church who could look to Peter of Blois for all types of letters of friendship and enmity, and teachers in clerical and monastic schools who knew their pupils would be interested in small tracts on friendship but who were themselves not concerned with personal statements of friendship. The spread of such a derivative or secondary literature of friendship in this period manifests the very popularity and success of the monastic ideal. Monastic friendship had become accessible to a much larger audience than ever before. It had become easier for members of this audience to capture the language of friendship because of the rich variety of models now available.

A CONTINUING ROLE FOR LETTERS OF FRIENDSHIP

Contemporary with the secondary expression of friendship in formularies and compilations, friendship continues to appear as a significant theme in letters and even poems. These provide evidence that, far from retreating from the surface of monastic life, friendship was alive and well at the end of the twelfth century. In this area, as in so much of medieval history, we are dependent for our information on chance. An Alan who was prior of Canterbury until 1186 wrote and preserved letters which until that date indicate almost nothing about friendship.[36] Once he had had to leave Canterbury to become abbot of Tewkesbury, however, he had an opportunity and a need to express himself in letters to his Canterbury friends.[37] What otherwise would have been lost in the current of orally expressed human bonds that leave no visible traces became part of a letter collection. Like the writing of histories, letter collections often emerge in periods of personal and social discontinuity in order to provide links with a better and more stable past and in order to preserve bonds with people who are loved and missed. Because Anselm's friends moved from Bec to Caen, he had an opportunity, even an obligation, to maintain bonds through letters. Similarly, in the summer of 1186, Alan had to continue his friendships at Canterbury by means of letter. Unlike Anselm, however, Alan seems to have had the same need for his friends that they did for him. His letters speak of pain at separation and longing for reunion. Here is the newcomer who, even though he is welcomed to a position of authority cannot help comparing his state with a happier and more familiar life where friends were within easy reach.

To Geoffrey, subprior at Christchurch, Alan spoke of the warm reception he had received at Tewkesbury. But his main purpose in writing the letter seems to have been to describe his yearning for his true home. Once love had been established, he could not be separated from his Canterbury friends: 'Perfect purity, which charity has joined in mutual embraces, does not allow us to be separate, even when we are separated'.[38] Probably a few months later, he described to a master Feramin at Canterbury his inner state. The separation from friends and his desire to return brought much sorrow: 'How much the more do I grieve in desiring, so that all the more I desire in grieving'.[39] The letter is a difficult one with many linguistic devices to make it attractive to the monastic rhetorical taste of the time. Such an element made the editor of these letters, Margaret Harris, uncertain to what extent they reflect 'genuine emotion'. 'Yet', she added, 'one cannot doubt the keen sense of loss and isolation which he felt throughout his first few months at Tewkesbury.'[40]

To a certain Philip, probably also a member of the Canterbury community, Alan asked how a friend could doubt the stability of his love for him. Apparently Philip had been peeved because no letter from Alan had been forthcoming. 'Are you thus removed from the faith and affection which you are obliged to offer to the one who loves you?' he asked.[41] Alan characterized himself as *dilector*, the person who loved Philip, an expression that suggests both friendship and closeness in a spiritual bond. He reminded Philip that they had been friends from the time they had entered the monastery. This bond could not be easily severed, even if they no longer lived together: 'Your love must not desert Alan'.[42]

The letter indicated that the sense of loss and deprivation was reciprocal. Alan wrote to the Canterbury community to express his own isolation, while individual monks such as Philip accused Alan of failing to given them the love or attention they expected. At Tewkesbury Alan had to identify with other ecclesiastical and political interests than he would have done if he had remained at Canterbury. The pain of separation was accentuated by a bitter conflict between the chapter of Christ Church and the ascetic and unwordly cistercian archbishop Baldwin of Ford, aggravated by Alan's criticism of the monks for not being willing to reform themselves, and culminating in the community's suspicion of Alan for betraying its interests.

During a short reconciliation in late 1189 or 1190, Alan was able to write again to Master Feramin and reassert the bond of friendship. 'In the Lord I most firmly hope that once friendship has been established between us, it can never again be weakened', he began his letter.[43] Alan rejoiced in the return of peace but his letter hints at fear that any criticism on his part would make the monks at Canterbury turn against him. The more he protests his friendship and loyalty, the clearer it is that his relationship to Canterbury was a difficult one. In the early 1190s he even compiled an account of the Canterbury case and wrote about his efforts to one of the monks in order to show his involvement and sympathy: 'Under this pledge of unity we have in good faith made for ourselves a bond of unsullied love'.[44] Such protestations suggest the vulnerability of Alan of Tewksbury's bond with Canterbury.

Alan's letters were usually meant not for individuals but for the entire community. To a few members, however, such as Geoffrey and Feramin, Alan gave special attention and devotion. As we have often seen in the literature of friendship, it is difficult to distinguish between a generalized impulse directed towards the community of friendship and a particularized message sent to an individual friend. But there is enough material in the letters to let us see Alan speaking to his friends in a personal manner. Writing to an unnamed friend, who had complained that Alan did not come to see him often enough, Alan asserted: 'my soul as an individual part of myself adheres to yours. I do not leave you but stay with you.'[45] These words express the kind of feelings Alan had for his friends at Canterbury.

Despite his reassurances, Alan's bond with Canterbury broke down. In a letter that can be dated only to some time between 1186 and 1202, he complained that he had obtained no sympathy from the very friends whom he once had consoled. These were probably his Canterbury friends who he claimed had forgotten his affection for them: *nostri affectus immemores*. Eventually the monks came to consider Alan their enemy because of his criticism and would not even allow him to visit them. Shocked and disappointed, Alan insisted on his good intentions: 'To this day we have not betrayed the bond made with our mother'.[46] Alan had sought community and friendship at Canterbury, but because he did not show complete loyalty to the cause of the monks in their opposition to the archbishop's plans for reforming them, they turned against him. 'Among friends one does not act with threats or terror or with reproaches', he wrote to the prior of Christchurch.[47] But it was too late. In the final letter in the collection, dated to 1199-1200, Alan made specific his charges against the monks: *livor et invidia, zelus et contentio, contemptus et irreverentia*.[48]

A disappointed man? Disillusioned with his ideal of friendship? It is impossible to say for sure, for here the number of letters is small in comparison with the Peter of Blois collection. But during this same period of controversy and disappointments, Alan was able to write a letter describing charity and friendship, showing how both exist in a monastic community where 'all things are in common . . . . one house, one family, one table, and so there are one heart and one mind'.[49] Alan was mainly thinking of the community as a whole, but he presupposed the love among its members. For him the two types of love can hardly be separated, the common state of loving and the individual bonds, 'for that very friendship which gave birth also nourishes those who love'.[50]

In Alan's constant association of the personal with the communal, he was faithful to the benedictine tradition represented by Saint Anselm himself. It is difficult if not impossible in the letters of Alan of Tewkesbury, as in those of Anselm, to pick out any single close friendship in which harmony and equality existed. In the very tensions that gave rise to the letters, however, we find a yearning for closeness in communty, for lasting bonds, for mutual understanding, and for regular contact.

Flowery language and tortuous metaphors reveal how much time, effort and devotion Alan of Tewkesbury invested in his letters of friendship. The same is true of the letters written by the augustinian abbot of Æbelholt in Denmark, William.[51] Care and concern for content point to an interest in friendship in letters and practice. A canon of Sainte Geneviève in Paris, he was summoned to Denmark by bishop Absalon in order to reform a monastic community apparently in decay. From about 1175 until his death in 1203, William remained loyal to the church in the cold North, despite many threats to return to Paris. Once again necessity, and exile from a beloved home, became the mother of a letter collection. The danish historian Nanna Damsholt has shown how William's collection corresponds to other twelfth-century collections, its contents faithful to the principle of providing variety and a portrait of the author's person and work through different types of letters: of friendship, of consolation, of advice to women, and of political affairs.[52] Damsholt sees William putting the greatest care into the letters of friendship, thus making it more difficult for us to penetrate his elegant prose (which is full of the stylistic device of *cursus*), but also pointing out how important such letters were for him as monuments of his life and work in Denmark. Once again we are dealing with a monastic author of the second rank who was compelled by circumstances as well as drawn by inclination to invest in letters much of his personal passion and involvement with people. William had the same concern with the reform of the church and especially of monasteries as Alan, but his personality is more flamboyant.

Three letters from William to Walbert, the abbot of cistercian Esrum in Denmark, reveal several facts about the abbot of Æbelholt's character. Since William's new augustinian house at Æbelholt was established in an area only about fifteen kilometres from the Cistercians at Esrum, the two monasteries were natural rivals for land, donors, and recruits. In one of his letters, William expressed regret that he had excoriated the monks of Esrum for their behaviour and had called them 'maneaters' for their attempt to recruit a certain Philip, an attractive and apparently wealthy young man. With a sigh of relief after getting the matter out into the open, William concludes:

> Friendships are sweeter after enmities than they were before when we experienced no problems with dissension.[53]

The phrase can in context sound like a convenient commonplace, the kind of felicitous piece of proverbial wisdom designed to wipe dark clouds off the horizon. Another such *sententia* is found in a second letter to Walter: 'Familiar conversation usually provides for friends a leaven in love and a remedy in sorrow'. [54] Once again William tries to explain away a tense situation by a facile remark. The remainder of the letter reveals the existence of a misunderstanding between the two monasteries. Walbert had returned from the cistercian General Chapter, and William was eager to reestablish good relations with him.

In a third letter, William expressed joy that Walbert had returned from yet another trip, apparently to France, but his main motive in writing only becomes evident at the end. He wanted to know the details of Walbert's situation: 'If it is not in conflict with your promises, we ask for letters from you, because with great desire we are suspended amid the uncertainty of events. . .'.[55] In all three letters the language of friendship is used in an elegant manner, even moreso than in Alan's letters, for William did not get lost in contorted images and biblical references. As so often in the literature of friendship, however, it is difficult to distinguish the pragmatic manipulation of phrases of friendship from the author's genuine desire for a friend. Once again one senses how by the end of the twelfth century even minor monastic writers had mastered the genre of the letter of friendship and could make the words say whatever they wanted. This very proficiency makes it difficult to determine with precision their attitude towards the importance of friendship in everyday life.

A consistent examination of all William's letters and their content dealing with friendship would probably indicate that much of what he said was literary artifice. For Anders Sunesen, royal chancellor, William used a *captatio benevolentiae* that borrowed from the language of the Song of Songs (3:3): *quem diligit anima mea*.[56] Most of this letter is not included in the collection in its present form, but from the medieval table of contents that summarizes the letters, it is clear that the letter was intended to arrange for a mass to be said once yearly for William. Another 'letter of friendship' which seems highly conventional is addressed to Count Bernard of Ratzeburg.[57] There are warm protestations of friendship to a man whom William had probably never seen or would ever meet. But William insisted that he could see the count with his 'inner eye' and thus loved him. William may have contacted Count Bernard because he was interested in a new monastic foundation under the Count's auspices.

William was at ease in the language of friendship that became widespread in clerical and monastic circles in Western Europe during the course of the twelfth century. To the abbot of Saint Victor he spoke of a law according to which one becomes sad at bad tidings from a friend but rejoices on hearing good news.[58] Similarly to the prior of an augustinian foundation at Konghelle in Norway he echoed the familiar sentiment that minds bound by laws of love cannot be separated by dangers of sea or great distances on land (*ep* II: 39). The theme *amoris leges* makes a fine opening, but the real purpose of the letter seems to have been a query about the state of the community and specifically concerning the possibility of sending a ship from Æbelholt to Konghelle.

It would be easy to continue in this manner and to reduce statements of friendship to pure window dressing, but there are some letters which clearly seem to have been written for the sake of friendship alone. In one entitled 'to an intimate friend', William claims that love does not know how to hide its affection. Therefore we write to each other to express this love. The letter expresses the sweet impulses of the mind.[59] William moves from the general to the specific: the friend should know that William wants the friend's virtue to increase through William's love for him. The friend is to be wary of the temptations of the flesh; thus he shall obtain a heavenly reward. At this point William closes the letter, for he says that by writing only a little he will make the friend want more. This would appear to be a letter of moral advice in the vein of Jerome or Peter of Blois. The care and precision used in formulating a language of love and friendship, however, once again manifest a monastic author concerned with expressing personal bonds in the christian life.

To Geoffrey, a canon at Sainte Geneviève, William wrote in the early spring of 1195 when he and the royal chancellor Anders Sunesen were on their way to Paris. William had come south to negotiate in the tortured affair of Philip the Fair's marriage with King Valdemar of Denmark's sister Ingeborg.[60] One of Philip's cronies had even briefly imprisoned William and Anders in order to teach them royal power. This tangled business is ignored in the letter, and William's thoughts concentrated on friendship. His concern prompted him to write Geoffrey, he says, and his love he describes as an impatient one. Geoffrey should know that his love had drawn William to him. Without you, he insists, life would be more like death: *sine uobis uiuere mors potius sit dicenda quam uita*. Geoffrey knew quite well that the sight of friends and their enjoyment of each other's presence causes joy. Soon William would be with his beloved, whose proximity he greatly needed (*quam valde requirimus*). The language borders on, and is probably influenced by, that of the Song of Songs.

Apparently Geoffrey did not respond to this passionate statement of William's love. In the *salutatio* of a second letter, William states his theme of disappointed loyalty, describing himself as one 'who never tries to go against the laws of love'.[61] Once again William underlines the presence of mutual obligations of love, which require personal contact. In an echo of Cicero, he says that nothing is sweeter than talk among lovers, nothing more joyful: *dulcius. . . iucundius*.[62] If Geoffrey had not answered his first letter because William had committed some offence against him, he was ready to make up for it. But if Geoffrey did not respond immediately, William would have to assume that he no longer was his friend: 'You are not the kind of friend that you claim to be'.[63]

Here is perhaps a hint of the importance friendship had in William's life. There can be little doubt that such a letter was included in the collection to provide readers with a model for the way a disappointed friend writes to the object of his affections in order to get some response. But this is only one dimension in the collection. Another is its deliberate reflection of the personality, desires, and hopes of a man who could not quite believe that in going to Denmark, he had lost his french monastic friends.

William seems to have believed firmly in the reality and obligations of friendship. When he wrote to Absalon, then archbishop of Lund, he called him his friend as well as his lord. Absalon, he reminded him, had brought William to Denmark and had preferred him 'above all other men'.[64] Now the archbishop had an obligation to that memory and friendship: he was obliged to help out William's community in hard times! Here, as so often in letters of friendship, practical needs are combined with the language of love.

To a monk named Stephen, William asserted a pact of equality between them because of friendship.[65] Life without him would be almost nothing or very little, he insisted. In the next lines, William asked him to provide Æbelholt with various seeds and cuttings of roots and trees! This is apparently the same brother Stephen of Esrum who had been sent to Æbelholt to lay waterpipes and who was so good at his work that William asked the abbot of Esrum if he could keep Stephen a few days longer.[66]

William's repeated assertion that there is some law governing human relationships indicates his own desire for friendship. In a letter to a monk named Goswin, William portrayed himself as an exile cut off from the men who knew and understood him. God bound him together with Goswin in a love that could not be dissolved. Through the messenger who bore the letter, William greeted Goswin 'with the title of a special love' and could be joined to him 'in our friendship'. The love William sought as his 'remedy in our exile' enabled him to cope with his imaginings and dark thoughts.[67] His one 'remedy in love' was the practice of writing letters to his friend: *Unum est igitur statuendum atque tenendum in amore remedium*.

William had a talent for communicating his own situation to his audience. His sense of self and of his difficult surroundings makes it easy for us to imagine what it must have been like for the highly educated french canon isolated in the barbaric North. But William's circle of friendship was not limited, as Alan's was, to the old friends at his native monastic house. William found friends among the leading families of the country he had adopted, especially the White (*Hviderne*) family, from which Archbishops Absalon and Anders Sunesen came. To Anders Sunesen's brother, Peder, William paid special attention because Peder was in Paris at his own Sainte Geneviève. William's letter to Peder is one of the longest in the collection. It was written before 1186, the year Peder's wealthy father Sune Ebbesen died.[68] William's salutation is more elaborate than almost any other in the collection: *Intimo suo, immo sibi alteri, immo non alteri, sed uerius sibi Petro* (to his intimate self, or rather his other self, or not the other, but the truer self, Peder). This balanced phrasing and wordplay makes one think of the language of Nicholas or of Bernard of Clairvaux, as well as that of Anselm and the benedictine tradition. The identity of the friends merges in a matching of self with the self of the friend. Two human beings become interchangeable, while their essential difference is still maintained. Rhetoric and affection are balanced carefully in a philosophical-religious statement that sets the tone for the rest of the letter.

William starts by asserting, as he does in so many other of his declarations of friendship, that his bond with Peder was regulated by the laws of love (*legibus amoris*).[69] They required that the friend concern himself with his companion's moral well-being and progress. Peder was to work hard at his studies and to fulfill the promise God had given him by birth and by ability. William had received Peder's letter sent the year before and had been happy with what he had said. The delay in his response had been due to difficulty in finding a messenger to bear it, a frequent (and quite believable) assertion in William's correspondence. As for the request Peder had made, William explains that he had done his best. He had conveyed it to Peder's father, but Sune Ebbesen had refused to grant it, not once but three times. William insisted, however, that he was doing all he could for Peder. He did not have contempt for the favour asked, nor did he neglect to act on it, but he had to follow the wishes of Sune, whose insight and wisdom he goes on to praise. William is quite frank about being afraid to offend a man whose wealth and support were important to the new monastery.

At this point in the letter the nature of Peder Sunesen's request becomes apparent. He had wanted some of his friends to join him at Sainte Geneviève, perhaps at the expense of his father. Sune had refused, according to William, because the 'rush of friends' would burden the church there with great expense,[70] and he was apparently unwilling to foot the bill himself. Dropping the subject, William concludes this section of the letter with news about his own community, which had grown in numbers to twenty-five. Its productivity had become so great that where as earlier it could daily feed eight or ten people, it could now provide for more than one hundred.[71]

The second part of the letter ends with a postscript to William's earlier remarks, apparently because in the meantime another letter from Peder Sunesen had arrived in which the youth reproached William for not responding and helping him. There are renewed assertions of love and devotion: 'For we love you in truth and what is yours we want to make prosper as if it were ours; in fact even more than if it were ours'.[72] William explains he would have liked to come to Paris to visit Peder and the other members of his community, but archbishop Absalon had refused to give him permission to do so. He closes the letter by one more statement of friendship that is couched in ciceronian terms: 'Nothing is sweeter in human affairs than to have intimate talk with a friend'.[73] At the very end he greets the community, but especially Master Andrew, 'whom in truth we also most affectionately love', as well as Master Jocelin, 'whose memory is blessed with us'.[74]

Peder thus served as a link between William and Saint Geneviève. William reveals his continuing devotion to the community, but he also shows his involvement in a danish family whose political, moral and financial support he needed. Protestations of friendship here could easily be dismissed as a sugar coating over the hard facts of life: William's need for Peder's father's support or land. Without denying this reality, however, I think one still can detect a dimension of friendship. In Peder Sunesen William had a bond linking his new life with his old one. Peder was the representative and hope of a new monastic and educated Denmark being trained at Sainte Geneviève. William had every reason to be concerned about the youthful and perhaps impetuous soul entrusted to his care through the vehicle of letters. This is one of the reasons why William devoted so much care to a long and ambitious letter. Like many letters of friendship, especially by William, there is an element of literary showmanship, but it is combined with fatherly concern for a potentially wayward spiritual son, and a man who William assumed would understand and respond to the language of spiritual friendship.

In almost any single letter of those Damsholt considers letters of friendship, we can find *topoi* or commonplaces that betray a skilled literary craftsman at work.[75] Abbot William's collection contains a group of letters of friendship because the inclusion of such a section was regular practice by the end of the twelfth century, as we have seen in the compilation of Transmundus of Clairvaux. But as in Alan of Tewkesbury's collection, the letters of friendship are sufficiently numerous to point to an author who was doing more than showing off his literary prowess. Even if any single letter can be dissected into familiar components, the totality of William's letters of friendship allows us to see him as a man who found in his self-chosen danish exile a means to convey a need for new friends and old. William was fascinated by the contact the letters provided. He insisted on the 'law' that friends keep each other informed. He made use of the familiar language of friendship because he wanted friends.

William participated in what can be seen as a network of friendship. This was not as extensive in its membership as that of Saint Bernard, but it still provides witness of how the *glutinum amoris* (love's glue!) was spread in letters of friendship. Another collection of letters from the same period which deals with the theme of friendship is that of Stephen, abbot of Sainte Geneviève during William's danish sojourn and later bishop of Tournai.[76] To Peder Sunesen after his return to Denmark, Stephen sent more a letter of fatherly advice and fraternal contact than an expression of individual friendship. Stephen nevertheless used the term *amicitiam* to describe the relationship he had formed with Peder at Sainte Geneviève. He claimed that this friendship persisted in spite of separation. He did not, he assured him, reproach Peder for leaving Paris. Another letter reveals that Peder had been allowed to go so he could be groomed to become a bishop.[77] Stephen was confident that those who cultivated charity could bridge geographical distances by their affection: 'By a certain artifice of nature they can speak to each other when absent'.[78] After this declaration of good will and lack of grudge, Stephen continued: 'Let these religious bonds extend between us, and what we are deprived of because of difficulty of contact should be made up for by a community of wills'.[79] Stephen was content that Peder had cast off the barbarism of his native land and had been made gentler by his training in Paris so that the 'pale offspring of glacial Denmark' could rejoice that such a person was given to them. Stephen asked to be kept informed of Peder's affairs and obviously expected him to continue living under monastic discipline. He sent greetings from all the brethren.

The link between Peder in Denmark and Stephen in Paris did not end with this letter. In about 1188 the abbot wrote to Peder to reassure him that none of the brothers had spoken ill of him:

> I grieve over you, my brother, so lovable beyond the love of Jonathan, that at the sound of one little false rumour you have been disturbed.[80]

Once again we have a statement of love linked to a model of friendship, this time Jonathan and David. The expression could be dismissed as the result of practical need, for at the same time Stephen was writing to prelates in Denmark to request their contributions for releading the roof of the church of Sainte Geneviève.[81] Stephen would not risk bad relations with a member of the leading family of Denmark and a primary link to the land, someone who knew his monastery and could speak for or against it. Toward the end of a letter to William at Aebelholt, Stephen describes the improvements being made on the church and emphasizes the healthy state of the community as a whole: the number of brothers had increased, buildings had been repaired, possessions multiplied, and, most importantly, he found peace among the brothers, observance of regular discpline, and devout rivalry in the observance of the church offices.[82] The pragmatic and even propagandistic aspect of this letter leaves room for showing a bond of fatherly concern for a former member of the Saint Geneviève community.

Some statements of friendship, just as in several of William of Aebelholt's letters, are meant merely as attractive openings. In thanking Archbishop Absalon in 1188 for promoting Peder Sunesen to a bishopric and asking him simultaneously for help in buying lead for his church roof, Stephen started with a *topos* of friendship: those of our lords and friends whom we cannot see, we keep in mind by frequent thought, embrace with fervent love, pursue in desire and venerate in service.[83] Likewise Stephen assured Bishop Omer of Ribe, that friendships are for four reasons: because of dialogue, mutual service, frequent exchange of letters, or the renown of virtue.[84] Since Stephen had no claim on any of the first three with Omer, he could appeal to the bishop's reputation to ask for his friendship and his financial assistance. This allusion to Omer's school training hints that he may have spent time in Paris, but aside from this the abbot of Sainte Geneviève seems to be writing to someone whom he had never seen. Stephen, like other monastic figures of the period, was willing to use the language of friendship in order to engage in fundraising and publicity for his church. Just as he often appealed to the Danes' historically troubled conscience by mentioning ninth-century viking attacks on Paris to legitimize his appeal, so too he sought to gain their good will by offering friendship.

By this point we are on our way out of the monastic world of intimate bonds and into a secular world in which friendship entails favours done for friends. Instead of looking down on this development as the imposition of something impure into an otherwise beautiful tradition, we ought to look at the persistence of friendship's language as a sign that monastic life in this period was flexible and adoptable. Even more frankly than William of Æbelholt, Stephen reveals his motives and needs. Writing to a master named Robert, who had been his friend in youth when they had studied together, Stephen makes use of their old bond to ask a favour for another friend. Robert is now at a court from whose lord Stephen's friend needs some help: 'in my absence', Stephen asks Robert, 'I ask that you provide for him through your presence'.[85] The actual problem is not mentioned and need not be. Stephen is appealing to Robert for old time's sake: 'For my love', he says. 'Necessity compels one to intercede for friend', he writes in another letter.[86] Here he appeals for forgiveness for a fugitive monk under whom he had once studied. Stephen emphasizes that the runaway is his friend and had once taught him at Orléans.

Before he came to Paris and became abbot at Sainte Geneviève, Stephen had been abbot at Orléans (1163-77) in a community of regular canons. During this period he wrote of one of his canons who had joined a community at Naples. Addressing the prior there, he said how he recalled the man's name because of 'the soul's true friendship'.[87] There is once again no particular indication that Stephen had seen the man face to face. The language of friendship provided a way of starting the letter and introducing the request that his brother be well provided for. As far as Stephen was concerned, the bonds of friendship between him and former teachers, youthful friends, monastic colleagues and young canons had many levels on which they could be expressed.

It is almost impossible for us to flush out a single intimate friendship in Stephen's correspondence, and yet there is no doubt that he considered friendship important:

> Some [of my friends] have too high an opinion of me, and others think that my abilities exceed what I know I can do, so that sometimes I can hate the confidence others have in me.[88]

By this 'modern' statement of self-awareness, Stephen sums up the dilemma of friendship when it is bound up with favours and expectations. His friends could come to him for help, but as he points out to his correspondent, he could not provide it on his own. He had to turn to other friends. In admitting his own limitations and then calling on a well-situated friend, Stephen conceded in this letter what probably had always been the case but what had now become acceptable to say aloud, as it were, in the literature: spiritual bonds among men can be seen in purely secular terms. There is no doubt that friendships of favouritism had earlier played a role in monastic life, but now they were spoken of with a matter-of-factness that indicates how universally they were accepted. A new word has entered the vocabulary of friendship here: *patrocinium* or patronage.[89]

Stephen did not feel obliged to justify his action. He acknowledged no gulf between the world of the monastery and that of the court when it came to helping out one friend by making use of another. It is hard to imagine such a frank admission of the commerce involved in friendship a few decades earlier.

The same Stephen who expressed so pragmatically the usefulness of friendship could also write from Southern France to Raymond, prior at Sainte Geneviève about his relationship to a leading church figure of his time:

> I shall follow the [cardinal] bishop of Albano through mountains and valleys, through vast wastes, through the madness of predators and the images of death, through burned towns and ruined houses, where there is no safety, no quiet, nothing which does not threaten salvation and does not lie in wait to ambush life. . . Beyond Toulouse, near the Spaniards, I shall find that man, as they say . . . [90]

In the light of the cardinal's circumstances in crusading against heretics and when contrasted with the court manners Stephen could manifest in letters from Paris, this declaration reveals another side to his character and his capacity for attachment to other men. Here is a true believer, ready to follow his spiritual leader through any valley of death. The word *amicitia* is not used, but the sense of loyalty and devotion is overwhelming.

Who was this cardinal of Albano? Henry of Marcy, formerly abbot of Clairvaux (1176-79) and then cardinal bishop, had been chosen by the pope to direct the attack on the albigensian heretics of the Midi. As papal legate in the area he had vast powers. His mission ultimately failed and the next attack against heresy came through a regular military crusade. As a prince of the church and a campaigner against heretics, Henry would appear at first an unlikely source for the ideal of friendship, to say nothing of its practice. His works, however, reveal that he too participated in the late twelfth-century flowering of friendship in a monastic context.

Most of Henry's letters that have been preserved are examples of diplomatic correspondence, but to an anonymous friend, he wrote what is entitled in Migne an *amicabilis epistola*. It opens with an assertion that the two friends had been separated by great geographical distance, so they were denied the possibility of speaking with each other and consoling each other in person. Yet their minds were capable of conversation and consolation, 'for when can my spirit forget yours, or when even for a moment can the memory of you, your love for me, and your tears because of me be torn out of me?'[91] The phrase is just as strong as any similar statement of need for a friend in contemporary letters of friendship. It reminds one of the letters of Nicholas and Bernard of Clairvaux, for it asserts with absolute certitude that friends who are physically separated cannot be spiritually parted. There is nothing original in the idea. It is one of the most common assertions in the literature of friendship. But such an intense formulation of need and union is typical of the cistercian world.

Wherever you go, Henry assures his friend, I will follow in spirit *illuc te sequar spiritu*:

> And so even if in this body it is not given that I can visit you, by these letters nevertheless I do not fail to visit you. . . as you were when you left us, as you were then beloved, also you now are no less beloved to me.[92]

The correspondent may have been a former monk of Clairvaux who had been transferred to another monastery. Henry says that he had learned from the friend's abbot that he was living an exemplary life 'acceptable to the Lord and commendable to men'. This echoes Bernard, blessing and encouraging his monks to leave his company and to spread the Order all over Europe. Henry wrote:

> My dearest, you have become a part of me and so you will not be easily removed; even if you should take on wings at dawn to fly further away and live on the borders of the ocean, I would follow you there in my spirit.[93]

The inspiration is drawn from the psalms (138:9): wherever the soul flees from the presence of God, he will follow. Any medieval monk who read these lines would think of the next verse: 'Even there your hand shall lead me and your right hand hold me'. Henry takes on an almost divine fatherly role, but he still expresses a personal need for the monk to whom he writes. This classic statement of friendship is a reminder of the continuity of a rich benedictine-cistercian tradition almost half a century after its zenith. In other letters Henry used a few commonplaces of friendship, but here, in writing a fellow monk, he drew on and enriched the entire tradition of requirements and pledges of monastic union in love and community.

A mystical streak in Henry implied in this letter is clearly demonstrated in his little-known treatise, *De peregrinante civitate dei*, which as cardinal he wrote to the monks of Clairvaux.[94] Its many layers of symbolism make it a difficult text. But is is important for us because he chose to describe the relationship of good men and especially good monks to Jesus in terms of friendship. We are bound to Christ, he says, as friends of the Spouse, *amici sponsi*, a relationship that evokes the language of the Song of Songs. We are not just servants of the Lord. We also are his friends.

Normally such a passage would be dismissed as one more example of a perception of the workings of Redemption. But Yves Congar has rightly pointed out the significance of the terminology as part of Henry's 'theology of mystical experience'.[95] Henry was interested not so much in what we could call interpersonal relationships as in the sublime status available to the friends of Christ. The language of friendship is nevertheless important to him here, as in some of his letters. His involvement with the albigensian crusade and politics are one aspect of the rich clarevallian inheritance, while his fascination with the language and meaning of friendship on a divine and human level is another part of this background. The cistercian commitment to fight heresy should thus be seen not as a departure from the tradition of Saint Bernard in terms of monastic friendship and ecclesiastical concerns but as a continuation and expansion of an old involvement.

From the barbarian North to the heretical South, friendship in the late twelfth century manifested itself as a european phenomenon. Stephen of Tournai's declaration of loyalty to Henry of Marcy, the latter's letter of friendship to a monk possibly from Clairvaux, William of Æbelholt's bond with Peder Sunesen and with his other friends in Paris: all these signs of human relationships are obviously nothing more than a poor relic of interlocking bonds of friendship and enmities that characterized the age. Similar friendships might be found in other periods, if the sources only made them accessible. What is significant for us, however, is a continuing view of friendship at the end of the twelfth century as a desirable state of affairs for men in the monastic life. We find no evidence of hesitation, doubts or second thoughts. The very frequency of *topoi* of friendship indicates the importance of the bond for monks and canons of the age. There may well be a development away from the spiritual dimension to a more secular one, as we shall see in the next section, but friendship is still something worth describing, discussing, debating and defending as one of the supreme values of human and especially monastic life.

THE GROWTH OF A SECULAR ETHIC OF FRIENDSHIP

Rievaulx is perhaps the last place in medieval Europe where one would look for signs of a change in the language of friendship from a spiritual to a more worldly type, without specific reference to the discipline of christian and monastic life. But within a few years after the death of Aelred, we find a monk, Matthew, writing about friendship in letters and poems in terms that owe nothing to Aelred. His aim seems to have been to imitate classical descriptions of friendship.

Matthew apparently joined Rievaulx shortly after the death of

Aelred.[96] Under Aelred's successor Silvain (1167-89), Matthew became precentor of Rievaulx, a post he tells us in his letters, he sometimes found thankless and burdensome. His works include historical poems which reflect on events occurring as late as 1218. Like his cistercian colleague on the continent, Matthew represents a new generation of monks who were actively and openly caught up in the affairs of the world and whose writings reflect this involvement. The age of monastic withdrawal had given way to a period when Cistercians engaged in an active and sometimes polemical dialogue with the surrounding world.[97] Helinand of Froidmont managed to enshrine cistercian *exempla* into a chronicle of world history, while Matthew speculated on english politics and mourned the effects of the papal interdict on his beloved country.[98] In Matthew there is even evidence of a sense of national pride, an attitude quite distant from international cistercian loyalties.[99]

Thanks to the brilliant detective work of André Wilmart, Matthew has emerged as an historical person in a clearly defined monastic context. Wilmart did not publish all his poems on friendship, but enough is available in his important article on Matthew to give us an impression of a monastic writer who expresses himself more as a writer who happens to be a monk than as a monk who writes:

> To a certain friend:
>
> There is no letter [from you], sweet bee full of honey.
> From a single sheep's hide this expense, I ask, provide.
> Give it quickly, avoid delay. It is shameful to delay the hour.
> You will seem unwilling if you give with no haste.
> Do you want to give? Give freely: This is the saying
> From Antiquity's wise man: it always harms to put off what is ready.[100]

My rough translation cannot convey the rhythm and elegance of this little poem. One notices immediately that there is no echo of christian doctrine or biblical language in these lines. The one reference is to Lucan, a pagan poet. The poem as a whole seems to owe most to the tradition of Horace. It is lithe, free, almost teasing.[101]

It is hard to imagine these lines being written at Rievaulx soon after

Aelred's death. For all his love of friends and friendship, Aelred would not have expressed his concerns in such playful language with no hint of the centrality of Christ in the bond of friendship. The poem may be considered to have been a pure literary exercise, a pen trial, with no serious intent at all. Certainly Matthew provided christian imagery when he wanted to do so. Another of his poems, whose full text Wilmart does not give, mentions the friendship of David and Jonathan, as well as that of the classical heroes Pylades and Orestes.[102]

In a third poem to a friend, Matthew expresses his pleasure in writing poetry and concludes with his delight in having a friend: 'Our love is solid; let it not be dissolved'.[103] Once again no christian element is apparent as is also the case with a shorter poem which uses images from nature and familiar devices of hyperbole and repetition in order to give an age-old assurance of lasting love:

> The winter will lose its cold, as the snow will be without whiteness,
> The night without darkness, the heavens without stars, the day without light,
> The flower will lose its beauty, all fountains their water, the sea its fish,
> The tree its birds, the forest its beasts, the earth its harvest—
> All these will pass before anyone breaks the bonds of our love,
> and before I cease caring for you in my heart.
> May your days be happy in number as flakes of snow,
> May your nights be peaceful, and may you be without
> troubles.[104]

According to Wilmart the most valuable part of Matthew's collection is his letters, for here he reveals his personality most clearly.[105] One gets the impression of a rather vain man, who took immense pride in his ability to express himself and who expects to be complimented on his talent. At the same time, however, he is just as fond of the idea and expression of friendship as his brethren on the Continent. To a certain Richard, addressed as his bosom friend (*precordiali amico*) he wrote a long and informative letter. Matthew described in great detail a recent illness and ascribes it to an excess of duties as precentor of Rievaulx. He blames himself, 'Bah, you wretch and rude ass, why do you take on and presume a burden that you cannot bear?' These words he claims to have said to himself when the attack came.[106] Such self-dramatization echoes the interior dialogues of an Otloh of Saint Emmeram two centuries earlier. Matthew betrays more awareness of himself and of his inner world than he does of other people.

In his suffering Matthew turned to the words both of Christ and of his friend. He quoted what appears to be the text of a letter he once had received from Richard, who had written, 'You are dear to me, dearer than all my friends, except for my father and mother and the other one who is our beloved'.[107] Only death will separate us, the friend had written, and now Matthew rejoiced over his comforting words and called it:

> . . . a message worthy of total acceptance, one that fills me with the drunken fervour of spiritual love. . . for how can it be that such a greeting of my friends should come to me?[108]

At this point Matthew again quotes from Richard's letter. The device of including the text of a friend's answer in one's answer is frequently applied in the letters of Bernard of Clairvaux as in those of Peter the Venerable. I have not noticed this practice as being especially prominent in other late twelfth-century writers. In Matthew's case, quotations from the friend's letter may have been included because they flattered him. At the same time, however, Matthew may have been making use of the friend's words in order to remind Richard of his commitment to Matthew. Even if two years had passed since the friends had heard from each other, the *fedus amicitie* or bond of friendship could not be broken. 'Love revives through the letter's page, affection flowers again and love takes fire. . . ,' he assured Richard.[109]

Much in this letter transcends the usual clichés about friendship. In a poetic passage encouraging the friend to write back, Matthew points out that one can express in writing what one would be embarrassed to say in speaking: *Queque loqui pudeat scribere multa licet*. This thought may have gone through the minds of many a letterwriter, especially those who tried to write love letters. But it is not a familiar expression in medieval friendship literature. Matthew sees the letter as a means to bind the friend more closely to him. For once we have a letter of friendship in which the epistolary genre is not seen as a substitute for personal, face-to-face contact, but as a fruitful means of deepening a friendship by making easier the intimate expression of the self that the letter can convey.

The letter ends in a playful manner. First Matthew solves a word puzzle sent by Richard. Then he asks Richard to greet 'our friends whom you well know and especially the man of God whose face I never saw'. Richard's monastery is described as his 'paradise'. In a final poem Matthew quips:

> Now write to me. What I demand you cannot deny.
> Here you are to say, 'Amen', but with brevity.
> I don't want you to say a lot or to be a burden to you;
> If you do write me, then you will surely be our friend.[110]

None of these details allows us to determine the whereabouts of Richard, but there is little doubt that he was a monk like Matthew.

This is Matthew's most attractive letter. In others, where he defends himself vitriolically against literary criticism and claims Vergil as his model, Matthew reveals the self-love of which Wilmart wrote.[111] Unlike the mid-century cistercian fathers, he conveys to his audience and to his correspondents his primary identity as that of writer, not monk. Like Peter of Blois, he comes across as an aspiring man of letters. Though Matthew apparently remained at Rievaulx, his letters and especially his poetry, suggest a development away from the world of the cloister to involvement with the secular world. If Aelred was an artist in being a spiritual author, Matthew of Rievaulx wanted only to be recognized and applauded as an artist in being an author.

Another witness to the continuity of monastic friendship and to a growing interest in the expression of human bonds in non-spiritual language is the benedictine abbot at Gembloux in today's Belgium, Guibert. A little-known writer who deserves more attention for a medium-sized and varied collection of letters, Guibert corresponded with the visionary Hildegard of Bingen and went to stay at her monastery in Rupertsberg in the late 1170s in order to have her visions written down.[112] Between 1189 and 1193 he was abbot at Florennes before being recalled to Gembloux, of which he had been elected abbot. He remained there until he resigned in 1203 or 1204.[113] Guibert had many interests. Besides Hildegard's visions, he was concerned with the cult of Saint Martin, and most of his writings concern this saint in one way or another, as does his *Apologia pro Sulpicio Severo*.[114] In Guibert we find some of the first indications that the language of friendship can be extended to women. He closes a letter to a nun named Gertrude, after describing the destruction of the town of Florennes and its monastery, with the words:

> Forgive me, I ask, most beloved sister, for pouring out such things to you and for provoking you with me to such sorrow, for the sad heart can never bring forth what is joyful, and the bitter mouth cannot make honey. I do not know by what instinct of nature it is that there seems to be some relief in one's sufferings if one can speak of them with a friend.[115]

In this passage Guibert addresses Gertrude as a friend with whom he can share his troubles. Here is the beginning of a development in european spiritual life whose importance I will consider a bit later in this chapter. For the moment it is enough to point out that Gertrude gets the same status of *amicus* as Gerbert's male friends.

The most explicit illustration of Gerbert's friendships comes in a letter to a certain *magister* named Joseph from the period during which Guibert was abbot at Gembloux (1193-1203). The collection also contains three letters from Joseph to him while he was still at Florennes. From Joseph's letters we gain the impression of an affectionate but traditional friendship expressed in christian terms between a young cleric and an older benedictine abbot. Thus it is a shock to turn to a letter from Guibert to Joseph from the 1190s and discover a passionate statement of disappointed love that contains no christian allusions at all.

In the first letter in the collection (not necessarily the earliest chronologically), Joseph addresses Guibert as someone he knows well, his 'father and lord, above all in singular affection beloved to him . . . the abbot of Florennes', and offers him, 'whatever he is, and if he can be anything, wholly his', a formulation which points to something more than a conventional relationship of respect for an abbot.[116] Joseph is grateful to God for being able to send a letter because he can show thereby that when he is 'absent in body' he is 'always present in heart'.[117] He had wanted to come to Guibert but had not had an opportunity. He asks for his prayers. Joseph had heard that Guibert had been elected abbot of Florennes and now hoped the best for him and his monastery. He himself intended to remain 'in my customary fashion' at Rheims, where he perhaps taught or was in the service of a prelate. At this point the letter breaks off, but enough has been preserved to indicate that the bond between the two probably went back to some time before Guibert's election to Florennes in the late 1180s.[118]

In the second letter, Joseph addressed Guibert as 'most beloved in Christ and most greatly to be loved lord', but not as Joseph's friend. Once again Joseph begins by stating his desire to see Guibert or else to enjoy his presence by letter: 'My spirit indeed is not with you as a guest. It dwells with you, so that it on the contrary cannot return to us, for it never went away'.[119] This formulation of a familiar idea is both elegant and clever. Joseph reveals himself in these few letters as a master of style and of the epistolary genre of friendship.

After this confident start, Joseph began to lament his own moral failings. His language hints that he was still rather young:

> But when I speak with you as if with myself out of complete trust in sincere love, and address you as friend and doctor, I wander about and feel impure in being distracted by my thoughts. I embrace wantonness studiously in my words; I commit acts which displease God, and I am always veering towards what is worse, so that now death on all sides knocks on my house. Death is outside the house, death in the tomb. Woe to me. What shall I do?[120]

The passage recalls to mind Anselm's first meditation, his lament on his sins.[121] But Anselm addressed God, while Joseph speaks to Guibert.

The friend has been entrusted with the role of counsellor and comforter to an extent that an earlier age (or a later one) might have considered almost blasphemous.

Joseph's somber tone is completely lacking in the third letter. For the first time Guibert is addressed as both lord and 'friend in Christ', someone 'singularly loved'.[122] This declaration of love is repeated in the body of the letter, where Joseph provides the news he is going to Jerusalem with the archbishop of Canterbury:

> You whom I love sincerely in the Lord and singularly, when we set out, then may you, my love, travel with me, so that we who are separated in body, at the same time be joined.[123]

The *topos* is the same as in the first letter, but as if to intensify his statement of loyalty and devotion to Guibert, Joseph expresses the wish to see him once more before he dies. Since this is not possible, he asks the abbot that when he in the future finds Joseph's writings among his own, Guibert call him to mind.[124] Joseph makes the theologically bold statement (but one that echoes the language of the Rule of Saint Benedict) that Guibert is ultimately responsible for Joseph's salvation: 'For those whose care you took on, you will have to render account to the strict judgment of God'.[125] In closing, a fearful Joseph asks that Guibert accept these his last gifts, his writings, so that Guibert will always remember him.[126]

Although Joseph's letters reveal linguistic vitality and intense emotional expression, they contain nothing about friendship that we have not already seen.[127] In Guibert's single letter to Joseph, however, we depart from the traditional language of spiritual friendship. Guibert describes their bond in a completely secular manner. By now he was abbot of Gembloux, so that the letter must have been written in or after 1193. Joseph's departure for Jerusalem can be dated to 1189, for in this year the archbishop of Canterbury, the learned cistercian Baldwin of Ford, left for the East. At least four years separate the two letters, and all we know about Joseph's adventures on the way to and from Jerusalem is that he survived. He is addressed as *scolasticus*, indicating that he had become a teacher. It was not the present, however, that concerned Guibert:

> A while ago I learned, most beloved, that you were staying in the town of Opgeldenaken near Gembloux, and when I considered the goodness and beauty of your face, the grace of your mouth, the elegance of your speech, the joy of your expression, the continence of your eyes, and when I looked over the gentleness of the movements of your whole body, I was delighted beyond belief with these qualities. I marvelled that a youth who was such an exemplar of goodness could be found, and so I took you to me in a totality of love, and my spirit found rest in you.[128]

In this remarkable passage Guibert, almost alone with Aelred in twelfth-century monastic circles, considered physical and moral beauty as complementary.[129] Guibert deliberately constructed a sentence which leads up to a dramatic climax, *requievit in te spiritus meus*, words that recall the soul's thirst for the Lord in the psalms, but actually not a literal biblical quotation. Although Guibert starts by recalling a single recent meeting with Joseph, his description covers the whole development of their friendship, which must have gone back several years:

> The habit of familiarity and its ensuing boldness enhanced our acquaintance, and the better I came to know you, the dearer and sweeter you became to me. I experienced in you what Saint Gregory said, that a friend is one who as it were is the guardian of the soul. . . . I saw, I regarded, and I came to love the face of your interior being, radiant with the beauty of virtues, and my soul clung to you [Ps 62:9]. Melted in the fire of charity, it ran, as it were, into yours.[130]

Guibert makes more specific use here of the language of the psalms, letting the soul's thirst for God become that of the friend for his beloved. He also borrows Pope Gregory's definition to describe his bond. But his love, even if it draws on biblical and patristic language, also has a basis in human nature:

> I do not know by what hidden instinct of nature it sometimes happens through the intermediary of a single vision of each other or one conversation, men can be bound together by the knots of an indissoluble friendship, in which the joy of internal beauty draws them away and fills them with the vitality of an interior beauty, so that in accord with the interior the exterior man is made up, as it is written, 'The wisdom of a man shines forth in his face' [Prov 17:24].[131]

Guibert used the phrase about natural instinct leading to friendship also in writing to a nun, Gertrude.[132] In Joseph's case the idea is linked to the connection between inner and outer man. Joseph's goodness of soul is reflected in the beauty of his visible features:

> So you, sweetest brother, when you consider and imitate in religious men who act with piety their disciplined ways, you make yourself admirable and worthy of imitation. You make the eyes of those who watch these men leave them by turning towards you, and you make your voice pleasing to those to whom you speak with a sweetness of discourse. You reveal a face that is desirable because it is brightened by the signs of virtues.
>
> Drawn by such attractions I desire and yearn to see you, to embrace you, to speak to you, but I do not grasp you, I do not get hold of you as I desire. Uncertain and changeable between faith and affection, between hope and fear I do not know what to choose or to obtain. Faithfulness which according to John Chrysostom preserves friendships, and joins holy associations, makes me certain of the indissoluble fraternity of your love, while affection, when the fullness of its fruit is denied, grieves that it is delayed from the favour of sharing life with you. What is even more serious, affection is afraid of being forever cheated. It grows anxious, sighs and groans. But amid

> these, sweetest brother, what are you to do? Are you not concealing something? Do you not have contempt for us who desire you, seek you, sigh for you?[133]

What is couched in terms of the psalms and the church fathers looks very much like a love getting out of control. We lack sufficient material to determine whether there was a jealous love or sexual attraction. But clearly Guibert felt his feelings were not being reciprocated. He wanted more of Joseph than he was being given. The letter seems to be an appeal to the young friend for contact and attention. Friendship has developed into a conflict between private-affectionate and collegial-fraternal bonds. On the one side is a calm faith in the goodness of the bond, while on the other a hint of loss of control.

In Guibert of Gembloux spiritual friendship seems to be on the way to losing its integrity and to becoming a frustrated or even disappointed attachment. For the early thirteenth-century Italian writer Boncompagno da Signa, spiritual friendship is still a goal but he did not give it much attention because he was primarily concerned with what blocks friendship: the self-serving pursuit of worldly gain, prestige and recognition. Boncompagno was master and teacher of rhetoric in Bologna and at other italian universities and celebrated for his works on rhetoric.[134] However much Boncompagno insisted that friendship at its ideal belongs to the spiritual life, his descriptions of the reality of friendship in his *Amicitia* brings his reader into a new setting for human bonds and divisions: the italian city state, and especially into a new class: secular masters, whose affiliation with the church was quite secondary to their identity as academics out to make a reputation for themselves. This group had been important in developing a language to express bonds of friendship since the wandering scholars of the eleventh century. In Boncompagno this group openly abandoned the ideals of spiritual friendship.

Boncompagno chose to write about friendship without acknowledging any debt at all to Cicero. Sarina Nathan, Boncompagno's modern editor, has in fact asserted that his *Amicitia*, written in 1205, was intended to replace Ciero's treatise, just as his *De malo senectutuis et senii* was intended as a slight to Cicero's *De senectute*.[135] With a new independence of mind and self-confidence in his abilities, this master at the University of Bologna provided anecdotes about friendship from his own life and experience instead of drawing exclusively on classical and biblical examples. Here he resembles Aelred of Rievaulx, but unlike Aelred, Boncompagno defied the classical tradition of friendship and introduced a new sense of limitations in friendship.

It would be unfair to claim that in Boncompagno the ideal of friendship is completely secularized. Boncompagno constructs a pious dialogue between Body, Soul, and Reason. These he sees as different parts of himself, and the purpose of the dialogue is to demonstrate to the Body that unselfish friendship based on equality is possible in human life. Of the twenty-nine different types of friendship that are presented in the course of the dialogue, however, only three have anything to do with what could be called genuine friendship. All the rest are base forms of opportunism parading under the name friendship. By them one man manipulates another for the sake of gain or recognition or out of jealousy.

Boncompagno's editor rightly calls him *une scrittore profondamente originale*.[136] The freshness of his vision lies not in his formulating of a new concept of friendship but in his admission of the friendships actually lived in his day in urban and academic life. The vitality of Boncompagno's approach is helped by examples which can at times be hilarious, illustrations of the absurd distance between what friends say to one another and the way they treat each other. Boncompagno delighted in clowning to his audience in order to imitate the ways of his colleagues. Such is the case in his description of the 'vocal friend', whose friendship consists solely in his talk and is never followed by action:

> In cities and many burghs there are many vocal friends who often go to castles and wealthy homes and receive gracious services from friends, but when any of them afterwards sees the friend, he embraces him tenderly and says with a happy voice: "Good that you have come, how are you? Is your wife in good health? And do your sons enjoy bodily health?"[137]

This back-slapping friend pretends to be offended when a friend visiting his town turns down his offer of lodging because he has already found shelter in someone else's home. But if the visiting friend says he has no place to go, then the vocal friend immediately suggests someone else's house and never his own. Masters and scholars, claimed Boncompagno, are for the most part vocal friends. When one greets another, he insists, 'Why did you not come to my house? You know that I am wholly yours and would do anything for you that should be done for a friend'', although he means not a word of it.

Even if the friend replies to the vocal friend, 'I was always tied to you by a bond of indissoluble friendship', he gets no advantages from such a relationship. The vocal friend will often extend invitations to come to his home for a meal. When one finally takes him up on it, he seems struck by terror, sighs and becomes the colour of ash: 'Many vocal friends often invite to lunch or dinner but would hardly give you a glass of cold water'. And yet such people claim 'I would most willingly take care not only of you but also of your dogs and cats!'[138]

Boncompagno's examples are timely and timeless. They are among the first illustrations of a new pattern of life that perhaps characterizes Western (and perhaps global) society to this day: collegial relationships based on the highest ideals but often lacking genuine sincerity. Boncompagno describes knights as well as scholars, but he is most acute in unveiling the hypocrisy of academic life in the competitive atmosphere of the italian city university. He describes the 'shady friend' (xxiii:*de umbratili amico*), who under cover of friendship does services to others until he has got what he wanted from them. Such people promise 'the mountains and the seas' to their teachers, but once they themselves mount the master's chair, do not hesitate to hold forth against their masters with 'the position of detraction which was hidden in their hearts'.[139] Boncompagno indicates his own experience of such treatment. In defining the 'turncoat friend', he provides a sample of gossip that may have circulated about his academic qualifications, his poor dress, even his womanizing: 'Be careful when your turncoat friend greets you with adulation', he warns, for he is winking one eye.[140]

This long list of abuses of true friendship ends with a pious statement that is intended to ensure the value of close human bonds. But here where we would expect some examples of true friendship, there are only weak illustrations from political history that further emphasize the rarity of any lasting trust among men. The only conclusion to be drawn is that we must put our hope in the 'heavenly friend', who will never let us down.[141] Boncompagno does not deny the possibility of human friendship, but his humorous illustrations are pessimistic in tone. His description of friendship in the context of urban and academic society points to a new sense of realism and a pragmatic mode of describing human bonds in early thirteenth-century society. His work appeared at the beginning of a period when spiritual friendship no longer had the same universal appeal as it had exercised in the twelfth century. We find growing scepticism about the real content of friendships. Monastic idealism had been replaced by the confident neo-aristotelian study of the world that was sweeping the university world in these years. Here friendship was seen not as an ideal but as a fact of human behaviour, for better or for worse.

A similar development can be seen in a surprisingly different source, the pious *Imitation of Christ*, whose author is now said to have been not the late medieval mystical writer Thomas à Kempis but an italian benedictine, John Gersenius, abbot of Saint Stephen of Vercelli, who wrote the work between 1220 and 1260.[142] According to Gersenius, we should guard against too close friendships with men (*de cavenda nimia familiaritate*, I 8): 'Seek to be close to God alone and his angels and avoid the intimate knowledge of men'.[143] Our one true friend is Jesus, 'who alone is good and faithful beyond all friends' (II 8). Thus we are not to be curious about the lives of other men (III:24)). The message seems almost a direct response to Boncompagno's vision of the limitations and hypocrisies of the northern italian urban world. Since men are not to be trusted and since God is our only friend, human friendships are to be minimized. Once again spiritual friendships are devalued. Neither Boncompagno nor the author of the *Imitation* denies the possibility of close friendships, but for the first time since the early christian centuries, friendship's contribution to the spiritual life was challenged.

INSTITUTIONAL CHALLENGES TO FRIENDSHIP

An increasing formalization and growing rigidity in institutions by the end of the twelfth century probably also undermined an earlier confidence that good men in the church could depend on each other for spiritual friendship. In monastic circles there grew up a sense that the expression of personal bonds gets in the way of discipline. Complaints appear about abuses in the writing of letters and excessive attention given to it.[144] In the Cistercian Order the statutes passed by the General Chapter at Cîteaux in the 1180s and 1190s show distrust of manifestations of affection. It was made clear that monks were to embrace each other only for very good reason, as after a long journey.[145] A brief absence of a few days did not provide sufficient reason for men to throw their arms around each other! Similarly, the abbots at the Chapter itself were to show restraint in demonstrating affection to each other when they were walking in the streets of nearby Dijon: 'They are to be very careful and keep from holding each other's hands or going about the streets in any other noticeable manner. . . ' .[146]

Such a short paragraph says more than a long treatise could have done about the practice of monastic friendship. When abbots saw each other on the way to or from the General Chapter, several years might have elapsed since they had been together. The statutes themselves reveal that many abbots did not obey the provision to come annually, and some monasteries were excused from the yearly journey because of great distance. One can imagine abbots who had been novices at Clairvaux and had then been sent to different parts of Europe. They must have looked forward to the General Chapter as a time of reunion with their dearest friends of youth. The meetings were social as well as business occasions. We know something of the way General Chapter was used for the telling of exemplary stories for the edification and enjoyment of the fathers.[147] At the same time the warning about holding hands shows how the meeting provided for the physical expression of friendship. Aelred in old age had accepted that his monks held each other's hands, but Cîteaux in 1181 could not permit the practice, at least not in public view.

At the same time as the General Chapter statutes show concern about demonstrations of affection, the literature of the Order was doing its best to revive the vitality of the earlier years and to recall monks to the founders' ideals. This is the period of gathering together monastic sources and ordering them in collections. The best known of these, and probably the most influential, was the *Exordium magnum cisterciense*, composed between about 1190 and 1210, and representative of the Clairvaux Cistercians' view of their past and present.[148] Despite its wealth of materials, this source says very little about interpersonal bonds among monks. Even in its rich use of legends about Bernard, it sheds little light on his friendships. It is probably by no means accidental that the *Exordium* leaves out some of the most passionate passages in Bernard's description of his love for his brother Gerard.[149] The eulogy in his *Sermon 26* on the Song of Songs is far more intense than its pale echo in the *Exordium magnum*, whose compiler, apparently deliberately, clipped the more personal edges of cistercian affective life. He sought to emphasize the aspects of the past that could easily be integrated into sound and well-functioning communities. Bernard's grief was acceptable, but only to a point, for an individual bond could easily detract from the collective life of the cloister and the Order.

The best illustration of the conflict between the requirements of a monastic institution and the needs of human friendship is provided by the benedictine chronicler of Bury Saint Edmunds in Norfolk, Jocelin of Brakelond. I have dealt elsewhere with Jocelin's magnificent account of life at Bury and especially of its first years under abbot Samson.[150] Here I want to touch only a few aspects of this rich narrative, which can be seen in terms of a friendship's failure. When Jocelin first started writing about Samson in the mid-1190s, he considered him as the man who had saved his monastery from the lax economic practices of his kind but weak predecessor, Hugh. As the new abbot's chaplain, Jocelin enjoyed privileged access to him, and he valued their conversations. But it became more and more difficult for Jocelin to talk to Samson on semi-equal terms. He might try to approach him with an intellectual problem in order to open the way to a more personal question, but Samson's increasing irritability eventually drove him away. After one outburst, directed against another former favourite, Jocelin describes his own reaction:

> . . . I marvelled that the abbot should have spoken thus and debated in my heart this way and that: but at length I was constrained to remain in doubt, since the legal Rule tells us and teaches us that all things are at the disposal of the abbot.[151]

Jocelin could find an explanation in the Rule of Saint Benedict, but his hope for a friendship had been quashed for good. In the latter part of the Chronicle, Samson is seen at a distance and Jocelin more and more identified himself with a faction in the monastery critical of the abbot. He managed somehow to rationalize for himself Samson's choice of a young and inexperienced man as prior, but his description sounds like an attempt to convince himself of something in which he did not really believe.

What can be called a monastic friendship between a resourceful Samson and the admiring, inquisitive Jocelin could not last once Samson had become abbot. His reform program for the administration of the abbey, its town of Bury, and for its vast country properties led to one confrontation after another, especially with the obedientiaries of the monastery. These officials guarded their rights jealously. Jocelin's chronicle has traditionally been used to illustrate the development of monastic economy in the period. It deserves also to be seen as a manifestation of the collapse of friendship when monastic institutions were torn apart by dissension over privileges and prerogatives. Aelred had as abbot believed in and cultivated friendships; Samson as abbot had no time or room in his busy life for the friendship Jocelin thought he had established with him.

Jocelin and the monks who wrote about the election of Samson's successor witness to a change in monastic mentality.[152] The preservation of material privileges and economic activities came to dominate the monks who were good at expressing themselves in writing. Late twelfth- and early thirteenth-century Bury literature reflects a high level of intellectual and even spiritual awareness at this abbey and so should not be used carelessly to point out some 'decline' from the monastic ideal. Events at Bury and the way they are described show how a human institution which comes to concentrate almost exclusively on maintaining itself and its privileges easily loses the flexibility and openness which is a prerequisite for making friendships.

The professionalization of life, attention to administration and to legal detail, and the rivalries and dissensions of community life go together with a general stiffening of literary forms. This was the case with the *Exordium magnum cisterciense*, which, despite its size and ambitious scope, says little about the Cistercians as human beings with weaknesses and strengths. Similarly the genre of *dictamen* or letter-writing took on a more impersonal quality in these same years. In the Clairvaux collection of Transmundus we can still detect an element of individuality, but in general the *topoi* of friendship failed to renew themselves during this period, except in such extraordinary writers as Guibert of Gembloux. There are the customary phrases about absence-separation-union through letters, an emphasis on the duties of friendship, and appeals to the sweetness of human life when friendship is present. In the poetry and letters of Matthew of Rievaulx, Aelred's devotion to friendship gives way to the display of literary brilliance. Even so sympathetic a writer as Alan of Tewkesbury drowns his correspondents (and us) in ambitious biblical images and complex metaphors which make it difficult to understand his meaning. Only in a writer such as Boncompagno can we be sure of his exact position on friendship. Otherwise the language of friendship has taken on an obscure and artificial quality.

A final element in this cultural development away from faith in the value of spiritual bonds between men is even harder to determine, for its presence can only indirectly be determined beneath the surface of medieval life. This is a fear that close friendships would turn into physical loves. Alan of Lille's *Plaint of Nature* several times mentions as a widespread phenomenon the practice of what we today call homosexuality.[153] This is poetic expression and not statistics, but Alan reveals an awareness that is also present in the scandal-collector of the late twelfth century, Walter Map, in a scurrilous anecdote about monks who show an interest in boys. Describing an attempt by Saint Bernard to revive a dead boy, he comments: 'He was surely the most unlucky of monks: for never have I heard of a man lying down upon a boy without the boy's arising immediately after the monk'.[154]

John Boswell, in his landmark work, has claimed that a climate of relative tolerance towards 'gay clerical sexuality' disappeared by the end of the twelfth century.[155] Open resistance and even persecution of clerics identified as homosexuals became more common. In this more repressive environment, which also brought an increased fear of heresy and heretics, the carefree poetry and passionate letterwriting of an earlier age needed to be qualified and put into a less intense and more impersonal context.

Fear of homosexuality is by no means a central motif in the movement away from close individual bonds in the monastic life. The problem seems to have been much broader: a loss of confidence in the possibility that a community's rich interior life could provide a sheltered and fertile ground for friendship. When the brotherhood of the group is challenged or corrupted, then its individual members cannot trust each other any more, nor can they seek each other out for comfort or help. As Nigel Longchamp of Christchurch, Canterbury, warned in about 1180 in his *Book of Burnel the Ass*: 'True brotherhood in act not name we see/Name without deed is unreality'.[156] If we remember the bitter controversies of the 1180s and 1190s at Canterbury between chapter and archbishop, Longchamp's words about fraternity seem almost prophetic. If Alan of Tewkesbury had read the *Book of Burnel* (and he could have done so), he might have identified with Longchamp's sense of defeat and disappointment. When he left Canterbury, he had tried to maintain his old bonds with the community through writing letters to some of its monks. But as soon as he criticized the rapacity and self-interest of his former community, he was informed that he had no right to speak as one of its members. Alan of Tewkesbury and Jocelin of Bury wanted to speak their minds and entrust their souls to other monks, but their contributions were not wanted. Too much fear, anger and suspicion existed to allow a sharing of hearts and minds in the community of brotherhood idealized in Acts 4:32, the christian *cor unum et anima una*.

Problems of this type are universal, and the historian can easily turn into a shallow moralist if he or she does not place these developments within the context of a given society and age. The end of the twelfth century and the beginning of the thirteenth witness a crisis of friendship not because the literature of friendship disappeared but because new social realities challenged friendship: the growth of formalized centres of learning, the establishment in them of rules and statutes, an end to the long period of monastic expansion, a proliferation of disputes over monastic privileges and property, an insistence on discipline in the 'old Orders', the Benedictines and Cistercians, now attacked for discarding their early values. Such changes in the mental, social and spiritual climate made it more difficult for men in the church to take the risk of showing frankness and honesty with each other.

Perhaps every human friendship requires an element of naïveté, a child-like belief that the other person wants to give the best of him- or herself. Once this trust has been eroded and human motives are perceived as based on selfishness and self-servingness, as in Boncompagno, friendship becomes an almost unattainable ideal. Either one ignores individual friendship and concentrates on the good of the community as a whole, as happened in late twelfth-century cistercian literature, or else one denies the value of human friendship and turns to Jesus as the only friend, as the *Imitation of Christ* requires. Either way, friendship is demoted to a subordinate and untrustworthy position in the intellectual and spiritual life. In the mid-twelfth century, friendship had seemed to be a way to achieve deeper individual expression in the christian community, but by the early thirteenth century, it no longer appeared in such a favourable light as a means of getting on with the business of monastic life.

An Opening to Women

Just at the time male friendships in the monastic life were becoming more difficult to establish (or at least were being seen as less easily attainable), we find a number of sources indicating the appearance of male-female friendships of spiritual content. This opening to women rose out of the *cura mulierum*, male clerical and monastic concern for the direction of women in religious life. This practice becomes visible to us in the years from about 1170 to 1240. The story of the relationship between celibate men and women is one that goes back to the earliest days of the church and beyond, to its prototype in the friendship between Christ and Mary Magdalene.[157] Once men were exclusively vested with sacerdotal powers, women were relegated to a subordinate position, where they were made to be dependent on men for spiritual guidance, physical protection and canonical recognition for the institutions in which they banded together. In turn women were allowed to share with some men their spiritual experiences and to listen and participate in men's spiritual and emotional problems. Such relationships frequently contained tensions and conflicts. In the story of Christina of Markyate, a mid-twelfth-century englishwoman who refused to get married and insisted on the life of recluse, men are heroes as well as villains.[158] Christina's flight from her family would not have been possible without the help and friendship of religious men. At the same time, however, she had to resist the advances of well meaning—or cynical—churchmen. There is nothing sentimental or romantic in the description of Christina's relationships with her benefactors. She made use of them as they did of her. Only with the rich and powerful but very human Geoffrey, abbot of Saint Albans, did she share moments of genuine affection and common spiritual revelation.[159]

In the literature surrounding the twelfth-century mystic and visionary Hildegard of Bingen, we find a similar environment of close relationships in the spiritual life, but since most of Hildegard's letters are descriptions of the contents of her vision, they say little about her bonds with men. When men's religious communities wrote her, they approached her from a distance as if she were some living relic or oracle and not a sensitive human being.[160] The men who contacted Hildegard made her into a phenomenon too formidable in knowledge and intensity to be described as a friend. When Guibert of Gembloux wrote Hildegard, he did not ask for her friendship, but for the privilege of becoming one of her *familiares*, those who were told of her revelations.[161]

A change in attitude from mid-twelfth century to early thirteenth century towards male-female spiritual bonds is apparent if we compare Aelred of Rievaulx's letter of advice for his sister with Jacques de Vitry's description of Mary of Oignies, the unofficial founder of the Beguine movement. Aelred told his sister that close bonds between men and women are dangerous and undesirable in the life of the recluse. He was convinced that, while male friendships can enrich the spiritual life, male-female spiritual bonds inevitably lead to sexual sin.[162] Jacques de Vitry did not theorize about such intimacy, but his biography of Mary reveals that he had come to know her as a friend whom he valued more highly than anyone else in the world.[163] His anecdotes about her show that he had had many conversations with Mary about her childhood and upbringing, and he hints that Mary was instrumental in his decision to leave university life and to become a preacher.

Elsewhere I have dealt in detail with what I called 'the transformation of monastic friendships'.[164] Today I would qualify that phrase by pointing to the evidence for the continuity of close bonds among men in the church at the same time as instances of male-female friendship appear. The problem with the literature about the latter phenomenon is that most of the male accounts concentrate on the virtues and visionary powers of the women, as in the case of Hildegard, and often we can only indirectly detect the existence of a personal friendship in which the man really comes to know the woman. As often as not, he was probably projecting some ideal image both of himself and of the virtuous woman on his subject and making her an object of religious devotion.[165] Often it seems to have been the women who did the hard work of forming friendships by seeking out men with whom they could share their visions and thus provide a basis of shared experience for the formation of friendship.

One of the best-known of the relationships in which a monk took the trouble to impart some of his own experience to a woman and to help her in practical and intellectual ways towards realizing her desire for the religious life is that between the Cistercian Adam, abbot of Perseigne, 1198-1221, and Agnes, a nun of Fontevrault. Adam apparently saw to it that Agnes was made abbess of a house for cistercian nuns at Les Clairets. The secular founder of this house was countess Mathilde of Perche, and it was not until the end of Adam's life that the monastery actually got underway.[166] The majority of Adam's letters to Agnes follow the usual formula; he begins by pointing out that the correspondent has long asked for some consolation through spiritual advice. After an apology for the delay in carrying out the request, with appropriate excuses, the writer proceeds to give a lengthy exposition of some spiritual topic, with rich biblical images and a language replete with mystical expressions.[167] The result is that it often is difficult to understand exactly what Adam is saying—and whether he was speaking to Agnes personally or merely using her as a receptacle for his teachings.

At times, Adam seems to be speaking to his female friend more intimately and personally. In about the year 1200, during a period when Agnes was sick, he wrote her a fairly succinct letter expressing the totality of his devotion to her:

> In my own way, most beloved, I wholly cling to you, and on your soul, mine depends. In this joining of individuals, the love of Christ has made itself our bond.[168]

The essence of christian spiritual friendship could hardly be expressed more purely. Completely bound up in each other, their two souls are still dependent on the love of Christ to glue them together.

In the body of the letter, Adam speaks of Agnes' illness in spiritual terms, instructs her not to overdo her penances, and reassures her of his own devotion. 'Truly I am yours,' he wrote, rejoicing in her spiritual progress and taking pity on her weakness. He was attached by a love both 'vehement and secure' *(et vehemens et indubitata mei dilectio te afficit)*. Almost as a postscript, Adam added that even though he had lately visited Fontevrault, the abbot of Cîteaux did not let him visit her.[169] In admitting that he did not have the right to do so, Adam revealed that male cistercian relationships with female religious were still at this time (about 1200) a delicate question. Adam nevertheless insisted he had a bond with Agnes and her community that was more than a general relationship of fraternity, for, as he said in closing, 'Greet for me that entire holy community, and do not fail to be sweeter and gentler to those who are more closely bound to me'.[170] Adam conceded different degrees of closeness with women. He loved them as individuals, not as anonymous members of a religious institution.

In many of his other letters to Agnes, Adam apologized for not seeing her:

> Surely if I had the wings of the winds, I would be present to you more often in body. But since the desired ability is not present to me, still my will in readiness will not be absent.[171]

All this is familiar language in the commerce of friendship. What is unusual is that a man is using it to address a woman in monastic life.

'Nothing is sweeter to me in life than that my heart find you happy in heavenly tasks', he tells Agnes, starting a letter that deals mainly, not with Adam and Agnes, but with Agnes and Christ.[172] The spiritualized language recalls some of Saint Bernard's sermons. The letter is actually a short treatise; its personal opening soon gives way to an impersonal edificatory exposition. Here, as in so much of the male cistercian monks' literature for and about women, men seem to have made use of women as a point of departure or source of inspiration for their own spiritual lives. Even with women they called friends, they did not display the same unreserved closeness apparent in many male-male relationships. Perhaps male-female relationships of real life were less reserved, but the literature still manifests distance. Fear of their own sexual impulses probably restrained many men.

Adam of Perseigne also wrote letters of friendship to men, and he did not show a similar restraint. In several which went to a monk in Normandy named Osmund, who was novicemaster, the vagueness and obscure symbolism of the letters of Agnes are replaced by a more direct manner.[173] Adam described Osmund as being 'importunate' in his request for instruction about how to fulfil his office. Nevertheless, Adam replied by writing a small treatise on the subject. He is the first cistercian author to specify the nature of the contact between master and novices. The novicemaster, he wrote, was to engage his charges in 'friendly and frequent talks. . .on spiritual matters'.[174] These talks, Adam indicated, were not to be one-sided instructions. By using the word *familiaritas*, he suggested that the novicemaster was to encourage the novices to express themselves. Together they were to engage in holy dialogues *(sanctis colloquiis)*:

> The attentive care of the master and the friendly interchange of spiritual conversation lead to shaping the desired obedience.[175]

The novice's experiences form his later monastic life. Adam took it for granted that novices were to be encouraged to express themselves verbally to one another and to their master. In the *probatorium* they would engage in fruitful conversation, openly admit their problems, and obtain spiritual guidance. This environment would have been ideal for the encouragement of friendships.

In another letter Adam is more specific about the talk of friends in a monastery: 'What except love should be the theme in the conversation of friends?' Adam qualifies his choice by saying that love is that which contains nothing suspect 'if it is called affection or charity'.[176] In a later letter, however, Adam warned Osmund against asking too much by telling Adam about his problems:

> . . . why. . . do you complain so bitterly to me about yourself, and set before me the different weaknesses of your soul, as if thus placing them as a cure?[177]

As far as Adam was concerned, the individual monk had to solve his own problems rather than turn to someone else for help. The aelredian delight in sharing the secrets of one's soul had vanished. Adam refused to provide the guidance for which Osmund asked: '. . . my son, do not be troublesome to me or ask from me anything more'.[178] The renowned abbot of Perseigne may have been wary about Osmund's notorious enthusiasm for publicizing his correspondence.[179] A final letter from Adam once again warned Osmund not to expect too much from their love, but still conceded the importance of individual friendships in the monastic life:

> . . . brotherly love is full of a tender anxiety and he who sincerely loves another hardly turns his eyes from looking upon the one of whom he is fond.
>
> See, my son, I have received your affectionate letters and have read them, and from the reading I have realized more clearly that love is really never idle. Where it plants its affection, there it directs its gaze and does not allow it to fail to see, with a gaze never satisfied, what it delights to love with constant and eager affection.[180]

By such lines Adam seems to be telling Osmund that pain is one of the consequences of loving another person. Love seeks the beloved, but, as Adam cited Ovid, 'Love is a thing full of anxious fear'. Adam maintained a certain distance from Osmund, while at the same time he gave Osmund a chance to admit his love. Osmund had claimed that he required nothing, but as Adam pointed out, the very writing of letters created an obligation, 'since I am, as it were, compelled to answer your letters, you seem indirectly to be asking for them'.[181]

Adam conceded the importance of 'frequent correspondence' as 'proof of an abiding affection'. He did not cut himself off from his enthusiastic correspondent, but he hinted that Osmund was making demands he could not honour. These few letters to Osmund provide us many more hints about Adam's friendships than to his literarily and spiritually more ambitious letters to Agnes. To the holy woman Adam wrote with great spiritual force and yet with cautious restraint so that he would not seem to promise too much. To the monk Osmund Adam wrote with greater openness about his feelings and reservations. In each case Adam defined the limits of what he was willing to offer, but only his correspondence with Osmund allows us to make out the outline of a personal relationship that contained elements of doubt, irritability and affection.

Not until we reach the letters of the Dominican Jordan of Saxony to the nun Diana of Andalò near Bologna from the 1220s and 1230s does the full flowering of male-female friendship become apparent.[182] This development goes together with greater expectations among urban middle class and noble women that the church would provide them with formalized ways of expressing their religious devotion. Jordan's attention to Diana can be explained in terms either of his own personal inclination or as the result of a new attitude towards women encouraged by Saint Dominic. Certainly the Dominicans (as well as the Franciscans) quickly made a commitment to women that had taken the Cistercians more than a century after their founding reluctantly to concede officially. Behind the institutional background, Jordan's own decision to befriend Diana seems to have been the central factor in their relationship. He saw to it that she was able to realize her wish to live in a religious community, in spite of the initial opposition of her father.[183] After she became a nun, Jordan visited Diana regularly every second year in connection with the Dominican General Chapter at Bologna. More importantly for us, he supplied Diana with a stream of magnificent letters whose simplicity, transparency and directness form a stark contrast to correspondence in monastic circles.

These letters are perhaps our finest medieval witness of a close friendship between a man and a woman in religious life. They have none of the literary pretensions of twelfth-century collections but instead convey a mixture of fresh news, spiritual advice, and declarations of love and friendship. Jordan's letters closely resemble what the personal letter has become in modern times, a concentrated statement of individual affections, hopes and fears that are conveyed in the context of one person's life and circumstances. Although none of Diana's letter is contained in the collection, Jordan refers to them often enough that from his letters we can get an idea of what Diana had asked for in terms of news and advice. Jordan's letters are at almost no time isolated statements that could as easily have been made to another audience. The pragmatic informativeness of such letters had not existed only a few decades earlier.[184]

The chronology of the letters remains an unsolved problem. Various editors have come up with vastly different solutions, and I would hazard only one general remark. The earliest letters are more epistles of spiritual advice than messages of personal friendship. In them Jordan often addresses the community of nuns as a whole. Later, in the 1220s, generalized letters of advice were still being sent to the community, but specific descriptions of Jordan's situation and his feelings were addressed to Diana. In one letter to her, Jordan directed Diana to share its contents with the community, thus hinting that some of the other letters were meant for Diana alone.[185]

Jordan's advice to the sisters and especially to Diana is consistent from the early 1220s until the mid-1230s, when the letters end. The nuns were advised to moderate their asceticism and not to tax their bodies excessively.[186] They were asked to pray for Jordan and his companions and for their success in converting young men, especially university students and masters, to the Dominican Order. The sisters are consistently described as spouses of Christ, while their friar correspondents are given the status of friends of the spouse. There are frequent references, especially after the 1230s, to Jordan's health, his bouts with fever, his movements and changes of plan which might keep him from a scheduled visit to Bologna. The most emotive letters concern the loss of Jordan's german friend and fellow Dominican, Henry, who died in 1229. 'O my brother Jonathan, so lovable,' he wept in a letter to Diana which shows a grief in intensity (if not literary quality) rivaling Bernard's eulogy for his brother Gerard.[187]

In this case a male-female correspondence reveals continuing close male-male bonds within the religious life. Another friendship, between Jordan and a brother Gerard, can be perceived only indirectly, for many letters have a postscript by brother Gerard, whom Jordan described as the companion of his journeys *(comes itineris nostri)*. Gerard calls himself Diana's son. One can construct here a figure of spiritual loves, uniting Gerard and Jordan with Diana, and through her with Christ himself.

A secular language of friendship, as seen earlier in this chapter, developed at the same time as the expression of spiritual friendships anchored in the events of everyday life. For Jordan, loving Diana meant telling her about himself, his sorrows and achievements, hopes and defeats. His letters do not hint at any potential conflict between his love for Diana and the love of Jesus. [188] His first words in a letter can concern Jesus Christ, but after them he turns to practical matters and ends by reassuring Diana of his affection for her. At times the language can seem so intense as to indicate that Jordan was in love with his Diana:

> You are so deeply imprinted on my heart, that I could never forget you; indeed I remember you all the more often, the more I have come to realise that you love me genuinely with all your heart. The affection you have for me inspires a more ardent affection in me, and stirs my mind all the more powerfully.[189]

In the tradition of spiritual friendships extending back to the church fathers and solidly supported in monastic literature, this statement of love can be seen for what it is: an assertion of the bonds which are formed when spiritual men and women share the same ideals and admit responsibility for each other's happiness and salvation. We must scrape away from our minds the accretions of two centuries of romantic idealization of male-female love and imagine a culture where the sensual language of the Bible and a tradition of celibacy could make such intense but chaste loves possible. The exact content of Jordan's love for Diana can elude us, despite the richness of our source. So too do her feelings for Jordan, which are only indirectly visible. Jordan may well have disappointed Diana at times by not coming to see her when she expected him.[190] In spite of the gaps in our knowledge, it is clear that these two Dominicans, male and female, expressed themselves to each other in a language of love that had been developing for centuries in christian monastic literature. These letters of friendship emerge fully-formed, unapologetic, and confident, not only because of Jordan's commanding personality but also because of his ability to draw on the tradition of spiritual friendship which elsewhere seems to have been drying up at this time. Without Jerome, Augustine, and Ambrose, without Bernard, Peter the Venerable, and Peter of Celle, the cultural soil would not have been prepared for this manifestation of close personal bonds between two human beings in religious life.

It is not my intention here to minimize an achievement of dominican spiritual literature and reduce it to a byproduct of cistercian-benedictine tradition. My point is that monks and friars, who traditionally have had their own interested public (also among historians) and have been kept separate from each other in the respective development of their Orders, have to be seen in terms of their interrelationship. The letters of Diana and Jordan were written in the wake of the Cistercians' institutional and interpersonal opening to women. The letters of friendship of Adam of Perseigne are almost contemporary with those of Jordan of Saxony. The two writers deal with the same subjects, and they often make use of the same images. They share a common cultural matrix of friendship. This is not the place for a close study and comparison of the *topoi* both writers use, but even this brief presentation shows that Jordan was clearly in the tradition of Bernard and Aelred when he wrote of his friend Henry:

> I grieve for my most faithful comrade, I grieve for my sweetest friend, I grieve for my most beloved brother, I grieve for my dearest son, Henry prior of Cologne.[191]

The great difference between cistercian and dominican letterwriting seems to lie in Jordan's willingness to be specific in defining Diana's spiritual function and in distinguishing it from his own. 'Do not worry about me,' he wrote her, 'you remain in peace and I go about amid diverse activities, while we do everything for the sole love (of Christ).'[192] The goal is the same, the means different. Diana's vocation is stability; Jordan's is to be on the move. Because Christ unites them, they can be each other's friends. The only aspect of friendship which Jordan admits he cannot accept is Diana's grief at separations and partings from him:

> For I see that you then were burdened in such an inconsolable manner that it was necessary for me to be sad not only because of our mutual separation, but also because of your special sense of abandonment. But why are you so anxious? Am I not yours, and am I not with you, yours in working, yours in resting, yours in presence as in absence. . .?[193]

Elsewhere Jordan wrote Diana that she loved him more than he loved her (another echo, intentional or not, of Bernard). He admitted his feelings for her and hers for him, without fear. Diana was his loyal supporter, eager for news, eager for his visits, but also insistent that he maintain contact and not forget her needs.

FRANCISCAN RESTRAINT AND A NEW RESERVE

The Dominicans quickly became the intellectuals of the reforming and educating thirteenth-century church, while the Franciscans clung at first to their identity as the companions of Francis, poor and simple. This self-definition might seem to make the Franciscans better suited than the Dominicans for living out friendships with each other, for the little brothers carried little or no intellectual baggage with them, only the image of their founder. On their journeys they went by twos, and so the distances and trials of travelling in medieval Europe promised many harrowing experiences to bring the two brothers together. From the very first, however, we detect a certain restraint in franciscan sources about the expression of friendship, as if individual relationships were looked upon as easily getting in the way of the mission of Saint Francis's company as a whole. Francis himself was described as a leader who knew his brothers intimately, at times because of prophetic insight, but he is also said to have given up having any special companions. While the dominican Jordan of Saxony had the company first of his beloved Henry and then of Gerard, Francis guarded himself against seeming to favour any of the brethren: 'I do not wish to appear singular because of a privilege, but let brothers go with me from place to place only as the Lord will inspire them'.[194] Francis was wary of *singularitas* in friendship in the same way the author of the *Imitation of Christ* suspected it. One is reminded of Anselm, as interpreted by Eadmer, reacting to a young friend's death by becoming 'all things to all men,' instead of permitting new special friends.[195]

In a very few instances Francis can be seen giving way to the desire of other brethren for a special bond with him. To Brother Leo, he wrote the one personal letter we have from him: '. . . if it is necessary to you for your soul's sake to have other consolation and come to me, then come'.[196] This is not the declaration of mutual affection that we know from Bernard or Jordan. It is the desire that the companion set the conditions for the relationship because Francis himself would rather leave the matter in God's hands. Francis did not himself seek, or apparently want, close friendships with other men.

Brothers Leo, Rufinus and Angelus, often called the 'intimate friends' or 'intimate companions' of Saint Francis,[197] probably knew him better than anyone else. Without intimate knowledge of him, they would not have been able in the mid-1240s to set down a number of anecdotes about Francis in their *scripta*, the freshest and most lively report of the founder's life and message we have outside his own few writings. But the man who emerges here was God's friend, not any man's. For a good friar the title *spirtualis homo et amicus Dei* was the highest tribute possible.[198] When the brothers walked together, Francis encouraged them to be silent until mid-afternoon:

> Let not idle or unprofitable words be uttered among you. For although you are walking, let your behaviour and life be as righteous as if you were in some hermitage or remaining in your cell, since wherever we are or wherever we walk we have our cell with us.[199]

Although we can assume *a priori* that brothers who went out together into the world would have formed close bonds with each other, their relationships are not described in such terms in early franciscan literature.

Rosalind Brooke assumes that 'deep and lasting friendships' were formed during these years, but this is a modern interpretation, not that of contemporary franciscan writers.[200] They were not interested in personal friendships, for these could be a distraction from zeal for the spread of the Order and the cult of Saint Francis, the Christ-like founder set apart from all other men. The memory of John on the bosom of Christ does not seem to have entered the franciscan tradition, which was more concerned with the figure of Judas and worried about betrayal of the content of the founder's message.

Francis himself seems to have encouraged this devaluation of special friendships. He exhorted the ministers of his Order to be men 'with no private loves', in order to make sure that the situation never arose where a minister 'shows favour to the one' and thus 'begets scandal in the whole group'.[201] This provision recalls the Rule of Saint Benedict (2:16), but in the Rule the abbot is allowed to prefer one monk to another because of his virtue. Francis left no such loophole. For him the minister was to be 'a man to whom zeal for prayers is a close friend'. Such language recalls the flight from human attachments engaged in by the desert fathers of Egypt. The Francis whom Brooke describes as never having been alone after his first conversions remains a lonely figure who preferred distances between friars to be bridged only by their common acceptance of life in the Order.[202]

We must, however, be careful about pinning down Francis to a single view. The saint by no means condemned friendships among the brethren. In his Rule (the so-called *Regula bullata)*, however, he made a provision which suggest how far he was willing to allow close personal bonds:

> Wherever the brothers are or happen to be, they shall act as members of a family to each other. Each shall show his brother confidently what he needs: for if a mother nourishes and loves her son after the flesh, how much more lovingly should not we love and nourish our brother in the spirit?[203]

Francis's term *domesticos* has to be seen in relationship to the image of the mother that follows. The brothers are to provide for each other's needs as if they were members of the same biological family. This implies a group solidarity rather than individual friendship. The mother is the loving provider who gives nourishment and love.

A second provision about relationships with other people is coupled with a warning that the brothers not enter the monasteries of nuns *(monasteria monacharum)*. The brothers are not to become godparents *(compatres)* for either men or women, a little-understood or -noticed warning that shows how Francis linked together contact with religious women with friendships or spiritual relationships with lay men and women. Francis wanted to establish a distance between the brothers and everyone else: nuns, laymen and laywomen, 'so that no scandal arise between brothers or on their account for any such reason'.[204]

In his relationship with Saint Clare, Francis maintained the same distance which he required of his brothers. From the start he was careful about meeting her at all.[205] In the *Scripta Leonis* it is emphasized that Francis's love was for Clare as a member of a religious community and was a 'fatherly affection'.[206] The last view that Clare and her sisters got of Francis was of him after death, already a relic 'for the consolation of his daughters and maidservants'.[207] Francis is seen to have maintained a distance from Clare, and even though there are elements in the tradition that emphasize their closeness, when the sources are examined they reveal very little about a personal relationship.

Such an interpretation of one of the most famed male-female 'friendships' of medieval life will undoubtedly cause dismay and perhaps even anger among those who rightly look upon Francis and Clare as patrons and guides. But if the early materials for Francis are taken as a whole, the *Scripta Leonis* and the *Lives* by Thomas of Celano, it seems to me that Francis had no enthusiasm for exclusive bonds inside or outside the community. He knew it was essential for the brothers to take care of each other as members of a loving family, and even to care for women in the religious life. At the same time, however, he hesitated at the thought of close relationships that might cause divisions among the brethren. Francis lacked Aelred's belief that close friendships strengthen community. With both male-female and male-male bonds, he feared conflict between individual affection and group solidarity.

The early Franciscans shared a daily intimacy on the road and yet were not encouraged to express themselves to each other in terms of friendship. In the franciscan ideal we meet the saint who went away to receive the stigmata or the brother Giles who said that only God is our friend:

> Therefore he withdrew himself not only from the society of seculars but even from that of the brothers and of other religious. 'It is easier to save one's soul among few than many,' he used to say. 'One must be alone and free to devote oneself to God and to one's soul. For the Lord alone, who created the soul, is its friend and no one else.'[208]

We have returned to the desert father who claimed that only by saying 'God and I are alone in the world' could one attain salvation.[209] While the optimistic and humanistic twelfth century saw the human friend as a way to salvation, he had become for thirteenth-century brother Giles the friend of the world described in the Epistle of Saint James, who leads the soul away from its only true friend in God. Here the message of a follower of Saint Francis meshes with that of the author of the *Imitation of Christ* and prepares the way for the intense but narrow spirituality of later medieval centuries, with reservations or outright suspicion about close friendships.

Why did the Franciscans show such reservation about personal friendships while the Dominicans did not? In the first place one should remember that Jordan of Saxony is a relatively isolated figure and that we do not meet a great number of friendships in the dominican literature.[210] Dominican friendships are for the most part invisible to us, but at the same time the Dominicans have nothing parallel to the franciscan concern about too-close bonds. The call of the desert is perhaps the closest we can come to explaining why the Franciscans held back: spiritually they sought the same isolation as their egyptian predecessors, even though their lives were completely different. At the same time, however, the Franciscans came from a completely different social background from the Cistercians.[211] The merchant class of northern Italy which gave so many of its sons, willingly or unwillingly, to the new Order, does not seem to have trained these youths in school with the same attachment to classical writers that the early Cistercians show. There are hardly any echoes in Francis's writings—or in those of the other early franciscan authors—of classical learning.

Whether or not Francis deliberately made grammatical mistakes in order to show humility, his way of expressing himself is close to the italian vernacular and not concerned with elegance of form or imitation of ciceronian *topoi*. The vast gulf between the finesse of Bernard and the directness of Francis in their letters is representative of the difference in the style of two groups of enthusiasts: for the Cistercians beauty of expression went together with the pursuit of friendships, while for the Franciscans clarity and simplicity of expression were desired to help in preaching to lay people. The Cistercians had 'world enough and time enough' to seek out each other, while the Franciscans gave friendships low priority. Like so many other social and religious groups in the thirteenth century, they specialized, almost from the very beginning, and had no desire for anything that might get in their way or provide a distraction.

The Dominicans recruited from the first young men who were fascinated with the type of learning that was built on knowledge of Cicero, while the Franciscans appealed to merchant and noble families whose sons' educations apparently were not so advanced. The Dominicans almost combed the schools of Italy, Germany, France and England in order to catch the best men. Jordan of Saxony's letters are full of news about how many young nobles and learned masters had gone over to the Order in each place he visited. The Dominicans, at least from the 1220s under Jordan of Saxony, sought the educated and cultivated men of the day. For the Dominicans there was no large gap between close human relationships and the new religious life, while the Franciscans concentrated on poverty and the imitation of their founder.

THE REALITY OF FRIENDSHIP: A DECLINE IN ITS CELEBRATION

The ideal and practice of friendship were still very much on the surface of monastic and religious life in the first decades of the thirteenth century. The franciscan literature provides a powerful indication of a new hesitation about the worth of individual friendships in the spiritual life. At times the franciscan sources indicate open scepticism about the value of friendship, but the main message seems to be that friendship was just not that important. In one story Francis gave way to a brother who required his special friendship, not because he himself found any particular positive or negative status in this bond, but because the brother apparently needed it.[212]

The dominican Jordan of Saxony provides a strong contrast. The daily experiences of his life he described in terms of friendship with both men and women. He used his letters and visits to Diana and her house at Bologna to recharge himself for the long voyages across the Alps to Paris, Oxford, and Germany. Jordan's letters warn us against making generalizations about a 'decline' in manifestations of friendship.

We can look back over the period 1180 to 1250 and contemplate a variety and diversity that is richer (if not literarily superior) to what appeared in the previous period. In terms of geography, social class, and the sexes, forms of friendship reveal themselves in many more areas than were visible in the mid-twelfth century. Increasing sophistication and diversification in the literature of friendships probably reflect the growth of Western European society: its new wealth, urbanization, and scholasticization, all of which manifested themselves in a sense of superiority to historical antecedents. In Boncompagno's decision to ignore Cicero in writing on friendship, we have the signal for a new confidence in one's native ability *without* standing on the shoulders of giants, even if one actually is doing so.

If there is any representative and spokesman for this new Europe and its ideal of friendship, it is the cistercian monk Caesarius of Heisterbach (c. 1180-c.1240) who was novicemaster at a house near Bonn founded in 1189. His *Dialogus Miraculorum*, with its hundreds of stories taken from monastic and secular life in the first decades of the new century, provides rich material for cultural history as well as conveying the content of spiritual values.[213] Caesarius almost never made use of the term *amicitia*, but the one time he did, he wrote about friendship so matter-of-factly that he perhaps revealed how friendship had become an accepted part of monastic life. It was nothing to get excited about, either positively or negatively. It was quite simply there. The term comes in a story about the monk Henry, who later became Caesarius's abbot at Heisterbach. Henry had asked a monk named

Christian about his revelations and could do so because 'he could count on a special friendship' *(de speciali praesumens amicitia)* with Christian.[214] Caesarius did not explain what he meant by such a friendship but assumed his audience would grasp the meaning. He did not defend the bond as legitimate or morally acceptable but took it for granted that it contributed to the fabric of cistercian life. Caesarius showed the same relaxed interest in describing close male-female relationships. He even speaks of a female friend, *amica*, of Henry, without bothering to explain what he meant by the word.[215]

There is no doubt that Caesarius himself had friends. He recorded many conversations he had, as with a monk of Heisterbach, Richwin, concerning the latter's temptation to leave the Order for the sake of a woman.[216] Caesarius knew monks and nuns well enough to ask them to confide in him about their visions. But he did not dwell on the nature of his relationships with them. It is what his friends said, not what he felt for them or they for him, that was important to him. A recent article about Caesarius I entitled, 'Friends and tales in the cloister', but these are friends by our perception, not in the language Caesarius used about them.[217] From his stories we can see his closeness to two men, Henry, Heisterbach's abbot, and Herman, who became abbot of a daughter house of Heisterbach, Marienstatt. These two monks alone provided a great number of edifying stories for Caesarius's pen. In telling them he makes us aware of the time he must have spent talking to friends and sharing secrets with them. Henry and Herman must be considered friends of Caesarius, as well as many of the novices whom he taught and to whom he told stories. They became his friends, and yet Caesarius never wrote about friendship itself.

With Caesarius we arrive at the end of our period of almost a thousand years. We have, I hope, gained an awareness of how men and women in the christian church could express themselves to each other in personal terms without the hesitations and reservations found in desert fathers, Jerome and Augustine. A reaction may have been setting in, however, visible in the pessimism of Boncompagno and the *Imitation of Christ*. Here friendship was seen either as virtually unattainable or as downright dangerous for those who sought the love of God. Because the world was so corrupt, men and women had to choose between being friends of each other in the world or friends of Jesus alone.

The twelfth-century cistercian celebration of friendship found an heir in the Dominican Order, but Jordan's letters to Diana are a byproduct of his life and work, exciting enough for us, but not a reflection of the central interests of his Order, to preach and to convert. Friendship lived on in the spiritual life of the Middle Ages, but the perception of friendship became less prominent in the literature of monastic and religious life, as we have seen in the case of Caesarius of Heisterbach. There were still and always will be friends and friendships, but the celebration of friendship had given way to second thoughts, silences and even doubts.

EPILOGUE:

ENDS AND BEGINNINGS IN COMMUNITY AND FRIENDSHIP

THE IDEA AND PRACTICE of spiritual friendship among medieval monks and clerics are usually seen in terms of the flowering of monastic life in the twelfth century.[1] Here, especially in the cluniac-cistercian axis, there grew up a literature of friendship most evident in the letter collections of Peter the Venerable, Bernard of Clairvaux, and Peter of Celle. Since the Second World War the most visible representative of this movement has been the yorkshire abbot Aelred of Rievaulx. Whatever Aelred's sexual identity may have been,[2] he summarizes the optimism of the middle decades of the twelfth century that close personal bonds among monks were not only desirable but also fruitful for the life of the monastery as a whole.

After Aelred, spiritual friendship as a visible phenomenon in monastic life and literature, as well as in the mainstream of church life in Western Europe, is thought to have 'declined'.[3] A few derivative treatises based on Aelred's work and the imitatory art of Peter of Blois are usually pointed out as indications that no one could live up to cistercian ideals of spiritual friendship. By the 1180s it is supposed to have passed away just as easily as other manifestations of twelfth-century culture.[4]

The history of spiritual friendship in fact continued into the later Middle Ages. The expression of such friendships still attracted writers. By the fifteenth century, however, there apparently came a flight from friendship because of a conviction that friendship among two or three spiritual men would undermine the integrity of life in religious community. This change in the Western view of friendship is of significance not only for medieval culture but also for our own time. This interpretation can only be suggested, not proven, but the rejection of spiritual friendship points to some of the modern dilemmas with which many of us live, especially with the separation of the individual from any enriching community.

Cicero defined friendship as harmony or agreement (*consensio*) in all areas of life, both divine and human, with goodwill and charity (*benevolentia et caritate*).[5] This *sententia* was the point of departure for medieval definitions of friendship, at least from the end of the tenth century. For the monks and clerics who dealt with the subject, however, there were underlying assumptions about spiritual friendship that went beyond the ciceronian definition. Friendship meant preferential love and close bonds with other human beings where these bonds enhance the spiritual life of the individuals involved and at the same time contribute to the community life they share. Usually we do not get to view friendships within a single monastery, for we have to depend on letters sent from one monastery to the next. Friendships among monks of different monasteries could, however, have grown out of bonds fashioned when monks lived together within a single monastery. The exchange of letters and the open expression of friendship could result from the departure of a monk from one monastery to another.

Here we encounter a perennial debate about links between literary form and historical reality. Without going into detail on the commonplace terms used to describe friendship, I can point out that the preceding pages have looked for textual evidence for emphasis on and even *celebration* of the value and desirability of personal friendship. When we find this celebration, we can assume that the practice of friendship was likely. When we find no evidence of such a concern to use terms of friendship, however, we cannot assume that friendship no longer existed. Friendship in one form or another is probably to be found in every human community and historical period, but we can conclude only on the basis of the sources we have, not from the silences.

Since most exchanges of friendship took place between men, at least the friendships which have left traces in our sources, it is appropriate to ask to what extent spiritual friendship in its actual manifestation might have been connected to gay love among men. In monastic life in the medieval West, there is little evidence of concern about physical love among men. The Rule of Saint Benedict assumed that in entering the monastery the novice left behind him all manifestations of what we might call genital sexuality. Thus the question of homosexual love is no more relevant in the realm of monastic friendship than that of heterosexual love. It is simply out of the question.[6]

The main question the sources give us reason to ask is not a narrowly sexual one but a broader social one: to what extent were preferential bonds among monks seen as strengthening or weakening the life of the community? The community was not just the individual monastery. For the Cistercians it could involve links among houses and extend to the Order itself. The monk or cleric who sought out others in friendship could at times be encouraged to do so, while in other periods he might be warned against close friendships as a potential danger to community life.

We briefly recall one representative of the late twelfth-century expression of friendship. The abbot of Clairvaux in the years 1176-1179, Henry of Marcy, who later became cardinal and led a crusade against the Albigensians, had no doubt that close personal bonds were important in the monastery. In a letter, probably to a monk who had been at Clairvaux and perhaps had been sent to another house, Henry used all the expressions of tenderness that Bernard could have summoned up.[7] Even if the letter functioned as a model and was not addressed to a 'real person', the production of such a document of friendship points to a continuing interest at Clairvaux in the literature of monastic friendship through the cultivation of the art of letterwriting, the *ars dictaminis*.[8]

Turning to the thirteenth century and leaving the monastic milieu for that of the university, we find continuing interest in friendship, at least on a theoretical level. In the writings of Thomas Aquinas, friendship was accepted as a natural and important part of human experience. Because Thomas turned to Aristotle, with his rich teaching on friendship in the *Nichomachean Ethics*, there could be no hesitation about the essential value of friendship.[9] Thomas saw no gap between greek and christian teaching on this point. It was merely a question of establishing that a link between friendship and virtue existed and then pointing to a bond between God and man in friendship. Thomas saw divine and human friendship as essentially the same, even though their objects he perceived as different. Thomas found no conflict between friendship as an individual goal and friendship as a part of community life. Like Aristotle, he thought that friendships were necessary for states to function. Virtuous men, he pointed out, seek each other's companionship and get to know each other in enjoying each other's company, in talking about philosophy and politics, and in influencing the course of events in their society.

This ideal of friendship does not in itself have any especially spiritual content, but it by no means excludes a spiritual element: what friends can be to each other would only be enhanced by placing their relationships in terms of a divine milieu. As late as the fifteenth century the prolific theologian Denis the Carthusian reasserted thomistic categories but also wrote almost lyrically about friendship in a way that would have delighted any twelfth-century writer on the subject: '. . . for in this vale of misery there is nothing so useful, comforting, desirable and salvific as having a faithful, pure, close, complete and constant friend'.[10] Only one's friend is able to see a person as he really is. To him all can be told, for in him there is one will, or one heart and mind in the sense of the passage from the Acts of the Apostles (4:32). These words, *cor unum et anima una*, originally applied to the unity of the first christian community in Jerusalem, but since the twelfth century have often been used to describe the bond of individual friendship. In fifteenth-century Denis, as in twelfth-century Aelred, friendship took a natural and inevitable place in human life, but also provided a link to other members of a spiritual community and a way to God.

In spite of this continuing interest in friendship, we detect by the end of the twelfth and the early thirteenth century a departure from spiritual language about friendship and a more secular view. This we noticed in the poetry and letters of the monk Matthew of Rievaulx, who showed no debt at all to his predecessor Aelred and worked within a world of classical *topoi* and literary self-assertiveness that was far from his cistercian predecessors.[11] Another pivotal figure we have considered, and a much more striking one, Boncompagno, tried in his *De amicitia* to outdo Cicero by providing a new and smarter tone to the language of friendship.[12] Boncompagno's exposé of the many types of fake friendship provides a hilarious tour of the snobbishness and hypocrisy of academic circles in Bologna and elsewhere in northern Italy. At the same time, however, Boncompagno shows that the monastic and clerical ideals of spiritual friendship were being replaced by a toughness and even cynicism of worldview based on a society that was ever more urban without becoming more urbane. The competitive element in academic and commercial life lies behind Boncompagno's descriptions of false friendships.

In the ascetic tradition of the late Middle Ages, friendship continued to be a concern, and at times the sweetness of twelfth-century expressions found an echo in spiritual writers usually categorized as 'mystics'. This is the case with Richard Rolle (d. 1349), an english hermit whose writings in both Middle English and Latin were easy to read and had some influence. His thoughts on friendship are by no means profound, but in his clear and direct manner, Rolle insisted on the usefulness and importance of friendship in the life of every good Christian. In Richard Rolle monastic friendship became available for all, whether lay or clerical, so long as they maintained the link to Christ. Friendship was not a distant ideal but a very human and enjoyable practice:

> . . . true friendship cannot exist without mutual enjoyment and pleasant fellowship and helpful conversation. And if this friendship is founded in God's grace, and is wholly his, related and directed to him, it can then be called a holy friendship, and it is very rewarding.[13]

Rolle's optimism about the value of friendship also included bonds between men and women. Despite some concern about sexual temptation, Rolle chose to believe in the spiritual value of such bonds:

> Familiarity between women and men is apt to turn to virtue's disadvantage. And yet that sort of friend-

> ship is not improper, but rewarding, it is practised with a good intention, and is loved for God's sake, and not for carnal delectation. . .There is a certain love that man has for woman and woman for man which none of us is without, not even the saint. It is both natural and 'instituted of God' in origin, and through it we exist, and fit in with each other, and enjoy instinctively each other's company. Indeed this delightful thing has its own pleasures, as for example in mutual conversation, or seemly contact, or a happy marriage.[14]

Rolle indicated that the best friendships in his life had been with women. With men he admitted he had failed to find the type of friend whom he had always sought: 'I would love him as I love my heart, nor would I dream of hiding anything from him'. This friend he asked Jesus to give him in a prayer that is passionate and personal, but Rolle indicated here that he had little hope that such a friend would materialize.

> If only you would send me a companion for my journey, so that the longing could be lightened by his encouragement, and the chain of my sighings loosed!
> . . .I would indeed rejoice to hymn you and live in happiness with the one you had given me with much positive and honest talk. Our very eating, to be sure, would be enjoyed in love. . .[15]

Richard Rolle never explained why he was unable to find this complete friend. His failure may have been due to purely personal idiosyncracies, and yet the problem is one we find elsewhere in the fourteenth and fifteenth centuries: a sense of the limitations, weakness or even impossibility of friendship. Rolle had no spiritual community in which he could seek his friend. For him the life of the ascetic Christian had to be lived as a hermit, even though this by no means required total separation from other human beings. But if we take his desire for close male friendship seriously then Rolle reflects a late medieval failure to accept the twelfth-century link between good friends and good communities.

THE FLIGHT FROM FRIENDSHIP

Richard Rolle believed in spiritual friendship but complained he could not attain it with another man. His life and writings manifest a continuing acceptance of the importance of spiritual friendship among later medieval writers. This point of view, however, was becoming that of a minority. From the early thirteenth century onwards, friendships in the religious life were being looked upon as problematic or even as undesirable. The crisis in friendship is connected with the urbanization of learned culture and the failure of small communities, the monasteries especially, to provide centres of religious and intellectual renewal. In the more competitive world of the city, despite all its charms, the sweet music of intimacy that Richard Rolle sought could no longer have the same resonance.[16]

The Franciscans, even if they were each other's friends, make up the first significant group in the medieval church that openly abandoned the pursuit of spiritual friendship. In the sparse writings of Saint Francis, we have noticed a rejection, however subtle, of the worth of close bonds among the brethren. They were to relate to each other as members of a family, not as special friends. Francis could be a friend when a brother asked him to be such, but he indicated little of the reciprocity or mutuality evident in William of Saint Thierry's descriptions of Bernard as his friend.[17] This interpretation of franciscan aloofness might be looked upon as a harsh one, but it is meant to point out that the new religious order had more important things on its agenda than the celebration in writing of close friendships. For those who described Francis, he had to be distant from all other men, just as another early franciscan saint we met in the last chapter, brother Giles, was seen as a hermit.[18] The idea that often lurks in christian ascetic life—that in seeking God one must get away from men—became quite explicit for the Franciscans:

> . . . . wherever we are or wherever we walk we have
> our cell with us . . .
> The Lord alone, who created the soul, is its friend
> and no one else.[19]

This view of friendship we have also noticed in the *Imitation of Christ*.

This work gained in the later Middle Ages, and continued to maintain afterwards, a tremendous influence on christian forms of piety. Usually ascribed to Thomas à Kempis, it apparently existed in an earlier form in the early decades of the thirteenth century.[20] The message of this powerful spiritual tract is that friends cannot be counted on to do anything except to distract each other from finding the only true friend, Jesus Christ. If you have a 'necessary and beloved friend', then you must 'learn to leave him for the love of God'! This is what the early martyr Saint Lawrence is said to have done in parting from the company of his friend, Pope Sixtus: 'In the love of his creator he overcame the love of creature'.[21]

A man is to concentrate all his being on God: *totum affectum suum in deum trahere*. Peace or trust are not to be placed in human beings.[22] In section after section the author warns against the fragility and brittleness of human bonds. He is sceptical about any closeness with women. A spiritual man is not to be their *familiaris*. In the twelfth century the term *familiaris* had been used to express the bond of spiritual friendship, but now when the *Imitation* applied it, the author meant what we today call the familiarity that breeds contempt. We are to be friends only of the saints and of Christ:

> Make yourself friends now by venerating the saints of God, and by imitating their acts, so that when you depart from this life, they may receive you in the eternal tabernacles.[23]

Richard Rolle had dreamed of going to heaven together with the male friend of whom he fantasized, while the author of the *Imitation* was sure that only by rejecting friends on this earth can we find them in heaven.

This attitude might be called christian stoicism. It had certainly been latent in christian thought ever since the fathers of Late Antiquity began reading Seneca's letters to Lucilius and saw in them elements of christian thought. For Seneca as for his christian descendants, human bonds must not become too pressing or immediate. Distance must be maintained (or in the *Imitation's* words, excessive familiarity was to be avoided). The Christian must be self-sufficient in the sense that he shows love to other people but does not become dependent on them for their love in return. Charity is required, but friendship is not desired, except as a one-way street, a mode of practising charity.

The *Imitation* teaches that each of us is on his own in the world and so we must forge our own individual bond with Christ without reference to any kind of loving or supportive community. If we think we can get a little help from our friends, we are deceiving ourselves and allowing ourselves to be distracted from the hard and necessary path ahead of us to heaven. Such an attitude is a point of departure for the self-reliance and sense of individuality which have been essential elements in modern western culture, especially in its anglo-american forms.

PESSIMISM ABOUT FRIENDSHIP AND COMMUNITY

The new humanism of the fourteenth century, when letterwriting spread and classical authors were seen as worth imitating in good latin style, by no means rejected friendship. Fourteenth century authors, however, no longer showed the same concern for friendship in terms of its place in enriching communities, as twelfth-century monks had done. For a writer such as Boccaccio male friendships were of great importance, and several of his stories develop on the basis of strong male bonds.[25] But when we examine these friendships more carefully, they are usually set in the context of some never-never land of courtly life or of Eastern exoticism, and not in the setting of the italian city-state that Boccaccio knew so well. His most memorable tale about the delights of friendship, that of the merchant Torello and sultan Saladin, combines fascination with Eastern opulence with an implicit criticism of the *ragion di mercatura*, the profit motive, which made it impossible for two merchants ever to let down their guard and to become each other's friends.[26] In Boccaccio's commercial world human bonds are sacrificed to cynical gain. Only the mythical figure of an Eastern potentate could practice friendship for friendship's sake.

Boccaccio was as sceptical about the possibility of friendship as the author of the *Imitation of Christ*. Neither of them believed that personal bonds could do much to improve the content of life. Their responses were different, but both authors had the same point of departure: the impotence of friendship. Christian friendship was foreign to both of them. Boncompagno had harboured a slight hope that a proper understanding of friendship would make possible embracing it in a realistic, attractive and spiritual form. This possibility no longer existed in Boccaccio's world, where friendship belongs in a fantasy land and not in the urban setting that erodes all trust among human beings.

Boccaccio was able to create individualized literary characters who are more believable to us than their typed medieval predecessors. But Boccaccio's 'real people' live in a city where there is no unity between personal bonds and those of community. The classical ideal based on Aristotle and Cicero of a society where good men make good alliances for the benefit of the community has been replaced by a view that virtuous friendships have to be isolated and protected from the realities of politics and power. In this setting we find Petrarch (1304-74), who knew his Cicero well and yet remained far from his model when it came to applying his teachings. Petrarch believed in the value of friendship and was concerned with showing posterity that he had made friends with some of the best men of his day, and especially with Boccaccio. At times Petrarch even played on the theme of christian friendship, as when he sent a treasured copy of Saint Augustine's *Confessions* to a young Carthusian and spoke affectionately of how he had received the book in his own youth from another Carthusian.[27]

Petrarch saw his friends as privileged members of an intimate circle to whom he could flee to escape from the evils of the world around him. Friends existed in order to sustain Petrarch in his literary production. He abandoned the greco-roman bond between friendship and community. He considered the community as an organism too complex, corrupt, difficult and frustrating with which to deal. This conviction appears in Petrarch's justly-famed last letter to Boccaccio, where Petrarch lamented the fact that he had spent so much time in the business of courts and kings. This was, he admits, lost time (*perditos dies voco*).[28] 'I lost seven months in the service of princes', he mourned, but this was not as bad as the time wasted in the preoccupations of adolescence! Even when he visited palaces on his delegation, Petrarch insisted, he had sought out quiet places to rest with his books.[29] He praised the quiet of the scholar in the same way that the *Imitation* lauded that of the ascetic. In both cases the individual must withdraw from the madding crowd in order to make sense of his life—and to be productive.

In Petrarch's description of his life in this remarkable letter, he looked back on his political activities as distractions from what really mattered:

> . . . in all earthly delights, as none is more complete than literary activities, and so none is more long-lasting, none more sweet, none more faithful . . .[30]

Friendship acts mainly as handmaiden to literary pursuits, which provide the basis for companionship and meaning in life that human attachments in themselves cannot provide. Petrarch saw friends as sounding boards for each other's ideas, and as such they could be helpful and necessary. One does not seek out a group of friends for their own sake, nor in order to cope with the evils of the day. Just as in the act of writing, the act of friendship requires withdrawal from community, a declaration of independence, and by no means leads to involvement in society.

Boccaccio had apparently told the aging Petrarch to cut back on his furious literary labours, and the latter answered that he could not imagine doing so, for this was the very stuff of his life:

> My reading and writing, which you order me to reduce, is a light task. Indeed it is a sweet rest which provides forgetfulness from heavy burdens.[31]

Friends could be reached through writing letters, and through this activity they took part in Petrarch's way of life. At the same time, however, they were to be kept at a certain distance. This attitude recalls the stoic ideal which required 'practising' friendship but not really needing it or getting too involved with other people. Petrarch had a great capacity for friendship, but what really mattered to him was his life as a writer.

In such a scholarly world political involvements had no recognized place, even if Petrarch was probably far more politically involved than he wanted to admit to most of his correspondents. But for Petrarch friendship was a very personal matter and not to be expressed in terms of community involvement. Here we see a point of departure for the modern european distinction between private and public life. Cicero also distinguished them, but in his mind they reflected and complemented each other, while Petrarch considered public life as merely a distraction and hindrance from his regular occupation of reading and writing.

Petrarch's description of himself in his letter of friendship to Boccaccio should by no means convince us that he had completely left the medieval tradition. The great master of letters regularly drew on the *ars dictaminis*: he owned and made marginal comments, for example, in a collection of model letters compiled in the thirteenth century.[32] Here as in his use of Cicero, Petrarch was in debt to the past but made use of it in his own way. Petrarch was an artist of words, a renewer of classical culture, the centre of a network of humanist friends. Most of all he wanted to be looked upon as man of letters who was on his own. 'I did it my way', he seems to be saying to Boccaccio in response to the friend's compliment that he, Petrarch, had renewed the study of classical letters in Italy.[33]

We can look at Petrarch as an early modern version of the desert father who withdrew into himself in order to produce the thoughts and sayings that were necessary for his own intellectual and spiritual life. Not accidentally he compared himself and Boccaccio with Anthony and Paul, desert dwellers who had known each other well but who also most of the time had kept a certain distance to one another. The desert fathers saw friendship only as a means to an ascetic end, not as an end in itself. Petrarch likewise used friends to reach his goal, a literary one. This new asceticism could take on christian garb but could also be without it. Christian vocabulary was welcome on occasion, but any ideal of making a christian community had disappeared.

FEAR OF PARTICULAR FRIENDSHIPS

In the late medieval process of cultural secularization, pessimism about the worth and strength of human bonds and a new emphasis on the prowess of the individual contributed to a minimalization of friendship as an ideal. Friendships doubtlessly continued to exist. Petrarch's friends were important for him and he needed them. But friendship was no longer seen as an integral part of the life of the community, as had been the case in the greco-roman tradition and again in medieval monastic life.

In the fifteenth century several brave attempts were made to reform monastic life and to reinvigorate it. If we look at the figures behind this little-known movement, their works show that the practice of friendship no longer was looked upon as an attractive goal in monastic life. We find in fact indications of fear that close personal bonds can give rise to physical expression in homosexual love. Ever since the sayings of the desert fathers had been translated into Latin in the fifth and sixth centuries, Western writers had only rarely openly admitted a fear of homosexual behaviour in the monasteries. A few cistercian decisions from the General Chapter in the late twelfth century and the early thirteenth indicate that there may have been a reaction against the open affectivity of some monks. In the monasteries as a whole however, we find no consistent reaction against 'gay clerical culture' which John Boswell finds elsewhere in the last decades of the twelfth century.[34] This may well be because it always had been obvious to monks that homosexual behaviour and spiritual friendship had nothing to do with each other. Here, however, we are arguing from what the texts do not say. They betray no open concern that close bonds of friendship would lead monks into sexual relationships.

An aristocratic bishop of Venice, Lawrence Justinian (d. 1455) was worried about such a development from friendship to sex when he wrote a treatise on the monastic life (*De disciplina et perfectione monasticae conversationis*). He was convinced that attractive friendships of the cloister easily can turn into homosexual involvement:

> How many are seduced and seduce under the appearance of charity. How many perish when love is feigned. Alas, how many live at first purely and without deception, then are slowly infected by excessive familiarity, and then have fallen down the huge cliff, all the more wretchedly, all the more filthily! For under the excuse of true charity the love of sensuality enters into the lives of such people.[35]

Lawrence Justinian chartered this process, from the attraction of the eyes to desire to be alone with the friend, followed by attacks of jealousy and finally the pursuit of physical intimacy. This development threatens not only the monastic vocation of the two persons involved but also the discipline of the cloister as a whole. Friends who involve themselves in each other in such a way do not respect silence, prayer or obedience, Justinian asserted. They undermine the entire community. He concluded that 'this type of assiduous and private contact is to be forbidden'. Even if it has no sexual element, it is not desirable because of the 'scandal' it gives to other members of the community.[36]

Lawrence Justinian conceded the worth of having companions, but he looked upon close, individual friendships as a danger to the community. Justinian provided an explicit monastic warning against a progression from close personal bonds to sexual relationships and the ruin of community life. Centuries before, John Cassian had warned against the conspiracies that can be cloaked with the name of friendship, but now Lawrence Justinian specifically pointed to sexual danger in such associations.

A descendant of Lawrence Justinian's family, Paul Justinian (1476-1528), spent a large part of his life in reforming a camaldolese house and in trying to bring his friends there.[37] Paul carried on earlier attempts at monastic reform and used as his model the hermit saint and churchman of the eleventh century, Peter Damian. By seeking out his friends, Paul Justinian admitted he needed them, but by bringing them to solitude and silence, he showed that the expression of friendship bonds in his life had to be restricted and transformed. As Jean Leclercq has put it so well, Justinian's life was divided between the desire to live a solitary life and the desire 'not to be alone there': *chercher la solitude et la peupler*.[38] The solution Paul Justinian reached is indicative of an age when affective bonds of daily life, so important to Bernard and to other twelfth-century monastic figures, no longer were seen as fruitful. Friendship was acknowledged and then put into a life-long state of abeyance.

Saint Francis de Sales (1567-1622) summarizes in his *Introduction à la Vie Devôte* this development in which friendship was seen as unnecessary or even as dangerous to the life of a religious community. He compared life in the world to the ascent of a steep mountain where we have to be able to take a friend by the hand in order not to slip. In a religious community, he claimed, we are on a flat plain and are surrounded by those who can help us, and so we do not need special friends:

> And as those who travel on the plain do not need to give each other a hand, but those who are on difficult and slippery paths ask one another for help so they can proceed more securely, so it is that those who are in religious life do not need particular friendships, while those who are in the world need to get assurance and to help each other, amid all the difficult passages they have to pass through.[39]

In simple, clear French appears a warning that would dominate the view of friendship in coming centuries: the spectre of particular friendships, a phrase that may have appeared earlier than in Francis de Sales but now was made prominent because of the book's tremendous success. It was outsold in catholic lands only by the Bible itself and our old friend, the *Imitation of Christ*.

Of all the prominent counter-reformation figures, Francis de Sales is perhaps the one best remembered for his friends and friendships, especially with Jeanne de Chantal.[40] But his recommendations did not always follow his own experience. Just as Paul Justinian, he used his authority as bishop and church reformer to provide new guidelines for the religious life, and here he saw no place for the friendships so important in his own life. Long after the friendships of Francis de Sales were half-forgotten, spiritual directors would continue to warn against the pitfalls of 'particular friendships.'

The phrase is logically corrupt, for it is a tautology. Every friendship is in itself a particular choice of another individual. But the very vagueness of the expression and its lack of definition made it serviceable for generations that were concerned about the possibility of a sexual element in friendship. The phrase could be used in speaking to young people in order to imply this possibility without ever being specific. Such a warning never made quite clear the exact 'danger'. The question of human affections was limited to that of sexual attachments, an association that medieval writers on friendship had not made. Even in postwar France, the american writer James Baldwin picked up the phrase 'les goûts particuliers' as an euphemism for homosexual preferences.[41] The word 'particular' had taken on a homosexual resonance. Clerical culture had lent its all-purpose expression to polite french society.

Saint Francis de Sales provided several careful definitions of virtuous friendship, but the phrase that was remembered in clerical and monastic folklore was 'particular friendship'. It implied both conspiracies against the authority of the abbot, against which John Cassian had warned, and the possibility of sexual attachments. At the same time monks and nuns nevertheless continued to be each other's friends regardless of all the warnings.[42] Human bonds have a marvellous way of disregarding the ideologies devised to strangle them.

The last full manifestation of a friendship celebrated and pursued in the religious life appears in the writings of Saint Teresa of Avila (1515-82), especially in her letters to her confessors. Of these Father Gracián is the most memorable, because of the almost passionate expressions of affection which Teresa sent him. She wanted to be with him as much as possible, she said, to kiss his hands, to tell him all the latest gossip of court life and church intrigues, and to defend her actions in spreading her group of religious houses.[43] Teresa combined politics and personal friendships in a way that recalls both Cicero and Bernard. The classical-medieval aristotelian practice of friendship becomes a living reality in her correspondence.

Teresa of Avila's experience of friendship, and especially her way of insisting on the importance of friendships in her life, point more to the continuity of medieval monastic culture in Spain than to any counter-reformation opening to this form of spiritual life. Teresa was faithful to the passions of her own life and in her autobiography remembered the bad friendships as well as the good ones of her early life.[44] Her great curiosity about other people meant that she insisted on letters in the same way that Anselm's friends at Canterbury in the eleventh century had required them. But Teresa even asked to see letters that her friends had been sending to each other. She had to know everything about them. As she wrote in 1576 to her beloved and beleaguered Gracián:

> Oh what a good time I have had today! Father Mariano sent me all the letters your Paternity had written him! You need not tell him to send me them: he is doing so because I asked him to, and, although they come late, they are a great comfort to me.[45]

Teresa made herself the centre of a network of friendship bonds where every letter counted and where one friend could be offended when he did not hear from her as often as another friend did:

> . . . I am told [Father Fray Antonio] is very much upset to find how many letters I write and how seldom I write to him. Oh Jesus, how wonderful it is when two souls understand each other! They never lack anything to say and never grow weary. . .[46]

Teresa seldom lacked a great deal to say, for she had so much to tell about herself, her efforts to further the interests of her convents, and her disapproval of political developments. She made no distinction in her letters between pious spiritual thoughts and cold political observations. Like Bernard, she lived in a world which held together because of the community she had made. Teresa combined affectivity with a fierce determination to support this community and all her friends who belonged to it.

If any explicit expression of friendship continued to manifest itself in monastic and religious life beyond the Reformation in roman catholic Europe, it was that between men and women rather than between men. Even the sombre Armand de Rancé, the founder of the Trappists, whose reputation is getting a new look thanks to the work of A.J. Krailsheimer, wrote affectionate letters to nuns in which personal friendship and not only spiritual counselling is evident.[47] Fear and hesitation about friendship seem to have been concentrated mainly on concern about homosexual bonds, but here more work needs to be done on manifestations of friendship in seventeenth- and eighteenth-century religious life.

MODERN FRIENDSHIP

Continuing interest in friendship, but as a secular phenomenon, appears in the writings of the philosopher Montaigne (1533-92). His essay on friendship shows hesitation about the possibility of friendship in a world of intrigue and falsity.[48] Like Petrarch, Montaigne cultivated his friends not as allies in a community network but as sharers of his solitude, comforters in time of need, and supporters in the solace of the intellectual life. His essay was written on the death of his best friend, whose loss he felt he never would get over or be able to compensate for. Montaigne remembered his Cicero in pointing out the uniqueness of friendship and its rarity in history, but he went further and made true friendship into an almost unattainable goal. In the twelfth century the Cistercians had looked upon friendship as available for any good monk, while in the sixteenth century it receded into the distance as a prize only for the highly learned and very sensitive man.

Here, as with the fourteenth-century humanists, Cicero was well known for his teaching on friendship but was hardly followed in his political dimension. For Montaigne friendship had nothing to do with the state, the community, or any common effort to change the conditions of society. It served as a refuge for the individual rather than as a point of departure for involvement in any community. In writing of the devotion that Caius Blossius in ancient Rome had shown to Caius Gracchus, Montaigne recalled how Blossius had said that if Gracchus asked him to set fire to the temples of Rome, he would have obeyed him. Blossius would have done so because he was the friend of Gracchus:

> They were friends before they were citizens, friends to one another before they were either friends or enemies to their country, or friends to ambition and revolt. Having absolutely given themselves up to one another, each had absolute control over the reins of the other's inclinations.[49]

When friendship in this manner comes absolutely first, we have arrived at a modern practice emphasizing the passionate and individual element in friendship and have left behind the classical-medieval ideal that considered friendship a personal bond integrated into commitment to the good of the community. Montaigne's uncompromising view provides a foundation for the twentieth-century Cambridge writer E.M. Forster's perhaps better-known assertion that if he had to choose between betraying his friend or betraying his country, he hoped he would have the guts to betray his country![51] For Aristotle, Aelred, and Thomas Aquinas, such a choice would have seemed self-contradictory, for they insisted on friends being made and kept as part of involvement in a community. For classical-medieval writers, the two allegiances of friendship and community belonged together. For Montaigne, however, as for E.M. Forster, friendship became a supreme value that sometimes had to be chosen exclusively of all others. This radical isolation of friendship helps explain why Montaigne claimed that all earlier writings on friendship seemed cold and lifeless to him. In the face of his own emotions for his dead friend, 'even the treatises which antiquity has left us on the subject seem flat to me in comparison with my own feeling'.[51] Montaigne's problem lay not only in his keen sense of loss but also in his view of friendship as an emotional involvement cut off from the world of rational choices in which the classical and medieval worlds had placed close human bonds.

In Montaigne friendship lost its place as a participant in the harmony and proportion of the good community in which friendship had been able to share in classical Rome and in twelfth-century monastic life. Montaigne, who in reality led an active life with political involvements, wrote about friendship as a lonely pursuit. He wanted to be a *homme de lettres* as Petrarch had been, commenting on the conditions of his time, writing poetry to his intimates, and harbouring boundless affection for one friend. In Montaigne we are only one step away from the nineteenth-century cult of romantic love which is at odds with a repressive social structure from which lovers have to flee.

When friendship becomes something attainable only for the few, when community is seen as either undesirable or all-encompassing, and when the salvation of the individual is seen in totally individual terms rather than in the context of a supportive community, we have left the classical-medieval synthesis and have entered the modern european world.[52] In the modern separation of the loves of the individual from the life of the community, private and public life no longer connect. It becomes necessary to follow E. M. Forster and choose one loyalty rather than another.

The recent appearance and enthusiastic reception of the study, *Habits of the Heart; Individualism and Commitment in American Life*, shows a contemporary interest in how individuals affect their surroundings by their beliefs about themselves and their actions in terms of community.[53] At the same time, modern monks, who see themselves more than ever as descendents not of seventeenth-century silence and enclosure but as heirs of twelfth-century affectivity, are seeking to open their way of life to young people for whom the experience of friendship is a necessary part of existence rather than something that has to be left behind in the world.[54]

Looking back over the experiences and modes of expression that have characterized community and individual life and loves, we can return to the words of Anselm of Canterbury:

> Wherever you are being loved, you cannot be, but wherever you are, you can be loved and be good.[55]

Anselm was writing to an unhappy monk at Canterbury who did not understand why he could not return to Bec to be with his friend Anselm, even though Anselm had claimed to love him greatly. Anselm's maxim was anchored in the teaching of the Rule of Saint Benedict on obedience and humility, as well as stability. These came first, but the structure they provided enabled a monk to participate in a community where love could be shown and where friendships were possible and even desirable. In this scheme social structure is not the enemy but the ally of human closeness. Since nineteenth-century romanticism, we have seen 'society' as the culprit in the separation of human beings from each other. In Anselm's mind, the society of the monastery was precisely what was necessary for monks who were each other's friends to grow and develop in these friendships.

The isolation of personal friendship from community life that took place in the late medieval and early modern world has led since the nineteenth century to a denial of the social and political dimension in human bonds. Bernard of Clairvaux insisted on this dimension, and yet generations of students have asked how he possibly could have been a good abbot and yet have traversed Europe in order to influence events. Bernard's answer would have been that he owed it to his friends to use the power he had at his command: to spread the Order, to bring more monks into it, and to secure its position in the world of his day.[56]

Monastic friendship may have been merely a peripheral cultural phenomenon that today is all but forgotten, despite increasing interest in the general subject of friendship.[57] But the experience of Anselm, Aelred and Bernard, as well as that of the lesser figures in their vicinity, points out that the great divide in our culture comes not between classical and medieval worlds but between medieval and modern times. Thomas Aquinas could use the language of Aristotle in defining friendship. Aelred could turn to Cicero. But when the *Imitation of Christ* insisted that the saintly man give up his friend in the world in order to become a friend of God, the author was making a distinction that would have seemed unnecessary and even perverse to many twelfth-century monks. When Francis de Sales distinguished between friendships among the laity and particular friendships among the religious and warned against these, he replaced the medieval belief in personal bonds as part of community life by open suspicion of close friendships.

The writings of Thomas à Kempis and Francis de Sales may have only limited influence in our own day, but for centuries they provided ammunition for confessors, vocational directors, and school teachers. In this sombre world view, which could easily revive in the coming years, we are alone with God, hermits in the desert of modern life, even within the religious community. Here we have come a long way from the twelfth-century synthesis which made the monastery into a paradise, a garden of friends, whose very existence provoked and transformed the world of which monastic community formed an integral part.[58]

NOTES

INTRODUCTION

1. *Dictionnaire de Spiritualité (DS)* (Paris, 1937) I.: 500 (G. Vansteenberghe).

2. *Laelius De amicitia* 6,20: *Est enim amicitia nihil aliud nisi omnium diuinarum humanarumque rerum cum beneuolentia et caritate consensio*. . . . My translation builds on that of Michael Grant in *Cicero: On the Good Life* (Penguin Classics, 1971) p. 187, but is more compact.

3. Gregory, *XL Homiliarum in Evangelia* II, *Homil.* 27.4= PL 176:1207: *Amicus enim quasi animi custos vocatur.* Isidore: *Etymologiarum sive Originum Libre XX*, ed. W. M. Lindsay (Clarndon Press: Oxford 1911) in Liber X, 'De Vocabulis': Amicus, per derivationem, quasi animi custos. Isidore also uses the image of the friend as hook or bond, one that was much less widespread: . . *amicus ab hamo, id est, a catena caritatis; unde et hami quod teneant.*

4. As Francesco Alberoni, *L'amicizia* (Garzanti: Milano, 1984) ch. 8:4: 'Una amicizia che non si reciproca è un non senso' (a friendship that is not reciprocal is nonsense).

5. Peter von Moos, *Consolatio* (Münstersche Mittelalter-Schriften 3: (Wilhelm Fink Verlag: München, 1971), a massive study for which I have great respect but which ends in reducing medieval writings to literary forms and clichés.

6. Liber I Regum (1 Samuel) 18:1: *Et factum est cum complesset loqui ad Saul, anima Ionathae conglutinata est animae David, et dilexit eum Ionathas quasi animam suam* (in the Vulgate): 'When he had finished speaking to Saul, the soul of Jonathan was knit to the soul of David, and Jonathan loved him as his own soul.'

7. 1 Sam 18:3: *Inierunt autem David et Ionathas foedus; diligebat enim eum quasi animam suam.*

8. *In Samuelem* prophetam allegorica expositio, PL 91:625: *Inierunt Christus et Ecclesia foedus mutuae charitatis et pacis. Diligebat enim eum ecclesia in membris suis perfectioribus, ita ut mori esset parata pro illo*. . .

9. 2 Sam. 1:26, which appears thus in the American Revised Standard Version: 'I am distressed for you, my brother Jonathan; very pleasant have you been to me; your love to me was wonderful, passing the love of women.' The sentence from the Vulgate, 'As a mother loves her only son, so I was loving you' is not included. The image of the friend as mother comes to play a central role in medieval spirituality, as shown powerfully in Caroline Walker Bynum, *Jesus as Mother* (University of California Press, 1982).

10. A phrase used repeatedly as in Sam. 18:1 and 20:17: *Et addidit Ionathas deierare David, eo quod diligeret illum: sicut enim animam saum ita diligebat eum.*

11. Despite Alberoni's interpretation of the bond (not 4 above) as '. . . probabilmente, un amore unilaterale non corrisposto' (p. 73).

12. See Michel Foucault, *Histoire de la Sexualité* 1: 'La volonté de savoir' (Gallimard, 1976) who sees the 'discovery' of the 'homosexual' in 1870 as the result of a nineteenth century concern with peripheral forms of sexuality. All this is part of a modern (post seventeenth century) discourse about sex, one in which the Middle Ages did not engage.

13. As 2 Sam. 3:12—*Misit ergo Abner nuntios ad David pro se dicentes: Cuius est terra? et ut loquerentur: Fac mecum amicitias, et erit manus mea tecum et reducam ad te universum Israël.* Also 1 Macc. 12:1: *Et vidit Ionathas, quia tempus eum iuvat, et elegit viros et misit eos Romam statuere et renovare cum eis amicitiam.*

14. Ps. 138:17: *Mihi autem nimis honorificati sunt amici tui, Deus; nimis confortatus est principatus eorum.* (The Revised Standard version has a totally different expression here, with nothing about friendship. Note that the Psalm numbers are the Vulgate enumeration.)

15. From *De amicitia spirituali* 2:26, trans. by Mary Eugenia Laker, *Spiritual Friendship* (Cistercian Publications, 1974) 76

16. *In Ecclesiasticum libri decem*, esp. the second book, ch. 1 and 2, PL109:795-8. Rhabanus uses Gregory's definition, col. 797: *Amicus dicitur quasi animi custos.* He is also highly dependent on Cicero, *De amicitia.* For Rhabanus's other works on friendship, see my section on the Carolingians in my chapter on early medieval friendship.

17. After a lecture on friendship to the cistercian monks of Holy Trinity Abbey in Utah in April 1986, one of them kindly pointed out to me the evidence for a close relationship between Paul and Timothy in 2 Tim 1:4 and in the greetings at the end of the letter. There is a tone of intimacy here, but as always in Paul, it is subordinated to the good advice in the body of the letter, advice of a general kind.

18. The classic study is that of L. Dugas, *L'Amitié antique* (Paris, 1894 and 1914). Also O. Gigon, *Grundprobleme der antiken Philosophie* (Bern and München, 1959), esp. pp. 302-14. I have also made use of J.-C. Fraisse, *Philia: La notion d' amitié dans la philosophie antique* (Paris, 1974), which has a rich bibliography and is excellent in tracing the theoretical structure of friendship but contains little about the actual practice of friendship.

19. For some of the relevant passages in english translation, John Burnet, *Early Greek Philosophy* (Meridian: Cleveland and New York, 1965) 207-212 (fragments § 20, 26, 35-36). See also, G. S. Kirk and J. E. Raven, *The Presocratic Philosophers* (Cambridge, 1957 and 1975) 326-31 and 345-46.

20. *De am.* (note 2 ABOVE) 7,24: . . .*quae in rerum natura totoque mundo constarent quaeque mouerentur, ea contrahere amicitiam, dissipare discordiam. Atque hoc quidem omnes mortales et intellegunt et re probant.*

21. I have used W. D. Ross's translation, *The Works of Aristotle,* Vol. IX: *Ethica Nichomachea* and will quote according to the standard paragraph sections he gives. For the Greek text, see the Loeb Classical Library edition, ed. H. Rackham.

22. Here the classic work is now K. J. Dover, *Greek Homosexuality* (Duckworth: London, 1979). I should like to thank Sir Kenneth Dover for a valuable conversation on the greek concept of *philia.* See also 'Pederasty in Classical Education' in H. I. Marrou, *A History of Education in Antiquity* (Sheed and Ward: London, 1956) 26-35.

23. Plato *Symposium,* ed. by Sir Kenneth Dover (Cambridge: London 1980), with a superb introduction. I use the Penguin Classics translation by W. Hamilton (Harmondsworth, 1951 and later).

24. Augustine seems to have been a key figure in this development. See Henri Marrou's *Saint Augustin et la fin de la culture antique* (Paris, 1937).

25. For a very readable translation and a helpful commentary, David Bolotin, *Plato's Dialogue on Friendship* (Cornell University Press: Ithaca and London, 1979).

26. This is nr. xxiii of the so-called Vatican Sayings, trans. Russel M. Geer, *Epicurus: Letters, Principal Doctrines and Vatican Sayings* (Bobbs-Merrill Co.: Library of Liberal Arts, 1964) 67

27. *De am.* 13.46.

28. Vatican Sayings 52 (note 25 above).

29. P.A. Brunt, '*Amicitia* in the late Roman Republic,' *Proceedings of the Cambridge Philological Society* N.S. II 191 (1965), 1-20.

30. Cicero claims that he is not going to deal with the problem of flattery because it does not pertain to friendship but he returns to it several times, thus indicating that it was a real problem in his social situation: *De am.* 24,88 and 26,97 and 98: 'Nulla est igitur haec amicitia, cum alter uerum audire non uult, alter ad mentiendum paratus est.' Finally in 26,100 Cicero admits: 'Sed nescio quo pacto ab amicitiis perfectorum hominum. . . . ad leues amicitias deflexit oratio.' But this *deflexio,* or going off on a tangent, is typical of the *De am.* as a whole, even if there is a certain structure in the essay.

31. One should give the friend as much assistance as one can provide and as much as he can bear; 20,73: 'Tantum autem cuique tribuendum, primum, quantum ipse efficere possis, dende etiam, quantum ille, quem diligas atque adiuues, sustinere.'

32. *De am. sp.* (note 15 above), Prologue; p. 45 in Laker.

33. *De am.* 3,10, trans. Grant pp. 180-81.

34. *Catilina* 20:4: *Idem uelle atque idem nolle ea demum firma amicitia est.* See Beryl Smalley, 'Sallust in the Middle Ages', R.R. Bolgar, ed., *Classical Influences on European Culture,* A.D. 500-1500 (Cambridge, 1971) 165-175, esp. 170. For a general treatment of how the classical heritage was maintained and exploited see L.D. Reynolds and N. G. Wilson, *Scribes and Scholars: A Guide to the Transmission of Greek and Latin Literature* (Second Edition: Clarendon Press, Oxford, 1974), especially ch. 3, 'The Latin West'.

35. Odes 3, line 8.

36. *Seneca ad Lucilium Epistulae Morales,* trans. Richard Gummere (Loeb Classical Library: Cambridge, Mass. and London, 1967) I, ep. 9. I use Gummere's translation.

37. *Ibid.*, p.45.

38. L.D. Reynolds, *The Medieval Tradition of Seneca's Letters* (Oxford, 1965).

39. See my chapter on late antiquity and especially on the tradition of the egyptian desert.

40. Seneca *Ep. mor.* I, 9, p. 55.

41. *Ibid.*, p. 52: *Nihilominus cum sit amicorum amantissimus. . . . saepe praeferat, omne intra se bonum terminabit.*

42. *S. Benedicti Regula,* ed. Gregorio Penco (Firenze, 1958), ch. 73. English translation by Anthony C. Meisel and M. L. del Mastro, *The Rule of Saint Benedict* (Image Books, Doubleday, New York, 1975), p. 106: 'Whoever you are, if you wish to follow the path to God, make use of this little Rule for beginners.'

43. This conviction is found not only in Seneca but also in Marcus Aurelius, as in his *Meditation* Bk. 5:33 (trans. in Gateway Edition, Henry Regnery Co. [Chicago, 1956] 59): 'Soon, very soon, thou wilt be ashes, or a skeleton, and either a name or not even a name, but name is sound and echo. And the things which are much valued in life are empty and rotten and trifling, and like little dogs biting one another, and little children quarrelling, laughing, and then straightaway weeping. . . . But to have good repute amidst such a world as this is an empty thing.'

44. *Regula,* Prologus (note 41 above), Penco, p. 10: *Constituenda est ergo nobis dominici scola servitii.* See Adalbert de Vogüé's magnificent exposition of this phrase and its implications in *The Rule of Saint Benedict: A Doctrinal and Spiritual Commentary* (Cistercian Publications: Kalamazoo, 1983), 25-30 esp. p. 27: 'The "school of the Lord's

service'' is therefore a complex metaphor which makes the monastery appear both as a teaching establishment and as a corps of soldiers or civil servants.'

45. *The Four Loves* (Collins, Fount Paperbacks: London 1960, 1985) p. 75.

46. As in Denis de Rougemont, *Love in the Western World,* first published in English in 1940 and reissued many times since (Harper and Row: New York, 1974). This book has had an immense influence on contemporary thinking about the medieval conception of love. Rougemont's ideas betray an almost total lack of understanding for medieval life and culture but have gained acceptance in our own age because of their appeal to mid-twentieth-century scepticism about the power and possiblity of spiritual love in human life.

47. In the mind of Caesarius of Heisterbach, a cistercian writer in about 1220, it was the prayers of his monks that kept the world from ending. The story was taken over by the Dominicans to their advantage. See *Dialogus Miraculorum* (ed. Joseph Strange, Cologne 1851 and reissued New Jersey 1966), dist. 12, ch. 58.

48. Here I think C.S. Lewis does not sufficiently point out the difficulty of combining friendship with charity.

49. One thinks again of the words of Christ in John 15:14; 'You are my friends, if you do what I order you.'

50. I, col. 500-530. For a more recent treatment, see Jean Leclercq's excellent entry 'Amicizia nella vita religiosa' in *Dizionario degli Instituti de Perfezione* (Edizioni Paoline: Roma, 1974) 1: col. 516-20.

51. Henri Dominique Noble, *L' Amitié avec Dieu:* Essais sur la vie spirituelle d'apres Saint Thomas d' Aquin (Desclée de Brouwer: Paris, 1932), esp. p. 497.

52. *Die Lehre von der Gottesfreundschaft in der Scholastik und Mystik des 12. und 13. Jahrhunderts* (Augsburg, 1928).

53. I am grateful to Chrysogonus Waddell, Trappist, Kentucky, and to Anthony Kenny, Balliol College, Oxford, for these recollections.

54. 'L' amitié dans les lettres au moyen âge', *Revue du Moyen-Age Latin* 1 (Lyon, 1945) 391-410.

55. *L' Amour des lettres et le désir de Dieu* was first published in Paris in 1957 and in English in 1961. The newest edition is by Fordham University Press, New York, 1982. See Leclercq's section on letter writing, p. 181.

56. From the essay, 'What I Believe,' In *Two Cheers for Democracy* (Penguin, 1965), p. 76.

57. *Ibid.*, pp. 76-77.

58. *L' amicizia* (Garzanti, Milano, 1984), p. 85: '. . . ha sempre diffidato dell'amicizia'.

59. *Friends and Friendship in the Monastic Tradition* (Cuernavaca, Mexico, 1970) esp. ch. 19, 1-24.

60. *Saint Anselm and his Biographer* (Cambridge, 1966). New edition 1986.

61. *The Life of Ailred of Rievaulx* by Walter Daniel (Clarendon Press; Oxford Medieval Texts, republished 1978).

62. 'Love, friendship and sex in the eleventh century: The experience of Anselm', *Studia Theologica* 28 (Oslo, 1974) 111-152.

63. *The Prayers and Meditations of Saint Anselm* (Harmondsworth, 1973 and later).

64. Dissertatio ad Lauream. Pontificia Facultas Theologica. Instititum Spiritualitatis Teresianum. Romae. I am very grateful to Paul Conner for sending me a copy of this work. See also his *Celibate Love* (Huntington, Indiana, 1978).

65. 'The Virtue of Friendship in Monastic Tradition - An Introduction,' *Tjurunga.* An Australasian Benedictine Review (October 1983) 21-35 I am grateful to Jean

Leclercq, who here as in so many other cases has supplied me with material that I would ordinarily not have been able to make use of; Basil Pennington, from the Trappist community at Spencer Massachusetts, has also sent me an unpublished article for which I am grateful, 'Friendship in the Monastic Life'.

66. 'Friendship and Love,' *Irish Theological Quarterly* (1983—84) 35-47. In the same spirit is Wilhelm Nyssen's chapter 'Amicitia Spiritualis' in *Irdisch hab' ich dich gewollt* (Occidens 6; Spee Verlag Trier, 1982) 217—33. For friendship in the Buddhist tradition, see Edmund F. Perry, 'Can Buddhists and Christians Live Together as Kalyanamitta?', *Buddhist Studies in Honour of Walpola Rahula* (Gordon Fraser, London and Vimamsa, Sri Lanka, 1980). I am indebted to David Bell, Memorial University of Newfoundland, for sending me this article.

67. McEvoy, 'Friendship and Love,' p. 42. The subject of friendship among women in the religious life will be given only a passing treatment in this book, for the available sources are so limited and scarce (and almost all supplied by men). So far the only studies I know are: Juan Maria de la Torre, 'La amistad en la vida monástica femenina. un camino de las amantes de Dios', *Mujeres del Absoluto* El Monacato Femenino. Historia, Instituciones, Actualidad, dir. Fray Clemente de la Serna Gonzalez (Abadia de Silos, Burgos, Spain, 1986) and Karen Glente, *Hellige Kvinder* (Middelaldercentret, K/obenhavns Universitet, Denmark, 1985). This book concerns for the most part the image of woman in their male biographers, but in the last chapter, which deals with the biographies of nuns written by the nuns at Unterlinden, Karen Glente provides a perspective of a community where there were individual friendships. At the Medieval Studies Congress at Kalamazoo in May 1986, Jane Schulenburg of the University of Wisconsin presented a lecture on male-female friendships in the early Middle Ages, and I look forward to the results of her research.

68. *Friendship. A Study in Theological Ethics* (University of Notre Dame Press: Notre Dame, London, 1981).

69. University of Chicago Press, Chicago and London, 1980 and later.

CHAPTER ONE
THE WISDOM OF THE EASTERN FATHERS

1. In what follows I am dependent on the interpretations and references which Peter Brown has generously provided for me in conversation and letters, as well as in his articles and books, especially *The Making of Late Antiquity* (Harvard, 1978) and 'The Rise and Function of the Holy Man in Late Antiquity,' *Journal of Roman Studies* 61 (1971) 80-101.

2. *Sancti Pontii Meropii Paulini Nolani Carmina*, ed. Guilelmus de Hartel, CSEL 30 (Wien, 1894) esp. carmina x and xi, pp. 24-42.

3. For a treatment of the poems in terms of friendship, see Pierre Fabre, *Saint Paulin de Nole et l'amitié chrétienne,* Bibliothéque des Ecoles Françaises d'Athenés et de Rome 167 (Paris, 1949) 155-66.

4. Boswell (1980) p. 133, missed the point completely. He seems to have been strongly influenced by Helen Waddell's introduction to some of the poems in *Mediaeval Latin Lyrics* and has no reference to Fabre's more careful evaluation of the poems in terms of the conversion of Paulinus to Christianity (note 3 above). The latin text of the

poem (included in Waddell, p. 46) is: *videbo corde, mente complectar pia, ubique praesentem mihi.*

5. Peter Brown, *The Cult of the Saints: Its Rise and Function in Latin Christianity* (Chicago, 1982), 53-4.

6. Paulinus *Carmina* (note 2 above) 11:18-19.

7. *Sancti Pontii Meropii Paulini Nolani Epistola*, ed. Guilelmus de Hartel, CSEL 29 (Vienna, 1894), ep 1.5: *Sit licet frater et amicus iunctior tibi dextera tua et carior lumine, si alienus est et inimicus in Christo, sit tibi ut extraneus et ut publicanus. Abscidatur ut inutilis dextera a corpore tuo, qui tibi in Christi corpore non cohaeret. . . .*

8. The Greek *Apopthegmata Patrum* are contained in PG 65: 71-439. I use the excellent translation by Benedicta Ward, *The Sayings of the Desert Fathers* (Mowbrays: London and Oxford, Cistercian Publications: Kalamazoo, 1975). The collection will be referred to as *G*, with the name of the father and the number of the saying. In this case G Olympios 2.

9. G Paphnutius 4.

10. Evelyne Patlagean, *Recherches sur les Pauvres et la Pauvreté dans l'Empire Romain d'Orient* (IV-VII Siècles) (Lille, 1974) 276-91.

11. *Ibid.*, p. 295.

12. G Carion 2. See Philip Rousseau, 'Blood-Relationships among Early Eastern Ascetics', *Journal of Theological Studies*, n.s. 23 (Oxford, 1972) 135-44: 'Close association between relatives seems to have taken place especially at the beginning of ascetical careers, or at moments of crisis and disruption'. A remarkable amount of evidence for the strength of family ties seen in a positive manner has been gleaned from papyrus letter collections by F. Joxe, 'Le Christianisme et l'Evolution des sentiments familiaux dans les lettres privées sur papyrus', *Acta Antiqua Academiae Scientiarum Hungaricae* 7 (1959) 411-20. Joxe uses the expressions of tenderness and affection in order to counter the traditional assertion that the rise of Christianity created a new tone of love in family life. For Joxe kinship warmth was already present in pagan culture. Aside from this polemic, the evidence presented here also shows that in *both* pagan and christian Egypt of Late Antiquity, family bonds were seen and interpreted by family members as being a central part of their existences.

13. For the question of how the sayings were collected and to what extent they represent the wisdom of single fathers, see Philip Rousseau, *Ascetics, Authority, and the Church* (Oxford, 1978) 11-14.

14. In the rivalry between Pachomius and his older brother John, Pachomius eventually got his way and turned an eremitical life into a cenobitic one. See the First Greek Life of Pachomius, 15, trans. by Armand Veilleux in *Pachomian Koinonia* I, Cistercian Studies 45 (Kalamazoo, Michigan, 1980) p. 307. To be referred to as *V. Pach.* G 1.

15. G An Abba of Rome, 2.

16. G Carion 2.

17. This is the finding of Derwas Chitty, *The Desert a City* (Blackwell, Oxford, 1966) 66-7, though I find it too easy to follow the judgment of the successors of the early fathers that their generation showed a decline from the high standards of their predecessors.

18. Homosexuality in G: Eudemon 1; John the Dwarf 4; Isaac priest of the Cells 4, 5; Carion 2, 3; Matoes 11; Poemen 176. Breaking family bonds: Cassian 8; Mark 3; Poemen 2, 3, 5, 7, 76, 180; Paphnutius 4: Sisoes 10. To the latter category could easily be added a great number of instances dealing with separation from one's neighbour, which includes family, and from worldly friendships, which are not indicated to have any sexual content.

19. Boswell (1980) pp. 159-60. The text is Basil's *Sermo asceticus* in PG 32: 880, most easily accessible in translation in *Saint Basil: Ascetical Works*, trans. Sister M. Monica Wagner (Fathers of the Church: New York, 1950) pp. 23-4.

20. The two sins are also linked in the Greek *Sayings*, as John the Dwarf 4: 'He who gorges himself and talks with a boy has already in his thought committed fornication with him'.

21. Greek version in PG 26:835-978. Latin version by Evagrius of Antioch, PL 73:15-70.

22. Cap. 59:, PL 73: 167 *Verba finierat, et osculantibus se discipulis, extendens paululum pedes, mortem laetus aspexit; ita ut ex hilaritate vultus ejus, angelorum sanctorum, qui ad perferendam animam ejus descenderant, praesentia nosceretur. His intuens, tanquam amicos videret, animam exhalavit*. . . .

23. *Ibid.* cap. 15, col. 135:. . .*si mutuis se invicem fratres sermonibus consolarentur*. . . .

24. G Anthony 9.

25. G Anthony 13, 27.

26. G Arsenius 13.

27. G Arsenius 32.

28. G Arsenius 34.

29. G Arsenius 15.

30. G Cyrus 1.

31. In a conversation with Armand Veilleux at his monastery in Conyers, Georgia, in the spring of 1986, we discussed several aspects of this chapter. Dom Armand was kind enough to point out that Arsenius characterizes the 'foreign' group that came to Egypt and became 'super-ascetic'. Arsenius is not typical for the egyptian monks themselves, but I would still contend that he makes explicit an extremism implicit in the very idea of the desert's call.

32. G Abba of Rome 1

33. *Ibid.*, also found in Patrologia Graeca 65:390:. . . factus est illius amicus et frequenter ad eum proficiscebatur, utilitatis causa. . . .The greek phrase for the formation of friendship leaves nothing in doubt: *Kai egeneto autou philos.*

34. Another instance is G Poemen 4, contained in the Latin Systematic Collection, PL 73:974.

35. G Ars. 38.

36. *Sayings* (note 7 above) p. 137.

37. G Poemen 2.

38. See Benedicta Ward, *The Lives of the Desert Fathers* (The *Historia Monachorum in Aegypto.* Oxford-Kalamazoo, 1980) p. 126, note 22: 'The goal of the struggle against the passions (by means of ascesis) is apatheia, a stripping away of the passions so that the soul, no longer bothered by impulses towards sin, can come to the direct knowledge of God'.

39. G Poemen 4.

40. Contained in the Systematic Collection, PL 73:974 (*Verba Seniorum* libellus 17.8. To be abbreviated as VS 17.8)

41. G Poemen 5.

42. G Poemen 6.

43. G Poemen 127.

44. G Poemen 7.

45. G Poemen 76.

46. As in the moving description of Pachomius, who founds a monastery for his sister: V. Pach. G 1.32 (note 14 above): 'The Great Man's sister heard (about him) and came to see him. He sent the brother attending the gate to tell her, 'Behold, you have heard that I am alive. Do not be distressed because you have not seen me. But if you too wish to share in this holy life, so that we may find mercy before God, examine (yourself). The brothers will make a monastery for you to live in quietly there, and perhaps the Lord will call others as well to be with you. For man has no other hope in the world than to do good for himself and for his neighbor before he departs from his body to the place where he shall be judged and rewarded according to his works.'

47. G Poemen 198.

48. G Poemen 206.

49. G Poem. 152.

50. G. Macarius 41.

51. G Joseph of Panephysis 3.

52. G Agathon 1.

53. For the Rule and letters of Pachomius, see *Pachomiana Latina* (abbreviated: *Pach. Lat.*), ed. Amand Boon, Bibliothèque de la Revue d'Historie Ecclèsiastique 7 (Louvain, 1932). The Rules of Pachomius and the regulations of his successor Horsiesios have been translated by Armand Veilleux in *Pachomian Koinonia* 2, Cistercian Studies 46 (Kalamazoo, Michigan, 1981). To be abbreviated as *Pach. Koin.*.

54. *Pach. Lat.* Praecepta § 2, 69.

55. *Pach. Lat.* Praecepta § 109.

56. *Pach. Lat.* Praecepta § 96. Other provisions concerned with physical contact and its avoidance are 88, 92, 93, 94, 95, 97. In the last provision, a prohibition against shaving one's head without the housemaster's permission and against shaving another man without being ordered to do so, Jerome did not include the second part in his latin translation.

57. This is the translation given in Veilleux, *Pach. Koin.* p. 177. *Pach. Lat.* Praecepta atque Iudicia § 7: *Si deprehensus fuerit aliquis e fratribus libenter cum pueris ridere, et ludere, et habere amicitias aetatis infirmae*. . . . I quote from the Latin because of its importance for western monasticism in the coming centuries.

58. *Pach. Lat.* Praecepta § 49:. . .*et utrum possit renuntiare parentibus suis et propriam contemnere facultatem.*

59. *Pach. Lat.* Praecepta atque iudicia § 16, trans. *Pach. Koin.* 2; 178-9.

60. *Regula Benedicti* (RB) § 69.

61. *tu et amici tui qui cognoverunt tecum voluntatem Dei: Pach. Lat.* Ep 4, p. 86.

62. *Pach. Lat.* Ep 7, p. 95: . . .*ut, cessantibus bellis, pacis tranquillitas redeat, et in ea ambulare possitis coram Deo et hominibus; ut omnes aequaliter diligatis, ut serviatis Deo atque concordiae.*

63. *Pach. Lat. Liber S. Orsiesii* 9, p. 113: *Ideo, o homo,. . .et cavere quam maxime ne alterum ames et alterum oderis; sed et cunctis exhibeas aequalitatem, ne forte quem tu diligis Deus oderit, et quem tu odisti Deus diligat. Nulli erranti pro amicitia consentias*. . .

64. *Ibid.*, 42, p. 136.

65. *Ibid.*, 23, p. 124.

66. *Ibid.*, 39, pp. 134-5: *Si quis in domo monasterii, sub praeposito manens, nulla re indigens quam in monasterio habere permissum est, et habet patrem fratremque et amicum*

carissimum, nihil ab eis penitus accipiat. . . . Notice how the close friend is placed in the same category as biological father or brother. All such intimate bonds are a threat to the good monk.

67. *Ibid.*, 50, p. 142: *In actibus apostolorum quoque idem legimus: Multitudinis autem credentium erat cor et anima una, et nullus suorum quid dicebat, sed erant eis universa communia.*

68. *V Pach.* G 1.104. Trans. in *Pach. Koin.* 1:369.

69. *V Pach.* G. 1.96. Trans. *Pach. Koin.* 1:363: 'It is a great evil not to confess one's temptation quickly to someone who has knowledge, before the evil has matured'.

70. *V. Pach.* G 1.42; p. 112. See the apt comments of Peter Brown, *The Making of Late Antiquity*, p. 96.

71. *V. Pach.* G 1.40,41. In the latin version by Denis the Little, this friend, Dionysios, is called *amicissimus sancti Pachomii* and censures Pachomius for not allowing monks from elsewhere to stay inside his monastery. Paradoxically enough, this special friend accuses Pachomius of not showing equal love to all the brethren: *Non recte facis, abba, charitatem fratribus deditam non aequaliter omnibus exhibens.* (PL 73: 252, cap. 33)

72. *V. Pach.* G 1.145. *Pach. Koin.* 1, p. 403.

73. See R. W. Southern, *Saint Anselm and His Biographer* (Cambridge, 1966) 320-25.

74. *V. Pach.* G. 1.37. *Pach. Koin.* 1:323.

75. *V. Pach.* G 1.65. *Pach. Koin.* 1:342.

76. *V. Pach.* G 1.66 *Pach. Koin.* 1:342.

77. *V. Pach.* G 1.67-68. *Pach. Koin.* 1:343-44.

78. G Alonios 1.

79. 'Saint Basil (ca. 330-79), who had occasion to become familiar with the Pachomian system while journeying in Egypt, set himself against these excesses of bodily austerity and perfected the coenobitic form of monastic life by declaring its theoretical supremacy over the eremitical form or the Pachomian syncretism.' Walter Horn and Ernest Born, *The Plan of St. Gall* Vol. 1, pp. 327-28 (Berkeley, 1979). See aslo E.F. Morison, *Saint Basil and his Rule: A Study in Early Monasticism* (Oxford, 1952).

80. David Hugh Farmer, *The Oxford Dictionary of Saints* (1978). The Long Rules (*Regulae Fusius Tractatae*) and Short Rules (*Regulae Brevius Tractatae*) as well as the *Constitutiones Monasticae* and a number of the so-called ascetical discourses are all contained in PG 31. I shall use the translations of Sister M. Monica Wagner, Saint Basil, *Ascetical Works,* Fathers of the Church (New York, 1950), to be referred to as *Asc. Wks.*.

81. *Asc. Wks.*, (Long Rules) p. 242 = PG 31:921.

82. *Asc. Wks.*, p. 254 = PG 31:936-37.

83. *Asc. Wks.*, p. 256 =PG 31:940.

84. *The Making of Late Antiquity*, p. 88: '. . . anger, a sin of human relations, bulked larger with the ascetics than did the "demon of fornication", which lurked in their bodies. In addition to sexual temptation, anger and the evils of speech were the stuff of village life.'

85. *Asc. Wks.*, p. 257 = PG 31:941.

86. *Asc. Wks.*, p. 295 = PG 31:996.

87. *Ibid.*

88. *Asc. Wks.*, p. 296 = PG 31:996.

89. *Asc. Wks.*, p. 297 = PG 31:997.

90. *Asc. Wks.*, p. 299 = PG 31:1000-1001.

91. *Asc. Wks.* (An Ascetical Discourse) p. 219 = PG 31: 885. Jean Leclercq asserts that the work is not authentic ('Amicizia nella vita religiosa', col. 516 in *Dizionario degli Istituti di Perfezione* 1 (Edizioni Paoline, Roma: 1974). See W.K.L. Clarke, *The Ascetic Works of Saint Basil* (London, 1925). John Boswell (1980) p. 160, n. 94, has pointed out another ascetic work that Clarke rejected as being Basil's product: 'The comments are certainly those of a contemporary of Basil's and were believed to be his'. This seems also to be the case here: whether or not the work is authentic, it reflects the thinking of Basil's 'school', to borrow from the art history concept.

92. *Constitutiones Monasticae* cap. 29 = PG 31: 1418. The latin chapter heading is: *Quod non decet in ascetico instituto peculiarem quandam amicitiam esse inter duos aut tres fratres.*

93. G. Poem. 206.

94. *Const. Mon.* cap. 29 = PG 31:1419.

95. *Asc. Wks.* (An Ascetical Discourse and Exhortation) p. 23 = PG 32:880.

96. *Asc. Wks.* (Long Rules) p. 253 = PG 31:936.

97. *Asc. Wks.* (Long Rules) p. 248 = PG 31:929.

98. *Asc. Wks.* (Long Rules) p. 252, where the text is based on Psalm 132:1, 'Behold, how good and pleasant it is, when brothers dwell in unity!'.

99. Quoted in Peter Brown, *The Making of Late Antiquity,* p. 63, from O. Neugebauer and H. B. van Hoesen, *Greek Horoscopes,* p. 126.

100. *Asc. Wks.* (Long Rules) p. 239 = PG 31:917.

101. See the letters of Saint Basil, as *ep* cxxiv written by him in 373 as bishop of Caesarea (PG 32:543-46). For Lecerlcq's evaluation, see his excellent 'amicizia nella vita religiosa' (note 91 above).

102. Leclercq, *Ibid.*, col. 520: 'Indubbiamente, gli autori dei primi secoli del monachesimo, piú che quelli del medioevo, avanzarono, a proposito dell'amicizia, princìpi piuttosto rigorosi; nella loro pratica, tuttavia, essi si mostrarono molto umani.'

103. As in the almost tender scene between Abba John the Dwarf and a prostitute (G John the Dwarf 40): 'Then John bent his head and began to weep copiously. She asked him, "Abba, why are you crying?" He raised his head, then lowered it again, weeping, and said to her, "I see Satan playing in your face, how should I not weep?" Hearing this, she said to him, "Abba, is it possible to repent?" He replied, "yes". She said, "Take me wherever you wish." '

104. As in the scene where John kisses an elder (G John the Dwarf 46), his external display of warmth is intended only to show that he internally has not felt offended by the elder's comparison of his function to that of a courtesan.

105. *Lives of the Desert Fathers* (note 28 above) p. 65. The latin text of Rufinus is in PL 21:407-8.

CHAPTER TWO
THE WESTERN FATHERS

1. Here as in the previous chapter I am greatly indebted to the guidance of Peter Brown, whose insights I often only reproduce and apply to the matter of friendship. See especially his *The Cult of the Saints: Its Rise and Function in Latin Christianity* (University of Chicago Press, 1981).

2. Derwas Chitty, *The Desert a City* (Blackwell, Oxford: 1966) pp. 49-50: '. . .a concept which became universal in Greek ascetic theology, while it was never made at home in Latin'.

3. This is one of the central theses of Philip Rousseau, *Ascetics, Authority and the Church* (Oxford, 1978).

4. John O'Meara, *The Young Augustine* (London, 1954) p. 88.

5. Rudolf Lorenz, 'Die Anfänge des abendländischen Mönchtums im. 4. Jahrhundert', *Zeitschrift für Kirchengeschichte* 77 (1966) 1-61, provides an excellent summary of this development, with full bibliography.

6. Marie Aquinas McNamara, *Friendship in Saint Augustine*, Studia Friburgensia, New Series 20 (Fribourg, 1958) provides a good treatment of the efforts of Augustine to provide a common life for his friends and contrasts the exclusivity of Thagaste with the openness of Hippo (pp. 97-101).

7. Venantius Nolte, *Augustins Freundschaftsideal in seinen Briefen, Cassiciacum VI* (Würzburg, 1939) p. 17.

8. In the entire section v of *Verba Seniorum* (PL 73), I cannot find a single story that refers to homosexual temptation. There is the abstract *cogitatio fornicationis*, but whenever the temptation is concretized, it deals with a woman. In lib. v, nr. 29 (col. 831), a brother is criticized for projecting his own sexual temptation on two brothers who lived together. Here, appropriately, the sin is not one of deed but of thought: 'Shut that brother into a cell by himself; for the passion which he would fasten on them he hath in himself.' (trans. Helen Waddell, *The Desert Fathers* [University of Michigan Ann Arbor Paperbacks, 1966] p. 80.

9. *Ep* 27.2: . . .*videtur a legentibus ibi coniunx non dux ad mollitiem viro suo, sed ad fortitudinem redux in ossa viri sui, quam in tuam unitatem redactam et redditam et spiritalibus tibi tanto firmioribus, quanto castioribus nexibus copulatam officiis vestrae sanctitati debitis in te uno resalutamus*. . . (ed. Al. Goldbacher, CSEL 34 [1895] pp. 97-8).

10. Text in PL 16:25-194.

11. M. Tulli Ciceronis, *De officiis libri tres* (Sumptibus Arnoldi, Rome: Mondadori, 1965).

12. For references, see McNamara (note 6 above) p. 74. She has a good section on the relationship between Augustine and Ambrose and how it never developed into a friendship, pp. 68-77.

13. *Ep* 47.1, PL 16: 1130: *Proxime cum veteris amoris usu familiaris inter nos sermo caederetur*. . .

14. *Ep* 47.5, PL 16: 1200: . . .*non solum animi conglutinari videntur per verae doctrinae profectum, sed etiam plenioris coloquii species et forma exprimi*. . .

15. *Ep* 49.1, PL 16: 1203: *Nunquam enim minus solus sum, quam cum solus esse videor; nec minus otiosus, quam cum otiosus*.

16. *De excessu fratris sui Satyri*, PL 16: 1345-1414.

17. *Sermo* 26:3-12 *super Cantica canticorum*, ed. J. Leclercq, C.H. Talbot, H.M. Rochais, *S. Bernardi Opera*, 1 (Roma, 1957).

18. *De virginibus*, PL 16: 197-244.

19. PL 34: 632: *interim quod ad me attinet, hoc in me egerunt cum scriberentur, et agunt cum leguntur.*

20. As in the studies of McNamara (note 6 above) and Nolte (note 7).

21. Augustine's classic statement here is his letter to Marcianus (*ep* 258), where he uses the ciceronian definition of friendship to state that since he and Marcianus as youths did not know the true God, they could not have been in harmony about

things divine. Thus their friendship was only on a human level. Even here Augustine admits that there were kindliness and affection in their relationship.

22. *Conf.* VI. 6, trans. R.S. Pine-Coffin (Penguin Classics: Harmondsworth, 1971) pp. 77-8.

23. *Conf.* IV. 14: *Beatus qui amat. . . amicum in te. . . solus enim nullum carum amittit, cui omnes in illo cari, qui non amittitur.*

24. *Serm.* 361.1: *In dedicatione ecclesiae* II.2 = PL 38: 1472.

25. *Ep* 73:10, CSEL 34: 276-7: *nec in hac mea securitate crastinum illud humanae fragilitatis incertum, de quo superius gemui, omnino formido cum enim hominem Christiana caritate flagrantem eaque mihi fidelem amicum factum esse sentio, quicquid ei consiliorum meorum cogitationumque committo, non homini committo sed illi in quo manet, ut talis sit: deus enim caritas est et, qui manet in caritate, in deo manet* (1 Jn 4:16).

26. *Ep* 130.4, CSEL 44: 44: *Nam sicut sibi quisque nemo alter alteri notus est, et tamen nec sibi quisque ita notus est, ut sit de sua crastina conversatione securus.* Also *En. in Ps.* lv. 9 (PL 36:652): *. . . omne cor omni cordi clausum est.*

27. See *ep* 205.1 (to Consentius; CSEL 57:323): *et ideo te magis videre desideramus, ut in his sis, quos et videmus et novimus.* Also, much more blatantly, *ep* 27.1 (to Paulinus: CSEL 34:96): *cum autem non aequo animo fero, quod te non video.* The opposite is indicated in *ep* 58.2 (to Pammachius: CSEL 34:217-8). Here there is no hint at the importance of Augustine's seeing the friend.

28. *Ep* 9.1 (CSEL 34:p. 20); *ep* 10.1 (pp. 22-23) *. . . quod recentissimis litteris legi, ubi nos arguis, quod consulere neglegamus, ut una nobis vivere liceat.*

29. As to Pammachius, a senator and important opponent of the Donatists, *ep* 58.2 (CSEL 34:217): *. . . tibique has gratulatorias litteras mitterem qualecumque specimen cordis amoris erga te mei.*

30. *Conf.* IV.7: *. . . vera amicitia, quia non est vera, nisi cum eam tu agglutinas inter haerentes sibi caritate diffusa in cordibus nostris per spiritum sanctum, qui datus est nobis.*

31. *Soliloquiorum Libri Duo* I,3: PL 32: 873.

32. *Ep* 10.3, CSEL 34: 24-5: *quae cum ita sint, restare unum vides, ut tu quoque in commune consulas, quo vivamus simul. quid enim cum matre agendum sit, quam certe frater Victor non deserit, tu multo melius calles quam ego. alia scribere, ne te ab ista cogitatione averterem, nolui.*

33. Peter Brown, *Augustine of Hippo* (Faber, London: 1969) 135-6.

34. For a discussion of Augustine's 'letters of art', H. I. Marrou, *Saint Augustin et la fin de la culture antique* (Paris, 1938) 95-104.

35. *Ep* 109.1, CSEL 34: 635: *deo ergo gratias, frater dulcissime, bene mihi tecum est, gaudeo tecum artius coniunctus et, ut ita dicam, unissime, quantum potest, adhaerens tibi redundantiam uberum tuorum suscipiens vires comparo. . . .*

36. Nolte (note 7 above), p. 91: 'Ein etwas geschmackloses, fast schmactendes Schreiben, das man nicht von einem Manne erwartete.'

37. *Ep* 110, CSEL 34:638-42. It may be of some significance that Augustine's salutation is to Severus and the whole community around him, from Augustine and the brothers with him: *Domino beatissimo atque dulcissimo venerabili nimiumque desiderabili fratri consacerdoti Severo et qui tecum sunt fratribus Augustinus et qui mecum sunt fratres in domino salutem.* Thus from the very first Augustine conveys himself as representing one episcopal community to another. In this sense he can accept the flowery language of Severus, addressed not to him as an individual but to his church. In classical rhetoric every nuance is important, and Augustine knows them all!

38. After the first was converted, he turned to his friend and said: 'I have torn myself free from all our ambitions and have decided to serve God. From this very moment, here and now, I shall start to serve him. If you will not follow my lead, do not stand in my way.' His friend answered '*that he would stand by his comrade*, for such service was glorious and the reward was great' (*Conf.* VIII. 6--p. 168 in Pine-Coffin's Penguin trans.).

39. Again I am indebted to Peter Brown for pointing out the significance of Augustine's characterization of Adam and Eve's relationship as *amicitia*. Adam's acceptance of the forbidden fruit from her is described by Augustine as a result of *amicali benevolentia*. (See Brown's forthcoming book on virginity and society in Late Antiquity).

40. *De Civitate Dei* XIX.8 (trans. Henry Bettenson: Pelican Classics, 1972) p. 862.

41. *Ibid.*, p. 863.

42. Douglas Roby, Introduction to *Aelred of Rievaulx, Spiritual Friendship*, CF 5 (1974) p. 15. I am very much indebted to this presentation of monastic friendship.

43. *De diversis quaestionibus*, PL 40: 82: *Et ideo amicorum mala fortius sustinemus, quia bona eorum nos delectant et tenent.*

44. PL 32: 65-6: . . .*cum quo ferme annis quadraginta Dei dono absque amara ulla dissensione familiariter ac dulciter vixi*. . .

45. *Ep* 2, ed. I. Hilberg, (CSEL 44: p. 10): *Quam vellem nunc vestro interesse conventui, et admirandum consortium, licet isti oculi non mereantur aspicere, tota cum exultatione complecti.*

46. *Ep* 3.1, CSEL 44: 13: *quam ego nunc arte tua stringerem colla complexibus, quam illud os, quod mecum vel erravit aliquando vel sapuit, inpressis figerem labiis!*

47. *Ep* 52.4, to Nepotian, from 394, CSEL 44: 420: *et per fines capitum singulorum acuta quaedam breviterque conclusa, quae plausus et clamores excitent audientum.* Trans. by F. A. Wright in *Select Letters of St. Jerome* (Loeb Classical Library: Camb., Mass. and London, 1975) p. 199.

48. For Jerome's background and person, the work of Ferdinand Cavallera is central: *S. Jérôme, sa vie et son oeuvre* (London, 1923) I-II, and 'The Personality of St. Jerome', *A Monument to Saint Jerome,* ed. James X. Murphy (New York, 1952) 15-34.

49. *Ep* 4.1, CSEL 54: 19: *non tantum laudandus sit ille, qui te amat, quam scelus putetur facere ille, qui non amat.* (Note the careful rhetorical opposition based on the two phrases 'he who loves you' and 'he who loves you not'.)

50. See R. W. Southern, *Saint Anselm and his Biographer* (Cambridge, 1966) pp. 72-3.

51. *Ep* 7.6 (CSEL 54: 30-31; trans. F. A. Wright, p. 27): *Et miremini forsitan, quod in fine iam epistulae rursus exorsus sim. Quid faciam? Vocem pectori negare non valeo. Epistulae brevitas conpellit tacere, desiderium vestri cogit loqui. Praeproperus sermo; confusa turbatur oratio; amor ordinem nescit.*

52. *Ep* 7.2 (CSEL 54:27; trans. F. A. Wright, p. 21): *Nunc cum vestris litteris fabulor, illas amplexor, illae mecum loquuntur, illae hic tantum Latine sciunt. hic enim aut barbarus seni sermo discendus est aut tacendum est.*

53. *Ep* 8, CSEL 54: 32: *tu modo a nobis abiens recentem amicitiam scindis potius, quam dissuis, quod prudenter Laelius vetat*. . . (*De amic.* 76).

54. *Ep* 14.1, CSEL 54: 45: *tacerem? sed quod ardenter volebam, moderate dissimulare non poteram. inpensius obsecrarem? sed audire nolebas, quia similiter non amabas*. . .

55. *Ep* 185.1, *S. Bernardi Opera* 7 (Roma, 1974).

56. *Ep* 14.10 (CSEL 54: 59; trans. Wright, p. 49).

57. As the rich roman matron Fabiola, who recited to Jerome by heart this very letter to Heliodorus (*ep* 77.9) as her incitement to monastic life.

58. *Ep* 52.1, CSEL 54: 414: . . .*dum essem adulescens, immo paene puer, et primos impetus lascivientis aetatis heremi duritia refrenarem, scripsi ad avunculum tuum, sanctum Heliodorum, exhortatoriam epistulam plenam lacrimis querimoniisque et quae deserti sodalis monstraret affectum. sed in illo opere pro aetate tunc lusimus et calentibus adhuc rhetorum studiis atque doctrinis quaedam scolastico flore depinximus.* (trans. Wright, p. 189).

59. For the manuscript tradition of Jerome's letters, Bernard Lambert, *Bibliotheca Hieronymiana manuscripta: La tradition manuscrite de S. Jerome,* Collectio Instrumenta Patristici (The Hague, 1969), Tome IA-1B. Also T. IVB, *Indices*, as on p. 178, references to the MSS of Jerome's letters at Clairvaux. I would like to thank Dom Jean Leclercq for supplying me with this reference.

60. See F. A. Wright, 'On Jerome's Correspondence with Roman Women', Appendix I in *Select Letters* (note 46 above), 483-97. Also Carolly Erickson, *The Medieval Vision* (New York, 1976) 189-94.

61. Contained in PL 23: 18-28. Trans. Helen Waddell, *The Desert Fathers* (note 8 above) 29-39.

62. 'Hieronymus Ciceronianus', *Transactions and Proceedings of the American Philological Association* (London, 1965) 119-38, reprinted in Fiske (1970) 1/1-1/20, esp. 1/17.

63. Pierre Fabre, *Saint Paulin de Nole et l'amitié chrétienne*, Bibliothèque des écoles françaises d'Athènes et de Rome, 167 (Paris, 1949), which I have found very helpful, even if I at times disagree with Fabre's interpretation of Paulinus's reactions to his friends. See also Pierre Courcelle, 'Paulin de Nole et saint Jérôme', *Révue des Etudes Latines* 25 (1947) 250-280. Joseph T. Lienhard, *Paulinus of Nola and Early Western Monasticism*, Theophaneia 28 (Cologne, 1977), and W. H. C. Frend, 'The Two Worlds of Paulinus of Nola', *Latin Literature of the Fourth Century*, ed. J. W. Binus (Routledge and Kegan Paul: London and Boston 1974) 100-133.

64. *Epistulae,* ed. de Hartel, CSEL 29 (Vienna, 1894) 1-10.

65. *Ep* 1.11, CSEL 29: 10: *verum quid de spatio agam? si nos desideras, via brevis est; longa si neglegis.*

66. *Ep* 5.1, CSEL 29: 24: *Et excusandum putasti, frater dilectissime, quod ad nos non ipse venisses secundum sponsionem tuam expectationemque nostram? tu vero potiore tui parte quam qua manseris, solo corpore domi residens, voluntate ad nos et spiritu et sermone venisti; quamquam ne corporaliter quidem penitus afueris, quando in pueris tuis sancta in domino tibi servitute conexis corporis ad nos tui membra venerunt*. . .

67. *Ep* 5.9, CSEL 29: 31: *ut quod volueras velle non desinas et immutabilem ad nos veniendi sententiam teneas.*

68. *Ep* 5.20, CSEL 29: 38: *in dictando enim dum te cogito et totus in te sum, quasi apud praesentem longo intervallo loquar, obliviscor inpositum finire sermonem.*

69. *Fuerint nobis fratres et amici et proximi boni et magni; sed non fuit placitum circa nos in eis domino, qui te elegit donare nobis in fratrem inseparabilem et in proximum dilectissimum, quem merito sicut nosmet ipsos diligamus, quia cor unum et unam animam tecum in Christo habemus. Ep* 11.4, CSEL 29: 63.

70. Pierre Fabre (note 62 above) p. 321: '. . . plus maî tre de lui, plus détaché des contingences, plus disposé à envisager les faits d'une façon objective.'

71. *Ibid.*, p. 451, 'un certain découragement', based on Paulinus's description of his spiritual state in *ep* 24.20.

72. As indicated in Sulpicius's inclusion of a painting of Paulinus in the shrine of Saint Martin (*ep* 32.2).

73. For the practice of celibate marriage at this time, see the excellent article by Jo Ann McNamara, 'Chaste Marriage and Clerical Celibacy', Vern L. Bullough and James Brundage, *Sexual Practices and the Medieval Church* (Prometheus Books: Buffalo, New York, 1982) 22-33.

74. Pierre Fabre (note 62 above) p. 336: 'Son affection pour son ami tout en demeurant très profonde se dépouille et se spiritualise de plus en plus.'

75. Cod. Lugdunensis 535 membr. 4°, 12-13c. from Bonnevaux, near Vienne in Southern France, founded in 1119 by one of the earliest abbots of Citeaux, Stephen Harding. (CSEL 29: p. x)

76. Ep. tertia, *Sulpicii Severi Libri qui supersunt*, ed. Car. Halm, CSEL 1 (Vienna, 1866) 146-51.

77. Sulpice Sévère, *Vie de Saint Martin*, t. 3, Sources Chrétiennes 135 (Paris, 1969), p. 1267.

78. *Vita S. Martini* 25 (CSEL 1:135). Trans. F. R. Hoare, *The Western Fathers* (Harper Torchbooks: New York, 1966) 41-2.

79. *Dialogues* I.1 (CSEL 1:152, trans. Hoare p. 68).

80. *Dial.* I.1. (p.153, Hoare p. 69): *Ego vero, inquam, etiam cum tu in Aegypto morareris, totus tecum semper animo et cogitatione versabar, meque de te dies ac noctes cogitantem totum tua caritas possidebat.*

81. *Dial.* I.1 (p. 154, Hoare, p. 70).

82. *Dial.* I.12 (p. 163, Hoare, pp. 81-2).

83. *Dial.* I. II.7-8, p. 189.

84. Hoare p. 112.

85. *Dial.* II (III) 18 (CSEL 1:216, Hoare p. 144): *quod si vel te quondam vel me semper audire voluisset, et Martinum magis quam illum, quem nominare nolo, fuisset imitatus, numquam me tam crudeliter disparatus ignoti pulveris syrte tegeretur. . . videant gloriam suam et vel nunc adversum me grassari desinant vindicati. . . Haec cum maxime flebili voce gemeremus, omnium lacrimis per nostra lamenta commotis. . .*

86. J. Leclercq, 'S. Martin dans l'hagiographie monastique du moyen âge', *Saint Martin et son Temps*, Studia Anselmiana 46 (Rome, 1961) 175-87.

87. *S. Benedicti Regula*, a cura di Gregorio Penso, Biblioteca di studi superiori 39 (Firenze, 1958): *Et ideo omni tempore sive ieunii sive prandii, si tempus fuerit prandii, mox surrexerint a cena, sedeant omnes in unum, et legat unus Collationes vel Vitas Patrum, aut certe aliud quod aedificet audientes.*

88. *De coenobitorum Institutis*, lib. II: *de nocturnis orationibus*, cap. 15 (ed. Michael Petschenig, CSEL 17 [Vienna, 1888] p. 30): *summa namque observantia custoditur, ne quisquam eum alio ac praecipue iuniores vel ad punctum temporis pariter substitisse aut uspiam secessisse, vel manus suas invicem tenuisse deprehendantur. . .*

89. Iohannis Cassiani *Conlationes*, xvi. 1; ed. Michael Petschenig, (Vienna, 1886) CSEL 13:439: . . . *nosque ab exordio renuntiationis nostrae tam in peregrinatione, quae ab utroque nostrum fuerat obtentu militiae spiritalis arrepta, quam in coenobii studio individua semper conjunctione sociatos. . .*

90. For the chronology of John Cassian's life, a difficult subject, see the helpful remarks in Philip Rousseau, *Ascetics, Authority and the Church* (Oxford, 1978) 169-76.

91. *John Cassian: A Study in Primitive Monasticism* (Cambridge, 1950) p. 107.

92. *Conlationes* xvi. 27, CSEL 13: 460: . . . *sed dilatamini in cordibus vestris, suscipientes adversus iracundiae fluctus in illis extentis sinibus caritatis, quae 'omnia suffert, omnia sustinet': et ita mens vestra amplitudine longanimitatis ac patientiae dilatata habeat in se consiliorum salutares recessus.*

93. *Ibid.*, ch. 6, p. 443: . . . *illud quod in Actibus apostolorum legimus de unitate credentium omni virtute custodiens.*

94. *Ibid.*, ch. 27, p. 460: . . .*damus locum irae, quotiens commotioni alterius humili atque tranquilla mente subcumbimus et quodammodo dignos nos qualibet iniuria profitentes inpatientiae saevientis obsequimur.*

95. *Ibid.*, ch. 15, p. 450: *Haec enim est vere charitas ordinata, quae odio habens neminem quosdam meritorum jure plus diligit: quaeque, cum generaliter diligat cunctos, excipit tamen sibi ex his quos debeat peculiari affectione complecti: et rursum inter ipsos qui in dilectione summi atque praecipui sunt aliquos sibi qui caeterorum affectui superextollantur excerpit.*

96. RB 2:16-17: *Non ab eo persona in monasterio discernatur. Non unus plus ametur quam alius, nisi quem in bonis actibus aut oboedientia invenerit meliorem.* I use Justin McCann's translation (London, 1976).

97. Boswell (1980) pp. 187-88, admits, however, that these provisions could be interpreted differently.

98. RB, ch. 69: *Praecavendum est ne quavis occasione praesumat alter alium defendere monachum in monasterio aut quasi tueri, etiamsi qualivis consanguinitatis propinquitate iungantur. Nec quolibet modo id a monachis praesumat, quia exinde gravissima occasio scandalorum oriri potest. Quod si quis haec transgressus fuerit, acrius coherceatur.*

99.*Reg. Pach.* nr. 176, PL 23: 88: *Qui consentit peccantibus, et defendit aliquem delinquentem, maledictus erit apud Deum et homines, et corripietur increpatione severissima.*

100. Can we not here in Benedict's words about protection and defence see the personal and social impulse behind the later formation of feudal society, in its classical early medieval development as described by Marc Bloch?

101. RB, 54:1: *Nullatenus liceat monacho neque a parentibus suis neque a quoquam hominum nec sibi invicem litteras, eulogias vel quaelibet munuscula accipere aut dare sine praecepto abbatis.*

102. *Gregorii Magni Dialogi Libri IV*, a cura de Umberto Moricca (Fonti per la storia d'Italia: Roma, 1924).

103. Trans. Odo John Zimmerman (Fathers of the Church: New York, 1959) Vol. 39: pp. 3-5.

104. I think especially of the friendship-hatred of Sichar and Chramnesind in *Historiae Francorum* (ix, 19), used so well by Erich Auerbach in *Mimesis* (Princeton, 1974), 77-95.

105. CSEL 29: 40: . . .*ut nobis non novam aliquam amicitiam sumere, sed quasi veterem caritatem resumere videremur*.

106. For John Crysostom on marriage, see John T. Noonan, *Contraception* (Harvard Univ. Press, 1965) 73, 139. For his fear of homosexuality, Vern L. Bullough, 'Formation of Medieval Ideals: Christian Theory and Practice', *Sexual Practices* (note 73 above) p. 18.

CHAPTER THREE
THE MONK AND THE WANDERER

1. *Historia Ecclesiastica Gentis Anglorum,* II.1, ed. Carolus Plummer (Oxford, 1946) p. 74. Abbreviated as *Plummer.* Peter is only called Gregory's deacon here, while Gregory calls him both dear friend and companion in the study of Sacred Scripture.

2. *Historia Abbatum*, ch. 4, ed. Plummer, p. 367: . . .*ad regem se Occidentalium Saxonum nomina Counvalh conferendum putavit, cuius et ante non semel amicitiis usus et beneficiis erat adiutus.*

3. As when a nun addresses her brother: '*Quid est, frater mi, quod tam longum tempus intermisisti, quod venire tardasti? Quare non vis cogitare, quod ego sola in terra et nullus alius frater visitet me, neque propinquorum aliquis ad me veniet?*' *Ep* 143 in Michael Tangl, *Die Briefe des heiligen Bonifatus und Lullus, Monumenta Germaniae historica: Epistolae Selectae in usum scholarum* (Berlin, 1916) - Abbreviated as Tangl. If we did not have further letters from the same woman, it would not be apparent that she was addressing her biological brother.

4. *Epistola ad Ecbertum* 9, Plummer, p. 412 in: . . .*firma protinus intentione adiuvare curabit, et maxime illa, quae tu, quum sis propinquus illius amantissimus*. . . . According to the notes here, it is likely that the king and the archbishop were first cousins once removed.

5. I am here greatly obliged to my teacher at Berkeley in 1964 who first brought me to this world and the sources for it: Robert Brentano, *The Early Middle Ages 500-1000* (Free Press: New York, 1964) provides a guide to early medieval stuctures and mentalities that I still find helpful. I am also grateful to Peter Brown, whose books and advice reach in their inspiration far beyond the realm of Late Antiquity.

6. Gavin Bone (trans.), *Anglo-Saxon Poetry* (Clarendon Press: Oxford, 1943) p. 68.

7. *Beowulf*, trans. David Wright (Penguin: Baltimore, Maryland, 1964) p. 60.

8. *Ibid*., p. 67.

9. I am aware of the long-standing debate on the date of the Beowulf poem. The best recent discussion is in Colin Chase ed. The *Dating of Beowulf* (Toronto, 1981) I am indebted to Walter Goffart of the University of Toronto for the guidance here and in many other points in this chapter.

10. Bertram Colgrave, *Two Lives of Saint Cuthbert* (Cambridge, 1940): Beda Vita Sancti Cuthberti, p. 248, ch. 28. Colgrave's text has *spiritualis*, but several of the manuscripts have *spiritalis*, which would become standard medieval usage. Bede's originality can be detected by a comparison to the Anonymous *Life* of Cuthbert which was his central source. Here there is no mention of spiritual friendship, only the term *conloquium spiritale* for the contact between the two holy men (Colgrave, p. 124). Spiritual friendship is thus Bede's own 'invention', a reflection of his own interest in bonds among men of holiness.

11. The term was also incorporated into the *Historia Ecclesiastica* (IV.27, p. 274 in Plummer). This would have contributed to its spread. But Bede's *Life* of Cuthbert was in itself quite popular. Boniface's successor Lull, for example, was sent a copy by the abbot of Jarrow and Wearmouth in 764 (Tangle, *ep* 116, p. 250).

12. . . . *set tui sodalis memineris*. . . . See the notes in the *Corpus Christianorum* edition of Ailred of Rievaulx, *De spiritali amicititia* (Turnhout, 1970) p. 290, where the letter of Boniface is cited.

13. Colgrave, (note 10 above) p. 250. In the *Historia Ecclesiastica* (p. 274), the phrase is *sui memor sis fidissimi sodalis*. Bede thus strengthened the concept of the bond with the idea of faithfulness.

14. *Vita Sancti Cuthberti*, cap. 24 (Colgrave, p. 234).

15. *Ibid*., cap. 23, p. 230: . . .*multo virum Dei semper excolebat amore.*

16. *Ibid*., cap. 34, p. 262.

17. For the letters, see PL 94. Most of the phrases seem to be essentially expressions of politeness (as *fratri dilectissimo et in Christi visceribus honorando Plegwino*, addressed to a monk of Hexham, *ep* 3, col. 669).

18. *Ep* 9, col. 689.

19. *Ep* 13, col. 698: *Unde tuo crebro, dilectissime ac desiderantissime omnium qui in terris morantum antistum, Acca, provocatus hortatu, tuis fretus orationibus*. . . .

20. One thinks, of course, of Gregory of Tours. See Peter Brown, *The Cult of the Saints* (University of Chicago, 1982).

21. Sidoine Apollinaire, Tome II, *Lettres*, ed. André Loyen (Société d'édition Les Belles Lettres: Paris, 1970), V. 18, p. 206: *Haeduae civitati te praesidere coepisse libens atque cum gaudio accepi. Laetitiae causa quadripertita est: prima quod amicus; secunda quod iustus es; tertia quod severus; quarta quod proximus.*

22. *Ibid.,: Quo fit, ut nostris nostrorumque contractibus plurimum velis, debeas, possis opitulari.*

23. See PL 59 for the letters, as one to a senator, Heraclius (col. 264), showing a general concern for his well-being: *Dum incessabilis de amicorum fide ac salute cura mihi est, nuper prosperitatis vestrae inter prima sollicitus agnovi.* See the Oxford D.Phil. thesis of I. N. Wood (1979, unpublished).

24. *Opera poetica*, ed. Fredericus Leo, contained in *Monumenta Germaniae Historica* (abbreviated MGH), *Auctorum Antiquissimorum*, t. IV (Berlin, 1881).

25. Richard Koebner, *Venantius Fortunatus: Seine Persönlichkeit unde seine Stellung in der geistigen kultur des Merovinger-Reiches* (Beiträge zur Kulturgeschichte des Mittelalters und der Renaissance: Band 22, Leipzig-Berlin, 1915) p. 46 'So ist der junge Mann, der am austrasischen Hofe als gefeirter Günstling unter den Grossen lebte, in Poitiers freiwillige Sklave einer Nonne geworden'.

26. See especially the poems translated by Helen Waddell in *Mediaeval Latin Lyrics* (Penguin: Harmondsworth, 1968) pp. 69-71.

27. Koebner (note 25 above) pp. 41-2.

28. As VIII.9, 195 in MGH Auct. Antiq. (note 24 above).

29. *Ibid.*, XI.22, p. 267: . . .*per quod mater amat, frater et ipse cupit / Ut, dum nos escam*
capimus, quodcumque loquaris,
quod si tu facias, his satiabor ego.

30. As XI. 21, p. 266, *De absentia sua:*
Si me non nimium pluviatilis aura vetaret
dum nesciretis, vos repetisset amans.
nec volo nunc absens nunc detenter ut hora,
cum mea tunc lux est quando videtur amans.

31. *Ibid.*, XI. 6, p. 260:
ac si uno partu mater Radegundis utrosque,
visceribus castis progenuisset, eram,
et tuamquam pariter nos ubera cara beatae
pavissent uno lacte fluente duos.

32. Even in the 'Versus in convivio factus' (XI. 23, p. 267).

33. IX. 8, p. 215: *'Ad baudoaldum episcopum'*: . . .*pignore amicitiae corde tenende meae*. . .

34. *Sequana te retinet, nos unda Britannica cingit: divisos terris alligat unus amor.* III. 26, p. 75. Full text of the poem and translation in Helen Waddell (note 26 above), pp. 72-3. One notices here that Rucco is called *care sodalis*, not *amice*, another indication that the roman word for friend still has a secular ring.

35. IX. 10, p. 216:
Summe pater patriae, dulci mihi nomine Rucco,
interiora mei cordis amore tenens:
quidquid amicitiae veteris collegimus ambo
crescit in affectum semper, opime, meum.

36. Koebner (note 25 above) p. 34. For an excellent account of the meeting of roman and barbarian cultures, see Walter Goffart, *Barbarians and Romans AD 418-584*: The techniques of accommodation (Princeton, 1980)

37. As in the Trinitarian ending of a poem to Radegund and Agnes: *et tribus in Christo sit precor una salus* (XI, 7, p. 261).
See the sections on carolingian writers, especially Alcuin. For the influence of Fortunatus in England, see R. W. Hunt and Michael Lapidge, 'Manuscript evidence for knowledge of the poems of Venantius Fortunatus in late Anglo-Saxon England', *Anglo-Saxon England* (1979) 279-95.

38. *Aldhelmi Opera*, ed. Rudolfus Ehwald (MGH, Auct. Antiq. XV: Berlin, 1919). See Michael Winterbottom, 'Aldhelm's prose style and its origins', *Anglo-Saxon England* 6 (1977) 39-76, and Michael Lapidge, 'The hermeneutic style in tenth-century Anglo-Saxon Literature ', Anglo-Saxon England 4 (1975) 67-111.

39. *Ibid.*: *De metris et enigmatibus ac pedum regulis* V, p. 75: *inextricabilis verae dilectionis ligatura tanto strictius et enixius per succiduas saeculorum aetates indisruptis restibus reliquum* nodetur in aevum. The last words here were used by the nun Lioba in writing to Boniface (*ep* 29, p. 53 in Tangl, note 3 above).

40. *Ibid.*, p. 75: *longa locorum intercapidine. . . indisruptae caritatis vinculum*. The first phrase is also used by Lioba, *ep* 29, p. 53, note 1.

41. *Saluto te diligenter, o Sigetyth, ex intimo cordis cubiculo subnixis obsecrans. . . . Ibid.*, p. 497: *Ep*, 6(8).

42. Compare Daniel of Winchester's: *Vale, vale, centupliciter carissime mihi* (*Ep* 64, p. 132 in Tangl).

43. As *Sermo* 335, 'De amore hominis in hominem' (PL 39:1692): *Amicus gratis amandus est, propter sese, non propter aliud.* This will be a point of departure for Aelred of Rievaulx's treatise on spiritual friendship.

44. The literature here is vast. I have been helped by John Ryan, *Irish Monasticism* (Talbot Press: Dublin, 1931). For the penitential literature, Ludwig Bieler, *The Irish Penitentials*, Scriptores Latini Hiberniae, Vol. 5 (Dublin Institute for Advanced Studies, 1963) for the texts with excellent English translations of the Latin materials. For more background information, J. T. McNeill and H. M. Gamer, *Medieval Handbooks of Penance*, Columbia Records of Civilization 29 (New York, 1938).

45. *Regula coenobialis*, PL 80:219: *Qui visitaverit alios fratres in cella seorsum sine interrogatione, simili modo poeniteat; aut in coquina post novam sine ordinatione vel jussione ierit, suppositione: aut extra vallum, id est, extra septum monasterii sine interrogatione ierit, suppositione.* For a full bibliography of Columban's life and writings, James F. Kenney, *The Sources for the early History of Ireland: Ecclesiastical* (Octagon: New York, 1966) pp.186-205.

46. P. 80: 224: *Si cum ullo qui cellae suae cohabitator non est, confabulari quantulumque praesumpserit, suppositione. Si alterius tenuerit manum, suppositione.* See the Precepts of Pachomius, § 95.

47. *Ibid.*: *Si parentum quempiam vel amicorum saecularium viderit, vel collocutus fuerit ei sine jussione; si epistolam cujuscunque susceperit, si tribuere praesumpserit sine suo abbate, suppositione.* (see RB, ch. 54)

48. PL 80: 218: *Si quis dicat ad consanguineum suum, sollicitans eum in alio loco habitantem: Melius est ut nobiscum habites aut cum aliquibus, tribus suppositionibus.*

49. *Illa ejulans et pavimenta prostrata denegat se permissurum; ille limen matremque transiliens, poposcit matrem ne maerore solvatur, dicens se numquam deinceps in hac vita videndum. . . . Vita S. Columbani*, ed. Mabillon, *Acta Sanctorum Ordinis Benedicti* II (Paris, 1669) p. 8. Also in PL 87.

50. *AA SS OSB*, p. 9: *Tanta pietas, tanta caritas omnibus inerat, ut unum velle, unum esset nolle.*

51. *Ibid.*, p. 15: *ab aliorum societate segregatus, et abditis locis receptus vel longiori spatio eremi secreta sectabatur, ut solida mente et absque curarum inquietudine solus orationi vacaret et religioni omni conatu intenderet.*

52. Maire and Liam de Paor, *Early Christian Ireland* (Thames and Hudson: London, 1961), Ch. II, 'The Monasteries'. Also Harold G. Leask, *Irish Churches and Monastic Buildings*, Vol. I (Dundalk, 1955), Ch. III.

53. *Irish Monasticism* (note 44 above) p. 357. For examples see C. Plummer, *Vitae Sanctorum Hiberniae* (Oxford, 1910) I, p. 72: *nescivit quem haberet patrem confessionis suae*. Also II, p. 147. Abbreviated as VSH.

54. See J. T. Fowler's introduction to *Adamnani Vita S. Columbae* (Clarendon Press: Oxford, 1894), pp. xlvi, lxxiii and the glossary, p. 167, for the term *anmchara.*

55. *Vita Sancti Maedoc*, ch. xx, VSH II: p. 147.

56. Whitley Stokes, *The Calendar of Oengus*, Transactions of the Royal Irish Academy I (Dublin, 1880) p. cxxix. The story, however, may be quite late and could be a high medieval idealization of the relationships of the early medieval irish saints.

57. *Vita Sancti Mochoemog*, ch. xxxi, VSH II: p. 180.

58. Plummer's introduction in VSH I: pp. cvi-cvii.

59. PL 80:225, §§ III, XV, XVII. Text and translation both in Bieler (note 44 above), who also includes the Penitential of Cummean, the most detailed of all the collections. Its section X: 1-21, deals with various forms of homosexual behaviour, as: 13:A man who practises masturbation by himself for the first offence one hundred days, if he repeats it, a year. 14. Men guilty of femoral intercourse, for the first offence, a year; if they repeat it, two years. 15. Those practising homosexuality (*in terga vero fornicantes*), if they are boys, two years; if men, three or four years; but if it has become a habit, seven years, and the manner of penance, moreover, shall be decided according to the judgment of a priest. 16. Those who satisfy their desires with their lips, four years. If it has become a habit, seven years.
It should be noted here that the penitentials are meant both for laymen and for monks, even though this literature emerges from a monastic milieu, inspired ultimately by the writings of John Cassian.

60. For a full treatment of this subject, which appeared too late for me to use it in preparing this chapter but with whose conclusions I agree (especially the section on homosexuality and the penitentials, pp 135-39) see Pierre J. Payer, *Sex and the Penitentials 550-1150* (University of Toronto Press, 1984).

61. *Adamnani Vita* (note 54 above) I.45, p. 58.

62. *Ibid.*, II. 22, p. 90: *Hic supradictum Columbanum, sancti amicum Columbae, persequebatur.*

63. *Ibid.*, II. 23, p. 91.

64. *Ibid.*, I. 49, p. 62: *nam mei congnationales amici et tui secundum carnem cognati, hoc est, Nellis Nepotes et Cruthini populi, in hac vicina munitione Cethirni belligerantes committent bellum.*

65. Contained in Wilhelm Levison, *Vitae Sancti Bonifatii*, ch. 1, MGH: Scriptores rerum Germanicarum in usum scholarum (Hannover, 1905), p. 7: *suis secum adstantibus amicis.*

66. *Ibid.*, ch. 2, p. 8.

67. *Ibid.*, ch. 6, pp. 34-5.

68. *Ibid.*, ch. 8, p. 45.

69. *Ibid.*, ch. 6, p. 33: *expulsis profani hostis amicis.*

70. *Ibid.*, ch. 8, p. 48: . . . *ut quibus iuxta apostolicae institutionis normam* cor erat unum et anima una, *una eademque et palma esset marteri et remuneratio triumphi.*

71. *Ibid.*, p. 46: *Cum enim praefatus tantae querellositatis antistes suspiria non ferens, sed statim se in lacrimas dedisset, iam sanctus Bonifatius, finito colloquio, ad alia rediit.*

72. Tangl (note 3 above), *Die Briefe. . . Bonifatius und Lullus.*

73. Tangl, *ep* 13, p. 18: *Abbate sancto veroque amico iure ac merito honorando divine scientiae ac religionis gratia repleto Uuynfrido. . . .*

74. See Tangl's notes for this letter, pp. 18-20, where Aldhelm's only competitor is Vergil.

75. Tangl, p. 19: *Et licet interim, ut nancta sum, aspectu corporali visualiter defraudata sim, sororis tamen semper amplexibus collum tuum constrinxero.*

76. *Ibid.*: *Iesum testor: ubique dolor, ubique pavor, ubique mortis imago.* Cf. *Aeneid* II, 369-70: *Crudelis ubique luctus, ubique pavor et plurima mortis imago.*

77. *Ibid.*, p. 20: *Quapropter crede mihi, non sic tempestate iactatus portum nauta desiderat, non sic sitientia imbres arva desiderant, non sic curvo litore anxia filium mater expectat, quam ut ego visibus vestris frui cupi*. Cf. Jerome *ep*. 3 to Rufinus, CSEL 54, for the same images and formulation.

78. Tangl, p. 21. The passage deserves full quotation, for it sums up the anglo-saxon concept of spiritual friendship: *Ego autem similiter Ealdeorcth pauperculus Christi in Domino cum omni affectu saluto te. Deprecor te, ut illius amicitiae quam olim spopondisti, in tuis deificatis orationibus recorderis, et licet corpore separemur, tamen recordatione iungamur.*

79. See Jean Nicholson, '*Feminae gloriosae*: Women in the age of Bede', *Medieval Women*, ed. Derek Baker, Studies in Church History. Subsidia I (Blackwell, Oxford, 1978).

80. Tangl, *ep* 14, p. 21.

81. CSEL 54, p. 45=*ep* 14 *ad Heliodorum*, which we have seen before!

82. Tangl. *ep* 14, p. 23: *tedebit nos vite nostrae et pene nobis pertesum est vivere. Omnis homo in sua causa deficiens et in suis consiliis diffidens querit sibi amicum fidelem in cuius consiliis confidat, qui in suis diffidet et talem fiduciam habeat in illo, ut omnem secretum sui pectoris pandet et aperiat, et ut dicitur: quid dulcius est, quam habeas illum, cum quo omnia possis loqui ut tecum.*

See Pseudo-Seneca, *De moribus* 20, for this last line.

Cf. Cicero *De amic.* 22: *Quid dulcius quam habere quicum omnia audeas sic loqui ut tecum.* Tangl did not identify this passage but the great scholar Wilhelm Levison traced it in his appendix 'On the Correspondence of Boniface', *England and the Continent in the Eighth Century* (Clarendon Press: Oxford, 1946) p. 283.

83. Tangl, *ep* 14, p. 26: *Amicus diu quaeritur, vix invenitur, difficile servatur*. See Jerome *ep* 3 to Rufinus, CSEL 54:18.

84. Wilhelm Levison (note 82 above) deals only with such Letters as manifestations of the level of learning (p. 150). Eleanor Duckett, *Anglo-Saxon Saints and Scholars* (New York: Macmillan, 1948) rephrases such letters but does not relate them to the ideal of friendship (pp. 370, 372).

85. Tangl, *ep* 27., p. 44: *Obsecro igitur per Deum sororem carissimam, immo matrem ac dominam dulcissimam, ut adsidue pro me dignetur. . .*

86. Ibid., Fidem antiquam inter nos numquam deficere scias.

87. *Ibid.*, *ep* 29, p. 52: *Rogo tuam clementiam ut memorare digneris prioris amicitiae quam iam dudum cum patre meo copulasti, cuius vocabulum est Dynne, in occiduis regionibus. . . .*

88. *Ibid.*, p. 53: *Ergo unica filia sum ambobus parentibus meis, et utinam licet sum indigna, ut merear te infratris locum accipere, quia, in nullo hominum generis mei tanta fiducia spei posita est mihi quanta in te.*

89. Tangl, *ep* 70, p. 143: *. . .caritas illa, quae inter nos est copulata spiritali germanitate.*

90. Tangl, *ep* 93, p. 212 (dated to 752). *Fraternae dilectionis tuae* **spiritalem amicitiam,** *quam sepe in necessitatibus meis pro Dei intuitu mecum fecisti, dignas gratias, quantas meruisti, persolvere non possum.*

91. Tangl, *ep* 98, p. 219: *per illam inmarcesibilem spiritalis amicitiae necessitudinem.* The Letter is dated to about 738, making it the earliest use of the term we have outside of Bede, whose *Life* of Cuthbert is dated to shortly before 721 (Colgrave, note 10 above, p. 16).

92. Tangl, *ep* 117, p. 252 (dated 759-65): *reminiscens videlicet, qualiter inter nos in civitate Romana de amicitiae conventione conloquium habuimus, quod etiam nos servare omnimodis confitemur.*

93. Tangl, *ep* 135, p. 274: *ad memoriam reducas antiquam amicitiam nostram qui inter nos habuimus in Maldubia civitate, quando Eaba abbas in amabile caritate nutrivit te. Et hoc signum, recordor, quod pro nomine vocabit te Lytel.* Boniface also writes of *antiquam amicitiam* in a letter to a former student in asking for help in sending some manuscripts (*ep* 34).

94. Tangl, *ep* 63, p. 128: *Consuetudo apud homines esse dinoscitur, cum alios triste et honerosum quid acciderit, ancxiate mentis solacium vel consilium ab illis querere, de quorum maxime amicitia vel sapientia et foedere confidunt.*

95. Still useful on this subject is Adalbert Ebner, *Die klösterlichen Gebets-Verbrüderungen bis zum Ausgange des Karolingischen Zeitalters* (Regensburg, 1810). See now especially the work of Karl Schmid, many of whose articles were collected in *Gebetsgedenken und adliges Selbstverständnis im Mittelalter* (Jan Thorbecke Verlag: Sigmaringen 1983).

96. Tangl, ep. 138, pp. 277-8: *Fateor enim tibi per Deum, quod contra voluntatem tuam nulla dignitas seculi, nulla secularis amicitia me hic ullo modo retinere potest; maxime quod te super omnes homines diligo, deus testis est.*

97. The fullest treatment is H. Hahn, *Bonifaz und Lull* (Leipzig, 1883). Also Levison (note 82 above).

98. Tangl *ep* 143, p. 282: *Quid est, frater mi, quod tam longum tempus intermisisti, quod venire tardasti? Quare non vis cogitare, quod ego sola in hac terra et nullus alius frater visitet me neque propinquorum aliquis ad me veniet?* We cannot be sure that this letter is from Berthgyth, but it is so close in theme and style to the ensuing letters from her that it is likely she wrote this one also.

99. Tangl *ep* 144, p. 285: *Nunc ergo rogo te, dilectissime frater me, ut venias ad me aut me facias venire, ut te conspiciam antiquam moriar, quia numquam descendit dilectio tua ab anima mea.*

100. I am especially indebted to Heinrich Fichtenau, *The Carolingian Empire*, trans. Peter Munz (Harper: New York, 1964) and Pierre Riché, *Daily Life in the World of Charlemagne*, trans. Jo Ann McNamara (University of Pennsylvania, 1978).

101. MGH *Epistolae* IV, ed. Ernestus Dümmler (Berlin, 1895), *ep* 14, p. 221: *Cum quadam die valde diligenda, honoranda atque laudanda devotio tua precipue mihi, cui gratis, id est absque merito, sola tua te benignitate instigante, piam amicitiam impendis, et manibus gestaret et ore proferret ea quae ad edificationem bonarum mentium pertinent, cognoverunt qui presentes aderant sollertissimam intentionem tuam velle secum semper habere de scripturis divinis aliqua.*

102. MGH *Epistolae* III (Berlin, 1899), ed. Karolus Hampe, *ep* 1, p. 109 dated to after 2 April 823. To Abbot Ansgisus of Fontenelles: *Obsecro dilectionem tuam, ut non graviter, sed potius misericorditer et amicabiliter accipere digneris, quod apud te pro necessitate N., quondam hominis nostri, nunc autem hominis domini Lotharii, intercedo, ut eum beneficium, quod ego illi dedi. . . .*

103. *Ibid., ep* 58, pp. 138-9, dated to 840: *N. comes rogavit me, ut te precarer de illis porcis, quos tu in eius ministerium ad pascendum misisti, ut ei liceret eosdem porcos sibi retinere, usque crassiores et meliores fierent, ut ille eos iusto pretio ad opus dominicum conparasset. Ille enim, sciens nostram amiciciam, putavit me hoc aput te impetrare potuisse*. . . .

104. For an extensive recent bibliography of works on Alcuin, see Peter Godman's introduction to *Alcuin: the Bishops, King and Saints of York*, Oxford Medieval Texts (Clarendon Press, 1982). For general biographical information I have used Eleanor Duckett, *Alcuin: Friend of Charlemagne* (Macmillan, New York: 1951). We need a good biography of Alcuin that could relate his personal and religious life to the development of Carolingian Empire. Fichtenau's treatment (note 100 above) is in many respects a description of the Empire on the basis of the alcuinian sources without ever letting Alcuin be understandable to us as a whole human being with contradictory traits.

105. MGH *Epist.* IV (Berlin, 1895), ed. Ernestus Dümmler, *ep* 10, p. 36: *O si mihi translatio Abacuc esset subito concessa, quam citatis manibus ruerem in amplexus paternitatis vestrae, et quam compressis labris non solum oculos aurea et os, sed etiam manuum vel pedum singulos digitorum articulos, non semel, sed multoties oscularer*. (The biblical reference is Daniel 14:35-38).

106. Riché, p. 265 (note 100): 'We must take care not to place more significance on these declarations than they deserve. Alcuin often borrowed expressions from Jerome's letter to Rufinus and from commonplaces in antique literature on friendship.' John Boswell (1980) p. 190.

107. The material of Alcuin's letters is so abundant that I have concentrated on them and only occasionally compared them with statements of friendship and love to be found in his poems.

108. *Ep* 31, *MGH Epistolae* IV, p. 72: *Spiritalis amicitiae cupidus, vestrae sanctitati parvitatis meae litterula dirigere curavi, ut et pactum antiquae familiaritatis innovarem et me vestris sacratissimis commendarem orationibus.*

109. *Ep* 24, p. 65: *amicitia fraternae dilectionis*. . . *olim inter nos quoque specialiter verbis est coniuncta pacifica.*

110. *Ep* 111, p. 159: To Megenfrid royal treasurer, he admonishes King Charles to send mild and abstinent priests to the pagans and not to collect tithes from among them (dated to 796). Here the bonds of friendship and church politics are enmeshed in each other:

Solet itaque cartula caritatis calamo perscripta inter amicales currere personas, ut ardorem sui pectoris litteris fraternis ostendat obtutibus, et quod intus latet in animo, foras videatur in scriptis. Unde ego tui memor, amice arissime, tibi hos tuae salutis, immo et multorum, ammonitorios dirigere curavi apices.

This preamble resembles the arengae of later medieval documents, or, more precisely, a *captatio benevolentiae* in an eleventh or twelfth century letter. Alcuin is quite aware how to use different types of letters (as here the letter of advice: *ammonitorios*. . . *apices*) in order to express his intentions. Alcuin's various types of letters could be looked upon as a source of inspiration for high medieval *ars dictaminis*. Note that most medieval letters were dictated to a secretary. Walter Goffart of the University of Toronto has pointed out to me in his helpful critical remarks to an earlier draft of this chapter that 'letter writing was an excercise in oratory, to one's secretary, not an interior meditation to a blank page'.

111. *Ep* 13, *MGH Epist.* IV, p. 39: *Ubi est dulcissimum inter nos conloquium. Ubi sacrarum litterarum studium desiderabile? Ubi laeta facies, quam conspicere solebam? Ubi communio caritatis, quam fraternus amor hinc inde exercuit?*

112. As Dümmler writes the first time Alcuin borrows Jerome's adage to Rufinus about the friendship which can end as never having been true: *'Proverbium Alcuino*

valde tritum ex Hieronymi epist. 3 . . . vide infra epp. 147, 170, 204, 212, 250'. This is a note to *ep* 18, p. 49. Alcuin's text is: *Quia amicitia, quae deseri potest, numquam vera fuit. Amicus fidelis diu quaeritur, vix Invenitur, difficile servatur.* Alcuin builds on this idea: *Vos quaerens inveni amicos, servabo amicos nec dimittam, quos amare coepi.* The letter is addressed to Ethelred king of Northumbria and his chief men who he admonishes to better lives after the attack by Northmen on Lindisfarne. It has to be taken into consideration that Alcuin would have deliberately used such simple epigrams in order to gain the attention and admiration of a lay audience here.

113. *Ep* 39, *MGH Epist.* IV, p. 82 (dated c. 793-95): *Amico antiquo novus non est similis. Amicus qui fortunam sequitur, et tempus observat, qui iuxta loci qualitatem mutatur, numquam verus fuit.*

114. *Ibid.*: *Quia in te, frater sanctissime, veram inveni caritatem, ideo nulla terrarum spatia me prohibent, secundum oportunitatem portantis cupiens te in Christo perenniter frui, cuius amor nostra utinam impleat corda, ut per eius dilectionem nobis inviolabilis permaneat fraternitas.*

115. See the Prooemium to *Alcuini Epistolae* (MGH *Epist.* IV, p. 4). The *MS* is Codex Bibl. Palatin. Vindobon. 808, written at Salzburg under Arno's direction in about 802-804 (Alcuin died in 804).

116. MGH *Epist.* IV, pp. 5-6. Here the development of the collection is not as clear as the Salzburg one.

117. *Ep* 146, p. 236: *Et dum hanc perlegas cartulam. Cito remitte alteram. Ut sciam, quid acturus sit Aquila cum aviculis suis. . .*

118. *Ep* 260, p. 418, which cannot be dated more precisely than sometime between 798 and 802, when the bulk of Alcuin's letters to Arno that we have through the Salzburg collection was composed. From *ep* 146 in 798 to *ep* 266, which may be from 803, I count 35 letters to Arno.

119. *Ep* 156, p. 254: *Per quoddam mentis excessum, o frater venerande, haec locutus sum, non tam ordinate quam epistolaris postulat angustia, sed tam affective quam intima cordis conpunctio exegit. Tu tamen, dulcissime pater et familiaris meus, patienter sustine cordis mei lacrimas. Et tecum reconde quod mecum audisti.*

120. *Ep* 265, p. 424: *Quod me tarditatis vel neglegentiae scribere vobis accusastis, ut fateor iuste: et hoc propter inopiam portitorum, qui vix fideles inveniuntur. Igitur longinquitas terrarum prohibet ex his partibus ad vos quemlibet, nisi raro transire.* Also *ep* 208, p. 346.

121. *Ep* 157, p. 255: *Et sollicitus fui in his litteris audire aliquid: unde eas dirigeres, vel qua die, vel de quo loco, vel quomodo dispositum habuisses facere secundum Dei voluntatem; et quando te sperarem in has venire partes.*

122. *Ibid.*: *Et utinam veniat volando aquila mea orare apud Sanctum Martinum: ut ibi amplecter alas illius suavissimas, et teneam, quem diligit anima mea, nec dimittam eum, donec introducam illum in domum matris meae, et osculetur me osculo oris sui; et gaudeamus ordinata caritate invicem.*

123. *The Carolingian Empire* (note 100 above) p. 101: 'Love of God, love of one's neighbour and profane love between friends were all utterly confused.' The statement reflects more Fichtenau's value system than Alcuin's.

124. MGH *Epist.* IV, *ep* 147, p. 236.

125. As *ep* 107, p. 154: *Tu vero pater sancte, amice fidelis, frater dilecte, fili carissime.*

126. As he tried to explain to the monks of York as a reason for not returning to them (*ep*42, p. 89): *Quia talis amicus mei cuilibet simili non est contemnendus. Dei enim gratia faciente plurimis profuit amicitia, quam deus mihi donavit cum illo.*

127. Fichtenau (note 100 above) p. 95, calls Alcuin 'in every respect a collector. . . He collected riches: he collected friends'. If so he was at least a collector who enjoyed collecting people and seems to have been concerned for them.

128. *Ep* 71, p. 114: *Omnibus in Christi caritate amicis.*

129. As *Ep* 218, p. 362, where he expresses a desire to see his friend Arno before he dies and to speak with him as a necessary preparation for death: *Quae fraterna conlocutione multum profierce nemini dubium esse debet decente ipsa veritate: 'Ubi sunt duo vel tres congregati in nomino meo, ibi sum in medio eorum'* (Matt 18:20). *Quid deerit boni consilii ubi tantum mediator interesse dinoscitur?* Here the presence of the friend and that of Christ are linked according to the passage in Saint Matthew.

130. *Ep* 294, p. 451: . . . *quatenus puras et liberas manus ad dominum deum tuum levare valeas* (Cf. 1 Tim 2:8).

131. *Ibid.*: *Quid est fili, quod de te audio, non uno quolibet in angulo susurrante, sed plurimis publice cum risu narrantibus: quod adhuc puerilibus deservias immunditiis, et quae numquam facere debuisses, numquam dimittere voluisses.* See Boswell (1980), p. 191, who has apparently misunderstood the tone and intention of this letter. His source of inspiration is apparently Fichtenau (note 100 above), p. 94, in referring to this letter: '. . . Several kinds of perversion were not unkown'.

132. *Ep* 65, p. 107.

133. He does, however call King Offa's daughter *dulcis amica* (*ep* 102, p. 149) and he speaks of his *amicali dilectione* for her (*ep* 103). But such variants of *amicus* are rare in Alcuin's addresses to women.

134. *Ep* 15, p. 40, dated to 793: . . . *ita ut ex eo die, quo pactum caritatis tecum inivi, dulcedine dilectionis tuae per singula pene momenta pascebar.*

135. *Ep* 196, p. 324: *Nam sicut loquentis lingua in aure audientis, ita scribentis calamus proficit in oculo legentis; et ad interiora cordis pervenit sensus dirigentis sicut verba instruentis.*

136. *Ibid.*, pp. 324-5: *Memento clarissimum in sancta ecclesia divinae scripturae doctorem, beatissimum siquidem Hieronimum, nobilium nullatenus spernere feminarum preces, sed plurima illarum nominibus in propheticas obscuritates dedicasse opuscula: saepiusque de Bethleem castello, Christi dei nostri nativitate consecrato, ad Romanas arces epistolares iisdem petentibus volare cartulas, nec terrarum longinquitate vel procellosis Adriatici maris fluctibus territum, quin minus sanctarum virginum petitionibus adnueret. Minore vadosum Ligeri flumen quam Tyrreni maris latitudo periculo navigatur. Et multo facilius cartarum portitor tuarum de Turonis Parisiacam civitatem, quam illius de Bethleem Romam, pervenire poterit.*

137. *Alcuin, Friend of Charlemagne* (note 104 above) p. 97: '. . . behind all can be felt in him now and again a hint of an inner uncertainty, of a lack of confidence in himself and his standing, which rarely allowed him to rest tranquil and secure. . .'.

138. *The Carolingian Empire* (note 100 above) p. 97: 'This newly found inwardness sprang from the terrifying thought of the Last Judgment, the fear of which made him tremble more and more'. I think it is wrong to label this a 'last-minute change of heart' in Alcuin, for we see his concern for death and requests for prayers through his letter collection. Fichtenau is far too harsh on Alcuin because the latter does not live up to the historian's own conception of Christianity as an ascetic, personal religion. He has little feeling for the community and liturgical experience the christian religion could provide in the carolingian age. Here Riché (note 100 above) is more generous and understanding. I am nevertheless indebted to Fichtenau for the clarity and forthrightness of his conceptions.

139. Contained in MGH *Epist.* V (Berlin, 1899) ed. Ernestus Dümmler.

140. MGH *Poetae* II (Berlin 1884), ed. Ernestus Dümmler, VI, pp. 169-70:
Vive, mea vires lassarumque anchora rerum,
Naufragio et litus tutaque terra meo,
Solus honor nobis, urbs in fidissima semper
Curisque afflicto tuta quies animo. . .

This is beautifully translated in Helen Waddell, *Mediaeval Latin Lyrics* (Penguin Classics: Harmondsworth, 1968).

141. *Ibid.*, X, p. 172, Versus ad Amicum:
Tu devota piis connectis vincula verbis,
Decantans placide pectora amica notans.

142. As Friduric of Utrecht, XVII, p. 181: Eigil was Rhabanus's predecessor at Fulda (817-22), XXII, pp. 186-7:
Te unum prae multis corde tenere volo
Sis mihi semper idem, quia sum tibi semper et idem.

143. XXV, p. 188:
Te mea mens sequitur, sequitur quoque carmen amoris
Expotans animo prospera cuncta tibi.
. . . Hocque, pater, monui, moneo te iterumque monebo,
Sis memor utique mei, sicut et ipse tui.
Ut deus in terris quos hic coniunxit amicos
Gaudentes pariter iungat in arce poli.

144. XXIX, p. 190:
Tu meus es placitus, placeas super aethera Christo.
Sis carus sanctis, tu meus es placitus.
Unicus esque meus, auctor te protegat unus
Unum cum multis unicus esque meus.

145. I have to disagree with Eleanor Duckett's evaluation of Rhabanus as not reaching the literary or human level of Alcuin (p. 311). This is certainly true in his letters but not in his poetry.

146. Adele Fiske, 'Alcuin and Mystical Friendship', *Studi Medievali* (1961) 551-75, p. 575: 'When one contrasts both the extent of Alcuin's correspondence and the intense vitality of his friendship with the meager collections of letters from contemporary writers and their matter-of fact, utilitarian or conventionalized attitude to friendship, one cannot help but wonder at the cause of this'.

147. MGH *Poet*. II (Berlin 1884), ed. Ernestus Dümmler: XXXD, p. 385
Ut ros graminibus, piscibus unda freti
Aer uti oscinibus, rivorum ut murmura pratis
Sic tua, pusiole, cara mihi facies.

148. Walter Horn and Ernest Born, *The Plan of Saint Gall* I (Berkeley, 1979) p. 343. Table II: List of the approximate number of monks in certain carolingian monasteries.

149. MGH *Poet*. II: XLV, 'Ad Probum Presbyterum', p. 394:
Sum tuus, esto meus, quod uterque habet alterius sit,
Sic ego tu sim alter tuque mihi alter ego.

150. *Ibid.*, XVIII, p. 364: *Sis mihi quam merui longe, rogo, maior amicus.*

151. See MGH *Poet*. I, p. 240, a poem of Alcuin to Paulinus of Aquileia: *Pars animae melior, nostrae pars inclyta vitae.* Cf. Horace *Carmina* III (to Vergil). . . *animae dimidium meae.*

152. Fiske (1970) ch. 12,1. From MGH *Poet*. II: XXIX, p. 386. For an evaluation of the poetry of Strabo as an indication of individual consciousness, see Georg Misch,

Geschichte der Autobiographie II:2 (Frankfurt am Main, 1955), pp. 442-51. For the difficulty of translating Carolingian diminutives like *pusiole*, see John Boswell (1980) p. 193.

153. MGH *Epist.* VI (Berlin, 1875) ed. Ernestus Dümmler, *epp.* 1-5. For a more sympathetic interpretation of these letters as indications of genuine warmth on the part of Lupus, see Adele Fiske (1970). Ch. 11,4.

154. See the buoyant evaluation of M. L. W. Laistner, *Thought and Letters in Western Europe* (Methuen: London, 1957) 252-59.

155. *Ep.* 6, MGH *Epist.* VI, p. 18: *annitentibus amicis.*

156. *Ep.* 6, p. 62: . . .*hac epistola meam offero et vestram expeto amicitiam, ut nobis vicissim cum in sacris orationibus, tum etiam in quibuslibet aliis utilitatibus prodesse curemus.*

157. *Ep.* 36, p. 45: Lupus to his friend the monk Altwin—he has taken charge of the monastery in the absence of the abbot—: *Namque ita me variis et inevitabilibus involutum offendisses negotiis, ut vix intra multos dies una hora vacuas tibi aures praebere potuissem; quin etiam abbatis absentia intentioni tuae plurimum derogasset.*

158. As *ep.* 50, p. 55. Lupus asks a friend to approach a certain lady to request money so that he can go to court. Money and friendship are intermeshed: *Pecunia nobis iam nulla est, quae tanto spatio vix potuit sufficere. . . non usquequaque inhonestum credidi opem ab amicis petere, quorum fides mihi non fluxa in similibus inventa est.*

159. As *ep.* 56, MGH *Epist.* IV, p. 99, dated between 782-96 and starting, 'Quia amicus in necessitate conprobatur'. Ardo's hagiography of Benedict of Aniane (MGH SS XV, 200-20) reveals nothing about any penchant to friendship (trans. Allen Cabaniss, *The Emperor's Monk* [Arthur Stockwell: Ilfracombe, Devon, 1979; distributed in North America by Cistercian Publications]). The fullest modern account is Josef Narberhaus, *Benedict von Aniane: Werk und Persönlichkeit*, Beiträge zur Geschichte des alten Mönchtums und des Benediktinerordens 16 (Münster in Westfalen, 1930).

160. Jean Leclercq, 'Les *Munimenta Fidei* de Saint Benoît d'Aniane', *Studia Anselmiana* 20, Analecta Monastica. Première Série (Vatican City, 1948) 21-74, esp. pp. 54-55: 'De Modis Amiciciarum et Vera Amicicia'. The sermon of Augustine is nr. 385 (PL 39.1691-92). For Leclercq's analysis, pp. 72-3, esp. note 49: 'Il est regrettable que cette partie du texte, peut-être parce qu'elle est la plus originale, soit la plus corrumpue'.

161. Now collected in Kassius Hallinger, *Corpus Consuetudinum Monasticarum* T. I: *Initia Consuetudinis Benedictinae*. Consuetudines Saeculi Octavi et Novi (Francis Schmitt, Siegburg: 1963), as in 'Memoriale Qualiter', p. 246: *Caveant se de saeculari vel superfluo risu, de frequenti locutione cum amicis et si necesse fuerit, ut aliter recte esse non possit, non loquatur solus cum viro nisi praesentibus et audientibus aliis fratribus de quorum fide certa sit fiducia; et hoc maxime in iuvenibus observetur.* This precept is for contact with laymen, but its spirit indicates that long and intimate conversations among monks would also have been discouraged.

CHAPTER FOUR
THE ECLIPSE OF MONASTIC FRIENDSHIP

1. As we can see if we compare one of Alcuin's letters with one of Ratherius of Verona's. Alcuin is almost always understandable in his mode of expression, while Ratherius

is contorted and obscure. The same could be said for the biography of John of Gorze by John of Metz. However informative it is, its latin is difficult to penetrate, and there seems to be an attempt at deliberate obscurity, a great contrast from carolingian lives, such as Einhard's of Charlemagne or Ardo's of Benedict of Aniane. However derivative these latter products are, they are written with a clarity and accessibility that disappear with carolingian culture.

2. Contained in MGH, *Poetarum Latinorum Medii Aevi* IV, fas. 2, rec. Karl Strecker (Berlin 1923), 'De caritate', pp. 526-29. The fourth and fifth stanzas can be seen as especially 'monastic' in application to harmony in community:

4. *Simul ergo cum in unum* *congregamur,*
Ne nos mente dividamus, *caveamus.*
Cessent iurgia maligna, *cessent lites,*
Vere medium sic nostrum *Christus erit.*
Ubi caritas est vera, *deus ibi est.*

5. *Nam ut caritas coniungit* *et absentes,*
Sic discordia seiungit *et praesentes.*
Unum omnes indivise *sentiamus.*
Ne et simul congregati *dividamur.*
Ubi caritas est vera, *deus ibi est.*

3. See the excellent article by Hugh Feiss, 'The Office for the Feast of the Trinity at Cluny in the late eleventh Century', *Liturgy O.C.S.O.* 17,3 (Trappist Kentucky, 1983) 39-66.

4. A comparison of the words *loqui* and *silentium* in the Index of Kassius Hallinger, *Corpus Consuetudinum Monasticarum* I (Siegburg 1963) reveals that there were far more instances in which silence was to be kept than when talking was allowed among the monks.

5. James Midgley Clark, *The Abbey of St. Gall as a Centre of Literature and Art* (Cambridge, 1926).

6. Walter Horn and Ernest Born, *The Plan of St. Gall* (University of California Press, 1979) I-III.

7. M.L.W. Laistner, *Thought and Letters in Western Europe* AD 500-900 (Methuen, London, 1957) p. 201.

8. As in Walafrid Strabo's dedication of his book 'Of Gardening' to Grimald, with its images of laughing boys in a happy school with huge apples. Trans. in Helen Waddell, *Medeiaval Latin Lyrics*, p. 127.

9. Contained in Ernst Dümmler, *Das Formelbuch des Bischofs Salomo III* (Leipzig 1857) p. 80, with commentary pp. 161-2. Also found in Wolfram von den Steinen, *Notker der Dichter und seine Geistige Welt* (A. Franke, Bern: 1948) p. 139 in Editionsband. (*defrudor* instead of *defraudor* is von den Steinen's reading).

10. *Ibid.*; *At nunc spernor ego, alter amatur homo.*
Sin magis ille senex odiis agitatus iniquis
Divisit socios corde furente locis,
Tum merore pari lugens et corde dolenti
Te sequor et lacrimis strata rigabo tua.

11. Dümmler, *Das Formelbuch* (note 9 above) p. 55: 'Epistola ad duos quosque'. For a treatment of the *Formelbuch* as a whole, see Wolfram von den Steinen's 'Notkers des Dichters Formelbuch', *Zeitschrift für Schweizerische Geschichte* 25 (1945) 449-90.

12. Dümmler, *Ibid.*; . . .*post dilectionem apostolorum et martyrum amicitiamque confessorum et virginum, familiaritatem patriarcharum et prophetarum et ipsius Domini quondam meditationem continuam, in quo omnes sancti fidelibus eius ubique praesentes assistunt, temporales et locales amicos habere didicerim, quamquam vos in Christo ipso teste diligam.*

13. I think especially of Bernard of Clairvaux's famed letter (*ep* 1) to his nephew Robert after the latter had left the Cistercian Order for the Cluniac, (*SBO p* 7). Also Jean Leclercq, 'Lettres de vocation à la vie monastique', *Studia Anselmiana* 37, Analecta Monastica. Troisieme Série (Herder: Rome, 1955) 169-97.

14. Dümmler (note 9 above) p. 62: *Et primum, quod opus habet professio vestra, quia literarum studiis ab infantia fuistis occupati obsecro, ut prosas orationes et strophas versuum congruas absque retractatione et dilatione texere curetis, quia, ut iam nunc advertere possumus, ita in posterum nos alloqui et salutare debemus, quando nos Alpium iuga, profunda vallium, rapidissimorum cursus omnium, lacuum procellae et nivalia frigora ab invicem separare coeperint*. . . .

15. Dümmler, p. 81.

16. According to LTK III (1931) col. 609, Ekkehard IV was born about 980 and died around 1060. His part of the *Casus Sancti Galli* covers the years 883 to 971. It is contained in *MGH SS* II (Hannover 1829, reprinted 1968) ed. G. H. Pertz, 78-147.

17. *MGH SS* II, p. 94: . . .*quantum a patribus audivimus, narrare incipimus*. . . . If Notker entered Saint Gall as a child in about the year 990, it is unlikely that there would have been many monks alive to tell about the doings of Notker the Stammerer, who died in 912. But there could have been a lively oral tradition about Notker and his circle.

18. *Ibid.*, p. 80.

19. *Ibid.*, p. 89: *Sed et amplius pace tua, sodes amande, loqui liceat. Bene enim et optime tecum actum noveris velim. Elemosinae enim, quae obitum praecedunt certiores et Deo sunt, quam quae sequuntur cariores*. . . .*Tandem in pristinam redeunt condicto mutuo sodalitatem, ut ultra neuter alterum nec serio deciperet nec ioco.*

20. *De Notkero, Ratperto, Tuotilone discipulis eius et Marcelli, quoniam quidem cor et anima una erant, mixtim, qualia tres unus fecerint, quantum a patribus audivimus, narrare incipimus* (p. 94).

21. *Erat tribus illis inseparabilibus consuetudo, permisso quidem prioris in intervallo laudum nocturno convenire in scriptorio collationesque tali horae aptissimas de scripturis facere* (p. 95). Notker calls the three 'senators for our republic'.

22. . . .*propter generis et propter ingenii nobilitatem semper amicus*. . . . (p. 112) The monk Victor asks permission to leave Saint Gall to see his friends outside: . . .*ut ad amicos foras eundi a decano licentiam Victor peteret* (p. 116). Knights provide insufficient safety against the friends of Victor: . . .*et iam sepe Victoris amicis milites sui securitatem frustra pro eo porrigerent* (p. 118).

23. *Audierant ne, mi anime, fratres omnia?* (p. 99); . . .*quod viderat, amabili suo aperuit* (p. 100).

24. *Enimvero hi tres, quamvis votis essent unicordes, natura tamen, ut fit, erant dissimiles.* (p. 94)

25. *Surgentibus a venia pariter omnes fratres occurrunt in amplexus et oscula, et quoniam incompetens hora esset, abbati decanum dirigunt, ut eis cum hospitibus incompetentia competere permitteret. Venit itaque laetus ipse, ut semper erat dulcissima caritatis anima, abbas, et meridiem usque nonam in sanctae hilaritatis gaudio perduxerant*. . . . *Ibi tanta hilaritate usque ad vesperum iam pene sonatum commanent ut senum qui adhuc hodie talia memorant, recordationem voluptas sit audire* (pp. 131-32—the event would have taken place in 966).

26. Ch. 38, *MGH SS* IV: pp. 269-70.

27. See G. Miccoli, 'Ratherio, un riformatore?', *Raterio di Verona* (Todi, 1971) 85-143.

28. MGH *Die Briefe der Deutschen Kaiserzeit* I: *Die Briefe des Bischofs Rather von Verona*, bearb. von Fritz Weigle (Herman Böhlaus Nachfolger, Weimar, 1949) nr. 1, p. 18.

29. *Ibid.*, p. 26: *Relinquere enim saeculum et sequi Deum non est aliud nisi ad certamen provocare diabolum, amicitias vero postea secularium ambire nil aliud quoque quam pacis dextras inimico dare. Scitis autem, domine, scitis, quia peius est cum inimico regis pacem facere quam terga prebere. Quod si aut dux ipse aut alius quilibet huius saeculi dives aut consanguineus vester confabulationem requisierit vestram, dicite, quod antiqui solebant dicere: Quid mihi et vobis? Ego mortuus sum. . . .*

30. *Itaque callidissime me affligebat, ut rarrissimus esset in regno, qui non aestimaret amicissimum eum esse mihi omnino* (*ep* 7, p. 39).

31. . . . *cum similitudo desideriorum aequalitatem gignat semper effectuum et humane amicitie pares animos et non dissimiles expetant voluntates.* (*ep* 16, p. 87—Cicero's *De amicitia* §§ 20, 61 and 74 are given as source, but it is just as likely that Ratherius is drawing on the statements on friendship in Ambrose's *De officiis* 3, ch. 22).

32. *Ep* 30, p. 175: *non est amici sed inimicissimi persuasio, fateor, talis.*

33. *Ep* 29, p. 163.

34. *Eadem namque velle atque nolle, ea demum amicitia, si iuxta illum, qui hoc primitus dixit, est firma, vel si iuxta alium humanae amicitiae pares animos et non dissimiles expetunt adeo voluntates, ut numquam diversitas morum ad firmam possit pervenire concordiam, numquam vel apud me vel apud illos stabilitatem amicitia semper contraria cupiens obtinere ut non valuit nostra. . .* (*ep* 29, p. 160). Once again it is not clear if Ratherius is drawing directly on Cicero and Sallust, or on Ambrose *De officiis* 3, c. 22.

35. Bertram Colgrave, *Felix's Life of Saint Guthlac* (Cambridge, 1956) ch. xxx, p. 98: *Quomodo illum zabulus pseudosodalitate ieiunium docere tentavit.* Guthlac, however, belongs very much to the Anglo-Saxon period when friendship could also be seen as a spiritual blessing. He finds a friend and helper in Saint Bartholomew, ch. xxix, p. 96: *Sanctus autem Guthlac, his auditis et creditis fidelissimi amici sui dictis, spiritali gaudio repletus. . . .* Thus friendship with a saint is possible, but it does not seem to lead to friendship with living men.

36. Ch. 1, MGH SS IV: p. 386: *Haec audita secretissimis fratribus intimavit, et eorum suasionem suavi colloquio mitigavit, totamque spem pristinae destinationis in sua mente deposuit, et ob hoc tamen discendi studium non omisit.*

37. Ch. 24, p. 409: *in turba, quod paucorum est, quasi solus erat. . . quasi solitarius vixit.*

38. Ch. 8, p. 257; ch. 30, p. 266.

39. Ch. 9, p. 257; . . . *nimiam . . . colloqui familiaritatem.*

40. Ch. 37, p. 269.

41. Ch. 20, p. 261: *Unum nos semper idemque sensisse, nec umquam vota nostra in quocumque negotio discrepasse, dici non potest, frater dilectissime, quantum delector. . . .*

42. 'Gerbert bénédictin', a paper given at the abbey of Bobbio in July 1983 and to be published in Italian. Other studies of Gerbert include: Fritz Eichengrün, *Gerbert (Silvester II) als Persönlichkeit*, Beiträge zur Kulturgeschichte des Mittelalters und der Renaissance, 35 (Leipzig, 1928), and F. Picavet, *Gerbert, un pape philosphe*, Bibliothèque de l'Ecole des hautes études, Sciences religieuses 9 (Paris, 1897).

43. I use the edition of Fritz Weigle, *Die Briefsammlung Gerberts von Reims*, MGH Die Briefe der Deutschen Kaiserzeit II (Herman Böhlaus Nachfolger, Weimar, 1966).

44. Contained in PL 139: *Epistolae et diplomata, Sectio secunda: Epistolae et decreta pontificia.*

45. Weigle (note 42 above) *ep* 12, p. 25: *O amicorum fidissime, ne deseras amicum consilio et auxilio.*

46. *Ibid.*, *ep* 22, p. 44: *Felicem me iudico tante femine agnitione et amititia.* Notice that the manuscripts use both forms *amititia* and *amicitia* almost indiscriminately.

47. *Ibid.*, *ep* 30, p. 43: *Sit ergo vestre prudentie amici causam agere, pro se stare, de eo, ut nostis et ut equum est, ex fide promittere.* See Godefroid Kurth, *Notger de Liège et la civilisation au xe siècle* 1 (Paris, 1905). Kurth sees Gerbert's letters as evidence of a ceaseless political activity: 'Les lettres de Gerbert, que nous avons conservées, s'en allaient dans toutes les directions, encourageant ou stimulant les uns, gourmandant, s'il le fallait, les autres, déjouant les intrigues françaises et les intrigues bavaroises, organisant et centralisant toutes les démarches. . .' (p. 72).

48. Weigle (note 42 above) *ep* 44, pp. 72-3. Gerbert is writing to Abbot Eberhard of Tours: *Sed quia non is sum, qui cum Panetio interdum ab utili seiungam honestum, sed potius cum Tullio omni utili admisceam, has honestissimas atque sanctissimas amicitias nulla ex parte suo cuique utili vacare volo.* Cf. Cicero *De off.* 3, 7-12, as pointed out by Weigle.

49. *Ep* 45, Weigle, p. 74: *Quanto amore vestri teneamur, noverunt Latini ac barbari, qui sunt participes fructus nostri laboris.* The translation is from Harriet Pratt Lattin, *The Letters of Gerbert*, Columbia Records of Civilization nr. 60 (New York 1961), p. 91 (Letter 51).

50. *Ep* 46, Weigle, p. 75: *An quicquam melius amicis divinitas mortalibus concesserit nescio, si modo ii sunt, qui digne expetiti digne que videantur habiti.* Trans. Lattin, *ep* 52, p. 92.

51. *Ep* 48, Weigle, p. 78: *Eius amicitiam si in commune expetissetis*. . . . We do not have the full text of the letter.

52. *Ep* 60, Weigle, p. 92: *Amicitia Hugonis non segniter expetenda, sed omnino conandum, ne bene coepta mala abutamur*. Trans. Lattin, *ep* 66, p. 107.

53. Trans. Lattin, *ep* 201, p. 236. The letter is not included in Weigle, who considered it to be more a treatise than a letter. Text in Julien Havet, *Lettres de Gerbert*, Collection de Textes pour servir a l'étude et a l'enseignement de l'histoire (Picard, Paris 1889), *ep* 217, p. 203: *Unde enim familiae, unde urbes et regna, nisi societate et amicitia stabiliuntur?* (=Cicero *De inventione* I-II, iii, according to Lattin).

54. Fiske (1970), 'Gerbert and Cosmic Friendship', does her best to distinguish between the letters Gerbert wrote for others and those in his own name. In the latter the political significance of expressions of friendship is supposed to be minimized. I do not find this to be the case. Except for the letters to the monastery at Aurillac, Gerbert's letters, whether in his own persona or not, usually have political content.

55. Shortly before Adalbero's death, Gerbert wrote of his desire to know how things were with him: *Nam cuius affectum participes sumus, eius certe progressus et exitus viarum ignorare minime debemus*. *Ep* 149, Weigle p. 176. To the abbot of Aurillac soon after Adalbero's death, Gerbert writes that he and the archbishop had one heart and one mind (Acts 4:32)—*ep* 163, Weigle p. 191. I think Adele Fiske makes a great more out of Gerbert's friendship with Adalbero than can be said on the basis of the few direct statements we do have from each side.

56. *Ep* 157, Weigle p. 186: *Magnum argumentum est in sanctissima amicitia ac firma societate nos in eternum mansuros*. . . . The letter is from Archbishop Arnulf of Rheims to the archbishop of Trier and is of purely political content. Gerbert is probably behind it.

57. *Ep* 166, Weigle p. 195: *Petimus ergo omni affectu caritatis vos affore Remis II kl. april, si iure amititie quicquam promeruimus aut promereri posse putamur.*

58. As *ep* 194, p. 237 to Abbot Raimund and the monks in which he seems to regret ever having left the monastery of Saint Gerald: *Que adulescens didici, iuvenis amisi, et que iuvenis concupivi, senex contempsi.*

59. The *Vita* is contained in MGH SS IV, ed. H. Pertz (Hannover, 1841, reprinted 1968). The passage is from ch. 9, p. 585. As in most saints' lives of the period before 1050, it is the ascetic practices that are foremost in the text, and friendships are present only to set off these heroic deeds.

60. *Ibid.*, ch. 15, p. 588: *repete urbem Romam. Quo cum angelo bono te ducente perveneris, domnum abbatem Leonem nobis amicissimum ex nostra omniumque persona salutes. . . .*

61. *Ibid.*, ch. 16, p. 588: . . . *qui etiam sibi carne et spiritu duplex germanus, et ab infantia semper fidissimus comes adhesit.*

62. *Ibid.*, ch. 18, p. 589: *Dilexerunt eum omnes, sed prae omnibus abbas suus qui et post se totis cohortibus fratrum praefecerat illum.*

63. *Ibid.*, ch. 23, p. 591: *Cum quo vir Dei mansit bonum tempus, quia valde familiarissimus sibi erat et nocte pariter ac die velut dulcissimus cubicularius imperiali camerae adhaesit.*

64. K. J. Leyser, *Rule and Conflict in an Early Medieval Society: Ottonian Saxony* (Edward Arnold: London, 1979) p. 1: 'The world of the tenth century is, or ought to be, strange to us, much stranger than that of the twelfth with its lyrical, individualistic, witty and rationalizing traits'.

65. In this part of the biography the term *amicissimus* is used for the favourable disposition of a secular ruler towards Adalbert (ch. 25, p. 593). This relationship is purely secular and has no religious overtones.

66. Ch. 29, MGH SS IV: p. 594: *Scias, dulcissime fili, quia amicus noster Adalbertus ambulat cum Spiritu sancto, et beatissimo fine praesentem vitam erit terminaturus.*

67. As Peter Brown pointed out to me in a letter in the autumn of 1983, the crucial turning point in friendship must come when the saints as friends provide the foundation for looking at one's earthly brethren as friends.

68. I cannot agree with Adele Fiske in her chapter on Adalbert of Prague (1970) that the saint's impulse to friendship is summed up in his friendship with Christ 'described in terms of human relations'. This theme I find mainly in Archbishop Bruno of Cologne's Vita of Adalbert, which is basically only a literary polish of John's Life. It adds the theme of Adalbert's closeness to Christ almost as a hagiographical *sine qua non* and not as a new dimension in any understanding of Adalbert. Mother Fiske's chapter on Adalbert is otherwise a sensitive treatment of an obscure representative for the ideal and practice of friendship in this period.

69. Contained in MGH SS IV, 337-77. A good treatment of this biography is contained in Ludwig Zoepf, *Das Heiligen Leben im 10. Jahrhundert*, Beiträge zur Kulturgeschichte des Mittelalters und der Renaissance 1 (Leipzig and Berlin, 1908) especially pp. 94-102. See also Stephanus Hilpisch, *Geschichte des Benediktinischen Mönchtums* (Herder: Freiburg im Breisgau, 1929), 144-48 and E. Sackur, *Die Cluniacenser* I (Halle, 1892), 150-61.

70. Zoepf (note 69 above) p. 95: 'Das Werk ist eine Propagandaschrift für die Askese, die in der Persönlichkeit des Johannes ihren glänzendsten Vertreter gefunden hat'.

71. MGH SS IV, p. 338: . . . *et qui licet immeritum, dum nobiscum esset, sancta familiaritate sui non iudicavit indignum, nunc pie operi sui amoris instantem, ope amicae olim pietatis pro gratia sua, ut libere praesumo, non deseret.* This is clearly a commonplace: the author asks assistance from the saint whose life he is describing. But even if the saint's loyalty is friendly (*amicae*) the biographer does not claim that John of Gorze was his friend (*amicus*).

72. Ch. 27, MGH SS IV: p. 346: *Apud se enim omnimodis latens, vitam. . . oculis hominum, ubi in publicum exierit, offerre, summa via atque arte dissimulat.* Ch. 49, p. 351: . . . *ut solitarius inter multitudines vixerit.*

73. 'quasi solitarius vixit'. See note 37 above. John of Gorze died in 976 and his biography was written shortly thereafter, while Bruno of Cologne's was composed within a year after his death in 968 (see Hatto Kallfelz, *Lebensbeschreibungen einiger Bischöfe des 10.-12. Jahrhunderts* (Wissenschaftliche Buchgesellschaft, Darmstadt 1973) p. 172.

74. Zoepf (note 69 above) p. 103: 'Ein reich entwickeltes Innenleben, das selbst dem Vertrautesten soviel wie verborgen bleibt'.

75. Ch. 45, MGH SS IV: p. 350.

76. Ch. 130, pp. 375: . . . *amicitiam pacemque de infestatione latrunculorum sarracenorum quoque pacto conficiat* . . .

77. As when John is recalled to the court, ch. 135: *post aliquantum tempus Iohannes a rege revocatus, familiaria multa cum eo conseruit.*

78. *Ibid.*, ch. 84, p. 361.

79. The Latin *Vita* is in PL 73, appropriately among the *Vitae Patrum*. A translation of the Greek version is available in Elizabeth Dawes and Norman H. Baynes, *Three Byzantine Saints* (Mowbrays: London and Oxford, 1977; rpt. St. Vladimir Press).

80. Ch. 89-93, MGH SS IV: pp. 362-64.

81. Ch. 76, p. 358: *Alii eum hypocritam, alii avarum, alii tenacem, alii fraudatorem publice appellabant.* Some of the monks even accused John of entering the monastery so he could be better off than at home: *Tua huc subdolus contraxisti, ut liberius ea hic possideres, et melius quam domi sufficeres hic procurares.*

82. Thus Zoepf (note 69 above) classified the account as a biography and not as hagiography. His distinction can seem forced, for John is made out to be a saint, miracles or not.

83. The *Occupatio* was ed. by Antonius Swoboda (Leipzig 1900). According to Raffaello Morghen, 'it is still far from having been exhaustively studied', (in an excellent article, 'Monastic Reform and Cluniac Spirituality', p. 21 in Noreen Hunt, *Cluniac Monasticism in the Central Middle Ages* (Archon Books: London, 1971). An important study of this period is Barbara H. Rosenwein, *Rhinoceros Bound: Cluny in the Tenth Century* (University of Pennsylvania Press: Philadelphia, 1982). The work was unfortunately not available to me when I wrote this chapter in 1983.

85. *Ibid.* III, 844-47: *Quisquis amat mundum, non patris amor replet illum.*
Cuius amicitia dignus fit iudicis ira
Quod turpem pulchro praeferet vile et precioso.
Huius amicus enim patris est inimicus . . .

86. *Ibid.* VI, 92-93: *Huius, ait, pulchrum quid erit vel quid preciosum?*
Frumentum et vinum generantia virginitatem.

87. Contained in PL 133 and translated by Gerald Sitwell, *Saint Odo of Cluny* (Sheed and Ward: London, 1958), which also includes John of Salerno's Life of Odo. Sitwell's translation is of high quality, with good notes, and one hopes that the work will be reprinted for the benefit of students of this difficult and obscure period.

88. Bk. I. ch. 35, PL 133:663: *Verum cum in amicitia Wilelmi devictus pacem habere videretur, ut homini in Christo viventi persecutio non deesset, praedictum comitem Ademarum illi Satanas instigavit.*

89. *Ibid.* II, 2, col. 670 = : *Etenim dominus iste Guisbertus viro Dei charissimus erat, et pro communi sanctitate, mutuum sibi invicem contubernium praestabant.*

90. Trans. Sitwell (note 87 above) p. 156 = Book II, ch. 30 (PL 133:687): . . . *quem post orationem deosculans, dixit, 'Quid nobis, Geralde frater, ad refectionem daturus es? En apud te prandere venimus.' Dicebat enim hoc pro familiari contubernio quod apud illum isdem sacerdos habebat.*

91. John of Salerno's Vita is in PL 133:43-86. The *Vita altera* by the cluniac monk Nalgod in the twelfth century is in col. 85-104, with the a harsh critique of its predecessor: *Tanta erat verborum confusio, tam dispersa prolixitas, ita inordinatus et praeposterus ordo narrandi, ut ipsa series relationis vix sibi aut ratione aut tempore cohaereret* (col. 85). All this is true. John's *Vita* nevertheless has a closeness to its subject that Nalgod's lacks.

92. Trans. Sitwell (note 87 above) p. 50, from II.7 (PL 133:65).

93. Bk. III.5, PL 133:79: *Infelix ego, qui nec duobus expletis annis illi merui famulari.*

94. II. 5, col. 63: . . .*spiritualis ejus hilaritas internum gaudium nostro cordi inserebat. Sed ego indignus quid de eo digne dicere potero, aut quid enarrare de tanto gaudio? Revera cum menti nostrae aliter nequibamus satisfacere, vestimenta ejus osculabamur occulte.*

95. John brought his father to Cluny itself, while the house his mother joined is not named (I.35).

96. Bk. I. ch. 27, PL 133:55: *familiariter sibi conferret. . . recordatus denique domnus Adhegrinus sodalitatis antiquae et mox inflammatus charitatis igne respondit.*

97. *Memorials of Saint Dunstan*, ed. William Stubbs (Rolls Series: London 1874).

98. After reading through the letters of Gerbert and of Fulbert I reread the sections on these men in Sir Richard Southern's *The Making of the Middle Ages* (Hutchinson: London, Yale: New Haven, 1953), esp. pp. 197-201, and I find that I am in complete agreement with Southern's contrast between the isolated Gerbert and the influential Fulbert. How much influence Southern's thesis exerted on my unconscious as I read the original sources is difficult to say, but here as in so much else I have no hesitation in conceding the immense debt I have to him as a guide in medieval studies.

99. . . .*perennem fidelitatis habitum amicitiae tuae rependo*. Text and translation in Frederick Behrends, *The Letters and Poems of Fulbert of Chartres*, Oxford Medieval Texts (1976) pp. 3-4. Behrends volume is an important piece of scholarship. I find, however, that he easily slips into the term 'friendship' in translating Latin expressions that are not equivalent to this usage, as when Fulbert addressed Abbot Odilo of Cluny (*ep* 49, p. 84) *suus ut ait*. Here it is making the relationship too definite to translate 'his friend, as he calls him'.

100. *Ep* 19, Behrends, pp. 34-5: *Ne turberis, fili me, nec decidat cor tuum ab amore et fiducia nostri, non enim dereliquit te anima mea.*

101. *Ep* 50, pp. 86-7: *Placuit, ut ipse fatetur, paternitati vestrae me licet indignum iudicem vitae vestrae, mandando mihi ut litteratim describerem vobis quid michi videretur de vestra quantum dici fas est inreprehensibili conversacione?*

102. *Ibid.*, pp. 90-91: *Quid illud sit, quam optime nosti.*

103. *Ibid.*: *Non enim potest a se quisquis recedere* (*Sententiae* ii. 26. 2).

104. *Ep* 64, Behrends, pp. 108-11.

105. Bk. I.11, PL 142:906.

106. *Ep* 64, Behrends, pp. 110-11: *Cuius etiam caritas singualiter afficiat animam meam aggrediar dicere, rem inerrabilem videar velle narrare.*

107. *Ep* 88, pp. 156-57: *Absencia tua sepe commemoror quam necessarius eras presens.*

108. As seen in *ep* 92, pp. 164-69.

109. *Ep* 67, pp. 114-15: *Dum apud nos morareris inter primos amicorum meorum habitus. . . .*

110. As Behrends points out in his notes, Hildegar's source is Cicero's *De officiis* iii. 33.118.

111. *Ep* 95, pp. 172-75: *Te enim cunctos mortales, quod simplicitas adulacionis ignara fatetur, animae meae visceribus diligendum mandavi. Sum namque divina procurante gratia*

disciplinae tuae vernaculus a puero; nec ulli unquam tanta meae conscientiae secreta, nam aliis quaedam, tibi omnia detexi.

112. *Ep* 105, pp. 190-91: *Salutate, precor, vice mea domnum meum Sigonem et Hilduinum, priorem animum meum, alterum animae meae dimidium* (Cf. Horace *Carmina* 1.3.8).

113. *Ep* 109, pp. 194-95: . . . *vitae nobis dulcedo pariter et gloria.* Again Behrends has caught the precise classical reminiscence: Macrobius, *Commentarium in Somnium Scipionis* i. 1.

114. *Ep* 114, pp. 204-207: *Cum sim tuorum minimus necque necessarii nomine dignus.*

115. *Ep* 115, pp. 206-209: *cum magis ex prompta fidelitate quam improba temeritate peccaverim.*

116. *Ep* 117, pp. 110-11: *In litteris amici tui G* [*uillelmi*] *comitis multum deprehendere potes erga te benignitatem, familiaritatem, amititiam, sustentiam, quae non opus est mihi exponere tibi optime scienti.*

117. Compare *ep* 39, Fulbert to Bishop Roger of Lisieux, with *ep* 88, to Hildegar on the administration of Saint-Hilaire of Poitiers. In both cases Fulbert gives advice, but in the first he is formal and distant, while in the second he is affectionate and didactic.

118. *Ep* 117, p. 210-11: *Nullatenus enim ferre possum nisi iussione tua coactus vel absentari penitus me vel abesse diutius obsequiis alme Dei genitricis et tuis, desiderans ut ceruus ad fontes aquarum* (Ps 41:2) *tuis plenius instrui documentis, omni auro et argento ipsa etiam vita mihi carioribus.*

119. Odilo's *Vita* of Maiol is in PL 142:943-62. It is full of generalities and perhaps the weakest of all the cluniac abbatial lives. For a full study, see Jacques Hourlier, *Saint Odilon abbé de Cluny*, Bibliothèque de la Revue d'Histoire Ecclésiastique 40 (Louvain, 1964).

120. PL 142:948.

121. *Ibid.*, 949: . . . *relicto saeculari et amicorum et parentum consortio.*

122. *Ibid.*, 956: . . . *quanto frequentius faciem ejus cernebant, tanto amplius in ejus amore crescebant.*

123. *Ibid.* 900-901 = Bk. I. ch. 5: *Vultus ipse plenus auctoritatis et gratiae: mansuetis hilaris et blandus; superbis vero et offensis ut vix sufferri posset, terribilis.*

124. I. 7=902,: . . . *quorum omnium amicitiis, officiis et imperialibus muneribus ita magnificatus est, ut sibi et illis cor unum et anima fuerit.*

125. *Ibid.*,: . . . *qui ita sibi in amicitiis adhaesit et copiosis muneribus deservivit ut ad eum etiam de tam longinquis regionibus veniret, et monachum se ab eo fieri decerneret.*

126. Again, how could one translate a phrase so rich in spiritual monastic associations, and exceeding by far the classical language of friendship? (PL 142:906,=I. 11: *Quocunque exibat, quocunque procedebat, tanta sequebatur eum frequentia fratrum, ut jam non ducem et principem sed revera putares eum esse archangelum monachorum. Hoc enim nomine censebat eum appellandum in suis sermonibus et epistolis Fulbertus ille sibi praecordialis amicus Carnotensis episcopus.*)

127. Jotsald I. 14, col. 909: . . . *istiusque nostri patris familiarissimus quorum uterque animus conglutinabatur individui amore spiritus.*

128. Jotsald I. 7, col. 902: *Quae enim persona undecunque locorum non cuperet habere Odilonem tanquam alterum Salomonem amicum et patrem, et pro se apud Deum intercessorem?*

129. Jotsald I. 14, col. 911: *Fuerunt enim inter se, dum viverent, amici indissolubiles, in sancta professione aequales, et in omni morum honestate non dispares.*

130. Ralph Glaber's *Vita* of William of Dijon is also contained in PL 1142:697-720. Born in 961 and dead in 1031, William spent his whole life as a monk. He spent some time at Cluny, and Ralph says the Abbot Maiol was especially devoted to him, but there is no mention of friendship here (ch. 9, col. 707). Ralph Glaber's celebrated Five Books of History are, as would be expected, concentrated on outward events and give no indication of inner life at Cluny.

131. As contained in the *Consuetudines Farfenses*, ed. Bruno Albers in *Consuetudines Monasticae* I (Stuttgart and Vienna, 1900) II, 2, p. 139: *Quomodo agendum sit novitiis* and especially in Ulrich's *Consuetudines Cluniacenses* from the 1080s, III, 8, 'De pueris et eorum magistris' (PL 149:742. The importance of these particular provisions is underlined by their inclusion in the biography of Odo of Cluny by John of Salerno, I. 30, which shows they went back to the tenth century.

132. Ulrich, *Cons. Clun.* (note 131 above) II. 20.

133. Here the work of Kassius Hallinger remains decisive: *Gorze-Kluny* I-II, Studia Anselmiana 22-26 (Herder, Rome 1950-51).

134. *Die Tegernseer Briefsammlung* (Froumund), herausgegeben von Karl Strecker, MGH Epistolae Selectae III (Berlin: Weidmannsche Buchhandlung, 1925). The manuscript is Tegernsee's Codex 1412, Clm. 19412. Strecker shows that the first part of the MS is divided up chronologically, according to the abbots of Tegernsee under whom Froumund worked.

135. As *ep* 28, p. 32, Abbot Gozpert to an unnamed count: *In maxima necessitate fideles amici merito queruntur et ut scriptum est sine dubio tunc comprobantur quando solatium adiutorii largiuntur,* or Gozpert to Arnold and his niece Adalheid (*ep* 26, p. 29): *Necessitate maxima compulsi amicorum nostrorum fida flagitamus auxilia, quia presenti anno minime sufficunt nobis victuum alimonia fructuum fertilitate agrorum sterilitate suffocata. . . .*

136. *Ep* 20, p. 20: . . . *lepidissimo fratrum colloquio paululum recreari desideramus:. . .*

137. Poem 32 in Froumunds codex, pp. 80-83, as lines 55-57: *Caris filolis Froumundus quicquid amoris,/Qui instatis nostro tempore sub studio./Te primum pono, mi frater amande Georgi. . . .*

138. *Salve confrater mihi dulcis semper amore;*
Dulcis es mihi tu quam mellis gustus in ore.
Nescit amare liquor, sed amor dulcescit et ad cor
Intrat et alterius coniungit foedere pectus. . . .

This is poem 7, 'Ad pabonem ypapanti facti', whose title seems to be the greek word for Candlemas (p. 28). At times the language to us might appear to be that of passionate love, and it is certainly indicative of the mode of expression that will become common in the next century:

Nusquam divellor, nunquam a te pector pellor.
Hec preclara dies merito vocitatur et omnes
Festos precellit, que te me cernere fecit.

139. *Ep* 33, pp. 35-36. My translation condenses terms that are much more lavish and verbose: *Ne creas parvitatis mee servitia de tue caritatis velle lassescere cura. . . . Adhuc, puto, calet apud te insopibilis circa me flamma caritatis, que fervida fomenta et inextinguibilia tui amoris fecerat accendi in precordiis meis. Oculo dilectionis illius vultum tuum iugiter intendo, quam dudum fixeras in cordis mei secreto, quo semper menti firmiter coagulato numquam te intueri desisto.*

140. Poem 27, p. 72, from the time of Abbot Eberhard, 1002-1003: *Si mihi versiculos faceres vel carmine ludos,/Ut quondam fletus, sic nunc volo gaudia risus,/Aspicerem gratumque foret tua cernere dicta,/Et quod non flebas, hoc nunc in carmine promas,/Tempora temporibus si mutas: hoc petit etas.*

141. *Ep* 89, p. 94: *Per cunctas namque regiones vagula mente te quesivimus merentes. Sed nimium gaudemus, quod te quiescere audimus in monasteriali quiete. . . . Quid multa? Ex quo homo indignus presbiter sum ordinatus, tui non sum oblitus: deinceps vero nunquam, nusquam, quando mei meorumve recordor, tui non obliviscor.*

142. *Ep* 102, p. 105: *Exterior meus homo quamvis longi temporis interstitio conspectu careat vestro, interior tamen intime dilectionis contemplatione vestri neutiquam recordatur.*

143. *Ep* 98, p. 102: *Sed ut ex hoc nulla ambiguitas subeat, quin vestri amor mei intima cubiculi semper exurat et de vestra prosperitate summe gaudeat, omnimodis deposco.*

144. Poem 28, p. 72: 'Man wird an Notkers Verse an Salomo erinnert'.

CHAPTER FIVE
REFORM AND RENEWAL

1. A source of inspiration for the remarks here is Benedicta Ward, 'The Desert Myth', *One Yet Two*, edited M. Basil Pennington (Kalamazoo, 1976) 183-99. Also Benedicta Ward's excellent *Miracles and the Medieval Mind* (Scolar Press: London, 1982).

2. For Dunstan in general, see David Knowles, *The Monastic Order in England* (Cambridge, 1976), as well as Eleanor Shipley Duckett, *Saint Dunstan of Canterbury* (W. W. Norton: New York, 1955), and the bibliography in David Hugh Farmer's helpful entry in his outstanding *The Oxford Dictionary of Saints* (Clarendon Press, Oxford: 1978) 111-13.

3. *Memorials of Saint Dunstan*, ed. William Stubbs (Rolls Series, nr. 63: London, 1874), 'Auctore B', ch. 9, p. 15.

4. *Ibid.*, Auctore Osberno, ch. 17, p. 89: . . .*quem puerum olim in corpore ipse puer noverat et sancta semper familiaritate dilexerat.*

5. *Ibid.*, Auctore Eadmero, ch. 9, p. 179.

6. *Ibid.*, Auctore Willelmo Malmesberiensi, ch. 10, pp. 263-64.

7. *Ibid.*, Epistola Arnulfi ad Dunstanum Archiepiscopum. pp. 359-60: . . .*quantum vobis cupiam esse in omnibus ubique amicus. . . . Caeterum obnixius oro ut amicitias inter me et inter dominum vestram regem tales nunc faciatis, quales habuerunt et antecessores nostri ad invicem foederatas.*

8. Here I am indebted to the classic studies of Leclercq (*Love of Learning*), R.W. Southern (*Making of the Middle Ages*), and Beryl Smalley (*Study of the Bible*) as well as several of the articles in *Renaissance and Renewal in the Twelfth Century*, edd. Robert L. Benson and Giles Constable (Clarendon Press, Oxford: 1982).

9. *Disticha Catonis*, ed. Marcus Boas (North Holland: Amsterdam, 1952).

10. William D. Patt, 'The Early *Ars Dictaminis* as Response to a Changing Society', *Viator* 9 (1978), 133-55, with rich bibliography. See also Giles Constable, *Letters and Letter-Collections*, Typologie des sources du moyen âge occidental 17 (Turnhout, 1976) as well as Constable's section on medieval letterwriting in *The Letters of Peter the Venerable* (Cambridge, Massachusetts., 1967), Vol. 2, pp. 1-44. Further bibliography is in James J. Murphy, *Medieval Rhetoric: A Select Bibliography*, Toronto Medieval Bibliographies 3 (1971).

11. As in Ludwig Rockinger, *Briefsteller und Formelbücher des elften bis vierzehnten Jahrhunderts*, (Quellen und Erörterungen zur bayerischen und deutschen Geschichte

9.1 (München, 1863, reprinted New York, 1961) 86-91. Also Jean Leclercq, 'L'amitié dans les lettres au moyen age', *Revue du Moyen Age Latin* 1 (1945) 391-410.

12. See Karl Pivec, 'Stil und Sprachentwicklung im mittellateinischen Briefen vom 8.-12. Jh.', *Mitteilungen des Osterreichischer Instituts für Geschichtsforschung* 14 (1931) 33-51. Despite some German nationalistic concerns in the article, Pivec is sensitive to how letters are reflections of the development of learning as well as of the ability to provide personal expression, as p. 47: 'Wir haben erst seit der Mitte des 11. Jh. im Briefstil eine Höhe der Entwicklung erreicht, auf der der Stilist sagen kann, was er sagen will, das heisst sein persönliches Denken und Fühlen in einer adäquaten Form zum Ausdruck bringen kann, die Sprache der Seele gehorcht'.

13. For the most accessible explanation of these terms in english translation, see Anonymous of Bologna, 'The Principles of Letter-Writing' (*Rationes dictandi*), trans. James J. Murphy, in his *Three Medieval Rhetorical Arts* (University of California: Berkeley, Los Angeles and London, 1971) 5-25.

14. Jean Leclercq has contrasted the 'real content' of medieval letters with the stiff pose of humanist letter-writing. The *caractère vivant* of the one gives way to *exercice littéraire*: 'Le Genre Epistolaire du Moyen Age', *Revue du Moyen Age Latin* 2 (1946), 63-70, esp. note 30, p. 70. I think this is going too far, but the opposition does emphasize how important it is to look at medieval letters not just in terms of form but also in terms of content and meaning.

15. E. Dümmler, 'Ueber den Mönch Otloh von St. Emmeram', *Sitzungsberichte der kgl. Preussischen Akademie der Wissenschäften zu Berlin* (1895) 2:1071-1102.

16. *Die ältere Wormser Briefsammlung*, bearb. von Walther Bulst, MGH Die Briefe der Deutschen Kaiserzeit 3: (Hermann Böhlaus Nachfolger, Weimar 1949).

17. *Ibid.*, *ep* 60, p. 101: *Amicitiam inter nos honeste fundamento inpositam non pure custodistis, quando inimicum meum de me omnia que potuit mala dicentem super mea criminatione audistis, et non solum audistis, sed multipliciter omnia que dixit confirmastis.*

18. *Ibid.* / *O Deus Deus, quo respiciam, quem mihi fidelem amicum inveniam?*

19. *Ibid.*, p. 102: *Hactenus quidem dilexi vos propter virtutem, propter quam Tullius docet nos* eos etiam diligere, quos numquam vidimus *(De am. 8:28).*

20. *Ibid.*, *ep* 61, 103: *Iohannes. . . super pectum suum recumbendo sui dulcedinem nectaris hauriente de dilectione imperavit.*

21. *Ibid.*, pp. 104-105: *Scio namque Salomonem de veris amicis elegendis, immo discernendis mirifice philosophantem. Scio Paulum de caritate terribiliter tonitruantem. Scio multos alios tam ex agiographis quam ex paganis sapienter et honeste de ea disputantes. . . .*

22. *Ibid.*, p. 7

23. *Ibid.*, p. 82, 45: **Ecce quam bonum et quam iocundum habitare fratres in unum** (Ps 132: 1) *licet in psalmo lectum sit, non minus tamen iocunda iure perhibetur fratrum et sororum in Deo cohabitatio et spiritalis in invicem dilectio, si in utrisque Deo semper medio et speculum castitatis et studium fervet caritatis. Sunt nimirum qui familiaritates et colloquia mulierum esse fugienda dicunt. Cur id ita sentiant, miror, cum facile inter eas discretio habeatur, que fugienda, que etiam sit diligenda.*

24. *Briefsammlungen der Zeit Heinrichs IV*, bearb. Carl Erdmann und Norbert Fickermann, MGH: Die Briefe der Deutschen Kaiserzeit, 5: (Hermann Böhlaus Nachfolger, Weimar, 1950). Also Erdmann's invaluable *Studien zur Briefliteratur Deutschlands im elften Jahrhundert*, Schriften des Reichsinstituts fur ältere deutsche Geschichtskunde I: (Leipzig 1938), which in many cases provides a running commentary on the letters in this collection.

25. Erdmann and Fickermann, *Briefsammlungen der Zeit Heinrichs IV*, p. 6

26. *Ibid.*, p. 29, *ep* 10: *Pauca verba amici, benivolentie indiciis, probatum sufficiunt ad amicum.*

27. *Ibid.*, p. 76, *ep* 36: *Recedens enim de te quasi in graves et exitiosas Egypti tenebras mente captivatus perducebar, et dum nihil de fortunis tuis, quas sepe et multum exquisivi, explorare quiveram, per iniqui et inimici deserti difficultates variis mentis incessibus oberrabam.*

28. *Ibid.*, p. 77: . . . *si quandoque corporali presentia tui me beaveris, ego te amplexando, tecum colloquendo iocunditate exultim congratuler, congratulanter exultaverim*. . . .

29. Thanks to R. W. Southern's *The Making of the Middle Ages*, the intellectual awakening of the twelfth century had to be pushed back far into the eleventh. Unfortunately our best narrative sources for the world of scholars belong for the most part to the twelfth century (as the letters of Abelard and Heloise, especially the *Historia Calamitatum*). But it is becoming ever more clear to medieval scholars that Abelard entered a world of learning that was not some frontier community, as he would like us to believe, but which had existed since the early eleventh century. Once more the teaching of Fulbert of Chartres and his assistants, as well as the learning of German cathedral schools, emerge as expressions of the same hunger for intellectual and ecclesiastical advancement. I have been influenced here by the work of Gavin Langmuir at Stanford University and especially by the lectures of R.W. Southern on the 'rise of scholastic thought' delivered at Copenhagen in 1975 and which one hopes will soon be published. Helpful is Alexander Murray, *Reason and Society in the Middle Ages* (Clarendon Press: Oxford, 1978).

30. *Ibid.*, *ep* 37, p. 79: *Miror vos me nominasse vobis unicum amicum, cum in re habuissetis despectissimum*. . . . *Tune, furcifer, ita te mihi subtraxisti, quem diu oris, non cordis, blanditiis lactasti?*

31. For the principle of *varietas* as a criterion for the selection of letters in a medieval collection, see Jean Leclercq, 'Recherces sur la collection des épitres de saint Bernard', *Cahiers de civilisation médiévale* 14 (1971) 205-19.

32. *Briefsammlungen der Zeit Heinrichs IV* (note 24 above), *ep* 48, p. 93: *Quotiens enim iocundum illud et amicum tempus nostre infantie, nostre adolescentie in memoriam reduxero, maxime cupio et desidero, ut dilectio, que nobiscum adhuc parvis suo modo bene excrevit, maturiori quodam robore modo nostro consolidetur.*

33. Once again my central obligation is to R.W. Southern, but also to Colin Morris, *The Discovery of the Individual* (London, 1972) and to Peter Brown, 'Society and the Supernatural: A Medieval Change', *Daedalus* 104 (1975) 133-151.

34. Jean Leclercq and Jean-Paul Bonnes, *Un maître de la vie spirituelle au xie siecle: Jean de Fécamp*, Etudes de théologie et d'histoire de la spiritualité 9 (Paris, 1946) and *The Prayers and Meditations of Saint Anselm*, trans. Benedicta Ward (Penguin Classics: London, 1973), especially the excellent introduction, including pp. 47-50 for Jean.

35. *Jean de Fécamp*, p. 185: 'Deploratio Quietis et Solitudinis Derelictae': . . . .*Quis te mihi abstulit, dilectam meam.* See p. 195: *Liberam animam servi tui ab his iurgiis et contentionibus, ab his causarum tumultibus et multiplici adventantium strepitu, ab hoc multo saeculo quod patior in monasterio, inter hanc frequentiam fratrum, ubi cotidie in multis offendo, et da mihi illud solitudinis secretum et spiritale opportunae ad te vacationis otium.*

36. As in Peter's description of how Romuald left his monastery: *Cumque in eius animo perfectionis amor magis ac magis in dies cresceret nullamque mens eius requiem inveniret audivit quia in Venetiarum partibus quidam spiritualis vir esset, Marinus nomine, qui heremiticam duceret vitam. Vita Beati Romualdi* ch. 4, p. 20, ed. Giovanni Tabacco, Fonti per la Storia d'Italia, nr. 94 (Roma, 1957).

37. *Jean de Fécamp*, the letter 'Tuae quidem', which cannot be dated but is thought to have been composed early in John's career: *Quid dulcius, quidve pulchrius quam inter tenebras huius vitae multasque amaritudines divinae dulcedini inbiare et aeternae beatitudini suspirare?* (p. 199—this could well be a conscious echo of Cicero's statement on friendship, *De amicitia* ch. 22: *Quid dulcius quam habere quicum omnia audeas sic loqui ut tecum?*—but John is very clearly linking every impulse of human charity to union with Christ.

38. *Ibid.*, p. 204: *Hanc scripsi epistolam et ad tuam misi caritatem ut me in meis litteris semper praesentem habeas et per eas quantum te diligo plenius certiusque cognoscas.*

39. Jean Leclercq, 'L'humanisme des moines au moyen age', *Studi Medievali A Giuseppe Ermini* (Spoleto 1970) 69-113, esp. 97-102. For a study of Otloh's theology, see Helga Schauwecker, *Otloh von St. Emmeram*, Studien und Mitteilungen zur Geschichte des Benediktiner-Ordens und seiner Zweige 74 (München 1964). For the autobiographical element in Otloh, see Georg Misch, *Geschichte der Autobiographie* III:2 (Frankfurt am Main, 1959), 57-107.

40. Jean Leclercq 'Modern Psychology and the Interpretation of Medieval Texts', *Speculum* 48 (1973) 476-90, esp. pp. 478-79.

41. Otloh's works are contained in PL 146. The description of Henry as friend is in the Prologue of Otloh's *Dialogus de tribus quaestionibus*, col. 59.

42. PL 146, col 58 (*Liber de suis scriptis*).

43. *Eadem velle et nolle ea demum firma amicitia est*: PL 146:309. See *Catilina* 20:4, *Idem velle atque idem nolle ea demum firma amicitia est*. For other medieval authors who use the phrase, Beryl Smalley, 'Sallust in the Middle Ages', *Classical Influences on European Culture*, A.D. 500-1500, ed. R. R. Bolgar (Cambridge, 1971) 170-71.

44. PL 146:353: . . . *an genibus flexis, ut placantur seniores? an tantum verbis, ut placatur minor aetas? siquidem flexis genibus utriusque damnum esse sum arbitratus; ejus, scilicet, propter elationem, quam forsitan sibi postmodum inde vindicaret; mei vero ideo quod arguendi illum post humilitatem hujusmodi exhibitam ulterius minor fiducia mihi restaret.*

45. PL 146:29.

46. *Ibid.*, col. 197: . . . *ne forte propter eius amicitiam vel aliquod temporale subsidium sibi cohaerentes in damnationem perpetuam veniamus.*

47. *Ibid.*, 259: . . . *adulationem amicorum aliorumque hominum.*

48. See MGH SS IV: 524.

49. PL 146:398: *Nam nisi amici precibus Heinrici, quo familiare habuit contubernium, retraheretur, omnimodo saecularibus renunciaret desideriis. Sed assidue tractans, quia caritas non quaerit quae sua sunt, sed quae alterius, ad tempus distulit quod postea devotus implevit.*

50. *Ibid.*: *At ille aliquandiu resistens, cum bene non posset, male noluit esse rebellis. Profectus est ergo cum amico.*

51. *Ibid.*, 399 (ch. 9). The letter of Jerome is *ep* 14, trans. by F. A. Wright: 'Though your little nephew hang on your neck, though your mother with dishevelled hair and torn raiment show you the breasts that gave you suck, though your father fling himself upon the threshold, trample your father underfoot and go on your way, fly with tears to the Cross. In these matters to be cruel is a son's duty.'

52. PL 146:401: *qui juvenilibus annis patria, parentes, feminam quoque sibi desponsatam relinquens, ad monasterium convolavit.*

53. See the introduction to the *Liber confortatorius of Goscelin of Saint Bertin*, ed. C. H. Talbot, *Studia Anselmiana* 37, Analecta Monastica 3 (Rome, 1955).

54. By *sentiment* I mean the ordered and careful expression of human feeling within an intellectual context, the marriage of emotion and reason in harmony, as it were.

This is light years away from *sentimentality*, an exclusive concentration on the impulses of the emotions with little or no attempt to provide any form of intellectual discipline or ordering. It can be argued that sentimentality does not at all exist in monastic texts, for by definition it would have been banned as the manifestation of egotism. Goscelin at times in the first book of his *Liber* may seem to verge on sentimentality, but the structure of the work as a whole saves him. Every time he seems about to concentrate exclusively on his own emotions, he turns to the message of Christ and salvation.

55. *Lib. confortatorius* (note 53 above) p. 27: *O luce dilectior anima, adest tibi Goscelinus tuus, inseparabili anime presentia; adest meliori parte, ea qua te diligere potuit, individua, qua nulla excludant terrarum interstitia.*

56. *Ibid. Sed ecce, dum scribo, grassans dolor non potuit dissimulari; cecidere manus et usus scriptorii; rugitus et eiulatus invasit me; corrui coram altari tui Laurentii, ut sedebam in eius ecclesia remotiori, clamabam frequens in diluvio lacrimarum quasi inter ictus et verbera Domini. . . .*

57. For John the friend p. 31; for worldly friendship, p. 40; for *beata sodalitas*, p. 44.

58. As in Karl Pivec (note 12 above), p. 46: 'Welch wunderbare Schriftstücke verdankt nicht die Briefliteratur dem lange dauernden Kampfe zwischen weltlicher und geistlicher Gewalt! Nie vorher in der abendländischen mittelalterlichen Geschichte waren Worte von gleicher packender Gewalt und Eindringlichkeit geschrieben worden wie etwa die Briefe von 1076 oder die, welche Heinrich IV. in den trüben Tagen nach seiner Flucht 1105 klagend und anklagend in die Welt hinausschickte. Die Intensivierung der Affekte, politischer und persönlicher, fand ihre Gegenspiegelung in der Intensivierung des sprachlichen Ausdruckes.'

59. *Ep* 34 (note 24 above): *Cum nihil in hac vita iucundius videatur honestorum virorum amicitia. . . Nolite hesitare defendere partem beati Petri!*

60. Note 26 above.

61. Lester Little, 'The Personal Development of Peter Damian', *Order and Innovation in the Middle Ages* (Princeton University Press, 1976) 317-41.

62. Contained in PL 144 and now being edited by Karl Reindel for the *Monumenta Germaniae Historica*. The first volume appeared in 1983.

63. I have benefited from Jean Leclercq's *Saint Pierre Damien: Ermite et homme de l'église* (Edizioni di Storia e Letteratura: Roma, 1960) and his 'Saint Peter Damian and Women', *Cistercian Studies* (1974) 354-65.

64. Lib. 6, *ep* 19 (PL 144:399). Dated to 1054-57 in Franz Neukirch, *Das Leben des Petrus Damiani* (Göttingen, 1875) p. 96: *Unanimis amicitiae proprium est ut cum fratre frater et prospera communicet et adversa, quatenus fideliter animus sicut referendi in adversitate compatitur, ita nihilominus et in prosperis unanimiter collaetetur.*

65. See *Opuscula* 45 and 46 (PL 145:695 and 703), addressed to Ariprand.

66. PL 144:402: *Haec vobis dilectissimi, tanquam complicibus et amicis, amicus exposuit, meaeque visitationis seriem, velut uterinis fratribus, unanimi familiaritate digessi.*

67. PL 145:326-27, *opuscula* 13, 'De perfectione monachi': *Quisquis vero se specietenus affabilem praebet, amicitiam simulat, sed in cordis occulto veritatem amicitiae non conservat, damnabiliter intus hiat. . . .*

68. PL 145:794, *opusc.* 53, 'De patientia', ch. 4: *. . . respondi ut, quod suum erat tollens, amicitiam nostram non more saecularium mercede redimere, sed quod inter fratres est legitimum gratuito possideret.*

69. Little (note 61) p. 332.

70. 'De perfectione monachi', PL 145:327.

71. Lib. 6, *ep* 5; PL 144:379.

72. *Ibid.*, col. 383: *Recte igitur sive mundi, sive principis ejus amicitias dedignamur, et cum eis simul societatis foedus habere contemnimus: ne dum tenebris jungimur, luce privemur.*

73. *Ibid.*, col. 384: *Audiat hoc Andreas, qui nuper de contubernio vestrae sanctitatis egrediens, cum Ammonitarum rege foedus amicitiae contulit: et nunc per Romana moenia tanquam rasus barba, et detruncatus habitu, non sine David pudore discurrit.*

74. *Sermo* 63; PL 144:863-65.

75. *Ibid.*, col. 863: *Qui nimirum nuptialis copulae thalamum deserens, omnem illecebrae carnalis ardorem in coelestium deliciarum transtulit voluptatem, arcetissimeque se in sui Redemptoris ac dilectoris amore conjunxit, propter quem scilicet conjugalis tori foedera abdicavit.*

76. *Ibid.*, col. 865: *Huc accedit, quod ille recubitus in pectore Salvatoris, ille divinus ardor, quem ex arcana ejus inspiratione concepit, ita in ejus visceribus omnium libidinum fomenta decoxit ut corpus ejus, tanquam revera Spiritus sancti templum, a cunctis vernaret aestuantis luxuriae squaloribus defaecatum; nec ullum in eo locum vindicabat flamma libidi. . . .*

77. *Christianity, Social Tolerance and Homosexuality*, pp. 210-213. The *Liber gomorrhianus* is in PL 145:159-90, and is available in an english translation by Pierre J. Payer, *Peter Damian: Book of Gomorrah.* (Waterloo, Ontario: Wilfrid Laurier University Press, 1982).

78. *Lib. Gomor.* ch. 17, PL 145:178: *Dic, vir evirate; responde, homo effeminate, quid in viro quaeris, quod in temetipso invenire non possis? quam diversitatem sexuum? quae varia lineamenta membrorum? quam mollitiem? quam carnalis illecebrae teneritudinem? quam lubrici vultus jucunditatem?*

79. J. Laporte, '*Epistulae Fiscannenses*: Lettres d'amitié, de gouvernement et d' affaires (XI-XIIe siecles)', *Revue Mabillon* 43 (1953) 5-31. The text of the letters is pp. 18-25. Laporte gives no final dating. The manuscript itself is from the last quarter of the twelfth century, but several indications point to the years around 1100.

80. *Saint Anselm and his Biographer*, pp. 67-76. Southern uses the term 'The Anselmian Revolution' to describe the way Anselm provided a personal and intense manner of praying, but this phrase could also be applied to his way of conveying himself to his friends in his letters from Bec—and to the response of his followers.

81. 'Saint Anselm', *Studia Monastica* 3 (1961) 259-80.

82. *Christianity, Social Tolerance and Homosexuality*, pp. 218-19. 'Love, friendship and sex in the eleventh century: The experience of Anselm', *Studia Theologica* 28 (Oslo, 1974) 111-52.

83. *S. Anselmi Opera Omnia*, ed. F. S. Schmitt 3 (Thomas Nelson: London, 1946). In *ep* 4, p. 104, to Gundulf he writes, *Qualiter namque obliviscar tui? Is enim qui cordi meo velut sigillum cerae imprimitur, quomodo memoriae meae subtrahitur?* while of Osbern he writes (p. 105): *Ubicumque Osbernus est, anima eius anima mea est.*

84. *The Life of Saint Anselm* by Eadmer, ed. and trans. R. W. Southern, Oxford Medieval Texts (1962: reprinted 1972) Book I, ch. 10.

85. *Ibid.*, p. 20 (in Southern's translation): 'From this time therefore several of them devoted themselves body and mind to Anselm's service, hoping to succeed to Osbern's place in his affections, but he, though he thanked God for their change of heart, "became all things to all men, that he might save all." (1 Cor 9:22)'—*omnibus omnia factus est, ut omnes faceret salvos.*

86. This interpretation excludes John Boswell's assertion (p. 219) that Anselm 'had extraordinary emotional relationships, first with Lanfranc and then with a succession of his own pupils'. There is no special evidence for emotional closeness with Lanfranc, and Osbern remains a unique love in Anselm's life. It is not to my liking to be polemical, but I find Boswell's characterization of Anselm indicative of a lack of

sensitivity to what Anselm is saying in his letters and theological works. His relationships to Gundulf, Osbern, Eadmer and Boso are all different from each other and cannot be stamped as 'emotional', for only with Osbern does he express a need for the presence of the friend, while with the others he exercises an intellectual discipline and an emotional distance of varying degrees.

87. The same originality of mind solidly based in patristic sources, especially Augustine, can be seen in Anselm's argument in *Cur Deus Homo*. See my Oxford D.Phil. thesis (1970, unpublished) *The History of Saint Anselm's Theology of the Redemption in the Twelfth and Thirteenth Centuries*, especially the early chapters. Also Gillian Evans, *Anselm and Talking about God* (Oxford, 1978) for the originality of thought and expression in other theological treatises.

88. *Ep* 59; Schmitt (note 83 above), vol. 3: 173: *Omnes quotquot veniunt a domno Gundulfo, referunt quod litteras meas desiderat domnus Gundulfus. In quibus bene novi quia nihil aliud expectas, nisi ut mutuum nostrae dilectionis affectum legas.*

89. *Ep* 16: *Et tamen tu instas mihi importune ut faciam quod fieri non potest. Sufficiant nobis conscientiae nostrae, quibus nobis invicem conscii sumus quantum nos diligamus.* For a more thorough review of the correspondence of Anselm and Gundulf, see my 'Love, friendship. . .' (note 82 above) 128-31.

90. *Ep* 69 (Schmitt 3:189): *Diu est quod nostris nos invicem litteris non visitavimus, quoniam de soliditate mutuae nostrae dilectionis non dubitavimus et quia nuntiorum sermonibus, cum opportunum fuit, nos salutavimus. Sed ne qua occasione amor ipse ab aliquo putetur tepere, expedire puto ut aliquando schedulis, quasi scintillis ab invicem emicantibus, videatur fervere. Hoc enim ipso quia desiderantem te desiderans habere mecum non possum, nequaquam minus, sed magis te diligo; quia cum te sic diligi a maioribus et melioribus me, ut te dimittere nolint, video, plus te diligendum intelligo. Unde fit ut paene dubium mihi sit, utrum quia sic te facis amabilem plus gaudeam, an quia tam amabili frui non possum plus doleam.* (The translation is my own.)

91. *Ibid.*: *Verum quoniam scio quia non tantum propter me quantum propter te a me debes amari, soluta quaestione certum est quia plus debeo de bonorum morum praesentia, quae tecum est, congratulari, quam de corporis tui absentia, quae mecum est, contristari.*

92. *Ibid.*: *Denique semper ut deo et bonis hominibus amabilies esses, desideravi et pro mea possibilitate, ut tu mihi conscius es, studui, quamdiu mecum fuisti; nec tamen desiderium idcirco tepuit, quia studium operari non potuit, postquam mecum non fuisti.*

93. *The Prayers and Meditations of Saint Anselm*, trans. Benedicta Ward (Penguin Classics, 1973), p. 67. The Prayer is found on pp. 157-162. *Oratio* 11 (Schmitt: 42-45).

94. *Domine et domine, credo, scio quia invicem vos diligitis: sed unde hoc ipse experiar, si quod peto propter invicem non conceditis? Oratio* 12, (Schmitt, 3:47). Benedicta Ward, *The Prayers*, p. 167.

95. For feudal language in the *Cur Deus Homo*, which Southern considers important but not essential for the argument, see *Saint Anselm and his Biographer*, pp. 107-14.

96. *Ep* 37, to Lanzio; Schmitt 3: 145: *Ingressus es, carissime, professusque Christi militiam, in qua non solum aperte obsistentis hostis violentia est propellenda, sed et quasi consulentis astutia cavenda.*

97. As *ep* 43 (Schmitt 3:155), where Anselm answers a letter from the monk Maurice at Canterbury and says he has not neglected him: *Absit enim ut, quem a puero et a prima cognitione tanto studio pro modulo meae possibilitatis te teste dilexi, nunc te negligam. . . .*

98. See my Oxford D.Phil. thesis (note 87 above).

99. For Lanfranc in general see the comprehensive study by Margaret Gibson, *Lanfranc of Bec* (Clarendon Press, Oxford 1978). His letters are in PL 150: 515-624, and

in Schmitt's *S. Anselmi Opera Omnia*, vol. 3. A new edition is Helen Clover and Margaret Gibson, *The Letters of Lanfranc* (Oxford, Clarendon Press 1979).

100. *Ep* 43; PL 150:534. Also contained in Schmitt's (*ep* 30) p. 137. Clover and Gibson, Letter 18.

101. *Ep* 44; PL 150:540, = Schmitt 3 (*ep* 32) p. 140: *quem vos pro vobis separatis ab illo, a quo plus amabatur quam ab alio, et quem plus amabat quam alium. . . .*

102. *Ep* 45; PL 150:541: *Charissimum mihi fratris mei filium, fratrem videlicet tuum, charitati tuae commendo, rogans, sicut rogari oportet a me jucundissimum filium fratremque meum, quatenus cum magna jucunditate animi tui eum diligas, et ad vitam laudabilem pro viribus tuis informare non desinas. . . . Crucem cum reliquiis, fraternitatis tuae oculis dum missam celebras conspiciendam, tibi transmitto: quam* ***perpetuae amicitiae monumentum inter te et ipsum*** *esse desidero.* (Letter 20 in Clover and Gibson)

103. *Ep* 45; PL 150:541 (*Ep* 20 in Clover and Gibson): *Quatenus in omni aetate tua sic me diligas, sicut in pueritia et adolescentia tue quondam diligere me solebas.*

104. *Ep* 47; PL 150:542: *Quia divinitus, ut credo, vos dilexistis in saeculo, rogo ut rogetis Deum quatenus, ipso cooperante, vos diligatis in eo quod assumpsistis sancto proposito.* (Letter 19 in Clover and Gibson)

105. *Ibid.* / *Alter alteri sit in tribulatione solatium: alter ab alterius vita sumat sanctae conversationis exemplum. Humilitatem omnibus ostendite, linguas vestras ab omni derogatione salubri censura compescite.*

106. *The Life of Gundulf Bishop of Rochester*, ed. Rodney Thomson, Toronto Medieval Latin Texts 7 (1977).

107. *Ibid.*, ch. 8: *Tanta Gundulfo est amicitia vinctus ut se alterum Gundulfum, Gundulfum vero alterum Anselmum diceret et vocari gauderet.*

108. Contrast the Vulgate text with the passage in the *Vita Gundulfi:*

Multitudinis autem credentium erat
cor unum et anima una;
nec quisquam eorum, quae possidebat,
aliquid suum esse dicebat;
sed erant illis omnia communia.

Erat enim illis in Deo
cor unum et anima una,
frequens de spiritualibus collocutio,
multa ut semper ad altiora
conscenderent exhortatio. . . .

Vita Gundulfi ch. 8, p. 30

109. *Vita Gundulfi* 8, p. 30: *Anselmus tamen, quia in Scripturis eruditior erat, frequentior loquebatur. Gundulfus vero, quia in lacrimis profusior erat, magis fletibus rigabatur. Loquebatur ille; plorabat iste.*

110. *Ibid.*, pp. 30-31: *Procul erat a cordibus eorum vel lingua priorum aut fratrum suorum detractio. Non eos vexabat, ut plerosque multotiens solet, cibi vel potus aut vestium murmuratio.* See Rodney Thomson's introduction, p. 7.

111. *Vita*, ch. 33, p. 55: *Sepius enim in diversis locis convenientes, mutuis se verbis inDei succendebant amorem, archiepiscopo tamen divini amoris ignem frequentius accedente loquendo, episcopo vero se ad ignem illum accensum propius calefaciente tacendo.*

112. *Epistolae herberti de Losinga*, ed. Robert Anstruther, Publications of the Caxton Society 5, Burt Franklin Research and Source Works Series 154 (New York, 1969). Even David Knowles (*The Monastic Order)* seems to have been unable to use the original 1846 edition (p. 624, n.1). This text leaves much to be desires: there is no information

tion about manuscripts or variants, and no attempt to date the letters, even on the basis of internal criteria.

113. *Ep* 57, Anstruther pp. 96-7: *Mea fuit hactenus consuetudo, ut a vobis corpore abiens, animo et verbis vobiscum remanerem, nec possent dividi alternatione locorum, quorum erat cor unum et anima una . . . Ubi omnes, ibi singuli, et ubi singuli, ibi omnes; omnia communiter fiant, ut nullus singularitati relinquatur locus.*

114. *Ep* 15, Anstruther, pp. 30-31: *Vado ad curiam, pene sine equis et sine pecunia, sed Deus erit comes meus. Norwicensensem ecclesiam et opus ecclesiae et meum commendo tibi, et te commendo Deo. Si quae tibi defuerint, adquire mutuo, et ego rediens, restituam omnia tuis creditoribus. Pax tecum et omnibus fratribus qui in humilitate et veritate tecum conservant nostrae regulae religionem in domo nostra.*

115. *Ep* 18, Anstruther, p. 36: *Oratio Reginae quam fecit Herbertus episcopus: Habeas tecum, o beate Johannes, in his meis anxietatibus relevandis, omnes socios amicos tuos quos negligenter vivendo mihi praeparavi inimicos.* The sentiment is very close to Anselm's own first prayer to John (Schmitt 3:43): *O vos misericordes amici dei, miseremini tam indigenti per illam misericordiam, quam vobis fecit deus. Succurrite, ne me obvolvat ira dei cum inimicis eius.*

116. Noreen Hunt, *Cluny under Saint Hugh* 1049-1109 (Edward Arnold: London, 1967) p. 14.

117. *Ep* 80, PL 159:241: *Quis enim unquam tam inhumanus fuerit, qui postquam expertus fuerit dulcedinem vestri colloquii, vos non recipiat et veneretur quasi angelum Dei.* See Southern, *Saint Anselm*, p. 218 for 'Anselm's Conversation'.

118. Contrast Schmitt's list of manuscripts for the prayers versus those for the letters in *Anselmi Opera Omnia* III.

119. Eadmer (*Vita Anselmi*, note 84 above) ch. 6, pp. 10-11.

CHAPTER SIX
THE AGE OF FRIENDSHIP

1. Jean Leclercq, *Monks and Love in Twelfth-Century France* (Clarendon Press: Oxford, 1979). Georges Duby, *The Three Orders: Feudal Society Imagined* (University of Chicago Press, 1980). See also Constance Brittain Bouchard, *Sword, Miter and Cloister: Nobility, Church and Reform in Burgundy, 980-1198* (Cornell University Press: Ithaca 1986), which provides much relevant information about social background.

2. See Leclercq, 'Lettres de vocation a la vie monastique', *Studia Anselmiana* 37, Analecta Monastica 3 (Roma 1955) 169-198.

3. A case in point is Bernard's embrace of the new monastic military order at some time in the period between 1128 and 1136 when he wrote his work in praise of the new knighthood: *Liber ad Milites Templi: de laude novae militiae* edd. J. Leclercq and H. M. Rochais, *S. Bernardi Opera* 3 (Editiones Cistercienses: Roma, 1963) 212-39.

4. The assembly-line quality of the phrases of friendship can be seen especially well in some of the letters that Nicholas of Montiéramey (see below) wrote as a monk at Clairvaux on behalf of other monks. In one (*ep* 47, PL 196:1649) he expresses the need to see the friend: *Conspectus enim et conversatio habent aliquid vivae voluptatis, quam mortui apices non loquuntur*. In the other (*ep* 50) he says that the sight of the friend is important only for the secular: *Scio ego quia conspectus et conversatio habent aliquid vivae voluptatis, sed hoc in saecularibus. Locorum enim vel temporis incommoda verus amor ignorat*. . .

5. For a full bibliography on the production of letters in the Middle Ages, see Giles Constable, *Letters and Letter-Collections*, Typologie des Sources du Moyen Âge Occidental, 17 (Editions Brepols, Turnhout, Belgium 1976) 42-48. Also Constable's section 'Medieval Letters and the Letter Collection of Peter the Venerable', *The Letters of Peter the Venerable* II (Harvard University Press: Cambridge, Massachusetts, 1967) 17-29; abbreviated as Constable (1967).

6. For Geoffrey of Auxerre's description of his first meeting with Bernard at Paris and his conversion to Clairvaux, see Robert Lechat, 'Les Fragmenta de Vita et Miraculis S. Bernardi', *Analecta Bollandiana* 50 (1932) p. 116.

7. As in a request from Peter the Venerable to his secretary and friend Peter of Poitiers, *ep* 129 in Constable, *The Letters* I, p. 327 (note 5 above). In another letter (*ep* 128, p. 326). Peter of Poitiers asked Peter the Venerable to keep his letters, for he did the same with the abbot's letters: *Nam et ego epistolas uestras diligentissime amplector et seruo.*

8. As letters from Bernard in Peter the Venerable's collection or from Nicholas of Montiéramey in Peter of Celle's collection. It is fascinating to note how the letters of the correspondent that are included in the letter-writer's own collection are used to justify the latter's own point of view—as can be seen by comparing the letters of Bernard Peter the Venerable had included in his collection with the letters of Peter that were put into Bernard's collection.

9. Southern (1966) pp. 271-73. I disagree that Elmer's 'expressions of friendship have the same ardent quality found in the early letters of Anselm', for Anselm's letters are more intense and personal than Elmer's.

10. 'Ecrits spirituels d'Elmer de Cantorbéry', *Studia Anselmiana* 31, Analecta Monastica 2 (Roma, 1953) p. 61: '. . .ces témoins obscurs nous disent comment, de fait, vivaient et enseignaient des moines ordinaires'. The text of the letters is pp. 62-117.

11. *Ibid.*, *ep* 1, p. 63: *Inter haec, dum ad cor reducitur quam dulcia de animarum nostrarum salute colloquia, cum nosmetipsos ad amorem supernae ciuitatis mutuis sermonibus excitaremus, habere consueuimus, augetur dolor. . . .*

Quid ergo? Si uobiscum, prout uellem, frequentius esse corporaliter nequeo, numquid uobis uel litteris adesse non debeo? Certe uel scripta nos iungant et nostrorum cordium interna ad amorem diuinum stilo simplici exaratus sermo pius accendat.

12. Ernst Robert Curtius, *European Literature and the Latin Middle Ages* (Routledge and Kegan Paul: London, 1953) pp. 407-13.

13. As *ep* 4. 23, p. 74: *Sed parcendum est infirmitati meae quae me saepe tanto doloris capite cruciat ut non solum dictare aut scribere, sed frequenter nec legere ualeam.*

14. *Ep* 9, p. 99: *Licet enim uerba cessent, numquam cessabit erga uos nostrae dilectionis affectus*. The idea of earthly friendships becoming heavenly ones is very strong in Anselm and his circle, as in Eadmer, his friend and biographer.

15. As *ep* 6, p. 87, to Nicholas, monk of St. Peter's benedictine abbey at Gloucester.

16. *Ep* 14, p. 106: *Dici non potest, dilectissime, qua dulcedine, quo spiritualis desiderii effectu, dulcissimam mihi animam uestram mens mea sancti amoris sinu complectitur, dum uestrae bonitatis suauiter recordatur.*

17. Jean Leclercq, 'Les lettres familières d'un moine du Bec', *Studia Anselmiana* 31, Analecta Monastica 2 (Roma 1953) 141-73.

18. *Ibid.*, p. 149: '. . . pour satisfaire aux exigences du silence claustral ou pour se dire avec plus de liberté, avec plus d'insistance aussi, des vérités qu'on éprouvait une certaine gêne à se communiquer de vive voix.' (See letter 5, for example, or letter 17).

19. *Ep* 3, p. 153: *O felix dilectio quae per singulos dies vel etiam horas prolixiori colloquio reficitur, sed o mirabilis quae per longa temporum intervalla vix aliquo modo se sibi repraesentans, nullam sustinendo patitur laesionem!*

20. *Ibid.*, p. 154: *Nonnullos enim video scripta quae in manus suas venerint tanta levitate discurrere, ut solam in illis dictorum elegantiam, si qua tamen est, examinando discutiant.*

21. *Ep* 4, p. 155: *Ad hoc accedit quod tecum duos habes quorum solatio non modice potes refoueri, quibus nostra parte salutationis uerba te mediante uolumus impendi.* There is perhaps here an echo of Si 4:11—*Et, si dormierint duo, fovebuntur mutuo: unus quomodo calefiet?*

22. *Ep* 5, p. 157.

23. *Ep* 7, p. 160: . . .*quantum ad saecularitatem pertinet, illis praecipue qui vitae propinquitatis mihi specialiter astringuntur manum consolationis teneor porrigere*. . . .

24. *Ibid.*: . . .*De cuius respectu sumpta fiducia tecum quasi cum altero me colloquor ut, etsi forte plurimos habeas in saeculo necessarios, in monachatu etiam unum, indubitanter me dico, verum te habere profitearis amicum*. . .

25. *Ep* 8, p. 162: . . .*ut ex animorum indissolubili consensu, fidelis oris consonante testimonio, in alterutro quasi in altero se ad inuicem confidamus.*

26. *Ep* 9, p. 163: *O utinam aliquem uel tandem ualeam reperire in cuius pectore totum me dubietate remota proiiciam!*

27. *Ibid.*, *Est enim mira uis pactae in Christo familiaritatis, dum idem uelle, idem nolle* [*Catil.* 20.5] *in duobus esse certum sit, et alter in altero citius quam in se uelle proprium recognoscat*. Notice how the sallustian definition is only part of a much fuller definition of friendship that has become fully christianized. This is typical for twelfth-century monastic thought on friendship: it draws on earlier expressions but is much richer and fuller in its breadth and depth of articulation.

28. *Ep* 13, p. 167: *Gemens ista dictaui, unde et confusum esse oportuit quod gemitus parturiuit: fraternitatem tuam, quam, sicut Christus omnium Dominus nouit, tenerrime diligo, manibus ut dicitur, protensis exoro, ne ulterius super falsis et incertis ambagibus erga me uultum induas indignantis.*

29. *Liber* 3, *ep* 6 (PL 171:287), written about 1107: *Odi verba, quae cum delectare incipiunt desinunt. Tuam vero prolixitatem amplector, ut epistolas longiores et occupatus suscipiam, et invitus deponam*. .: *Vale, atque id potius age, ut aliquando obliviscaris me, quam ut aliquando cogites de me.* Chronologically most of Hildebert's letter-writing belongs in the previous chapter, but I have deliberately placed him in this one because he expresses the same need and desire for individual friendships as the anonymous of Bec does.

30. *Lib.* 3, *ep* 10 (PL 171:289): *Haec enim est inter amicos animorum concordia, ut nihil ab altero sit alienum, nihil alteri singulare. Omnia facit eis unam rempublicam voluntas una. Hic amicitiae legibus actum noveris ut memoria reverterer ad te, compassione essem juxta te, orationibus agerem pro te.*

31. *Lib.* 3, *ep* 18, col. 294 . . .*desiderio desideramus* [Cf. Luke 22:15] *in sacrarium tuae familiaritatis recipi.* Bernard mentions Gebuin in *ep* 17 (*SBOp* 7:65). Nicholas of Montiéramey does so in his *ep* 5 (PL 196:1598). For Gebuin and Bernard, see Leclercq, *Recueil d'Etudes sur Saint Bernard et ses écrits* I (Edizioni di Storia et Letteratura: Roma, 1962) 83-94.

32. *Ep* 123, SBOp 7: p. 304: *Verumtamen quod sum tuum est; et si quid melius Dei umquam munere fuero, tuum fore confidito, reverendissime atque amantissime Pater.* There is also a letter from Bernard to Hildebert (*ep* 124) in which he demands that the archbishop of Tours go over to Innocent as pope. A full study of Hildebert is provided by Peter von Moos, *Hildebert von Lavardin* 1096-1133 (Stuttgart, 1965).

33. *Lib.* 1, *ep* 23; PL 171: 203. The monk was apparently having involuntary seminal emissions when he was prostrate in prayer.

34. See Herbert's *Moralis Philosophia*, a collection of classical quotations, which has a section (col. 1023) *De amicitia*, with definitions from Cicero and Seneca.

35. PL 171:873 = Sermo 116, which takes as its theme Ps 132:1—*Ecce quam bonum et quam jocundum habitare fratres in unum.*

36. The subject needs more detailed study, but recent research emphasizes how more and more monks in the twelfth century, not just Cistercians, were recruited as adults or near-adults. The oblate system was disappearing. See J. H. Lynch, 'Monastic Recruitment in the Eleventh and Twelfth Centuries: Some Social and Economic Considerations', *American Benedictine Review* 36 (1975) 425-47. Also Pierre Riché, 'L'enfant dans la société monastique au xiie siéle', *Pierre Abélard Pierre le Vénerable*. Les courants philosophiques, littéraires et artistiques en Occident au milieu du xiie siècle (Paris, 1975) 689-701.

37. *Ep* 11: PL 171:218: *Si enim propter Deum, ut illi placeamus, inimicos, multos magis, ne illi displiceamus, diligere debemus amicos.* Also in F. S. Schmitt, *S. Anselmi Opera Omnia* 4 (Thomas Nelson, Edinburgh, 1949) *ep* 241.

38. *Ep* 39: PL 171:263: . . .*scitote in eo me vobis loqui, vos etiam precari. quatenus in eo mihi subveniatis, scientes me pro eo loqui devotius quam pro meipso.*

39. As in some of the language of a letter of thanks to Anselm for sending his treatise on the procession of the Holy Spirit (about 1102), *Ep* 13 (PL 171:220): *Susceperam prius benedictionem tuam, servus ego, servus tuus, et egit gratias Deo et tibi devotus effectus, affectus meus.* The wordplay could be anselmian. But it also reminds one of Bernard's style.

40. Boswell (1980), especially ch. 9, 'The Triumph of Ganymede: Gay Literature of the High Middle Ages', 243-66. Much of this literature is now available in an excellent Latin-English edition in Thomas Stehling, *Medieval Latin Poems of Male Love and Friendship* (Garland Publishing: New York and London, 1984).

41. Phyllis Abrahams, *Les oeuvres poétiques de Baudri de Bourgueil* (Paris, 1926) xx-xxii. I have used Abrahams' edition, but there is a new one by Karlheinz Hilbert, *Baldricus Burgulianus Carmina* (Heidelberg, 1979).

42. Baudri, p. 112, l. 102: *Hoc scelus est majus, natura quidem violatur*. . . .

43. As Baudri, p. 123, ll. 38-40: *Crede mihi, non vera loquor, magis omnia fingo./Nullus amor foedus mihi quidlibet associavit,/Sed modus iste mihi dictandi plus inovelit*. . . .

44. As in the poem better known for its mention of Ganymede (cxxxix), with its lines about the advantages of Bourgueil as an ideal place for study:

Sed libri desunt fortassis, et otia desunt.
Ipse locum novi qui floridus otia gignit,
Libros et cartas, et cuncta studentibus apta. (p. 113, ll.157-59)

In another invitation to studies at the monastery (p. 114, ll. 202-203), Baudri promises that the friend can take with him his brother and friends: *Nec tibi nec fratri nec amicis ipse deessem/Susciperemque omnes qua conditione juberes.* This could be called a poem of conversion, but it is a different type of conversion to monastic life from that which Elmer of Canterbury or Anselm of Bec would have recognized.

45. Baudri, p. 128: poem 151—*Ad eum cujus colloquium expectabit:*

O si colloquium nos nobis contiguaret,
Prospera colloquii me commoditas recrearet.

46. This ranking is especially obvious in a trilogy of poems to a friend given the nickname of Teucer. He has come to see Baudri and in poem 180 he moves up from being the fifth in rank among Baudri's friends to fourth place, because number four did not come on time. In the next poem, p. 172, Baudri laments that he had rejoiced too quickly in Teucer, who has let him down. Finally in poem 182, p. 173, Teucer is replaced to fourth rank and forgiven for having 'transgressed the bond of friendship' (p. 174—*transgressus erat foedus amicitiae*).

47. The poem is a perfect expression of a timeless frustration of the friend or lover with the beloved who does not keep his promises:

Ut venias, venias ego mando et saepe remando,
Quod venies venies mandas et saepe remandas.
Verborum satis est, fidei nihil: aut tua verba
Committam ventis, aut verba fides tueatur. (poem 166, p. 161)

48. Poem 167, p. 162:

Suscepi gaudens quicquid mihi rettulit ex te,
Jamque rependo tibi foedus amicitiae.

49. Poem 169: *Ad eum qui sibi inimicabatur* (p. 162)

Sim saltim decimus vel quilibet inter amicos,
Sim cui digneris huc ades innuere. . .

50. Poem 120, p. 163: *Ad amicum cui cartam mittebat:*

. . . Tunc explorarem vultumque animumque legentis,
Si tamen et possem me cohibere diu.

51. Poem 179, p. 171:

Interea quod vis nostra de parte jubeto,
Indigus esse tibi, Maiole, non potero.

52. *Ibid.*: *Ergo salutatis Hugone, priore, Blaino,*
Fratribus et reliquis amplius impse vale.
Immo magis valeat quem plus amo, verius et qui
De vobis poterit dicere: plus amo te.

53. Although Marbod was not a monk before he became bishop, he knew enough about monasticism to write a poem in praise of it (*Laus vitae monasticae*, PL 171:1656).

54. *Qui vitio morum corpus vetat esse decorum:* PL 171: 1717-1718, based on Horace *Odes* IV.10. See Boswell (1980) pp. 248, 371. Boswell entitles the poem 'The Unyielding Youth' (p. 370). It would be more accurate to stick to Horace's term, *superbia*, and speak of the arrogant youth. This may seem like quibbling, but the change in emphasis alters the entire interpretation of the poem.

55. Boswell (1980), p. 248. Marbod PL 171:1655.

56. Note 53 above.

57. Marjorie Chibnall, *The Ecclesiastical History of Orderic Vitalis*, Vol. II (Oxford Medieval Texts: Clarendon Press, 1969) Bk. 4, p. 244.

58. *Ibid.*, p. 296.

59. Orderic, Vol. III, Bk. 5 (1972), p. 118: *. . . et amicos ac parentes suos ad simile propositum monitis et precibus compellebant. . . .*

60. Orderic, Vol. V, Bk. 10 (1975): p. 242: *Paganus de Montedublelli, Normannis olim familiaris amiciciam cum rege firmauit et fortissimam quam apud Balaonem possidebat motam regi tradidit.*

61. Orderic, Vol. 6, Bk. 13 (1978), p. 426.

62. *Ibid.*, p. 552: *. . . patriam et parentes omnemque cognationem et notos et amicos reliqui. . . inter exteros omnem mansuetudinem et familiaritatem reperri.*

63. Michel Aubrun, *Vie de Saint Étienne d'Obazine*, Publications de l'Institut d'Etudes du Massif Central, 6 (Clermont-Ferrand, 1970), I (2), p. 48.

64. *Ibid.*, I (6), p. 52. *. . . in quo die ac nocte una cum venerabili socio, continuis orationibus et psalmorum decantationibus insistebat.* Note that here and elsewhere Peter is called *socius*, not *amicus*.

65. *Ibid.*, I (14) p. 64.

66. *Ibid.* II (10) p. 108: *Qui cum esset religiosus et sanctus, in tantum simplex dicitur extitisse ut ei persuaderetur a quibusdam prave mentis quod eum vellet domnus abbas in quodam ex his qui edificabantur loco abbatem constituere....*

67. *Ibid.*, p. 110.

68. As seen in Bernard's attempt to regain for Clairvaux his former prior Raoul, whom Pope Eugenius III had summoned to Rome. Bernard wrote Raoul about how much he missed him, and how much he was troubled by Raoul's sadness in his new post: *Satis superque afflixit nos absentia tua, Rualene carissime; sed longe magis comperta tua tristitia turbati sumus.* (*ep* 260; SBOp 8:169).

69. Southern (1966), pp. 68-69.

70. As Adele Fiske, 'Saint Bernard of Clairvaux', *Citeaux* 11 (1960) 3-4. The article is reprinted in Fiske (1970), 16/1-41. Father Chrysogonus Waddell of Trappist, Kentucky, has very kindly sent me the draft of his article 'Cassian and the *Carta Caritatis*'.

71. The best text of the *Carta Caritatis Prior* is contained in Jean de la Croix Bouton and Jean Baptiste Van Damme, *Les plus anciens textes de Citeaux, Citeaux—Commentarii Cistercienses*: Studia et Documenta II (Achel, 1974) 89-102.

72. Chrysogonus Waddell, 'Notes Towards the Exegesis of a Letter by Saint Stephen Harding', *Noble Piety and Reformed Monasticism*, Studies in Medieval Cistercian History VII, CS 65 (1981) 10-39.

73. S. Bernardi *Vita Prima* I. 10 (PL 185:232): . . .*sic ignis quem miserat Dominus in cor servi sui volens ut arderet, primo fratres ejus aggreditur, solo minimo ad conversionem adhuc minus habili, seniori patri ad solatium derelicto, deinde cognatos, et socios, et amicos, de quibuscunque poterat esse spes conversionis.* Also I. 15: col. 236: *Ipsi vero quasi mensibus sex post primum propositum in saeculari habitu stabant, ut proinde plures congregarentur, dum quorumdam negotia per id temporis expediebantur.*

74. *Vita Prima* I, ch.13-14, col. 235. Cf. *Les Fragmenta* (note 6 above) p. 94-5. For an analysis of this passage, see my 'Was Bernard a Friend?', *Goad and Nail*, Studies in Medieval Cistercian History, X (Kalamazoo, 1985) pp. 206-207.

75. Ep 85; *SBOp* 7: p. 221. Translated Bruno Scott James, *The Letters of Saint Bernard* (Burns and Oates: London, 1953) p. 125: 'You may be right when you say that you cannot be certain. "My affection for you is greater than yours for me". These are your very words, and I could wish they were not, for I do not know if they are true.'

76. According to a tradition at Clairvaux written down after Bernard's death, he had claimed in a sermon made to the monks a Clairvaux that even Judas, if he had become a Cistercian, would have been able to gain heaven. See my 'A Lost Clairvaux Exemplum Found: The *Liber visionum et miraculorum* compiled under Prior John of Clairvaux, 1172-79', *Analecta Cisterciensia* 39 (1983) 43. At the end of the century the story was incorporated into the *Exordium Magnum Cisterciense* (II, 5, p. 101), ed. Bruno Griesser, Series Scriptorum S. Ordinis Cisterciensis, II (Rome, 1961).

77. Remo Gelsomino, 'S. Bernardo di Chiaravalle e il *De Amicitia* di Cicerone', *Studia Anselmiana* 43, Analecta Monastica V (Roma, 1958) 180-86.

78. Birger Munk Olsen, 'The Cistercians and Classical Culture', *Cahiers de l'Institut du Moyen-Age Grec et Latin* 47 (Copenhagen, 1984) 64-102.

79. A.H. Bredero, 'The Controversy between Peter the Venerable and Saint Bernard of Clairvaux', *Petrus Venerabilis* (1156-1956). Studies and Texts Commemorating the Eighth Centenary of His Death, edd. Giles Constable and James Kritzeck, *Studia Anselmiana* 40 (Rome, 1957). For the friendship of Peter and Bernard, Jean Leclercq, *Pierre le Vénérable* (Saint Wandrille, 1946). Leclercq is severely criticized for his interpretation of a friendship between the two monks by J. Lortz, *Bernhard von Clairvaux, Mönch unde Mystiker* (Internationaler Bernhardcongress: Mainz 1953—Wiesbaden, 1955)

xxxiv-xxxv. See the rejoinder by J. B. Auniord, 'L'ami de S. Bernard, quelques textes', *Collectanea Ordinis Cisterciensis Reformatae* 18 (1956) 88-99.

80. *Ep* 28, Constable (1967) I; p. 52, much more a treatise than a letter; I, ep 65, p. 194. See also Constable (1967) II, Appendix E, for the date of letter 28.

81. Constable (1967) II, p. 141.

82. *Ep* 74, Constable (1967) I; p. 207 = ep 147, *SBOp 7, p. 350.*

83. Constable (1967) ep 110, p. 272 = ep 228, *SBOp* 8: 98-99: *Itane iocari libet? Dignanter sane atque amicabiliter, sed si ita luditis, ut non illudatis. Nolite mirari hoc. Nam suspectum id mihi facit vestra ipsa tam subita et inopinata dignatio. Non enim multum temporis est quod scribens ad vos debita reverentia vestram magnitudinem salutavi, et non respondistis mihi verbum. Nec multo ante rursum scripseram ad vos ex urbe Roma, et nec tunc quidem vel unum iota recepi. Modo miramini quod revertenti nuper de Hispania nugas meas denuo ingerere non praesumpsi?*
I use the translation of Bruno Scott James (note 75 above), who lists the letter as 305, p. 374.

84. *Ibid.*, p. 273 = *SBOp* 8:99 = James p. 375. *Si forte intepueram, ut arguitis, haud dubium quin velociter recalescam, fotus vestrae caritatis visceribus. 2. Et nunc quod placuit scribere, obviis manibus suscepi. Legi avide, libenter relego, et placet saepius repetitum. Placet fateor iocus. Est enim et iucunditate gratus, et serius gravitate.*

85. *Ep* 111, Constable (1967) I: p. 274: *Tam dulcibus et iocundis amici litteris.*

86. *Ibid.*, p. 275: *Tractus inquam sicque tractus est, ut quod nunquam, nisi sacrorum reuerentia librorum me fecisse memini, perlectam epistolam mox exosculatus sim.*

87. *Ibid: Quod si ita est, culpa michi imposita me deserens, uos incipit intueri, quia inculpabilem culpare, et sarcina aliena ne dicam uestra aggreuare humeros fratris innocentis uoluistis.*

88. *Ibid.*, p. 276: *Unde dulce michi est semper uobiscum loqui, et melleam inter nos caritatis dulcedinem iocundis sermonibus conseruare.*

89. *Ibid.*, p. 277: *Praesumo et ego hoc idem de uobis, nec a cordis uestri penetralibus me cuiuslibet impulsus posse excludi confido.*

90. *Ibid.*, p. 276-77: *Nam quantum ad eam caritatem spectat, quam uobis in abdito cordis mei iam ab intiquo reseruo, uidetur michi quod aqua multae ut scriptum est non poterunt eam extinguere, nec flumina obrurere* (Cant. 8:7).

91. *Ep* 26, Constable (1967) I: pp. 48-50, and II: P. 113.

92. Constable I: p. 49: *Tu autem nullam huic nostrae beniuolentiae uicem reddere curans, quod saluo amicitiae priuilegio dixerim, uideris tibi uiuere, tua curare, ea quae sunt aliorum et quod est deterius amicorum uilipendere. . . . Sed absit ut sic de corde tuo sentiam, de quo non aliud quam quod de meo sentire consueui.*

93. *Ibid.*, p. 50: *Veni ergo ad me celeriter, ut tutis amici auribus credere possim, quae cartis plerumque infidelibus committere non praesumpsi.*

94. *Ep* 58, Constable I: p. 180: *Ibi ergo positus et tui recordatus, immo nunquam uel breuissimo temporis spacio oblitus, quanto tuam cum adest iocundius amplector praesentiam, tanto molestius tolero absentiam.*

95. *Ibid.*, p. 181: *Quo enim aut quanto praecio ut de ceteris virtutibus tuis taceam, michi uel moribus meis consimilem uel conformem potero aliquando mercari? Si scripturarum sanctarum libuit abdita rimari, te semper paratissimum repperi. Si de saecularis litteraturae scientia gratia tamen diuinae aliquid conferre placuit promptum et perspicacem inueni.*

96. *Ibid.*, p. 182: *O quotiens clausis ianuis, nullo nobiscum admisso mortalium, illo tantum teste qui de se cogitantibus aut conferentibus nunquam deest, formidolosus sermo inter nos habitus est de cordis humani caecitate atque duritia, de diuersis peccatorum laqueis, de*

uariis demonum insidiis, de abysso iudiciorum dei, quam terribilis sit in consiliis super filios hominum, quod quibus uult miseretur et quos uult indurat, et quod nescit homo utrum amore an odio dignus sit, de incerta et formidabili uocatione nostra, de dispensatione salutis humanae per incarnationem filii dei ac passionem facta, de tremendo ultimi iudicii die, de incomprehensibili diuini examinis seueritate qua ain perpetuum malos punit, de inenarrabili misericordia, qua aeterna bonis praemia reddit.

97. Cf. the outstanding work of Caroline Walker Bynum, 'Jesus as Mother and Abbot as Mother: Some Themes in Twelfth-Century Cistercian Writing', *Jesus as Mother* (University of California Press: Berkeley, 1982) 110-69.

98. *Ep* 58, Constable I: p. 183: . . . *ut in te uno et pene solo illam uerae amicitiae diffinitionem expertus sim, idem scilicet uelle, et idem nolle, ut nunquam michi potuerit placere, quod tibi displicebat, nec displicere, quod tibi placebat, et iuxta id quod dictum a quodam legitur, non duobus corporibus duae sed una utrique corpori uideretur inesse anima.*

99. *Ibid.*, p. 194: *Ecce me laborante, tu quiescis; me vigilante, tu dormis; me clamante tu taces; me pugnante, tu vacas, me orbem lustrante, tu in tuo monte resides.*

100. *Ibid.*, p. 188. The language is beautiful, passionate, controlled, perhaps the most perfect formulation of the desire for sharing in a friendship that I find in the twelfth-century literature. At the same time the tone is quintessentially monastic, with its reminder of the call of the desert, but now interpreted in a manner where the solitude of one is replaced by the solitude-sharing of two: *Et uelut intra septa montium, sic intra archana cordium nobis solitudines aedificemus, ubi a ueris mundi contemptoribus, uera tantum heremus inuenitur, ubi nullus externus admittitur, ubi mundanorum tumultuum turbo fragorque sopitur, ubi sine ullo corporeae uocis sono in sibilo aurae tenuis uox dei loquentis auditur.*

101 *Ep* 123, Constable I: p. 317. For dating and circumstances, see Constable II (1967), pp. 181-82.

102. *Ep* 126, Constable I: p. 322-23: *Tantum hic sursum cucullatos poetas quaere, coloratos nigro monachos mirare, religionis, orationis, lectionis amatores fratres desidera. Nichil fucatum penes hos existimes, nichil admixtum uicio formides. Custos etenim uirtutum iustitia, nichil fluctuare sinit in monte nostro, caritate magistra.*

103. *Ep* 128, Constable I: p. 325 *Vere dulcis et pie iocosa epistola, in qua sic uestram de siluestri uel heremitico uocabulo iniuriam uindicatis, ut ualde sic me peccasse delectet, qui pro uerberibus laudes accipio.*

104. *Ibid.*, pp. 325-26: *Hinc est quod et modo et quotienscumque non adestis, solus sum. Etsi multi assint, et totus orbis obstrepat, sine uobis in ueritate solum esse me sentio. Sciatis etiam Cluniacum, urbem uestram clarissimam totam unanimiter imperialem ac piissimum uultum uestrum cotidie desiderare.*

105. Constable II: p. 15. For more on Peter of Poitiers, Constable's appendix Q in II, 331-43, gathers all the facts.

106. *Ep* 69, Constable I: p. 200. Peter here reveals a concern that is apparent in many of his letters: obtaining authenticity in conveying himself to a loved one: *Sic uerba per aures alienas aliorum cordibus committenda, referentium inscitia, incuria, industria, aut non intellectam, aut neglectam, aut deprauatam, quandoque augent, mutant, minuuntque ueritatem. Vnde quia certius quisque cor suum quam alter agnoscit, uerius se ipsum quam alter exponit.*

107. The closest I can come to Peter's idea of the importance of a personal letter is in one of Seneca's letters to Lucilius (40), where he at the beginning points out how a friend's letter is more precious than his portrait: *quanto iucundiores sunt litterae, quae uera amici absentis uestigia, ueras notas afferunt? nam quod in conspectu dulcissimum est, id amici manus epistulae impressa praestat, agnoscere.*

108. *Ep* 71, Constable I: p. 204: *Volo linguam retinere, sed ipsa non permittit, stilum manu dimittere, sed ipsa interedicit* [the *ipsa* is *caritas*]. *Timeo sermonem prolixum et incompositum, sed ipsa dicit, fac quod uis, quia singulari amico singulariter scribis.* See Constable I, p. 60, note z for full references.

109. *Ep* 81, Constable I: p. 217: *Quo enim pacto manet amicus, qui diligi se nescit? Aut quomodo stabit lilla antiqua amicitiae diffinitio, qua dictum est quod 'amicitia nichil sit aliud quam diuinarum humanarumque rerum cum beniuolentia et caritate consensio'* [*De amic.* VI, 20]. *Quae consensio, uel sicut ait quidam doctorum caritas, ad minus quam inter duos haberi non potest* [Gregory the Great, *In Ezech.* II. iv.3]. *Sed neque iuxta Tullium, neque iuxta Gregorium, conuenire in una beniuolentia uel caritate, duo uel plures poterunt, dum alternos animorum suorum affectus nesciunt, dum ad inuicem sensa sua sibi non communicant, dum utrum sese diligant aut odiant ignorant.*

110. *Ep* 85, Constable I: p. 222: *Vera enim amicitia obliuionem nescit, interruptionem non patitur.* Compare Jerome's maxim: *amicitia quae desinere potest, vera nunquam fuit* (CSEL 44, p. 18). Also Cassian, *Conlat.* 16:3 (CSEL 13, 440), as pointed out by Constable.

111. *Ep* 85, p. 222: *His amicitiae legibus agitur, ut in uobis gaudeam, assidue cogitem de uobis. . . Beatus ego qui eandem amoris uicem in uobis esse confido. . . . Sed est quod amplius dissimulare nequeo, amicitia compellente ut proferam. . . ubi frequentes epistolae, ubi crebra consolatio, ubi illa solita eloquentia, qua amicum senem releuare solebatis?*

112. *Ep* 86, Constable I:223: *. . .ubi est deuotio illa, ubi est affectus ille caelo approprians. . . .*

113. *Ep* 121, Constable I: p. 314: *Legitur in Salomone: Vinum nouum amicus nouus ueterascat, et cum suauitate bibes illud* [Si 9:15]; p. 315: *Sic plane carissime sic prorsus in te hoc Salomonicum uerbum impleri cognosco.*

114. *Ep* 106, Constable, p. 269: *Inter uarias pectoris mei curas, ingessit se aliquando cogitatio de amicitia, et quem cui amicum uel praeponere uel subponere deberem, sollicita perquisiuit.* Notice here there is, as in Baudri, a suggestion of the idea of ranking friends.

115. *Ibid.*: *. . .et uere Christus ipse ad universa mutui amoris primordia se medium exhibens, indiuisibiliter coniunxit.*

116. As so often, Jean Leclercq's work marks the point of departure for post-war studies in this field: *La Spiritualité de Pierre de Celle (1115-83)* (J. Vrin: Paris, 1946). In recent years a monk of Solesmes, Gérard de Martel, had edited several of Peter's works, as *L'Ecole du cloître*, SCh 47 (Editions du Cerf: Paris, 1977) and *Petrus Cellensis: Commentaria in Ruth; Tractatus de Tabernaculo*, CC CM 54 (Turnholt, 1983). I am grateful to Brother Gerard for his letters and suggestions. His article 'Pierre de Celle à Reims', *Memoires de la Sociéte d'agriculture, commerce et arts du département de La Marne*, Châlons-sur-Marne, 89, (1974) 71-105, provides a faithful review of Peter's activities during these years and a bibliography.
See also G. Wellstein, 'Die freundschaftlichen Beziehungen des Benediktiners Petrus Cellensis zu den Cisterciensern (1150-1183)', *Cistercienser-Chronik* 38 (1926) 213-18.

117. PL 202, a reprint of the Maurist edition of Paris, 1671. Jean Leclercq has published further letters of Peter, one of which (V) deals specifically with friendship (Leclercq calls it a 'lettre d'amitié' because 'it has no other goal than to renew with a correspondent who is not named the assurance of affection that Pierre de Celle has for him'—'Nouvelles lettres de Pierre de Celle', *Studia Anselmiana* 43, Analecta Monastica 5 (Roma 1958) 160-79.

118. *Liber* I, *ep* 9, PL 202:411: *Pereat omnis casus, a quo amicitiae infertur occasus. Sit solitarius, nec laude dignus qui venas interrumpens dilectionis inimicitiarum conglomerat virus.*

119. *Lib.* I, *ep* 10, col. 413: *Non facerem hoc, nisi auroram resurgentis amicitiae per concessam et recognitam in litteris vestris culpam aspicerem.*

120. *Lib*. I, *ep* 13, col. 415: *Charitas patiens, quod mirum dictu est, pene impatientiam me impellit.*

121. *Ibid*.: *Estne, inquam, in Britannia consecutivum, ut ubi sterilitas panis, sequatur et defectio cordis?*

122. *Lib*. I, *ep* 14; PL 202:416: *Quem enim sine fine diligo, nunquam satis ei scribere, nunquam satis loqui valeo. Conventus noster vester est populus, noster populus vester est, anima mea vestra est.*

123. Bk I, *ep* 15, PL 202:416: *Haec inter nos mediatrix, unico amore dulciter, fortiter et sapienter animas nostras conglutinavit.* [Cf. 1 Sam. 18:1—*anima Ionathae conglutinata est animae David*. . .].

124. I.15, 416-17: *Nisi autem justa occasione inventa ad nos veneritis, satis de integritate amoris nostri diminuetis.*

125. *Lib*. 1, *ep* 16, PL 202:417: *Clamamus tandem post vos. Volumus enim suscitare compassionem in vobis passionibus nostris.*

126. *Ibid*.: *Amicus nempe tam omnium consiliorum dicitur esse conscius quam coadjutor in omnibus voluntarius.*

127. *Lib*. I, *ep* 17, PL 202:418: *Valet dominus meus? Vivitne? Ut credo, aut est alteratus episcopus S. Maclovii, aut alter a meo est substitutus.*

128. *Ibid*.: *Doleo, Pater, excessum memoriae vestrae jam per biennium suspensae, decessum quoque amicitiae quatriduanae multo tempore quasi sepultae.*

129. *Ibid*., col. 419: *Suntne montes interjacentes? Estne mare interjacens? Estne chaos magnum firmatum inter nos et vos, ut hi qui volunt hinc transire non possint, neque inde huc transmeare? Sed charitas omnem altitudinem exsuperat, sed aquae multae non possunt exstinguere charitatem; sed non est qui se abscondat a calore ejus, sed attingit usque ad finem fortiter, et disponit omnia suaviter.*

130. *Ep* I.18, PL 202:420.

131. *The Letters of John of Salisbury* I: *The Early Letters (1153-61)*, ed. by W. J. Millor and H. E. Butler, revised by C.N.L. Brooke (Thomas Nelson: London, 1955) p. xix. See the superb analysis of *ep* 112 to Peter of Celle as 'the sort of nonsense which "the lunatic, the lover and the poet" have poured forth in every age, but has only rarely been used as a normal mode of expression between intimate friends: it is an elaborate, almost a romantic conceit, with something of the sixteenth and something of the nineteenth century about it, and it is built up on a card-house of word-play indescribably medieval. It is the expression of an age when the deepest purely human emotion was the love of man for man' (p. xlvii). I would take exception to the last statement and say that the letter's style and content illustrate an age when the human emotion most openly and clearly expressed in latin literature was the love of man for man. Several of the articles in *The World of John of Salisbury*, ed. Michael Wilks, Studies in Church History, Subsidia 3 (Blackwell, Oxford, 1984) shed new light on John, but there is little about friendship as such.

132. *Ep* 19 (The Letters. . .I, p. 31), dated to autumn 1156 (See Appendix II); *epp* 31-35 (pp. 49-65), all dated to 1157 or later; *epp* 111-112 (pp. 180-84), dated to 1159 or later. A letter of John 'to an intimate friend' was once thought to be for Peter of Celle, but recent editors reject the attribution, and I agree—*ep* 97 (p. 149). The language borders tantalizingly on a christian conception of friendship but could just as well be seen in classical pagan terms: *De moribus enim amicorum sanctum semper esse debet uenerandumque iudicium, et peruersi ingenii est de eis facile. . . iudicare.* Some of the language, however, sounds very much like a perfect mixture of Cicero, Peter of Celle, and the Bible: *Quid ergo dulcius quam talem thesaurum frequenter inuisere ubi et anima iocundatur et alios iocunditatis suae facit esse participes? 'Ubi est amor' inquit*

'Ibi oculus; et ubi thesaurus, ibi est et cor tuum' [cf. Matt 6:21 and Luke 12:34, but also association to Qo 6:14].

133. *Lib.* I, *ep* 69, PL 202:515, perhaps an answer to John's *ep* 33 about wine and drinking. The affection is pure joy: *tu autem pars magna deliciarum mearum*, but for Peter the bond in Christ is always present: *ut nam corporum eadem semper mediante Christo propinquitas esset, quae animorum*. See Ronald E. Pepin, *Amicitia Jocosa*: Peter of Celle and John of Salisbury, *Florilegia* 5 (1983) 140-56, an excellent treatment.

134. Bk I, *ep* 72, col. 518: addressed to 'Suo clerico suus abbas'—*Tibi an occupationibus tuis visitationum tuarum raritatem imputare debeam, non plane discerno. Hoc unum perpendo, quod litterarum tuarum ad nos rarissima pervenit salutatio.*

135. Bk II, *ep* 118, PL 202:568: *Hactenus unice amicos fuisse quis dubitat? Hujus rei testis est acervus epistolarum, marina pericula non timentium, cum familiarissimo recursus et brachiali complexu nostra quondam sese revisitabat amicitia.*

136. Bk II, *ep* 120, col. 570: *Facile est amicorum erratibus ignoscere, qui contingunt casu, non deliberatione.*

137. *Ep* 121, *Ibid.*, dated to soon after the murder of Becket, so *c.* 1171: *Ecce mi dulcissime Richarde, proruo in osculis faciei tuae, non sine affectu viscerali, attendens mutatum habitum, nescio si melioratum animum.*

138. Bk II, *ep* 124, col. 573.

139. The letters John wrote to Peter as abbot of Saint Rémi are contained in W. J. Miller and C. N. L. Brooke, *The Letters of John of Salisbury* II: *The Later Letters (1163-80)*, Oxford Medieval Texts (Clarendon Press, 1979), 304 (p. 714) and 310 (p. 754).

140. Bk II, *ep* 72, PL 202:606: *Admittendi tamen salvo silentio sunt amici illi, cum quibus omnia sunt communia, qui non invident, sed congaudent fortunis prosperis.* Elsewhere (I, *ep* 67, col. 513) Peter, in writing to John, speaks of the *leges amicitiae*, as other writers of the period so often also did.

141. Bk II, *ep* 97, col. 547: *Chariora mihi forte et utiliora sunt spatia nocturnalia quam diurna. Siquidem diurna accersitis hinc inde et contra ductis copiosarum occupationum catervis, animam meam de manibus meis tollunt, et me mihi tam violenter quam fraudulenter assidue subtrahunt: hiemales autem noctes sua prolixitate non fastidium, aut taedium, sed interdum duplex beneficium conferunt. Tribuunt etenim corpori requiem, et animae renovant vetustatem.*

142. *Ibid.*: *Plura de hac materia vobis libenter scriberem, sed scriptor noster frater Hugo, abrepta brevi chartula, propter finem chartae finem fecit scripturae nostrae.*

143. Bk II, *ep* 98, col. 548: . . . *ecce symphonia et chorus, ecce amicorum ibi sanctus conventus, et ubi ego, et quid ego?*

144. Bk II, *ep* 102, col. 553: *Mira veri amoris natura: ignea siquidem est, et tamen contra ignis naturam acrius fervet in amicis remotis, quam sub oculis constitis. Quaeris quare? Quia sollicitudo ministra dilectionis quasi jacet, dum quod amat videt: currit vero cum assiduo impetu mordens animum propter absentem amicum. Ubi est, inquiens, quem diligit anima mea? Vivitne? sospesne est? estne tristis an laetus? estne timens, an securus? estne de me sollicitus, an ad se intentus? estne indigens, an copiosus?* Some of these are precisely the questions Peter put to John of Saint Malo in his letters to him after John had failed to write him.

145. As defined by R. W. Southern in 'Medieval Humanism', *Medieval Humanism and other Studies* (Basil Blackwell: Oxford, 1970) 29-60.

146. 'The Cistercians and Classical Culture' (note 78 above) pp. 75-6. Also L. D. Reynolds, *The Medieval Tradition of Seneca's Letters* (Oxford, 1965).

147. P. Augustin Steiger, 'Nikolaus, Mönch in Clairvaux, Sekretär des hl. Bernard', *Studien und Mitteilungen zur Geschichte des Benediktiner Ordens*, 38. Neue Folge 7 (1917)

41-50, which concludes harshly: 'Nikolaus infolge seiner ungezügelten Selbstsucht und verwerflichen Falschheit seinem Orden und der Kirche zur Unehre gereichte, und sich selbst nur eine traurige Berühmtheit erworben hat.' See also Jean Leclercq, 'Les collections de sermons de Nicolas de Clairvaux', *Revue bénedictine* 56 (1956) 269-302, reprinted in *Recueil d'Etudes sur Saint Bernard et ses écrits* I (Edizioni di Storia e Letteratura: Roma, 1962) 47-82, esp. pp. 74-76, concerning a letter from Nicholas to Peter of Celle. A thorough review of Nicholas' life and work in connection with Peter the Venerable is contained in Constable (1967) II, 316-30. I am immensely grateful to John Benton at the California Institute of Technology for letting me see the text of his unpublished article 'Nicholas of Clairvaux's Second Letter Collection' and for an exchange of letters concerning the problem of Nicholas' 'sincerity'. Much of what I write about Nicholas comes directly or indirectly from this exchange with John Benton. See also Benton's invaluable article 'Nicholas de Clairvaux', *Dictionnaire de Spiritualité 11* (Beauchesne: Paris, 1981) col. 255-59.

148. As Benton points out in his introduction to his article on Nicholas' second letter collection (note 147 above), the first letter collection was compiled by Nicholas at Clairvaux ostensibly on the request of the prior Gerard of Péronne, another secretary of Bernard's, and Henry of France, the brother of Louis VII, whose spectacular conversion to Clairvaux had caught Nicholas' attention. See the first letter of the collection, printed in PL 196:1595. Some of the letters are probably from before Nicholas' final entrance at Clairvaux, but the chronology of the letters needs a new study. Because of Nicholas' expulsion from Clairvaux, generally agreed as having taken place in 1152, the collection must have been drawn up before that date. It can be pushed back even further, to 1149, the date of the election of Henry of France as bishop of Beauvais. See Constable (1967) II, 195-96.

149. Bk I, *ep* 50, PL 202:475: *Furtum enim feceram propter vos, nunc furatus sum me mihi pro vobis: ego enim, qui stylum abjuraveram, dignus latebris et omni solitudine, postquam aviditatem vestram praesensi et persensi quam habetis de verbis et pro verbis hominis illius, cujus eloquentia et sapientia, vita et fama non immerito per totam latinitatem decucurrit, accepi tabulas et quod habuit et feci.* Nicholas is of course referring to Bernard of Clairvaux.

150. 'La Lettre à Pierre de Celle' in *Recueil d' Etudes* (note 147 above) p. 75.

151. PL 202:475: *Festinate et haec festinanter rescribere, et exemplaria remittite mihi et sic ad opus meum, secundum pactum meum rescribi facite....*

152. Bk I, *ep* 61, PL 202:489: *Ipse autem etsi imperitus sum stylo rescribendi, non tamen scientia redamandi. Scio quem amare debeam, quare et quantum et quandiu.*

153. Bk I, *ep* 62, col. 490: *Antequam vos viderem, dilexi vos, et fuit principium dilectionis testimonium religionis, quod a religiosis de vobis audieram.*

154. *Ibid.*: *Postquam vero auditui visus accessit, successit mutuae familiaritatis arcanum, et de personis imparibus pares animos amicitia fecit,* [Cf. Cicero *De amic.* 71].

155. Bk I, *ep* 63, col. 491.

156. *Ibid.*, col. 494: *Validissimum tibi tamen argumentum sit quam profundius in viscerum meorum abdita descendisti....*

157. Bk I, *ep* 64, col. 495.

158. Bk I, *ep* 65, col. 499: *Absconderam enim me a facie quaerentium me in loco secretissimo et remoto, hic autem brevibus et interruptis spatiolis, ut hoc magis dicerem quam dictarem.*

159. *Ibid.*, col. 505. Nicholas calls Peter *melior pars animae meae* (col. 498), clearly a reference to and improvement on Peter's assertion that Nicholas is *dimidium animae meae* taken from Horace (*Odes* I, 3). The two are competing with each other in the same language of friendship, with its patristic and classical antecedents. In this exchange one thinks frequently of the early letters of Jerome, with their passionate rhetoric

combined with definitions of the monastic life and the requirements of solitude in conflict with intellectual production. Nicholas, I think, was very much aware of Jerome's letters, but the subject would require closer study.

160. Bk I, *ep* 66, PL 202, col. 505: *Satis namque superque quod mihi scripsisti dulce, utile et honestum fuit. Quid enim dulcius amore? Quid utilius divinarum et humanarum rerum subtili et compendiosa descriptione?* [cf. *De amic.* 20 and 22]. For language taken from the Song of Songs (ch. 1), see col. 507: *Haec osculata est me osculo oris sui. Haec digito manus suae tenens animam meam voce propria, ne declinarem ab ea. Hujusmodi attractus et delinitus blanditiis, an ulterius progrediendum sit haesito.*

161. *Ibid.*, col. 512: *O dulcissime! Dormiebas quando epistolam nostram legebas? Forte eras occupatus, et ideo non es culpandus.*

162. M.-D. Chenu, 'Platon à Citeaux', *Archives d'histoire doctrinale et litteraire du moyen-âge* 29 (1954) 99-106.

163. *Vita Prima*, I. 14. 68, PL 185:264: *Novi ego clericum quemdam, Nicolaum nomine, saeculo pene desperabiliter deditum, sed per eum de saeculo liberatum: qui cum in Clara-Valle monasticae conversationis habitum et ordinem suscepisset, videns eos qui de saeculi naufragio illuc confugerant, naufragii sui damna continuis redimere lacrymis, idem ipse facere volens, nec valens prae duritia cordis sui, rogabat eum cum magno cordis dolore, ut impetraret sibi a Deo gratiam lacrymarum.*

164. *Ep* 148, Constable, p. 363 = *ep* 387, *SBOp* 8: p. 355.

165. *Ep* 389, *SBOp* 8: pp. 356-57: *Abripui tamen me, et eripui votis et responsionibus omnium, et inclusi me cum Nicolao illo, quem diligit anima vestra.* Constable (1967) I, *ep* 181, p. 423: *Tuus quidem est, sed dilectus michi est. An non placet tibi si diligo quae tua sunt? An non placet tibi, ut eum quem tu ut arbitror, multis tuorum tenerius diligis, ipse affectuosius diligam? Et quae maior probatio uerae amicitiae, quam amare quod amicus amat? Diligo eum causa tui, diligo et causa sui.*

166. From Nicholas, *ep* 43, PL 196:1642: . . . *sublatus est mihi homo una nimis secundum cor meum, dulcis ad gratiam, suavis ad mores. . . Quam ardentissima charitate ipse in me, et ego in eum irruimus.* From Bernard, who emphasizes Raoul's feelings and not his own, *ep* 260; SBOp, 8: p. 169: *Satis superque afflixit nos absentia tua, Rualene carissime; sed longe magis comperta tua tristitia turbati sumus. Etenim iustius te quam nostram de te desolationem seu destitutionem plangere nobis videmur.*

167. Bk I, *ep* 49, PL 202:474: *Dignatio enim vestra fecit me vobis familiarem, familiaritas amicum, amicitia unum animum ex duobus effecit. . . Neminem habeo tam unanimem in visceribus Jesu Christi: testis est mihi Christus. . . Quid enim? Suspiciosus vobis factus sum, sicut etiam in litteris vestris apparet. Hoc signum est quia aut non diligitis, aut minus diligitis quod in veram amicitiam nec cadit nec cadere potest.* See note 154 above for another letter in which Nicholas compares *familiaritas* and *amicitia*.

168. One of the most obvious cases is Bernard's letter to Eskil, archbishop of Lund, *ep* 390, (SBOp 8: pp. 358-59) with phrases such as: *Audax sum, sed non mendax* = Nicholas *ep* 34 (PL 196:1626): *quasi si audax sum, non tamen mendax.* Also: *Utinam mihi datum esse desuper haec dicere, non dictare* (the desire to speak face to face instead of through the dictation of a letter) = Nicholas *ep* 47, col. 1648: *Utinam datum esse nobis desuper haec dicere, non dictare. And Oculi quippe loquentis fidem facerent dictis* = Nicholas *ep* 29 (col. 1620). *oculi quippe loquentis fidem proferrent vel facerent* (the chance to see the eyes of the one speaking lends credibility to him). Finally, the word *affectus* is one shared by Bernard and Nicholas in expressing something close to what we would call an emotional impulse, a feeling—as Bernard's closing of letter 390: *Actum excludunt a me, non affectum*, or Nicholas (in the person of brother Matthew of Clairvaux) apologizing for ending a letter because of the requirements of style, which cannot be restrained because of his feelings for his correspondent: *Excessi, fateor, epistolarem*

modum, sed currentem stylum plurimus instigavit affectus. (*ep* 50, col. 1650). A further examination of Bernard's, Nicholas's, Peter of Celle's, Peter the Venerable's and other letter collections of the age would certainly reveal many more parallels in expression. These, I think, do not necessarily mean that letters of friendship can be reduced to catalogues of appropriate phrases. The shared language of friendship can just as well point to its living reality in a monastic context where identity of language hints at similarity of experience and actual expression of friendship.

169. *Neque enim quia in Clarevalle sum vel exui vel exivi: affectus humanus: ep* 31, PL 196:1622, in the person of brother Walter of Clairvaux to his brother. The same sentiment in *ep* 15 (col. 1609) to a friend: *Nec enim quia in Clarevalle sum, affectus humanos vel exui vel exivi: sed testis mihi est Deus quomodo vos omnes habeam in visceribus meis.* The friend had apparently charged Nicholas with not caring about others: *Quod dicis quia non est cura mihi de aliquo; aliter est.* This is a fascinating accusation, which perhaps goes to the heart of Nicholas's paradox: wanting so much to be involved with other people and at the same time being so caught up in himself.

170. For abba Alonios, Benedicta Ward, *The Sayings of the Desert Fathers* (Mowbrays, London 1975), p. 30.

171. *Ep* 35, PL 196:1626-27: *Est mihi scriptoriolum in mea Clarevalle, vallatum undique officinis coelestibus et celantibus illud. Ostium ejus aperitur in cellam novitiorum, ubi frequens numerositas tam nobilium quam litteratorum novum hominem in novitate vitae parturiunt, gemitibus coelos, fletibus angelos inclinantes. . . . A dextra parte claustri monachorum excrescit. . .*

172. *Ibid.*, col. 1628: *Cum igitur eam attentius et intentius perlegissem cogitavi dies antiquos inter nos, secundum saeculum, et quae saeculi sunt, animae duae, animus unus excitarat. . . et videam dimidium animae meae vivere voluntati tuae in medio meorum Clarevallensium.*

173. *Ibid.*, col. 1630: *Nec tamen, si non veneris ideo putes me ab amore tuo vel transverti vel averti posse, sed amicitiam semel ceptam atque receptam usque ad mortem et post mortem etiam retinebo in visceribus Jesu Christi, unde, et quidquid habeo, quidquid sum, quidquid possum, tuum est. . . .*

174. *Ibid.*, col. 1630-31: *Intolerabiles enim essent amicorum absentiae, si non intervenirent remedia litterarum.*

175. As *ep* 38 (col. 1652): *Audacter, fateor, tam secure loquens tecum, quam mecum, quippe qui credebam cor unum et animam unam* (cf. Acts 4:32).

176. Constable (1967) II, p. 325. See *ep* 182, pp. 425-26, where Peter the Venerable seems to be expressing a desire to have Nicholas with him all the time: *Volui, immo tot corde optaui, te semper mecum esse, nec datum est. Volui saltem sepe nec concessum est.*

177. At moments Peter the Venerable (as in the last letters in his collection) does seem to have been 'in love' with Nicholas in the modern sense. As a handsome, bright and able monk who could play up to whomever he wanted to please, Nicholas must have been an enormously attractive personality. For our purposes, it is not necessary, however, to 'psychoanalyze' Peter the Venerable, only to point to the apparent intensity of his affection and need for having Nicholas with him. Such a need can be seen in a totally human sense without our having to pretend to pass judgment on its possible erotic element. If love in our own surroundings is difficult to define and describe, how much more so for the twelfth century. And yet it is definitely there.

178. Bk II, *ep* 170, PL 202, col. 615, entitled 'Ad Nicolaum alium' to distinguish the correspondent from Nicholas of St. Albans. The main joke of the letter is based on the changing habit of Nicholas—from the natural colour (Cistercian) to black for the Cluniac Benedictine: *Nescio utrum modo sis melior, quam tunc, vetustior tamen et nigrior es, et terrae propinquior* (his arrogance is gone?). Peter asks his Nicholas to pay

back his jokes 'with interest': *Exspecto facetias istas nostra a te cum usura statim solvi.* He wants this Nicholas to come 'to our feast', for his 'most beautiful and holy face' will illuminate the festivities, while his mouth with its truth will cure Peter of his worries and wounds. There is no conclusive evidence that the recipient is Nicholas of Montiéramey, but the recipient is someone who once was Cistercian who used to write Peter while he was in the Cistercian habit: (*reciprocae salutationes quas tu bonus sub ovina pelle mihi solebas mittere. . .*). This is precisely what happened to Nicholas.

179. As can be seen in a letter to Henry count of Champagne from the early 1160s *ep* 56; PL 196: 1651, but especially in a letter to Roland Bandindelli edited by John Benton. 'Second Letter Collection', (note 147 above), from Berlin MS Phillipps 1719, ff. 117v-118. Some of the old phrases of friendship are there, but in a new context: *Nichil enim in me sentio eligendum, sed multum michi placeo, quia placeo tibi. . . Tuus fui, tuus sum, tuus ero quamdiu fuero, et singulariter tuus.*

180. *Ep* 175, Constable, I: p. 417: *Videbo te sancte frater in illo, audiam te per illum. . . .*

181. *Epp* 183-84, I: p. 427.

182. *Vita Prima* I.12.59, PL 185:259.

183. *Ep* 506, *SBOp* 8: 464: *Sicut depinxi me in epistola, sic sum, nisi quod minus valuit exprimere manus ut affectus est animus.*

184. *Ibid.*: *Quoniam tamen dignamini, vester sum et ero quamdiu ero.* Compare Nicholas' *ep* 23 (PL 196:1619): *Ego autem vester fui, vester sum, et vester ero, quandiu fuero.*

185. *SBOp* 8:464:185. *Ep* 506, *Novum ex antiquo amplector amicum, quia verae amicitiae non veterascunt, aut verae non fuerunt. 'Tenebo eum dimittam, donec introducam illum in domum matris meae et in cubiculum genitricis meae'* (Cant. 3:4). Compare Jerome (*ep* 3): *Amicitia quae desinere potest, vera nunquam fuit.* See also Cicero *De amic.* 19.67 for the same thought in less precise terms. The letter is addressed to a W, whom the editors think might be William of Saint Thierry.

186. *Ep* 7, PL 196:1602: *. . . vallis abundans, paradisus deliciarum, gratiarum hortus, in quo si non fuero et vixero moriar. . . . Clarevallis in affectu, Clarevallis in sensu, Clarevallis in praesentia, Clarevallis in memoria, Clarevallis in ore, Clarevallis in corde est, et teneram animam tenerrima meditatione succendit.*

187. Cicero *De amic.* 21.80, trans. Michael Grant (Penguin Classics: Harmondsworth, 1971) p. 216.

188. *De Civitate Dei* 19.8, trans. Henry Bettenson (Pelican Classics: Harmondsworth, 1972).

189. 'The Wanderer', trans. Gavin Bone, *Anglo-Saxon Poetry* (Oxford, 1943) 68-71.

190. Bk I, *ep* 73, PL 202:519: *Satis amoenum delegisti, mi charissime, exsilium, ubi superabundant gaudia licet vana, ubi exuberat plus quam in patria panis et vini copia, ubi amicorum frequens affluentia, ubi sociorum non rara contubernia. Quis praeter te alius sub coelo Parisius non aestimavit locum deliciarum, hortum plantationum, agrum primitiarum?* [see note 186 above] *Ridendo tamen verum dixisti, quia major et amplior voluptas corporum, ibi verum exsilium animarum: et ubi regnat luxuria, ibi miserabiliter ancillatur et affligitur anima. O Parisius, quam idonea es ad capiendas et decipiendas animas!*

191. For social backgrounds of early Cistercians, see R. Fossier, 'La fondation de Clairvaux et la famille de Saint Bernard', *Mélanges Saint Bernard* (Association des amis de Saint Bernard: Dijon, 1954) 19-27. For the Cistercians of the Rhineland, my 'Friends and Tales in the Cloister: Oral Sources in Caesarius of Heisterbach's *Dialogus Miraculorum*', *Analecta Cisterciensia* 36 (1980) 167-245. esp. 201-17.

CHAPTER SEVEN
AELRED OF RIEVAULX

1. For Aelred's life and works, Aelred Squire, *Aelred of Rievaulx: A Study*, (SPCK: London, 1969, Kalamazoo, 1981). For his theology, Amédée Hallier, *The Theology of Aelred of Rievaulx: an Experimental Theology*, CS 2 (1969). For a full treatment of the historical background for Aelred's life, F.M. Powicke's introduction to *The Life of Aelred of Rievaulx by Walter Daniel* (Thomas Nelson: London, 1950) is still invaluable. Almost all aelredian research until the early 1960s, together with a valuable review of manuscripts and printed editions of his writings, is to be found listed in *Instrumenta Patristica II*, Anselm Hoste, *Bibliotheca Aelrediana* (Steenbrugge, 1962). In the last decades the amount of publications on Aelred has been enormous, and I make no attempt in these notes to account for all of it, only to give credit to the studies which have been an immediate help in forming my interpretation of Aelred's friendships and view of friendship.

2. For the new intimacy of the twelfth century, Colin Morris, *The Discovery of the Individual* (SPCK: London, 1972). For Aelred's share in this development, Georg Misch, 'Die Selbstbekenntnisse des Zistercienser-Abtes Aelred von Rievaulx', *Geschichte der Autobiographie* 3: *Das Mittelalter* 2 (Frankfurt, 1959) 464-504.

3. Fiske (1970) 18, 1. The article is also printed as 'Aelred of Rievaulx' in *Citeaux* 13(1962) 5-17, 97-132. Although Fiske does not deal at length with Aelred's actual friendships, her interpretation of his doctrine of friendship is valuable becaue she takes into account what Aelred says in his sermons, a source for his teaching that has not otherwise received sufficient attention.

4. For Cassian and Augustine, see above, my chapter 'The Western Fathers and the Search for Community'.

5. Phillippe Delhaye, 'Deux adaptations du *De Amicitia* de Cicéron au xxie siecle', *Recherches de théologie ancienne et médiévale* 15 (1948) 307.

6. *De amicitia spiritali*, Prologus 3: *amicitiae formulam*. 6: *regulas mihi castae sanctaeque dilectionis*. This treatise will be abbreviated as *Sp am*, while the *Speculum Caritatis* as *Spec car*. In both instances I use the standard edition in CC CM 1, ed. A.Hoste and C.H.Talbot (Turnholt, 1971).

7. Sr. Eugenia Laker's translation (CF5, 1974) p. 45; CC CM 1, p. 287: *Cum adhuc puer essem in scholis, et sociorum meorum me gratia plurimum delectaret, et inter mores et uitia quibus aetas illa periclitari solet, totam se mea mens dedit affectui, et deuouit amori; ita ut nihil mihi dulcius, nihil iucundius, nihil utilius quam amari et amare uideretur.* See the notes here for the various references to Augustine, especially to his *Confessions*.

8. See *Spec car* 3:31-39, CC CM 1, pp. 119-123.

9. 'Notes on the Prologue of St. Aelred of Rievaulx's *De Spirituali Amicitia*, with a Translation', *Traditio* 37 (1981) 396-411, esp. p. 400.

10. Pierre Courcelle, 'Ailred de Rievaulx a l'école des *Confessions*', *Revue des Etudes Augustiniennes* 3 (1975) 163-74. Something of the augustinian influence may have of course been filtered through Bernard of Clairvaux. See Jean de la Croix Bouton, 'La doctrine de l'amitié chez saint Bernard', *Revue d'ascétique et de mystique* 29 (1953) 3-19. There is no doubt, however, of Aelred's fondness for Augustine, also witnessed in Walter Daniel.

11. Courcelle, p. 174: '. . .un cistercien si profondément nourri des Confessions d'Augustin peut revivre avec lui les épisodes de sa propre existence et les présenter en conformité avec les chapitres augustiniens. . . .'

12. *Sp am* 3.69, *Ipse Dominus ac Saluator noster uerae nobis amicitiae formam praescripsit: Diliges, inquiens, proximum tuum sicut te ipsum*. [Matt 22:39] *Ibid.* 2.30, *Vnde aliquam certam mihi in amicitia metam a te opto constitui*. Often Aelred also speaks of the rights of friendship, *amicitiae iura* (as 3.94).

13. *The Life of Ailred of Rievaulx by Walter Daniel* (note 1 above) pp. xxxiv-xxxv. Also Aelred Squire, *Aelred*, pp. 3-14.

14. *Inst incl*, ch. 32, ed. C.H.Talbot, CC CM 1: p. 674: *Recole, si placet, illas foeditates meas pro quibus me plangebas et corripiebas saepe puella puerum, femina masculum. . . . Recole nunc, ut dixi, corruptiones meas cum exhalaretur nebula libidinis ex limosa concupiscentia carnis et scatebra pubertatis, nec esset qui eriperet et saluum faceret*. Translated as A *Rule of Life for a Recluse* by Mary Paul Macpherson in *Aelred of Rievaulx, Treatises* CF 2 (1971) p. 94.

15. *Spec car* 1.79, p. 47 in CC CM 1: *Vinculabat me catena pessimae consuetudinis meae, uinciebat amor sanguinis mei, stringebant uincula socialis gratiae, maxime nodus cuiusdam amicitiae, dulcis mihi super omnes dulcedines illius uitae meae. . . . Placebat amicitiae gratiae connexio, sed semper timebatur offensio, et certa erat futura quandoque diuisio. Consideraui iucunditatem illarum initia, attendi processus, finem prospexi. Vidi nec initia reprehensione, nec media offensione, nec finem carere posse damnatione. Mors suspecta terrebat, quia talem animam post mortem certa poena manebat. Et dicebant homines, attendentes quaedam circa me, sed nescientes quid ageretur in me: O quam bene est illi! O quam bene est illi!*

16. For Aelred's position at court, Powicke (note 1 above) pp. xxxix-xli, has a helpful discussion of the term Walter Daniel uses for Aelred, *dapifer*.

17. See Augustine's *Confessions* VI.15: . . . *morbus animae meae satellitio perdurantis consuetudinis*. . . Also VIII.5: *dum seruitur libidini, facta est consuetudo, et dum consuetudini non resistitur, facta est necessitas*.

18. *Inst inc* 18, CC CM 1: 653 . . . uiolentia uitiosae consuetudinis. cf. *Oratio Pastoralis*, CC CM 1: 759: ch. 5, *Et contra uitia et passiones malas quae adhuc impugnant eam* [*animam meam*] *siue ex antiqua consuetudine mea pessima*. . . . *The Pastoral Prayer* is translated in CF 2 (note 14 above) by Penelope Lawson.

19. *Inst inc* 16, p. 652: . . . *illum qui scrutatur corda et renes scito esse praesentem, et sub eius esse oculis quidquid agis uel cogitas*.

20. Boswell (1980) p. 223, note 48.

21. *Inst inc* ch. 15, p. 651: *Nec sic hoc dictum aestimes, quasi non uir sine muliere, aut mulier sine uiro possit foedari, cum detestandum illud scelus quo uir in uirum, uel femina furit in feminam, omnibus flagitiis damnabilius iudicetur*. Such a passage provides one more indication of Aelred's keen awareness of homosexuality as a danger for those in the religious life, a subject that, as we have seen, was not normally broached in Western monastic circles.

22. *Spec car* 3.38 on '*carnalis affectus*' (CC CM 1: 122-23): *Facile quippe alicuius et forma elegantior, et sermo suauior, et maturus incessus, et uenustus aspectus, etiam ignorantis qualis ipse homo sit, prouocat et perstringit affectum*.
3.43, pp. 125-26: *Cum igitur iste, cui animus meus dulci quadam inclinatione mouetur, etsi minus perfectus, non sit tamen uitiosus, immo multis uirtutibus adornatus; cur non iste affectus ex uirtute credatur habere principium, ac proinde non timendus sit, sed potius amplectendus?*

23. *De bello Standardii*, in PL 195:703.

24. *Life* (note 1 above) p. 15.

25. As in the scene of the servants of the rich cleric Henry of Trier weeping when he left them for Heisterbach, in Caesarius of Heisterbach, *Dialogus Miraculorum* I, ch. 23 (p. 30 in Joseph Strange's edition (Cologne, 1851: reprinted New Jersey, 1966):

. . . mane familiam suam flentem cum nave remisit, et habitum regulariter induens nobiscum permansit.

26. As in Caesarius's first distinction, which is dedicated to conversion to the monastic life, ch. 19, the conversion of Henry, brother of the king of France. See also Aelred's own remarks about the conversion of his friend Simon: *Vere stupenda conuersio tua!* (*Spec car*, 1:100, CC CM 1:58.

27. *Inst incl* 18, CC CM 1:653: *Noui ego monachum, qui cum in initio suae conuersionis, tum naturalibus incentiuis, tum uiolentia uitiosae conseutudinis, tum suggestione callidi tentatoris, pudicitiam suam periclitari timeret, erexit se contra se, et aduersus carnem suam immanissimum concipiens odium, nihil magis quam quod eam afflictaret expetebat.*

28. *Ibid.*, p. 654: *Deus meus quas cruces, quae tormenta tunc pertulit miser ille, donec tanta ei infusa est delectatio castitatis, ut omnes quae sentiri possunt uel cogitari uinceret uoluptates.*

29. *Life* (note 1 above), ch. 16, p. 25.

30. *Spec car* 1.76, CC CM 1:44-45: *Supprimo multa silentio, quae mihi contra hanc immundissimam luem animo suggeruntur, uerens nimirum pudicissimos oculos tuos, mi amantissime et desideratissime cui praesens opusculum destinaui.*

31. *Inst incl* 22, CC CM 1:655: *Vidi hominem qui cum in pueritia sua, ui consuetudinis oppressus, continere non posset, tandem in se reuersus supra modum erubuit. . . .*

32. As Charles Dumont points out, *La Vie de Recluse*, p. 96, n. 1. Both Dumont and Powicke think the name of this friend was Geoffrey of Dinant (*Life*, p. lxvii), even though Powicke admits he is guessing.

33. As in his description of the love he experienced at Rievaulx (*Sp am* 3.82, p. 334): *Sentiebam quippe meum spiritum transfusum in omnibus, et in me omnium transmigrasse affectum, ut dicerem cum Propheta: Ecce quam bonum et quam iucundum, habitare fratres in unum.*

34. *Spec car* 3.64, p. 135: *Procedunt quidam capillati et effeminati seminudis natibus cultu meretricio, de qualibus Scriptura: Et posuerunt inquit, pueros in prostibulo.* (Joel 3:3)

35. *Ibid.*, 3.67, p. 137: *Noui ego uiris pudicissimis et abstinentissimis omnemque spurcitiam summo horrore detestantibus, accidisse, ut dum quosdam in tenera adhuc aetate summis uirtutibus cernerent accessisse, ac mirabili morum grauitate ac uitae sanctitate in quosdam canos, ut ita dixerim, spiritales incredibiliter profecisse; deuotissimo eos ac dulcissimo colerent simul et amplecterentur affectu. Quibus dum sui copiam pronius indulgerent, ac in eorum aspectu et, ut ita dicam, amplexu suauius requiescerent, uitioso quodam affectu subtilius irrepente plurimum fatigati sunt. . . uix sine quadam uitii titillatione frequentari potuerint.* Once again one can take Aelred's general statement both as an assertion about his own problem of physical attraction and as an indication of an awareness in his own time that close bonds between older men and youths could have a sexual element in them.

36. See *Sp am* 1.35-38.

37. As *Sp am* 2.57 on puerile friendship (pp. 312-13): *Est amicitia puerilis, quam uagus et lasciuiens creat affectus; diuaricans pedes suos omni transeunti; sine ratione, sine pondere, sine mensura, sine alicuius commodi uel incommodi consideratione.* Notice that this description of youthful friendship is close to that found in the Prologue of the work, indicating the possibility of a sexual element in these attractions.

38. *Inst incl* 20, p. 654: *Te, soror, nunquam uolo esse securam, sed timere semper, tuamque fragilitatem habere suspectam . . . .*

39. *Spec car* 1.109: *Dilexi te, qui me ab ipso initio conuersionis meae in amicitiam suscepisti, qui te mihi prae caeteris familiarem exhibuisti, qui in ipsis uisceribus animae tuae tuo me Hugoni associasti. Tanta enim tibi era circa utrosque dilectio, tam similis affectio, tam una*

deuotio, ut, sicut mihi uidetur ex uerbis tuis collegisse, neutrum alteri tuus praeferret affectus, quamuis eius sanctitatem mihi omnino praefferendam certa ratio iudicaret.

40. *Spec car* 1.100, CC CM 1:58: . . .*quis non miretur puerum tenerum et delicatum, clarum genere, forma conspicuum*. . . .

41. *Sp. Car. praefatio*, CC CM 1:6: *Sane autem praesentis operis suscipiendi propositum, quaedam ipse mecum meditando, quaedam uero quasi mecum, immo magis mecum, quia illi unanimi meo reuerendissimo priori Hugoni, qui plus mecum quam ego ipse mecum, communicanda epistolarum more sparsim dictaueram*. . . .

42. Bernard's letter is included in CC CM 1, pp. 3-4. In *SBOp* (8) it is *ep* 523. See 'L'instigateur du *Speculum Caritatis*', *Revue d'Ascétique et de Mystique* 14 (1933) 369-94.

43. *Sp am* 3.67. See J. Dubois, *Aelred de Rievaulx. L'amitié spirituelle* (Bruges, 1948) 139, n. 1. For Gerard the sacristan, see *Exordium Magnum Cisterciense*, III, 14, ed. Bruno Griesser, Series Scriptorum S. Ordinis Cisterciensis 2 (Rome, 1961) p. 179.

44. See Peter von Moos, *Consolatio. Studien zur mittelalterlichen Trostliteratur über den Tod und zum Problem der christlichen Trauer*. Darstellungsband (Vilhelm Fink Verlag: München, 1971) pp. 340-97, esp. pp. 342-43.

45. *Spec car* 1.98-114. *Sermones super Cantica Canticorum* 26, *SBOp* 1:3-14.

46. *Sp am* 3.119, CC CM 1:345: *nihil exigens, nihil praestans praeter affectum, et ipsius affectus suaue quoddam prout caritas dictabat indicium*.

47. *Life*, ch. 9, p. 18. Knowles (1966) p. 244, n. 3.

48. Powicke (*Life*, p. lxvi) hazards the guess that 'This model young man, well born, beautiful and holy, may possibly have been the Simon de Sigilllo, whose psalter was preserved in the following century in the library. . . '.

49. *Spec car* 1.107, p. 60: *Simul quidem loqui Ordinis nostri prohibebat auctoritas, sed loquebatur mihi aspectus eius, loquebatur mihi incessus eius, loquebatur mihi ipsum silentium eius. Aspectus pudicus, maturus incessus, grauitas in sermone, silentium sine amaritudine.*

50. *Sp am* 3.65. Fiske (1970) 18/12, n. 23: 'It is not wholly comprehensible how these two elements can belong to Cistercian friendship unless the monks had more intercourse than the written rule suggests and than the novice in the *Speculum* mentions, or unless Aelred conceives friendship as possible only to those in office.'

51. *Sp am* 3.87. Laker's translation (note 11 above) p. 113.

52. As pointed out by Douglass Roby, 'Chimaera of the North: The active life of Aelred of Rievaulx', *Cistercian Ideals and Reality*, ed. John R. Sommerfeldt, CS 60 (1978) 152-69, esp. p. 164: '. . .Aelred was still very much the member of a special class of feudal society: in spite of the conscious rejection by the Cistercians of so many ties to the feudal world. Aelred's life was a round of visits to his relatives and peers'. This same volume also has a brief but penetrating analysis of *Spiritual Friendship* by Charles Dumont (pp. 187-98).

53. *Spec car* 3:60-61.

54. *Spec car* 1.109, CC CM 1:61: *Ecce quid perdidi; ecce quid amisi. Quo abisti, o exemplar uitae meae, compositio morum meorum? Quo abisti, quo recessisti? Quid faciam? Quo me uertam?. . .Quomodo auulsus es ab amplexibus meis, subtractus osculis meis, subductis oculis meis? Amplexabar te, dilecte frater, non carne, sed corde. Osculabar te, non oris attactu, sed mentis affectu.*

55. *Sp am* 2.24-25, CC CM 1:307.

56. *Sic osculari nihil alind sit quam adulterari: Ibid.*, Laker, p. 76.

57. *Ibid.*, 2.21, CC CM 1:306: *Itaque amicus in spiritu Christi adhaerens amico, efficitur cum eo cor unum et anima una* (Acts 4:32).

58. *Ibid.*, 2.30, p. 309: *Vnde aliquam certam mihi in amicitia metam a te opto constitui.*

59. *Ibid.*, 3.67 and 122.

60. *Ibid.*, 3.123, Laker, p. 128.

61. *Ibid.*, 3.8, CC CM 1:319: *Cernitis ergo quatuor gradus, quibus ad amicitiae perfectionem conscenditur; quorum primus est electio, secundus probatio, tertius admissio, quartus rerum diuinarum et humanarum cum quadam caritate et beneuolentia summa consensio* (Cicero *De am* 20).

62. *Sp am* 3.125. *Circuitus nullus, nullus angulus, sed omnina nude et aperta.*

63. *Ibid.*, 3.127, Laker p. 129.

64. *Ibid.*, 3.82, Laker, p. 112.

65. As we shall see in the next chapter in dealing with Jocelin of Brakelond. Even in cistercian houses, internal divisions would have made friendships impossible, as occurred in the increasingly frequent laybrother revolts after about 1180. See James S. Donnelly, *The Decline of the Medieval Cistercian Laybrotherhood* (Fordham University Press: New York, 1949).

66. *Sp am* 3.14 = *De am* 76. The line that reappears in Aelred even more often than Jerome's maxim is the Vulgate of Proverbs 17:17—*Omni tempore diligit qui amicus est*.

67. *Sp am* 3.18, Laker p. 95.

68. *Sp am* 3.20, Laker p. 95.

69. *Ibid.*, 3.16-17.

70. *Ibid.*, 3.37, Laker p. 100.

71. Powicke on Walter Daniel in his introduction to the *Life*, pp. xi-xxvii, is excellent, but he does not go into detail about what Walter reveals about himself through Aelred, except 'he was not able to control his feelings' (p. xvi).

72. *Sp am* 2.1, Laker p. 69, CC CM 1:302: . . .*et nunc oculos huc illucque uertebas, nunc frontem confricabas manu, nunc capillos digitis attrectabas, nunc iram ipsa facie praeferens*. . . .

73. *Ibid.*, 1.2, Laker p. 51.

74. See the *Rules* of Saint Pachomius, *Precepts* 7: 'Let no one look at another twisting ropes or praying; let him rather be intent on his own work with eyes cast down'. Trans. Armand Veilleux, *Pachomian Koinonia* 2 CS 46 (Kalamazoo, 1981) p. 146.

75. *Sp am* 3.89, Laker, p. 114, CC CM 1:336: *Accedat huc in sermone iucunditas, hilaritas in uultu, suauitas in moribus, in oculorum etiam nutu serenitas in quibus haudquaquam mediocre in amicitia condimentum*. The following lines, about how friendship ought to be 'somewhat relaxed at times', come from Cicero *De am* 66, but those quoted here are Aelred's own formulation.

76. *Ibid.* 3.1, CC CM 1:317: *Gratianus: Habebo ei fidem. Nam et praesentiam eius mihi reor necessariam, cui et sensus est acutior ad intellegendum, et lingua eruditior ad interrogandum, et memoria tenacior ad retinendum*. For these kind remarks Gratian gets nothing but a slight from Walter! 'How could he fail to be my friend, since he is everybody's friend?' (Laker, p. 91).

77. *Sp am* 3.92:. . .*praeclarissimum uerae amicitiae speculum*.

78. 1 Sam 20:41: . . .*et osculantes se alterutrum fleverunt pariter, David autem amplius*.

79. *Sp am* 3:69: *inter amplexus et oscula, cum se mutuis lacrymis perfudissent, ac pio fletu pium protestarentur affectum, renovato rursus foedere intulit Jonathas*. . . .

80. *Sp am* 3.117.

81. *Sp am* 1.30.

82. *Sp am* 3.80.

83. Amédée Hallier (note 1 above) esp. p. 164.

84. For the general applicability of Aelred's concept of friendship outside the cloister and its humanistic ideal, see Letterio Mauro, 'L'amicizia come compimento di umanità nel *De Spirituali Amicitia* di Aelredo di Rievaulx', *Rivista di Filosofia Neo-Scolastica* 66 (1974) 89-103. My only criticism of this illuminating article is that the author ignores what always is Aelred's point of departure: the life of the cloister.

85. *Sp am* 3.119 and 134.

86. *Sp am* 3.60 trans. Laker p. 105.

87. *Sp am* 2.71, trans. Laker p. 87.

88. See Aelred Squire (note 1 above) p. 120.

89. PL 195:361-64.

90. *Ibid.*:364:. . .*ita tui avidus effectus sum ut non solum ad tuae serenitatis notitiam, sed etiam, quod in inspientia dicam, ad ipsam audeo aspirare amicitiam.*

91. For the *De officiis*, see chapter 2, 'The Western Fathers'.

92. The borrowings are well documented in the CC CM 1 edition of *Sp am*, but even such a sensitive observer as Douglass Roby, in his introduction to Laker's translation in the CF series, writing on 'Sources of the Spiritual Friendship', pp. 29-35, virtually ignores Ambrose.

93. Delhaye (note 5 above) p. 307.

94. Mauro (note 84 above) esp. p. 103.

95. Aelred indicates that he still felt involved with the world of princes, politics and secular tales in a passage in *Spec car* 2.72, CC CM 1:101 . . .*pro ineptissima uanitate noctes ducimus insomnes regum praelia, victorias ducum*. . .*omnia regni negotia in ipsa psalmodia uel orationibus nostris otiosis discurribus ordinamus*.

96. *De Iesu puero duodenni*, ed. A. Hoste in CC CM 1. English trans. in *Treatises 1* (Cistercian Publications, CF 2) as 'On Jesus at the Age of Twelve', trans. Theodore Berkeley. SCh edited by A. Hoste and translated Joseph Dubois: *Quand Jésus eut douze ans*. . . (Editions du Cerf: Paris, 1958).

97. *De Iesu*, ch. 5, CC CM 1:253.

98. Trans. Berkeley (note 96) p. 9.

99. *De Iesu*, ch. 6, CC CM 1:254: *Quis tibi cibum ministrauit ac potum? Quis lectulum strauit? Quis detraxit calceamenta? Quis membra puerilia unguentis fouit et balneis?*

100. *Ibid.*, ch. 26, p. 273: *Osculare, osculare, osculare, o beata peccatrix, osculare pedes illos dulcissimos, suauissimos, speciosissimos* . . . .

101. *Ibid.*, ch. 8, p. 256: . . .*brevis eius absentia maximi doloris materia sit.* cf. Ch. 24, p. 271.

102. *Spec car* 3.16: *Igitur ut homo se diligat, nulla se carnis delectatione corrumpat. Ut uero carnali concupiscentiae non succumbat, omnem affectum suum ad suauitatem Dominicae carnis extendat.*

103. Knowles (1966) p. 241: 'It is not easy to think of another in that age—unless it be Abelard—who so arouses and baffles all our endeavours to comprehend what comes so near to us and yet remains so far away.'

104. For the presence of the letters at Rievaulx in the fifteenth century, see Powicke (note 1 above) p. *c* in his Introduction, and Walter Daniel's comment on the content and recipients of the letters, p. 42: *Inter hec epistolas ad dominum papam, ad regem Francie, ad regem Anglie, ad regem Scocie, ad archiepiscopos Cantuariensem et Eboracensem, et fere ad omnes episcopos tocius Anglie atque ad illustrissimos uiros regni eiusdem et maxime ad comitem Leicestrie, illustri stilo exaratas transmisit, et ad omnen ordinem ecclesiastice*

dispensacionis, in quibus uiuentem sibi reliquit imaginem. . . .

Anselm's later letters, from his time as archbishop, had a similar audience and could have been described in a similar manner. Similarly Aelred's contemporary and friend, Gilbert Foliot, though he writes extremely vivid letters, limits himself to the same high-powered milieu in the letter collection we have from him and reveals little or nothing about any monastic friendships, though he was an abbot. See Adrian Morey and C.N.L. Brooke, *Gilbert Foliot and his Letters* (Cambridge, 1965) and Z.N. Brooke, Adrian Morey, C.N.L. Brooke, *The Letters and Charters of Gilbert Foliot* (Cambridge, 1967).

105. For the manuscripts of the *Sp am*, CC CM 1:281-85. As Talbot points out, 'There appear to be no copies of the work amongst the many Cistercian abbeys of Germany and Austria'.

106. As told by Chrysogonus Waddell at the Cistercian Conference at Kalamazoo, May 1984.

107. Douglass Roby in his excellent introduction to Mary Eugenia Laker's translation of *Spiritual Friendship*, CF 5 (Cistercian Publications, 1974) pp. 21-22. Fiske (1970), briefly in footnote 63 in 18/36. Boswell (1980), 221-26, shows great sensitivity in his use of Aelred but perhaps makes the question of Aelred's sexual development almost too straightforward. He distinguishes, for example, between Aelred's early 'casual sexuality' and then a 'more stable relationship' (p.222). Aelred's references are just not that clear about exactly what happened in his early life. See also Kenneth C. Russell, 'Aelred, The Gay Abbot of Rievaulx', *Studia Mystica* 5 (Sacramento, California: 1982) 51-64.

108. Boswell (1980) 43-44.

109. In the early 1970s Dom Alberic Stacpoole, in an introduction to a translation of the *Mirror of Charity* that unfortunately has not appeared, dealt with Aelred's sexuality in a frank manner that emphasizes this problem of personal integration. These remarks have been of great help to me, and with Dom Alberic's permission, I quote from his typescript:

> Man, when he has to compensate for a defect or guard against an over-strong drive, will move in one of two directions: he will either become unnecessarily severe upon himself, creating a puritanical taboo around the area of his characteristic which he will come to regard as a weakness; or he will embrace it for what it is, a characteristic capable of being fruitfully absorbed into his whole psyche. It is a sign of his sanctity that Aelred achieved the latter building on the nature he was given, to produce a most gracious and loving personality.

My only disagreement with this interpretation is the use of the word 'defect' to characterize Aelred's homosexuality. In my mind human sexual identity has nothing to do with defects or imperfections. Still, Dom Alberic's term is helpful in understanding Aelred's sexuality in terms that Aelred himself would have used.

110. *Inst incl*, ch. 19, CC CM 1: p. 654. For this central work, see the introduction to the French translation by Charles Dumont, *La Vie de Recluse*, SCh 76: (Cerf, Paris, 1961). English translation as *A Rule for a Recluse* in *Treatises. The Pastoral Prayer*, CF 2 (Cistercian Publications, 1971).

111. See my 'The Cistercians and the Transformation of Monastic Friendships', *Analecta Cisterciensia* 37 (1981) 1-63, esp. pp. 10-13. Also Louis Lekai, *The Cistercians: Ideals and Reality* (Kent State, Ohio, 1977) 347-49. Sally Thompson 'The Problem of the Cistercian Nuns in the twelfth and early thirteenth centuries', *Medieval Women*, ed. Derek Baker (Ecclesiastical History Society: Basil Blackwell, Oxford, 1978) 227-52.

112. Fiske (1970) 18/1: 'It [Aelred's teaching] seems even to mark a final stage of positive development, for it is perhaps significant that Van Steenberghe's article in the *Dictionnaire de Spiritualité* [1:500-529] on spiritual friendship presents Aelred's doctrine with little or no further development.' Fiske is correct about this important article. My objection is that Aelred is not the natural culmination of the development!

113. *Life* (note 1 above) pp. 33-34.

114. *Ibid.*, p. 40. What has not been understood about this much-quoted passage and the reference to holding hands is that Aelred was going against a very specific provision in John Cassian's *Institutes*: . . . *summa namque obseruantia custoditur, ne quisquam cum alio ac praecipue iuniores uel ad punctum temporis pariter substitisse aut uspiam secessisse uel manus suas inuicem tenuisse deprehendantur. Inst.* 2.15, p. 30 in CSEL 17, ed. Michael Petschenig (Vienna, 1888). This provision in turn can be traced to the Rule of Pachomius, *Praecepta* 95: 'No one may clasp the hand or anything else of his companion'. (*Pachomian Koinonia*, CS 46, p. 161). Walter Daniel was thus aware of a specific prohibition against physical contact which Aelred flaunted. This would indicate that Aelred himself knew he was going against a strong tradition, one more sign that in practicing monastic friendship he realized he was functioning on the borderline of established monastic practice.

115. *Life*, p. 79.

116. 'Epistola ad Mauricium', *Life*, pp. 66-81.

117. *Life*, p. 77.

118. *Life*, pp. 62-3.

119. *Ibid.*, pp. 53-4.

120. As pointed out by Fiske (1970), 18/45-6: 'Sometimes indeed it seems as if his teaching on friendship could hardly apply to any simple monk who would not, one would think, have the right to have such contact with others.'

121. We actually know very little about the conversations average cistercian monks might have been allowed with each other in the twelfth century. For the thirteenth century, however, there was some official recognition of the need for pious conversations 'for the sake of comfort' (*causa solatii*) as indicated in a General Chapter statute for 1232 (J.M. Canivez, *Statuta Capitulorum Generalium Ordini Cisterciensis*, Bibliothèque de la Revue d'Histoire ecclésiastique 9: [Louvain, 1933] I, 1232, nr. 5—*Propter collationes illicitas de medio tollendas, statuitur ut quando monachi causa solatii ad colloquium ab ordinis custode vocantur, illud colloquium sit de sanctorum miraculis, de verbis aedificatoriis, et de his quae pertinent ad salutem animarum, exclusis detractionibus, contentionibus et aliis vanitatibus*.

122. Only Adele Fiske has integrated the teachings of the sermons into a consideration of Aelred on friendship. The footnotes to her article (note 3 above) provide an excellent introduction to Aelred's sermons *De oneribus*, printed in PL 195, as well as his sermons *De tempore et sanctis*, also there. She does not, however, make use of C.H. Talbot, *Sermones Inediti B. Aelredi Abbatis Rievallensis*, Series Scriptorum S. Ordinis Cisterciensis 1 (Rome, 1952). Aelred's sermon here on the Assumption of Mary is especially informative about problems of monastic life (pp. 161-75).

123. For the newly found sermons of Aelred, Gaetano Raciti, 'Deux collections de Sermons de Saint Aelred', *Collectanea Cisterciensia* 45 (1983), 165-84. I should like to thank Dom Alberic Stacpoole for pointing out this article to me. His own 'The Public Face of Aelred', *Downside Review* (1967) 183-99 and 318-25, had helped shape my own view of Aelred as amazingly successful in combining public duties with his personal needs.

124. William of Newburgh, *Historia rerum Anglicarum*, in *Chronicles of the Reigns of Stephen, Henry II and Richard I*, ed. Richard Howlet (Rolls Series, 1884-89). William's work is commented on by Antonia Gransden in *Historical Writing in England c.550 to c. 1307* (Routledge and Kegan Paul: London, 1974) pp. 263-68. She calls Abbot Ernald of Rievaulx 'a pupil of Ailred' (p. 263), but this is only in the sense that Ernald like Ailred was interested in the writing of history. A venerable but still useful translation of William is that of Joseph Stevenson in *The Church Historians of England* IV2 (Seeleys: London, 1856).

125. *Historia rerum anglicarum* I, ch. 14.

126. See the *Cartularium abbatiae de Rievalle* (Surtees Society: Durham, 1889) n.261, p. 194, a mandate from Pope Alexander III to the heads of churches in the province of York because of runaways from Rievaulx, issued in the 1170s, an indication that Aelred's tolerant regime did not outlast his death. See Powicke's commentary in *Life*, p. 40, n. 3.

CHAPTER EIGHT
CONTINUITY AND CHANGE

1. Still invaluable for the details of this development is Hastings Rashdall, *The Universities of Europe in the Middle Ages*, I-III, edd. F. M. Powicke and A. B. Emden (Oxford, 1936). This can be supplemented by several articles in Robert Benson and Giles Constable, *Renaissance and Renewal in the Twelfth Century* (Cambridge, Massachusetts: 1982), as well as by Alexander Murray, *Reason and Society in the Middle Ages* (Clarendon Press, Oxford: 1978) esp. pp. 213-233 'The University Ladder'. Also A. B. Cobban, *The Medieval Universities* (Methuen: London, 1975) and J. I. Catto, ed., *The History of the University of Oxford*, Vol I: The Early Schools (Clarendon Press: Oxford, 1984).

2. John Baldwin, *Masters Princes and Merchants: The Social Views of Peter the Chanter and his Circle*, I-II (Princeton, New Jersey, 1970).

3. Fiske (1970) stops with Aelred. Douglass Roby comments in his introduction to *Spiritual Friendship*, CF 5 (Cistercian Publications, 1974), p. 38, that Aelred's 'work seems. . . to have inspired no successors in the monastic tradition, either because it was found to be a completely adequate treatment of the subject or because the subject was no longer regarded with the same favor'. It is the last part of this statement with which I disagree.

4. Here the point of departure for later studies remains Herbert Grundmann, *Religiöse Bewegungen im Mittelalter* (Berlin, 1935, reprinted with additional bibliography in 1977 by Wissenschaftliche Buchgesellschaft, Darmstadt).

5. CC CM 1:352-634: *Abbreviationes de Spiritali Amicitia.*

6. 'Le *Speculum Spiritalis Amicitiae*. . .' , *Analecta Monastica* 3 (1961) 291-96: 'Toutefois d'un dialogue plein de saveur et vibrant de vie, il n' a su faire qu'un traité aride' (p. 294).

7. Also illustrated in the contemporary cistercian passion for classification of sources. See Richard H. Rouse, 'Cistercian Aids to Study in the Thirteenth Century', *Studies in Medieval Cistercian History* II, ed. John R. Sommerfeldt, CS 24 (Kalamazoo, 1976) 123-34. Edmé Smits of Groningen, Holland is studying Hélinand of Froidmont, the cistercian writer, also in terms of this development.

8. 'Peter of Blois: A Twelfth Century Humanist?', *Medieval Humanism and Other Studies* (Basil Blackwell, Oxford: 1970) 105-132. The last few pages of this article provide an outline for dating Peter's letters, a vexed problem which still requires study. I have followed Southern's conclusions. Ethel Cardwell Higonnet, 'Spiritual Ideas in the Letters of Peter of Blois', *Speculum* 50 (1975) 218-244, provides a good characterization of the collection as a whole.

9. Printed in PL 207:871-958, with a modern edition by M.M. Davy, *Un traité de l'amour du XIIe siècle* (Paris, 1932). As Southern points out ('Peter of Blois', note 8 above), Davy did not realize Peter's debt to Aelred (p. 124, n.1).

10. According to Philippe Delhaye (RTAM 15, [1948,] p. 309), 'Il veut tromper son lecteur', but this is hard to reconcile with Peter's statement (PL 207:871: *ut mellificarem mihi plurium tam veterum quam modernorum sententias de amicitia et dilectione Dei et proximi*. This should be a signal for the attentive reader that Peter lays claim only to the thoughts and expressions of other writers.

11. *Ep* 32, PL 207:108: *Momentanea itaque collocutio, et notitia brevis, sed me vobis in glutino charitatis univit, ut vestrum omnino me censeam.*

12. *Ibid.*: *Fortasse decipior, nec meis ex aequo respondetis affectibus; sed inurbanum foret vos in amicitia claudicare, quem verba, quem opera, quem facies, quem incessus, quem quaelibet alia, amicum efficacem et stabilem pollicentur.*

13. *Ep* 39, PL 207:119: *Praefationibus coloratis, et picturato fastu verborum, sincera non eget affectio: unde et certissimus de mutua inter nos unione affectuum compendiosae orationi deservio, atque ab epistola praesenti, et venativas adulationum blanditias, et omne taedium prolixitatis abscindo.*

14. As *ep* 137, col. 405, to Master Alexander of Saint Albans, addressed as *dilecti et praedilecto socio et amico*, where there is a long opening statement about friendship and then a great deal of moral advice about conversion to the monastic life.

15. *Ep* 49, col. 146: *Nonne viscera mea amici mei sunt, quos foveo et qui me fovent in obsequiorum dulci commercio, in identitate affectuum sine quibus omnis cogitatio mihi esset taedium, omnis operatio labor, omnis terra peregrinatio, omnis vita tormentum?*

16. *Ep* 57, col. 171: *Ea inter nos ab adolescentia coaluit dilectionis affectio, quam in cognationibus nec vincere sanguis nec natura transcenderet.*

17. *Ibid.*, col. 172: *Quod autem amatoria juventutis et adolescentiae vestrae ludicra postulas ad solatium taediorum, consiliorum non arbitror, cum talia tentationes excitare soleant, et fovere. Omissis ergo lascivioribus cantilenis, pauca quae maturiore stylo cecini tibi mitto, si te forte relevent a taedio, et aedificent ad salutem.*

18. *Ep* 162, col. 457: *Inter amicos et fratres te solum experientia mihi fratrem exhibuit et amicum, cujus beneficio respondere non sufficerem, si totus auro effulgerem et argento.*

19. Southern (note 8 above) pp. 112-115.

20. Criticism of Cîteaux for taking tithes from clerics and others; see *ep* 82; the woman's right to decide, *ep* 54; praise of a woman who chose to become a nun, *ep* 35.

21. *Ep* 129 to the archdeacon of Orleans, who is addressed as *amice charissime* and then attacked for simony. With John of Salisbury he is more diplomatic in treating the bishop of Chartres' favour towards his nephew (*ep* 130).

22. *Ep* 118, to the archdeacon of York. He criticizes a prior for pleasing princes and being a friend of the world (*ep* 131), while in *ep* 40 he is horrified that a friend had criticized the english king in his sermons.

23. *Ep* 164, col. 459: *Legimus magnum Gregorium et alios reverendos ecclesiae patres, non solum ratione humilis poenitentiae aut supplicatione principum, sed ob simplicem amicorum gratiam quandoque in his et similibus et majoribus multiformiter dispensasse.*

Noli ergo in domino meo detestabiliter accusare quod quotidiana in hominibus benignitas consuevit.

24. *Ep* 111, col. 334: *Quodam jure naturae in contractum amicitiae venit, ut amici se ipsos mutua consolatione praeveniant, et onera tentationum, quae alterutrum nimis premunt, communicatae charitatis beneficio patientius ferant.*

25. *Ep* 121, col. 354: . . . *rogo vos in ea fide sociali et amicitia quam contraximus ab antiquo*. . . .

26. *Ep* 127, col. 378: . . . *in commercium mutuae charitatis et contractum amicitiae fortius convalescat.*

27. *Ibid.*, col. 380: *Quia igitur secundum nomen magnorum, qui sunt in terra, magnificavit vobiscum Deus misericordiam suam, qui fuistis magnus in minimis, sitis major in magnis; nunquam vestra nobilitas ab avita magnanimitate degeneret.*
Peter reminded Odo earlier that he was related to the english king.

28. *Ep* 132, col. 391.

29. *Ibid.*: *Licet, testimonio Hieronmyi, nescio quid latentius energie viva vox habeat, et efficacior sit vox viva quam scripta.* See Jerome, *ep.* 53 (PL 22:541): *Habet nescio quid latentis energiae viva vox; et in aures discipuli de auctoris ore transfusa fortius sonat.*

30. *Ep* 137, col. 405: *Totis medullis animae conversioni et conversationi vestrae congratulor. A prima enim vestri notitia dilexi vos, non ad faciem, non ad quaestum, sed pro virtutibus vestris in Domino virtutum. Litteratura siquidem vestra, et famae commendabilioris celeberrimus odor multos vobis conciliavit ad amicitiam, salva Tulii sententia, qui in libro De amicitia scribit, vix a pluribus saeculis quatuor amicorum paria exstitisse. Hodie vero amici multiplicati sunt super numerum. Charitas enim diffusa est in cordibus nostris, quae sola est vera amicitiae condimentum.*

31. *Ep* 143, col. 429.

32. *Ep* 149, col. 439: . . . *pia compassio, quae venire frequenter in contractum amicitiae consuevit*. . . .

33. Southern (note 8 above) p. 107.

34. Sheila J. Heathcote, 'The Letter Collections attributed to Master Transmundus', *Analecta Cisterciensia* 21 (1965) 35-109 and 167-238, esp. pp. 195-97 for the letters of friendship.

35. *Ibid.*, p. 65.

36. These letters are printed in PL 190:1475-88.

37. Margaret A. Harris, in 'Alan of Tewkesbury and his Letters' provides an excellent introduction I, *Studia Monastica* 18 (Montserrat, 1976) 77-108. The letters from Tewkesbury are in II: 299-351. I would like to thank Margaret Harris for her kindness in sending me offprints, and to remember our common teacher and inspirer, Beryl Smalley, for making us aware of each other's work.

38. *Ep* 16, *Studia Monastica* 18 (1976) p. 303: . . . *perfecta puritas mutuis amplexibus quos coniunxit caritas, separari non sineret, etiam separatos.*

39. *Ep* 17, p. 304: *Quanto igitur magis doleo in desiderando, tanto magis desidero in dolendo.*

40. Harris, p. 85.

41. *Ep* 18, *Studia Monastica* 18, p. 305: *Et iccirco abduceris a fide et affectu quem teneris rependere tuo dilectori?*

42. *Ibid.*, p. 306: . . . *non erit de cetero, ut credo, ut debeat dilectio tua de Alan dissidere*. . . .

43. *Ep* 36, p. 315: *In Domino firmissime spero, quod olim inter nos firmata amicitia de cetero nullatenus possit infirmari.*

44. *Ep* 30, p. 319: *Sub hoc quidem unitatis pignore in spe bona subarravimus nobis dilectionis fedus inmaculate*. . . .

45. *Ep* 37, p. 330: . . . *et quia anima mea tue adheret individua, a te non recedo sed tecum maneo.*

46. *Ep* 45, p. 334: *nec usque in hunc diem adulteravimus cum matre nostra fedus initum* . . . .

47. *Ep* 48, p. 340: . . . *inter amicos non agitur minis vel terroribus, nedum conviciis.*

48. *Ep* 50, p. 345.

49. *Ep* 47, p. 339: *omnia in communi* . . . *una domus, una familia, mensa una, denique cor unum et anima una* [Acts 4:32] . . . .

50. *Ibid.*, *Ipsa siquidem amicitia quos genuit nutrit amantes.*

51. The letters are printed in PL 209. A better edition is that of *Diplomatarium Danicum*, I Raekke, 3 Bind, ed. C.A. Christensen, Herluf Nielsen, and Lauritz Weibull (C.A. Reitzel: Copenhagen, 1976-77): *Epistolae abbatis Willelmi de Paraclito*. A hagiography of William, probably written in connection with his canonization process, is printed in *Vitae Sanctorum Danorum*, ed. M. Cl. Gertz, Selskabet for udgivelse af kilder til dansk historie (Copenhagen 1908-12). It was probably written by a canon of Sainte Geneviève in Paris and is not a dependable or informative source for his abbacy in Denmark.

52. 'Abbed Vilhelm af Aebelholts brevsamling', *Historisk Tidsskrift* 78 (Copenhagen, 1978) 1-22, with a summary in English, p. 22. For Abbot William's letters and the Cistercians, see my *The Cistercians in Denmark*, CS 35 (1982) pp. 92-98.

53. *Dip. Dan.* (note 51 above) I, 3: *epp.* I.38, p. 484: *Dulciores siquidem sunt amicitiae post inimicitias, quam ante fuerant cum nullas pateremur dissensionis augustias.*

54. *Ibid.* I.37, p. 483: *Solet enim inter amicos esse in amore leuamen et in dolore remedium familiare colloquium.*

55. *Ibid.* I.36, p. 483: . . . *si uotis non obuiat, uestris nobis litteris exarari deposcimus, quod desiderio multo sub uario rerum euentu suspendimur* . . . .

56. *Ibid.*, II.3, p. 488: *Certe dilecto meo, quem diligit anima mea, sine quo uiuere iam non est uiuere, sed dolor et gemitus.*

57. *Ibid.*, II.15, p. 494.

58. *Ibid.*, II.32, p. 523: *Haec enim, ut nostis, lex constituitur in amore, ut mentes amantium sinister rumor exulceret et de feliciori successu abundantior materia iucunditatis exuberet.*

59. *Ibid.*, II.38, p. 528: *Quia ergo scribimus, amore morem gerimus, ut tenore litterarum nostrarum expressos animi nostri dulces experiantur excessus.*

60. *Ibid.*, II.63, pp. 555-56. For the Ingeborg affair, see John W. Baldwin, The *Government of Philip Augustus* (University of California 1986) pp. 80-86.

61. *Ibid.*, II.29, p. 516: . . . *qui nunquam amoris legibus nititur obuiare.*

62. Cf. *De am* 22: *Quid dulcius quam habere quicum omnia audeas sic loqui ut tecum?*

63. *Dip.Dan.* I,3, *epp.* II 29, p. 516: . . . *amicus quidam diceris, sed non esse comprobaris.*

64. *Ibid.* II.21, p. 500: *Et certe super omnes homines, qui cognitioni uestrae possunt occurrere, decreuistis ut amicus et dominus amoris gratiae respondere.*

65. *Ibid.* II.76, p. 566: *Quod si uerum est, immo quia uerum est, sic ueri amatores foedere pari iunguntur, ut nulla disiunctionis detrimenta in amoris terminos irrumpere patiantur.* The language here is almost anselmian in its strictness: Sic ergo *necessario* concludimus *argumento*, quod a nobis nullo disiungi poteris necessitatis aut aduersitatis articulo.

66. *Ibid.*, II.35, p. 526, addressed to Walbert, abbot of Esrum: *Sed ad hoc quis idoneus nisi frater Stephanus?*

67. *Ibid.*, II.56, p. 547: *Inde est, quod et te salutamus et specialis amoris tytulo te amicitiis nostris adiungimus.* . . . *Est enim nonnullum in exilio nostro remedium, ubi tot occurrunt illusiones phantasmatum et uana simulationum umbracula, ut habeas, quem diligas.*

68. *Ibid.*, II.30, pp. 516-20.

69. *Ibid.*, p. 517: *Quod autem te, carissime, diligamus, te dubitare nullatenus arbitramur, uerum cum te diligimus, legibus amoris obsequimur.*

70. *Ibid.*, pp. 518-19: *Hoc etiam diligenter attendas, quod tamen ex consilio et condicto patris tui esse non dubites, ne ad te notis et amicis tuis concurrentibus ecclesiam graues uel in expensis uel in ordinis institutis.*

71. *Ibid.*, p. 519. This information is of great value and unique for danish monastic history. We have no similar figures, for example, for cistercian monasteries at the time in Denmark.

72. *Ibid.*: . . . *cum te in ueritate diligamus et tuis sicut et nostris, immo certe plus quam nostris profectibus prosperos successus inesse uelimus; intelligis, quae dicimus.*

73. *Ibid.*, p. 520: . . . *nichil est dulcius in rebus humanis quam cum amico familiare colloquium.* Cf. Cicero *De am* 22 (note 62 above).

74. *Ibid.*: *Magistrum Andream quem in ueritate et affectuosissime diligimus ex parte nostra salutabis et magistrum Iocelinum cuius memoria est apud nos in benedictione. Uiuas et ualeas.*

75. 'Abbed Vilhelm af Aebelholts brevsamling' (note 52 above) esp. pp. 14-17. I am grateful to Nanna Damsholt for her guidance on this point. My only disagreement is with her statement (p. 17) that William's concept of friendship seems 'traditional, dry and containing few nuances' in comparison to that of Peter of Blois. William is in my mind able at moments to reach and exceed the literary level of Peter, and he is helped by his emotional involvement not just in his own situation (as Peter is) but also in the predicament of the friend. Here I am in accord with Dr. Damsholt that William 'was emotionally very much engaged' in his friends.

76. I have used the collection in PL 211 as well as the letters in *Dip.Dan.* I:3. See also Jules Desilve, *Lettres d'Etienne de Tournai* (Paris, 1893).

77. *Ep* 136, PL 211:418, in *Dip.Dan.* I,3,nr.132, dated to 1185.

78. *Ep* 139, PL 211:420, in *Dip.Dan.* I.3,nr.133, dated to 1185: . . . *et artificioso quodam naturae colloquio sibi confabulantur absentes.*

79. *Ibid.*: *Current inter nos haec religiosa commercia, et quod invidet commeantium raritas, communio suppleat voluntatum.*

80. *Ep* 145, PL 211:431, (according to *Dip.Dan.* I,3,nr.153, this letter is dated to 1188): *Doleo super te, frater mi, amabilis valde super amorem Jonathae, quod ad unius falsi rumusculi sonum turbatus es* . . . .

81. As to Archbishop Absalon (*ep* 146, col. 432, dated in *Dip.Dan.* I.3 [154] to 1188).

82. *Ep* 145, PL 211:432: *Augetur fratrum numerus, renovantur aedificia. multiplicantur possessiones, et, quod majus est, pax et tranquillitas inter fratres, disciplinae regularis observantia, in officiis ecclesiasticis devota contentio* . . . .

83. *Ep* 146, PL 211:432: *Dominos et amicos nostros quos uidere non possumus, frequenti cogitatione recolimus, ferventi dilectione complectimur, desiderio prosequimur. obsequi ueneramur.*

84. *Ep* 149, col. 436 = *Dip. Dan.* I,3,nr.157: *Quatuor sunt quae aut nouas conciliant amicicias aut ueteres colunt. alternae confabulationes. obsequia mutua. litterarum frequens excursus. uirtutum fama consentiens ueritati.*

85. *Ep* 30, PL 211:332: *Causam habet coram domino meo, in qua quoniam mei copiam facere non possum ad eumdem, absentia, precor, mea per tui praesentiam suppleatur.*

86. *Ep* 28, col. 330: *Intercedere pro amicis et necessitas urget, et charitas persuadet.*

87. *Ep* 16, col. 322 (notice the word play here): *Ea jucunditate simul et laetitia, frater amantissime, nominis tui recordor, quae animae veram amicitiam degustanti non minus afferat dilectionis commodum, quam delectationis condimentum.*

88. *Ep* 30, col. 332: *Opinantur aliqui de me supra me, et aliorum aestimatio sic excedit conscientiam meam, ut exosam habeam quandoque confidentiam alienam.*

89. *Ibid.*: *Talium est unus praesentium lator amicus meus, et in curia domini mei in qua negotium habet, me posse aliquid confidens, et confidens, ut vos et caeteros amicos meos pro ipso sollicitem, sollicite me compellit. Dilectionis vestrae preces fundo, ut ei pro amore meo, et in agendo dictetis consilium, et in postulando patrocinium praebeatis.*

90. *Ep* 73, col. 371-72: *Sequor Albanum episcopum per montes et valles, per vastas solitudines, per praedonum rabiem et mortis imaginem, per incendia villarum et ruinas domorum, ubi nihil tutum, nihil quietum, nihil quod non minetur saluti et non insidietur vitae. . . ultra Tolosam, prope Hispanos, hominem illum inveniam, sicut dicunt.*

91. *Ep* 25, PL 204:232: *Quando enim mihi meus spiritus tui poterit oblivsci? quando vel ad momentum recordatio tui et dilectionis tuae circa me, et lacrymarum propter me a visceribus meis poterit avelli?*

92. *Ibid.*: *Denique, etsi in hoc corpore te visitare non datur quemadmodum placeret, his tamen apicibus te visitare non negligo, per quos veraciter insinuo, quia talis in eis hodie, qualis eras cum a nobis discessisti, charus utique tunc, et nunc non minus charus.*

93. *Ibid.*: *Charissime, invisceratus es, non tam facile erueris; etiamsi assumpseris pennas tuas diluculo, ut longius avoles et habites in extremis maris, illuc te sequar spiritu.* [Cf. Psalm 138:9]

94. Contained in PL 204. See Yves Congar, 'Henry de Marcy, Abbé de Clairvaux, cardinal évêque d'Albano et légat pontifical', *Studia Anselmiana* 43 (Analecta Monastica 5: Herder, Roma, 1958) 1-90, for an excellent treatment.

95. *Ibid.*, p. 65.

96. André Willmart, 'Les Mélanges de Mathieu Préchantre de Rievaulx au début du XIII siècle', *Revue Bénédictine* 52 (1940) 15-84, esp. pp. 29-30.

97. For contemporary criticism of the Cistercians, see Jean Leclercq, 'Epitres d'Alexandre III sur les cisterciens', *Revue Bénedictine* 64 (1954) 68-82. Despite his attraction to cistercian spirituality, Peter of Blois also criticized the white monks. In a letter to the abbot and monks of Cîteaux on behalf of the archbishop of Canterbury, he excoriated them for usurping tithes on properties that had once gone to monks or clerics (*ep* 82, PL 207:252).

98. See E.R. Smits, 'Helinand of Froidmont and the A-Text of Seneca's Tragedies', *Mnemosyne* 36 (1983) 324-58, esp. 328-37, for an invaluable introduction to what is known about this elusive but important figure.

99. Matthew's 'De interdicto' is printed by Wilmart (note 96 above), pp. 83-4.

100. Wilmart, p. 53 (II): *Cuidam amico*
Scedula deest, o dulcis apis plenissima melle:
Ex una pelle iacturam, queso, repelle.
Da cito, tolle moram; pudor est, si protrahis horam.
Par erit inuito, qui dabit absque cito.
Vis dare? Da gratis: hec est sententia uatis
Antiqui: Semper nocuit differre paratis (Lucan *Bel.Civ.*I,281)

101. One of Matthew's favourite authors according to Wilmart (p. 29) is Hildebart of Lavardin. There is thus the possibility that his classical background comes via Hildebert. A more careful study of Matthew's antecedents, taking into account all the poems in Paris Bibl. Nat. MS lat. 15157, is needed. The Matthew collection is in a MS that once belonged to the augustinian house of Saint Victor, which thus takes pride of place in the preservation of one of the unique witnesses of medieval friendship. A careful review of all the Saint Victor MSS might shed light on the subject.

102. Wilmart p. 37, nr. 50, ff. 66-66v, *Amicus amico: David amat Ionathan: res hoc notissima Nathan;/ Sunt plures testes: Piladem dilexit Orestes/. . .*

103. Wilmart, p. 68, nr. XXIV: *Noster amor solidus, set non sit dico solutus.*

104. Wilmart, p. 69, nr. XXV: *Amicus amico*

Frigore bruma prius, ut nix candore carebit,
Nox tenebris, celum sydere, luce dies,
Flos spetie, fons omnis aqua, mare piscibus, arbor
Alite, silua feris, fruge carebit humus,
Vincla quam nostri quisquam disrumpat amoris,
Quam tua labatur pectore cura meo.
Sit tibi leta dies niues numerata lapillo;
Sint placide noctes, tedia nulla. Vale.

105. Wilmart, p. 30.

106. Wilmart, p. 75, XXXI: *His ita accidentibus, me ipsum agrediens, ego ipse taliter affatus sum apud me: 'Vath, miselle/et rudis aselle/, quid assumis/et presumis/pondus tibi importabile?. . .*

107. Wilmart, p. 76, lines 70-74: *Karus michi es. . . carior amicis omnibus, excepto patre et matre et alio quod* [*am*] *dilecto nostro:*

Quo tamen inferior nullatenus ipse teneris.
A te me solum disiungent funera mortis.

Although Wilmart sets the last two lines off from the preceding ones, I think they go together as one complete statement from the friend Richard to Matthew. After *Karus michi es* Wilmart does not include the words *aqua set et sic*, which is written in by another hand in an erasure. Wilmart has *quod dilecto nostro*, which does not make sense. If it is changed to *quodam*, then the word refers to a third person who is more beloved than the friend. Jørgen Raasted and Sten Ebbesen of my Institute provided help with this obscure passage.

108. Wilmart, p. 77, 1.75-78: *O uerbum omni acceptione dignum. O uerbum inebrians omnia interiora mea spiritualis amore feruore, uiscera replens nimis dulcore, uelud calix uini meri de botro Cipri aut de uineis Angadi. Et unde hoc michi ut ueniat hec salutatio amici mei ad me?*

109. Wilmart, p. 77, 1. 105-108: *Biennium est enim ex quo fames cepit in terra nostra, idest ex quo uicaria rescriptio inter nos non cucurrit. Nosti uero quod epistolari pagina coalescit rediuiuus amor, reflorescit affectus, dilectio ignescit,/ k(a)ritas pinguescit.*

110. Wilmart, p. 79, 1. 151-54:

Iam michi rescribis. Quod posco negare nequibis.
Hic dicas: 'Amen', sub breuitate tamen.
Vt multum dictes nolo, ne forte graueris;
Si facis hoc, certe amicus noster eris.

111. Wilmart, p. 81, XXXIII, 1. 32-34: *Minor digitus eius maior est dorso tuo, cuius fungor tuitione ad tuendum nostrum problema, quod tu acute non defendis/, set uilipendis; et si uis scire, ipse est Virgilius, et non alius, doctissimus omnium poetarum in omni poemate.*

112. See J.B. Pitra, *Analecta Sacra Spicilegio Solesmensi Parata* VIII: *Sanctae Hildegardis Opera* (Monte Cassino, 1882), esp. pp. 328-34, as p. 330, where Guibert asks for Hildegard's intimacy (. . . *ut me inter familiares tuos computare digneris*), so she will tell him about her visions.

113. *Lexikon für Theologie und Kirche* X: 856 (under Wilbert).

114. A full review of Guibert's hagiographical works, with many excerpts, is to be found in *Catalogus Codicum Hagiographicorum Bibliothecae Regiae Bruxellensis,* I, ed. Hagiographi Bollandiana (Bruxelles: 1886) 484-582.

115. *Ep* 13, PL 211:1301: *Indulgete, obsecro, soror dilectissima, talia vobis profundenti, et vox mecum ad dolorem incitanti, quia et cor triste nunquam laeta proferre, et os amarum mel non potest spuere, et nescio quo naturae instinctu etiam de miseriis suis cum amico loqui remedium aliquod esse videtur.*

116. *Ep* 18, PL 211:1305: *Patri et domino prae omnibus singulari affectione sibi dilecto G. Dei gratia Florinensi abbati, Joseph quidquid est, et si quid potest totus suus. . . .*

117. *Ibid.*: *. . . ut illuc devotionis meae currat epistola, ubi corpore absens, corde semper praesens sum.*

118. The rest of this letter and of the other Joseph-Guibert letters not complete in Migne are to be found in Bibliothèque Royale Bruxelles MS 5527-34, ff. 221r-225v.

119. *Ep* 19, PL 211:1306: *Meus quidem animus vobiscum non hospitatur, sed moratur, ut jam vicissim ad nos redire non possit qui nunquam discedit.*

120. *Ibid.*: *Sane cum ex summa dilectionis sincerae fiducia vobiscum loquar ut mecum, non erubesco ulcera mea detegere, amico praesertim et medico. Vagus et pollutus cogitationibus distrahor, verborum lasciviam studiosius amplector, opera quae Deo displicent operor, semper in deteriora vergens, ut jam me undique pulset mors in domo, mors extra domum, mors in sepulcro. Vae mihi! quidnam faciam?*

121. 'Studium Sacrae Scripturae' by Burcht Pranger, in the collection *Les Mutations socio-culturelles au tournant des xie-xiie siecles* (CNRS éditions: Paris, 1984) 469-90, provides a superb analysis of logic and method in Anselm's first meditation.

122. *Ep* 20, PL 211:1307: *Reverendo domino suo et amico sibi in Christo singulariter dilecto G. Dei providentia abbati Florinensi, Joseph semper suus, ubique suus, totus suus, salutem et se totum ex toto.*

123. *Ibid.*: *Vos autem quem sincere in Domino et singulariter diligo, mihi cum proficiscimur sic vestra mecum properegrinetur dilectio, ut qui corpore sejungimur, simul copulemur.*

124. Here the Migne version leaves out a passage that is included in Brussels BRB MS 5527-34, f. 222, from Gembloux, 13th c., printed *Cod.Cat.Hag.*, p. 546 (note 114 above). Joseph indicates that one of the main links between him and Guibert had been the cult of Saint Martin and writings about him. Guibert has apparently been Joseph's guide and inspirer: *Praeterea prosam de sanctissimo et dilectissimo patrono nostro, beato scilicet Martino, versusque aliquot de laudibus virginitatis, secundum materiam quam mihi praescripseratis, nuper compositos, vestrae nunc judicio prudentiae examinandos transmitto.*

125. *Ep* 20, PL 211:1307: *. . . quia non solum de vobis, sed et de his quorum curam suscepistis districto judici Deo rationem reddituros estis. . . .* Y.RB 2:34: *sed semper cogitet quia animas suscepit redditurus est.*

126. This is followed in the Gembloux MS (note 124 above) by Joseph's 'Prosa de sancto Martino' and his 'Metra de virginitate'.

127. As Joseph's description of the love between him and Guibert, not found in the Migne edition, but included in the Gembloux MS: *. . . si, inquam, haec tanta virtus per Spiritum sanctum diffundatur in cordibus nostris, quantocumque locorum dirempti fuerimus interstitio, dulcissimi ejus nexu colligati, unum velle, unum nolle habentes, id ipsum in invicem sentiendo vel sapiendo unum erimus, alter alterius onera portabimus, et ita et quod patet et quod latet in divinis sermonibus tenentes in moribus. . . .* Joseph made use of perhaps the most popular definition for friendship in the Middle Ages, that of Sallust, *Catilina* 20, but otherwise this is the language of the Gospels and of Paul.

128. *Ep* 21, PL 211:1308: *Dudum te amantissime, in Geldorensi oppido commorantem cognoscens, considerata vultus tui honestate et venustate, oris gratia, elegantia sermonis, frontis hilaritate, continentia oculorum, et gestuum totius corporis tui moderatione inspecta, ultra quam credi possit super his delectatus et admirans in juvene tantae specimen honestatis reperiri, totis te dilectionis visceribus suscipiens, requievit in te spiritus meus.*

129. Cf. Aelred, *Spec car* 1100, CC CM 1, p. 58.

130. *Usus familiaritatis et ausus deinceps auxit notitiam, et quanto notior, tanto charior et dulcior mihi esse coepisti, et expertus sum in te quod ait beatus Gregorius, quia amicus quasi animi custos dicatur, eo quod amor ipse notitia sit. Vidi, consideravi, et adamavi faciem interioris hominis tui, multo virtutum decore radiantem, et adhaesit post te anima mea* [Ps 62:9], *et igne charitatis liquefacta, ut sic dicam, cucuurit in tuam.*

131. *Et nescio quo occulto naturae instinctu nonnunquam fit ut ex solo mutuae visionis vel collocutionis intercessu plerique indissolubilis nexibus amicitiae foederati constringantur, abstrahente et afficiente eos exuberantia internae pulchritudinis, qua etiam secundum interiorem exterior homo interdum componitur, sicut scriptum est: Sapientia hominis lucet in facie ejus.* The phrase *nescio que occulto naturae instinetu* is also used in letter 13 in the collection. See note 115 above.

132. See note 115 above.

133. *Unde tu, frater dulcissime, dum in viris religiosis et devote se habentibus disciplinatos mores consideras et imitaris, mirabilem te et imitabilem praebes, oculosque intuentium convertendo in te avolare facis, vocem quoque tuam quibus loqui dignaris gratam et colloquium tuum dulce reddis, et faciem multis decoratam virtutum insignibus desiderabilem exhibes.*

Quibus tractus incitamentis desidero et afficior videre te, amplecti te, et loqui tibi sed non capio, nec assequor quod cupio: dubius ac varius inter fidem et affectum, inter spem et metum positus quid eligam aut diffiniam ignoro. Fides quae secundum Chrysostomum amicitias servat, sanctaque collegia copulat, de indissolubili dilectionis tuae fraternitate certum me reddit; affectus, dum ei copia fruitionis denegatur, et se differri a gratia cohabitationis tuae dolet, et quod gravius ducit, fraudari perpetim veretur, angitur, suspirat et ingemiscit. Sed inter haec, dulcissime frater, quid facies? Nunquid omnino dissimulabis? Nunquid nos te desiderantes et quaerentes te, suspirantes, despicies. . . .

Here the letter breaks off in Migne with an *etc.*; a fuller text is available in the Gembloux MS, f. 224r-225r.

This text is more than twice as long, but does not contain the last dramatic sentences of the PL version. Together with John Benton, I have published an edition, in *Cahiers de l'Institut du Moyen-Age grec et latin* 53 (1986) 3-14. This version only underlines the passionate quality of Guibert's longing for Joseph. Professor Albert Derolez of Ghent, Beigium, wrote after we published this letter that he is completing a critical edition of Guibert's letters contained in Brussels B.R.MS 5527-34, in the *Corpus Christianorum* series. He also pointed out the edition of the correspondence between Joseph and Guibert by F. Gompf, *Joseph Iscanus. Werke und Briefe*, Mittellateinische Studien und Texte, IV (Leiden-Cologne, 1970).

134. *Amicitia di Maestro Boncompagno da Signa*, Miscellanea di Letteratura del Medio Evo 3, ed. Sarina Nathan (Roma 1909).

135. *Ibid.*, pp. 24-5.

136. *Ibid.*, p. 21.

137. *Ibid.*, p. 57, xix: *Item in civitatibus et in magnis burgis multi sunt vocales amici qui sepe vadunt ad castella et villas et grata obsequia recipiunt ab amicis, set cum eorum aliquis amicum postea viderit, eum tenerrime amplexatur et inquid voce iocunda: Bene veneritis, quomodo vos habetis? est uxor vestra incolumis? et filii vestri potiuntur corporea sanitate?*

138. *Ibid.*, pp. 58-9: *Item multi sunt vocales amici qui ad prandium vel ad cenam cum summa instantia plures invitant, quibus calicem aque frigide vix preberent. Dicitur etiam multotiens ab eisdem: Certe non solum vobis verum etiam canibus et gattis vestris, dilectionis vestre intuitu, libentissime deservirem.*

139. *Ibid.*, pp. 61-2: *Umbratiles etiam amici sunt scolares qui ad magisterium promoventur. Nam cum sub aliquorum ferula militant addiscendo, suis doctoribus montes et maria pollicentur, utendo iugiter blanditiis venativis, set postquam ascendunt cathedram magistralem,*

venenum detractionis, quod in precordialibus latitabat, contra suos magistros fundere non desistunt et ad ipsorum vituperium et exitium expendere vires et operas pre ceteris adnituntur.

140. *Ibid.*, pp. 67-9: xxx, *de versipelli amico.*

141. *Ibid.*, p. 88: *Illam igitur amicitiam que girum celi circuit et domesticos aule ipsius studeatis votivis affectionibus et gratis obsequiis venerari, spem accuratius in superno amico ponentes qui stat super omnes celos celorum, nec desinit esse ubique, qui dat escam omni carni et solem suum oriri facit super bonos et malos, quia fragilitatis subiacet omnis amicitia mundanorum.*

142. T. Lupo, *De Imitatione Christi libri quattuor* (Rome, 1982). I owe thanks for this information to Jean Leclercq.

143. Thomae Hemerken à Kempis, *Opera Omnia* 2: *De Imitatione Christi* ed. Michael Joseph Pohl (Freiburg, 1904) p. 15: *Soli Deo et angelis eius opta familiaris esse: et hominum notitiam devita.*

144. Giles Constable, *Letters and Letter-Collections*, Typologie des sources du moyen age occidental 17 (Editions Brepols: Turnhout, 1976) p. 37: 'It is possible that letters had become almost too much of a good thing in the twelfth century and that the fashion for writing letters brought its own reaction, especially among monks, who had been among the most ardent practitioners of the art.' Constable quotes Robert of Bridlington, writing about 1150 (*The Bridlington Dialogue* [London, 1960] p. 145a, a commentary on the Rule of Saint Augustine).

The same problem can be seen among Cistericians in a decision from the General Chapter of 1195, nr. 35, printed in J.-M. Canivez, *Statuta Capitulorum Generalium Ordinis Cisterciensis*, 1, Bibliothèque de la Revue d'Histoire Ecclesiastique, 9 (Louvain, 1933): *Secundum Regulam, non licet monachis litteras vel eulogias alicui mittere, vel ab aliquo accipere; immo statuimus ut nulli de cetero liceat litteras patri abbati vel alteri personae, sine conscientia et voluntate proprii abbatis, dirigere.* The prohibition in the Rule of Saint Benedict against sending letters without the permission of the abbot occurs in chapter 54.

145. Canivez, 1195, 9: *Indecens est consuetudo in quibusdam abbatiis vel abbatibus de via regressis, etiam non post longas moras, pacis osculum petant; quod ne ulterius fiat omnino his probibemus.*

146. Canivez, 1181, 5: *Apud Divionem quando veniunt ad Capitulum vel redeunt abbates, omnino caveant ne manibus se invicem tenentes, vel alio notabili modo per vicos incedant, nec sine certo negotio se invicem visitent, nec species alicubi emant, sed nec alia aliqua extra hospitia sua.* I am grateful to Chrysogonus Waddell for pointing this provision out to me.

147. See my 'Friends and Tales in the Cloister', *Analecta* 36 (1980) 224-25.

148. Ed. Bruno Griesser, in Series Scriptorum S. Ordinis Cisterciensis II (Roma, 1961). Abbreviated *Ex. Mag.*.

149. *Ex. Mag.* dist. 3, ch. 1. Compare with *Sermones super Cantica* 26 (SBOp 1:177), where the following passage appears and is not included in the *Ex. Mag.* (p. 151 in Griesser for the context): *Ego, ego illa portio misera in luto iacens, truncata parte sui, et parte potiori, et dicitur mihi: 'Ne fleveris?' Avulsa sunt viscera mea a me, et dicitur mihi: 'Ne senseris?' Sentio, sentio vel invitus, quia nec fortitudo lapidum fortitudo mea, nec caro mea aenea est; sentio prorsus et doleo, et dolor meus in conspectu meo semper.*

See also my 'Structure and Consciousness in the *Exordium Magnum Cisterciense*', *Cahiers de l'Institut du Moyen Age grec et latin* 30 (1979) 33-90.

150. 'The Collapse of a Monastic Friendship: The Case of Jocelin and Samson of Bury', *Journal of Medieval History* 4 (1978) 369-97.

151. *The Chronicle of Jocelin of Brakelond*, ed. H. E. Butler (Nelson Medieval Texts: London, 1962) p. 75.

152. *The Chronicle of the Election of Hugh*, ed. R. M. Thomson (Oxford Medieval Texts: 1974).

153. *De planctu Naturae*, ed. N.M. Häring, in *Studi Medievali* 19 (1978) 797-879; translated by James J. Sheridan, Medieval Sources in Translation 26 (Pontifical Institute of Medieval Studies: Toronto, 1980). See pp. 67-68, 'The active sex shudders in disgrace as it sees itself degenerate into the passive sex', and p. 71: 'No longer does the Phrygian adulterer chase the daughter of Tyndareus but Paris with Paris performs unmentionable and monstrous deeds'.

154. *De Nugis Curialium: Courtiers' Trifles*, ed. and trans. M. R. James (Cymmrodorion Record Series, 1923) p. 49.

155. Boswell (1980), ch. 10, 'Social Change: Making Enemies', pp. 269-302. One type of evidence that Boswell leaves out but which could contribute to his thesis is from the cistercian statutes. In 1195 (Canivez, 1195, nr. 19) there is a provision for the treatment and expulsion of any monk caught *in manifesto contagio carnis*, which could be any form of explicit genital sex, whether alone or with others of either sex. In the 1220s, however, (Canivez, 1221, 9, and 1224, 21) statutes were issued dealing specifically with sodomy, to make sure that anyone expelled for this reason would never be allowed to return to the order. Interestingly enough, the general statute on sexual acts was included in the codifications of cistercian statutes from 1202, 1237 and 1252, but the statute on sodomy did not appear in 1237 or later. See Bernard Lucet, *La codification cistercienne de 1202 et son évolution ultérieure*, Bibliotheca Cisterciensis 2 (Roma, 1964) X, 18, p. 122 and Lucet, *Les codifications cisterciennes de 1237 et de 1257* (Centre National de la Recherche Scientifique: Paris, 1977) X:10, pp. 317-18.

156. *A Mirror for Fools*, trans. J. H. Mozley (University of Notre Dame Press, 1985) p. 72. Again I am grateful to Chrysogonus Waddell for this reference.

157. Rosemary Rader, *Breaking Boundaries: Male/female Friendships in Early Christian Communities* (Paulist Press: New York, 1983). Jo Ann McNamara, *A New Song: Celibate Women in the First Three Christian Centuries* (Haworth Press: New York, 1983).

158. *The Life of Christina of Markyate*, ed. C.H. Talbot (Clarendon Press: Oxford, 1959).

159. A relationship that seems to have caused some problems: 'Before they had become spiritual friends, the abbot's well-known goodness and the maiden's holy chastity had been praised in many parts of England. But when their mutual affection in Christ had inspired them to greater good, the abbot was slandered as a seducer and the maiden as a loose woman' (Talbot, p. 175).

160. C. Damen, 'De quodam amico spirituali beatae Hildegardis Virginis', *Scaris Erudiri* 10 (1958) 162-9, presents the *Vita* of Gerlac the hermit as indicative of a spiritual friendship. Closer inspection, however, reveals only a single instance of indirect contact between the hermit and the visionary. See *Acta Sanctorum* Januarii I (Venice, 1734) ch. 8, p. 309, where Hildegard sends Gerlac a crown as a *signum perpetuae. . . societatis et felicitatis*.

161. See note 112 above.

162. Charles Dumont, ed., *La Vie de Recluse*, ch. 7, SCh 76 (Paris, 1961) p. 58: *Nunquam inter te et quemlibet virum quasi occasione exhibendae caritatis, vel nutriendi affectus, vel expetendae familiaritatis aut amicitiae spiritalis discurrant nuntii. . . .*

163. *Acta Sanctorum* Jun. IV (1707) 630-84.

164. *Analecta* 37 (1981) 1-63. An abridged and revised version of this paper appears in *Hidden Springs: Medieval Cistercian Women* III edd. John A. Nichols and Lillian Thomas Shank (CS *forthcoming*).

165. Karen Glente, *Hellige kvinder: Om kvindebillede og kvindebevidsthed i middelalderen* (Holy Women: On the image of woman and consciousness of woman in the Middle Ages) (Middelaldercentret: Copenhagen University, 1985).

166. J. Bouvet, *Correspondance d'Adam, abbé de Perseigne*, Archives Historiques du Maine 13 (Le Mans, 1951) I, Lettres à ses Correspondants du Maine, pp. 569-70.

167. *Ep* 58, Bouvet, pp. 587-90, is a good example.

168. *Ep* 57, p. 582: *More meo, amantissima, totus tibi inhaereo, et ex anima tua pendet anima mea, cui conjunctioni individuae se fecit glutinum Christi amor.*

169. *Ibid.*, p. 583: *Ceterum, novit dilectio tua me quidem nuper fuisse apud Oratorium, sed quia penitus mei juris non eram, omnino ad te transire non potui, nec domini Cisterciensis auctoritas hoc permisit; hoc idcirco dixerim ne te forte contemptam putes si hoc tibi innotuerit.*

170. *Ibid.*, p. 584: *Saluta mihi totum sanctum illud collegium, et illas dulcius et suavius, quas mihi adstrictas familiarius non ignoras.*

171. Ep 59, p. 594: *Certe si pennis ventorum pennatus forem, me vobis corporaliter saepius repraesentarem. Sed quoniam mihi non adest desiderata facultas, non abest tamen prompta voluntas.*

172. *Ep* 60, p. 596: *Nihil mihi est in vita dulcius quam ut cor meum te hilarem experiatur in disciplinis caelestibus.*

173. Jean Bouvet, *Adam de Perseigne, Letters* 1, SCh 66 (Paris, 1960). Latin text and french translation. *The Letters of Adam of Perseigne* I, trans. Grace Perigo, (Kalamazoo, 1976), the english translation, which I use here.

174. Letter 5.55, *Letters*, p. 103, *Lettres*, p. 118: *. . . ac per hoc amica et frequens de spiritualibus collocutio magistri.*

175. Letter 5.61, *Letters*, p. 108, *Lettres*, p. 126: *Intenta sollicitudo magistri et amica confabulatio spiritualis colloquii ad exhibendae obedientiae pertinent informationem.*

176. Letter 6.66, *Letters*, p. 112, *Lettres*, p. 130: *Et quae in amicorum colloquiis debet esse nisi de amore materies; de illo, inquam, amore quem nulla notat suspicio, si dilectio vel caritas nominetur?*

177. Letter 7.79, *Letters*, p. 122, *Lettres*, p. 144: *Sed quid est, obsecro, quod tantum de teipso mihi conquereris, et varias mentis tuae aegritudines mihi proponis quasi ad remedium et exponis?*

178. Letter 7.86, *Letters*, p. 127. *Lettres*, p. 152: *De cetero, fili, noli mihi molestus esse, nec a me aliquid amplius quaeras.*

179. Letter 8.89-90, *Letters*, p. 130-31, *Lettres*, pp. 155-57.

180. Letter 9.91-92, *Letters*, p. 135, *Lettres*, pp. 158-60: *Sed nihilominus pia plenus est sollicitudine amor fraternus; et qui sinceriter alterum diligit, a dilecto respectus sui oculum vix reflectit.*

Ecce, fili, dilectionis tuae suscepi litteras, et mihi lectae sunt, et ex earum lectione cognovi apertius quod revera amor nunquam est otiosus. Ubi enim infigit affectum, illuc dirigit oculum, nec insatiabili oculo patitur non videre quod affectu tenaci et avido delectat amare.

181. Letter 9.96, *Letters*, p. 137. *Lettres*, p. 162: *Sed quid est, obsecro, mihi scribere, nisi alicuius responsi rescriptum requirere, ut, dum quasi compellor respondere litteris, indirecte litteras expetere videaris.*

182. *Beati Iordani de Saxonia Epistolae*, ed. Angelus Walz, Monumenta Ordinis Fratrum Praedicatorum Historica 23 (Roma, 1951). There are several english translations, including Kathleen Pond, *Love among the Saints: A Translation of the Letters of Blessed Jordan of Saxony to Blessed Diana d'Andalo* (London, 1958), and Norbert Georges, *Blessed Diana and Blessed Jordan of the Order of Preachers* (Rosary Press: Somerset, Ohio,

1933). See also Gerald Vann, *To Heaven with Diana! A Study of Jordan of Saxony and Diana d'Andalo* (Pantheon: New York, 1960). I am grateful to Paul M. Conner for sending me his two books dealing with Jordan and Diana in terms of the tradition of male-female relationships in the christian church: *Friendship between Consecrated Men and Women and the Growth of Charity* (Pontificia Facultas Theologica Insititutum Spiritualitatis Teresianum: Romae 1972) 91-106, and *Celibate Love* (Our Sunday Visitor: Huntington, Indiana, 1979).

183. See the Chronicle of Saint Agnes, Bologna, *Analecta Sacri Ordinis Praedicatorum* 1 (Roma, 1893) 181-84, and translated in Simon Tugwell, *Early Dominicans: Selected Writings*, Classics of Western Spirituality (Paulist Press: New Jersey, and SPCK: London, 1982) 395-400. The dominican commitment to women in their Order was not immediate, however, and emerged only after controversy. For background see W. A. Hinnebusch, *History of the Dominican Order* II (New York, 1973) pp. 387 ff. I should like to thank Simon Tugwell OP for this reference.

184. I think especially of the letters of Hildegard of Bingen, where the concreteness of the other-world visions, not information from this world, forms the main impulse and content of her letters.

185. *Iordani... Epistolae* (note 182 above) 29, p. 35: *Omnibus sororibus potestis legere litteras.*

186. As *ep* 31, from summer 1225, p. 37: *Noli nimis abstinere a cibo, potu et somno, sed moderate et patienter in omnibus age.* Jordan also recommended bodily exercise: *ep* 39, p. 45: *...exercitatio corporalis ad modicum est utilis et vigiliarum et abstinentiarum lacrimarumque facile modus exceditur.*

187. *Ep* 53, p. 64, which starts with a literary device of repetition and distinction of roles of the friend-beloved that reminds one of the phrases of Bernard and Aelred: *Unde et ego lugeo amicum dulcissimum, lugeo fratrem amantissimum, lugeo filium meum carissimum, Henricum, priorem Coloniae.... Erat enim vere angelus Domini exercituum et loquens magis linguis angelorum quam hominum, non aes sonans aut cymbalum tinniens, sed cymbalum iubilationis, omni spiritu suo laudens et praedicans Dominum* [1 Cor 13:1]. Here the language departs from monastic practice in order to emphasize the preaching of the good Dominican. But Jordan never leaves his own personal bond to Henry: *Hic erat a cunctis fratribus amatus... O frater mi Ionatha, amabilis valde! Eras enim mihi donum columbae gloriosae virginis Mariae. Dum enim in corde meo firmaveram ingressum ordinis, postulavi a Domina mea, ut ipsa daret mihi eum in fratrem. Quod et fecit....* Here Jordan makes clear what one would suspect but can rarely confirm from autobiographical or hagiographical writings about the religious life: that the time of conversion to the new Order is crucial to the formation of close friendships that subsequently last a lifetime.

188. As *ep* 41, p. 47, in speaking first of Diana's love for Christ, and then of her love for Jordan: *Hoc verbum lege in corde, replica in mente et dulcescat in ore tuo sicut mel. Hoc verbum cogita et revolve, maneat in te et habitet semper tecum. Est et aliud verbum breve et modicum, affectus scilicet et cor vestrum, quod tuae dilectioni pro me in corde tuo satisfaciet et loquetur.*

189. *Ep* 12, p. 14 (trans. Tugwell [note 183 above] p. 402): *Ita enim medullis cordis mei impressa es, ut tantum oblivisci non valeam, immo ut tui tanto saepius et memoriam agam, quanto cognovi, quod me sine fictione diligas et totis visceribus cordis tui. amor siquidem tuus, quem erga me habes, ardentius provocat caritatem meam in te et afficit vehementius mentem meam.*

190. As in *ep* 2, from Milan in spring 1233 or 1234, pp. 4-5: *Scio, quod desiderabas, ut venirem Bonoiam, et hoc ipsum mihi quoque consolationi magis fuisset, si congrue potuissem. Sed nimis longum esset me debilem ad praesens venire Bonoiam et redire.*

191. *Ep* 44, p. 49 (from Germany in autumn 1229): *Lugeo socium fidelissimum, lugeo amicum dulcissimum, lugeo fratrem amantissimum, lugeo filium carissimum, Henricum priorem Coloniensem.* See note 187 above for almost the same formula in another letter about the death of Henry.

192. *Ep* 4, p. 7: *De me noli esse sollicita, quia ille idem, qui te custodit Bononiae remanentem, ipse, ut spero, me quoque custodiet in diversis itineribus ambulantem; quoniam, quod tu in quiete permanes et quod ego in diversa perambulo, totum pro sola ipsius facimus caritate.*

193. *Ep* 46, p. 52: *Video enim te tam inconsolabiliter tunc gravari, ut non solum de separatione mutua, sed etiam de tua speciali desolatione necesse habeam contristari. Sed quare sic angeris? Nonne tuus suum, vobiscum sum, tuus in labore, tuus in quiete, tuus in praesentia, tuus absens. . . ?*

194. Thomas de Celano, *Vita Secunda*, ch. 105, nr. 144: *Hac libertatis praerogativa singularis videri nolo, sed fratres me de loco ad locum associent, sicut Dominus inspiraverit eis.* Text in *Analecta Franciscana* X: Legendae S. Francisci Assisiensis (Quaracchi-Firenze, 1926-41) p. 213. Translated by Placid Hermann, *St. Francis of Assisi: First and Second Life of St. Francis* (Franciscan Herald Press: Chicago, 1963) p. 253.

195. *The Life of St. Anselm* by Eadmer, Bk I, ch. 10, ed. R. W. Southern (Oxford Medieval Texts, 1972) p. 20: From this time therefore several of [the brethren] devoted themselves body and mind to Anselm's service, hoping to succeed to Osbern's place in his affections, but he, though he thanked God for their change of heart, "became all things to all men, that he might save all." (1 Cor 9:22]

196. Text in Bibliotheca Franciscana Ascetica Medii Aevi 1: *Opuscula Sancti Patris Francisci Assisiensis* (Quaracchi, 1904) p. 116, and translation in Rosalind B. Brooke, *Scripta Leonis, Rufini et Angeli Sociorum S. Francisci* (Oxford Medieval Texts, 1970) p. 9. The Latin deserves quotation in full: *Ita dico tibi, fili mi, et sicut mater, quia omnia verba, quae diximus in via, breviter in hoc verbo dispono et consilio, et si te post oportet proper consilium venire ad me, quia ita consilio tibi: In quocumque modo melius videtur tibi placere Domino Deo et sequi vestigia et paupertatem suam, faciatis cum benefictione Domini Dei et mea obedientia. Et, si tibi est necessarium propter animam tuam aut aliam consolationem tuam, et vis, Leo, venire ad me, veni.*

197. As in John R. Moorman, *A History of the Franciscan Order to 1517* (Oxford, 1968) p. 280, and on the jacket of OMT edition of the *Scripta Leonis* (note 196 above).

198. *Scripta Leonis*, ch. 31, p. 142.

199. *Ibid.*, ch. 80, pp. 228-29: *Et uerba otiosa uel inutilia non nominentur in uobis. Licet enim ambuletis, tamen conuersatio uestra sit honesta, quemadmodum in heremitorio aut in cella permaneretis; quoniam ubicumque sumus et ambulamus, habemus cellam nobiscum. . . .*

200. *Ibid.*, p. 10.

201. *Vita Secunda* (note 194 above) ch. 139, nr. 185, *Anal. Fran.* X p. 236: *Homo qui privatis amoribus careat, ne dum in parte plus diligit in toto scandalum generet. Homo cui sanctae orationis studium sit amicum.* Trans. p. 284.

202. *Scripta Leonis*, p. 9.

203. Text in *Opuscula. . . Francisci* (note 196 above) ch. 6, p. 69: *Et ubicumque sunt et se invenerint fratres, ostendant se domesticos invicem inter se. Et secure manifestet unus alteri necessitatem suam, quia, si mater nutrit et diligit filium suum carnalem, quanto diligentius debet quis diligere et nutrire fratrem suum spiritualem?* Translation in Rosalind B. Brooke, *The Coming of the Friars* (Allen & Unwin: London, Barnes and Noble: New York, 1975) p. 123, except that I have removed the phrase 'intimate friends one to another' and replaced it with 'members of a family to each other', which better brings out the sense of the word *domesticos* and indicates that Francis was thinking in terms not of friendship but of the family bond.

204. *Opuscula Francisci* (note 196 above) ch. 11, p. 63: *Quod fratres non ingrediantur monasteria monacharum: Nec fiant compatres virorum vel mulierum, ne hac occasione inter fratres vel de fratribus scandalum oriatur. Coming of the Friars* (note 203 above) p. 125.

205. *The Life of Saint Clare*, ascribed to Thomas of Celano, ed. Paschal Robinson (Dolphin Press: Philadelphia 1910) p. 10: Francis visited Clare and she more often visited him, so ordering the times of their visits that their holy meetings might neither become known by man nor disparaged by public rumor.

206. *Scripta Leonis* (note 196 above) nr. 109, p. 280: *Beatus Franciscus hoc audiens cum diligeret eam ac eius sorores paternali affectione propter earum sanctam conuersationem, motus est ad pietatem....*

207. *Ibid.*, ...*ut impleretur sermo quem Dominus locutus est in sancto suo, ad consolandum filias et ancillas suas.*

208. *Vita Beati Fratris Egidii*, in *Scripta Leonis*, ch. 11, pp. 334-45: *Proinde subtraxit se non solum a familiaritate secularium, sed etiam a fratribus suis et aliis religiosis. Dicebat enim: 'Securius est hominibus saluare animam suis cum paucis quam cum multis: hoc est esse solitarium et uacare Deo et anime sue: quia* **solus Deus qui creauit animam, est amicus eius et non alius**.' (emphasis mine)

209. *Vitae Patrum*, Verba Seniorum, Bk 11, ch. 5 (PL 73:934).

210. A significant exception is Petrus de Dacia, whose *Vita Christinae Stumbelensis*, ed. Johannes Paulson in Scriptores Latini Medii Aeui Suecani I (Gothenburg, 1896) provides a fascinating account of a male-female relationship in the later thirteenth century. I owe thanks to Karen Glente (note 165 above) for introducing me to this source.

211. See Lester K. Little, *Religious Poverty and the Profit Economy in Medieval Europe* (Paul Elek:London, 1978) 160-61.

212. *Vita Secunda* (note 194 above) ch. 15, nr. 44a, *Anal. Fran.* X, pp. 158-9. The story is entitled: 'Quomodo fratrem Ricerium a tentatione liberavit'. The point is that Francis helped the brother out of a temptation concerning his own inadequacy, and not that friendship is a valuable asset for a friar: *Cumque ad obtinendum familiaritatis illius beneficium vehementius aspiraret, timuit valde ne quid occulte in ipso vitii fore sanctus deprehenderet.... Cuius adventu simul et animum vir Dei cognoscens, ei benigne ad se vocato, sic ait: 'Nullus te timor de caetero, nulla te, fili, conturbet tentatio, quoniam carissimus mihi es, et inter praecipue caros speciali charitate te diligo. Securus ad me, cum tibi placuerit, venias, et a me libere pro tua voluntate recedas'.* Trans. pp. 176-77.

213. Abbreviated as DM with distinction and chapter. Ed. Joseph Strange in two volumes (Köln, 1851, reprinted Gregg Press: Ridgewood, New Jersey, 1966). For full bibliography of work on Caesarius to the early 1970s, see Fritz Wagner, 'Studien zu Caesarius von Heisterbach', *Analecta* 29 (1973) 79-95. Also my 'Written Sources and Cistercian' Inspiration in Caesarius', *Analecta* 35 (1979) 227-82, and 'Friends and Tales in the Cloister', *Analecta* 36 (1980) 167-247.

214. DM IV. 30 = Strange I: 199-200.

215. DM IX. 36 = Strange II: 192. See 'The Cistericians and the Transformation of Monastic Friendship' *Analecta* 37 (1981) 1-63, esp. 29-31.

216. DM IV. 94 = Strange I: 260-61: *Requisitus a me, si adhuc aliquas de supradictis cogitationibus sentiret reliquias, respondit: Vere, frater, tentationes quae tunc temporis sciderunt cor meum, modo vix vestimenta mea foris attingunt.* For Caesarius in an almost humorous conversation with one of his fellow monks, see IV. 49 = Strange I: 215-16, which I have translated in 'Friends and Tales' (Note 213 above) p. 192.

217. Note 213 above.

EPILOGUE

1. This epilogue is based on a lecture given in California in April 1986. I wish to thank the following for their comments and criticism: John Benton, Will Jones, and Eleanor Searle at the California Institute of Technology; Mary Stroll, Constance Bouchard, and Stanley Chodorow at the University of California at San Diego; Robert Brentano and Gerry Caspary at Berkeley; Gavin Langmuir and George Brown at Stanford.

2. 'Aelred, the Gay Abbot of Rievaulx', *Studia Mystica* 5 (Sacramento, California, 1982) 51-64.

3. See Douglas Roby's introduction to *Aelred of Rievaulx: Spiritual Friendship*, CF 5 (Kalamazoo, 1974) 38-40.

4. See Robert L. Benson and Giles Constable, *Renaissance and Renewal in the Twelfth Century* (Clarendon Press: Oxford, 1982), especially their introduction, p. xxvii: '. . . the renaissance was mainly bracketed in the century from the 1060s or 1070s to about the 1160s and . . . the early twelfth century was its center of gravity'. This chronology fits well with the period when monastic friendship is most evident: from Anselm's early letters in the 1060s, as it were, to Aelred's completion of his *Spiritual Friendship* in the 1160s.

5. *De amicitia* 20: *Est anim amicitia nihil aliud nisi omnium diuinarum humanarumque rerum cum beneuolentia et caritate consensio*. . .

6. Even John Boswell, whose interpretation of latin texts sometimes makes them more explicit than they actually are, speaks of 'gay clerical culture' rather than of any 'gay monastic culture'.

7. *Ep* 25, PL 204:232.

8. Among the best recent studies: William D Patt, 'The Early *Ars Dictaminis* as response to a changing society', *Viator* 9 (1978) 133-55, and Giles Constable, *Letters and Letter-Collections*, Typologies des sources du moyen âge occidental 17 (Turnhout, 1976).

9. *Sancti Thomae de Aquino Opera Omnia* 47: *Sententia Libri Ethicorum*, cura et studio Fratrum Praedicatorum, Vol II: Libri iv-x (Roma, 1969) § 12, pp. 541-47. See also *Summa Theologiae* 2. 2ae, quae. 23, art. 3 and quae. 28, art 6.

10. *Doctoris Ecstatici D. Dionysii Cartusiani Opera Omnia*, t. 40: *Opera Minora* VIII (Tornaci, 1911), p. 347: 'De passionibus animae', art. 16, 'quam salubre atque beatum sit habere fidelem amicum': . . . .*propterea in hac valle miseriae nihil tam utile, solatiosum, desiderabile et salubre, sicut habere fidelem, purum, familiarem, perfectum itemque constantem amicum*. .

11. André Wilmart, 'Les Mélanges de Mathieu Préchantre de Rievaulx au début du XIIIe siecle', *Revue Bénédictine* 52 (1940) 15-84.

12. Sarina Nathan, ed., *Amicitia di maestro Boncompagno da Signa*, Societa filologica romana: Miscellanea di letteratura del medio evo 3 (Roma, 1909).

13. Richard Rolle, *The Fire of Love*, trans. Clifton Wolters (Penguin Classics: Harmondsworth, 1972 and later) p. 175.

14. *Ibid.*, pp. 175-76.

15. *Ibid.*, pp. 154-55.

16. As in the warning by Peter of Celle to John of Salisbury against the allurements of Paris, which provided friendship and enjoyment, but these were still a form of exile for the soul: *O Parisius, quam idonea es ad capiendas et decipiendas animas!* PL 202: 519.

17. PL 185:33, for William on his first meeting with Bernard and the impression he made on him. See my 'Was Bernard a Friend?' *Goad and Nail:*, Studies in Medieval Cistercian History X (Kalamazoo, 1985) 201-27.

18. *Vita Beati Fratris Egidii*, text and trans. in Rosalind B. Brooke, *Scripta Leonis, Rufini et Angeli Sociorum S. Francisci* (Clarendon Press: Oxford, 1970)

19. *Ibid.*, ch. 80, pp. 228-29 and *Vita Egidii, Ibid.*, ch. 11, pp. 334-35: . . .*solus Deus qui creauit animam, est amicus eius et non alius.*

20. T. Lupo, *De Imitatione Christi libri quattuor* (Roma, 1982). The edition I quote from is that by Friedrich Eichler, Thomas von Kempen, *De Imitatione Christi* (Kösel Verlag: München, 1966).

21. *Ibid.*, II, 9, p. 156: *Amore igitur creatoris amorem hominis superavit, et pro humano solacio diuinum beneplacitum magis elegit. Ita et tu aliquem necessarium et dilectum amicum pro amore Dei disce relinquere* . . . .

22. *Ibid.*, III, 42, p. 322: *Quod pax non est ponenda in hominibus.*

23. *Ibid.*, I, 23, p. 108: *Fac nunc tibi amicos venerando Dei sanctos, et eorum actus imitando; ut cum defeceris in hac vita: illi te recipiant in aeterna tabernacula.*

24. See especially *Seneca ad Lucilium Epistulae Morales*, trans. Richard Gummere (Loeb Classical Library, 1967), I, *ep* 9, on how the wise man bears the loss of a friend with equanimity, for he can always make another friend.

25. Here I am indebted to my student Kirsten Grubb Jensen for her interpretation of Boccaccio in *Mennesker og idealer i Giovanni Boccaccios Decameron* (Center for Europaeiske Middelalderstudier: Københavns Universitet, 1985).

26. This is the ninth story on the tenth day in *Decameron*. For a tragic tale of murder of a lover because he was considered unsuitable for marriage into an upcoming merchant family, see IV, 5, concerning Lisabetta, who buried her lover's head in a pot of basil.

27. *Senilium Rerum Libri* (contained in *Letteratura Italiana Storia et Testi*, vol. 7, pp. 1132-34) xv:7: *Ad fratrem Lodovicum Marsilium, cum libro Confessionum Sancti Augustini.*

28. *Ibid.*, xvii, 2: *Ad Iohannem de Certaldo, de non interrumpendo per etatem studio*, p. 1148.

29. *Ibid.*: *Itaque cum palatium omnes, ego vel nemus petebam vel inter libros in thalamo quiescebam.*

30. *Ibid.*, p. 1156: . . .*omnium terrestrium delectationum ut nulla literis honestior, sic nulla diuturnior, nulla suavior, nulla fidelior* . . . .

31. *Ibid.*, pp. 1155-56: *Legere hoc meum et scribere, quod laxari iubes, levis est labor, imo dulcis est requies, que laborum gravium parit oblivionem.*

32. Jean Leclercq, 'L'amitié dans les lettres au moyen age', *Revue du Moyen Age Latin* 1 (1945) 391-410.

33. *Senilium* xvii, 2 (note 27 above), p. 1144: *Illud plane preconium quod michi tribuis non recuso: ad hec nostra studia, multis neglecta seculis, multorum me ingenia per Italiam excitasse et fortasse longius Italia* . . . .

34. The one author who clearly indicates a fear of homosexuality is Alan of Lille, but his bonds to the Cistercians, and the monastic milieu, had little influence on his writings. Since he entered the Order very late in life, his moralization reflects not so much monastic culture as clerical life.

35. *Sancti Laurentii Justiniani Opera Omnia* I (Venice, 1751) p. 156: *O quot sub specie charitatis seducuntur et seducunt! O quanti simulata pereunt dilectione! Heu quam multi in principio pure et sine deceptione conversantes, et nimia familiaritate paulantim infecti, immane praecipitium dilapsi sunt: eo miserabilius, quo fedius! Sub verae charitatis namque praetextu in tales subintrat amor sensualitatis* . . . .

36. *Ibid.*: *Proinde interdicenda est assidua et privata conversatio in collegiis servorum Christi: quae quanquam in nullo alio reprehensibilis sit: sine proximorum tamen scandalo fieri nequit.*

37. Jean Leclercq, *Un humaniste ermite: Le bienheureux Paul Giustiniani* (Edizioni Camaldoli: Roma, 1951).

38. *Ibid.*, p. 131.

39. *Oeuvres de Saint François de Sales* III (Annecy, 1893), p. 204. The Introduction was first published in 1609. By 1656 it had already been published in seventeen languages:

> Et comme ceux qui cheminent en la plaine n' ont pas besoin de se prester la main mais ceux qui sont es chemins scabreux et glissans s'entretiennent l'un l'autre pour cheminer plus seurement, ainsy *ceux qui sont es Religions n' ont pas besoin des amitiés particulières*, mais ceux qui sont au monde en ont nécessité pour s'asseurer et secourir les uns les autres, parmi tant de mauvais passages qu'il leur faut franchir.

40. Wendy Wright, *Bond of Perfection: Jeanne de Chantal and Francois de Sales* (Paulist Press: Mahwah, New Jersey, 1986). Also Paul M. Conner, *Friendship between Consecrated Men and Women and the Growth of Charity* (Pontificia Facultas Theologica Instititum Spiritualitatis Teresianum: Rome, 1972) 137-48. Still useful is Maurice Henry-Coüannier *Saint François de Sales et ses amitiés* (Casterman: Paris, Tournai, 1954).

41. *Giovanni's Room* (first published 1956; Dell, New York 1964) 196-97: 'Most of the men picked up in connection with this crime were not picked up on suspicion of murder. They were picked up on suspicion of having what the French, with a delicacy I take to be sardonic, call *les goûts particuliers*. These "tastes", which do not constitute a crime in France, are nevertheless regarded with extreme disapprobation by the bulk of the populace. . . .'

42. When I mentioned 'particular friendships' at a cistercian session at the medieval conference in Kalamazoo, Michigan in May 1986, one elderly nun made the marvellous comment that she had been brought up with such warnings and yet had always formed and enjoyed friendships with no regard for whether or not they were 'particular'. The expression seems to have received its deathblow after the Second Vatican Council in the 1960s, but there is still a middle-aged and older generation of monks and nuns that keenly remembers such warnings. This I experienced on a trip to cistercian houses throughout the United States in spring 1986. I am very grateful to the monks I met for their frank and thoughtful response to my presentation of the development of friendship in monastic communities.

43. *The Letters of Saint Teresa of Jesus*, trans. E. Allison Peers, Vol. 1 (Sheed and Ward: London, 1951 and 1980), esp. Letter 145 (p. 364) and 147 (p. 368) to Gracián.

44. *The Life of Teresa of Jesus*, trans. E. Allison Peers (Image Books: Doubleday and Co.: Garden City, New York, 1960) ch. 3 (p. 73): 'As I began to enjoy the good and holy conversation of this nun, I grew to delight in listening to her. . . .This good companionship began to eradicate the habits which bad companionship had formed in me, to bring back my thoughts to desires for eternal things, and to remove some of the great dislike which I had for being a nun. . . .'

45. *Letters* (note 43 above) nr. 147, p. 368.

46. *Letter* 146, p. 368.

47. *The Letters of Armand-Jean de Rancé* 1-2, CSH 80-81 (Kalamazoo, 1985).

48. Montaigne, *Essays* (Penguin Classics: Harmondsworth, 1967) Book 1, ch. 28, p. 92: '. . .a friendship so complete and perfect that its like has seldom been read of, and nothing comparable is to be seen among the men of our day. So many circumstances are needed to build it up that it is something if fate achieves it once in three centuries.'

49. *Ibid.*, p. 98.

50. Contained in his justly-famed essay, 'What I Believe', from 1939, in *Two Cheers for Democracy* (Harmonsdworth, 1961) p. 76.

51. Montaigne (note 48 above) p. 102.

52. Here my thinking on the unity of classical and medieval culture and concerning the great divide between them and the modern world is akin to that of C.S. Lewis in his 'De Descriptione Temporum', based on his inaugural lecture to a chair of Medieval and Renaissance Studies at Cambridge. See *Selected Literary Essays*, ed. Walter Hooper (Cambridge, 1967). Lewis, however, moved the boundary right up to the mid-nineteenth century: '. . . I have come to regard as the greatest of all divisions in the history of the West that which divides the present from, say, the age of a Jane Austen and Scott' (p. 7).

53. Robert N. Bellah et alii (Harper and Row: Perennial Library, 1986). See especially the section on 'The Therapeutic Quest for Community', which is said to 'grow out of an old strand of American culture that sees social life as an arrangement for the fulfillment of the needs of individuals' (p. 134).

54. Again, the american trip in 1986 and many conversations with monks, young and old, gave me a chance to participate in the contemporary debate on friendship. One of the unresolved questions seems to be how novices are to deal with the friendships they have with people outside the monastery: whether they are to stop writing to them completely or to allow themselves to maintain contacts. This is a question on which medieval experience can shed only some limited light, for the answer of Bernard and other Cistercians was to bring their friends with them into the monastery.

55. Anselm to Maurice, Ep 69: *Verum non ubicumque amaris, esse potes; sed ubicumque sis, amari et bonus esse potes.* In F.S. Schmitt, *Sancti Anselmi Cantuariensis archiepiscopi Opera Omnia* iv, p. 189 (Edinburgh, 1938).

56. Adriaan H. Bredero, 'Saint Bernard and the Historians', *Saint Bernard of Clairvaux*, ed. M. Basil Pennington (Kalamazoo, 1977) 57-62.

57. The italian sociologist Francesco Alberoni's popular treatment of friendship, *L'amicizia* (Garzanti: Milano 1984) reveals careful reading of classical texts on friendship but total ignorance of the medieval tradition of spiritual friendship in monasteries and clerical life.

58. Adele M. Fiske, 'Paradisus homo amicus', *Speculum* 40 (1965) 426-59.

ABBREVIATIONS

Anal. Cist.	*Analecta Sacri Ordinis Cisterciensis* (Rome 1945-64). Since 1964, *Analecta Cisterciensia*
Asc. Wks.	Basil the Great. *Ascetical Works*. Fathers of the Church. New York, 1950.
Boswell (1980)	John Boswell. *Christianity, Social Tolerance and Homosexuality*. Chicago, 1980.
Brown (1969)	Peter Brown. *Augustine of Hippo. A Biography*. London, 1969.
Canivez	J.M. Canivez. *Statuta Capitulorum Generalium Generalium Ordinis Cisterciensis*. Bibliothèque de la Revue d'Histoire Ecclésiastique 9-14B. Louvain, 1933-41.
CC CM	*Corpus Christianorum. Continuatio Mediaevalis*. Turnhout, 1971-
CF	Cistercian Fathers series. 1970-
Constable (1967)	*The Letters of Peter the Venerable* 1-2. Cambridge, Massachusetts, 1967.
CS	Cistercian Studies series, 1970-
CSEL	*Corpus Scriptorum Ecclesiasticorum Latinorum*. Vienna, 1866-
De am.	Cicero, *De amicitia*.
Dip. Dan.	*Diplomatarium Danicum*. Det danske Sprog og Litteraturselskab. Copenhagen 1938-
DS	*Dictionnaire de Spiritualité*. Paris, 1937-
Ex. Mag.	*Exordium Magnum Cisterciense*, ed. Bruno Griesser. Series Scriptorum S. Ordinis Cisterciensis 2: Rome, 1961.
Fiske (1970)	Adele M. Fiske, *Friends and Friendship in the Monastic Tradition*. Cidoc Cuaderno 51 Cuernavaca, Mexico, 1970.

Inst. inc.	Aelred of Rievaulx. *De institutione inclusarum*. ed. C.H. Talbot in CC CM 1 (1971) 637-82.
Knowles (1966)	*The Monastic Order in England*, David M. Knowles. Cambridge, 1966.
Leclercq (1961)	Jean Leclercq, *The Love of Learning and the Desire for God*. New York, 1961; 1982.
LTK	*Lexikon für Theologie und Kirche*. Freiburg 1957- . (Sometimes the earlier edition from the 1930s is used).
MGH	*Monumenta Germaniae Historica*.
Pach. Koin.	*Pachomian Koinonia, 1-3*, trans. Armand Veilleux. CS 45-47. Kalamazoo, 1980-82.
Pach. Lat.	*Pachomiana Latina*, ed. Amand Boon. Bibliothèque de la Revue d'Histoire Ecclésiastique 7. Louvain 1932.
PG	*Patrologia Graeca*, ed. J.P. Migne. Paris 1857-
PL	*Patrologia Latina*, ed. J.P. Migne. Paris 1844-
RB	*Regula Benedicti*
RTAM	*Recherches de Théologie Ancienne et Médiévale*. Louvain, 1929-
SBOp	*Sancti Bernardi Opera* 1-8, ed. Jean Leclercq, Henri Rochais, C.H. Talbot. Editiones Cistercienses. Rome, 1957-77.
SCh	Sources Chrétiennes. Paris, 1942-
Sp.am.	Aelred of Rievaulx. *De spiritali amicitia*, CC CM 1:287-350.
Sp.car.	Aelred of Rievaulx, *Speculum Caritatis.* CC CM 1:3-161.
Southern (1966)	R.W. Southern. *Saint Anselm and his Biographer.* Cambridge, 1966.
Tangl	Michael Tangl, *Die Briefe des Heiligen Bonifatius und Lullus*. MGH: Epistolae Selectae 1. Berlin, 1916.
VSH	C. Plummer, *Vitae Sanctorum Hiberniae* 1-2. Oxford, 1910.

BIBLIOGRAPHY

PRINTED SOURCES

(note that Cambridge means Cambridge, England, unless otherwise noted)

Adam of Perseigne. *Correspondance d'Adam abbé de Perseigne*, I ed. Jacques Bouvet. Archives Historiques du Maine 13: Le Mans, 1951.

___. *Adam de Perseigne, Lettres*, ed. J. Bouvet. SCh 66. Paris 1960.

___. *The Letters of Adam of Perseigne* 1, trans. Grace Perigo. CF 21. 1976.

Adalbert of Prague. *Vita*. See John Canaparius.

Aelred of Rievaulx. *De Bello Standardii*. PL 195: 701-711.

___. *Sermones de Oneribus*. PL 195: 361-501.

___. *L'amitie spirituelle*, trans. Joseph Dubois. Bruges 1948.

___. *The Life of Aelred of Rievaulx by Walter Daniel*, ed. F.M. Powicke. London: Thomas Nelson, 1950.

___. *Sermones Inediti B. Aelredi Abbatis Rievallensis*, ed. C.H. Talbot. Series Scriptorum S. Ordinis Cisterciensis 1. Rome 1952.

___. *Quand Jésus eut douze ans*, ed. Joseph Dubois. Editions du Cerf. Paris. 1958.

___. *La Vie de Recluse*, ed. Charles Dumont. SCh 76. Paris 1961.

___. *Aelredi Rievallensis Opera Omnia 1: Opera Ascetica*, ed. Anselm Hoste and C.H. Talbot. CC CM 1. Turnholt 1971. (includes *Amicitia spiritalis* and *Speculum caritatis* together with abbreviated versions)

___. *Spiritual Friendship*, trans. Mary Eugenia Laker. CF 5. Kalamazoo, 1974.

Agobard of Lyons. *Epistolae*, in MGH Epistolae V: 150-239 ed, Ernestus Dümmler. Berlin, 1895.

Alan of Lille. *De planctu naturae*, ed. N.M. Häring. *Studi Medievali* 19 (1978) 797-879.

___. *The Plaint of Nature*, trans. James J. Sheridan. Medieval Sources in Translation 26: Pontifical Institute of Medieval Studies. Toronto, 1980.

Alan of Tewkesbury. *Letters*, ed. by Margaret A. Harris. *Studia Monastica* 18 (1976) 299-351.

Albers, Bruno, ed. *Consuetudines Monasticae* I. Stuttgart and Vienna, 1900.

Alcuin. *Epistolae*. MGH Epistolae IV: 1-481 ed. Ernest Dümmler. Berlin, 1895.

___. MGH Poetae I:160-351, ed. Ernest Dümmler. Berlin, 1881.

___. *Alcuin: The Bishops, Kings and Saints of York*, ed. and trans. Peter Godman. Oxford Medieval Texts. 1982.

Aldhelm. *Aldhelmi Opera*, ed. Rudolf Ehwald. MGH Auctores Antiquissim XV. Berlin, 1919.

Ambrose of Milan. *Epistulae* PL 16:913-1346.

___. *De officiis ministrorum*. PL 16:25-194.

___. *De virginibus*, PL 16: 197-244.

___. *De excessu fratris sui Satyri*, PL 16:1345-1414.

___. English trans. by John J. Sullivan and Martin R.P. McGuire, *Funeral Orations*. Fathers of the Church 22. Washington D.C. 1953/1968.

Anselm. *S. Anselmi Opera Omnia*, I-VI, ed. F.S. Schmitt. London: Thomas Nelson, 1938-61.

___. *The Prayers and Meditations of Saint Anselm*, trans. Benedicta Ward. Penguin Classics, 1973 and later.

Anthony. *Vita* in Greek by Athanasius of Alexandria. PG 26:835-978. *Vita* in Latin trans. by Evagrius of Antioch. PL 73-15-70.

Apophthegmata Patrum. PG 65:71-439.
trans. by Benedicta Ward, *The Sayings of the Desert Fathers* The Alphabetical Collection. London-Kalamazoo, 1975.

Ardo. *Vita* of Benedict of Aniane. MGH SS XV:200-220.
trans. Allen Cabaniss, *The Emperor's Monk*. Arthur Stockwell. Ilfracombe, Devon, 1979.

Aristotle. *The Works of Aristotle*, trans. W. D. Ross IX: *Ethica Nichomachea*. Oxford, 1949.

Augustine of Hippo. *City of God* (*Civitas Dei*). Harvard: Loeb, I (1957); II (1963); III (1968); IV (1966); V (1965).

___. *City of God*, trans. Henry Bettenson. Pelican Classics 1972.

___. *Confessions*. Loeb, Harvard I-II (1960-61).

___. *Confessions*, trans. R. S. Pine-Coffin. Penguin Classics, 1971 and later.

___. *De diversis quaestionibus*. PL 40:11-100.

___. *Epistulae*, ed. Al. Goldbacher. CSEL 34, 44, 57-58. Vienna, 1895-1923.

___. *Sermones*. PL 38.

___. *Retractiones* PL 32: 586-656.

Avitus of Vienne. *Epistolae* PL 59:199-290.

Basil the Great. *Regulae Brevius Tractatae. Regulae Fusius Tractatae* PL 31: 890-1320.

___. *Sermo Asceticus*. PG 32:880.

___. *Saint Basil: Ascetical Works*, trans. Sister M. Monica Wagner. Fathers of the Church. New York, 1950.

Baudri of Bourgueil. *Les oeuvres poétiques de Baudri de Bourgueil*, ed. Phyllis Abraham. Paris, 1926.

___. *Baldricus Burgulianus Carmina*. Karlheinz Hilbert. Heidelberg, 1976.

Bede the Venerable. *Historia Ecclesiastica Gentis Anglorum*, ed. Ch. Plummer. Oxford, 1946.

___. *In Samuelem prophetam allegorica expositio* PL 91:499-714.

Benedict of Aniane. 'Les *Munimenta Fidei* de Saint Benoît d'Aniane', ed. Jean Leclercq, *Studia Anselmiana* 20. Analecta Monastica I. Vatican City, 1948.

___. *Vita* = MGH SS XV:200-20, trans. by Allen Cabaniss, *The Emperor's Monk*. See above under 'Ardo'.

Benedict of Nursia. *S. Benedicti Regula*, ed. Gregorio Penco. Florence, 1958.

___. *The Rule of Saint Benedict*, trans. Anthony C. Meisel and M.L. del Mastro. Garden City, New York, 1975.

Beowulf. trans. David Wright. Penguin Classics, 1964 and later.

Bernard of Clairvaux. *S. Bernardi Opera*, ed. Jean Leclercq, C.H. Talbot, H.M. Rochais: I-VIII. Editiones Cistercienses. Rome, 1957-77.

___. *'Les Fragmenta de Vita et Miraculis S. Bernardi'*, ed. Robert Lechat, *Analecta Bollandiana* 50 (1932) 82-122.

___. *Vita S. Bernardi (Vita Prima)*. PL 185:225-350

___. *The Letters of Saint Bernard*, trans. Bruno Scott James. Burns and Oates. London, 1953.

Bieler, Ludwig. *The Irish Penitentials*. Scriptores Latini Hiberniae. V. Dublin Institute for Advanced Studies, 1963.

Boas, Marcus, ed. *Disticha Catonis*. Amsterdam, 1952.

Boncompagno da Signa. *Amicitia di Maestro Boncompagno da Signa*, ed. Sarina Nathan. Miscellanea di Letteratura del Medio Evo 3. Rome, 1909.

Bone, Gavin, trans. *Anglo-Saxon Poetry*. Oxford: Clarendon, 1943.

Boniface. *Die Briefe des heiligen Bonifatius und Lullus*. MGH Epistolae selectae in usum scholarum, ed. Michael Tangl. Berlin, 1916.

___. *Vitae Sancti Bonifatii*, ed. Wilhelm Levison. MGH: Scriptores rerum Germanicarum. Hannover, 1905.

___. trans. C.H. Talbot, *The Anglo-Saxon Missionaries in Germany*. London, 1954, 1981.

Bouton, Jean de la Croix and Van Damme, Jean Baptiste. *Les plus anciens textes de Citeaux*. Cîteaux. Commentarii Cistercienses. Studia et Documenta 2. Achel, Belgium, 1974.

Brooke, Rosalind B. *Scripta Leonis, Rufini et Angeli Sociorum S. Francisci*. Oxford, 1970.

___. *The Coming of the Friars*. London, New York, 1975.

Bruno, Archbishop of Cologne, See Ruotger.

Bulst, Walter, ed. *Die ältere Wormser Briefsammlung*. MGH Die Briefe der Deutschen Kaiserzeit 3. Weimar, 1949.

Burnet, John. *Early Greek Philosophy*. Cleveland, Ohio, 1965.

Caesarius of Heisterbach. *Dialogus Miraculorum*, ed. Joseph Strange 1-2. Cologne 1851, reissued Ridgewood, New Jersey, 1966.

Canivez, J.M. *Statuta Capitulorum Generalium Ordinis Cisterciensis* 1. Bibliothèque de la Revue d'Histoire ecclésiastique 9: Louvain, 1933.

Cicero. *L'amitié: Laelius de Amicitia*, trad. Robert Combès, Budé. Paris, 1975.

———. *On the Good Life*, trans. Michael Grant. Penguin Classics 1971 and later.

———. *De officiis libri tres*. Sumptibus Arnoldi Mondadori. Rome, 1965.

Denis the Carthusian. *Doctoris Ecstatici D. Dionysii Cartusiani Opera Omnia* 40. Opera Minora 8. Tournai, 1911.

Dümmler, Ernst, ed. *Das Formelbuch des Bischofs Salomo III*. Leipzig, 1857.

Dunstan of Canterbury. *Memorials of Saint Dunstan*, ed. William Stubbs. Rolls Series (Chronicles and Memorials of Great Britain and Ireland in the Middle Ages), 63. London, 1874.

Eadmer. *The Life of Saint Anselm*, ed. R.W. Southern. Oxford, 1972.

Ekkehard IV. *De Casibus Monasterii*, ed. G.H. Pertz in MGH Scriptores rerum Germanicarum II:78-147. Hannover, 1829; reprinted 1968.

Text and trans. by Hans F. Haefele in *St. Galler Klostergeschichten*. Wissenschaftliche Buchgesellschaft. Darmstadt, 1980.

Elmer of Canterbury. 'Ecrits spirituels d'Elmer de Cantorbéry', ed. Jean Leclercq, *Studia Anselmiana* 31. Analecta Monastica 2. Rome, 1953.

Epicurus. *Letters, Principal Doctrines and Vatican Sayings*, trans. Russell M. Geer. Indianapolis, 1964.

Erdmann, Carl and Fickermann, Norbert. *Briefsammlungen der Zeit Heinrichs IV.* MGH: Die Briefe der Deutschen Kaiserzeit 5: Weimar, 1950.

Forster, E.M. *Two Cheers for Democracy*. Penguin, 1961.

Francis of Assisi. *Opuscula Sancti Patris Francisci Assisiensis*. Bibliotheca Franciscana Ascetica Medii Aevi 1. Quaracchi, 1904.

François de Sales. *Oeuvres* 3. Annecy, 1893.

Froumund. *Die Tegernseer Briefsammlung*, ed. Karl Strecker. MGH Epistolae Selectae III. Berlin, 1925.

Fulbert of Chartres. *The Letters and Poems of Fulbert of Chartres*, ed. and trans. Frederick Behrends. Oxford, 1976.

Gerhard. *Vita Sancti Oudalrici Episcopi Augustani*. MGH Scriptores rerum Germanicarum IV. 1841.

___. *Vita* of Bishop Ulrich of Augsburg, trans. Hatto Kallfelz in *Lebensbeschreibungen einiger Bischöfe des 10.-12. Jahrhunderts.* Wissenschaftliche Buchgesellschaft. Darmstadt, 1973.

Gerbert of Aurillac (Pope Silvester II). *Lettres de Gerbert*, ed. Julien Havet. Collection de Textes pour servir à l'étude et à l'enseignement d'histoire. Paris, 1889.

___. *Die Briefsammlungen Gerberts von Reims*, ed. Fritz Weigle. MGH. Die Briefe der Deutschen Kaiserzeit 2. Weimar, 1966.

___. *The Letters of Gerbert*, trans. Harriet Pratt Lattin. Columbia Records of Civilization 60. New York, 1961.

Gilbert Foliot. *The Letters and Charters of Gilbert Foliot*, ed. Z.N. Brooke, Adrian Morey, C.N.L. Brooke. Cambridge, 1967.

Goscelin of Saint Bertin. *Liber confortatorius*, ed. C.H. Talbot. *Studia Anselmiana* 37. Analecta Monastica 3. Rome, 1955.

Gregory the Great. *Gregorii Magni Dialogi Libri IV*, ed. Umberto Moricca. Fonti per la storia d'Italia. Rome, 1924.

___. *Dialogues*, trans. Odo John Zimmerman. Fathers of the Church. New York, 1959.

___. *XL Homiliarum in Evangelia*. PL 76:1075-1312.

Griesser, Bruno, ed. *Exordium Magnum Cisterciense*. Series Scriptorum S. Ordinis Cisterciensis 2. Rome, 1961.

Guibert of Gembloux. *Catalogus Codicum Hagiographicorum Bibliothecae Regiae Bruxellensis* I (pp. 484-582). Brussels, 1886.

___. *Epistolae*. PL 211:1288-1312.

___. 'A Letter of Passionate Friendship', edd. John Benton and Brian McGuire. *Cahiers de l'Institut du Moyen-Age grec et latin* 53, pp. 3-14, Copenhagen, 1986.

Gundulf of Rochester. *The Life of Gundulf Bishop of Rochester*, ed. Rodney Thomson. Toronto Medieval Latin Texts, 7. 1977.

Hallinger, Kassius, ed. *Corpus Consuetudinum Monasticarum* I. Initia Consuetudinis Benedictinae. Francis Schmitt. Siegburg, 1963.

Henry of Marcy. *Epistolae* PL 204: 215-251.

___. *Tractatus de Peregrinante Civitate Dei.* PL 204:251-402

Herbert of Losinga. *Epistolae*, ed. Robert Anstruther. Publications of the Caxton Society V. 1846. Reprinted Burt Franklin Research and Source Works Series, 154. New York, 1969.

Hildebert of Lavardin. *Epistolae* PL 171:135-311.

Hildegard of Bingen. *Sanctae Hildegardis Opera*, ed. J.B. Pitra. Analecta Sacra Spicilegio Solesmensi Parata 8. Monte Cassino, 1882.

Hoste, Anselm. 'Le Speculum Spiritalis Amicitiae. . .', *Analecta Monastica* 3 (1961) 291-96.

Isidore of Seville. *Etymologiarum sive Originum Libri XX*, ed. W. Lindsay. Oxford, 1911.

Jerome. Epistolae, ed. I. Hilbert. CSEL 54. Vienna, 1910.

Select Letters of Saint Jerome, trans. F.A. Wright. Loeb Classical Library. Cambridge, Mass., 1975.

Jocelin of Brakelond. *The Chronicle of Jocelin of Brakelond*, ed. H. E. Butler. Nelson Medieval Texts. London, 1962.

John the Almsgiver (Johannes Elemosinarius). *Vita* (in Latin) PL 73:339-384.

___. *Life* trans. from Greek by Elizabeth Dawes and Norman H. Baynes. *Three Byzantine Saints*. London/Crestwood, New York, 1948/1977.

John Canaparius. *Vita* (of Bishop Adalbert of Prague) in MGH Scriptores Rerum Germanicarum IV, ed. H. Pertz. Hannover, 1841; rep. 1968.

John Cassian. *Conlationes*, ed. Michael Petschenig. CSEL 13, 17. Vienna, 1886.

___. *De Institutis Coenobiorum* ed. Michael Petschenig. CSEL 17. Vienna, 1888.

John of Fécamp. *Un maître de la vie spirituelle au xie siècle: Jean de Fécamp*, ed. Jean Leclercq et Jean-Paul Bonnes. Etudes de théologie et d'histoire de la spiritualité 9. Paris, 194 .

John of Gorze. *Vita* by John of Metz, ed. G.H. Pertz. MGH Scriptores rerum Germanicarum IV:337-77. Hannover, 1841.

John of Salisbury. *The Letters of John of Salisbury I: The Early Letters* (1153-61), ed. W. J. Millor and H.E. Butler, rev. C.N.L. Brooke. London, 1955.

___. *The Letters II: The Later Letters 1163-80*, ed. W. J. Millor and C.N.L. Brooke. Oxford, 1979.

Jordan of Saxony. *Beati Iordani de Saxonia Epistolae*, ed. Angelus Walz. Monumenta Ordinis Fratrum Praedicatorum Historica 23. Rome, 1951.

___. *Love among the Saints*, trans. Kathleen Pond. London, 1958.

___. *Blessed Diana and Blessed Jordan of the Order of Preachers*. Somerset, Ohio: Rosary Press, 1933.

Kenney, James F. *The Sources for the early History of Ireland: Ecclesiastical*. New York, 1966.

Kirk, G.S. and Raven, J.E. The *Presocratic Philosophers*. Cambridge, 1957 and 1975.

Lanfranc. *Epistolae* PL 150:515-624.

The Letters of Lanfranc, ed. and trans. Helen Clover and Margaret Gibson. Oxford, 1979.

Laporte, J., ed. 'Epistulae Fiscannenses: Lettres d'amitié, de gouvernement et d'affaires xie-xiie siècles', *Revue Mabillon* 43 (1953) 5-31.

Lawrence Justinian. *Sancti Laurentii Justiniani Opera Omnia*. Venice, 1751.

Lechat, Robert, 'Les *Fragmenta de Vita et Miraculis S. Bernardi*', *Analecta Bollandiana* 50 (1932) 83-122.

Leclercq, Jean. 'Les lettres familières d'un moine du Bec', *Studia Anselmiana* 31: 141-73. Analecta Monastica 2. Rome, 1953.

Lucet, Bernard. *La codification cistercienne de 1202 et son évolution ultérieure*. Bibliotheca Cisterciensis 2. Rome, 1964.

___. *Les codifications cisterciennes de 1237 et de 1257*. Centre National de la Recherche Scientifique. Sources d'Histoire Médiévale. Paris, 1977.

Lupo, T. *De Imitatione Christi libri quattuor*. Rome, 1982.

Lupus of Ferrières. *Epistolae*, ed. Ernest Dümmler. MGH Epistolae VI: 1-126. Berlin, 1875.

Marcus Aurelius. *Meditations*. Chicago, 1956.

Matthew of Rievaulx. See 'André Wilmart'.

Montaigne. *Essays*. Penguin, 1967 and later.

Moorman, John. *A History of the Franciscan Order to 1517*. Oxford, 1968.

Murphy, James J. *Three Medieval Rhetorical Arts*. University of California Press, 1971.

Nicholas of Clairvaux (or Montiéramey). *Epistolae*. PL 196: 1593-1654.

Nigel Longchamp. *A Mirror for Fools*, trans. J.H. Mozley. University of Notre Dame Press, 1985.

Notker the Poet. *Das Formelbuch des Bischofs Salomo III*, ed. Ernest Dümmler. Leipzig, 1857.

Odilo of Cluny. *Vita* by Jotsald. PL 142: 897-940.

___. *Vita* of Saint Maiol. PL 142: 943-62.

Odo of Cluny. *Occupatio*, ed. Antonius Swoboda. Leipzig, 1900.

___. *Vita* by John of Salerno. PL 133:43-86.

___. *Saint Odo of Cluny*, trans. Gerard Sitwell. London, 1958.

Olsen, Birger Munk. 'The Cistercians and Classical Culture', *Cahiers de l'Institut du Moyen-Age grec et latin* 47:64-102. Copenhagen, 1984.

Orderic Vitalis. *The Ecclesiastical History*, ed. Marjorie Chibnall. Oxford Medieval Texts. II, 1969. III, 1972. IV, 1973. V, 1975. VI, 1978.

Otloh of Saint Emmeram. *Liber de suis temptationibus*; PL 146:29-58.

Pachomius. *Pachomian Koinonia*, trans. Armand Veilleux. CS 45. Kalamazoo, I, 1980. II, 1981. III, 1982.

___. *Pachomiana Latina*, ed. Amand Boon. Bibliothèque de la Revue d'Histoire Ecclésiastique 7. Louvain, 1932.

Paulinus of Nola. *Epistulae*, ed. Guilelmus de Hartel. CSEL 29. Vienna, 1894.

___. *Carmina*, ed. Guilelmus de Hartel. CSEL 30. Vienna, 1894.

Peter of Blois. *Epistolae* PL 207:1-560.

___. *De amicitia christiana* and *De charitate dei et proximi*. PL 207:807-958.

___. *Un traité d'amour au xiie siècle*, ed. M.M. Davy. Paris, 1932.

Peter of Celle. *L'école du cloître*, ed. Gérard de Martel. Sources chrétiennes 47. Paris, 1977.

___. *Petrus Cellensis: Commentaria in Ruth. Tractatus de Tabernaculo*, ed. Gérard de Martel. CCCM 54. Turnhout, 1983.

___. *Epistolae* PL 202: 405-636.

Peter of Dacia. *Vita Christianae Stumbelensis*, ed. Johannes Paulson. Scriptores Latini Medii Aevi Suecani I: Gothenburg, 1886.

Peter Damian. *Epistolae* PL 144. *Opuscula* PL 145.

___. *Liber gomorrhianus* PL 145:159-90. Trans. Pierre J. Payer. *Peter Damian: Book of Gomorrah*. Waterloo, Ontario, 1982.

___. *Die Briefe des Petrus Damiani*, ed. Kurt Reindel. MGH. Die Briefe der Deutschen Kaiserzeit IV:1. Munich, 1983.

Peter the Venerable. *The Letters of Peter the Venerable* 1-2, ed. Giles Constable. Cambridge, Massachusetts, 1967.

Petrarch. *Senilium Rerum Libri*, in Guido Martellotti et alii. *Francesco Petrarca Prose*. Letteratura Italiana Storia e Testi 7. Ricciardo Ricciardi editore: Milan, 1955.

Plato. *Dialogue on Friendship* (*Lysis*), trans. David Bolotin. Ithaca and London, 1979.

___. *Symposium*, ed. K. J. Dover. Cambridge, 1980.

___. *The Symposium*, trans. W. Hamilton. Penguin, 1951 and later.

Plummer, C. *Vitae Sanctorum Hiberniae* 1-2. Oxford, 1910.

Rancé, Armand-Jean de. *The Letters*, 1-2, trans. A.J. Krailsheimer. CS 80-81. Kalamazoo, 1984.

Ralph Glaber. *Vita* of William of Dijon. Pl 142:697-720.

Ratherius of Verona. *Die Briefe des Bischofs Rather von Verona*, ed. Fritz Weigle. MGH Die Briefe der Deutschen Kaiserzeit 1. Weimar, 1949.

Rhabanus Maurus. *Epistolae*. MGH Epistolae V:379-516 ed. Ernestus Dümmler. Berlin, 1899.

___. *Poems* in MGH Poetae II:214-258 ed. Ernestus Dümmler. Berlin, 1884.

Riché, Pierre. 'L'enfant dans la société monastique au xiie siecle', *Pierre Abélard. Pierre le Vénerable*: 689-701. Paris, 1975.

Robert of Bridlington. *The Bridlington Dialogue*. London, 1960.

Rockinger, Ludwig. *Briefsteller und Formelbücher des elften bis vierzehnten Jahrhunderts*. Quellen und Eröterungen zur bayerischen und deutschen Geschichte 91. Munich, 1863; rep. New York, 1961.

Rolle, Richard. *The Fire of Love*, trans. Clifton Wolters. Penguin, 1972 and later.

Romuald. *Vita beati Romualdi*, ed. Giovanni Tabacco. Fonti per la Storia d'Italia 94. Rome, 1957.

Rufinus. *Historia Monachorum in Aegypto*; PL 21. Trans. Norman Russell, *The Lives of the Desert Fathers*, London-Kalamazoo, 1981.

Ruotger. *Vita* of Archbishop Bruno of Cologne. MGH SS IV, ed. G.H. Pertz, 1841.

___. *Vita* with German trans. by Hatto Kallfelz in *Lebensbeschreibungen einiger Bischöfe des 10.-12. Jahrhunderts*. Wissenschaftliche Buchgesellschaft. Darmstadt, 1973.

Sallust. *Caii Sallustii Crispi Catilina*, ed. Charles Merivale. London, 1870, 1974.

Seneca. *Ad Lucilium Epistulae Morales*, trans. Richard Gummere. Cambridge, Massachusetts; Loeb Classical Library, 1967.

Sidonius Apollinaris. *Sidoine Apollinaire II: Lettres*, ed. André Loyen. Société d'edition Les Belles Lettres. Paris, 1970.

Stehling, Thomas. *Medieval Latin Poems of Male Love and Friendship*. New York-London, 1984.

Stephen of Obazine. *Vie de Saint Etienne d'Obazine*. Publications de l'Institut du Massif Central 6. Clermont-Ferrand, 1970.

Stephen of Tournai. *Epistolae* PL 211: 309-562.
Lettres d'Etienne de Tournai, ed. Jules Desilve. Paris, 1893.

Stokes, Whitley. *The Calendar of Oengus*. Transactions of the Royal Irish Academy I. Dublin, 1880.

Strecker, Karl, ed. MGH Poetarum Latinorum Medii Aevi IV:2. Berlin, 1923.

Sulpicius Severus. *Sulpicii Severi libri qui supersunt*, ed. Carolus Halm. CSEL 1. Vienna, 1866.

___. *The Life of Saint Martin* and other writings, in F.R. Hoare, trans. *The Western Fathers*. New York, 1966; rep. London, 1980.

___. *Vie de Saint Martin*, ed. Jacques Fontaine I-III. Sources chrétiennes. Paris, 1967-69.

Talbot, C.H., ed. and trans. *The Anglo-Saxon Missionaries in Germany*. London, 1954, 1981.

___. *The Life of Christina of Markyate*. Oxford, 1959.

Teresa of Avila. *The Letters of Saint Teresa of Jesus*, trans. E. Allison Peers 1. London, 1951, 1980.

——. *The Life of Teresa of Jesus*, trans. E. Allison Peers. Garden City, New York, 1960.

Thomas of Aquinas. *Opera Omnia* 47. *Sententiae Libri Ethicorum*, cura et studio Fratrum Praedicatorum II. Rome, 1969.

Thomas of Celano. *Vita Secunda* of Saint Francis: Analecta Franciscana X. Legendae S. Francisci Assisiensis. Quaracchi-Firenze, 1926-41.

——. *First and Second Life of Saint Francis*, trans. Placid Herman. Chicago: Franciscan Herald Press, 1963.

——. *The Life of Saint Clare* (ascribed to Thomas of Celano) ed. Paschal Robinson. Philadelphia, 1910.

Thomas à Kempis. *De Imitatione Christi*, ed. Michael Pohl *Opera Omnia* 2. Freiburg, 1904.

——. Thomas von Kempen, *De Imitatione Christi*, ed. Friedrich Eichler. Munich, 1966.

Thomson, R.M., ed. *The Chronicle of the Election of Hugh*. Oxford, 1974.

Ulrich of Augsburg. *Vita* in MGH Scriptores rerum Germanicarum IV: 377-428. ed. Georg Waitz. 1841.

——. *Vita* trans. to German by Hatto Kallfelz, *Lebensbeschreibungen einiger Bischöfe des 10.-12. Jahrhunderts*. Wissenschaftliche Buchgesellschaft. Darmstadt, 1973.

Ulrich of Cluny. *Consuetudines Cluniacenses*. PL 149:643-778.

Venantius Fortunatus. *Opera poetica*, ed. Fredericus Leo. MGH Auctorum Antiquissimorum IV. Berlin, 1881.

Verba Seniorum (The Latin Systematic Collection of the Sayings of the Desert Fathers) PL 73: 739-1062.

Vitae Patrum = *Verba Seniorum*

Waddell, Helen. *Mediaeval Latin Lyrics*. London, 1929; Penguin, 1952 and later.

Walafrid Strabo. MGH Poetae II, 259-423 ed. Ernestus Dümmler. Berlin, 1884.

Walter Daniel. *The Life of Ailred of Rievaulx*, trans. F.M. Powicke. Oxford, 1950, 1978.

Walter Map. *De Nugis Curialium. Courtiers' Trifles*, ed. M.R. James Cymmrodorion Record Series, 1923. Revised by C. N. L. Brooke and R. A. B. Mynors. Oxford, 1983.

Ward, Benedicta. *The Sayings of the Desert Fathers*. London-Kalamazoo, 1975.

——. *The Lives of the Desert Fathers*. London-Oxford-Kalamazoo, 1980.

William of Æbelholt. *Epistolae* PL 209:635-728.

——. *Epistolae abbatis Willelmi de Paraclito*, ed. C.A. Christensen, Herluf Nielsen and Lauritz Weibull. *Diplomatarium Danicum* I:3. Copenhagen, 1976-77.

——. *Vita* in *Vitae Sanctorum Danorum*, ed. M.Cl. Gertz, 300-369. Selskabet for udgivelse af kilder til dansk historie. Copenhagen 1908-1912.

William of Newburgh. *Historia Rerum Anglicarum* in *Chronicles of the Reigns of Stephen, Henry II and Richard* I, ed. Richard Howlett. Rolls Series I (1884) II-408. II (1889) 416-583.

——. *The History of William of Newburgh*, trans. Joseph Stevenson. IV:2. London, 1856.

Wilmart, André. 'Les mélanges de Mathieu Préchantre de Rievaulx au début du xiiie siècle', *Revue Bénédictine* 52 (1940) 15-84.

SECONDARY WORKS

Alberoni, Francesco. *L'amicizia*. Milan: Garzanti, 1984.

Auerbach, Erich. *Mimesis*. Princeton, 1974.

Auniord, J.B. 'L'ami de Saint Bernard, quelques textes', *Collectanea Ordinis Cisterciensis Reformatae* 18 (1956) 88-99.

Baldwin, John. *Masters, Princes and Merchants*. The Social Views of Peter the Chanter and his Circle 1-2. Princeton, 1970.

——. *The Government of Philip Augustus*. University of California, 1986.

Bellah, Robert *et alii*. *Habits of the Heart:* Individualism and Commitment in American Life. New York: Harper and Row, 1986.

Benson, Robert L. and Constable, Giles. *Renaissance and Renewal in the Twelfth Century*. Oxford: Clarendon Press, 1982.

Benton, John. 'Nicholas of Clairvaux', DS 11 (1981) 255-59.

Bethune, Brian. 'Personality and Spirituality: Aelred of Rievaulx and Human Relations', *Cistercian Studies* (1985) 98-112.

Boswell, John. *Christianity, Social Tolerance and Homosexuality*. University of Chicago, 1980 and later.

Bouchard, Constance B. *Sword, Miter and Cloister*: Nobility, Church and Reform in Burgundy 910-1198. Ithaca, New York: Cornell University Press, 1986.

Bouton, Jean de la Croix. 'La doctrine de l'amitié chez saint Bernard', *Revue d'ascetique et de mystique* 29 (1953) 3-19.

Bredero, A.H. 'The Controversy between Peter the Venerable and Saint Bernard of Clairvaux', *Petrus Venerabilis 1156-1956*, ed. Giles Constable and James Kritzeck. *Studia Anselmiana* 40. Rome, 1957.

___. 'Saint Bernard and the Historians', *Saint Bernard of Clairvaux*, ed. M. Basil Pennington. CS 28: 27-62. Kalamazoo, 1977.

Brentano, Robert, ed. *The Early Middle Ages*. New York, 1964.

Brooke, C.N.L. and Morey, Adrian. *Gilbert Foliot and his Letters*. Cambridge, 1965.

Brown, Peter. *Augustine of Hippo*. London: Faber, 1969.

___. 'The Rise and Function of the Holy Man in Late Antiquity', *Journal of Roman Studies* 61 (1971) 80-101.

___. 'Society and the Supernatural: A Medieval Change', *Daedalus* 104 (1975) 133-51.

___. *The Making of Late Antiquity*. Cambridge, Massachusetts: Harvard, 1978.

___. *The Cult of the Saints*: Its Rise and Function in Latin Christianity. Chicago, 1982.

Brunt, P.A. '*Amicitia* in the late Roman Republic', *Proceedings of the Cambridge Philological Society* N.S. II 191 (1965) 1-20.

Bynum, Caroline Walker. *Jesus as Mother*. University of California, 1982.

Cambria, M.G. *Il Monastero Dominicano di S. Agnese in Bologna*. Bologna, 1973.

Casey, Michael. 'The Virtue of Friendship in Monastic Tradition—An Introduction', *Tjurunga* (1983) 21-35.

Catto, J.I., ed. *The History of the University of Oxford* 1: *The Early Schools*. Oxford, 1984.

Cavallera, Ferdinand. *S. Jérôme, sa vie et son oeuvre* 1-2. London, 1923.

Chadwick, Owen. *John Cassian*: A Study in Primitive Monasticism. Cambridge, 1950 and later.

Chase, Colin, ed. *The Dating of Beowulf*. Toronto, 1981.

Chenu, M.-D. 'Platon à Citeaux', *Archives d'histoire doctrinale et littéraire du moyen-âge* 29 (1954) 99-106.

Chitty, Derwas. *The Desert a City*. Oxford: Blackwell, 1966.

Clark, James Midgley. *The Abbey of Saint Gall as a Centre of Literature and Art*. Cambridge, 1926.

Cobban, A.B. *The Medieval Universities*. London, 1975.

Congar, Yves. 'Henri de Marcy, abbé de Clairvaux, cardinal évêque d'Albano et légat pontifical', *Studia Anselmiana* 43. Analecta Monastica 5: 1-90. Rome, 1958.

Conner, Paul. *Friendships between Consecrated Men and Women and the Growth of Charity*. Pontificia Facultas Theologica Institutum Spiritualitatis Teresianum. Rome, 1972.

———. *Celibate Love*. Huntington, Indiana: Our Sunday Visitor, 1978.

Constable, Giles. *Letters and Letter-Collections*. Typologie des sources du moyen-age occidental 17. Turnhout, 1976.

Courcelle, Pierre. 'Paulin de Nole et saint Jérôme', *Revue des Etudes Latines* 25 (1947) 250-80.

———. 'Ailred de Rievaulx à l'école des *Confessions*', *Revue des Etudes Augustiniennes* 3 (1957) 163-74.

Curtius, Ernst Robert. *European Literature and the Latin Middle Ages*. London: Routledge and Kegan Paul, 1953.

Damen, C. 'De quodam amico spirituali beatae Hildegardis Virginis', *Sacris Erudiri* 10 (1958) 162-69.

Damsholt, Nanna. 'Abbed Vilhelm af Æbelholts brevsamling', *Historisk Tidsskrift* 78. 1-22. Copenhagen, 1978.

Delhaye, Philippe. 'Deux adaptations du *De Amicitia* de Cicéron au xii siècle', *Recherches de Théologie ancienne et médiévale* 15 (1948) 304-31.

Donnelly, James S. *The Decline of the Medieval Cistercian Laybrotherhood*. New York: Fordham, 1949.

Dover, J.K. *Greek Homosexuality*. London: Duckworth, 1976.

Duby, Georges. *The Three Orders: Feudal Society Imagined*. University of Chicago Press, 1980.

Duckett, Eleanor Shipley. *Anglo-Saxon Saints and Scholars*. New York: Macmillan, 1948.

___. *Alcuin: Friend of Charlemagne*. New York: Macmillan, 1951.

___. *Saint Dunstan of Canterbury*. New York: W.W. Norton, 1955.

Dugas, L. *L'amitié antique*. Paris, 1894, 1914.

Dümmler, E. 'Über den Monch Otloh von St Emmeram', *Sitzungsberichte der kgl. Preussischen Akademie der Wissenschaften zu Berlin* 2 (1895) 1071-1102.

Ebner, Adalbert. *Die klösterlichen Gebets-Verbrüderungen bis zum Ausgangs des Karolingischen Zeitalters*. Regensburg, 1810.

Egenter, R. *Die Lehre von der Gottesfreundschaft in der Scholastik und Mystik des 12. und 13. Jahrhunderts*. Augsburg, 1928.

Eichengrün, Fritz. *Gerbert (Silvester II) als Persönlichkeit*. Beiträge zur Kulturgeschichte des Mittelalters und Renaissance 35. Leipzig, 1928.

Erdmann, Carl. *Studien zur Briefliteratur Deutschlands im elften Jahrhundert*. Schriften des Reichsinstituts für ältere deutsche Geschichtskunde 1. Leipzig, 1938.

Erickson, Carolly. *The Medieval Vision*. New York, Oxford, 1976.

Evans, Gillian. *Anselm and Talking about God*. Oxford: Clarendon, 1978.

Fabre, Pierre. *Saint Paulin de Nole et l'amitié chrétienne*. Bibliothèque des Ecoles Françaises d'Athènes et de Rome 167. Paris, 1949.

Farmer, David Hugh. *The Oxford Dictionary of Saints*. Oxford, 1978.

Feiss, Hugh. 'The Office for the Feast of the Trinity at Cluny in the late eleventh century'. *Liturgy OCSO 17* (Trappist, Kentucky, 1983) 39-66.

Fichtenau, Heinrich. *The Carolingian Empire*, trans. Peter Munz. New York: Harper, 1964.

Fiske, Adèle. 'Alcuin and mystical Friendship', *Studi Medievali* (1961) 551-75.

___. 'Saint Anselm', *Studia Monastica* 3 (1961) 259-80.

___. 'Saint Bernard of Clairvaux', *Cîteaux* (Westmalle, Belgium) II (1960) 1-41.

___. 'Aelred of Rievaulx', *Cîteaux* 13 (1962) 5-17, 97-132.

___. 'Hieronymus ciceronianus', *Transactions and Proceedings of the American Philological Association* (London, 1965) 119-38.

___. '*Paradisus homo amicus*', *Speculum* 40 (1965) 426-59.

___. *Friends and Friendship in the Monastic Tradition*. Civoc Cuaderno, 51. Cuernavaca, Mexico, 1970.

Forster, E.M. *Two Cheers for Democracy*. Penguin, 1965.

Foucault, Michel. *Histoire de la Sexualité*. Paris: Gallimard, 1976.

Fraisse, J.-C. *Philia. La notion d'amitié dans la philosphie antique*. Paris, 1974.

Frend, W.H.C. 'The Two Worlds of Paulinus of Nola', *Latin Literature of the Fourth Century*, ed. J. W. Binns: 100-133. London: Routledge and Kegan Paul, 1974.

Gelsomino, Remo. 'S. Bernardo di Chiaravalle e il *De Amicitia* di Cicerone', *Studia Anselmiana* 43. Analecta Monastica 5: 180-86. Rome, 1958.

Gibson, Margaret. *Lanfranc of Bec*. Oxford: Clarendon, 1978.

Gigon, O. *Grundprobleme der antiken Philosophie*. Bern and Munich, 1959.

Glente, Karen. *Hellige Kvinder*. Center for Europaeiske Middelalder-studier. Copenhagen: Københavns Universitet, 1985.

Goffart, Walter. *Barbarians and Romans AD 418-584*: The Techniques of Accommodation. Princeton, 1980.

Gransden, Antonia. *Historical Writing in England c. 550 to c. 1307*. London: Routledge and Kegan Paul, 1974.

Grundmann, Herbert. *Religiöse Bewegungen im Mittelalter*. Berlin, 1935, Darmstadt, 1977.

Hahn, H. *Bonifaz und Lull*. Leipzig, 1883.

Hallier, Amédée. *The Monastic Theology of Aelred of Rievaulx*. CS 2. Spencer, Massachusetts, 1969.

Hallinger, Kassius. *Gorze-Kluny* 1-2. Studia Anselmiana 22-26. Rome, 1950-51.

Harris, Margaret A. 'Alan of Tewkesbury and his Letters', *Studia Monastica* 18 (Montserrat, 1976) 77-108, 299-351.

Henry-Couannier, Maurice. *Saint François de Sales et ses amitiés*. Paris, 1954.

Higonnet, Ethel Cardwell. 'Spiritual Ideas in the Letters of Peter of Blois', *Speculum* 50 (1975) 218-44.

Hilpisch, Stephen. *Geschichte des Benediktinischen Mönchtums*. Freiburg im Breisgau, 1929.

Hinnebusch, W.A. *History of the Dominican Order*. New York, 1973.

Horn, Walter and Born, Ernest. *The Plan of Saint Gall* 1-3. Berkeley: University of California Press, 1979.

Hoste, Anselm. *Bibliotheca Aelrediana*. Instrumenta Patristica 2. Steenbrugge, 1962.

Hourlier, Jacques. *Saint Odilon abbé de Cluny*. Bibliothèque de la Revue d'Histoire Ecclésiastique 40: Louvain, 1964.

Hunt, Noreen. *Cluny under Saint Hugh 1049-1109*. London: Edward Arnold, 1967.

Cluniac Monasticism in the Central Middle Ages. London: Archon Books, 1971.

Hunt, R.W. and Lapidge, Michael. 'Manuscript evidence for knowledge of the poems of Venantius Fortunatus in late Anglo-Saxon England', *Anglo-Saxon England* 8 (1979) 279-95.

Jensen, Kirsten Grubb. *Mennesker og idealer i Giovanni Boccaccios Decameron*. Copenhagen: Center for Europaeiske Middelalderstudier, Københavns Universitet, 1985.

Joxe, F. 'Le christianisme et l'evolution des sentiments familiaux dans les lettres privées sur papyrus', *Acta Antiqua Academiae Scientiarum Hungaricae* 7 (1959) 411-20.

Laistner, M.L.W. *Thought and Letters in Western Europe 500-900*. London: Methuen, 1957.

Lambert, Bernard. *Bibliotheca Hieronymiana manuscripta*. La tradition manuscrite de S. Jerome. Collectio Instrumenta Patristici. 1A-B. The Hague, 1969.

Lapidge, Michael. 'The hermeneutic style in tenth-century Anglo-Latin literature', *Anglo-Saxon England* 4 (1975) 67-111.

Leask, Harold G. *Irish Churches and Monastic Buildings* 1. Dundalk, 1955.

Leclercq, Jean. 'L'amitié dans les lettres au moyen-âge', *Revue du Moyen Age latin* 1 (Lyon, 1945) 391-410.

——. 'Le genre epistolaire au moyen-âge', *Revue du Moyen Age latin* 2 (1946) 63-70.

——. *Pierre le Vénerable*. Saint Wandrille 1946.

——. *La spiritualité de Pierre de Celle 1115-83*, Paris: J. Vrin, 1946.

——. (with Jean-Paul Bonnes) *Un maître de la vie spirituelle au xie siècle: Jean de Fécamp*. Études de théologie et d'histoire de la spiritualité 9. Paris, 1946.

——. *Un humaniste ermite: Le bienheureux Paul Giustiniani*. Rome, 1951.

——. 'Epîtres d'Alexandre III sur les cisterciens, *Revue Bénédictine* 64 (1954) 68-82.

——. 'Lettres de vocation à la vie monastique', *Studia Anselmiana* 37. Analecta Monastica 3: 169-97. Rome: Herder, 1955.

——. 'Les collections de sermons de Nicolas de Clairvaux', *Revue Bénédictine* 56 (1956) 296-302.

——. '*L'amour des lettres et le désir de Dieu*. Paris, 1957. Trans. Catherine Musrahi, *The Love of Learning and the Desire for God*. New York: Fordham University Press, 1982.

——. 'Nouvelles lettres de Pierre de Celle', *Studia Anselmiana* 43. Analecta Monastica 5 (1958) 160-79.

——. *Saint Pierre Damien: Ermite et homme de l'église*. Rome: Edizioni di Storia e Letteratura, 1960.

——. 'Saint Martin dans l'hagiographie monastique du moyen-âge', *Saint Martin et son Temps, Studia Anselmiana* 46 (Rome, 1961) 175-87.

——. *Recueil d'Etudes sur Saint Bernard et ses écrits* 1-3. Rome: Edizioni di Storia et Letteratura, 1962-68.

——. 'L'humanisme des moines au moyen-âge', *Studi Medievali A Giuseppe Ermini* 69-113. Spoleto, 1970.

___. 'Recherches sur la collection des épitres de saint Bernard', *Cahiers de civilisation médiévale* 14 (1971) 205-19.

___. 'Modern Psychology and the Interpretation of Medieval Texts, *Speculum* 48 (1973) 476-90.

___. 'Saint Peter Damian and Women', *Cistercian Studies* (1974) 354-65.

___. 'Amicizia nella vita reliogiosa', *Dizionario degli Instituti di Perfezione*, I:516-20. Rome: Edizioni Paoline, 1974.

___. *Monks and Love in Twelfth-Century France*. Oxford: 1979.

Levison, Wilhelm. *England and the Continent in the Eighth Century*. Oxford: Clarendon, 1946.

Lewis, C.S. *The Four Loves*. London: Collins, 1960, 1985.

___. *Selected Literary Essays*, ed. Walter Hopper. Cambridge, 1967.

Leyser, K. J. *Rule and Conflict in an early Medieval Society: Ottonian Saxony*. London: Edward Arnold, 1979.

Lienhard, Joseph T. *Paulinus of Nola and Early Western Monasticism*. Theophaneia 28. Cologne, 1977.

Little, Lester. 'The Personal Development of Peter Damian', *Order and Innovation in the Middle Ages*. Essays in Honor of Joseph R. Strayer, ed. William C. Jordan *et alii*: 317-41. Princeton, 1976.

___. *Religious Poverty and the Profit Economy in Medieval Europe*. London: Paul Elek, 1978.

Lorenz, Rudolf. 'Die Anfänge des abenländischen Mönchtums im 4. Jahrhundert', *Zeitschrift für Kirchengeschichte* 77 (1961) 1-61.

Lynch, J.H. 'Monastic Recruitment in the Eleventh and Twelfth Centuries. Some Social and Economic Considerations', *American Benedictine Review* 36 (1975) 425-47.

McEvoy, James. 'Notes on the Prologue to Saint Aelred of Rivaulx's *De Spirituali Amicitia*, with a Translation', *Traditio* 37 (1981) 396-411.

___. 'Friendship and Love', *Irish Theological Quarterly* (1983-84) 35-47.

___. '*Philia* and *Amicitia*: The philosophy of friendship from Plato to Aquinas', *Sewanee Medieval Colloquium. Occasional Papers* 2 (1984) 1-23.

McGuire, Brian Patrick. 'Love, friendship and sex in the eleventh century: The experience of Anselm', *Studia Theologica* 28:111-52. Oslo, 1974.

——. 'The Collapse of a monastic Friendship: The Case of Jocelin and Samson of Bury', *Journal of Medieval History* 4 (1978) 369-97.

——. 'Structure and Consciousness in the *Exordium Magnum Cisterciense*., *Cahiers de l'Institut du Moyen Age grec et latin* 30 (1979) 33-90.

——. 'Written Sources and Cistercian Inspiration in Caesarius of Heisterbach', *Anal. Cist.* 35 (1979) 227-82.

——. 'Friends and Tales in the Cloister: Oral Sources in Caesarius of Heisterbach,' *Anal.Cist.* 36 (1980) 167-245.

——. 'The Cistercians and the Transformation of Monastic Friendships', *Anal. Cist.* 37 (1981) 1-63.

——. *The Cistercians in Denmark*: Attitudes, Roles and Functions in Medieval Society. CS 35. Kalamazoo, 1982.

——. 'A Lost Clairvaux Exemplum Found: The *Liber Visionum* compiled under Prior John of Clairvaux 1171-79', *Anal. Cist.* 39 (1983) 26-62.

——. 'Was Bernard a Friend?', *Goad and Nail*, ed. E. Rozanne Elder. Studies in Medieval Cistercian History X. CS 84:201-27. Kalamazoo, 1985.

——. 'Monastic Friendship and Toleration in Twelfth-Century Cistercian Life', *Monks, Hermits and the Ascetic Tradition* Studies in Church History 22, ed. W.J. Sheils: 147-60. Oxford, Blackwells, 1985.

——. 'Looking Back on Friendship: Medieval Experience and Modern Context', *Cistercian Studies* (1986) 123-42.

McNamara, Jo Ann, 'Chaste Marriage and Clerical Celibacy', *Sexual Practices and the Medieval Church*, ed. Vern L. Bullough and James Brundage: 22-33. Buffalo, New York: Prometheus, 1982.

——. *A New Song: Celibate Women in the First Three Christian Centuries*. New York: The Institute for Research in History and the Haworth Press, 1983.

McNamara Marie Aquinas. *Friendship and Saint Augustine*. Studia Friburgensia. New Series 20. Fribourg, 1958.

Marrou, Henri I. *Saint Augustin et la fin de la culture antique*. Paris, 1937.

——. *A History of Education in Antiquity*. London, 1956.

Martel, Gérard de. 'Pierre de Celle à Reims', *Memoires de la Société d'agriculture, commerce et arts du département de la Marne* (Châlons-sur-Marne, 1974) 71-105.

Mauro, Letterio. 'L'amicizia come compimento di umanità nel *De Spirituali Amicitia*', *Rivista di Filosofia Neo Scolastica* 66 (1974) 89-103.

Meilaender, Gilbert C. *Friendship. A Study in theological Ethics*. University of Notre Dame, 1981.

Misch, Georg. *Geschichte der Autobiographie* II:2 (Frankfurt am Main, 1955), III:2 (1959).

Moos, Peter von. *Hildebert von Lavardin 1096-1133*. Stuttgart, 1965. *Consolatio. Studien zur mittelalterlichen Trostliteratur*. Münstersche Mittelalter Schriften 3. Wilhelm Fink Verlag, Munich, 1971.

Morison, E.F. *Saint Basil and his Rule*: A Study in Early Monasticism. Oxford, 1952.

Morris, Colin. *The Discovery of the Individual*. London: SPCK, 1977.

Murphy, James A. *A Monument to Saint Jerome*. New York, 1952.

Murphy, James J. *Medieval Rhetoric: A Select Biography*. Toronto Medieval Bibliographies 3. 1971.

Murray, Alexander. *Reason and Society in the Middle Ages*. Oxford: Clarendon Press, 1978.

Narberhaus, Josef. *Benedict von Aniane: Werk und Persönlichkeit,* Beiträge zur Geschichte des altes Mönchtums und des Benediktinerordens 16. Münster in Westfalen, 1930.

Neukirch, Franz. *Das Leben des Petrus Damiani*. Göttingen, 1875.

Nicholson, Jean. '*Feminae gloriosae*: Women in the age of Bede', *Medieval Women*, ed. Derek Baker. Studies in Church History. Subsidia I: 15-30. Oxford: Blackwell, 1978.

Noble, Henri Dominique. *L'amitié avec Dieu*. Paris, 1932.

Nolte, Venantius. *Augustins Freundschaftsideal in seinem Briefen*. Cassiciacum VI. Würzburg, 1939.

Noonan, John T. *Contraception*. Cambridge, Massachusetts: Harvard, 1965.

Nyssen, Wilhelm. *Irdisch hab' ich dich gewollt*. Trier: Spee Verlag, 1982.

O'Meara, John. *The Young Augustine*. London, 1954.

Paor, Maire and Liam de. *Early Christian Ireland*. London: Thames and Hudson, 1961.

Patlagean, Evelyne. *Recherches sur les Pauvres et la pauvreté dans l'Empire romain d'Orient* (IV-VII siècles). Lille, 1974.

Patt, William D. 'The Early *Ars Dictaminis* as response to a changing society', *Viator* 9 (1978) 133-55.

Payer, Pierre J. *Sex and the Penitentials 550-1150*. University of Toronto Press, 1984.

Pepin, Ronald E. '*Amicitia Jocosa*: Peter of Celle and John of Salisbury', *Florilegia* 5 (1983) 140-56.

Perry, Edmund F. 'Can Buddhists and Christians Live Together as Kaly–ā a-mittā', *Buddhist Studies in Honour of Walpola Rahula*. London: Gordon Fraser, 1980.

Picavet, F. *Gerbert, un pape philosophe*. Bibliothèque de l'Ecole des hautes études. Sciences religieuses 9. Paris, 1897.

Pivec, Karl. 'Stil und Sprachentwicklung im mittellateinischen Briefen vom. 8.-12. Jahrhundert', *Mitteilungen des Österreichisches Instituts für Geschichtsforschung* 14 (1931) 33-51.

Pranger, Burcht. '*Studium Sacrae Scripturae*', *Les mutations socio-culturelles au tournant des xie - xiie siècles*: 469-90. Paris: CNRS, 1984.

Raciti, Gaetano. 'Deux collections de sermons de Saint Aelred', *Collectanea Cisterciensia* 45 (1983) 165-84.

—— 'Une allocution familière de S. Aelred conservée dans les mélanges de Matthieu de Rievaulx', *Coll. Cist.* 47 (1985) 267-80.

Rader, Rosemary. *Breaking Boundaries: Male/Female Friendships in early Christian Communities.* New York: Paulist Press, 1983.

Rashdall, Hastings. *The Universities of Europe in the Middle Ages*, 1-3, ed. F.M. Powicke and A.B. Emden, Oxford, 1936.

Reynolds, L.D. *The Medieval Tradition of Seneca's Letters*. Oxford, 1965.

and Wilson, N.G. *Scribes and Scholars*. Oxford, 1974.

Riché, Pierre. *Daily Life in the World of Charlemagne*, trans. JoAnn McNamara. Philadelphia: University of Pennsylvania, 1978.

Roby, Douglass. 'Chimaera of the North: The active Life of Aelred of Rievaulx', *Cistercian Ideals and Reality*, ed. John R. Sommerfeldt. CS 60: 152-169. Kalamazoo, 1978.

Rosenwein, Barbara H. *Rhinoceros Bound: Cluny in the Tenth Century*. Philadelphia: University of Pennsylvania, 1982.

Rougemont, Denis de. *Love in the Western World*. New York, 1940; New York: Harper and Row, 1974.

Rouse, Richard H. 'Cistercian Aids to Study in the 13th Century', *Studies in Medieval Cistercian History* 2, ed. John R. Sommerfeldt. CS 24: 123-134. Kalamazoo, 1976.

Rousseau, Philip. 'Blood-Relationships among early Eastern Ascetics', *Journal of Theological Studies* N. S. 23 (Oxford 1972) 135-44.

___. *Ascetics, Authority and the Church*. Oxford, 1978.

Russell, Kenneth C. 'Aelred. the Gay Abbot of Rievaulx', *Studia Mystica* 5 (Sacramento, California, 1982) 51-64.

Ryan, John. *Irish Monasticism*. Dublin, 1931.

Sackur, E. *Die Cluniacenser* 1-2. Halle, 1892.

Schauwecker, Helga. *Otloh von St. Emmeram*. Studien und Mitteilungen zur Geschichte des Benediktiner-Ordens und seiner Zweige 74. Munich, 1964.

Smalley, Beryl. *The Study of the Bible in the Middle Ages.* Oxford: Blackwell, 1952; University of Notre Dame 1964 and later.

___. 'Sallust in the Middle Ages', *Classical Influences on European Culture AD 500-1500*, ed. R.R. Bolgar: 165-175. Cambridge, 1971.

Smits, E.R. 'Helinand of Froidmont and the A-text of Seneca's Tragedies' *Mnemosyne* 36 (1983) 324-58.

Southern, R.W. *The Making of the Middle Ages*. London: Hutchinson; 1953 and later.

___. *Saint Anselm and his Biographer*. Cambridge, 1966.

___. *Medieval Humanism and Other Studies*. Oxford: Blackwell, 1970.

Squire, Aelred. *Aelred of Rievaulx: A Study*. London, 1969; London-Kalamazoo, 1981.

Stacpoole, Alberic. 'The Public Face of Aelred', *Downside Review* (1967) 183-99, 318-25.

Steiger, P. Augustin. 'Nikolaus, Mönch in Clairvaux, Sekretär des hl. Bernhard', *Studien und Mitteilungen zur Geschichte des Benediktiner Ordens* 38. Neue Folge 7 (1917) 41-50.

Steinen, Wolfram von den. 'Notker des Dichters Formelbuch', *Zeitschrift für Schweizerische Geschichte* 25 (1945) 449-90.

———. *Notker der Dichter und seine geistige Welt*. Bern: A. Francke, 1948.

Thompson, Sally. 'The Problem of the Cistercian Nuns in the Twelfth and early Thirteenth Centuries'', *Medieval Women*, ed. Derek Baker. Ecclesiastical History Society. Oxford: Blackwell, 1978.

Torre, Jan Maria de la. 'La amistad en la vida monástica femenina. Un camino de las amantes de Dios', *Mujeres del Absoluto*, dir. Fray Clemente de la Serna Gonzalez: 323-39. Burgos, Spain, 1986.

Vann, Gerald. *To Heaven with Diana*. A Study of Jordan of Saxony and Diana of Andalo. New York: Pantheon, 1960.

Vansteenberghe, G. 'Amitié', *Dictionnaire de Spiritualité* I (Paris, 1937) 500-529.

Vogüé, Adalbert de. *The Rule of Saint Benedict: A Doctrinal and Spiritual Commentary*. CS 54. Kalamazoo, 1983.

Waddell, Chrysogonus. 'Notes towards the Exegesis of a Letter by Saint Harding', *Noble Piety and Reformed Monasticism*. CS 65. Studies in Medieval Cistercian History 7: 10-39. Kalamazoo, 1981.

Wagner, Fritz, 'Studien zu Caesarius von Heisterbach', *Anal. Cist.* 29 (1973) 79-95.

Ward, Benedicta. 'The Desert Myth', *One Yet Two*, ed. Basil Pennington. CS 29: 183-99. Kalamazoo, 1976.

———. *Miracles and the Medieval Mind*. London: Scolar Press, 1982.

Wellstein, G. 'Die freundschaftlichen Beziehungen des Benediktiners Petrus Cellensis zu den Cisterciensern 1150-1183', *Cistercienser-Chronik* 38 (1926) 213-18.

Wilks, Michael, ed. *The World of John of Salisbury*. Studies in Church History. Subsidia 3. Oxford: Blackwell, 1984.

Winterbottom, Michael. 'Aldhelm's Prose Style and its Origins', *Anglo-Saxon England* 6 (1977) 39-76.

Wright, Wendy. *Bond of Perfection: Jeanne de Chantal and François de Sales*. Mahwah, New Jersey: Paulist, 1986.

Zoepf, Ludwig. *Das Heiligen Leben im 10. Jahrhundert*. Beiträge zur Kulturgeschichte des Mittelalters und der Renaissance 1. Leipzig, 1908.

INDEX

Most names before 1500 are arranged according to forename, e.g. John Cassian under *John*

CISTERCIAN PUBLICATIONS INC.

Kalamazoo, Michigan

TITLES LISTING

THE CISTERCIAN FATHERS SERIES

THE WORKS OF BERNARD OF CLAIRVAUX

Treatises I: Apologia to Abbot William, On Precept and Dispensation . . . CF 1

On the Song of Songs I–IV . . . CF 4,7,31,40

The Life and Death of Saint Malachy the Irishman . . . CF 10

Treatises II: The Steps of Humility, On Loving God . . . CF 13

Magnificat: Homilies in Praise of the Blessed Virgin Mary [with Amadeus of Lausanne] . . . CF 18

Treatises III: On Grace and Free Choice, In Praise of the New Knighthood . . . CF 19

Sermons on Conversion: A Sermon to Clerics, Lenten Sermons on Psalm 91 . . . CF 25

Five Books on Consideration: Advice to a Pope . . . CF 37

THE WORKS OF WILLIAM OF SAINT THIERRY

On Contemplating God, Prayer, and Meditations . . . CF 3

Exposition on the Song of Songs . . . CF 6

The Enigma of Faith . . . CF 9

The Golden Epistle . . . CF 12

The Mirror of Faith . . . CF 15

Exposition on the Epistle to the Romans . . . CF 27

The Nature and Dignity of Love . . . CF 30

THE WORKS OF AELRED OF RIEVAULX

Treatises I: On Jesus at the Age of Twelve, Rule for a Recluse, The Pastoral Prayer . . . CF 2

Spiritual Friendship . . . CF 5

The Mirror of Charity . . . CF 17†

Dialogue on the Soul . . . CF 22

THE WORKS OF GILBERT OF HOYLAND

Sermons on the Song of Songs I–III . . CF 14,20,26

Treatises, Sermons, and Epistles . . . CF 34

THE WORKS OF JOHN OF FORD

Sermons on the Final Verses of the Song of Songs I–VII . . . CF 29,39,43,44,45,46,47

Texts and Studies in the Monastic Tradition

OTHER EARLY CISTERCIAN WRITERS

The Letters of Adam of Perseigne, I . . . CF 21

Alan of Lille: The Art of Preaching . . . CF 23

Idung of Prüfening. Cistercians and Cluniacs: The Case for Citeaux . . . CF 33

Guerric of Igny. Liturgical Sermons I–II . . . CF 8,32

Three Treatises on Man: A Cistercian Anthropology . . . CF 24

Isaac of Stella. Sermons on the Christian Year, I . . . CF 11

Stephen of Lexington. Letters from Ireland, 1228–9 . . . CF 28

Stephen of Sawley, Treatises . . . CF 36

Baldwin of Ford. Spiritual Tractates . . . CF 38,41

Serlo of Wilton & Serlo of Savigny . . . CF 48†

** Temporarily out of print*

† Forthcoming

THE CISTERCIAN STUDIES SERIES

MONASTIC TEXTS

Evagrius Ponticus. Praktikos and Chapters on Prayer . . . CS 4
The Rule of the Master . . . CS 6
The Lives of the Desert Fathers . . . CS 34
The Sayings of the Desert Fathers . . . CS 59
The Harlots of the Desert . . . CS 106
Dorotheos of Gaza. Discourses and Sayings . . . CS 33
Pachomian Koinonia I–III:
The Lives . . . CS 45
The Chronicles and Rules . . . CS 46
The Instructions, Letters, and Other Writings of St Pachomius and His Disciples . . . CS 47
Besa, The Life of Shenoute . . . CS 73
Menas of Nikiou: Isaac of Alexandria & St Macrobius . . . CS 107
The Syriac Fathers on Prayer and the Spiritual Life (S. Brock) . . . CS 101
Theodoret of Cyrrhus. A History of the Monks of Syria . . . CS 88
Simeon Stylites: The Lives . . . CS 112†
Symeon the New Theologian. Theological and Practical Treatises and Three Theological Discourses . . . CS 41
The Venerable Bede: Commentary on the Seven Catholic Epistles . . . CS 82
The Letters of Armand-Jean de Rancé (A.J. Krailsheimer) . . . CS 80, 81
Guigo II the Carthusian. The Ladder of Monks and Twelve Meditations . . . CS 48
The Monastic Rule of Iosif Volotsky . . . CS 36
Anselm of Canterbury. Letters . . . CS 94,95†
Br. Pinocchio, Rule of St Benedict . . . CS 99
Peter of Celle: Selected Works . . . CS 100

CHRISTIAN SPIRITUALITY

The Spirituality of Western Christendom . . . CS 30
Russian Mystics (Sergius Bolshakoff) . . . CS 26
In Quest of the Absolute: The Life and Works of Jules Monchanin (J.G. Weber) . . . CS 51
The Name of Jesus (Irénée Hausherr) . . . CS 44
The Roots of the Modern Christian Tradition . . . CS 55
Abba: Guides to Wholeness and Holiness East and West . . . CS 38
Sermons in a Monastery (Matthew Kelty–William Paulsell) . . . CS 58
Penthos: The Doctrine of Compunction in the Christian East (Irénée Hausherr) . . . CS 53
The Spirituality of the Christian East. A Systematic Handbook (Tomas Spidlik SJ) . . . CS 79
From Cloister to Classroom . . . CS 90
Fathers Talking. An Anthology (Aelred Squire) . . . CS 93
Friendship & Community (Brian P. McGuire) . . . CS 95

MONASTIC STUDIES

The Abbot in Monastic Tradition (Pierre Salmon) . . . CS 14
Community and Abbot in the Rule of St Benedict I (Adalbert de Vogüé) . . . CS 5/1–2
Consider Your Call: A Theology of the Monastic Life (Daniel Rees et al.) . . . CS 20
The Way to God According to the Rule of St Benedict (E. Heufelder) . . . CS 49
The Rule of St Benedict. A Doctrinal and Spiritual Commentary (Adalbert de Vogüé) . . . CS 54
Serving God First (Sighard Kleiner) . . . CS 83
Monastic Practices (Charles Cummings) . . . CS 75†
St Hugh of Lincoln (David Hugh Farmer) . . . CS 87

CISTERCIAN STUDIES

The Cistercian Way (André Louf) . . . CS 76
The Cistercian Spirit (M. Basil Pennington, ed.) . . . CS 3
The Eleventh-Century Background of Cîteaux (Bede K. Lackner) . . . CS 8
Cistercian Sign Language (Robert Barakat) . . . CS 11
The Cistercians in Denmark (Brian P. McGuire) . . . CS 35
Athirst for God. Spiritual Desire in Bernard of Clairvaux's Sermons on the Song of Songs (Michael Casey) . . . CS 77†
Saint Bernard of Clairvaux: Essays Commemorating the Eighth Centenary of His Canonization . . . CS 28
Bernard of Clairvaux: Studies Presented to Dom Jean Leclercq . . . CS 23
Bernard of Clairvaux and the Cistercian Spirit (Jean Leclercq) . . . CS 16
Another Look at St Bernard (Jean Leclercq) . . . CS 105
Women and Womanhood in the Works of St Bernard (Jean Leclercq) . . . CS 104
Image and Likeness. The Augustinian Spirituality of William of St Thierry (David N. Bell) . . . CS 78
William, Abbot of St Thierry . . . CS 94
Aelred of Rievaulx: A Study (Aelred Squire) . . . CS 50
Christ the Way: The Christology of Guerric of Igny (John Morson) . . . CS 25
The Golden Chain: The Theological Anthropology of Isaac of Stella (Bernard McGinn) . . . CS 15

** Temporarily out of print*

† Forthcoming

Nicolas Cotheret's Annals of Citeaux (Louis J. Lekai) . . . CS 57

The Occupation of Celtic Sites in Ireland by the Canons Regular of St Augustine and the Cistercians (G. Carville) . . . CS 56

The Finances of the Cistercian Order in the Fourteenth Century (Peter King) . . . CS 85

Rancé and the Trappest Legacy (A. J. Krailsheimer) . . . CS 86

Fountains Abbey and Its Benefactors, 1132–1300 (Joan Wardrop) . . . CS 91

Medieval Religious Women

Distant Echoes: MRW, I (L.T. Shank and J.A. Nichols, edd.) . . . CS 71

Peace Weavers. MRW II (L.T. Shank and J.A. Nichols, edd.) . . . CS 72

Studies in Medieval Cistercian History sub-series

Studies I . . . CS 13

Studies II . . . CS 24

Cistercian Ideals and Reality (Studies III) . . . CS 60

Simplicity and Ordinariness (Studies IV) . . . CS 61

The Chimera of His Age: Studies on St Bernard (Studies V) . . . CS 63

Cistercians in the Late Middle Ages (Studies VI) . . . CS 64

Noble Piety and Reformed Monasticism (Studies VII) . . . CS 65

Benedictus: Studies in Honor of St Benedict of Nursia (Studies VIII) . . . CS 67

Heaven on Earth (Studies IX) . . . CS 68

Goad and Nail (Studies X) . . . CS 84

Erudition in God's Service (Studies XI) . . . CS 98

Studies in Cistercian Art and Architecture

Studies in Cistercian Art and Architecture, I (Meredith Lillich, ed.) . . . CS 66

Studies in Cistercian Art and Architecture, II (Meredith Lillich, ed.) . . . CS 69

Studies in Cistercian Art and Architecture, III (Meredith Lillich, ed.) . . . CS 89

THOMAS MERTON

The Climate of Monastic Prayer . . . CS 1

Thomas Merton on St Bernard . . . CS 9

Thomas Merton's Shared Contemplation: A Protestant Perspective (Daniel J. Adams) . . . CS 62

Solitude in the Writings of Thomas Merton (Richard Anthony Cashen) . . . CS 40

The Message of Thomas Merton (Brother Patrick Hart, ed.) . . . CS 42

Thomas Merton Monk (revised edition/ Brother Patrick Hart, ed.) . . . CS 52

The Legacy of Thomas Merton (Brother Patrick Hart, ed.) . . . CS 92

Thomas Merton and Asia: His Quest for Utopia (Alexander Lipski) . . . CS 74

Towards an Integrated Humanity (M.B. Pennington, ed.) . . . CS 103

Thomas Merton: Monk & Artist (Victor Kramer) . . . CS 102

THE CISTERCIAN LITURGICAL DOCUMENTS SERIES

The Cistercian Hymnal: Introduction and Commentary . . . CLS 1

The Cistercian Hymnal: Text and Melodies . . . CLS 2

The Old French Ordinary and Breviary of the Abbey of the Paraclete: Introduction and Commentary . . . CLS 3

The Old French Ordinary of the Abbey of the Paraclete: Text . . . CLS 4

The Paraclete Breviary: Text . . . CLS 5–7

The Hymn Collection of the Abbey of the Paraclete: Introduction and Commentary . . . CLS 8

The Hymn Collection of the Abbey of the Paraclete: Text . . . CLS 9

The Molesme Summer-Session Breviary . . . CLS 10–14

STUDIA PATRISTICA

Papers of the Oxford Patristics Conference 1983 (Elizabeth A. Livingstone, ed.)

1. Historica-Gnostica-Biblica
2. Critica-Classica-Ascetica-Liturgica
3. The Second Century-Clement and Origen-The Cappodocian Fathers †
4. Augustine-Post Nicene Latin Fathers-Oriental Texts-*Nachleben* of the Fathers †

FAIRACRES PRESS, OXFORD

The Wisdom of the Desert Fathers

The World of the Desert Fathers

The Letters of St Antony the Great

The Letters of Ammonas, Successor of St Antony

A Study of Wisdom. Three Tracts by the author of *The Cloud of Unknowing*

The Power of the Name. The Jesus Prayer in Orthodox Spirituality (Kallistos Ware)

Contemporary Monasticism

The Influence of St Bernard

Theology and Spirituality (Andrew Louth)

Prayer and Holiness (Dumitru Staniloae)

Saint Gregory Nazianzen: Selected Poems

** Temporarily out of print*

† Forthcoming

Eight Chapters on Perfection and Angel's Song (Walter Hilton)

Creative Suffering (Iulia de Beausobre)

Bringing Forth Christ. Five Feasts of the Child Jesus (St Bonaventure)

Gentleness in St John of the Cross

Distributed in North America only for Fairacres Press.

DISTRIBUTED BOOKS

St Benedict: Man with An Idea (Melbourne Studies)

The Spirit of Simplicity

Benedict's Disciples (David Hugh Farmer)

The Emperor's Monk: A Contemporary Life of Benedict of Aniane

A Guide to Cistercian Scholarship (2nd ed.)

North American customers may order through booksellers or directly from the publisher:

Cistercian Publications
WMU Station
Kalamazoo, Michigan 49008
(616) 383-4985

Cistercian Publications are available in Britain, Europe and the Commonwealth through A. R. Mowbray & Co Ltd St Thomas House Oxford OX1 1SJ.
For a sterling price list, please consult Mowbray's General Catalogue.

A complete catalogue of texts-in-translation and studies on early, medieval, and modern Christian monasticism is available at no cost from Cistercian Publications.

Cistercian monks and nuns have been living lives of prayer & praise, meditation & manual labor since the twelfth century. They are part of an unbroken tradition which extends back to the fourth century and which continues today in the Catholic church, the Orthodox churches, the Anglican communion, and, most recently, in the Protestant churches.

Share their way of life and their search for God by reading Cistercian Publications.